Words of the True Peoples

Anthology of Contemporary Mexican Indigenous-Language Writers

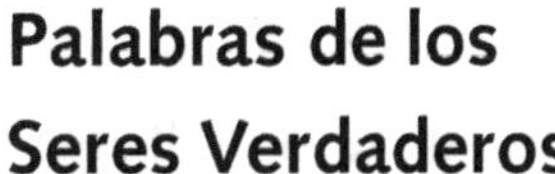

Palabras de los Seres Verdaderos

Antología de Escritores Actuales en Lenguas Indígenas de México

Joe R. and Teresa Lozano Long Series in
Latin American and Latino Art and Culture

Words of the True Peoples

Anthology of Contemporary Mexican Indigenous-Language Writers

VOLUME ONE: PROSE

A Multilingual Volume

Edited by
Carlos Montemayor and Donald Frischmann

Photography by
George O. Jackson, Jr.

Palabras de los Seres Verdaderos

Antología de Escritores Actuales en Lenguas Indígenas de México

TOMO UNO: PROSA

Edición Multilingüe

Editado por
Carlos Montemayor and Donald Frischmann

Fotografía de
George O. Jackson, Jr.

University of Texas Press Austin

First edition, 2004
First paperback edition, 2017

♾ The paper used in this book meets the minimum requirements of ANSI/NISO Z39.48-1992(R1997) (Permanence of Paper).

Library of Congress Cataloging-in-Publication Data

Words of the true peoples : anthology of contemporary Mexican indigenous-language writers / edited by Carlos Montemayor and Donald Frischmann ; photography by George O. Jackson, Jr. = Palabras de los seres verdaderos : antología de escritores actuales en lenguas indígenas de México / editado por Carlos Montemayor and Donald Frischmann ; fotografía por George O. Jackson, Jr.—1st ed.

v. cm. — (Joe R. and Teresa Lozano Long series in Latin American and Latino art and culture)
English, Mayan, and Spanish.
"A multilingual volume/Edición multilingüe"—V. 1.
Includes bibliographical references.
Contents: v. 1. Prose = Prosa
ISBN 0-292-70580-8 (cloth : alk. paper)
1. Indian literature—Mexico—History and criticism. 2. Maya literature—History and criticism. 3. Indians of Mexico—Languages—Texts. 4. Mexican literature—History and criticism. I. Title: Palabras de los seres verdaderos. II. Montemayor, Carlos, 1947– III. Frischmann, Donald H. IV. Series.
PM3082.W67 2004
897'.0972—dc22 2004017345

ISBN 978-1-4773-1526-2, paperback

*To Patricia Urbina and Susana de la Garza,
for your radiant and constant presence*

*A Susana de la Garza y Patricia Urbina,
por su luminosa y constante presencia*

Contents/Contenido

Acknowledgments/Agradecimientos

We wish to offer our thanks to the following institutions and individuals whose valuable support has made this project possible:

The Texas Christian University Research and Creative Activities Fund, Department of Spanish and Latin American Studies, and AddRan College of Humanities and Social Sciences; Universidad de las Américas-Puebla, Escuela de Humanidades, Departamento de Filosofía y Letras, and Decanatura de Asuntos Internacionales; the Council for International Exchange of Scholars; the Mexico-U.S. Commission for Educational and Cultural Exchange (COMEXUS); the International Bank of Commerce, Laredo, Texas; the Fondo Nacional para la Cultura y las Artes (FONCA); the U.S.-Mexico Fund for Culture and the National Endowment for the Humanities, for having supported the preparation of the subsequent volumes of this work; George O. Jackson, Jr., for his rich visual enhancement of these volumes; Anne Luna Fleck, M.A., for her English translations of "Past and Present Writing in Indigenous Languages" and the appendices by Carlos Montemayor; Juan de la Torre López, for his translation into Tzotzil of the essay by Jacinto Arias Pérez; Dr. Juan Hernández, for having generously recommended this work to the University of Texas Press; John Christopher Drake, M.A., for his valuable stylistic suggestions; Lucelva Jácome Lara, for having recorded on computer the voluminous multilingual material presented here; and particularly the Indigenous-language writers, for their steadfast collaboration on this historic project.

Deseamos agradecer el apoyo invaluable de las siguientes instituciones y personas que hicieron posible la realización de este proyecto:

Texas Christian University Research and Creative Activities Fund, Department of Spanish and Latin American Studies y AddRan College of Humanities and Social Sciences; la Universidad de las Américas-Puebla, Escuela de Humanidades, Departamento de Filosofía y Letras, y Decanatura de Asuntos Internacionales; el Council for International Exchange of Scholars; la Comisión México-Estados Unidos para el Intercambio Educativo y Cultural (COMEXUS); el International Bank of Commerce, Laredo, Texas; el Fondo Nacional para la Cultura y las Artes (FONCA); el Fideicomiso para la Cultura México-E.U.A. (Contacto Cultural) y la National Endowment for the Humanities, por haber apoyado la preparación de los siguientes tomos de este trabajo; George O. Jackson, Jr., por el rico realce visual que le ha dado a estos tomos; Anne Luna Fleck, M.A., por sus traducciones al inglés de "Past and Present Writing in Indigenous Languages" y los apéndices de Carlos Montemayor; Juan de la Torre López, por su traducción al tzotzil del ensayo de Jacinto Arias Pérez; el Dr. Juan Hernández, por haber recomendado generosamente esta obra a la University of Texas Press; John Christopher Drake, M.A., por sus valiosas sugerencias estilísticas; Lucelva Jácome Lara, por haber capturado todo el inmenso material multilingüe de la presente obra; y en particular, los escritores en lenguas indígenas, por su colaboración constante en este histórico proyecto.

Abbreviations/Abreviaturas

a.n.—author's note
CNCA—Consejo Nacional para la Cultura y las Artes
DGCP—Dirección General de Culturas Populares
FCE—Fondo de Cultura Económica
INI—Instituto Nacional Indigenista
n.a.—nota del autor
PACMYC—Programa de Apoyo a las Culturas Municipales y Comunitarias
Sedesol—Secretaría de Desarrollo Social
SEP—Secretaría de Educación Pública
TRF—The Rockefeller Foundation

Words of the True Peoples

Anthology of Contemporary Mexican Indigenous-Language Writers

Palabras de los Seres Verdaderos

Antología de Escritores Actuales en Lenguas Indígenas de México

Past and Present Writing in Indigenous Languages

Carlos Montemayor

1

I have explained on another occasion that Mexican literature encompasses at least three great branches of literary production,[1] each important and possessing a complex and abundant history. It includes, of course, the literature written in Spanish from the sixteenth century until the present day. Also included is the literature written in Latin, a language used continually from the 1500s until the eighteenth-century apogee of the humanists, who included for the first time the concept of *mestizaje* as part of Mexican identity and reassessed pre-Hispanic culture: Francisco Xavier Clavijero, José Luis Maneiro, Manuel Cavo, Diego José Abad, Francisco Xavier Alegre, Rafael Landívar, and Rafael Campoy, among others. And, finally, it includes the literature which was written in Indigenous languages before the conquest and during the colonial period and which is now reemerging in various parts of Mexico, despite persistent discrediting of these languages and widespread ignorance of the artistic composition of such literature.

The Mayan expert Silvanus G. Morley affirmed, for example:

> The Mayas are essentially conservative and opposed to progress; in this way they have managed to conserve their own language during four centuries of Spanish domination, to such a degree that today they continue to employ it in place of Spanish in the henequen works and in their daily occupations, in all the small cities and villages of Yucatan.[2]

It is odd that for an expert in Mayan culture the idea of conserving the Mayan language means being opposed to progress. In the same vein, we find a Chontal narrative which justifies the elimination of the native language on supernatural grounds:

> . . . before, they couldn't go out at midday because the *chibompan,* as he is called, would carry them off. That one takes the children, the young girls, the men that go to work in the mangrove swamp . . . he puts a spell on them there . . . he carries them off. The one that knows how to speak Chontal, he grabs him right away! And the one that doesn't know how to speak his language, he can't be with him, because he doesn't understand what he's saying! What the ancestors did was teach the children to speak Spanish so that the *chibompan* wouldn't take them.[3]

The artistic discrediting of these languages is more far-reaching. At the beginning of the twentieth century, as he was considering the history of Spanish-American poetry, Spanish philologist Marcelino Menéndez y Pelayo addressed the theme of American Indigenous-language poetry. At that time, he disdainfully stated that it was pointless to concern oneself

> with the few obscure literary fragments surviving from those primitive languages . . . rather, [one should turn one's attention to] the languages that the Spanish colonists brought to America and their descendants still use. If some component of American primitivism managed to infiltrate this poetry (which is very doubtful), it would only be in this sense that such barbaric and exotic elements could have influenced the body of Latin American literature, which has followed the path of general Spanish literature in all its vicissitudes, receiving influences from the Italian classicism of the sixteenth century, the *culteranismo* of the seventeenth, the neoclassic reaction of the eighteenth, the romanticism of the present century, and the most avant-garde foreign literature, especially French and English. This does not exclude a considerable degree of originality in the particulars; but the basis of this originality, rather than in the opaque, incoherent, and mysterious traditions of barbaric and degenerate peoples . . . should be looked for in the contemplation of the marvels of a New World.[4]

Menéndez y Pelayo never had the chance to become acquainted with the ancient Nahuatl, Maya, Quechua, or Guarani poetry that became known around the middle of the last century or with the new poetry that, in more than twenty-five Indigenous languages, would burst forth everywhere on the Latin American continent at the beginning of the twenty-first century. Neither could he have imagined that notable authors writing in Spanish would construct their narratives based on the influence of an Indigenous language, as is the case with Guarani in the writings of Augusto Roa Bastos, with Quechua in José María Arguedas, or with Zapotec from the Isthmus of Tehuantepec in Andrés Henestrosa. What is astonishing is that there are still authors who think like Menéndez y Pelayo.

Various imprecisions, historical oversights, and ingenuous beliefs have tended to confuse what should be understood by Indigenous and traditional literature: for instance, the belief that languages can be differentiated by degrees of development and that developed languages are the "real" languages whereas the others are just "dialects." Another example is the belief that developed languages are spoken in first-world countries and dialects in subjugated ones. Perhaps it will come as a surprise to many to know that there are no superior languages; that all alike consist of linguistic systems definable in the same terms, with the grammatical structures necessary for a complex range of abstract, symbolic, metaphorical, imperative, and ludic communication, based on a unique phonological system. Nahuatl is a linguistic system just as complete as German; Mayan and French are equally complete, as are Zapotec and Italian, Purepecha and Greek, or Spanish and English and Ñahñu and Mazatec. Dialectal variation is a linguistic concept that refers to the regional uses of a language. In the case of the Spanish language, regional variations at the lexical, phonetic, and syntactic levels may be observed, for example, in Andalucía, Buenos Aires, Bogotá, Yucatán, or Mexico City.[5] In the same way, different dialects of English are spoken in various regions of England itself (Scotland, London, Wales) as well as in Ireland, Australia, Jamaica, Boston, and California. The French spoken in Normandy differs from that spoken in the south of France, Algeria, Canada, or Haiti. Only in this sense is it correct to speak of linguistic "dialects."

Another error, perhaps arising from the different criteria applied to European and Indigenous cultures, is the belief that languages with a written tradition possess a literature, while Indigenous languages or those from nonliterate societies have only an oral tradition. Certainly, the term "literature" as a *writing technique* comes from the Latin word *littera* (letter), but the concept today refers more to the notion of art than to the writing itself. In contrast, the concept of "oral tradition" in the anthropological sense does not recognize divisions between *the art of language* (whether written or not) and *oral communication.* I have explained elsewhere,[6] in detail, the *art of composition* in both the Indigenous languages and the Homeric epics as a complex construct that does not require writing to concretize or to transmit it. Hence I have reiterated on several occasions that the Indigenous cultures of Mexico have retained their vigor, among other reasons, because their languages have served as essential supports for their cultures, through the role they play in the ritualization of civil, agricultural, and religious life—and that, in those contexts of cultural resistance or continuity, the Indigenous languages are used in a specific manner that is in itself a type of *composition,* distinguished from colloquial use in the same way that in any other language artistic composition is distinguished from everyday expression. It is necessary to begin with this concept of the *art of language* to understand the role of literature in the Indigenous languages of yesterday and today.

2

Recalling some elements of the historical and linguistic oppression to which the Indigenous languages of Mexico have been subjected can help us to understand the important social function performed by modern-day Indigenous literature. Foreign dominion over Indigenous languages has often been an instrument of destruction or cultural control. The talent of the sixteenth-century Spanish friars is surprising: in a very few years, they managed to learn the numerous Indigenous languages of the New World as well as prepare grammars and glossaries, adapt practical alphabets, and write numerous songs, plays, prayers, and catechisms. This was an extraordinary achievement, especially when added to their pedagogical efforts during a number of years among the members of the Indigenous aristocracy. The result of this erudition, however, was that the numerous Indian scribes remained in the shadow of their civil or religious masters as informants; and the literature thus produced in the Indigenous languages was not exactly written in the interest of the languages themselves but rather that of the conquering religion, for purposes of instruction in the Christian doctrine.[7]

The mastery achieved by the sixteenth-century Spanish friars over the Indigenous languages can only be compared to a twentieth-century linguistic phenomenon, also religious in nature: the Summer Language Institute, which carried out an admirable and detailed study of many languages for the purpose of translating the Bible and other Protestant evangelizing tracts into these languages. Again, the ultimate goal was Christianization.[8] This institute produced grammars and primers that were extremely useful in the Indigenous literacy programs which the Mexican government began to promote at that time. This was a positive step, even if it did represent a type of "lay" catechism, whose ultimate goal was to replace the Indigenous languages, considered a barrier to national unification, with Spanish.[9] It is significant that, because of these programs, texts in the same language have often been printed using alphabets that vary according to the institutions or the specialized linguists who created them.[10]

On the other hand, we should also remember that the evolution of pre-Hispanic writing in Mesoamerica was remarkable. For peoples, such as the Mayas, who achieved advanced levels of mathematical, astronomical, botanical, and historical knowledge (and whose vast territory included large areas of Central America and Mexico), writing could not have been unknown. Perhaps the sheer number of Mesoamerican languages used at the time prompted the Mayas to develop a form of written expression which, rather than being phonetic and by its very nature regional, was ideographic and therefore universal. This writing suffered the onslaught of the conquest in multiple ways, ranging from the physical destruction of books, to the imposition of the Latin alphabet for use in the writing of their languages, to, finally, the elimination of the Indigenous intelligentsia and the permanent refusal to recognize learned Indians as genuine authors.

It is precisely from one of the greatest destroyers of pre-Hispanic books, Friar Diego de Landa, that we learn that before the arrival of the Spaniards, for example, among the Mayas of Yucatán,

> the sciences they taught were the counting of years, months, and days, the celebrations and ceremonies, the administering of their sacraments, the ill-fated days and times, their ways of divining, remedies for ills, their antiquities, reading and writing with their own letters and characters in which they wrote with figures that constituted their writings . . . They wrote their books on long sheets that folded up, enclosing everything between two attractively made covers, and where they wrote on both sides in columns, in accordance with the folds; and this paper they made from the roots of a tree, and they gave it a glossy white finish on which they were able to write easily, and some of the principal noblemen knew about these sciences because they were interested in them, and these men were highly esteemed, although they did not use them openly.[11]

Bernal Díaz del Castillo affirms that in a town located in the present-day state of Veracruz, which at that time was subject to Cempoala, "many books of paper, folded in the manner of cloths of Castilla," were found in a temple.[12] Pedro Mártir refers to these, saying that the

> characters they use are very different from ours and consist of squares, tildes, loops, curves, and other objects placed in a line, as is common among ourselves and very similar to Egyptian writing. Between the lines they draw figures of men and animals, principally of kings and magnates, which is why it is believed that in these writings the epic achievements of the ancestors of each king are recorded, so that the printers often, in order to lure potential customers, insert in the general histories, and even in books for entertainment, illustrations representative of the protagonists . . . They also make beautiful book covers of wood. Their books, when closed, are like ours and contain, it is believed, their laws, the order of their sacrifices and ceremonies, their accounts, their astronomical annotations, and the methods and times for planting.[13]

As J. Eric. S. Thompson suggests, these books on *paper* were Mayan.[14] The Nahuas, the Mixtecs, and the Zapotecs also had books written on deerskin in various formats.[15] Other instances of writing are to be found on the Mayan stelae and, in general, in the inscriptions carved on stones from the rocky beds of rivers. To these sculpted testimonies we owe the knowledge, for example, that certain features of Mayan writing already existed before 400 B.C.: the numerical use of bars and dots and various glyphic elements with astronomical associations defined among the Olmecs and Mayas, such as the character *U,* which represented the moon; *kin,* the sun; *lamat,* the stars; and the crossed-bar motif, representing the intersection of the Milky Way with the ecliptic.[16] The glyphs on some of the stelae in Monte Albán I are even older, dating from the seventh century B.C.[17]

Without this tradition of Mesoamerican writing, the immediate Indigenous response to the teaching of alphabetical writing in the schools established by the various religious orders in Mexico City, Oaxaca, and Yucatán would have been inexplicable. At the beginning of 1547, for example, Friar Luis de Villalpando persuaded Governor Francisco de Montejo that all the Mayan chiefs in Yucatán who so desired could send their children to a monastery school to learn to read and write. The response was immediate: more than a thousand children attended the first school, directed by Friar Juan de Herrera. From that school came teachers who in turn educated other Indigenous groups in Yucatán towns with monasteries or visitations. J. Francisco Molina Solís names as among the most enthusiastic the towns of Camkal, Maní, Izamal, Cancenote, Tihosuco, Cochuah, Chikinconot, Tikuch, Ichmul, Xocen, and Yalcón. He also mentions as learned Indians notable for their eloquence Francisco Eván, of the town of Comcel, who in the San Francisco monastery, at more than fifty years of age, learned to read and write as well as learning "all the Christian doctrine and ethics"; Nakuk Pech, author of the chronicle of Chicxulub in 1562; and Gaspar Antonio Xiu, grandson of Chief Tutul Xiu de Maní, who wrote in Spanish, Mayan, and Latin and who was entrusted by the Mérida City Council, together with Martín de Palomar, to write the report sent to the king in 1597. Molina Solís clarifies that of course

> there was no Indigenous town without a certain number of literate inhabitants who were able to compose not just letters, but documents, and even some chronicles: it was essential for the *caciques,* mayors, and aldermen to know how to read and write, and since the latter could not be re-elected, it was necessary that every town include a certain number of literate individuals.[18]

At present we are experiencing a reemergence of the literary arts in these languages and analysis of Indigenous cultures by the Indians themselves. This resurgence of Indigenous intellectuals and of writing in Indigenous languages represents one of the most profoundly important cultural events in Mexico at the end of the twentieth and beginning of the twenty-first century. From the perspective of non-Indigenous researchers or state and federal government cultural workers, an understanding of the literature written in Indigenous languages will require an understanding of the various levels, phases, and objectives contributing to its complex resurgence. To stimulate the development of this new literature, it will also be necessary to have reading materials available in Indigenous languages, with a diverse literary production both traditional and contemporary in the form of books, pamphlets, collections, periodicals, and comic books, not just textbooks.

Of course, there exists a powerful acculturation process that accelerates the loss of ethnic values in many individuals and groups. But another process is gaining strength now, which is also powerful and profoundly aware of its objectives: to reinforce and consolidate these ethnic values throughout the course of the twenty-first century. These new writers may be said to represent a dual process: a national one, corresponding to ethnic development and empowerment; and a personal one, consisting of their commitment to their bloody histories of oppression, to their individual cultures, and to their own languages that describe our territory in a fresher and more natural way. Many languages have managed to survive and even now continue to be the repositories of their cultures' religious heritage. Those religious heritages are based, among other things, on an idea current among the ancient Greeks and Romans which is no longer understood by Westernized peoples: that our planet is not something inert and inanimate, but a living being.

3

This important cultural phenomenon—the emergence of writers in several Indigenous languages—began to take place in Mexico during the 1980s. The concurrent appearance of these writers in practically all areas of the country, albeit not coordinated in the beginning, was a result of the evolution of the Indigenous organizations themselves and of the educational programs promoted in Mexico by different and at times contradictory language policies.[19] During the last five hundred years non-Indigenous national and foreign researchers have defined Indigenous groups and explained what they think, how they behave, and in what they believe. With these new writers we have the possibility for the first time of discovering, through the Indigenous groups' own representatives, the natural, intimate, and profound face of a Mexico that is still unknown to us. Many of these writers, working as bilingual specialists in regional or national government offices, have participated in, stimulated, or confronted government educational and cultural programs. Since 1990 some government departments have decided to support them, but their specific emergence was the result of individuals or independent projects rather than of government policies.

The development of these Indigenous writers and the individual nature of their texts vary widely throughout the country. Some areas and languages have a greater degree of activity and even several generations of Indigenous literature. Four essays are instrumental in understanding this phenomenon: "La flor de la palabra" (The Flower of the Word) by Víctor de la Cruz (Zapotec); "Vivencias de nuestra palabra: El resurgimiento de la cultura maya en Chiapas" (Our Word's Life Experiences: The Resurgence of Mayan Culture in Chiapas) by Manuel Pérez Hernández (Tzotzil); "La computadora y sus aplicaciones en la escritura de las lenguas indígenas" (The Computer and Its Applications in Indigenous-Language Writing) by Jesús Salinas Pedraza (Ñahñu); and "La formación de escritores en lengua maya" (The Development of Mayan-Language Writers) by Miguel May May (Maya).[20] These essays demonstrate the different ways in which these processes evolved among the Mayas of Yucatán, the Tzotziles and Tzeltales of Chiapas, the Zapotecs of the Isthmus of Tehuantepec, and several writers of different tonal languages for whom Jesús Salinas Pedraza has designed computer programs.

For example, the support of retired military personnel and Juchitec artists was an integral part of the growth of Zapotec literature in the Isthmus; the Harvard University project directed by Evon Z. Vogt, the persistence and goodwill of Robert Laughlin, and the consulting of North American theatre director Ralph Lee were essential in the evolution of the Tzeltal and Tzotzil literature of Chiapas;[21] the University of Florida at Gainesville and Professor H. Russell Bernard provided support to Jesús Salinas Pedraza and his wife, Josefa Leonarda González Ventura;[22] and in the case of Yucatán, my own participation facilitated the formation of an important group of writers. To these four evolutionary processes we must add one more, which predated all the rest: the one promoted by Miguel León-Portilla from the National Autonomous University of Mexico, which has been of importance for the pre-Hispanic, colonial, and contemporary history of literature in the Nahuatl language.

I have worked with Mayas from Yucatán and Campeche; with Tzotzil and Tzeltal groups from Chiapas; with Zapotec poets from the Isthmus of Tehuantepec; with Zapotecs, Mixes, and Chinantecs from the Sierra de Oaxaca; with Mixtecs in Guerrero and Purepechas in Michoacán. I have dealt personally with other writers from the Huasteca regions and from the Sierra Tarahumara and collaborated in the organization of the First and Second National Congress of Writers in Indigenous Languages,[23] as well as in the creation of the Association of Indigenous-Language Writers.[24] These experiences have allowed me to appraise and weigh some elements of this evolutionary process. For example, the strong collective nature of some literary genres—narratives, drama, and songs—makes these genres interesting not so much as individual expressions of their authors but as group participations which include the spectators. Popular songs are heard during festivities; storytelling and plays take place at community gatherings. These arts are collective because they represent a process of linguistic reaffirmation in which the strengthening of the language and the collective memory of the community are more important than the subjective vision of an individual author.

The development of the Indigenous writer is a more laborious and delayed process than that of the Mexican authors who write in Spanish. Not only is it an individual vocation; it is also a project with collective consequences, influenced by many aspects of an educational and social nature and by the choice of which alphabet to use. Up to now, the definition of these alphabets for Indigenous languages has been done solely by official institutions, based on the opinions of Indigenous specialists who no longer form an integral part of their communities or those of non-native linguists and specialists. The agreements about unifying the use of different alphabets in diverse official publications have doubtless been somewhat useful, but they are not comparable to the real, productive literary use of those alphabets by authors who are neither "official" nor subject to the guidelines laid down by government programs.

Because of these factors, the Indigenous writers are confronted by a cultural commitment that obliges them to rethink almost everything having to do with their language from the very moment when they decide which alphabet to use. Other challenges, such as their formal literary training, come later. Among the Zapotecs of the Isthmus one finds highly sophisticated poets, masters of an art which contains national and regional references. Authors like Gerardo Can Pat (Maya), Juan Gregorio Regino (Mazatec), Librado Silva (Nahua), Víctor de la Cruz and Javier Castellanos (Zapotec), and Gabriel Pacheco (Huichol) are individual cases whose work shows a great deal of sharpness and elegance.

4

Generally speaking, contemporary Indigenous authors tend to write drama, essays, narratives, songs, and poetry. As I have pointed out elsewhere, the genres of the essay and the short story are often confused in certain languages, since short stories are considered to consist of the cultural, religious, historical, or geographical information possessed by a community or a region; they contain information that can be verified and that is compiled from diverse testimonial or documentary sources, very similar, in short, to historical research.

Similarly, the authors who write about customs, history, or traditions exercise their craft in a manner very like that used by the story writers. Both transmit information about probable facts or those related to invisible entities or prodigies which in themselves constitute "historical" information. When I was preparing the two volumes of *Escritores indígenas actuales,* I asked various authors for stories and essays; some gave me, under the heading of stories, what to me seemed more like essays, while others gave me as essays works that were closer to my idea of stories. This was the case with "*Alux,*" by Santiago Domínguez Aké (which I included in the short-story section),[25] and "El temascal," by Librado Silva Galeana (which I placed in the essay section).[26] On that occasion I remarked that the considerable weight of oral tradition has led to the emergence of a narrative art with a historical, medicinal, or religious content that makes artistic narrative similar to historical or anthropological research. In reality, from the Indigenous perspective there is no clear demarcation between a short story and the medical, religious, or historical *information* contained in a communal tradition. That is to say, it is not always possible to speak of fiction writing, since all narrative writing is based on traditional information and is therefore of historical and social value: in other words, nonfiction.

The criterion that I employed in order to distinguish between the two types of narrative was the idea of narrative sufficiency or autonomy: if a story was self-sufficient based on its *episodic, objectual,* or *character motifs,*[27] it was considered to belong to the genre of short story; if its composition required supplementary information or elements of research which were distinct from its narrative *motifs,* it was considered an essay or a chronicle. Nonetheless, the essayists (chroniclers and historians) partake of the literary art just as much as the "creators" (poets, short-story writers, playwrights) do. Such was the case with the classic Greeks and Romans: literature was everything that was written—science and poetry.

Narrative exercises a great attraction among writers of Indigenous languages. The majority of the narrators work with traditional materials; very few attempt fiction, perhaps because the traditional themes are extensive and still provoke a powerful feeling of cultural commitment.

The authors included in this volume are examples of these diverse trends in contemporary literature in Indigenous languages. Each of them has broad experience as a writer, researcher, or cultural promoter. From 1993 to 1999, I coordinated the publication of the Colección Letras Mayas Contemporáneas (Contemporary Mayan Letters Collection), which contained fifty bilingual volumes written by authors from Yucatán, Campeche, Quintana Roo, and Chiapas. The collection was financed by the Rockefeller Foundation and the Instituto Nacional Indigenista. This project gave me the opportunity to be close to the authors and to some traditional ritual officiants or priests. I met Javier Castellanos in Oaxaca around 1980, along with other young Zapotec, Mixe, and Chinantec writers. Those meetings are described in a book I published later.[28] I have worked frequently with Purepecha authors during several periods of residency in the lakes and mountainous regions of Michoacán.

In the annotations to the texts in Indigenous languages, the reader will find pertinent information about the alphabet and the approximate number of speakers of the language. These data are taken from the map *La diversidad cultural de México,* published in 2000 by the Consejo Nacional para la Cultura y las Artes (National Council for Culture and the Arts) through the Dirección General de Culturas Populares (National Popular Cultures Office). These notes do not always correspond to the annotations for the Spanish and English texts. For various reasons, I have included more lexical and grammatical information in the notes for the original texts. One reason is that at times the authors have chosen to present concepts in the Spanish versions that are different from the ones originally expressed in the Indigenous languages. This is the case with Jorge Echeverría, who uses the Spanish word *cenote* to express the Mayan word *ch'e'en;* with Enrique Pérez López, who has translated the Tzotzil word *ch'upak'* as *amole,* a nahuatlism, in the Spanish version; and with Román Güemes, who uses the Spanish word *huacalitos* for the Nahuatl *pilatekontsij.* Finally, I have attempted to make the published versions of the texts in Indigenous languages correspond to Spanish and English typographical customs, so that the comparison of the original text with the translations will be easier for the reader. In no case have I altered the original text or the type of alphabet that each author decided to use.

In regard to the Spanish texts, I have left almost intact the versions of five authors: Librado Silva Galeana and Román Güemes, who write in Nahuatl; the Mayan writer Jorge Echeverría; the Chontal writer Isaías Hernández Isidro; and the Tzeltal writer Diego Méndez Guzmán. In the other cases I have participated in varying degrees and circumstances in the editing of the material, whether in the actual writing in Indigenous languages or in the first or final versions in Spanish. During the editing stage of the publication of the Colección Letras Mayas Contemporáneas, I translated or revised the final versions of translations for almost all the works. For the present book I have newly revised the texts of the chosen works both in their original languages and in their translations to Spanish to such a degree that readers familiar with both books will find numerous changes. The most recent revisions of the texts anthologized here are the following three: the one written by Joel Torres, with which I have worked since it was a draft in Purepecha; the text written by Gabriel Pacheco, at his request; and the one by Javier Castellanos, who did not accept my revisions willingly, as he considered the final version "too Spanish." On certain occasions and in some specific passages, the authors have considered their narratives in the vernacular and the corresponding Spanish versions to be independent of each other. Nevertheless, Donald Frischmann and I have attempted in all cases to remain as faithful as we could to the original text, evoking as far as possible the unique mode of expression characteristic of the Indigenous language. In some of the notes for the Indigenous texts, we have also resorted to grammatical explanations in an attempt to clarify those passages where the translation was not successful in expressing the original meaning.

Finally, I would like to mention the case of Tzotzil author Jacinto Arias, which differs somewhat from the others. Given the importance of his actions in Chiapas and his numerous cultural, political, and literary contributions, we have included here, rather than a narrative in an Indigenous language, an excerpt from one of his works which is vital to the understanding of the religious nature of the Mayan communities.[29] This work is, among other things, the first approach to Western religion (Christianity) from the perspective of Mayan spirituality. It was originally written in English as a master's thesis in anthropology at the Catholic University of America (Washington, D.C.); the Spanish version is from the first Mexican edition.

In addition, Donald Frischmann and I decided to include in the Appendices the cultural, religious, or symbolic information that was impossible to summarize in the notes. We believe that the annotations to the texts, Appendices, lexical variants, versions, and preliminary studies will serve to provide the reader with a broad spectrum of information about the new literature in Indigenous languages being written and discovered today. This literature is making a place for itself in early twenty-first century Mexico and constitutes a significant part, though by no means all, of the literature in Indigenous languages appearing throughout the entire continent.

Mexico City
July 2002

Notes

1. See Carlos Montemayor, *La tradición literaria en los escritores mexicanos* (Mexico City: Universidad Autónoma Metropolitana–Azcapotzalco, 1985); "Los poetas neolatinos de México en el siglo XVIII y su contribución ideológica e histórica" by Carlos Montemayor, in *Congresso Internacional as Humanidades Greco-Latinas e a Civilização do Universal* (Coimbra, Portugal: Instituto de Estudos Clássicos da Faculdade de Letras de Coimbra e Livraria Minerva, 1988); "La revaloración del indio como origen de México," in C. Montemayor, *Los pueblos indios de México hoy* (Mexico City: Editorial Planeta, 2001), pp. 57–64.

2. S. G. Morley, *La civilización maya,* translated by Adrián Recinos (Mexico City: FCE, 1965).

3. Carlos Inchaústegui, *Las márgenes del Tabasco Chontal,* Anthropology Series (Villahermosa: Government of the State of Tabasco, 1987), pp. 276–277.

4. Marcelino Menéndez y Pelayo, "Introducción," in *Antología de poetas hispano-americanos,* vol. 1: *México y América Central* (Madrid: Real Academia Española, 1983), pp. viii and ix.

5. See Rafael Lapesa, *Historia de la lengua española* (Madrid: Escelicer, 1965), pp. 123–137, 209–293, and 341–364; Alonso Zamora Vicente, *Dialectología española* (Madrid: Gredos, 1960); and José Joaquín Montes Giraldo, *Dialectología general e hispanoamericana: Orientación teórica, metodológica y bibliográfica* (Bogotá: Instituto Caro y Cuervo, 1987).

6. Carlos Montemayor, "A manera de introducción" and "El cuento tradicional," in *Arte y trama en el cuento indígena* (Mexico City: FCE, 1998); and Chapter 1 of *Arte y plegaria en las ceremonias de tradición oral* (Mexico City: FCE, 1999).

7. The Nahuatl language, as Miguel León-Portilla has stressed, has a different history, since it has been practiced in its written form without interruption since the first years of the colony. See Miguel León-Portilla, *Literaturas de Mesoamérica,* Colección Cien de México (Mexico City: SEP, 1984), pp. 26ff. See also the catalogue of manuscripts in this language recorded by Ángel María Garibay in *Historia de la literatura náhuatl,* 2 vols. (Mexico City: Editorial Porrúa, 1953–1954), vol. 1, pp. 51–56.

8. For the case of Mexico, see Gonzalo Aguirre Beltrán, *Lenguas vernáculas, su uso y desuso en la enseñanza: La experiencia de México* (Mexico City: Ediciones de la Casa Chata, 1983); and Shirley Brice Heath, *La política del lenguaje en México: De la colonia a la nación* (Mexico City: INI, 1986), pp. 223–224; for information about the continent as a whole, see David Stoll, *Fishers of Men or Founders of Empire?* (London: Zed Press; Cambridge, Mass.: Cultural Survival, 1982).

9. See Aguirre Beltrán, *Lenguas vernáculas,* pp. 311–331.

10. For a more detailed discussion of this point in the works of contemporary authors, see my book *La literatura actual en las lenguas indígenas de México* (Mexico City: Universidad Iberoamericana, 2001), pp. 33ff.

11. Diego de Landa, *Relación de las cosas de Yucatán* (Mérida: Consejo Editorial de Yucatán, 1986), Chapter 7, pp. 21–22.

12. Bernal Díaz del Castillo, *Historia verdadera de la Conquista de la Nueva España*, ed. Joaquín Ramírez Cabañas, 3 vols. (Mexico City: Editorial Pedro Robredo, 1944), vol. 1, Chapter 44, p. 181.

13. Pedro Mártir de Anglería, *Décadas del Nuevo Mundo* (Mexico City: José Porrúa e Hijos, 1964), vol. 1, *Cuarta década*, Book 8, p. 426.

14. J. Eric S. Thompson, *Un comentario al Códice de Dresde*, translated by J. Ferreiro (Mexico City: FCE, 1988), pp. 14–19, particularly his allusion to Antonio de Ciudad Real.

15. See Víctor de la Cruz, "La flor de la palabra," in *Los escritores indígenas actuales*, edited and coordinated by Carlos Montemayor, 2 vols. (Mexico City: Editorial Tierra Adentro, CNCA, 1992), vol. 2, pp. 57–60.

16. See M. D. Coe, "Olmecas y mayas: Estudio de relaciones," in *Los orígenes de la civilización maya*, edited by R. E. W. Adams, translated by S. Mastrangelo (Mexico City: FCE, 1989), pp. 211–212.

17. León-Portilla, *Literaturas de Mesoamérica*, p. 19.

18. J. Francisco Molina Solís, "Historia de Yucatán durante la dominación española," in Carlos Castillo Peraza, *Historia de Yucatán: Antología* (Mérida: Consejo Editorial de Yucatán, 1986), pp. 192–194.

19. In addition to the previously cited texts by Shirley Brice Heath and Gonzalo Aguirre Beltrán, the following works may be useful: "Oralidad y escritura de la literatura indígena: Una aproximación histórica" by Dora Pellicer, in *Situación actual y perspectivas de la literatura en lenguas indígenas*, ed. Carlos Montemayor, Colección Pensar la Cultura (Mexico City: CNCA, 1993), pp. 15–54; and "La literatura indígena: Una mirada desde fuera" by Gabriela Coronado, in ibid., pp. 55–76.

20. "La flor de la palabra," by Víctor de la Cruz; "Vivencias de nuestra palabra: El resurgimiento de la cultura maya en Chiapas," by Manuel Pérez Hernández; "La computadora y sus aplicaciones en la escritura de las lenguas indígenas," by Jesús Salinas Pedraza; and "La formación de escritores en lengua maya," by Miguel May May, in Montemayor, *Los escritores indígenas actuales*, vol. 2, pp. 51–81, 83–102, 103–112, 113–127.

21. Donald H. Frischmann, "New Mayan Theatre in Chiapas: Anthropology, Literacy, and Social Drama," in *Negotiating Performance: Gender, Sexuality and Theatricality in Latin/o America*, edited by Diana Taylor and Juan Villegas (Durham, N.C., and London: Duke University Press, 1994), pp. 213–238.

22. See H. Russell Bernard, "Microcomputación y preservación de las culturas," *Anuario Indigenista* (Mexico City: Instituto Indigenista Interamericano) 48 (1988): 71ff.

23. See *Memoria: Primer Encuentro de Escritores en Lenguas Indígenas* (Mexico City: DGCP/CNCA, 1990); and *Memoria: II Encuentro Nacional de Escritores en Lenguas Indígenas*, San Cristóbal de las Casas, Chiapas, November 13–16, 1991 (Mexico City: DGCP, 1992).

24. This association was constituted in Texcoco, State of Mexico, on November 26, 1993, with sixty-four founding members.

25. "*Alux*," by Santiago Domínguez Aké, in Carlos Montemayor, prologue, literary selection, and notes, *La voz profunda: Literatura mexicana en lenguas indígenas* (Mexico City: Joaquín Mortiz, 2004), pp. 54–59.

26. "El temascal," by Librado Silva Galeana, in Montemayor, *La voz profunda*, pp. 190–195.

27. See Carlos Montemayor, "El cuento tradicional," in *Arte y trama en el cuento indígena*, Chapter 1, pp. 24ff.

28. Carlos Montemayor, *Encuentros en Oaxaca*, Colección Torre Inclinada (Mexico City: Editorial Aldus, 1995).

29. Jacinto Arias, *El mundo numinoso de los mayas*, 2nd ed. (Tuxtla Gutiérrez, Chiapas: Gobierno del Estado de Chiapas/Instituto Chiapaneco de Cultura, 1991).

Pasado y presente de la escritura en lenguas indígenas

Carlos Montemayor

1

He explicado en otro momento que la literatura mexicana comprende por lo menos tres grandes ramas de producción literaria,[1] todas importantes y de compleja y abundante historia. Comprende, por supuesto, la escrita en lengua española desde el siglo XVI hasta nuestros días. También la escrita en latín, lengua que se empleó ininterrumpidamente desde el siglo XVI hasta el apogeo de los humanistas del siglo XVIII, quienes formularon por vez primera el mestizaje en la idea de México y revaloraron la cultura prehispánica: Francisco Xavier Clavijero, José Luis Maneiro, Manuel Cavo, Diego José Abad, Francisco Xavier Alegre, Rafael Landívar, Rafael Campoy, entre otros. Y comprende, finalmente, la que proviene de las lenguas indígenas: la que se escribió antes de la conquista, durante la colonia y la que ahora resurge en varias zonas del país, a pesar de la constante descalificación de las lenguas y del generalizado desconocimiento de su composición artística.

El mayista Silvanus G. Morley afirmó, por ejemplo:

> Los mayas son esencialmente conservadores y opuestos al progreso; de esta manera han logrado conservar su propio idioma durante cuatro siglos de dominación española, al grado de que hoy en día lo siguen empleando en los trabajos del henequén y en las ocupaciones de la vida diaria, en todas las ciudades pequeñas y aldeas de Yucatán, en lugar del castellano.[2]

Curioso que para un mayista conservar la lengua maya sea oponerse al progreso. En esta misma línea de descalificación se sitúa un relato chontal, que justifica por razones sobrenaturales la eliminación de la lengua indígena:

> . . . antes, a las 12 del día no podían salir porque se los llevaba el *chibompan,* como le dicen. Se lleva ése a los niños, las muchachas, los hombres que se van a trabajar en el manglar . . . allí los encanta . . . los lleva . . . ¡Al que sabe hablar el chontal rapidito lo lleva! ¡Y al que no sabe hablar su lengua no puede estar con él, porque no le entiende lo que dice! Lo que hicieron los antepasados es enseñarle a hablar el español a los niños para que así no los lleve.[3]

La descalificación artística es más amplia. Al referirse a la poesía en las lenguas indígenas de América, a principios del siglo XX al reseñar la historia de la poesía hispanoamericana, el filólogo español Marcelino Menéndez y Pelayo expresó con desdén que no tenía caso ocuparse

> de los pocos y obscuros fragmentos literarios que de esas lenguas primitivas quedan . . . sino solamente de las que llevaron a América los colonos españoles y conservan sus descendientes. Si algo del americanismo primitivo llegó a infiltrarse en esta poesía (lo cual es muy dudoso), sólo en este sentido podrán tener cabida tales elementos bárbaros y exóticos en un cuadro de la literatura hispano-americana, la cual, por lo demás, ha seguido en todo las vicisitudes de la general literatura española, participando del clasicismo italiano del siglo XVI, del culteranismo del siglo XVII, de la reacción neoclásica del XVIII, del romanticismo del presente y de las influencias de la novísima literatura extranjera, especialmente de la francesa y de la inglesa. Esto no excluye gran originalidad en los pormenores; pero el fundamento de esta originalidad, más bien que en opacas, incoherentes y misteriosas tradiciones de gentes bárbaras y degeneradas . . . ha de buscarse en la contemplación de las maravillas de un Mundo Nuevo.[4]

Menéndez y Pelayo no alcanzó a conocer la vieja poesía náhuatl, maya, quechua o guaraní que se difundió a mediados del siglo XX, ni la nueva poesía que en más de veinticinco lenguas indígenas surgiría en todo el continente en los albores del siglo XXI. Tampoco pudo suponer que autores notables de la lengua castellana construyeran su narrativa a partir del influjo de una lengua indígena, como ocurre en Augusto Roa Bastos con el guaraní, en José María Arguedas con el quechua o en Andrés Henestrosa con el zapoteco del Istmo. Lo asombroso es que haya autores que sigan pensando como Menéndez y Pelayo.

Varias imprecisiones, olvidos históricos e incluso creencias ingenuas tornan confuso a menudo lo que debemos entender por literatura indígena y tradicional. Por ejemplo, creer que los idiomas pueden diferenciarse por grados de crecimiento y que las lenguas con desarrollo son los idiomas propiamente dichos y los otros tan sólo "dialectos." También, creer que las lenguas desarrolladas se hablan en los países hegemónicos y los dialectos en los pueblos sojuzgados. Quizás sorprenderá a muchos saber que no hay idiomas superiores; que todos son sistemas lingüísticos definibles en los mismos términos, con el ordenamiento gramatical necesario para una compleja gama de comunicación abstracta, simbólica, metafórica, imperativa, lúdica, a partir de un sistema fonológico particular. El náhuatl es un sistema lingüístico tan completo como el alemán; el maya es un sistema tan completo como el francés; el zapoteco lo es como el italiano, el purépecha como el griego, o el español y el inglés lo son como el ñahñu y el mazateco. Variación dialectal es un concepto lingüístico que se aplica a los usos regionales de un idioma. En el caso de la lengua española, se observan variaciones regionales a nivel léxico, fonético y sintáctico en, pongamos por caso, Andalucía, Buenos Aires, Bogotá, Yucatán o la ciudad de México.[5] De igual manera hay diferencias dialectales del inglés en la misma Inglaterra (Escocia, Londres, Gales) o en Irlanda, Australia, Jamaica, Boston o California, y del francés en Normandía, el sur de Francia, Argelia, Canadá o Haití. Sólo así es posible hablar de "dialectos" en lingüística.

Otro error, acaso relacionado con los divergentes criterios que se aplican a las culturas europeas y a las indígenas, es creer que las lenguas con tradición escrita tienen literatura y que las lenguas indígenas o de sociedades ágrafas tienen sólo tradición oral. Ciertamente, el término "literatura" como *técnica de escribir* proviene de la voz latina *littera* (letra), pero el concepto se refiere actualmente más a la noción de arte que a la de redacción. En cambio, el concepto de "tradición oral" en el contexto antropológico no distingue fronteras entre *arte de la lengua* (escrita o no) y *comunicación oral.* He explicado en otra parte,[6] pormenorizadamente, el *arte de composición* en las lenguas indígenas y en los poemas homéricos como una construcción compleja que no requiere de la escritura para fijarse ni transmitirse. Por ello he señalado reiteradas veces que las culturas indígenas de México permanecen vivas entre otras causas por el soporte esencial del idioma, por la función que desempeña en la ritualización de la vida civil, agrícola y religiosa. Y que en esos contextos de resistencia o continuidad cultural, las lenguas indígenas suponen un uso específico que es en sí mismo un tipo de *composición* que se destaca del uso coloquial en la misma medida que en cualquier otro idioma se distingue la composición artística de la expresión común. De este *arte de la lengua* es necesario partir para entender la dimensión de la literatura en lenguas indígenas de ayer y de hoy.

2

Recordar algunos elementos del opresivo contexto histórico y lingüístico que se ha impuesto sobre las lenguas indígenas de México podría ayudarnos a entender la relevante función social de la actual literatura. El dominio extranjero de las lenguas indígenas ha sido a menudo un instrumento de aniquilación o control cultural. Sorprende el talento de los frailes españoles del siglo XVI que en pocos años lograron aprender las numerosas lenguas indígenas del nuevo mundo y preparar gramáticas y vocabularios, aplicar alfabetos prácticos y escribir numerosos cantos, dramas, rezos y catecismos. Un trabajo portentoso, es cierto, sobre todo si añadimos su labor educativa durante varios años entre la aristocracia indígena. Pero esta erudición propició que los numerosos escribas indios quedaran a la sombra de sus patrones civiles o religiosos como informantes y que la escritura en las lenguas indígenas no estuviera precisamente al servicio de las lenguas mismas, sino al de la religión de los conquistadores, al de la catequización.[7]

El dominio de las lenguas indígenas que alcanzaron los frailes españoles del siglo XVI sólo es comparable con otro despliegue de lingüistas del siglo XX, también religiosos: el Instituto Lingüístico de Verano, que desarrolló un estudio admirable y minucioso de muchas lenguas otra vez para cristianizar, para traducir en ellas la Biblia y documentos de la evangelización protestante.[8] Este instituto produjo gramáticas y cartillas utilísimas para los programas de alfabetización indígena que el gobierno mexicano alentó desde entonces. Esto fue positivo, aunque por su orientación final representó otra especie de catequesis "cívica": la castellanización se propuso desaparecer las lenguas indígenas por considerarlas una barrera para la unificación nacional.[9] Por ello es significativo que a menudo se impriman textos en una misma lengua con alfabetos que varían según las instituciones o los lingüistas especializados.[10]

Por otra parte, debemos recordar también que la evolución de la escritura prehispánica en Mesoamérica había sido notable. Para pueblos que alcanzaron un conocimiento matemático, astronómico, botánico e histórico, como el de los mayas (y con ellos me refiero a un amplísimo territorio de Centroamérica y de México), la escritura no podía ser extraña. Quizás la abundancia de las lenguas mesoamericanas los persuadió a utilizar una escritura no fonética, que sería forzosamente regional; sino ideográfica, que podría ser universal. Esta escritura sufrió el embate de la conquista en múltiples formas, ya con la destrucción material de libros, ya con la imposición del alfabeto latino para escribir en sus lenguas, ya, finalmente, con la eliminación de la intelectualidad indígena y con el desconocimiento permanente de los letrados indios como autores reales.

Precisamente por uno de los mayores destructores de libros prehispánicos, Fray Diego de Landa, sabemos que antes de la llegada de los españoles, por ejemplo, entre los mayas de Yucatán

> las ciencias que enseñaban eran la cuenta de los años, meses y días, las fiestas y ceremonias, la administración de sus sacramentos, los días y tiempos fatales, sus maneras de adivinar, remedios para los males, las antigüedades, leer y escribir con sus propias letras y caracteres en los cuales escribían con figuras que representaban las escrituras . . . Escribían sus libros en una hoja larga doblada con pliegues que se venían a cerrar todos entre dos tablas que hacían muy galanas, y que escribían de una parte y de otra a columnas, según los pliegues; y que este papel lo hacían de las raíces de un árbol y que le daban un lustre blanco en que se podía escribir bien, y que algunos señores principales sabían de estas ciencias

por curiosidad, y que estos eran más estimados aunque no las usaban en público.[11]

Bernal Díaz del Castillo afirma que en un pueblo situado en el territorio del actual estado de Veracruz y en aquel tiempo sujeto al poder de Cempoala encontraron en un templo "muchos libros de papel, cogidos a dobleces, como a manera de paños de Castilla."[12] Acerca de ellos Pedro Mártir se refirió diciendo que los

> caracteres de que usan son muy diferentes de los nuestros y consisten en dados, ganchos, lazos, limas y otros objetos dispuestos en línea como entre nosotros y casi semejantes a la escritura egipcia. Entre las líneas dibujan figuras de hombres y animales, sobre todo de reyes y magnates, por lo que es de creer que en esos escritos se contienen las gestas de los antepasados de cada rey, y a la manera que los impresores actuales suelen muchas veces, para estímulo de compradores, intercalar en las historias generales, e incluso en los libros de entretenimiento, láminas representativas de los protagonistas . . . También disponen con mucho arte las tapas de madera. Sus libros, cuando están cerrados, son como los nuestros, y contienen, según se cree, sus leyes, el orden de sus sacrificios y ceremonias, sus cuentas, anotaciones astronómicas y los modos y tiempos para sembrar.[13]

Como sugiere J. Eric S. Thompson, estos libros en *papel* eran mayas.[14] Los nahuas, los mixtecos y los zapotecos contaban también con libros en piel de venado en distintos formatos.[15] Otros documentos escriturarios fueron las estelas mayas y, en general, las inscripciones talladas en piedras de lechos rocosos de ríos. A estos testimonios esculpidos debemos la noticia, por ejemplo, de que antes del año 400 a.C. habían aparecido algunos rasgos de la escritura maya, el uso numérico de barras y puntos y varios elementos glíficos con asociaciones astronómicas definidos ya entre los olmecas y mayas como el signo *U* para la luna, el *kin* para el sol, *lamat* para las estrellas y el motivo de barras cruzadas para el cruce de la Vía Láctea con la eclíptica.[16] Los glifos de algunas estelas de Monte Albán I son más antiguos aún, pues datan del siglo VII a.C.[17]

Sin este pasado de la escritura mesoamericana hubiera sido inexplicable la respuesta inmediata indígena en el aprendizaje de la escritura alfabética en escuelas que diversas órdenes religiosas establecieron en México, Oaxaca y Yucatán. A principios del año 1547, por ejemplo, Fray Luis de Villalpando persuadió al adelantado Francisco de Montejo para que todos los jefes mayas de Yucatán que lo desearan pudieran enviar a sus hijos a una escuela del monasterio para que aprendieran a leer y escribir. La respuesta fue inmediata: más de mil niños acudieron a esa primera escuela, que dirigió Fray Juan de Herrera. De ahí surgieron maestros que a su vez formaron a otros grupos de indígenas en pueblos de Yucatán que contaban con monasterios o visitas. J. Francisco Molina Solís señala entre los pueblos más aventajados a Camkal, Maní, Izamal, Cancenote, Tihosuco, Cochuah, Chikinconot, Tikuch, Ichmul, Xocen y Yalcón, y menciona como letrados indígenas notables por su elocuencia a Francisco Eván, del pueblo de Comcel, que en el monasterio de San Francisco, y con más de cincuenta años de edad, aprendió a leer y escribir y "toda la doctrina y moral cristiana"; a Nakuk Pech, autor de la crónica de Chicxulub en 1562; y a Gaspar Antonio Xiu, nieto del jefe Tutul Xiu de Maní, que escribía en español, maya y latín, y a quien el Ayuntamiento de Mérida le encomendó redactar, en compañía de Martín de Palomar, la relación que se dirigió al rey en 1597. Molina Solís aclara que desde luego

> no había pueblo de indios en donde no existiese cierto número de ellos que supiese leer y escribir y que pudiese redactar no solamente cartas, sino documentos, y aun algunas crónicas: los caciques, alcaldes y regidores por necesidad debían saber leer y escribir, y como estos últimos no podían ser reelectos, forzosamente había que contar en cada pueblo con cierto número de individuos que supiesen leer y escribir.[18]

Pues bien, estamos ahora ante el resurgimiento del arte literario en estas lenguas. Ante el resurgimiento de un análisis de las culturas indígenas provenientes de los indios mismos. Este despertar de los intelectuales indígenas y de la escritura en sus lenguas es uno de los hechos culturales de mayor relevancia en el México de finales del siglo XX y principios del XXI. Desde la perspectiva de investigadores no indígenas o de funcionarios culturales de los gobiernos estatales y federales, entender esta literatura escrita en lenguas indígenas supondrá entender los varios niveles, fases y objetivos que intervienen en su complejo resurgimiento. Impulsar esta nueva literatura supondrá también contar con obras de lectura en lenguas indígenas, con una producción literaria tradicional y nueva que esté diversificada en libros, folletos, colecciones, periódicos, historietas de colores y no sólo en libros de texto.

Cierto, hay un proceso de aculturación muy poderoso que acelera la pérdida de valores étnicos en muchos individuos y grupos. Pero resurge otro proceso, también poderoso y con una profunda conciencia de sus objetivos, que se propone fortalecer esos valores y consolidarlos a lo largo del siglo XXI. Podemos decir que estos nuevos escritores son muestra de un doble proceso: uno nacional, que corresponde al desarrollo y fortalecimiento étnico; otro personal, de compromiso con su historia de sangre y opresión, con su cultura, con sus lenguas indígenas que describen con mayor frescura y naturalidad nuestro territorio. Muchas lenguas han logrado sobrevivir y mantener aún el patrimonio religioso de sus pueblos. Entre otras cosas, ese patrimonio tiene como sustrato un pensamiento que el hombre occidental no entiende ya, pero que poseyeron los griegos y romanos de la antigüedad: que el planeta no es algo inerte, inanimado, sino un ser viviente.

3

Durante la década de los ochenta del siglo XX comenzó a darse en México este proceso cultural relevante del surgimiento de escritores en varias lenguas indígenas. La aparición simultánea, aunque no coordinada en sus inicios, de estos escritores en prácticamente todos los rumbos del país fue resultado de la evolución de las organizaciones indígenas mismas y de las acciones educativas provocada en México por las diferentes y a veces contradictorias políticas del lenguaje.[19] A lo largo de quinientos años otros investigadores nacionales o extranjeros han dicho qué son, qué piensan, cómo se comportan, en qué creen los grupos indígenas. Con estos escritores tenemos la posibilidad, por vez primera, de acercarnos, a través de sus propios protagonistas, al rostro natural e íntimo, al profundo rostro de un México que aún desconocemos. Muchos de estos escritores, laborando como técnicos bilingües en dependencias gubernamentales regionales o nacionales han participado, impulsado o enfrentado programas de educación y cultura. Desde 1990 algunas dependencias decidieron apoyarlos, pero el surgimiento específico de ellos no fue el resultado de políticas de gobierno, sino de personas o proyectos independientes.

La formación de estos escritores y el artificio de sus textos no son semejantes ni uniformes en todo el país. Algunas zonas e idiomas cuentan con mayor actividad e incluso con varias generaciones literarias. Cuatro ensayos son necesarios para entender este proceso: "La flor de la palabra" del zapoteco Víctor de la Cruz; "Vivencias de nuestra palabra: El resurgimiento de la cultura maya en Chiapas" del tzotzil Manuel Pérez Hernández; "La computadora y sus aplicaciones en la escritura de las lenguas indígenas" del ñahñu Jesús Salinas Pedraza y "La formación de escritores en lengua maya" del escritor maya Miguel May May.[20] Estos ensayos señalan las modalidades que fueron asumiendo estos procesos entre los mayas de Yucatán, los tzotziles y tzeltales de Chiapas, los zapotecos del Istmo y varios escritores de diversas lenguas tonales para quienes Jesús Salinas Pedraza ha diseñado programas de computación.

En el proceso de la literatura zapoteca del Istmo, por ejemplo, han sido esenciales los apoyos de militares retirados y de artistas juchitecos; en el de los tzeltales y tzotziles de Chiapas el proyecto de la Universidad de Harvard dirigido por Evon Z. Vogt, la tenacidad y amistad de Robert Laughlin y la asesoría del director de teatro norteamericano Ralph Lee;[21] con Jesús Salinas Pedraza y su esposa Josefa Leonarda González Ventura lo han sido la Universidad de Florida, en Gainesville, y el profesor H. Russell Bernard;[22] en el caso de Yucatán, mi participación aceleró la formación de un grupo importante de escritores. A estos cuatro procesos hay que añadir uno más, anterior a todos: el que desde la Universidad Nacional Autónoma de México impulsó Miguel León-Portilla y que ha sido relevante para la historia prehispánica, colonial y contemporánea de la literatura en lengua náhuatl.

He trabajado con mayas de Yucatán y Campeche; con grupos tzotziles y tzeltales de Chiapas; con poetas zapotecos del Istmo de Tehuantepec; con zapotecos, mixes y chinantecos de la Sierra de Oaxaca; con mixtecos en Guerrero y con purépechas en Michoacán. He tratado personalmente a otros escritores de las Huastecas y de la sierra Tarahumara y colaboré en la organización del Primer y Segundo Congreso Nacional de Escritores en Lenguas Indígenas,[23] así como en la formación de la Asociación de Escritores en Lenguas Indígenas.[24] Esto me ha permitido apreciar y aquilatar algunos elementos de este proceso. Por ejemplo, el fuerte sentido colectivo de algunos géneros literarios: los relatos, el teatro o la canción interesan no como expresiones individuales de los autores, sino como participaciones colectivas de los espectadores. Las canciones populares se escuchan en festividades; los relatos y el teatro ocurren en reuniones de la comunidad. Estas artes son un hecho colectivo porque se trata de un proceso de reafirmación lingüística en el que importa más el fortalecimiento del idioma y la memoria de la comunidad que la visión subjetiva de un autor individual.

El desarrollo del escritor indígena es más laborioso y dilatado que el de los escritores mexicanos que escriben en español. No es sólo una vocación individual, sino un proyecto de consecuencias colectivas, pues concurren muchos aspectos de orden educativo y social y una evaluación sobre el alfabeto a utilizar. Hasta ahora la perspectiva única que ha afectado la definición de estos alfabetos para las lenguas indígenas ha sido la de instituciones oficiales a través del juicio de técnicos indígenas ya no integrados en sus comunidades o de lingüistas y especialistas no nativos. Los acuerdos para unificar el uso de alfabetos en la variada producción editorial oficial es algo provechoso, sin duda, pero no equivale a la utilización real, productiva, literaria, de esos alfabetos por autores no oficiales ni supeditados al encuadramiento de programas públicos.

Por ello el escritor indígena se enfrenta con un compromiso cultural que lo obliga a replantearse prácticamente todo lo que tiene que ver con su idioma desde el momento mismo en que decide qué alfabeto utilizar. Después enfrentará otro tipo de aspectos. Por ejemplo, el de su formación literaria propiamente dicha. Entre los zapotecas del Istmo se encuentran poetas altamente sofisticados, dueños de un gran oficio y con referencias nacionales o regionales asimiladas en sus obras. Autores como el maya Gerardo Can Pat, el mazateco Juan Gregorio Regino, el nahua Librado Silva, los zapotecos Víctor de la Cruz y Javier Castellanos o el huichol Gabriel Pacheco, por su parte, son casos individuales de escritores de mucha agudeza y elegancia.

4

En términos generales, los escritores indígenas contemporáneos cultivan el teatro, el ensayo, el relato, la canción y la poesía. Como he apuntado en otro momento, el ensayo y el cuento a menudo se confunden en ciertas lenguas, ya que el cuento es considerado como la información cultural, religiosa, histórica o geográfica que posee una comunidad o una región; se trata de un material comprobable, de una información que debe integrarse por diversas fuentes testimoniales o documentales y que se asemeja mucho, en suma, a la investigación histórica.

Por otra parte, los autores que escriben sobre costumbres, historia o usos tradicionales operan de una manera muy semejante al escritor de relatos. Ambos transmiten una información de hechos probables o relacionados con entidades invisibles o prodigios que en sí mismos son información "histórica." Cuando preparaba los dos tomos de *Escritores indígenas actuales* pedí cuentos y ensayos a diversos autores; algunos me dieron como cuento lo que para mí se acercaba más al ensayo, y otros me dieron como ensayo lo que se aproximaba más a mi idea de cuento. Ocurrió así con "*Alux*" de Santiago Domínguez Aké (que incluí en la sección de cuentos)[25] y con "El temascal" de Librado Silva Galeana (que incluí en la sección de ensayos).[26] En esa ocasión señalé que la fuerte carga de tradición oral propicia el surgimiento de un arte narrativo de contenido histórico, medicinal o religioso, que aproxima la narración artística a la investigación histórica o antropológica. En realidad, desde la perspectiva indígena no hay una clara demarcación entre lo que es un cuento literario y la *información* médica, religiosa o histórica de una tradición comunitaria. Es decir, no siempre es posible hablar de un relato de creación, ya que toda fabulación es una información tradicional y, por lo tanto, de valor histórico y social, esto es, no ficticio.

El criterio que empleé para distinguir ambos tipos de narración fue el de la suficiencia o autonomía narrativa: si una historia era autosuficiente en sí misma por sus *motivos episódicos, objetuales* o de *personajes,*[27] pertenecería al género del cuento; si la historia requería una información suplementaria o elementos de investigación diversos a sus *motivos* narrativos, sería un ensayo o una crónica. Pero del arte literario participan tanto los "creadores" (poetas, cuentistas, dramaturgos) como los ensayistas (cronistas e historiadores). Así fue en el caso de los griegos y romanos clásicos: la literatura fue todo lo escrito, la ciencia y la poesía.

La narrativa ejerce una gran atracción entre los escritores de lenguas indígenas. Gran parte de los narradores trabajan materiales tradicionales y muy pocos se proponen relatos de ficción, quizás porque los temas tradicionales son muy amplios y aún ejercen un poderoso sentimiento de compromiso cultural.

Los autores incluidos en este volumen son ejemplo de estas vertientes diversas de la literatura actual en lenguas indígenas. Cada uno de ellos tiene una amplia trayectoria como escritor, investigador o promotor cultural. De 1993 a 1999 coordiné la publicación de la Colección Letras Mayas Contemporáneas, compuesta por cincuenta títulos bilingües de escritores de Yucatán, Campeche, Quintana Roo y Chiapas. La colección fue financiado por la Rockefeller Foundation y el Instituto Nacional Indigenista. Con ese motivo estuve cerca de los autores y de algunos oficiantes o sacerdotes tradicionales. A Javier Castellanos lo conocí en Oaxaca hacia el año de 1980, con otros jóvenes escritores zapotecos, mixes y chinantecos. Describí esos encuentros en un libro que publiqué más tarde.[28] Con los autores purépechas he trabajado con frecuencia en varias estadías por las zonas montañosas y por las regiones lacustres de Michoacán.

En las notas a los textos en lenguas indígenas el lector encontrará la información pertinente sobre el alfabeto y el número aproximado de hablantes de la lengua según los registros censales del mapa *La diversidad cultural de México,* publicado en el año 2000 por el Consejo Nacional para la Cultura y las Artes a través de la Dirección General de Culturas Populares. No siempre las notas a los textos en lenguas indígenas se corresponden con las notas a los textos en español e inglés. He dado una mayor información léxica y gramatical en las notas a los textos originales por diversos motivos, incluso porque a veces los autores optan por un concepto distinto al de su lengua cuando hablan en español. Es el caso de Jorge Echeverría, que usa en maya la palabra *ch'e'en* y en español la palabra *cenote;* o el de Enrique Pérez López con la palabra tzotzil *ch'upak'* que traduce al español como *amole,* que es un náhuatlismo; o el de Román Güemes cuando emplea en nahuatl *pilatekontsij* y en español *huacalitos.* He tratado que la edición de los textos en lenguas indígenas se corresponda, por último, con los usos tipográficos del español y el inglés a fin de que se facilite más al lector el cotejo del texto original con las traducciones. En ningún caso he alterado el texto original ni el tipo de alfabeto que cada autor decidió emplear.

En cuanto a los textos en español, he dejado casi intactas las versiones de cinco autores: de Librado Silva Galeana y Román Güemes, autores de lengua náhuatl, del maya Jorge Echeverría, del chontal Isaías Hernández Isidro y del tzeltal Diego Méndez Guzmán. En los otros casos, he participado en diversos grados y circunstancias, ya sea en los inicios de la redacción en lengua indígena, ya sea en las primeras versiones o en la última a la lengua española. Durante los trabajos editoriales de la Colección Letras Mayas Contemporáneas preparé traducciones o versiones finales de traducciones de casi todas las obras. Para esta edición he vuelto a revisar los textos en lenguas indígenas y las traducciones al español de las obras seleccionadas, de tal manera que el lector de ambas publicaciones podrá encontrar numerosos cambios. Tres han sido las revisiones más recientes de los textos aquí antologados: el de Joel Torres, que trabajé desde que era un borrador el texto en purépecha; el de Gabriel Pacheco, a petición del autor, y el de Javier Castellanos, que no aceptó de buen talante la propuesta por considerar demasiado castellana la versión final. En ocasiones y en ciertos pasajes, los autores ven como textos independientes el relato en lengua vernácula y su versión española. Sin embargo, Donald Frischmann y yo nos propusimos en todos los casos la mayor fidelidad posible al texto original y la mayor evocación de los giros de la lengua indígena. En ciertas notas a los textos indígenas intentamos resolver también con explicaciones gramaticales los pasajes donde la traducción no logró expresar el sentido original.

Finalmente, un caso aparte es el del autor tzotzil Jacinto Arias. Por la relevancia de su trayectoria en Chiapas y por sus numerosas aportaciones culturales, políticas y literarias hemos incluido de él no un relato en lengua indígena, sino un fragmento de una obra esencial en el conocimiento de la religiosidad de los pueblos mayas.[29] Entre otras cosas, esta obra constituye el primer acercamiento a la religiosidad cristiana occidental desde la perspectiva de la espiritualidad maya. Fue escrita originalmente en inglés como tesis de maestría en antropología en la Catholic University of America (Washington, D.C.); la versión española corresponde a la primera edición mexicana.

Por otra parte, Donald Frischmann y yo decidimos que la información cultural, religiosa o simbólica que fue imposible sintetizar en las notas se concentrara en los Apéndices. De esta manera, las notas, Apéndices, variantes léxicas, versiones y estudios preliminares suponemos que proporcionarán al lector una muy amplia información de lo que actualmente es la nueva literatura que en lenguas indígenas se escribe, se descubre y se abre paso en el México de los inicios del siglo XXI—una parte importante, ciertamente, pero no total, de la literatura en lenguas indígenas que emerge en el continente entero.

México
julio de 2002

Notas

1. Véase Carlos Montemayor, *La tradición literaria en los escritores mexicanos* (México, D.F.: Universidad Autónoma Metropolitana-Azcapotzalco, 1985); "Los poetas neolatinos de México en el siglo XVIII y su contribución ideológica e histórica" de Carlos Montemayor, en *Congresso Internacional as Humanidades Greco-Latinas e a Civilizaçao do Universal* (Coimbra, Portugal: Instituto de Estudos Clássicos da Faculdade de Letras de Coimbra e Livraria Minerva, 1988); "La revaloración del indio como origen de México," en C. Montemayor, *Los*

pueblos indios de México hoy (México, D.F.: Editorial Planeta, 2001), pp. 57–64.

2. S. G. Morley, *La civilización maya*, trad. Adrián Recinos (México, D.F.: FCE, 1965).

3. Carlos Inchaústegui, *Las márgenes del Tabasco Chontal*, Serie Antropología (Villahermosa: Gobierno del estado de Tabasco, 1987), pp. 276–277.

4. Marcelino Menéndez y Pelayo, "Introducción," en *Antología de poetas hispano-americanos*, tomo 1: *México y América Central* (Madrid: Real Academia Española, 1983), pp. viii y ix.

5. Véase Rafael Lapesa, *Historia de la lengua española* (Madrid: Escelicer, 1965), pp. 123–137, 209–293 y 341–364; Alonso Zamora Vicente, *Dialectología española* (Madrid: Gredos, 1960); y José Joaquín Montes Giraldo, *Dialectología general e hispanoamericana: Orientación teórica, metodológica y bibliográfica* (Bogotá: Instituto Caro y Cuervo, 1987).

6. Carlos Montemayor, "A manera de introducción" y "El cuento tradicional," en *Arte y trama en el cuento indígena* (México, D.F.: FCE, 1998); y Capítulo 1 de *Arte y plegaria en las ceremonias de tradición oral* (México, D.F.: FCE, 1999).

7. La lengua náhuatl, como lo ha destacado Miguel León-Portilla, tiene una historia aparte, pues se le ha cultivado ininterrumpidamente desde los primeros años de la colonia. Véase Miguel León-Portilla, *Literaturas de Mesoamérica*, Colección Cien de México (México, D.F.: SEP, 1984), pp. 26 y ss. Ver también el catálogo de manuscritos en esta lengua que registró Ángel María Garibay en *Historia de la literatura náhuatl*, 2 tomos (México, D.F.: Editorial Porrúa, 1953–1954), t. 1, pp. 51–56.

8. Para el caso de México, véase Gonzalo Aguirre Beltrán, *Lenguas vernáculas, su uso y desuso en la enseñanza: La experiencia de México* (México, D.F.: Ediciones de la Casa Chata, 1983); y Shirley Brice Heath, *La política del lenguaje en México: De la colonia a la nación* (México, D.F.: INI, 1986), pp. 223–224; para una información a nivel continental, véase David Stoll, *Fishers of Men or Founders of Empire?* (London: Zed Press; Cambridge, Mass.: Cultura Survival, 1982).

9. Véase Aguirre Beltrán, *Lenguas vernáculas*, pp. 311–331.

10. Para una exposición más amplia de este punto en la obra de los autores contemporáneos, véase mi libro *La literatura actual en las lenguas indígenas de México* (México, D.F.: Universidad Iberoamericana, 2001), pp. 33 y ss.

11. Diego de Landa, *Relación de las cosas de Yucatán* (Mérida: Consejo Editorial de Yucatán, 1986), Capítulo 7, pp. 21–22.

12. Bernal Díaz del Castillo, *Historia verdadera de la Conquista de la Nueva España*, ed. Joaquín Ramírez Cabañas, 3 tomos (México, D.F.: Editorial Pedro Robredo, 1944), t. 1, Capítulo 44, p. 181.

13. Pedro Mártir de Anglería, *Décadas del Nuevo Mundo* (México, D.F.: José Porrúa e Hijos, 1964), tomo 1, *Cuarta década*, Lib. 8, p. 426.

14. J. Eric S. Thompson, *Un comentario al Códice de Dresde*, trad. J. Ferreiro (México, D.F.: FCE, 1988), pp. 14–19, particularmente su alusión a Antonio de Ciudad Real.

15. Véase Víctor de la Cruz, "La flor de la palabra," en *Los escritores indígenas actuales*, ed. y coord. Carlos Montemayor, 2 tomos (México, D.F.: Editorial Tierra Adentro, CNCA, 1992), t. 2, pp. 57–60.

16. Véase M. D. Coe, "Olmecas y mayas: Estudio de relaciones," en *Los orígenes de la civilización maya*, ed. R. E. W. Adams, trad. S. Mastrangelo (México, D.F.: FCE, 1989), pp. 211–212.

17. León-Portilla, *Literaturas de Mesoamérica*, p. 19.

18. J. Francisco Molina Solís, "Historia de Yucatán durante la dominación española," en Carlos Castillo Peraza, *Historia de Yucatán: Antología* (Mérida: Consejo Editorial de Yucatán, 1986), pp. 192–194.

19. Además de las obras citadas de Shirley Brice Heath y de Gonzalo Aguirre Beltrán, pueden consultarse "Oralidad y escritura de la literatura indígena: Una aproximación histórica" de Dora Pellicer, en *Situación actual y perspectivas de la literatura en lenguas indígenas*, coord. Carlos Montemayor, Colección Pensar la Cultura (México, D.F.: CNCA, 1993), pp. 15–54; y "La literatura indígena: Una mirada desde fuera" de Gabriela Coronado, en ibídem, pp. 55–76.

20. "La flor de la palabra" de Víctor de la Cruz; "Vivencias de nuestra palabra: El resurgimiento de la cultura maya en Chiapas" de Manuel Pérez Hernández; "La computadora y sus aplicaciones en la escritura de las lenguas indígenas" de Jesús Salinas Pedraza; y "La formación de escritores en lengua maya" de Miguel May May en Montemayor, en *Los escritores indígenas actuales*, t. 2, pp. 51–81, 83–102, 103–112, 113–127.

21. Donald H. Frischmann, "New Mayan Theatre in Chiapas: Anthropology, Literacy, and Social Drama," en *Negotiating Performance: Gender, Sexuality and Theatricality in Latin/o America*, ed. Diana Taylor y Juan Villegas (Durham, N.C., y London: Duke University Press, 1994), pp. 213–238.

22. Véase H. Russell Bernard, "Microcomputación y preservación de las culturas," *Anuario Indigenista* (Instituto Indigenista Interamericano, México) 48 (1988): 71 y ss.

23. Véase *Memoria: Primer Encuentro de Escritores en Lenguas Indígenas* (México, D.F.: DGCP/CNCA, 1990); y *Memoria: II Encuentro Nacional de Escritores en Lenguas Indígenas*, San Cristóbal de las Casas, Chiapas, del 13 al 16 de noviembre de 1991 (México, D.F.: DGCP, 1992).

24. Esta asociación se constituyó en Texcoco, Estado de México, el 26 de noviembre de 1993, con sesenta y cuatro miembros fundadores.

25. "*Alux*" de Santiago Domínguez Aké, en Carlos Montemayor, prólogo, selección y notas, *La voz profunda: Literatura mexicana en lenguas indígenas* (México, D.F.: Joaquín Mortiz, 2004), pp. 54–59.

26. "El temascal" de Librado Silva Galeana, en Montemayor, *La voz profunda*, pp. 190–195.

27. Véase Carlos Montemayor, "El cuento tradicional," en *Arte y trama en el cuento indígena*, Capítulo 1, pp. 24 y ss.

28. Carlos Montemayor, *Encuentros en Oaxaca*, Colección Torre Inclinada (México, D.F.: Editorial Aldus, 1995).

29. Jacinto Arias, *El mundo numinoso de los mayas*, 2a ed. (Tuxtla Gutiérrez, Chiapas: Gobierno del Estado de Chiapas/Instituto Chiapaneco de Cultura, 1991).

The Indigenous Word in Mesoamerica

Orality, Writing, and Contemporary Prose

Donald Frischmann

From Monk's Mound to Cholula's Tlachihualtepetl: The Story of a Cultural Voyage

A long and fascinating road has led me to be a student of Mexican Indigenous literatures. I was born and lived the first twenty-two years of my life in a multiethnic neighborhood of European immigrants in Saint Louis, Missouri. In that part of the American Midwest, the harsh reality of most U.S. Native Americans was far removed. During my formative years, my image of "Indians" came from Western movies that my family and I saw on television or at the local movie house. In those predictable Hollywood productions, the Caucasians were the faithful bearers of "reason" and "civilization" and therefore were always able to triumph over the "Indians," who were invariably portrayed as barbarian savages whose speech and behavior appeared ridiculous in comparison to that of the whites. It would take me a few years still to discover that things were not really so.

The present-day city of Saint Louis was founded by French explorers at the point of confluence of the Missouri and Mississippi Rivers. Those black, fertile bottomlands were first inhabited by agricultural societies over 1,000 years ago. Saint Louis was formerly known as Mound City due to the proliferation of ancient ceremonial mounds. By the mid-twentieth century there remained but one reminder of those times past: the imposing Monk's Mound complex located on the opposite shore of the Mississippi in Cahokia, Illinois.[1] My family, however, never went to visit that ancient oddity. Even as a state park, it remained minimally maintained (despite several scientific studies carried out there) until 1989, when the State of Illinois added an excellent interpretive museum to the site.

I finally came to discover that wonder of the past during one day of curious wandering about in a friend's car. By that time, the Cultural Revolution of 1968 had instilled in many of my contemporaries an appreciation for worldviews that differed from Western or Christian perspectives. For my friends and I, the latter no longer provided satisfactory responses to our existential questions. Our searching for new, substitute values led us to study not only the Far East but also the marginalized cultures of Native Americans in the United States, as nearby as they were distant. Thus, I became aware of place names such as Taos, New Mexico, which had become a Mecca for young pilgrims in their anxious search for alternative values.

During the following two years my small world opened up enormously, and forever, as I took part in two high school cultural excursions to Mexico City. I was awestruck by that metropolis, the grandeur of Teotihuacán, and the cultural treasures in the National Museum of Anthropology and History. Although I still knew very little regarding contemporary Indigenous peoples, I had found another world that beckoned to me through its antiquity and the language of my maternal grandfather: español.

My Spanish-language studies and independent readings on Mexico acquired greater importance for me than my other high school subjects; this was due in great measure to the boundless enthusiasm of a young teacher, James Wiswall, who remains a dear friend. Later, as an undergraduate university student majoring in Hispanic Literatures and Linguistics, the demands of my studies and after-school jobs prevented me from again venturing south of the Rio Grande.

A few years later, following the advice of my mentor Dr. Enrique Noble, of the University of Missouri, I would enroll in the master's program in Latin American Studies at the Universidad de las Américas (UDLA) in Cholula, Puebla; this was another decisive step in my development. While in my literature courses we studied the great Mexican mestizo writers, my anthropology courses led me to carry out fieldwork in the Nahuatl-speaking communities near the Popocatépetl volcano. A year later, I returned to my place of origin due to a prolonged labor dispute at the university; nevertheless, I would never lose my interest in exploring ancient Mesoamerican wisdom through the Indigenous word itself. Interestingly, I had already experienced a cultural journey that would continue to repeat itself until the present day: from the largest Indian mound in the United States to Mesoamerica's largest pre-Hispanic mound or pyramid, Cholula's Tlachihualtepetl, "Hand-Made Mountain." Both have left a strong and indelible imprint on my psyche, and they cyclically demand my presence.

Throughout my M.A. and Ph.D. studies in Hispanic Literatures and Linguistics at the Ohio State University and the University of Arizona, respectively, the views of the vast Latin American Indigenous world were invariably filtered through *indigenist,* not Indigenous writers, who continued being passive objects rather than active subjects of the literary process. During the years when I lived and studied in Tucson, Arizona, my desire to go beyond the limitations of the degree program grew along with my presence at the celebrations and rituals of the neighboring Yoreme (Yaqui), Tono Ooh'tam (Papago), and Otam (Pima) peoples.

Some years later, I would renew that journey through my doctoral dissertation.[2] As a researcher of urban, *campesino,* and Indigenous grassroots theatre, I established friendships with some Yucatec Mayan actors and writers: Carlos Armando Dzul Ek, Feliciano Sánchez Chan, Miguel May May, and María Luisa Góngora Pacheco, among others.[3] In Volumes 1 and 3 of this anthology, works by these experienced writers are presented for the first time in English-language versions.[4]

My involvement with grassroots theatre has since grown ever stronger; the result has been two decades of rich experiences throughout Mexico's central, south, and southeastern regions. Through the National Association of Community Theatre (TECOM) and the Volcanoes Region Community Theatre Council I have come to share experiences with Nahuas, Yucatec Mayas, Tzotziles, Tzeltales, Purepechas, Totonacs, and Zapotecs (from both the Isthmus and the Sierra). I have learned about their histories, traditions, and problems, while sharing in days and nights of workshops, round-table discussions, performances, meals, and social interaction. Volume 3 of this anthology is dedicated to Contemporary Indigenous Theatre, with a special emphasis on that of Mayan peoples.

My professional ties to Dr. Carlos Montemayor also resulted from my involvement with Indigenous theatre. We were both working with Sna Jtz'ibajom, A.C.[5] (the House of the Writer), a nonprofit collective of Tzotzil and Tzeltal Mayan writers and actors based in San Cristóbal de las Casas, Chiapas. I had recently published studies on their work in the United States and in London. Carlos was editing their collective dramatic works, which later appeared as Volumes 1–3 of the second series of the Colección Letras Mayas Contemporáneas: Chiapas.[6] Carlos would subsequently accept two invitations to lecture and read from his own poetry at my base, Texas Christian University. It was then that we began to explore the concept of a multilingual, annotated anthology of contemporary Mexican Indigenous writers, featuring Indigenous-language texts, Spanish-language versions prepared by the authors and Montemayor, and my versions in English. All texts would be annotated, and the volume would contain introductory studies by both editors. The first trial was preparing in a similar format some fifty poetic texts that were to appear in a Mexican cultural journal. Six months of careful editorial work, combined with interviews with the poets, resulted in an excellent corpus of material that was never published, for reasons unknown to us. That material forms the basis of our Volume 2, to which we have added a considerable number of additional works by these and other poets, representing a total of nine Mexican Indigenous peoples and languages.

Simultaneously, I initiated a relationship with the national organization known as ELIAC or Escritores en Lenguas Indígenas, A.C. (Indigenous-Language Writers). I began to frequent its Mexico City headquarters, where I participated as a guest in special events and interviewed the first generation (1996–1999) of resident writers in what was still known as the House of Indigenous-Language Writers, located at Antonio Caso #33 in the San Rafael neighborhood. There I established an excellent working relationship with director Natalio Hernández (Nahua); Juan Gregorio Regino (Mazatec), ELIAC president; Feliciano Sánchez Chan (Yucatec Maya), publications coordinator; Apolonio Bartolo Ronquillo (Mazatec), coordinator for research and professional development; Isaías Hernández Isidro (Tabasco Chontal), library coordinator; and María Roselia Jiménez (Tojolabal), finance secretary. Natalio Hernández and Jiménez subsequently appeared as distinguished lecturers in my Seminar on Contemporary Indigenous Literatures. During those years of great effervescence for ELIAC and its "House," a solid working base and a constant media presence were achieved at the national level.

How This Project Was Born

In July 2000 I arrived at the Universidad de las Américas–Puebla as a Fulbright–García Robles Senior Scholar. My project was two-pronged: to teach a graduate seminar on Contemporary Indigenous Literatures and to prepare the multilingual anthology. Twenty-two students from the School of Humanities enrolled in the seminar; all were eager to explore this topic that was being offered as a first-time special course by the Department of Philosophy and Literature. The students were a fascinating, heterogeneous group: a Mexican majority, hailing from Mexico City to Chiapas, was joined by other young people from the United States, Canada, Nicaragua, Korea, and Chile. Our joint exploration began with pre-Hispanic and colonial-period Nahuatl and Yucatec Mayan literatures; our pathway then traversed the contemporary literatures of major Indigenous peoples, with particular emphasis on the Mayan family: Yucatecs, Tzotziles, Tzeltales, and Tojolabales. The seminar produced a good corpus of research papers; the students applied a variety of analytical models, including feminist, postmodern, and ethnoliterary criticism, that they adjusted to the cultural specificity of the Indigenous writers and literatures.

In August 2000 Carlos Montemayor and I sat down in the living room of his Mexico City residence to work out the plan and contents of our anthology. At that moment, a work emerged that was no longer one volume but three. That shift sprang from our decision to present each work in three languages and from our calculation of the resulting volume of material; there were many writers of great merit whose work demanded attention, and a multilingual format would respond to the needs of a broad Pan-American readership. From the start, we established a standard of academic and literary excellence for this pioneering anthology. We decided to present writers with decades of development and experience and a long-term commitment to promoting their native languages. Nearly all of the anthologized writers have authored books published by nationally prominent publishing houses. They are no longer *promising* writers whose work has appeared solely in cultural periodicals but dedicated, very *experienced* professionals. There is not an equal gender balance within this leading group of Indigenous-language writers. The preponderance of male writers in this anthology reflects this reality. Given the dramatic increase in fledgling women writers today, a future anthology of this type will undoubtedly include a greater number of distinguished women writers. Our present focus is not *recent* writing in Mexican Indigenous languages, however, but the work of writers who have already excelled in their craft.

One of the main tasks I assumed was to prepare English-language versions of all the selected works.[7] In January 2001, having concluded the seminar at UDLA and following a research tour of Yucatán and Chiapas, I started this phase of the project, beginning with the works in prose. Upon finishing our first version of this volume, Montemayor and I sought additional support in order to dedicate all of 2002 to preparing the following two tomes. For that purpose, we were awarded a grant from the U.S.-Mexico Fund for Culture, while I received a National Endowment for the Humanities Fellowship. Since then, our plan for the volumes has expanded further to include Spanish and English Glossaries of Indigenous-language terms and Appendices presenting essential elements of the Mesoamerican worldview.

In March 2002 I traveled to Austin, where upon arrival I joined cultural photographer George O. Jackson, Jr., in a dinner with Ann Hartness, the head of the University of Texas Library's Benson Latin American Collection. The following morning I personally offered our work to Theresa May at the University of Texas Press. Despite the fact that her desk was covered with impressive piles of work, she graciously received me and within a few days enthusiastically offered us a contract to publish this anthology. In mid-2003 my dream of Jackson's becoming the portrait photographer of the anthologized writers came true; a grant from the International Bank of Commerce of Laredo, Texas, enabled Jackson and I to travel over 4,000 miles by car throughout Mexico, photographing the writers and sharing a meal and brief but warm exchange with each. As a result, their words acquire here *a face.*

My starting point in preparing the English-language versions has generally been the Spanish-language versions. These were prepared by the writers themselves, by other writers from the same language group, or by Montemayor. To resolve some challenges of interpretation, I have also consulted the Indigenous-language versions, particularly those written in the Mayan languages (Yucatec Mayan, Tzotzil, Tzeltal, Tojolabal, Tabasco Chontal, and Totonac). In the course of their passage into English, those works whose discourse remains close to their oral roots have offered little resistance; others have constituted greater challenges due to their syntactic and stylistic complexity. These complex works surpass, to varying degrees, what Iván Carrasco calls *oralidad inscrita* (inscribed orality), to achieve excellent degrees of literary originality or *escritura propia* (original writing), while solidly rooted in the maternal culture's collective literary orality.[8]

I have also personally consulted with most of the writers, seeking numerous clarifications regarding linguistic and culture-specific elements in their works and their own professional development. To shake the writer's hand and become his or her student has been the most stimulating phase of this project. I offer my thanks to each and every one of them for their open-mindedness; this process has awakened new interests and concerns not only in me but, many times, in them as well.

Orality and Indigenous Texts: From Ancient Times to the Present

Since pre-Hispanic times, orality has been intimately related to the written expression of Mesoamerican peoples. Complex systems of writing existed among the Aztecs, Mixtecs, Zapotecs, Otomis, Purepechas, and Mayas. These cultures, inheritors and producers of Mesoamerican civilization, created a considerable number of painted texts in the form of folding books known as codexes, from the Latin *codex* (manuscript book).[9] These texts recorded and transmitted information of a ceremonial, divinatory, scientific, and historical nature; this content was rendered through ideograms—predominant among the Aztecs and Mixtecs[10]—and logosyllabic glyphs, predominant among the Mayas.[11]

The notion that oral expression has always enjoyed a privileged status among Mesoamerican peoples will serve as our starting point for this discussion. In its more elevated forms, oral verbal expression has been considered *sacred.* As Gary H. Gossen points out, most Mesoamerican Indian communities link language and dialogue to the dawn of consciousness in their creation narratives. Among the Tzotzil Mayas of San Juan Chamula, Chiapas, beautifully executed speech and song are considered to be the maximum human offering to the gods. Language is the metaphorical "heat of the heart" of the person who offers it up.[12]

This privileged status enjoyed by the spoken word is clearlyobservable in the Popol Vuh, the Quiché Maya cosmogonic text inscribed in the Latin alphabet in the mid-sixteenth century based upon previous glyphic texts. Here the primordial gods' successive creations of beings (from mud and clay and from wood) are considered finally successful when those fashioned from corn exhibit the linguistic ability to offer verbal praise to their creators.[13]

The ideographic texts have been compared to a sort of script for actors: the images were conceived as references or signs for a narrated or sung performance before an audience. For those who were able to read the painted manuscripts, they were "familiar roads" that their interpreters had memorized.[14]

Regarding orality and the Popol Vuh, Dennis Tedlock observes that at times the writers of the alphabetic Popol Vuh seem to be "describing pictures," with phrases like "this is" and verbs in the Quiché present tense. "At one point they themselves take the role of a performer, *speaking directly to us* as if we were members of a live audience rather than mere readers."[15]

With respect to the ancient Maya and Nahua peoples, David S. Stuart observes that common terms for "governor" or "noble," *ajaw* in Maya and *tlatoani* in Nahuatl, literally mean "he who shouts" and "one who is accustomed to saying things"; these titles may refer to leaders' fundamental role in public oral reading and not simply to ordering.[16] Thus oral expression enjoyed a sacred, ritual status in ancient Mesoamerica, where those who ruled defined themselves as their gods' earthly representatives and spokespersons.

Contemporary Echoes of Ancient Orality

This tradition of the public reading of texts still continued in the early 1980s; Allan F. Burns describes the annual readings of the Mayan books of Chilám Balám,[17] in ceremonial centers such as X-cacal, Quintana Roo. In massive public events, two "scribes" (*ah dzibo'ob*), responsible for keeping the books, took turns reading passages aloud and "improvising" on the "words of God" (*thaan hahaldios*) transmitted in these texts.[18]

More recently, the project Continuity of the Yucatec Mayan Collective Memory has followed this ancient tradition. Writer and cultural promoter Feliciano Sánchez Chan and his team of collaborators have collected numerous Mayan-language oral narrative texts. They have transcribed these texts, translated them into Spanish, and published them in bilingual format in the volume entitled *Del sabucán del abuelo* (From Grandfather's *Sabucán*).[19] In this project, orality and writing enter into a dynamic relationship in which the latter serves to reinforce the former. Sánchez Chan explains:

> In our attempt to bring the oral tradition back to the realm of everyday orality, publishing a book is not the

end, but just a way to place Mayan knowledge on an equal footing with modern forms of learning. The book, therefore, is an important tool in our attempt to permeate the Mayan children's sector with the contents of our social memory.

The project's aim is to "restore the important role of adults in cultural transmission and continuity" through the oral tradition. The tradition is resown and reinforced in the community through public readings carried out by youth; children are asked to summarize narratives they hear in the form of drawings, a mnemonic device that has given positive results in the retransmission of the cultural content. *Del sabucán del abuelo* includes mainly texts belonging to a specific Mayan discourse category, *jadzutz tzikbalo'ob,* that includes "fables, stories, and narratives regarding spooks, complemented with real-life tales that are very common to the region."[20]

Sánchez Chan explains that the presence of the book in the public readings lends special status and prestige to the narratives and attracts greater attention; he additionally reports that the project has had very good results: despite problems of intergenerational communication, children, young people, and adults have come together as links in the process of cultural transmission through oral narrative. Furthermore, in transcribing the recorded narratives, a process of "restoration" is carried out: those lexical and syntactic elements that have infiltrated the Mayan language from Spanish are replaced with neglected or forgotten elements of the maternal tongue. At the same time, the transcriptions retain basic elements of the narrators' oral discourse (formulae, repetitions, pauses, etc.). The public readings, therefore, have as an additional goal "restoring" Mayan-language oral expression to its fullest forms.[21]

The Progressive Loss of Indigenous Writing

The imposition of alphabetic writing, a pillar of the Western Renaissance, began with the Spanish conquest. The Franciscans and other religious orders appropriated the written Indigenous word—now represented in Latin characters—to spread the faith and make Mesoamerican religious practices known among the clergy. This process was motivated in part by the intellectual curiosity of true ethnographer-humanists such as Friar Bernardino de Sahagún; but more importantly, its purpose was to facilitate the imposition of the new faith.

Faced with this situation, the intelligentsia of the diverse Indigenous cultures began to create strategies of adaptation and resistance. One such strategy consisted in the creation of new "colonial" codices, which were produced in considerable numbers in the eighteenth century; their updated content was rendered through glyphs as well as alphabetic writing. In the alphabetic *Títulos primordiales* (The Supreme Titles), of Nahuatl, Mayan, Zapotec, Mixtec, and Otomi origin, among others, Indigenous peoples established the history of their varied lineages to assure and recover lands and privileges within the new colonial order. At the same time, a more clandestine appropriation of the alphabet resulted in works such as the Mayan Chilám Balám books.

With respect to Indigenous orality and literature during the colonial period, Dora Pellicer points out:

> While Christian thought limited Indigenous languages to an instrumental and informative role, they nevertheless maintained their own space in the everyday life of Indo-American communities; and from the seventeenth century on, they were vigorously tied to Indian resistance movements against the sociocultural order of the vice-royalty. *Indigenous literary creation* continued to reproduce itself, linked to *orality.*[22]

As a consequence of the linguistic policies of the colonial period and later the postindependence period that favored Spanish as the hegemonic and supposedly "unifying" tongue, the realm of communication became split into two distinct spheres: *native languages–orality,* on one hand, and *Spanish-writing,* on the other. Pellicer observes that "the latter erased from Indigenous linguistic consciousness the memory of writing in their languages and granted an ahistoric recognition to the absence of a written social practice in these languages."[23]

Regarding the effects of colonialism on Indigenous writing, Walter Mignolo comments:

> The conflict of literacies in the colonial period went hand in hand with a redistribution of forces according to which European languages became the language of the empire, and Amerindian languages survived in oral form, in marginal adaptations of alphabetic script, and in the decreasing influence (and eventual disappearance) of Amerindian writing systems.[24]

Indeed, Indigenous literatures became *marginal* even though they were expressed in languages of a *majority.*

As León-Portilla points out:

> With few exceptions, the oral tradition became the only vehicle for that which had been preserved and continued to be conceived within the boundaries of the community. The native word lived on only in the hearts of those who viewed it as a treasure. Thus survived deep-rooted forms of narrative, including some concerning ancient beliefs; chants that were generally intoned in public; and varied forms of acting with dance and music, some of which may qualify as drama.[25]

This predominant orality remains today a product of the chronic illiteracy found among Mexico's Indigenous peoples; Laughlin comments:

> Since few Zinacantecos read or write in their own language, tales are the sole means for relating the deeds of the past. If storytelling is not appreciated as an art in itself, nevertheless folktales are valued as part of the town's treasure.[26]

In addition to these tales and narratives, numerous ritual texts live on in oral form in Mesoamerican Indigenous cultures and are the dominion of ceremonial officiants.[27] These texts are extremely detailed and precise in their content and are transmitted without visual aids (such as that formerly provided by the painted books). The concept of *escrituralidad,* a term we might translate as "the condition of that which approximates writing," has been applied to this phenomenon. *Escrituralidad* places forms of orality on the same level as a type of "nongraphic writing." The authors of the book *Función gramática didáctica del huichol* (Grammatical-Didactic Function of Huichol) explain:

> We might imagine that there are other forms of writing that are not materialized in an external physical medium, but rather [in] . . . the ability to elaborate and formulate complex thoughts in complex semantic and grammatical structures.[28]

Within the realm of spoken language, a distinction is therefore drawn between *oral language,* "characteristic of everyday communication,"[29] and

> *escritural*[30] *language,* the sacred language of the *mara'akate* in which the ancient history of the ancestors is narrated. This is a complex language (register) that is not used in everyday life but rather in fiestas and rituals. *Escritural* texts are stored in biological memory; that is, in the memory of some individuals who, from childhood, learn them to pass them on to subsequent generations.[31]

This *escritural* language is learned in special ways, by "participating in the fiestas, in the hunts, in the rituals of the agricultural cycle, and in the peyote pilgrimages."[32]

One of the responsibilities assumed by the writers that we present in this volume is the expression, dissemination, and continuity of their peoples' traditional knowledge, which they have inherited largely through the spoken word. The following discussion examines the nature of this task and the various ways in which contemporary Indigenous writers reflect this heritage in their works.

New Indigenous Literatures

It is natural that in their quest to establish a new *written* literature the starting point for today's new writers has been their existing literary tradition. As we have seen, this tradition has existed in the form of writing and/or orality.

Montemayor points out that "the sources of Indigenous peoples' oral tradition are not 'primitive': they include at least Spanish written and oral tradition and the *written* and oral tradition of pre-Hispanic civilization."[33] Furthermore: "In the case of Mexico's Indigenous languages, the narrator is relaying to the audience a story regarding the community's most profound reality: its history, geography, religion, or cultural tradition."[34]

While a non-Indigenous receptor would probably interpret such stories as fantastic and fictitious, the Indigenous receptor generally would not doubt their veracity.[35] Events that a Western receptor would term "magical" fit perfectly within the Indigenous concept of everyday reality; this reality is characterized by the coexistence of planes or levels of reality: that of human beings and that of the ancient and contemporary deities, both pre-Hispanic and Catholic. The two worlds touch, are interdependent, and are expressed through oral and written literature. With regard to the Tzotziles of Zinacantán, in the Chiapas Highlands, Laughlin observes that "often the course of history is shaped by the intervention of spirits drawn from Zinacantán's pantheon."[36] In fact, this coexistence between the human and supernatural communities is a central motif in the narratives of Mayan writers María Luisa Góngora Pacheco, Miguel May May, and Jorge Echeverría Lope as well as in those of Diego Méndez Guzmán (Tzeltal), Jacinto Arias (Tzotzil), Joel Torres Sánchez (Purepecha), Román Güemes Jiménez (Nahua), María Roselia Jiménez (Tojolabal), and Isaías Hernández Isidro (Tabasco Chontal).

In this volume we include two narratives that are very close to the model of *inscribed orality* proposed by Carrasco with respect to the literature of Chile's Mapuche people.[37] When transcribed, the oral texts surpass their state of *absolute orality:* their oral textuality is adapted to the written medium, and the texts are often translated into Spanish or some other modern language. This "trans-encoding" grants a double mode of existence to these narratives: both oral and written form, in their original language and in other secondary languages. In this way, they transcend intraculturality and enter into the context of national and world literature. In moving from orality to writing, however, the narratives become decontextualized from their original linguistic and extralinguistic situation and meaning.[38] Certainly, reading a narrative that has been transcribed and perhaps translated to another language is not the same as listening to the Indigenous narrator while sharing in the warmth of the family's cooking fire in the mountains of Oaxaca or Chiapas. Gestures, intonation patterns, facial expressions, and perhaps a ritual context become lost in the transcription and translation. Oral narrative is not the same as inscribed orality; nor is it what we seek to present in this volume. Nevertheless, we must not underestimate the great value of partially decontextualized texts or original Indigenous writing as included in this anthology, as they all constitute intercultural bridges in their own right.

Perhaps the closest example to what at first glance may seem to be "inscribed orality" is "Poverty" by Mayan cultural promoter and actress *María Luisa Góngora Pacheco.* This narrative begins in the following manner: "Señor Aurelio Zumárraga tells that there was once a certain elderly woman whose name was Poverty, and she lived on the outskirts of town."[39] This narrative did not pass from the narrator's mouth to the written page without changes, however. The author modified at least two motifs: she substituted the native *huaya* for the exotic fig tree; and the allegorical protagonist assumed the name "Pobreza" (Poverty) rather than "Miseria" (Extreme Poverty), because the latter does not exist in her cultural environment.[40] Therefore, this narrative, which has appeared in similar forms around the world,[41] underwent a typical adjustment to its medium as it was filtered through the writer's pen.

In a similar manner, Tojolabal bilingual teacher and cultural promoter *María Roselia Jiménez* places the following epigraph to "A Tale from Our Grandfathers and Great-Great-Grandfathers": "As told by Señora Trinidad Pérez García, from the town of Lomantam, Municipality of Las Margaritas, Chiapas."[42] This narrative takes place in an ancient, mythic time, when marvelous occurrences still took place, such as those retold here. Oral history serves to preserve and transmit such occurrences, which are not included in historical discourse written from a Western perspective. One of the greatest responsibilities assumed by these two writers is to adjust the oral texts that they have collected to their new written form, which in itself is a contribution to their preservation and future retransmission.

Oral material also serves as a starting point for what Carrasco calls *escritura propia* (original writing). In these cases, the success of the writer, like that of all good traditional narrators, is measured by his/her ability to employ specific motifs; these motifs, according to Indigenous narrative tradition, are considered the *sine qua non* of a legitimate narration.[43] In my experience, the use of certain character motifs generally determines which object and episodic motifs are appropriate or inappropriate. Around this nucleus, the narrators often leave their original mark, be it within an oral or a written mode of transmission. Regarding the orality of Tzotzil narrators in Zinacantán, Chiapas, Laughlin observes:

> Despite enormous variations in style and content, Zinacantec narrators emphasize that they are merely repeating the ancient words handed down by their parents, grandparents, and, rarely, great-grandparents. Innovations are frequent, but they are never acknowledged. A tale speaks time-honored truths; conscious alterations are deemed lies.[44]

Thus, in his original story "The Secret of the Zutz'baläm," Tabasco Chontal (Yokot'an) writer *Isaías Hernández Isidro* makes good use of motifs common to the cycle of narratives regarding an ancient protective deity of the Yokot'an people, the Zutz'baläm (literally, Bat-Jaguar). True to traditional episodic motifs, the Zutz'baläm in this story is born of a human mother; lives in darkness by day and flies by night; is omniscient regarding the personal lives of all humans with whom he has contact; leaves his human home at age twelve to join the other Zutz'baläms on a mythical island homeland; indicates imminent weather and disasters through his behavior; and severely punishes anyone who does not maintain respect and secrecy regarding contact with him.

While this is not a strict example of inscribed orality, the writer's sources of inspiration do not go without due recognition. On the dedication page to his volume *Cha' jop'e t'ok chap'e älkan/Las doce verdades* (The Twelve Truths), Hernández Isidro acknowledges: "In this work appear the names of my grandfathers, grandmothers, my father, my mother. They raised me immersed in my people's tales."[45]

In the volume's final narrative, "El viejo y la Zutz'baläm" (The Old Man and the Zutz'baläm), the grandfather, finding himself face to face with the deity, receives the following charge:

> "Go and tell them, you know who, so they do not forget that we exist." The old man left. Only he had the fortune of meeting a Zutz'baläm, there in Tecolutilla.
>
> Ever since, every Monday Celestino made an offering to the Zutz'baläm, who took him away when he had finished telling these stories: "The Twelve Truths."[46]

This brief narrative is in fact a personal testimony. The Yokot'an-language title of the volume, *Cha' jop'e t'ok chap'e älkan,* literally means "The Twelve Experiences" or "The Twelve Truths";[47] that is, the book is presented as a collection of writings based on the author's personal experiences and those of others, particularly those of his primary source, his grandfather Celestino. Celestino, when narrating these experiences to his grandson, always first requested the permission of the Zutz'baläm. The author admits that throughout the creative process he was fearful of writing on this theme, since he himself had personally witnessed a Zutz'baläm that was born in his hometown;[48] he felt blocked and that his writing was not progressing. Finally one night he dreamt that he "was flying very high" on the back of a Zutz'baläm. Upon landing, he encountered his grandfather standing next to several Zutz'baläms. The following day his grandfather assured him that the deities he had dreamt about had given him permission to continue with his book. From then on, Hernández Isidro's writing flowed; and within a month the volume was complete. Once he had delivered it for publication, his grandfather Celestino passed away, as if he had fulfilled his mission.[49]

I have a very fond memory of my interview of August 14, 1998, with Isaías in a classroom within Mexico City's Casa de los Escritores en Lenguas Indígenas. Daylight was fading away as the interview progressed; Isaías continued to talk. He demonstrated a strong impulse to set forth the facts behind his stories; not even the invading darkness could interrupt his telling of the most intimate details behind his book. At that moment, I realized that I had gained access to very privileged information that I had to take quite seriously. These were not tales from the remote past or of fantastic creatures, but rather the experiences and profound beliefs of a very sane person whom I was facing; to the present day I share his respect for the Zutz'baläm.

The figure of the grandfather as a privileged source of knowledge once again appears in "A Story about Yum Tziles," by Mayan writer and cultural promoter *Miguel Ángel May May.* This writer also makes good use of traditional motifs, in this case those common to the cycle of narratives regarding the Mayan Nature Guardians. True to traditional episodic motifs, the Yum Tziles appear to individuals whom they specially choose to perform the task of *jmeno'ob* (see Appendix A) and whom they invite to enter into a type of apprenticeship. It is the Mayan *jmeno'ob* who perform the all-important Ch'a' Cháak ceremonies in which they implore the Yum Tziles to provide rain for the crops.

The protagonist of this narrative, Clavio, relays to another person his extraordinary encounter with four supernatural beings. The other man tells him: "Yes, it was the Yum Tziles who took you away. I now remember my grandfather told me that they had taken another person away."[50] This reference is yet another homage to the most important bearers of community history: the elders.

In the text by Tzeltal narrator and actor *Diego Méndez Guzmán* entitled "Saint Ildefonso's Pilgrimage," he acknowledges "the elders" of Tenejapa collectively as his source. As in the two previous examples, this narrative is not presented as an exact transcription of any particular version of the tale but rather as an original literary work. It is apparent from studying Tzeltal narrative tradition, however, that Méndez Guzmán has introduced no substantive changes with respect to the versions he has heard throughout his life. Beginning with the first paragraph, we observe a character motif common to Tzotzil and Tzeltal oral narrative: *the bad priest,* who "one day disappeared forever and, according to the elders, took with him Tenejapa's statue of Saint Ildefonso."[51] The collective Sna Jtz'ibajom, A.C. (The House of the Writer), in which Méndez Guzmán has served as writer, actor, and president, has staged the Tzotzil narrative *El cura diablo* (The Devil Priest) for puppet theatre. In this piece, a priest sends the town's men far away to deliver messages; in their absence, he seduces their wives. When he is finally discovered, he is banished from the community. With regard to this typical character motif, Laughlin points out that the Tzotziles of Zinacantán "do not bear fools or priests lightly . . . Here the vagaries of priests, their amorous adventures, are the subject not of humor, but outrage."[52]

While this motif is not central to Méndez Guzmán's narrative (which takes place in the Tzeltal municipality of Tenejapa not in Zinacantán) and the narrator stops short of such condemnation, it is nevertheless a priest whose act of thievery unleashes the tale's misadventures. This motif aids us in identifying this narrative as clearly being from the Chiapas Highlands. The central episodic motif, which we might call "the saint chooses his town," has obvious Christian and European roots; according to my experience, it is one of the most common leitmotifs in Mexico's Indigenous and mestizo oral tradition.

The volume *Narrativa P'urhepecha* (Purepecha Narrative) by *Joel Torres Sánchez,* is a watershed for the Purepecha people of Michoacán's *zona lacustre* or "lakes region" in their transition from orality to writing. The author explains that he prepared this volume in response to

> the fact that, in the communities that make up the Purepecha region, our mother tongue is being lost . . . mainly due to the loss of ethnic identity; the negative influence of the mass media; emigration to Mexican urban centers or abroad; and the lack of educational programs and their implementation.

At the same time, he remains hopeful for "a new dawn" prophesied some time ago, "the day when the oral tradition will be spread in written form among the new generations of Purepechas." The author also points out that

> [c]ontained in these four works there is a permanent recognition and tribute to the greatness of Purepecha oral tradition; from generation to generation, this tradition has managed to reach us as an ancestral tradition turned present-day reality in writing.[53]

The fragment we include here of the narrative "I'm Not a Witch, I'm a Healer!" is presented as a personal testimony of extraordinary experiences. The author acknowledges its resemblance to the Western genre of the fantastic short story and clarifies:

> Outsiders, knowing nothing of the Purepecha people, do not believe [all this], they say it isn't true, that they are just stories; but we know to what extent the inexplicable is real, and the point where reality becomes the fantastic.[54]

Torres recounts the life of Nana Delfina, a renowned healer of remarkable feats from his hometown of San Jerónimo Purenchécuaro, Michoacán. The author establishes himself as an eyewitness to events that were inexplainable, even for his fellow townspeople:

> What we saw was astonishing indeed: stuck up amongst the four electric wires was Nana Delfina, whose only article of clothing consisted of pieces of an old *petate* . . . She was elderly, and that was why my eye was drawn to her hair: very long, black, and shiny.[55]

At the end of his piece Torres manifests his intention to establish himself as a primary source of events and people from his town:

> I believed it fitting to write something about her; that way, those who know nothing of her existence will realize that *señora* lived, that she was there, she was part of the history of a town, and that many of us are indebted to her.[56]

In 2001 the second volume of *Narrativa P'urhepecha* appeared in print; it was given to me by the author during my March 2002 visit to Michoacán's lakes region. I came to know Purepecha hospitality firsthand as Joel invited me to eat native white fish at his Lake Pátzcuaro shoreside home; his mother, over ninety years old, cooked for us that day and impressively displayed the agility and sharpness of someone forty years her junior.

While May May and Méndez Guzmán practice what Carrasco calls "original writing"—making use of the memory (and not the accurate transcription) of narratives heard from their grandparents and parents—Torres, like Hernández Isidro, bases his original writing upon *original experiences.*

The title piece from *Tatei Yurienaka y otros cuentos huicholes* (Our Mother Yurienaka and Other Huichol Stories) by Huichol narrator *Gabriel Pacheco* is yet another example of original writing linked overtly and intentionally to orality.[57] Pacheco, recipient of the Nezahualcóyotl Prize for Literature in Indigenous Languages (1998), presents the stream of consciousness of a child whose worldview is entirely conditioned by his grandfather's words. The narrative is marked by the constant repetition of "my grandfather tells me" and "my grandfather tells me everything." Orality is recognized as fundamental for the transmission of ancestral knowledge: "He tells me that he teaches me the same things that were taught to him."[58] The child's Huichol identity—with a strong emphasis on the relationship to Mother Earth (Tatei Yurienaka)—is constructed through the contact with his grandfather.

Pacheco's prose is extraordinary and reflects a degree of formal preparation uncommon in his medium. In his "Prologue" to Pacheco's volume, Dr. José Luis Iturrioz points out:

> His studies toward the bachelor's in literature have allowed him to acquire a broad overview of world literature and to become familiar with techniques used in other literary traditions, oral and written, as well as different methods of literary analysis. Still unsatisfied, he decided one day to produce his own literary texts . . . gradually developing a personal style inspired by the traditional short story, but incorporating elements from both traditions.[59]

Cantares de los vientos primerizos (Songs of Bezelhao) by *Javier Castellanos Martínez* has the distinction of being the first novel produced by a Mexican Indigenous writer. We present here selections from Chapter 5, "Second Revelation," and Chapter 6, "Third Revelation." Castellanos' novel is narrated in first person and exhibits a certain resemblance to the Western *Bildungsroman.* The narrator is a young Sierra Zapotec who retells his adventures as a salaried researcher of his own cultural roots for a state cultural agency. The monologues of the enigmatic Trhon Lia stand out as true moments of "revelation": her heavy consumption of mezcal induces in her a type of trance state; from this state, with extraordinary clarity, she orally narrates the history of her Zapotec people, before and after the arrival of the Spanish. Her ancestor, Lia Kaxhon, assumed the extraordinary role of organizing the Indigenous towns against the Spanish oppression. She personally stood up to commander Reynozo, though she subsequently faced torture and death. Trhon Lia's orality, inscribed within the fictitious framing of the novel, emerges as a privileged source of historical information.

Our selection from Chapter 6 includes a distinctly humorous episode of cultural conflict: the Zapotec narrator recounts how his attempt to seduce a mestizo anthropologist earned him a jail term.

"Ancient Rope Marks" by Mayan writer *Jorge Echeverría Lope* presents a child protagonist,[60] a motif shared by several of the narratives in this volume. Young Súulub Chan Ek' (Little Star Bit) walks in search of a cenote or natural well called "Ancient Rope Marks" of which he has repeatedly dreamt. He encounters a series of personified natural elements along his way, some divine, who guide him in his search through Yucatán's wilderness. He finally arrives at the cenote, whose ancient and nearly forgotten waters will enlighten him.

While Echeverría Lope includes numerous motifs from his Mayan oral literary heritage, he pursues several objectives: to "practice writing in the Mayan language"; "make known the names of some cenotes found in this region"; and "make known that my town exists." The author clarifies his relationship to the oral literary tradition:

> I created this story, but based upon my experience of having heard many oral tales since my childhood from the mouth of my grandmother and others. The influence of the oral tradition is undeniable, but this was my creation. The stretch of forest the protagonist travels I have often traveled on bicycle since my childhood. Because I had gone up and down that path so many times, it suggested many things to me. All the place names are real, only I turned them into the names of characters.[61]

Through this outstanding example of contemporary Indigenous writing, the Chunkanán henequen plantation has been inscribed into Mexico's national literary memory. This little-visited area of the Yucatán Peninsula abounds in natural treasures, particularly the cenotes that are the central motifs in Echeverría Lope's tale. I cannot help but recall my visit to Chunkanán in February 2002. Jorge arranged for myself, my wife, Patricia, and two friends to travel part of "Little Star Bit's" route on a wooden, steel-wheeled "truck," mounted on narrow-gauge rails and pulled by a small but able horse named Jorobado (Hunchback). This was still the means of hauling henequen from the fields to the plantation's rustic processing plant, located several miles away. (The plant was destroyed in the October 2002 hurricane, and there are no plans to rebuild it.) We stopped several times along the way to descend fifty feet or more beneath Yucatán's limestone crust on metallic ladders; there we witnessed the magnificence of turquoise-blue underground cenotes. With respectful awe we recalled how, since ancient times, the Mayas have held their waters to be sacred. We conversed over dinner in the writer's open-air dining room, and I carried out an interview. When we left Chunkanán for Mérida, by then in total darkness, I had gained a firsthand appreciation of how a small boy might come to commune and dialogue with the wonders of the Yucatán wilderness.

"Chicomexóchitl: The Child the Church Devoured," by anthropologist, linguist, and Nahuatl-language writer *Román Güemes Jiménez,* narrates another child's search. The protagonist here is the divine Corn-Child, who seeks to find the only human being who still observes his memory: the *tlapopochuijketl* or "incenser," the "officiant at all the great ceremonies."[62] Child Chicomexóchitl or "Seven Flower" desires that the incenser tie his feet to the pathway of death; he is dying of neglect, "devoured by the Church" or by the imposition of Catholic practices that have replaced his traditional feast. In the end the narrator, the *fandanguero,* discovers a ranch where Chicomexóchitl's feast is still observed; he adds the sound of his guitar to the celebration. Though the child has already perished, the hope of reviving him lives on among ancient rituals in which sacred words are adorned in song.

Güemes' story transpires in "Temikiloyan, the place where one truly dreams"; "the place where a true dream might seize one"; "where those who are able to see, dream"; where "those who are able to conquer the darkest and most fearful distance" are found; "the place of the most desired eventuality."[63] And it is in a solemn tone of ritualistic repetitions and visions that the narrator names and remembers the sacred places and entities of these lands of the Veracruz Huasteca. To remain alive the deity requires the *tlapopochuijketl*'s incense, along with "those who know to name us with their speech, flowery and profound."[64] Once again, the written word serves to underline the vital importance of the spoken word in the survival of an entire age-old worldview, if not the continuation of life itself.

"K'ox and the Lord of the Water" by Tzotzil writer *Enrique Pérez López* also has a child as its central character motif: K'ox, "the smallest one," "the youngest brother." This character, also known as Xut, figures in an entire cycle of narratives well known to Chiapas Tzotziles and Tzeltales. Though in other narratives he is a child-god, in the version by Pérez López the child's human condition predominates, as a result of the author's decision to remove him from his divine role. Nevertheless, the character exhibits special powers when he establishes direct contact with the Lord of the Water. At the end of the narrative, however, the author refers us back to the child's human condition: "At home we have a little one; the latest in the family. He is our K'ox."[65]

In other narratives, K'ox is typically mistreated by his older brothers; he makes use of his cleverness to rid himself of them. By magical means, he makes them fall to earth along with a tree that they have climbed greedily to consume its fruits or a honeycomb. He then turns their inert bodies into animals, while he becomes the sun, and his mother, the moon. This narrative reminds us of the Popol Vuh episode where the Divine Twins take advantage of their characteristic cleverness: they first manage to make their older brothers also climb a tree and then punish them by turning them into monkeys. Once the Twins have also defeated the evil Lords of Xibalbá, they also transform themselves into the sun and the moon. In another version written by Pérez López, K'ox's greedy brothers are transformed into pigs and their clothing, into turkeys.[66]

In Zinacantán, Laughlin has collected several narratives regarding the Xut. In one version, the character is identified as "Our Holy Father"; he also typically turns his brothers into pigs. Laughlin entitles these versions "The Three Suns," since Xut and his two brothers are identified in one version as the three suns that took turns in remote times when there was no darkness.[67] The Popol Vuh contains a great number of narrative episodes that have been perpetuated orally by Tzotzil and Tzeltal Mayas in Chiapas, along with innovations and expansions.

The divine figure of Juan López from the Tzeltal area of Chiapas is central to the inscribed orality contained in the book *Jwan Lopes: Bats'il Ajaw/Juan López: Héroe Tzeltal* (Juan López: Tzeltal Hero) by *Domingo Gómez Gutiérrez.* In the author's words, this volume consists of

> the narratives of seven elders who, for many years, carried intheir hearts the story of an immortal man, the God of the "TrueMen [and Women]," the Tzeltal people; he who did not call himself the "Indian King," but simply *jwe' ijk'al xbojt'il chenek',* he who eats the large black bean. But in reality, he is the Ajaw or God of the Bats'il or the True Men [and Women], the Tzeltales. Those who, as children, lent their ear to their grandparents' talk have remembered him. Here in the town of Bachajón, Juan López was born and grew up, an orphan child of an undetermined father.[68]

The "Versión conjuntada" (Combined Version) by Gómez Gutiérrez follows. This is the most complete of the volume's texts in the sense that he includes all of the character, object, and episodic motifs present in the other versions, which were collected and transcribed by the author from oral narrators whose names are included at the beginning of each piece. In "Juan López, the Tzeltal *Ajaw* and Shepherd (Manuel Hernández, Swijlibjá, Chilón)," we find both an example of inscribed orality and the motif of the child or youth-god, extensively commented upon by Montemayor.[69] Furthermore, this book is presented as the true chronicle of a local god, an Indigenous version of history, which, to the present-day, has barely transcended the Tzeltal area of Chiapas.

Finally, two significant characteristics that Iván Carrasco observes with respect to original writing by Chile's Mapuche people are also present in Mexico: the creation of bilingual texts (in Indigenous languages and in Spanish) and the appearance of new genres in Indigenous languages.[70]

The ethnographic essay by Indigenous specialists strongly linked to orality began in Mexico with today's writers. We present here selections from two works that are fundamental for understanding the Yucatec and Tzotzil Mayas, respectively: *La milpa en Muxupip* (The Cornfield in Muxupip), by *Santiago Domínguez Aké,* and *El mundo numinoso de los mayas* (The Numinous World of the Mayas), by *Jacinto Arias Pérez.* In the case of these authors, the ethnographic genre came about as a product of the writers' professional training. Jacinto Arias Pérez (Tzotzil) has completed doctoral studies in anthropology at Princeton University. His book is based on his master's thesis, written in English at the Catholic University of America. Here we include his original English-language version extracted from his thesis, in which he attempts to reveal the profound differences in Mayan and *ladino* worldview, using as his point of departure the concept of the "numinous." Arias Pérez goes on to examine the uniquely Mayan interpretation given to the Catholic sacraments, such as baptism.

Santiago Domínguez Aké holds a bachelor's degree in anthropology from the Universidad Autónoma de Yucatán; he works as a bilingual cultural promoter for the Yucatán Regional Popular Cultures Office and has a marked interest in his Mayan people's complex agricultural science. Domínguez Aké states: "Here we must emphasize the highly important role played by the oral tradition in the making of this book."[71] He similarly gives thanks for the collaboration of over forty men and women, many of them already deceased, "who accepted with pleasure being interviewed in order to obtain the information that made possible this work regarding the cornfield in Muxupip."[72] His work contains extensive quotations from these individuals; they often reveal, in first person, the ancient wisdom of the Mayas, who are now divided between, on the one hand, traditional organic agriculture and, on the other, agrichemical products, whose effects are as swift as they are harmful to the environment and humans. Domínguez Aké promotes Mayan agrarian science actively by oral means, giving practical talks to groups of farmers.[73]

We also include the essay "The *Temascal*" by distinguished Nahua writer and paleographer *Librado Silva Galeana,* who was the first recipient of the Nezahualcóyotl Prize for Literature in Indigenous Languages (1994). This text is also related to Mesoamerican science, orally transmitted; it details how the traditional sweat lodge is constructed and made use of in his Nahua home community of Santa Ana Tlacotenco, which presently forms part of southeastern Mexico City's Milpa Alta Delegación. The *temascal* continues to be a living cultural element throughout Mesoamerica, though it varies with respect to the materials used in its construction, its shape, and the medicinal herbs utilized therein.

In conclusion, in this volume and those that will follow, we attempt to fill a gap in Mexican and Latin American literary and cultural studies. Carlos Montemayor and I have also been guided by the desire to inspire other people, Indigenous and non-Indigenous, to pay due attention, both critical and human, to the contemporary voices that address us from the depths of time—voices that resound in numerous tongues to create bridges of understanding, so necessary for the survival of age-old wisdom that is a critical part of our cumulative collective human experience.

Personal Acknowledgments

I give thanks for the constant support received from my parents, Harry Frischmann and Thelma Carril, so that I might achieve an education far beyond their wildest dreams; to my grandparents George and Catherine Hogan, who made that first journey to Mexico economically possible; and to my grandfather Esteban Carril, whose memory inspired me to master his maternal tongue, Spanish. May they all rest in peace.

I also offer my thanks to James Wiswall, M.S., for having taught me my first letters in Spanish and for having passed on to me his enormous enthusiasm for Mexican culture; to the late Dr. Enrique Noble of the University of Missouri–St. Louis, who inspired me to pursue graduate studies in Latin American Literatures; and to Dr. Carlos Montemayor, for having inspired me with his professional and personal commitment to contemporary Mexican Indigenous literatures and for having agreed to enter into this stimulating and fruitful partnership.

Finally, I especially thank all the writers who have so generously shared their work and time. Their Word is our best pathway for coming to know other cultural universes. The knowledge they share with us through this volume enriches all of humanity in a profoundly global sense.

Universidad de las Américas, Cholula, Puebla,
and San Miguel Nepantla de Sor Juana Inés de la Cruz,
Estado de México
2000–2003

Notes

1. A large ceremonial mound that measures some 100 feet high and whose volume equals some 22 million cubic feet. Monk's Mound corresponds to the Mississippian culture that reached its peak of urban development at Cahokia from A.D. 1000 to 1400. Some sixty-five smaller mounds today still surround this mound. Monk's Mound was crowned by a massive ceremonial and administrative structure that dominated an urban center of 10,000–20,000 inhabitants. In 1735 French priests built a small chapel, now gone, on one corner of the mound's first terrace; in 1809 French Trappist monks built another chapel on the same site, which they abandoned in 1813 (thus the modern name "Monk's Mound"). See *Cahokia, City of the Sun.*

2. Revised and published as *El nuevo teatro popular en México.*

3. Their works in theatre, poetry, and prose have been published and disseminated due in great measure to the effort of distinguished writer and linguist Dr. Carlos Montemayor. I have published texts and analysis of the work of Dzul Ek.

4. May May and Góngora Pacheco in Vol. 1 (*Prose*); Dzul Ek and Sánchez Chan in Vol. 3 (*Theatre*).

5. A.C.: Asociación Civil, a legally registered nonprofit organization.

6. Mexico City: Instituto Nacional Indigenista and Rockefeller Foundation, 1996.

7. The only exception is Tzotzil writer Jacinto Arias, whose work was written originally in English.

8. Carrasco has applied both terms to the literature of Chile's Mapuche people. *Oralidad inscrita* (inscribed orality) is the accurate transcription of the oral narrative. *Escritura propia* (original writing) is "made up of texts shaped by Mapuche categories in both their enunciation and content, though non-Mapuche categories may be included in the texts' conception" (Iván Carrasco, "Etnoliteratura mapuche y literatura chilena: Relaciones," *Actas de Lengua y Literatura Mapuche* 4 [1990]: 19–27). I thank Paulina Barrenechea for having introduced me to Carrasco's work.

9. There are also texts with a variety of dimensions and functions in the form of painted murals and texts on ceramic bowls, jewelry, and bone brooches; others were sculpted on stone as public monuments, many of which have survived the passage of millennia to give testimony to the complexity of Mesoamerican worldview and social structures.

10. See Elizabeth Hill Boone, *Stories in Red and Black: Pictorial Histories of the Aztecs and Mixtecs.*

11. See Michael D. Coe and Mark Van Stone, *Reading the Maya Glyphs.*

12. Gary H. Gossen, *Telling Maya Tales: Tzotzil Identities in Modern Mexico,* p. 84.

13. See Dennis Tedlock, prologue, translation, and notes, in *Popol Vuh: The Definitive Edition of the Mayan Book of the Dawn of Life and the Glories of Gods and Kings,* p. 169.

14. Elizabeth Hill Boone, "Aztec Pictorial Histories: Records without Words," in *Writing without Words: Alternative Literacies in Mesoamerica and the Andes,* ed. Elizabeth Hill Boone and Walter D. Mignolo, pp. 71–72.

15. Tedlock, *Popol Vuh,* pp. 31–33.

16. David S. Stuart. "Lectura y escritura en la corte maya," *Arqueología Mexicana* 8, no. 48 (2001): 52.

17. Books in the Yucatec Mayan language written after the Spanish conquest in the Latin alphabet. Their broad content includes materials of a religious (pre-Hispanic with a few Christian elements), historical, astrological, astronomical, ritualistic, and literary nature. Barrera Vásquez and Rendón point out that their sources are ancient hieroglyphic books, Indigenous oral tradition, and European printed texts. See Alfredo Barrera Vásquez and Silvia Rendón, *El libro de los libros de Chilám Balám.*

18. Burns presents the hypothesis that since the ancient glyphs were usually written in pairs, public presentations of those texts may have been carried out by two readers or performers: Allan F. Burns, *An Epoch of Miracles: Oral Literature of the Yucatec Maya,* pp. 22–23. With respect to the writing of Mayan glyphs in pairs, see Coe and Van Stone, *Reading the Maya Glyphs,* pp. 17–18.

19. Feliciano Sánchez Chan, prologue and ed., *Del sabucán del abuelo.* The *sabucán* is a sack made of henequen fiber in which the Mayan farmer traditionally carries food items and tools to the fields.

20. Ibid., no pagination.

21. Frischmann interview with Sánchez Chan, Mérida, Yucatán, February 22, 2002.

22. Dora Pellicer, "Oralidad y escritura de la literatura indígena: Una aproximación histórica," in *Situación actual y perspectivas de la literatura en lenguas indígenas,* ed. Carlos Montemayor, p. 31.

23. Ibid., p. 41.

24. Walter D. Mignolo. "Afterword," In *Writing without Words: Alternative Literacies in Mesoamerica and the Andes,* ed. Boone and Mignolo, pp. 301–302.

25. Miguel León-Portilla, *Literaturas indígenas de México,* p. 311.

26. Robert M. Laughlin, compiler and trans., and Carol Karasik, ed., *Mayan Tales from Zinacantán: Dreams and Stories from the People of the Bat,* p. 16.

27. The names applied to these officiants vary from culture to culture; see Appendices A and H.

28. José Luis Iturrioz Leza, Julio Ramírez de la Cruz, and Gabriel Pacheco Salvador, *Función gramática didáctica del huichol,* p. 125.

29. Ibid., p. 264.

30. The adjective form of the noun *escrituralidad.* We have decided, for practical reasons, to leave this adjective untranslated.

31. Iturrioz Leza et al., *Función gramática didáctica del huichol,* p. 265.

32. Ibid., p. 125; also see Appendix H.

33. Carlos Montemayor, *Arte y trama en el cuento indígena,* p. 22.

34. Ibid., pp. 20–21.

35. Nevertheless, today this division is spreading within the Indige-

nous community itself: young people tend to believe less and less in tales of transformations, nature deities, and so forth.

36. Laughlin and Karasik, *Mayan Tales,* p. 13.

37. See note 8.

38. Carrasco, "Etnoliteratura mapuche," pp. 21–22.

39. María Luisa Góngora Pacheco, *U tzikbalilo'ob Oxkutzcab yéetel Maní,* p. 15/*Cuentos de Oxkutzcab y Maní,* p. 13.

40. The author explains that the narrator, Aurelio Zumárraga, used both Spanish words in his narration. Frischmann interview with Góngora Pacheco, Oxkutzcab, Yucatán, February 18, 2002.

41. As Montemayor points out, this story has a long history that goes back to Greek and Hebrew antiquity; it subsequently passed through Italy and France before taking root among the Yucatec Mayas. See Montemayor, *Arte y trama,* p. 139.

42. María Roselia Jiménez, *Jna'jeltik/Vivencias tojolabales,* p. 48.

43. Montemayor points out that "the preserving of traditional tales is explained by the securing of a group of episodic, object, or character *motifs,* whose deletion or neglect would be equivalent to the death of the story itself" (*Arte y trama,* p. 42).

44. Laughlin and Karasik, *Mayan Tales,* p. 15.

45. Isaías Hernández Isidro, *Cha' jop'e t'ok chap'e älkan/Las doce verdades,* p. 7.

46. Ibid., p. 64.

47. Frischmann interview with Hernández Isidro, Mexico City, Casa de los Escritores en Lenguas Indígenas, May 22, 1998.

48. This experience is the basis of the narrative entitled "Dz'aji"/ "Cuento" (Story) (Hernández Isidro, *Cha' jop'e t'ok chap'e älkan /Las doce verdades,* pp. 21–22, 23–24). The Spanish-language title is deceiving, however, since it attempts to translate the Yokot'an word *dz'aji,* which means "that which you are saying about what you just experienced." Frischmann interview with Hernández Isidro, Casa de los Escritores en Lenguas Indígenas, Mexico City, August 14, 1998.

49. Frischmann interview with Hernández Isidro, August 14, 1998.

50. Miguel Ángel May May, *Lajump'éel maaya tzikbalo'ob/Diez relatos mayas,* p. 125.

51. Diego Méndez Gúzmán, *A'yejetik yu'un jtzeltaletik ta Tenejapa/ Relatos tzeltales de Tenejapa,* p. 51.

52. Robert M. Laughlin, compil., trans., prologue, and notes, *Of Cabbages and Kings: Tales from Zinacantán,* p. 9.

53. Joel Torres Sánchez, *P'urhepecha Uandatskuecha/Narrativa P'urhepecha,* vol. 1, pp. 9–10.

54. Ibid., p. 175.

55. Ibid., p. 187.

56. Ibid., pp. 194–195.

57. Gabriel Pacheco, "Nuestra Madre Yurienaka," in *Tatei Yurienaka y otros cuentos huicholes,* pp. 153–159.

58. Ibid., p. 157.

59. Ibid., p. 9.

60. Jorge Echeverría Lope, *X-Lá-Boon-Suumij/Vieja huella de soga.*

61. Frischmann interview with Echeverría Lope, Unidad Regional Yucatán de Culturas Populares, Mérida, March 19, 2001.

62. Román Güemes Jiménez, "Chicomexóchitl: El niño devorado por el templo," in *Narrativa Náhuatl contemporánea/Yancuic Nahuasasanili: Antología,* pp. 165–180.

63. Ibid., pp. 165, 166, 169, 180.

64. Ibid., p. 169.

65. Enrique Pérez López, "K'ox y el Dueño del agua," in *Alperes: Te'tikal mut/El pájaro alférez,* p. 151.

66. Enrique Pérez López, *El K'ox: El niño que se transformó en sol.*

67. "The Three Suns," #T13, T155, T162. In Laughlin, *Of Cabbages and Kings.*

68. Domingo Gómez Gutiérrez, "Conclusión: Versión conjuntada," in *Jwan Lopes: Bats'il Ajaw/Juan López: Héroe Tzeltal,* p. 117.

69. Carlos Montemayor, *Chiapas: La rebelión indígena de México,* pp. 117–130.

70. Carrasco, "Etnoliteratura mapuche," p. 25.

71. Dominguez Aké, *La milpa en Muxupip,* p. 131.

72. Ibid., p. 7.

73. Frischmann interview with Domínguez Aké, Mérida, Yucatán, March 20, 2001.

Works Cited

Arias Pérez, Jacinto. *El mundo numinoso de los mayas.* 2nd ed. Tuxtla Gutiérrez, Chiapas: Gobierno del Estado de Chiapas/Instituto Chiapaneco de Cultura, 1991.

Barrera Vásquez, Alfredo, and Silvia Rendón. *El libro de los libros de Chilám Balám.* Mérida, Yucatán: Producción Editorial Dante, 1989.

Boone, Elizabeth Hill. "Aztec Pictorial Histories: Records without Words." In *Writing without Words: Alternative Literacies in Mesoamerica and the Andes,* ed. Elizabeth Boone and Walter D. Mignolo, pp. 50–76. Durham, N.C.: Duke University Press, 1994.

———. *Stories in Red and Black: Pictorial Histories of the Aztecs and Mixtecs.* Austin: University of Texas Press, 2000.

Burns, Allan F. *An Epoch of Miracles: Oral Literature of the Yucatec Maya.* Austin: University of Texas Press, 1983.

Cahokia, City of the Sun. Collinsville, Ill.: Cahokia Mounds Museum Society, 1992 (revised 1999).

Carrasco, Iván. "Etnoliteratura mapuche y literatura chilena: Relaciones." *Actas de Lengua y Literatura Mapuche* 4 (1990): 19–27.

Castellanos Martínez, Javier. *Wila che be ze lhao/Cantares de los vientos primerizos: Novela zapoteca.* Colección Letras Indígenas Contemporáneas. Mexico City: Editorial Diana/CNCA/DGCP, 1994.

Coe, Michael D., and Mark Van Stone. *Reading the Maya Glyphs.* London and New York: Thames & Hudson, 2001.

Domínguez Aké, Santiago. *La milpa en Muxupip.* Colección Letras Indígenas Contemporáneas. Mexico City: DGCP, 1996.

Echeverría Lope, Jorge. *X-Lá-Boon-Suumij/Vieja huella de soga.* Colección Letras Mayas Contemporáneas, 3rd series, vol. 8. Series ed. C. Montemayor. Mexico City: INI/TRF, 1998.

Frischmann, Donald H. *El nuevo teatro popular en México.* Mexico City: Instituto Nacional de Bellas Artes/Centro de Investigación y Documentación Teatral Rodolfo Usigli, 1990.

———. Interview with Santiago Domínguez Aké (unpublished). Mérida, Yucatán, March 20, 2001.

———. Interview with Jorge Echeverría Lope (unpublished). Mérida, Yucatán, March 19, 2001.

———. Interview with María Luisa Góngora Pacheco (unpublished). Oxkutzcab, Yucatán, February 18, 2002.

———. Interviews with Isaías Hernández Isidro (unpublished). Mexico City, May 22 and August 14, 1998.

———. Interview with Feliciano Sánchez Chan (unpublished). Mérida, Yucatán, February 22, 2002.

Gómez Gutiérrez, Domingo. *Jwan Lopes: Bats'il Ajaw/Juan López: Héroe Tzeltal.* Colección Letras Mayas Contemporáneas: Chiapas, 2nd series, vol. 4. C. Montemayor, series ed. Mexico City: INI/TRF, 1996.

Góngora Pacheco, María Luisa. *Cuentos de Oxkutzcab y Maní.* Colección Letras Mayas Contemporáneas, 1st series, vol. 4. C. Montemayor, series ed. Mexico City: INI/Sedesol, 1993.

———. *U tzikbalilo'ob Oxkutzcab yéetel Maní.* Colección Letras Mayas Contemporáneas, 1st series, vol. 3. C. Montemayor, series ed. Mexico City: INI/Sedesol, 1993.

Gossen, Gary H. *Telling Maya Tales: Tzotzil Identities in Modern Mexico.* New York and London: Routledge, 1999.

Güemes Jiménez, Román. "Chicomexóchitl: El niño devorado por el templo." In *Narrativa Náhuatl Contemporánea/Yancuic Nahuasasanili: Antología*, pp. 165–180. Colección Letras Indígenas Contemporáneas. Mexico City: Editorial Diana/CNCA/DGCP, 1994.

Hernández Isidro, Isaías. *Cha' jop'e t'ok chap'e älkan /Las doce verdades.* Mexico City: Dirección General de Culturas Populares, 1997.

Iturrioz Leza, José Luis, Julio Ramírez de la Cruz, and Gabriel Pacheco Salvador. *Función gramática didáctica del huichol.* Guadalajara: Departamento de Estudios en Lenguas Indígenas, Universidad de Guadalajara, 1999.

Jiménez, María Roselia. *Jna'jeltik/Vivencias tojolabales.* Colección Letras Mayas Contemporáneas: Chiapas, 2nd series, vol. 5. C. Montemayor, series ed. Mexico City: INI/TRF, 1996.

Laughlin, Robert M., compil., trans., prologue, and notes. *Of Cabbages and Kings: Tales from Zinacantán.* Smithsonian Contributions to Anthropology no. 23. Washington, D.C.: Smithsonian Institution Press, 1977.

Laughlin, Robert M., compil. and trans., and Carol Karasik, ed. *Mayan Tales from Zinacantán: Dreams and Stories from the People of the Bat.* Washington, D.C.: Smithsonian Institution Press, 1988.

León-Portilla, Miguel. *Literaturas indígenas de México.* 2nd ed. Mexico City: Editorial Mapfre/FCE, 1992.

May May, Miguel Ángel. *Lajump'éel maaya tzikbalo'ob/Diez relatos mayas.* Letras Mayas Contemporáneas, 3rd series, vol. 10. C. Montemayor, series ed. Mexico City: INI/TRF, 1998.

Méndez Guzmán, Diego. *A'yejetik yu'un jtzeltaletik ta Tenejapa/Relatos tzeltales de Tenejapa.* Colección Letras Mayas Contemporáneas: Chiapas, 2nd series, vol. 7. C. Montemayor, series ed. Mexico City: INI/TRF, 1996.

Mignolo, Walter D. "Afterword." In *Writing without Words: Alternative Literacies in Mesoamerica and the Andes,* ed. Elizabeth Hill Boone and Walter D. Mignolo, pp. 293–313. Durham, N.C.: Duke University Press, 1994.

Montemayor, Carlos. *Arte y trama en el cuento indígena.* Mexico City: FCE, 1998.

———. *Chiapas: La rebelión indígena de México.* Mexico City: Joaquín Mortiz, 1997.

Narrativa Náhuatl Contemporánea/Yancuic Nahuasasanili: Antología. Colección Letras Indígenas Contemporáneas. Mexico City: Editorial Diana/CNCA/DGCP, 1994.

Pacheco, Gabriel. *Tatei Yurienaka y otros cuentos huicholes.* Colección Letras Indígenas Contemporáneas. Mexico City: Editorial Diana/CNCA/DGCP, 1994.

Pellicer, Dora. "Oralidad y escritura de la literatura indígena: Una aproximación histórica." In *Situación actual y perspectivas de la literatura en lenguas indígenas,* ed. Carlos Montemayor, pp. 15–53. Mexico City: Conaculta, 1993.

Pérez López, Enrique. *Alperes: Te'tikal mut/El pájaro alférez.* Colección Letras Mayas Contemporáneas: Chiapas, 2nd series, vol. 11. C. Montemayor, series ed. Mexico City: INI/TRF, 1996.

———. *El K'ox: El niño que se transformó en sol.* San Cristóbal de las Casas: Universidad Nacional Autónoma de México/Centro de Investigación Humanística de Mesoamérica y el Estado de Chiapas, 1995.

Sánchez Chan, Feliciano, prologue and ed. *Del sabucán del abuelo.* Mérida and Xaya, Tekax: Miatzil Maayáa, A.C., 2001.

Stuart, David S. "Lectura y escritura en la corte maya." *Arqueología Mexicana* 8, no. 48 (2001): 48–53.

Tedlock, Dennis, prologue, trans., and notes. *Popol Vuh: The Definitive Edition of the Mayan Book of the Dawn of Life and the Glories of Gods and Kings.* New York: Touchstone/Simon & Schuster, 1985.

Torres Sánchez, Joel. *P'urhepecha Uandatskuecha/Narrativa P'urhepecha.* Vol. 1. Morelia: INI/PACMYC, 1997.

———. *P'urhepecha Uandantskuecha/Narrativa P'urhepecha.* Vol. 2. Morelia: SEP, 2001.

La Palabra indígena mesoamericana

Oralidad y escritura y la prosa contemporánea

Donald Frischmann

De Monk's Mound al Tlachihualtepetl de Cholula: Historia de una travesía cultural

Llegar a ser estudioso de las culturas y las letras indígenas mexicanas ha significado para mí una larga y fascinante trayectoria. Nací y viví mis primeros veintidós años en un barrio multiétnico de inmigrantes europeos en la ciudad de Saint Louis, Missouri. En aquel lugar del centro o Midwest de Estados Unidos, nos quedaba lejos la dura realidad que vivía la mayor parte de los indígenas estadunidenses. Durante mis años formativos mi imagen de los "indios" provenía de las películas sobre el Viejo Oeste que veía con mi familia por televisión o en el cine local. En aquellas producciones formulaicas de Hollywood, los blancos eran los fieles portadores de la "razón" y la "civilización" y, por ello, siempre lograban triunfar sobre los "indios," que invariablemente eran representados como bárbaros, salvajes y ridículos en su forma de hablar y de comportarse ante aquéllos. Tardaría todavía algunos años en descubrir que las cosas no eran así, en realidad.

La ciudad actual de Saint Louis fue fundada por exploradores franceses en el punto de confluencia del Río Missouri y el Mississippi, lugar de fértiles tierras antes habitadas desde hacía más de mil años por pueblos agrícolas. En las cercanías de Saint Louis, antes apodada Mound City por la proliferación de antiguos montículos ceremoniales, a mediados del siglo pasado quedaba sólo un recuerdo significativo de aquella época ya pasada: el imponente complejo de Monk's Mound ubicado en la otra orilla del Mississippi en Cahokia, Illinois.[1] Pero mi familia nunca iba a visitar aquella curiosidad antigua; aun como parque estatal, recibió un mínimo de mantenimiento (no obstante varios estudios científicos realizados allí) hasta 1989, cuando el Gobierno del Estado de Illinois construyó allí un excelente museo de sitio.

Descubrí por fin aquella maravilla del pasado en un día de curiosidad vagabunda en la carcacha de un amigo. Para aquel entonces, la revolución cultural de 1968 nos había impregnado de una apreciación por otras cosmovisiones que no fueran la del Occidente cristiano. A muchos de mi generación ésta ya no nos proveía de respuestas satisfactorias a nuestras interrogantes existenciales; nuestra búsqueda recorrió no sólo el Oriente, sino también las cercanas—y a la vez tan distantes—culturas marginalizadas de los indígenas norteamericanos. Así llegaron a mi conocimiento nombres de lugares como Taos, Nuevo México, que se había convertido en una especie de *mecca* para jóvenes peregrinos en su ansiosa búsqueda de valores alternativos.

Durante los dos años siguientes mi pequeño mundo se abrió enormemente—y para siempre—cuando participé en dos excursiones culturales estudiantiles a la ciudad de México. Quedé maravillado de aquella metrópoli, así como de la grandeza de Teotihuacán y los tesoros culturales del Museo Nacional de Antropología e Historia. Aunque todavía sabía muy poco acerca de los pueblos indígenas contemporáneos, había encontrado otro mundo que me llamaba a través de su antigüedad y la lengua de mi abuelo materno: el español.

Mis estudios de lengua española y mis lecturas independientes sobre México adquirieron para mí mayor importancia que las demás materias de *high school,* debido en gran medida al entusiasmo desbordante de un joven maestro, James Wiswall, con quien todavía mantengo amistad. Después, como estudiante universitario en la carrera de licenciatura en Letras y Lingüística Hispánicas, el rigor de los estudios y el trabajo no me permitían emprender otro viaje al sur del Río Bravo.

Pero pocos años después, siguiendo los consejos de mi mentor el Dr. Enrique Noble en la Universidad de Missouri, me lanzaría en coche con un amigo para Cholula, Puebla, para cursar la maestría en Estudios Latinoamericanos en la Universidad de las Américas (UDLA); ése fue otro paso decisivo para mi formación. Mientras en mis cursos de letras estudiábamos a los grandes escritores mestizos mexicanos, las materias antropológicas me llevaban a realizar estudios de campo en las comunidades de habla náhuatl cercanas al volcán Popocatépetl. Aunque un año después volví a mi lugar de origen debido a un prolongado conflicto laboral en aquella universidad, jamás perdería mi interés por explorar la antigua sabiduría mesoamericana a través de la misma palabra indígena. Curiosamente, ya había vivido una travesía cultural que seguiría repitiéndose hasta la actualidad: desde el montículo indígena más grande de Estados Unidos, hasta el montículo más grande de Mesoamérica, el Tlachihualtepetl, el "cerro hecho a mano" de Cholula. Ambos han dejado una fuerte e indeleble huella y atracción en mi psique y reclaman mi presencia cíclicamente.

Al seguir la carrera de posgrado en Letras Hispánicas en la Ohio State University (maestría) y posteriormente en la University of Arizona (doctorado), las visiones del vasto mundo indígena latinoamericano se filtraban invariablemente a través de los escritores *indigenistas,* no indígenas; éstos seguían siendo objetos pasivos en vez de sujetos activos del quehacer literario. Durante los años que viví y estudié en Tucson, Arizona, mi deseo de superar las limitaciones curriculares de la carrera crecía al par de mi presencia en las fiestas y los ritos de los vecinos pueblos *yoreme* (yaqui), *tono ooh'tam* (pápago) y *otam* (pima).

Algunos años después, retomaría aquel camino a través de la disertación doctoral.[2] Como investigador de teatro popular urbano, campesino e indígena llegué a entablar amistad con algunos teatristas y escritores Mayas de Yucatán: Carlos Armando Dzul Ek, Feliciano Sánchez Chan, Miguel May May y María Luisa Góngora Pacheco, entre otros.[3] En los tomos 1 y 3 de esta antología se presentan por primera vez versiones en inglés de textos de estos escritores experimentados.[4]

Desde entonces, mi compromiso con el teatro indígena y comunitario se ha vuelto cada vez más fuerte, dando como resultado dos décadas de ricas experiencias por el centro, sur y sureste del país. Mi participación con TECOM (la Asociación Nacional de Teatro Comunidad) y el Consejo de Teatro Comunitario de la Región de los Volcanes me ha llevado a convivir con nahuas, mayas yucatecos, tzotziles, tzeltales, purépechas, totonacos y zapotecos del Istmo y de la Sierra. He aprendido sobre su historia, tradiciones y problemática, compartiendo días y noches de talleres, mesas redondas, presentaciones teatrales y convivios. El Tomo 3 de esta antología se dedica al Teatro Indígena Contemporáneo, con un énfasis particular en la familia lingüística y cultural mayanse.

Mi relación profesional con el Dr. Carlos Montemayor también resultó de mi participación con el teatro indígena. Cada quien realizaba un proyecto con Sna Jtz'ibajom, La Casa del Escritor, A.C., un colectivo de escritores y teatristas mayas tzotziles y tzeltales basado en San Cristóbal de las Casas, Chiapas. Yo acababa de publicar en Estados Unidos y en Londres sendos estudios sobre su trabajo; Carlos estaba preparando para la publicación su obra teatral colectiva que aparecería como los Tomos 1–3 de la 2a serie de Colección Letras Mayas Contemporáneas: Chiapas.[5] Carlos aceptaría luego dos invitaciones a dictar conferencias y a leer de su propia obra poética en la Texas Christian University (TCU). Fue entonces cuando empezamos a explorar el concepto de una antología multilingüe anotada de escritores indígenas contemporáneos, que incluyera los textos en lengua indígena, versiones en español preparadas por los autores y Montemayor y mis versiones en inglés. Todos los textos aparecerían ampliamente anotados, y el tomo contendría estudios introductorios nuestros. La primera prueba se dio cuando asumimos la tarea de preparar en ese formato unos cincuenta textos poéticos que aparecerían en una revista cultural mexicana. Seis meses de trabajo editorial meticuloso y entrevistas a los poetas rindieron un excelente cuerpo de material que nunca conoció la luz pública por razones que desconocemos. Ese material es la base de nuestro Tomo 2, que hemos aumentado considerablemente con nuevas creaciones de los mismos poetas y de otros, representando a nueve pueblos y lenguas indígenas de México.

Simultáneamente empezó mi relación con Escritores en Lenguas Indígenas, A.C. (ELIAC). Empecé a visitar con frecuencia su sede en el Distrito Federal, participando como invitado en eventos especiales y entrevistando a la primera generación (1996–1999) de escritores-residentes de lo que todavía se conocía como la Casa de los Escritores en Lenguas Indígenas, ubicada en Antonio Caso #33 de la Colonia San Rafael. Entablé una excelente relación profesional con Natalio Hernández (nahua), director; Juan Gregorio Regino (mazateco), presidente de ELIAC; Feliciano Sánchez Chan (maya yucateco), coordinador de publicaciones y difusión; Apolonio Bartolo Ronquillo (mazateco), coordinador de investigador y formación profesional; Isaías Hernández Isidro (chontal de Tabasco), coordinador de la biblioteca; y María Roselia Jiménez (tojolabal), secretaria de finanzas. A Natalio Hernández y a Jiménez los recibí posteriormente como conferencistas en la TCU, y junto con Carlos Montemayor participaron como conferencistas distinguidos en mi Seminario sobre Letras Indígenas Contemporáneas que yo impartía. Durante esos años de gran efervescencia para ELIAC y su "Casa" se lograron a nivel nacional una base sólida de trabajo y una presencia constante en los medios de comunicación.

De cómo nació este proyecto

En julio del 2000 llegué a la Universidad de las Américas–Puebla como Becario Fulbright–García Robles de la COMEXUS. Mi proyecto consistía en impartir un seminario de posgrado sobre Letras Indígenas Contemporáneas y preparar la antología multilingüe. En el seminario de la UDLA se inscribieron veintidós estudiantes de la Escuela de Humanidades, todos deseosos de explorar este tema que por primera vez se ofrecía como materia especial del Departamento de Filosofía y Letras. Los alumnos constituían un grupo fascinante y heterogéneo: una mayoría de mexicanos, provenientes del Distrito Federal hasta Chiapas, más otros jóvenes de Estados Unidos, Canadá, Nicaragua, Corea y Chile. Nuestra exploración conjunta empezó con la literatura náhuatl y la maya yucateca de la época prehispánica y la colonial; nuestro camino luego avanzó a través de las literaturas contemporáneas de los principales pueblos indígenas, con un énfasis particular en la familia mayanse: yucatecos, tzotziles, tzeltales y tojolabales. El seminario rindió un buen conjunto de trabajos de investigación; los alumnos aplicaron esquemas de análisis varios desde la crítica feminista hasta la posmoderna y la etnoliteraria, siempre intentando adecuar aquellos esquemas a la especificidad cultural de los escritores y literaturas indígenas.

En agosto del 2000 nos sentamos Carlos Montemayor

y yo en la sala de su residencia en la ciudad de México para detallar el plan y contenido de esta antología; en ese momento surgió una obra en tres tomos, ya no en uno solo. Ese cambio resultó de nuestra decisión de presentar cada obra en tres lenguas, y de haber calculado el volumen de material que ese formato representaría. Había muchos escritores y escritoras de gran calidad cuya obra merecía atención, y un formato multilingüe respondería a las necesidades de un amplio público lector panamericano. Desde el inicio, establecimos un criterio de excelencia académica y literaria para esta antología pionera: decidimos presentar a escritores que poseían décadas de desarrollo y experiencia y un compromiso de largo plazo con la promoción de su lengua. Ellos ya no son escritores *prometedores* cuyo trabajo ha aparecido sólo en periódicos culturales, sino profesionales muy *experimentados* y autores de libros publicados a nivel nacional por casas editoriales prestigiosas. No existe dentro de esta vanguardia un equilibrio cuantitativo entre escritores hombres y mujeres; la preponderancia de escritores masculinos en esta antología refleja esta realidad. Sin embargo, una futura antología de este tipo indudablemente incluirá a más escritoras distinguidas ya que en los últimos años, se ha dado un aumento dramático en el número de mujeres que se han iniciado en el quehacer literario. Sin embargo, nuestro enfoque actual no es la escritura *reciente* en lenguas indígenas mexicanas, sino la obra de escritoras y escritores que ya han sobresalido en su oficio.

Una de las tareas principales que yo asumí fue la preparación de versiones en inglés de todas las obras seleccionadas.[6] En enero del 2001, luego de concluir el seminario en la UDLA y después de una gira de trabajo por Yucatán y Chiapas, inicié esta fase del proyecto comenzando por las obras en prosa. Al terminar nuestra primera versión de este tomo, Montemayor y yo solicitamos nuevos apoyos para poder dedicarnos durante el 2002 a la preparación de los siguientes dos. Para ello nos fue otorgada una beca del Fideicomiso para la Cultura México-EUA; y por mi parte, una National Endowment for the Humanities Fellowship de Estados Unidos. Desde entonces, nuestro plan de los tomos expandió aun más, para incluir también Glosarios de términos en lenguas indígenas al español y al inglés y Apéndices que examinan elementos esenciales de la cosmovisión mesoamericana.

En marzo del 2002 viajé a Austin donde al llegar gocé de la hospitalidad del fotógrafo cultural Jorge Jackson de Llano (George O. Jackson, Jr.). Esa noche cenamos con Ann Hartness, la directora de la Colección Latinoamericana Benson de la Biblioteca de la Universidad de Texas. A la mañana siguiente, ofrecí personalmente nuestro trabajo a Theresa May de la University of Texas Press. A pesar de que su escritorio estaba cubierto de montones impresionantes de trabajo, Theresa me recibió amablemente y dentro de un par de días con entusiasmo nos ofreció un contrato para publicar esta antología. A mediados del 2003, mi sueño de que Jackson se convirtiera en retratista de los escritores antologados se realizó: una beca del Internacional Bank of Commerce de Laredo, Texas, nos permitió viajar más de 7,000 kilómetros por carro, retratando a los escritores y compartiendo una comida y un breve pero cálido intercambio con cada uno de ellos. Como resultado, sus palabras adquieren aquí *un rostro.*

Mi punto de partida para la elaboración de las versiones en inglés ha sido generalmente las versiones en castellano; éstas son obra de los mismos escritores, de otros escritores del mismo grupo lingüístico o de Montemayor. Para resolver varias dudas de interpretación también he consultado las versiones en lengua indígena, particularmente aquéllas de la familia mayanse (maya yucateco, tzotzil, tzeltal, tojolabal, chontal de Tabasco y totonaco). Las obras que se han dejado pasar al nuevo idioma con mayor facilidad son aquéllas que menos se han apartado de sus fuentes orales inmediatas; otras han constituido un mayor desafío debido a su complejidad sintáctica y estilística. Éstas rebasan, en mayor o menor grado, la condición de *oralidad inscrita* (Carrasco), alcanzando excelentes niveles de originalidad literaria o *escritura propia,*[7] aunque siempre sólidamente cimentadas en la oralidad literaria colectiva.

He consultado personalmente también con la gran mayoría de los autores, pidiendo aclaraciones sobre numerosos elementos de su obra, de tipo lingüístico, de cosmovisión, o bien sobre la génesis, el desarrollo y el sentido más profundo de su obra. Estrechar la mano del escritor o la escritora y volverme alumno suyo ha sido la fase más estimulante del proyecto. Le doy las gracias a cada uno de ellos por su actitud siempre abierta durante este proceso, que ha despertado nuevas inquietudes no sólo en este investigador, sino también en algunos entrevistados.

Oralidad y textos indígenas: Desde la antigüedad hasta la actualidad

Desde tiempos prehispánicos, la oralidad ha estado íntimamente relacionada a las expresiones escritas de los pueblos mesoamericanos. Los aztecas, mixtecos, zapotecos, otomíes, purépechas y mayas, culturas herederas y productoras de la civilización mesoamericana, desarrollaron sistemas complejos de escritura que resultaron en una cantidad considerable de textos pintados en libros plegables: códices, del latín *codex* (libro manuscrito).[8] A través de ideogramas, predominantes entre los aztecas y mixtecas,[9] y en glifos logosilábicos, que predominaban en la escritura maya,[10] se grababa y transmitía información de orden ceremonial, divinatorio, científico e histórico.

Como punto de partida para la presentación que sigue, afirmamos que la palabra enunciada en el plano de la oralidad siempre ha gozado de un estatus privilegiado entre los pueblos mesoamericanos, considerándose *sagrada* en sus expresiones más elevadas. Como señala Gary H. Gossen, la mayoría de las comunidades indígenas mesoamericanas relacionan el lenguaje y el diálogo al albor de la conciencia en sus narrativas cosmogónicas. Entre los mayas tzotziles de San Juan Chamula, Chiapas, el lenguaje oral y el canto, realizados con belleza, se vuelven la máxima ofrenda humana a los seres divinos. El lenguaje es considerado metafóricamente "el calor del corazón" de la persona que lo ofrenda.[11]

Este lugar privilegiado de la palabra hablada se observa claramente en el Popol Vuh, texto maya quiché plasmado en alfabeto latino a mediados del siglo XVI en base a libros glíficos anteriores. Allí, la creación sucesiva de los seres humanos (de lodo y barro, y de madera) de parte de los dioses primordiales es considerada exitosa sólo cuando aquéllos—ya seres de maíz—demuestran la capacidad lingüística de ofrendar una alabanza verbal a sus creadores.[12]

Los textos ideográficos han sido comparados a una especie de guión de actuación: las imagénes se concebían como referencias o signos para una representación narrada o cantada ante un público. Los que sabían leer los manuscritos pintados ya los habían memorizado y para ellos eran "caminos conocidos."[13]

A propósito de la oralidad y el Popol Vuh, Dennis Tedlock observa que a veces los autores del Popol Vuh alfabético parecen estar "describiendo dibujos" mediante frases en quiché como "éste es" y verbos en el tiempo presente. "En un momento dado ellos mismos asumen el papel de un intérprete, *hablándonos directamente* como si fuéramos miembros de un público en vivo y no simples lectores."[14]

Con respecto a los mayas y nahuas antiguos, David S. Stuart observa que los términos comunes para "gobernante" o "noble," *ajaw* en maya y *tlatoani* en náhuatl, podrían traducirse literalmente como "el que grita" y "uno que acostumbra decir cosas"; estos títulos tal vez se refieren a una función muy antigua e importante de los nobles como lectores orales ante un público, más que quienes simplemente ordenaban.[15] Así la expresión oral gozaba de un estatus sagrado ritual en la Mesoamérica antigua, donde los gobernantes se definían a sí mismos como los representantes y portavoces terrenales de sus dioses.

Ecos contemporáneos de la oralidad antigua

Esta tradición de las lecturas públicas de textos escritos seguía todavía a principios de los 1980s; Allan F. Burns informa que se realizaban lecturas anuales de los libros mayas de Chilám Balám,[16] en el centro ceremonial de Xcacal, Quintana Roo. Allí, en eventos públicos masivos, dos "escribanos" (*ah dzibo'ob*), responsables de guardar los libros, se turnaban leyendo pasajes en voz alta e "improvisando" en base a las "palabras de Dios" (*thaan hahaldios*) que transmiten estos textos.[17]

En fechas más recientes, el proyecto Continuidad de la Memoria Colectiva Maya de Yucatán sigue esta tradición antigua. El escritor y promotor cultural Feliciano Sánchez Chan y su equipo de colaboradores han recogido diversas expresiones de narrativa oral en lengua maya que han transcrito, traducido al español y publicado en forma bilingüe en el tomo titulado *Del sabucán del abuelo*.[18] En este proyecto, la oralidad y la escritura entran en un juego dinámico en el cual ésta sirve para reforzar aquélla. Sánchez Chan explica:

> Para nuestra búsqueda por regresar a la tradición oral al plano de la oralidad, publicar un libro no es el fin, es sólo una manera de equiparar los conocimientos mayas con las formas modernas de aprendizaje. Tenemos al libro entonces, como una importante herramienta para intentar permear a la población infantil maya con los contenidos de la memoria social.

El proyecto se propone "restituir a los adultos su importante función en la transmisión y continuidad cultural" a través de la "tradición oral," la cual se vuelve a sembrar y se refuerza en la comunidad a través de lecturas públicas hechas por jóvenes; y entre los niños, a través de resúmenes en dibujos que realizan luego de escuchar una narración. Este procedimiento mnemotécnico también ha resultado exitoso en la retransmisión del contenido cultural. *Del sabucán del abuelo* abarca mayormente *jadzutz tzikbalo'ob,* una categoría discursiva maya que engloba "fábulas, cuentos y narraciones sobre espantos, complementados con relatos vivenciales muy comunes en la región."[19]

Sánchez Chan explica que la presencia del libro en las

lecturas públicas le otorga al relato un estatus y prestigio especiales y por ello atrae mayor atención. Se reporta que hasta la fecha el proyecto ha dado muy buenos resultados: pese a problemas de comunicación intergeneracional, se ha logrado involucrar a niños, jóvenes y mayores como eslabones en la transmisión cultural por la vía oral. Es más, en el proceso de la transcripción, se realiza una "restauración": aquellos elementos léxicos y sintácticos que han infiltrado a la lengua maya del español son reemplazados por elementos casi olvidados de la lengua materna. Al mismo tiempo, las transcripciones reflejan elementos básicos del discurso oral (fórmulas, repeticiones, pausas, etc.). Las lecturas públicas, por lo tanto, tienen como fin adicional "restaurar" la expresión oral en lengua maya a sus formas más plenas.[20]

La pérdida progresiva de la escritura propia

El proceso de imposición de la escritura alfabética, pilar de la Civilización Occidental renacentista, empezó a partir de la conquista española. Los franciscanos y otras órdenes religiosas se apropiaron de la palabra indígena escrita—ahora en caracteres latinos—para divulgar la fe y dar a conocer (entre religiosos) las prácticas religiosas mesoamericanas; este proceso respondía en parte a la curiosidad intelectual de verdaderos etnógrafos humanistas como fray Bernardino de Sahagún; pero más importante, se destinaba a facilitar la imposición de la nueva fe.

Como respuesta a esta situación, la *intelligentsia* de las diversas culturas indígenas empezó a crear estrategias de adaptación y resistencia, una de las cuales consistía en la creación, ya en el siglo XVIII, de numerosos códices "coloniales," cuyo contenido actualizado se plasmaba en glifos así como en escritura alfabética. En los textos alfabéticos conocidos como *Títulos primordiales* de origen náhuatl, maya, zapoteco, mixteco y otomí, entre otros, los indígenas plasmaban la historia de sus varios linajes para afianzar y recobrar tierras y privilegios dentro del nuevo orden colonial. Al mismo tiempo, la apropiación más clandestina del alfabeto resultó en obras como los libros mayas de Chilám Balám.

Con respecto a la oralidad y la literatura indígena durante el período colonial, Dora Pellicer señala:

> En contraste con el papel instrumental e informativo al que los limitó el pensamiento cristiano, los idiomas indígenas mantuvieron sus espacios propios en la vida cotidiana de las comunidades indoamericanas y, a partir del siglo XVII, estuvieron vigorosamente atados a los movimientos de resistencia india contra el orden sociocultural del virreinato. La *creación literaria indígena* siguió reproduciéndose ligada a la *oralidad.*[21]

A consecuencia de las políticas lingüísticas de la colonia y posteriormente del México independiente que favorecían al español como idioma hegemónico y supuestamente "unificador," se dividió el mundo de la comunicación en dos espacios distintos: el territorio de los *idiomas nativos–oralidad* por un lado, y por otro, el del *español-escritura.* Pellicer observa que "esta última borró de la conciencia lingüística indígena la memoria de la escritura de sus lenguas, y otorgó un reconocimiento ahistórico a la ausencia de una práctica social escrita de estos idiomas."[22]

A propósito de los efectos del colonialismo en la escritura indígena, Walter Mignolo señala:

> El conflicto entre alfabetismos en el período colonial estuvo íntimamente ligado a la redistribución de fuerzas según la cual las lenguas europeas se volvieron la lengua imperial, y las amerindias sobrevivieron en forma oral, en adaptaciones marginalizadas de la escritura alfabética, y en la influencia menguante (y la eventual desaparición) de los sistemas de escritura amerindios.[23]

Efectivamente, las literaturas indígenas se vuelven *marginales* aunque se expresan en lenguas *mayoritarias.*

León-Portilla observa:

> Con contadas excepciones, la tradición oral vino a ser la única portadora de lo que se había preservado y se seguía concibiendo en el ámbito de las comunidades. La palabra nativa pervivió tan sólo en el corazón de los que veían en ella un tesoro. Perduraron así arraigadas formas de narrativa, entre ellas algunas referentes a las creencias ancestrales, cantares que solían entonarse en público, variadas formas de actuación con danzas y música, algunas de las cuales pueden calificarse como pertenecientes al género dramático.[24]

Esta oralidad preponderante sigue siendo hoy en día producto del analfabetismo crónico de los pueblos indígenas mexicanos; Laughlin señala:

> Dado que pocos zinacantecos saben leer o escribir en su lengua materna, la narración oral es el único modo de transmisión de los hechos del pasado. Si la narración oral no se valora como un arte en sí, los cuentos sí se aprecian como parte del tesoro comunitario.[25]

Aparte de estos cuentos y narraciones, en las culturas indígenas mesoamericanas todavía existen en forma oral numerosos textos rituales que son el dominio de los ejecutantes ceremoniales.[26] Estos textos son sumamente detallados y precisos en su contenido, y se transmiten sin ningún soporte visual (como el que prestaban antiguamente los libros pintados). Con respecto a este fenómeno se ha aplicado el concepto de la *escrituralidad,* el cual equipara formas de oralidad a una "escritura no gráfica." Los autores del libro *Función gramática didáctica del huichol* explican:

> Podemos pensar que existen otras formas de escritura no materializadas en un soporte físico externo, sino [en] . . . la capacidad de elaborar y formular pensamientos complejos en estructuras semánticas y gramaticales complejas.[27]

Dentro del plano de la lengua hablada, se distingue por lo tanto entre *la lengua oral,* "característica de la comunicación cotidiana,"[28] y

> *la lengua escritural,* a saber el lenguaje sagrado de los mara'akate en el que se narra la historia antigua de los antepasados, un lenguaje (registro) complicado que no se utiliza en la vida cotidiana, sino en las fiestas y en los ritos. Los textos escriturales se guardaban en la memoria biológica, es decir en la memoria de algunos individuos que desde niños los aprendían para poderlos transmitir después a las generaciones siguientes.[29]

Esta lengua escritural se aprende de una manera especial, "participando en las fiestas, en las cacerías, en los rituales del ciclo agrícola y en las peregrinaciones de los hikuritamete."[30]

Una de las responsabilidades que asumen los escritores que presentamos en este tomo es la expresión, difusión y continuidad de la sabiduría tradicional de su pueblo, la cual han recibido principalmente a través de la palabra oral. A continuación, examinaremos la naturaleza de este quehacer y las diversas maneras en que los escritores indígenas contemporáneos plasman esta herencia en sus obras.

Las nuevas literaturas indígenas

Es natural que para la creación de una nueva tradición literaria *escrita,* los nuevos escritores contemporáneos han tomado como punto de partida su propia tradición literaria existente; ésta, como hemos visto, ha existido en forma escrita y/u oral.

Montemayor señala que "las fuentes de la tradición oral de los pueblos indígenas no son 'primitivas': son al menos la tradición escrita y oral española y la tradición *escrita* y oral de la civilización prehispánica."[31] Es más: "En el caso de las lenguas indígenas de México el narrador está refiriendo a su auditorio un relato sobre la realidad más profunda de la comunidad: sobre la historia, la geografía, la religión o su tradición cultural."[32]

Mientras un receptor no indígena interpreta tales historias como fantásticas y ficticias, el indígena generalmente no duda de su veracidad.[33] Hechos que un receptor occidental llamaría "mágicos" caben perfectamente dentro de la concepción indígena de la realidad cotidiana, la cual es caracterizada por la co-existencia de planos o niveles de realidad: el de los seres humanos y el de las deidades antiguas y contemporáneas, pre-hispánicas y católicas. Ambos mundos se tocan, son interdependientes y se expresan a través de la literatura oral y la escrita. Laughlin observa con respecto a los tzotziles de Zinacantán que "frecuentemente el curso de la historia adquiere su forma debido a la intervención de espíritus del panteón de Zinacantán."[34] De hecho esta convivencia entre la comunidad humana y la sobrenatural es un motivo central en las narraciones de los escritores mayas María Luisa Góngora Pacheco, Miguel May May y Jorge Echeverría Lope, así como en las de Diego Méndez Guzmán (tzeltal), Jacinto Arias (tzotzil), Joel Torres Sánchez (purépecha), Román Güemes Jiménez (nahua), María Roselia Jiménez (tojolabal) e Isaías Hernández Isidro (chontal de Tabasco).

Incluimos en este tomo dos narraciones muy cercanas al modelo de *oralidad inscrita* propuesta por Carrasco con respecto a la literatura mapuche de Chile.[35] Los textos orales, al ser transcritos, rebasan la condición de *oralidad absoluta.* Su textualidad oral se adecua a las posibilidades de la escritura y son frecuentemente traducidas al español u otra lengua moderna. Así, la transcodificación otorga a estas narraciones un doble modo de existencia: en forma oral y escrita, en su lengua original así como en otras lenguas secundarias. De esta manera van más allá de la intraculturalidad para incorporarse al contexto de la literatura nacional y universal. Sin embargo, en su paso de la oralidad a la escritura quedan descontextualizados de la situación lingüística y extralingüística que les dio origen y su sentido original.[36]

No cabe duda de que el acto de leer una narración transcrita y quizás, traducida a otra lengua, no es igual al acto de escuchar al narrador indígena mientras se comparte el calor del fogón de su familia en las montañas de Oaxaca o

Chiapas. Los gestos, la entonación, las expresiones faciales y tal vez un contexto ritual se pierden en el proceso de la transcripción y traducción. La narrativa oral no es lo mismo que la oralidad inscrita, ni es lo que pretendemos ofrecer en este tomo. Sin embargo, no debemos subestimar el gran valor de textos parcialmente descontextualizados, ni de los textos de *escritura propia* que presentamos aquí ya que todos constituyen en sí puentes interculturales.

Tal vez el ejemplo más cercano a lo que podría parecer "oralidad inscrita" a primera vista es la narración "La Pobreza," de la promotora cultural y teatrista Maya *María Luisa Góngora Pacheco,* que comienza de la siguiente manera: "El señor Aurelio Zumárraga cuenta que hubo una vez cierta viejita cuyo nombre era Pobreza y que vivía en las afueras de la población."[37] Sin embargo, esta narrativa no pasó de la boca del relator a la página escrita sin cambio alguno. La autora modificó por lo menos dos motivos: colocó el árbol nativo de *huaya* donde antes había una exótica higuera; y la protagonista alegórica ahora se llama "Pobreza," ya no "Miseria," ya que esta condición extrema se desconoce en su medio.[38] Por consiguiente, esta narración, la que se ha dado en formas parecidas por todo el mundo,[39] sufrió una adecuación típica a su medio al filtrarse a través de la pluma de la escritora.

De una manera semejante, la maestra bilingüe y promotora cultural tojolabal *María Roselia Jiménez* coloca el siguiente epígrafe a "Lo que contaron nuestros abuelos y tatarabuelos": "Narrado por la señora Trinidad Pérez García de la Colonia Lomantam, Municipio de las Margaritas."[40] Esta narración transcurre en un tiempo mítico, antiguo, cuando todavía se daban hechos maravillosos como los que se narran acá. La historia oral sirve para guardar y transmitir tales hechos, que no serían recogidos por un discurso histórico concebido desde una perspectiva occidental. Una de las mayores responsabilidades que asumen estas dos escritoras es adecuar los textos orales que recogen a su nueva forma escrita, la cual es en sí una contribución a su preservación y retransmisión futura.

La materia prima oral sirve también como punto de partida para lo que Carrasco llama *escritura propia.* En estos casos el éxito del escritor, así como el de todo buen narrador tradicional, se mide según su habilidad de manejar, según la tradición narrativa indígena propia, los varios motivos que son los *sine qua non* de una narración.[41] De acuerdo a mi experiencia, el aprovechamiento de ciertos motivos de personajes generalmente determina qué motivos objetuales y episódicos son apropiados o bien, inapropiados. Alrededor de este núcleo, los narradores imprimen frecuentemente su huella original sea dentro de la modalidad de transmisión oral, o bien la escrita. Laughlin observa con respecto a la oralidad de los narradores tzotziles de Zinacantán, Chiapas:

> A pesar de enormes variaciones en estilo y contenido, los narradores zinacantecos subrayan que simplemente están repitiendo las palabras antiguas que han recibido de su padres, abuelos y, en raros casos, bisabuelos. Son frecuentes las innovaciones, pero nunca son reconocidas. Una narración comunica verdades ancestrales; alteraciones concientes son consideradas mentiras.[42]

Así, el escritor chontal de Tabasco (yok'ot'an) *Isaías Hernández Isidro* aprovechó motivos comunes al ciclo de narraciones sobre el/la Zutz'baläm (literalmente "murciélago-jaguar")—una antigua deidad protectora de su pueblo chontal—para crear un historia original, "El secreto del Zutz'baläm." Fiel a los motivos episódicos tradicionales, el Zutz'baläm de este cuento nace de madre humana; vive en la oscuridad de día y sale a volar sólo de noche; demuestra omnisciencia con respecto a la vida personal de toda persona con la que tiene contacto; deja el hogar humano a los doce años para reunirse con los demás Zutz'baläm en una isla mítica; predice el tiempo y las catástrofes inminentes a través de su comportamiento; y castiga severamente a cualquier persona que no maneja con sumo respeto y discreción el hecho de haberlo conocido.

Sin ser ejemplo de oralidad inscrita, las fuentes de inspiración del escritor no pasan sin su reconocimiento debido. En la dedicatoria a su tomo *Cha' jop'e t'ok chap'e älkan/Las doce verdades,* Isaías Hernández Isidro señala: "En este trabajo va el nombre de mis abuelos, mis abuelas, mi padre, mi madre. Ellos me crecieron nadando en las historias de mi pueblo."[43]

En la última narración del tomo titulada "El viejo y la Zutz'baläm," el personaje del abuelo, al encontrarse cara a cara con la deidad, recibe el siguiente encargo:

> —Cuéntale, tú sabes a quién, para que no se olvide de nuestra existencia. El anciano salió. Sólo él tuvo la fortuna de conocer a una Zutz'baläm allá en Tecolutilla.
>
> Desde entonces, cada lunes, Celestino hacía ofrendas al Zutz'baläm. Éste lo recogió cuando había terminado de contar estas historias: *Las doce verdades.*[44]

Esta brevísima narración es de hecho un testimonio personal. El título del tomo en lengua chontal, *Cha' jop'e t'ok chap'e älkan,* significa literalmente "Las doce vivencias" o "Las doce verdades";[45] es decir, se presenta como una colección de escritos que tienen su base en la experiencia personal del autor y de otros, particularmente de su fuente primaria y abuelo Celestino. Éste, al contárselas a su nieto, siempre les pedía permiso primero a los Zutz'baläm. Durante el proceso creativo el autor admite que sentía miedo al abordar el tema ya que había sido testigo ocular de una Zutz'baläm nacida en su pueblo;[46] sentía que se bloqueaba y que no le salían bien sus escritos. Finalmente una noche soñó que "volaba muy alto" sobre la espalda de un Zutz'baläm; al aterrizar, encontró a su abuelo parado junto con varios Zutz'baläm. Al otro día el abuelo le aseguró que aquellas deidades soñadas le habían dado licencia para proseguir con su libro. A partir de entonces, Hernández Isidro escribía con fluidez y dentro de un mes, el tomo ya estaba listo; al entregarlo para su publicación, su abuelo Celestino falleció, ya habiendo cumplido con su misión.[47]

Guardo como recuerdo muy especial aquella entrevista de 14 de agosto de 1998 con Isaías; en un salón de clase de la Casa de los Escritores en Lenguas Indígenas del Distrito Federal, se nos iba la luz del día mientras la entrevista avanzaba. Isaías no paraba de hablar, mostrando un impulso fuerte de externar datos sobre el trasfondo de sus narraciones; ni la creciente obscuridad pudo interrumpir su plática sobre los detalles más íntimos que yacen detrás de su libro. En ese momento, me di cuenta de que yo había ganado acceso a información muy privilegiada, cuyo conocimiento no podía tomar sino muy en serio. No se trataba de cuentos de un pasado remoto ni de criaturas fantásticas, sino de vivencias y creencias profundas de la persona muy cuerda a quien tenía delante, cuyo respeto por los Zutz'baläm comparto hasta el presente.

La figura del abuelo como fuente de información privilegiada surge también en "Una narración sobre Yum Tziles" del escritor y promotor cultural maya *Miguel Ángel May May.* Él también aprovecha bien los motivos tradicionales, en este caso aquéllos que son comunes al ciclo de narraciones sobre los guardianes mayas de la naturaleza. De acuerdo a los motivos episódicos tradicionales, los Yum Tziles se aparecen a individuos que ellos escogen especialmente para desempeñar el cargo de *jmeno'ob* (véase Apéndice A) y que invitan a entrar en una especie de aprendizaje con ellos. Son los *jmeno'ob* mayas quienes realizan la tan importante ceremonia de Ch'a' Cháak en la cual les ruegan a los Yum Tziles a que regalen lluvias para los sembradíos.

El protagonista de esta narración, Clavio, le cuenta a otra persona la experiencia extraordinaria que acaba de vivir con cuatro personajes sobrenaturales. El otro le advierte: "Sí, son los Yum Tziles quienes te llevaron. Ahora recuerdo que mi abuelo platicaba que se habían llevado a otra persona."[48] Esta referencia sutil es un reconocimiento más a los portadores más importantes de la historia de los pueblos: los ancianos.

En el texto del narrador y teatrista tzeltal *Diego Méndez Guzmán* titulado "Peregrinar de San Ildefonso," se reconoce en su conjunto a "los viejos" de Tenejapa como sus fuentes. Igual que en los dos ejemplos anteriores, no se pretende que ésta sea una transcripción fiel de ninguna versión en particular sobre este hecho, sino un trabajo literario propio. Sin embargo, según las normas narrativas tzeltales, Méndez Guzmán no introduce cambios substanciales con respecto a las versiones que ha escuchado a lo largo de su vida. Desde el primer párrafo, se observa un motivo-personaje común a la narrativa oral tzotzil y tzeltal: *el sacerdote malo,* quien "un día desapareció para siempre, llevándose la imagen de San Ildefonso, según cuentan los viejos."[49] El colectivo Sna Jtz'ibajom, A.C., en el cual Méndez Guzmán ha fungido como escritor, actor y presidente, ha montado para el teatro guiñol una narración tzotzil titulada "El cura diablo"; en ésta, un sacerdote manda a los hombres del pueblo lejos a entregar mensajes para aprovecharse de sus mujeres en su ausencia; finalmente es descubierto y como castigo es desterrado de la comunidad. Con respecto a este motivo-personaje típico, Laughlin señala que los Tzotziles de Zinacantán "apenas toleran a tontos o a curas . . . Allá los delices de sacerdotes y sus aventuras amorosas no son objeto de humor (como en cuentos españoles similares), sino de indignidad."[50]

Mientras este motivo no es el central al relato de Méndez Guzmán (cuya acción transcurre en el municipio tzeltal de Tenejapa, no en Zinacantán) y el narrador no llega a expresar tal condenación, es sin embargo un cura cuya acción censurable "motiva" las desgracias del relato. Al mismo tiempo, este motivo nos ayuda a identificar esta narración claramente como perteneciente a la tradición oral indígena de los Altos de Chiapas, aunque el motivo episódico central que podríamos llamar "el santo escoge su pueblo" es obviamente de influencia cristiana y de origen europeo; y según mi experiencia, es uno de los más comunes a la narrativa oral de los pueblos indígenas y mestizos de México.

El tomo *Narrativa P'urhepecha* de *Joel Torres Sánchez* marca la transición contemporánea de la oralidad a la escritura del pueblo purépecha y representa una contribución al acervo histórico de la zona lacustre de Michoacán. El autor explica que preparó este tomo como respuesta al

> hecho de que en las comunidades que conforman la zona P'urhepecha nuestra lengua materna se esté perdiendo . . . principalmente por la pérdida de la identidad étnica y la influencia negativa de los medios de comunicación, la emigración a los centros urbanos nacionales y al extranjero [y] la falta de programas educativos y su adecuada aplicación.

Al mismo tiempo, guarda la esperanza de "un nuevo amanecer" profetizado desde tiempo atrás, "el día en que la tradición oral, ahora escrita, se esparcirá entre la nueva generación P'urhepecha." El autor señala también:

> En estos cuatro trabajos está presente el reconocimiento y homenaje permanente a la grandeza de la tradición oral P'urhepecha que de generación en generación ha logrado llegar a nosotros con la actualidad propia de una costumbre ancestral convertida en realidad escrita.[51]

El fragmento que incluimos aquí de la narración "No soy hechicera, ¡soy curandera!" se presenta como testimonio de vivencias personales e insólitas. El autor está consciente de su parecido con el género occidental del cuento fantástico, y aclara:

> Las personas ajenas a nosotros, las que no saben nada del P'urhepecha, no creen, dicen que no es cierto, que son cuentos; pero nosotros sabemos hasta dónde lo inexplicable es realidad, y en dónde, la realidad se convierte en fantasía.[52]

Al narrar la vida de Nana Delfina, una curandera de gran fama y hazañas extraordinarias de su pueblo, San Jerónimo Purenchécuaro, Michoacán, Torres se presenta como testigo ocular de hechos inexplicables, aun entre sus paisanos:

> Lo que vimos era en realidad asombroso. Atorada entre los cables de los postes estaba Nana Delfina. Como única vestimenta colgaban de sus brazos pedazos de petate viejo . . .
>
> Era una señora de edad y por eso me llamó la atención su cabello: muy largo, negro y brilloso.[53]

La intención de Torres de constituirse en fuente primaria de hechos y personajes de su pueblo la manifiesta al final de su escrito:

> Creí justo escribir algo sobre ella, para que quienes no saben de su existencia, se den cuenta que esa señora vivió, estuvo ahí, fue parte de la tradición de un pueblo y muchos le debemos mucho.[54]

En el 2001 apareció el volumen dos de *Narrativa P'urhepecha* del mismo Torres Sánchez, el cual me fue entregado por el autor durante mi visita a la zona lacustre de Michoacán en marzo de 2002. Conocí de primera mano la hospitalidad purépecha cuando Joel me invitó a comer el nativo pescado blanco en su casa a orillas del lago de Pátzcuaro, preparado por la madre del escritor, quien a pesar de sus noventa y tantos años de edad, demostró la agilidad y lucidez de una mujer de unos cuarenta años más joven.

Si bien May May y Méndez Guzmán ejercen lo que Carrasco llama la *escritura propia,* aprovechando la memoria (ya no la transcripción fidedigna) de narraciones oídas a sus abuelos y padres, Torres, igual que Hernández Isidro, lo realiza a través de *experiencias propias.*

La pieza que le da título al tomo *Tatei Yurienaka y otros cuentos huicholes*[55] del narrador *Gabriel Pachecho* es otro ejemplo de escritura propia que se vincula en forma manifiesta e intencional a la oralidad. Pacheco, ganador del Premio Nezahualcóyotl de Literatura en Lenguas Indígenas (1998), presenta el monólogo interior de un niño cuya visión de mundo está completamente condicionada por las palabras de su abuelo. La narración está marcada por la constante repetición de: "mi abuelo me cuenta" y "todo me platica mi abuelo." La oralidad es reconocida como fundamental para la transmisión del conocimiento ancestral: "Él me cuenta que lo que me enseña ahora, eso mismo se lo enseñaron a él."[56] La identidad del niño como Huichol—con un fuerte énfasis en la relación con la Madre Tierra (Tatei Yurienaka)—se va construyendo gracias al contacto con el abuelo.

La prosa de Pacheco es extraordinaria, reflejando un nivel de preparación formal no común en su medio. Como señala el Dr. José Luis Iturrioz en su "Prólogo" al tomo:

> Los estudios de licenciatura en letras le han permitido adquirir un panorama general de la literatura universal y conocer técnicas utilizadas en otras tradiciones literarias, orales y escritas, así como diferentes métodos de análisis literario. Pero no contento con esto, decidió un día ponerse a producir él mismo textos literarios . . . desarrollando paulatinamente un estilo personal, inspirado en el cuento tradicional, pero incorporando elementos de ambas corrientes.[57]

La novela *Cantares de los vientos primerizos* de *Javier Castellanos Martínez* tiene la distinción de ser la primera producida por un escritor indígena en México. Acá presentamos selecciones del Capítulo 5, "Segunda revelación," y del Capítulo 6, "Tercera revelación." Obra que presenta cierto parecido con el género occidental del *Bildungsroman,* la novela de Castellanos narra en primera persona las peripecias de un joven zapoteco de la sierra quien se convierte en investigador asalariado de sus propias raíces culturales para una dependencia cultural estatal. Sobresalen los monólogos de la enigmática Trhon Lia como verdaderos momentos de "revelación": el consumo fuerte del mezcal le induce cierto estado de trance desde el cual, con extraordinaria lucidez, narra oralmente la historia de su pueblo zapoteco, antes y después de la llegada de los españoles. Sobresale el papel de su antepasado Lia Kaxhon quien organizó a los pueblos indígenas en contra de la opresión española, enfrentándose personalmente al comandante Reynozo, para luego sufrir la tortura y la muerte. La oralidad de Trhon Lia, inscrita dentro del marco ficticio de la novela, surge como fuente privilegiada de información histórica.

Nuestra selección del Capítulo 6 abarca un episodio humorístico de choque cultural: el protagonista zapoteco recuenta cómo su intento de seducir a una antropóloga mestiza le ganó un tiempo en la cárcel.

"Vieja huella de soga" del maya yucateco *Jorge Echeverría Lope* presenta a un protagonista niño,[58] motivo común a varias de las narraciones que incluimos. El pequeño Súulub Chan Ek' (Pequeño Pedazo de Estrella) camina en búsqueda del cenote X-La'-Boon-Suumij (Vieja huella de soga) con el cual ha soñado repetidamente. Se encuentra con una serie de elementos de la naturaleza personificados, algunos de carácter divino, que lo van guiando en su búsqueda por el monte de Yucatán. Finalmente llega al cenote cuyas aguas antiguas, ya casi olvidadas, lo han de iluminar.

Aunque Echeverría Lope incluye en su narración múltiples motivos de la tradición literaria oral de su pueblo maya, su motivación, además de "practicar la escritura en lengua maya," incluye "dar a conocer los nombres de algunos cenotes que hay en esta tierra" y "dar a conocer que mi comunidad vive." Con respecto a su relación a la tradición literaria oral, el autor aclara:

> Esta historia yo la creé, pero basándome en la experiencia que tengo de haber escuchado muchas historias orales de mi abuela y de otros desde mi infancia. La influencia de la tradición oral es innegable, pero fue creación mía. Este tramo que recorre el protagonista lo he recorrido mucho en bicicleta desde mi infancia. De tanto pasar y pasar, me dio muchas cosas por conocer ese camino. Todos los nombres de lugares son reales, sólo que los convierto en nombres de personajes.[59]

A través de este ejemplo sobresaliente de escritura indígena contemporánea, la hacienda henequenera de Chunkanán ha quedado inscrita en la memoria literaria nacional de México. En esta zona poco visitada de la Península de Yucatán abundan los tesoros naturales, particularmente los cenotes que son los motivos centrales al relato de Echeverría Lope. Debo recordar mi visita a Chunkanán en febrero del 2002. Jorge hizo los arreglos para que unos amigos de Mérida, mi esposa Patricia y yo recorriéramos parte de la ruta del pequeño Súulub Chan Ek' sobre un *truck* o carreta de ruedas de acero; ésta iba montada sobre unas vías estrechas y fue jalada por "Jorobado," un caballo pequeño pero fuerte. Ésta es la manera en que todavía se transportaba el henequén de los campos de cultivo a la planta procesadora rústica de la hacienda, que queda a una distancia de varios kilómetros. (Esta planta fue destruida en el huracán de octubre de 2002, y no se prevee su reconstrucción.) Paramos varias veces en nuestro recorrido y descendimos quince metros o más en escaleras metálicas bajo la capa caliza de la Península. Allí presenciamos la magnificencia de los cenotes subterráneos de color azul turquesa. Con una actitud de asombro reverencial y de deleite recordamos cómo desde tiempos antiguos los mayas han considerado sagradas sus aguas. Durante una cena en el comedor al aire libre del escritor, conversamos, y yo le hice una entrevista. Cuando salimos de Chunkanán para Mérida, ya en plena oscuridad, me llevé conmigo una apreciación de primera mano de cómo un niño podría llegar a entrar en contacto y hasta dialogar con las maravillas del monte yucateco.

"Chicomexóchitl: El niño devorado por el templo" del antropólogo, lingüista y escritor en lengua náhuatl *Román Güemes Jiménez* narra otra búsqueda de parte de un niño, sólo que ahora es el divino Niño-Maíz quien busca al único ser humano que todavía lo recuerda: el *tlapopochuijketl* o incensador, "el oficiante de todas las grandes ceremonias."[60] El niño Chikomexóchitl, el niño Siete-Flor, quiere que éste le amarre los pies al camino de la muerte ya que se está muriendo de olvido, ya "devorado por el templo"; o sea, por la imposición de las prácticas católicas que han puesto fin a su fiesta tradicional. Al final el narrador, el fandanguero, descubre un rancho donde todavía se observa la fiesta tradicional a Chikomexóchitl, y une el sonido de su guitarra al festejo. Aunque el niño ya ha desaparecido, persiste la esperanza de resucitarlo mediante ritos antiguos en los cuales la palabra sagrada se adorna del canto.

El cuento de Güemes transcurre en un lugar llamado "Temikiloyan: el lugar donde se sueña verdaderamente"; "el lugar donde algún sueño verdadero te puede apresar"; donde "sueñan los que saben ver"; donde están "los que saben vencer a la distancia más oscura y temerosa"; "el lugar de la posibilidad mejor deseada."[61] Y es en tono solemne, de repeticiones ritualísticas y de ensueño que el narrador va nombrando y recordando los espacios y los personajes sagrados de esta tierra de la Huasteca Veracruzana. Para seguir viva la deidad requiere del incienso del *tlapopochuijketl*, así como a "quienes saben nombrarnos con sus discursos floridos y profundos."[62] Nuevamente a partir de la palabra escrita, resalta la vital importancia de la palabra hablada para la sobrevivencia de toda una cosmovisión ancestral, y de la vida misma.

"K'ox y el Dueño del agua" del escritor tzotzil *Enrique Pérez López* tiene también como motivo central un niño, K'ox o Xut—"el más pequeño," el "hermano menor." Este personaje figura como motivo-personaje central a todo un ciclo de narrativas muy conocidas entre los tzotziles y tzeltales de Chiapas. En la versión que nos entrega Pérez López, predomina en el protagonista su carácter de niño humano, mientras en otras narrativas es un niño-dios; este hecho corresponde a una decisión del autor de sacarlo de su papel divino. Sin embargo, el personaje exhibe aquí poderes especiales cuando establece contacto directo con el Dueño del agua. Pero al cerrar la narración, Pérez López nos remite a su condición humana: "En casa tenemos un pequeño, el último de la familia. Ahí está el K'ox."[63]

En otras narraciones, el K'ox es típicamente maltratado por sus hermanos mayores y aprovecha su astucia para deshacerse de ellos. Mediante la magia, hace que caigan a tierra junto con un árbol al que se han subido donde se consumen golosamente sus frutos o un panal de miel. Luego convierte sus cuerpos inertes en animales mientras él se transforma en el sol, y su madre en la luna. Esta narrativa nos recuerda el episodio del Popol Vuh en el cual los Gemelos Divinos aprovechan su astucia característica: primero logran que sus hermanos mayores también se trepen a un árbol, y luego como castigo los convierten en monos. Los Gemelos, luego de vencer a los temibles Señores de Xibalbá, se transforman también en el sol y la luna. En otra versión de Pérez López, los hermanos golosos de K'ox se convierten en puercos y su ropa, en guajolotes.[64]

Por su parte, Laughlin ha recogido varias narrativas sobre el Xut en Zinacantán. El personaje, identificado en una versión como "Nuestro Santo Padre," convierte a sus hermanos malvados también en cochinos. Laughlin titula estas versiones "The Three Suns" (Los Tres Soles), ya que Xut y sus dos hermanos son identificados en una versión como los tres soles que se turnaban en tiempos remotos cuando no había obscuridad.[65] El Popol Vuh encierra gran número de episodios narrativos que se han perpetuado a través de la vía oral entre los mayas tzotziles y tzeltales de Chiapas, con innovaciones y ampliaciones.

La figura divina de Juan López de la zona tzeltal de Chiapas es central a la oralidad inscrita del libro de *Domingo Gómez Gutiérrez* titulado *Jwan Lopes: Bats'il Ajaw/Juan López: Héroe Tzeltal.* El autor dice que éste consiste en

> los relatos de siete ancianos que durante muchos años conservaron en sus corazones la historia de un hombre inmortal, Dios de los verdaderos hombres del pueblo tzeltal, aquel que no dijo llamarse Rey Indio, sino simplemente *jwe' ijk'al xbojt'il chenek'*, hombre que se alimenta de gran frijol negro. Pero en otra realidad es el Ajaw o Dios del *bats'il* o verdadero hombre, el dios de los tzeltales. Lo han recordado quienes de niños inclinaron sus oídos a las pláticas de sus abuelos. En este pueblo de Bachajón se vio nacer y crecer a Juan López, niño huérfano, de padre desconocido.[66]

Sigue la "Versión conjuntada" de Gómez Gutiérrez en la que presenta la versión más completa ya que incluye todos los motivos de personaje, de objeto, y los episódicos presentes en las demás versiones; el autor las recoge y transcribe de narradores orales que cita al principio de cada pieza. En "El Ajaw Tzeltal Juan López, el Pastor (Manuel Hernández, Swijlibjá, Chilón)" confluyen la oralidad inscrita y el motivo del dios niño-joven, ya ampliamente comentado por Montemayor.[67] Además, este libro se presenta como una crónica real de un dios propio, una versión indígena de la historia que hasta la actualidad apenas se ha llegado a conocer fuera de la zona tzeltal de Chiapas.

Finalmente, dos de los hechos significativos que Iván Carrasco observa con respecto al fenómeno de la escritura propia entre los mapuches de Chile se han dado también en México: la producción de textos de doble registro (en lengua indígena y en español) y la aparición de géneros nuevos en lenguas indígenas.[68]

Con los escritores actuales se estrena en México el ensayo etnográfico escrito por especialistas indígenas y muy ligado a la oralidad. Presentamos acá selecciones de dos obras fundamentales para el estudio de los mayas yucatecos y los tzotziles: *La milpa en Muxupip* de *Santiago Domínguez Aké* y *El mundo numinoso de los mayas* de *Jacinto Arias Pérez*. En el caso de estos autores, el género etnográfico surge como producto de la preparación profesional del escritor: El tzotzil Jacinto Arias Pérez terminó los estudios para el doctorado en antropología en la Princeton University. Su obra se basa en su tesis de maestría escrita originalmente en inglés en la Catholic University of America; incluímos aquí su versión original en este idioma donde intenta revelar las profundas diferencias entre la visión de mundo maya y la de los ladinos, usando como punto de partida el concepto de lo "numinoso." Arias además examina la interpretación peculiar que los maya les dan a los sacramentos católicos, como el bautizo.

Por su parte, Domínguez Aké es egresado de la carrera en antropología de la Universidad Autónoma de Yucatán, trabaja de promotor cultural bilingüe en la Unidad Regional Yucatán de Culturas Populares y tiene un marcado interés en la compleja ciencia agrícola de su pueblo maya. Domínguez Aké subraya que "aquí cabe destacar el papel tan importante que juega la tradición oral en la realización de este trabajo."[69] Asimismo, agradece la colaboración de una cuarentena de hombres y mujeres, muchos de ellos ya fallecidos, "quienes gustosamente accedieron a ser entrevistadas para obtener la información que hizo posible este trabajo sobre la milpa en Muxupip."[70] Obra que contiene citas extensas de estos individuos, *La milpa en Muxupip* revela muchas veces en primera persona la sabiduría antigua del pueblo maya que hoy se debate entre la agricultura orgánica tradicional, por un lado, y por otro, los productos agroquímicos de efecto tan rápido como nocivo para el medio ambiente y los seres humanos. Domínguez Aké promueve la ciencia agrícola maya activamente por la vía oral al ofrecer pláticas de tipo práctico a grupos de agricultores.[71]

Incluimos también el ensayo "El temascal" del distinguido escritor y paleógrafo nahua *Librado Silva Galeana*, primer recipentiario del Premio Nezahualcóyotl de Literatura en Lenguas Indígenas (1994). El texto se relaciona también con la ciencia mesoamericana de transmisión oral, ya que explica cómo se construye y se aprovecha el baño de vapor tradicional en su comunidad nahua de Santa Ana Tlacotenco, que actualmente forma parte de la Delegación de Milpa Alta, en el sureste del Distrito Federal. Aunque varía de material, forma y en cuanto a las hierbas medicinales aprovechadas, el temascal sigue como elemento cultural vivo por toda Mesoamérica.

En conclusión, en el presente tomo y los que seguirán, pretendemos llenar una laguna en los estudios literarios y culturales mexicanos y latinoamericanos, e inspirar a otros, tanto indígenas como no indígenas, a prestar la debida atención—crítica y humana—a las voces contemporáneas que nos hablan desde las profundidades del tiempo; voces que se proyectan en múltiples lenguas para crear puentes de comprensión que son tan necesarias para la sobrevivencia de su sabiduría milenaria, que es parte de nuestra experiencia humana acumulativa y colectiva.

Agradecimientos personales

Agradezco el apoyo constante de mis padres, Harry Frischmann y Thelma Carril, para que yo pudiera educarme más de lo que ellos jamás soñaron posible; a mis abuelos George y Catherine Hogan, quienes hicieron económicamente posible aquel primer viaje a México; y a mi abuelo Esteban Carril, cuya memoria me inspiró a estudiar su lengua materna, el español. Que descansen en paz.

También agradezco al maestro James Wiswall, M.S., por haberme enseñado mis primeras letras en español, y por haberme contagiado su enorme entusiasmo por la cultura mexicana; al doctor Enrique Noble (q.e.p.d.) de la University of Missouri–Saint Louis, quien me inspiró a seguir la carrera de posgrado en Letras Latinoamericanas; y al Dr. Carlos Montemayor por haberme inspirado con su compromiso profesional y humano con las literaturas indígenas contemporáneas de México, y por haber aceptado entrar en esta mancuerna tan estimulante como fructífera.

Finalmente agradezco de manera particular a todos los escritores quienes han compartido tan generosamente su obra y su tiempo; su Palabra se convierte en nuestro mejor guía para el conocimiento de otros universos culturales, conocimiento que a su vez enriquece a la humanidad en un sentido profundamente global.

Universidad de las Américas, Cholula, Puebla,
y San Miguel Nepantla de Sor Juana Inés de la Cruz,
Estado de México
2000–2003

Notas

1. Un gran montículo ceremonial que mide unos 33 metros de alto y cuyo volumen abarca unos 22 millones de pies cúbicos. Monk's Mound corresponde a la cultura Mississippian cuyo auge de desarrollo urbano se dio en Cahokia entre los años 1000–1400 d.C. Este montículo se encuentra todavía rodeado de otros sesenta y cinco más pequeños. En su apogeo, Monk's Mound estuvo coronado de un edificio ceremonial y administrativo masivo que dominaba un centro urbano de diez a veinte mil habitantes. En 1735 curas franceses construyeron una pequeña capilla, ya desaparecida, en una esquina de la primera terraza del montículo; en 1809 frailes franceses de la orden *trappist* construyeron otra capilla en el lugar, que abandonaron en 1813 (de ahí su nombre moderno, que significa "Montículo del Fraile"). Véase *Cahokia, City of the Sun.*

2. Revisada y editada como *El nuevo teatro popular en México.*

3. Su obra teatral, poética y narrativa ha sido editada y difundida debido en gran medida al esfuerzo del Dr. Carlos Montemayor; por mi parte, he publicado textos y análisis de la obra de Dzul Ek.

4. May May y Góngora Pacheco en Tomo 1 (Prosa); Dzul Ek y Sánchez Chan en Tomo 3 (Teatro).

5. México, D.F.: INI/TRF, 1996.

6. La única excepción es la del tzotzil Jacinto Arias, cuya obra fue escrita originalmente en inglés.

7. Ambos términos han sido aplicados por Carrasco a la literatura de los mapuches de Chile. *Oralidad inscrita* es la transcripción fiel de la narración oral. Con respecto a *escritura propia*, "se trata de textos conformados con categorías mapuches en su enunciación y su enunciado, aunque en la concepción de texto estén incluidas categorías no mapuches" (Iván Carrasco, "Etnoliteratura mapuche y literatura chilena: Relaciones," *Actas de Lengua y Literatura Mapuche* 4 [1990]: 19–27). Agradezco a la maestra Paulina Barrenechea el haberme introducido al trabajo de Carrasco.

8. Se produjeron textos de diversas dimensiones y funciones también en pinturas murales, vasijas de cerámica, joyas y alfileres de hueso; otros fueron esculpidos en piedra como monumentos públicos. Muchos han sobrevivido el paso de milenios para atestiguar la complejidad de la cosmovisión y las estructuras sociales mesoamericanas.

9. Véase Elizabeth Hill Boone, *Stories in Red and Black: Pictorial Histories of the Aztecs and Mixtecs.*

10. Véase Michael D. Coe y Mark Van Stone, *Reading the Maya Glyphs.*

11. Gary H. Gossen, *Telling Maya Tales: Tzotzil Identities in Modern Mexico*, p. 84 (traducción nuestra).

12. Véase Dennis Tedlock, prólogo, traducción y notas, *Popol Vuh: The Definitive Edition of the Mayan Book of the Dawn of Life and the Glories of Gods and Kings*, p. 169.

13. Elizabeth Hill Boone, "Aztec Pictorial Histories: Records without Words," en *Writing without Words: Alternative Literacies in Mesoamerica and the Andes*, compil. Elizabeth Hill Boone y Walter D. Mignolo, pp. 71–72 (traducción nuestra).

14. Tedlock, *Popol Vuh*, pp. 31–33 (traducción nuestra).

15. David S. Stuart, "Lectura y escritura en la corte maya," *Arqueología Mexicana* 8, no. 48 (2001): 52.

16. Libros en lengua maya yucateca redactados después de la conquista española en alfabeto latino; su contenido heterogéneo abarca lo religioso (pre-hispánico con unos pocos elementos cristianos), histórico, astrológico, astronómico, ritualístico y literario. Barrera Vásquez y Rendón señalan que sus fuentes son los antiguos libros jeroglíficos, fuentes orales indígenas e impresos europeos. Véase Alfredo Barrera Vásquez y Silvia Rendón, *El libro de los libros de Chilám Balám.*

17. Burns presenta la hipótesis de que antiguamente los textos glíficos eran objeto de presentaciones públicas que alternarían también entre dos lectores, lo cual reflejaría la forma generalizada de pintar los glifos en pares: Allan F. Burns, *An Epoch of Miracles: Oral Literature of the Yucatec Maya*, pp. 22–23 (traducción nuestra). Con respecto a la disposición en pares de los glifos mayas, véase Coe y Van Stone, *Reading the Maya Glyphs*, pp. 17–18.

18. Feliciano Sánchez Chan, prólogo y compil., *Del sabucán del abuelo.* El *sabucán* es una bolsa hecha de fibra de henequén en la que el campesino maya tradicionalmente lleva sus alimentos e instrumentos de trabajo al campo.

19. Ibid., s.p.

20. Entrevista de Frischmann a Sánchez Chan, Mérida, Yucatán, 22 de febrero de 2002.

21. Dora Pellicer, "Oralidad y escritura de la literatura indígena: Una aproximación histórica," en *Situación actual y perspectivas de la literatura en lenguas indígenas*, compil. Carlos Montemayor, p. 31.

22. Ibídem, p. 41.

23. Walter D. Mignolo, "Afterword," en *Writing without Words: Alternative Literacies in Mesoamerica and the Andes*, comp. Boone y Mignolo, pp. 301–302 (traducción nuestra).

24. Miguel León-Portilla, *Literaturas indígenas de México*, p. 311.

25. Robert M. Laughlin, comp. y trad., y Carol Karaskik, comp., *Mayan Tales from Zinacantán: Dreams and Stories from the People of the Bat*, p. 16.

26. Éstos varían de nombre dependiendo de la cultura; véase Apéndices A y H.

27. José Luis Iturrioz Leza, Julio Ramírez de la Cruz y Gabriel Pacheco Salvador, *Función gramática didáctica del huichol*, p. 125.

28. Ibídem, p. 264.

29. Ibídem, p. 265.

30. Ibídem, p. 125; véase también Apéndice H.

31. Carlos Montemayor, *Arte y trama en el cuento indígena*, p. 22.

32. Ibídem, pp. 20–21.

33. Sin embargo, hoy en día esta disyuntiva se está extendiendo dentro de la comunidad indígena misma: los jóvenes tienden a creer cada vez menos en las historias de transformaciones, deidades de la naturaleza, etc.

34. Laughlin and Karasik, *Mayan Tales*, p. 13.

35. Véase nota 7.

36. Carrasco, "Etnoliteratura mapuche," pp. 21–22.

37. María Luisa Góngora Pacheco, *U tzikbalilo'ob Oxkutzcab yéetel Maní*, p. 15/*Cuentos de Oxkutzcab y Maní*, p. 13.

38. La autora explica que el narrador, Aurelio Zumárraga, empleaba ambas palabras en español en su narración. Entrevista de Frischmann a Góngora Pacheco, Oxkutzcab, Yucatán, 18 de febrero de 2002.

39. Como señala Montemayor, este cuento tiene una larga historia que se remonta a la antigüedad griega y hebrea; pasó posteriormente por Italia y Francia antes de arraigarse entre los Mayas de Yucatán. Véase Montemayor, *Arte y trama*, p. 139.

40. María Roselia Jiménez, *Jna'jeltik/Vivencias tojolabales*, p. 48.

41. A propósito, Montemayor señala que "la conservación de los cuentos tradicionales se explica por la fijación de un grupo de *motivos* episódicos, objetuales o de personajes cuya supresión u olvido equivaldría a la desaparición del relato mismo" (*Arte y trama*, p. 42).

42. Laughlin and Karasik, *Mayan Tales*, p. 15.

43. Isaías Hernández Isidro, *Cha' jop'e t'ok chap'e älkan/Las doce verdades*, p. 7.

44. Ibídem, p. 64.

45. Entrevista de Frischmann a Hernández Isidro, México, D.F., Casa de los Escritores en Lenguas Indígenas, 22 de mayo de 1998.

46. Esta experiencia es la base de la narración titulada "Dz'aji"/"Cuento" (Hernández Isidro, *Cha' jop'e t'ok chap'e älkan/Las doce verdades*, pp. 21–22 and 23–24). El título resulta engañoso en español, ya que intenta traducir la palabra yok'ot'an *dz'aji*, que quiere decir "lo que

tú estás diciendo de lo que acabas de vivir." Entrevista de Frischmann a Hernández Isidro, Casa de los Escritores en Lenguas Indígenas, México, D.F., 14 de agosto de 1998.

47. Entrevista de Frischmann a Hernández Isidro, 14 de agosto de 1998.

48. Miguel Ángel May May, *Lajump'éel maaya tzikbalo'ob/Diez relatos mayas*, p. 125.

49. Diego Méndez Gúzmán, *A'yejetik yu'un jtzeltaletik ta Tenejapa/Relatos tzeltales de Tenejapa*, p. 51.

50. Robert M. Laughlin, compil., trad., prólogo y notas, *Of Cabbages and Kings: Tales from Zinacantán*, p. 9 (traducción nuestra).

51. Joel Torres Sánchez, *P'urhepecha Uandatskuecha/Narrativa P'urhepecha*, t. 1, pp. 9–10.

52. Ibídem, p. 175.

53. Ibídem, p. 187.

54. Ibídem, pp. 194–195.

55. Gabriel Pacheco, "Nuestra Madre Yurienaka," en *Tatei Yurienaka y otros cuentos huicholes*, pp. 153–159.

56. Ibídem, p. 157.

57. Ibídem, p. 9.

58. Jorge Echeverría Lope, *X-La'-Boon-Suumij/Vieja huella de soga.*

59. Entrevista de Frischmann a Echeverría Lope, Unidad Regional Yucatán de Culturas Populares, Mérida, 19 de marzo de 2001.

60. Román Güemes Jiménez, "Chicomexóchitl: El niño devorado por el templo," en *Narrativa Náhuatl Contemporánea/Yancuic Nahuasasanili: Antología*, pp. 165–180.

61. Ibídem, pp. 165, 166, 169, 180.

62. Ibídem, p. 169.

63. Enrique Pérez López, "K'ox y el Dueño del agua," en *Alperes: Te'tikal mut/El pájaro alférez*, p. 151.

64. Enrique Pérez López, *El K'ox: El niño que se transformó en sol.*

65. "The Three Suns," #T13, T155, T162, en Laughlin, *Of Cabbages and Kings.*

66. Domingo Gómez Gutiérrez, "Conclusión: Versión conjuntada," en *Jwan Lopes: Bats'il Ajaw/Juan López: Héroe Tzeltal*, p. 117.

67. Carlos Montemayor, *Chiapas: La rebelión indígena de México*, pp. 117–130.

68. Carrasco, "Etnoliteratura mapuche," p. 25.

69. Dominguez Aké, *La milpa en Muxupip*, p. 131.

70. Ibídem, p. 7.

71. Entrevista de Frischmann a Domínguez Aké, Mérida, Yucatán, 20 de marzo de 2001.

Obras citadas

Arias Pérez, Jacinto. *El mundo numinoso de los mayas.* 2a ed. Tuxtla Gutiérrez, Chiapas: Gobierno del Estado de Chiapas/Instituto Chiapaneco de Cultura, 1991.

Barrera Vásquez, Alfredo, y Silvia Rendón. *El libro de los libros de Chilám Balám.* Mérida, Yucatán: Producción Editorial Dante, 1989.

Boone, Elizabeth Hill. "Aztec Pictorial Histories: Records without Words." En *Writing without Words: Alternative Literacies in Mesoamerica and the Andes*, comp. Elizabeth Boone y Walter D. Mignolo, pp. 50–76. Durham, N.C.: Duke University Press, 1994.

———. *Stories in Red and Black. Pictorial Histories of the Aztecs and Mixtecs.* Austin: University of Texas Press, 2000.

Burns, Allan F. *An Epoch of Miracles: Oral Literature of the Yucatec Maya.* Austin: University of Texas Press, 1983.

Cahokia, City of the Sun. Collinsville, Ill.: Cahokia Mounds Museum Society, 1992 (edición revisada, 1999).

Carrasco, Iván. "Etnoliteratura mapuche y literatura chilena: Relaciones." *Actas de Lengua y Literatura Mapuche* 4 (1990): 19–27.

Castellanos Martínez, Javier. *Wila che be ze lhao/Cantares de los vientos primerizos: Novela zapoteca.* Colección Letras Indígenas Contemporáneas. México, D.F.: Editorial Diana/CNCA/DGCP, 1994.

Coe, Michael D., y Mark Van Stone. *Reading the Maya Glyphs.* London y New York: Thames & Hudson, 2001.

Domínguez Aké, Santiago. *La milpa en Muxupip.* Colección Letras Indígenas Contemporáneas. México, D.F.: DGCP, 1996.

Echeverría Lope, Jorge. *X-La'-Boon-Suumij/Vieja huella de soga.* Letras Mayas Contemporáneas, 3a serie, vol. 8. C. Montemayor, coordinador de la colección. México, D.F.: INI/TRF, 1998.

Frischmann, Donald H. *El nuevo teatro popular en México.* México, D.F.: Instituto Nacional de Bellas Artes/Centro de Investigación y Documentación Teatral Rodolfo Usigli, 1990.

———. Entrevista a Santiago Domínguez Aké (inédita). Mérida, Yucatán, 20 de marzo de 2001.

———. Entrevista a Jorge Echeverría Lope (inédita). Mérida, Yucatán, 19 de marzo de 2001.

———. Entrevista a María Luisa Góngora Pacheco (inédita). Oxkutzcab, Yucatán, 18 de febrero de 2002.

———. Entrevistas a Isaías Hernández Isidro (inédita). México, D.F., 22 de mayo y 14 de agosto de 1998.

———. Entrevista a Feliciano Sánchez Chan (inédita). Mérida, Yucatán, 22 de febrero de 2002.

Gómez Gutiérrez, Domingo. *Jwan Lopes: Bats'il Ajaw/Juan López: Héroe Tzeltal.* Colección Letras Mayas Contemporáneas: Chiapas, 2a serie, vol. 4. C. Montemayor, coordinador de la colección. México, D.F.: INI/TRF, 1996.

Góngora Pacheco, María Luisa. *Cuentos de Oxkutzcab y Maní.* Colección Letras Mayas Contemporáneas, 1a serie, vol. 4. C. Montemayor, coordinador de la colección. México, D.F.: INI/Sedesol, 1993.

———. *U tzikbalilo'ob Oxkutzcab yéetel Maní.* Colección Letras Mayas Contemporáneas, 1a serie, vol. 3. C. Montemayor, coordinador de la colección. México, D.F.: INI/Sedesol, 1993.

Gossen, Gary H. *Telling Maya Tales: Tzotzil Identities in Modern Mexico.* New York y London: Routledge, 1999.

Güemes Jiménez, Román. "Chicomexóchitl: El niño devorado por el templo." En *Narrativa Náhuatl Contemporánea/Yancuic Nahuasasanili: Antología*, pp. 165–180. México, D.F.: Editorial Diana/CNCA/DGCP, 1994.

Hernández Isidro, Isaías. *Cha' jop'e t'ok chap'e älkan/Las doce verdades.* México, D.F.: DGCP, 1997.

Iturrioz Leza, José Luis, Julio Ramírez de la Cruz y Gabriel Pacheco Salvador. *Función gramática didáctica del huichol.* Guadalajara: Departamento de Estudios en Lenguas Indígenas, Universidad de Guadalajara, 1999.

Jiménez, María Roselia. *Jna'jeltik/Vivencias tojolabales.* Colección Letras Mayas Contemporáneas: Chiapas, 2a serie, vol. 5. C. Montemayor, coordinador de la colección. México, D.F.: INI/TRF, 1996.

Laughlin, Robert M, compil., trans., prólogo y notas. *Of Cabbages and Kings: Tales from Zinacantán.* Smithsonian Contributions to Anthropology 23. Washington, D.C.: Smithsonian Institution Press, 1977.

Laughlin, Robert M., compil. y trans., y Carol Karasik, comp. *Mayan Tales from Zinacantán: Dreams and Stories from the People of the Bat.* Washington, D.C.: Smithsonian Institution Press, 1988.

León-Portilla, Miguel. *Literaturas indígenas de México.* 2a ed. México, D.F.: Editorial Mapfre/FCE, 1992.

May May, Miguel Ángel. *Lajump'éel maaya tzikbalo'ob/Diez relatos mayas.* Colección Letras Mayas Contemporáneas, 3a serie, vol. 10. C. Montemayor, coordinador de la colección. México, D.F.: INI/TRF, 1998.

Méndez Guzmán, Diego. *A'yejetik yu'un jtzeltaletik ta Tenejapa/Relatos tzeltales de Tenejapa.* Colección Letras Mayas Contemporáneas: Chiapas, 2a serie, vol. 7. C. Montemayor, coordinador de la colección. México, D.F.: INI/TRF, 1996.

Mignolo, Walter D. "Afterword." En *Writing without Words. Alternative Literacies in Mesoamerica and the Andes,* comp. Elizabeth Hill Boone y Walter D. Mignolo, pp. 293–313. Durham, N.C.: Duke University Press, 1994.

Montemayor, Carlos. *Arte y trama en el cuento indígena.* México, D.F.: FCE, 1998.

———. *Chiapas: La rebelión indígena de México.* México, D.F.: Joaquín Mortiz, 1997.

Narrativa Náhuatl Contemporánea/Yancuic Nahuasasanili: Antología. Colección Letras Indígenas Contemporáneas. México, D.F.: Editorial Diana/CNCA/DGCP, 1994.

Pacheco, Gabriel. *Tatei Yurienaka y otros cuentos huicholes.* Colección Letras Indígenas Contemporáneas. México, D.F.: Editorial Diana/CNCA/DGCP,1994.

Pellicer, Dora. "Oralidad y escritura de la literatura indígena: Una aproximación histórica." En *Situación actual y perspectivas de la literatura en lenguas indígenas,* comp. Carlos Montemayor, pp. 15–53. México, D.F.: Conaculta, 1993.

Pérez López, Enrique. *Alperes: Te'tikal mut/El pájaro alférez.* Colección Letras Mayas Contemporáneas: Chiapas, 2a serie, vol. 11. C. Montemayor, coordinador de la colección. México, D.F.: INI/TRF, 1996.

———. *El K'ox: El niño que se transformó en sol.* San Cristóbal de las Casas: Universidad Nacional Autónoma de México/Centro de Investigación Humanística de Mesoamérica y el Estado de Chiapas, 1995.

Sánchez Chan, Feliciano, prólogo y comp. *Del sabucán del abuelo.* Mérida y Xaya, Tekax: Miatzil Maayáa, A.C., 2001.

Stuart, David S. "Lectura y escritura en la corte maya." *Arqueología Mexicana* 8, no. 48 (2001): 48–53.

Tedlock, Dennis, prólogo, trad. y notas. *Popol Vuh: The Definitive Edition of the Mayan Book of the Dawn of Life and the Glories of Gods and Kings.* New York: Touchstone/Simon & Schuster, 1985.

Torres Sánchez, Joel. *P'urhepecha Uandatskuecha/Narrativa P'urhepecha.* Tomo 1. Morelia: INI/PACMYC, 1997.

———. *P'urhepecha Uandantskuecha/Narrativa P'urhepecha.* Tomo 2. Morelia: SEP, 2001.

María Luisa Góngora Pacheco

Maya

María Luisa Góngora Pacheco. Photographed at her home in Oxkutzcab, Yucatán.

María Luisa Góngora Pacheco is one of today's foremost Mayan writers. In Yucatán's Oxkutzcab region, she has supported and carried out numerous activities related to Mayan culture, including language, traditional medicine, and historical research. In 1984 in Yucatán she published *Jo'op'óol baaxalo'ob* (Five Children's Stories) (Mérida: DGCP). As part of the first series of the Colección Letras Mayas Contemporáneas (C. Montemayor, series ed.) she published *U tzikbalilo'ob Oxkutzcab yéetel Maní* (vol. 3; Mexico City: INI/Sedesol/TRF, 1993) and *Cuentos de Oxkutzcab y Maní* (Stories from Oxkutzcab and Maní) (vol. 4; Mexico City: INI/Sedesol/TRF, 1993) and co-authored *U Yum Santísima Kruuz Tuunil Xocén* (vol. 25; Mexico City: INI/Sedesol/TRF, 1993) and *Yum Santísima Cruz Tun* (The Very Holy Lord *Tun* Cross of Xocén) (vol. 26; Mexico City: INI/Sedesol/TRF, 1993). In the third series of the same collection she published *Chan Mosón/Pequeño remolino* (Little Whirlpool) (vol. 11; Mexico City: INI/TRF, 1998).

María Luisa Góngora Pacheco es una de las más relevantes escritoras entre los mayas actuales. Ha impulsado en la región de Oxkutzcab numerosas actividades relacionadas con la cultura maya tanto a nivel del idioma como de la medicina tradicional y la investigación histórica. En 1984 publicó en el estado de Yucatán *Jo'op'óol baaxalo'ob* (Cinco cuentos infantiles) (Mérida: DGCP). En la primera serie de la colección Letras Mayas Contemporáneas (C. Montemayor, coord. de la colección) publicó *U tzikbalilo'ob Oxkutzcab yéetel Maní* (vol. 3; México, D.F.: INI/Sedesol/TRF, 1993) y *Cuentos de Oxkutzcab y Maní* (vol. 4; México, D.F.: INI/Sedesol/TRF, 1993) y fue coautora de *U Yum Santísima Kruuz Tuunil Xocén* (vol. 25; México, D.F.: INI/Sedesol/TRF, 1993) y de *Yum Santísima Cruz Tun* (vol. 26; México, D.F.: INI/Sedesol/TRF, 1993). En la tercera serie de la misma colección publicó *Chan Mosón/Pequeño remolino* (vol. 11; México, D.F.: INI/TRF, 1998).

X-ootzilil

María Luisa Góngora Pacheco

Maya[1]

[From *U tzikbalilo'ob Oxkutzcab yéetel Maní*, pp. 15–18. Maya dziibo'ob bejla'e, 1st series, vol. 3, C. Montemayor, series ed. Mexico City: INI/Sedesol/TRF, 1993.]

Yum Aurelio Zumarragae' ku tzikbaltike', anchaj bin juntéenake', juntúul x-chiich ku k'aba'tike' X-óotzilil, leti' bin kaja'an jo'kaaj. Tu joonajil u yootoche' u pak'maj junkúul wayúum[2] ku dzaik sen ya'ab u yich láaj ja'ab. Ba'ax beetik u k'úuxil le nojoch ko'olelo', tumen tuláakal le máax ken u yil u yich le wayúumo' ku taaktal u yéensik u jaant kex ma' u k'áatiko'ob ti'.

Junp'éel k'iine', le nojoch ko'olelo' tu yilaj tu k'íiwikil le kaajo' juntúul nojoch wíinik táan u k'áatik u máat kex junp'íit ba'al u jaantej, ba'ale' mixmáak dzaik ti'. Le nojoch ko'olelo' tu ch'a'aj óotzilil ti'e', ka tu bisaj tu yotoch ti'al u síikt ti' kex junp'íit ki'iwaj; ka dzo'ok u janal le nojoch wíiniko', ka tu ya'alaj ti' le nojoch ko'olel beya':

—Beora dzo'ok a síik ba'al in jaante', k'aat ti' ten je ba'axake', tene' kin dzaik ti' tech.

—Utzil máak—tu ya'alaj le nojoch ko'olelo'—chéen ba'ax in k'áate', ka wa'al ti' le wayúum ma' u cha'ik u yéemel je máax ka na'akak tu k'abe', tak le ma' in wa'al ti' ka béeychajaki'.

—Béeychajak ba'ax a k'áatij—tu ya'alaj le nojoch wíiniko', ka binij.

Le nojoch ko'olelo', ki'imakchaj u yóol ka tu yilaj táan u béeytal ba'ax tu ya'alaj le nojoch wíiniko'.

Máanik ya'ab ja'abo'obe', ma' túun junp'éel k'iin ti' lelo' k'uch Yum Kíimil[3] tu yiknaal le nojoch ko'olelo', ka tu ya'alaj ti' beya':

—Dzo'ok u k'uchul u k'iinil ka talakech tin wéetel X-ma Ootzilil, yo'olal lelo', taalen in ch'a'ech.

Bey túun ma' taak u bin tu yéetelo' ka tu jan tukultaj bix úunchak ma' u bisa'al tumen Yum Kíimile', ka tu ya'alaj ti'e':

—Je'el in bin ta wéetele', ba'ale' k'abéet ka wéens jayp'éel wayúum ka in nóolej.[4]

—Ma'alo'ob túun, beora ken in beete'—tu núukaj Yum Kíimil.

Bino'ob tu yáanal le che'o'. Ti' yano'obe' ka tu ya'alaj X-ma Ootzilil ti' Yum Kíimil beya':

—Na'aken tak te tu jach ka'analilo', te tu'ux yan u nuuktakilo'obo', leti'ob in k'aato'obo'.

Yum Kíimile' jach topa'an u yu'ubikubae' ka na'ak tu k'ab le che'o', ba'ale ma' páajchaj u yéemeli', tumen ti' táak'i'.

Le X-Ootzilil ka tu yilaj ba'ax ku yúuchule' ka ook tu yotoch.

Bey máanik ya'ab ja'abo'obo', Yum Kíimile' ma' táan u bisik mixmáak, kex ka jach k'oja'anchajak. Le aj Dzaako'obo' jak'a'an u yóolo'ob u yiliko'ob ma' táan u kíimil mix máak, kex leti'ob taak u kíimilo'ob.

Junp'éel k'iine', juntúul ti' le Aj Dzaako'ob bin tu yotoch le nojoch ko'olelo', ba'ax yáax tu yilaj le ka k'uche' leti' le che' jach piin u yicho', ka taakchaj u jaantik jayp'éeli'. Na'ake', ma' páajchaj u yéemeli'. Tu k'ab le che'o' ti' tu yiluba yéetel Yum Kíimile' ka tu k'áataj ti':

—Baáx ka beetik weye', tuláakal máak kaxtikech, tumen u k'áato'ob kíimil; teche' ma' táan a k'uchul a ch'a'ob.

—Ba'ax úuche' le u x-nuk meejenxulub u yuumil le naja' tu topen, taalen in ch'ae', ma le x-che'ek'a'anpeelo' tu ya'alaj je'el u bin tin wéetele', ba'ale', táanile' ka in wens ti' jayp'éel wayúum; ka na'akene' ma' páajchaj in wéemeli', ma túun je'elena'. Tuláakal máak ku na'akale' ku p'áatal weye', tak teech ken p'áatakech—tu núukaj Yum Kíimil.

—Yo'olal túun lelo' ma' táan u kíimil le máako'obo'—tu ya'alaj le Aj Dzaako'—ba'ax k'abéet k-beetike' k-éemel te'ela'—ka júup awat:

—¡Ko'otene'ex weye'! ¡Ko'oteneéx weye'! ¡Yum Kíimile' tin wéetel yan! ¡Ko'otene'ex a wile'ex!

Jach k'a'am awatnajike' ka káaj u much'ikuba máako'ob te yáanal le che'o'.

—Eemene'ex—ku ya'alal ti'ob.

—Ma' táan k-páajtal, tuláakal máax ku na'akale', wey ku p'atalale'—tu núukaj le Aj Dzaako'.

Le máako'obo' tu ya'alajo'ob u ch'akiko'ob le che'o',

ti'al ka éemek Yum Kíimil yéetel le Aj Dzaako'. Ma túun tu yoorail nuka'aj u ch'ako'obe', ka tíip' le nojoch ko'olelo'.

—¡Ba'ax ka tukultik a beetike'ex! Wa k'aat a wéense'ex le máako'ob yano'ob te che'o', ba'axten ma' táan a walike'ex ten.

—¡Sa'as to'on!—Tu ya'alajo'ob le máako'obo'.

Le X-Ootzililo' tu sutuba aktáan ti' le che'o' ka tu ya'alaj ti':

—¡Che' cha' u láaj éemelo'ob!

Le ka dzo'ok u laaj éemelo'obe', Yum Kíimile' tu ya'alaj beya':

—X-nuk Ootzilil, tu yo'olal ma' ta cha'aj in wéemel te che'o', bejlae' jach taj ya'ab meyaj yan ten; ma' táan u páajtal in bisikech, tu láak' k'iin wale'.

—Bin Yum Kíimil. Le X-óotzilo' p'aat wey yóok'ol kaabe'; le o'olal tak bejla' ti' yan ichilo'one'—dzo'ok u ya'alik Yum Aurelio.

Notes

1. At the end of the twentieth century the Mayan language or Yucatec Mayan was Mexico's second largest Indigenous language in number of speakers: nearly 1.5 million, living primarily on the Yucatán Peninsula, in the states of Campeche, Yucatán, and Quintana Roo, in addition to some areas of the Republic of Belize. The alphabet used by María Luisa Góngora Pacheco is based on the Practical Literacy Alphabet for Adult Mayan Speakers, established by several government institutions in August 1984, in Mérida, Yucatán. The author's orthographic variations vis-à-vis this alphabet reside in the use of *tz* and *dz* rather than *ts* and *ts'*, respectively.

2. *Talisia olivaeformis:* this Mayan word has become hispanicized in two forms: *huaya* and *guaya.*

3. Here the term "Yum" does not imply the sacred, as it does when used with the names of other spiritual entities (see Appendix E). Rather than designating this character as the "Owner," "Guardian," or "God" of Death, "Yum" should be interpreted here as a reverential form of address for a male adult, which might be rendered into English as "Sir Death" or, more literally, as "Sir Dying."

4. Verb rendered in Spanish as *anolar.* (See note 3 of the English-language text.)

Notas

1. La lengua maya, o mejor, el maya yucateco, era a finales del siglo XX la segunda lengua indígena con más hablantes en México: cerca de millón y medio de individuos asentados primordialmente en la Península de Yucatán en los estados de Campeche, Yucatán y Quintana Roo, y también en algunas zonas de Belice. El alfabeto empleado por María Luisa Góngora Pacheco tiene como referente básico el Alfabeto Práctico para la Alfabetización de los Adultos Hablantes de Maya que diversas instituciones oficiales de México acordaron en Mérida, Yucatán, en agosto de 1984. Las diferencias ortográficas de la autora con el alfabeto acordado institucionalmente son dos: el empleo de *tz* en lugar de *ts* y el de *dz* en lugar de *ts'*.

2. *Talisia olivaeformis:* esta voz en maya se ha castellanizado bajo dos formas: *huaya* y *guaya.*

3. El término "Yum" no tiene aquí el sentido sagrado que otras entidades espirituales (véase Apéndice E). Más que el "Dueño," "Guardián" o "Dios" de la muerte, debe entenderse como la forma de respeto o distinción con que se trata a una persona adulta de género masculino: "El Señor Muerte," o quizás, más literalmente, "El Señor Morir."

4. Verbo que se castellaniza como *anolar.* (Véase la nota 3 del texto español.)

Poverty

María Luisa Góngora Pacheco

Maya[1]

[From *U tzikbalilo'ob Oxkutzcab yéetel Maní,* pp. 15–18, and *Cuentos de Oxkutzcab y Maní,* pp. 13–15. Colección Letras Mayas Contemporáneas, 1st series, vols. 3 and 4, C. Montemayor, series ed. Mexico City: INI/Sedesol/TRF, 1993.]

Señor Aurelio Zumárraga tells that there was once a certain elderly woman whose name was Poverty, and she lived on the outskirts of town. She had planted a huaya[2] tree just outside her front door, and it bore fruit all year long. What bothered the old woman was that anyone who saw the fruit was enticed by it and would climb the tree and suck[3] on the huayas without asking permission.

One day, when the old woman arrived in the center of

town, she saw an elderly man begging. He was asking for food, if not money, but no one paid any attention to him. The old woman was moved, seeing him in such a pitiful state, and took him home to feed him. When the little man finished eating, he said to the old woman: "Now that I have eaten what you have given me, tell me what you want, that I may give it to you."

"Good man," said the old woman, "all I can wish for is that you tell the huaya tree not to let anyone down who climbs up its limbs, until I command it to."

"Your wish is fulfilled!" answered the old man, and he went away satisfied.

The old woman was very pleased to see that what the old man promised came true.

Many years passed, and one day the Lord of Death came to see the old woman and ordered her: "It is time for you to come with me, old woman Poverty. That is why I have come for you."

She thought quickly how she might rid herself of Death and said to him: "I will go with you, but first I want you to pick some huayas so I may suck on them."

"All right, I shall do it right away," answered Death.

They went over to the tree; and once they were underneath it, the old woman said to Death: "Climb up to the highest part, for there you will find the biggest and most beautiful huayas: those are the ones I want."

Death, very sure of himself, climbed the tree but was unable to climb down.

Poverty, seeing what had happened, went back into her house and went about her business.

Many years passed, and Death could not get to anyone, even if someone fell ill. The doctors were astonished that old woman Poverty could not die, even if she tried.

One day, one of the doctors went to the old woman's house and the first thing he saw was the huaya tree, full of fruit. He had such an urge to eat some that he climbed the tree and then could not climb down. Among the branches, he encountered the Lord of Death and asked him: "What are you doing here? Everyone is looking for you; people are ready to die and you no longer come to take them away."

"Look, what happened is this: that crazy old woman tricked me. I came to take her away, and the old shrew said she would go with me but asked me to pick her some huayas first. Once I climbed up, I could not climb down again, and here I am. Whoever climbs up becomes stuck; even you will stay up here," responded Death.

"So that is why no one is dying," said the doctor. "What we should do is get down"; and he began to yell: "Come, come, Death is in my power, come and see!"

He shouted so much and so loudly that the townspeople gathered under the tree.

"Come down!" they said.

"We cannot; everyone who climbs up here stays," answered the doctor.

Then the people agreed to cut down the tree so that the doctor and Death could get down. When they were ready to start cutting, old woman Poverty appeared.

"What are you doing? If you wanted to get them out of the tree, why did you not tell me?"

"Pardon us," said the townspeople.

Old woman Poverty turned to the tree and said: "Let everyone down!"

Once everyone was down, the Lord of Death said to her: "Old woman Poverty, because you did not let me down out of the tree, I have so much work that I am unable to take you away today. I will see you another day."

The Lord of Death left, and Poverty remained in the world. For that reason she is still among us.

Notes

1. At the end of the twentieth century the Mayan language or Yucatec Mayan was Mexico's second largest indigenous language in number of speakers: nearly 1.5 million living primarily on the Yucatán Peninsula, in the states of Campeche, Yucatán and Quintana Roo, in addition to some areas of the Republic of Belize.

2. *Talisia olivaeformis: huaya* is the Hispanicized version of the Mayan *wayúum*, a tree native to the Yucatán Peninsula and several regions of the states of Tabasco and Chiapas. It reaches a height of up to 20 meters and produces an edible elliptical fruit 2–4 centimeters in diameter.

3. The Mayas often hold the large pit of the huaya fruit between the tongue and the hard palate for some time, without chewing on it, as if it were a candy or a type of game. In the Spanish of Yucatán, this action is called *anolar,* from the Mayan verb *nóol,* "to play with an object in the mouth."

La Pobreza

María Luisa Góngora Pacheco

Maya[1]

[De *Cuentos de Oxkutzcab y Maní,* pp. 13–15. Colección Letras Mayas Contemporáneas, 1a serie, vol. 4, C. Montemayor, coord. de la colección. México, D.F.: INI/Sedesol/TRF, 1993.]

El señor Aurelio Zumárraga cuenta que hubo una vez cierta viejita cuyo nombre era Pobreza y que vivía en las afueras de la población. En la puerta de su casa había sembrado una mata de huaya[2] y ésta le daba frutos todo el año. Lo que le molestaba a la viejita es que aquel que veía el fruto le daban ganas de comérselo y sin pedirle permiso se subía a la mata y se anolaba[3] las huayas.

Un día, cuando la viejita llegó al centro del poblado, vio que un viejito pedía limosna, pedía aunque sea le dieran algo de comer en vez de unas monedas, pero nadie lo tomaba en cuenta. A la viejita le dio pena verlo en ese estado tan lastimoso y se lo llevó a su casa para darle de almorzar. Cuando el hombrecito terminó de comer, le dijo a la viejita:

—Ahora que ya comí lo que me diste, pídeme lo que quieras, que yo puedo concedértelo.

—Buen hombre—dijo la viejita—lo único que quiero es que le digas a la huaya que no deje bajar al que suba a sus ramas, hasta que yo lo mande.

—¡Que se cumpla lo que pides!—contestó el viejito y se fue satisfecho.

La viejita quedó muy complacida al ver que se cumplía la promesa del viejito.

Pasaron muchos años y un día llegó con la viejita el señor de la Muerte, quien le ordenó:

—Ya es tiempo de que vengas conmigo, vieja Pobreza, por eso te vine a buscar.

Ella pensó rápidamente la forma de deshacerse de la Muerte y le dijo:

—Me voy contigo, pero primero quiero que bajes unas huayas para que yo anole.

—Bien, en seguida lo haré—contestó la Muerte.

Se dirigieron al árbol y ya debajo, la viejita le dijo a la Muerte:

—Sube hasta allá en lo más alto, ahí se encuentran las más grandes y hermosas huayas, de esas quiero.

La Muerte, muy segura de sí misma, trepó a la mata, pero no pudo bajarse.

La Pobreza, al ver lo que sucedía, se metió a su casa y se desentendió de todo.

Así pasaron muchos años y la Muerte no llegaba a nadie, aunque se enfermara la persona. Los doctores veían con asombro que la viejita Pobreza no moría aún buscando alguna manera de hacerlo.

Un día, uno de los doctores fue a la casa de la viejita y lo primero que vio fue la mata llena de frutos; se subió para comer algunos y no pudo bajar. En las ramas encontró al señor de la Muerte y le preguntó:

—¿Qué haces aquí? Todos te andan buscando, pues ya quieren morirse y tú no llegas para llevártelos.

—Mira, lo que pasó fue que esa mentecata de viejita de la casa me fregó; pues vine a buscarla y la muy taimada me dijo que se iría conmigo, pero antes le bajara unas cuantas huayas. Al subir no pude bajarme y aquí me tienes, y todo aquel que se sube, se queda y hasta tú te quedarás—contestó la Muerte.

—Entonces, a eso se debe que no mueran las personas—dijo el doctor.—Lo que debemos hacer es bajar—y empezó a gritar ¡vengan aquí, vengan aquí, la Muerte está en mi poder, vengan a verla!

Fue tanto lo que gritó y tan fuerte, que la gente de la población se reunió debajo del árbol.

—Bajen—les decían.

—No podemos, todo el que se sube se queda aquí—contestó el doctor.

Entonces la gente acordó cortar el árbol para que bajaran el doctor y la Muerte. Cuando iban a comenzar, se asomó la viejita Pobreza.

—¿Qué pretenden hacer? Si quieren bajar a los que están en la mata de huaya, ¿por qué no me lo dicen?

—Discúlpenos—dijeron los ahí reunidos.

La vieja Pobreza se volvió hacia el árbol y le dijo:

—¡Deja que todos bajen!

Cuando todos bajaron, el Señor de la Muerte le dijo:

—Vieja Pobreza, por no dejarme bajar del árbol, ahora tengo mucho trabajo y no te puedo llevar, otro día será.

Se fue el señor de la Muerte y la Pobreza se quedó en la tierra. Por eso hasta ahora la tenemos con nosotros.

Notas

1. La lengua maya, o mejor, el maya yucateco, era a finales del siglo XX la segunda lengua indígena con más hablantes en México: cerca de millón y medio de individuos asentados primordialmente en la Península de Yucatán en los estados de Campeche, Yucatán y Quintana Roo, y también en algunas zonas de Belice.

2. *Talisia olivaeformis: huaya* es la españolización de la voz maya *wayúum,* árbol de la península de Yucatán y de varias regiones de Tabasco y Chiapas. Puede medir hasta 20 metros y produce un fruto elíptico de 2 a 4 centímetros, comestible.

3. Los mayas suelen mantener en la boca mucho tiempo, entre el paladar y la lengua, sin masticar, la semilla interior del fruto de la huaya como dulce o juego. Le llaman a esa acción *anolar,* del verbo maya *nóol,* "jugar con un objeto en la boca."

Jorge Echeverría Lope

Maya

Jorge Echeverría Lope. Photographed at Hacienda Chunkanán, Cuzamá, Yucatán.

Jorge Echeverría Lope was born on September 4, 1947, on the Chunkanán Hacienda in Cuzamá, Yucatán. He studied telegraphy and radio electronics in the city of Mérida from 1967 to 1969. He presently works as a small merchant. Since 1984, he has been an independent short-story writer in the Mayan language and a consultant to a Mayan language reading/writing workshop. In 1990, 1992, and 1995 Echeverría Lope earned first place in the annual Mayan-language literary contests organized by Mérida's Instituto de Cultura. In 1993 the Yucatán Instituto de Cultura published his book *Buukinte Nook'a'/Ponte esta ropa* (Put on These Clothes). In the third series of the Colección Letras Mayas Contemporáneas he published the volume entitled *X-La'-Boon-Suumij/Vieja huella de soga* (Ancient Rope Marks).

Jorge Echeverría Lope nació el 4 de septiembre de 1947 en la Hacienda Chunkanán, de Cuzamá, Yucatán. Estudió telegrafía y mecánica de radio en la ciudad de Mérida entre 1967 y 1969. Actualmente se desempeña como comerciante en pequeño. Desde 1984, de manera independiente, escribe cuentos en lengua maya y asesora un taller de lectoescritura en esa lengua. Ha obtenido el primer lugar en los concursos anuales de literatura en lengua maya organizados por el Instituto de Cultura de Yucatán en 1990, 1992 y 1995. En 1993 el Instituto de Cultura de Yucatán le publicó *Buukinte Nook'a'* (Ponte esta ropa). En la tercera serie de la Colección Letras Mayas Contemporáneas publicó *X-La'-Boon-Suumij* (Vieja huella de soga).

X-La'-Boon-Suumij

Jorge Echeverría Lope

Maya[1]

[From *X-La'-Boon-Suumij/Vieja huella de soga,* pp. 7–22. Maya dziibo'ob bejla'e, 3rd series, vol. 8, C. Montemayor, series ed. Mexico City: INI/TRF, 1998.]

—Hey, hey, tu'ux ka bin paal ma' ta wilik ta'itak u chíini k'iin ts'ookole' a kajal náach p'aata', ki' suut paach ka suunakech tanaj. Tumen k'áaxe', yéetel ak'abe' ku jo'osik u yáayam je' ti' máa sajake', bey xan ku náaktsentik máax jach ts'íik u ts'ikuba.

—Tech wa ka t'an noj lu'um.

—Ma' wa ta k'ajóoltik in t'aan. Pakteni', ten u nojochil Ya'axche'.[2]

—Ba'an túun ka béetik weyé, masak' k'aja'anten chéen ich káj p'ata'anech kajtá'.

—Le ba'ax ka wa'aliko' ma' beyi', a woje', chéen jujuntúul ti' in páalal yéetel jujuntúul ti' in wáabilo'ob bisa'an kájtál ich kaaj, ts'o'okole', Jajal-K'uj k'ubmi ti' maya t'aan wíinik u tia'al u k'ajóolko'ob u bejil ka'an. U páay ti' le je'elo' ma' a wa'a'len wa saatalech' wa yaan ba'ax ku máan a kaxant', ts'ookole' mix a k'aaba' a wa'alen.

—Ma' wa ta k'uuxi ka in t'anech, "Yum Ya'axche'," [3] wa k'abéet in t'ankech "U Nojoch Yum Ya'axche'." [4]

—Mejen ma'alob a t'anken yoolá "Yum Ya'axche' " ma' k'as in wu'uyik. Teche' ts'o'ok a ts'ik ulaak' unp'éel in k'aaba', ts'ookole' ma' a wa'aten máakalmáak a tia'al, wa x-ma' k'aaba'ech.

—A woje, yaax kin in wa'atech, in k'aaba' Súulub, in k'a' k'aaba' yo'ola in tatae', Chan, in ka' k'aaba' yo'ola in mamae', Ek', tuulis in k'aabae', Súulub Chan Ek', chen baale' ma suuka'an in t'aana beyo', chen Súulub in t'aana.

—Mina'an a wiits'ino'ob máasi'ma'.

—Mina'an, ba'axten.

—Tin na'ata ilie'.

—Wa a woje na'at, a'axten tuun ma' taan a na'atik ba'ax kin beetik weye'.

—Le ba'ax ka k'aatik ooli' k'as talám tumen mina'an in sáastún kin ch'ene'et, K'abeet a wáalik ten.

—Maalo' tuun, a woje, taan in kaxtik unp'eel ch'e'en[5] k'aba' ta'an "X-La'-Boon-Suumij" chen baale', ma' tulakal máak u k'aat u ts'aten t'an, "Yum Aak" tu K'as k'eyen, ma bey u "Yum Sak Néj Keej," le tie' tu chan tsoláj ten un p'iit ba'a, chen yoola le jeelo' koojen weye', tu aaláj ten xane': "Yum Ya'axche' úts, le tie' wa ka luubu uutsíj ti' je' u tsolik tech ulaak' un p'iit ba'a ka' nájkech tu'ux a k'aat bin."

—Jáj u t'an u Yum Sak Nej Keej, chen báale' yaan in k'aatik tech jujunp'iit ba'a k'abeet a nuukik ten, wa maalob a nuukik je' u pájtáj in waankech ka' kojkech un p'éel tu'ux je' u ts'aba tech uláak' un p'iit ántaj, Wa ma' taan a nuukik in t'an tu tu beele', tanxá tu'ux kin in tuuxtech. Yáax ba'a kin in k'ajtech, jach tu jajil, a woje waa ba'ax táan u máan a kaxtik, tumen wa mae', k'as ánilech.

—Tene' kin tukultike' bey xan in wáalik: Tene' in k'aat bin in k'ajoolt u ch'e'eni X-La'-Boon-Suumij.

—Ko'ox aalik ma'alo'ob ta nukkilak, je' wa ta t'an u k'a'ajá tech máax oks ta pool a k'ajooltik le ch'e'eno.

—Mix máak oks tin pool in k'ajooltik, jach yaaxe', chen wayak' bil tin beetaj, u yox páak in wayak'tik ka' tin tsikbaataj ti in Yum, leti' tuune' tu áala ten: "Le k'iin ka chukik oxlajun (trece) ja'ab ka bin a kaxant u X-Nuuki Ka'-Lóot'Kóom, chen baale' bik tájkech ka' xiikech tu k'iinil ja'aja'al wa ma' a woje báab, tumen Ka' Lóot Kóom ka'atul mosonij-ja' u alak'tmáj." Ma' in chuk ka'lajun ja'ab (doce años) ka' p'aten tin jun wey yook'ol kab, le ka' tu chuká ten le oxlajun (trece) ja'ab ts'ook xan in kanik báab, le k'iin xano' jupen in kaxant tu'ux kaja'an u X-Nuuki Ka'Lóot-Kóom, ma' xancháj ka' tin kaxtáj, u jajile', chen kan p'éel k'iin tu bisáj ten in kaxtik, tumen ma' jach náach ti in kaajal kaja'an, letie' tu k'aat-chi'ten je'x a béetik, leili' tin nuukáj ti', yoola le jeelo'tu aala ten ka' in kaxant u Yum Sak Néj Keej, Keeje' tu tsolcikin ten ka' taaken in kaxtech, tumen teche' utséch, jé bin a waankene', u yalab a láj woje.

—In láj woje, teche' chik'iin a táj lak'iin xan a bin a kaxant u Yum Kosonij Ja' ku ts'atech t'an ti' X-La'-Boon-Suumij.

—Chen wa le kan a tsolten.

—Ba'ax uláak' a k'áat a wojéet tumen ts'o'ok in wáalik tech máax kan a kaxtéj, yéetel mu'ux.

—Chen in k'aa in wojeet ba'ax k'iin k'abéet in kojo tu yiknaj.

—Chan Súulub, uuts u bin tech, jach tu k'iinil yano'on, u k'iinil xamánka'an, k'abéet a p'ilik a wich kin waalik tech, ma' jach naach p'aataj tu'ux ka bin, chen baale' ma' ki saasak ken líikech a kaxant un p'éel ek' tu naa' ka'an lak'iin, le ken a wile' ka bin tu tojil, jach xaanile' tia'al u piik'bal ken kojkech iknaj Yum Kosonij Ja'.[6]

—Yan wa tuun in p'aata wenéj weye'.

—Bix tuun wa ma', k'abéet a paatik u jok'oj ek' tu naa' ka'an.

—Maalo' tuun, bey ts'o'k u chan ak'abtáj, mi un puli' kin in ch'uy in k'ann tu chun le kaa' p'éel che'a.

—Chan Súulub, wa ma' ta koojo te' tu'ux a k'aat bin, le ken suunakech ka' maankech tsikbáj tin weete, tumen in k'aat in wojéet bix kun bin tech.

—Je' bixák ka' xi'ik ten je' in máan in tsikbaatech, baaxe' teche', ma' taan a naachtaj jaal béj.

—Ma' tukultik, mina'an ten tuukul in bin kajtaj yaana tu'ux.

—Maalo' tuun je'e k-tsikbáj ti' ulaak' k'iin.

• • •

—Pik' saastáj ku beetik ka' kooj ti un nojoch wool chak'an, ti' tu k'ajooltáj u yiits'in Yum Ya'axche'. "Ka' xáak'ab u bin u k'uchul Yum Kosonij Ja'."

• • •

—Eey, eey, chan xiipaal tu'ux ka bin, saatalech waa, tumen teche' ma' weyilech.

—Kiimak ooláj tech nojoch máak yéetel un p'éel maalo' saatal a tia'tej, ja ja t'an ma' wuyilen.

—Báan tuun iik'il taaskech weye'.

—Taan in máan in kaxtik Yum Kosonij Ja' tia'al u tsolxikin ka en ka' paatak in koojo tu'ux in k'aat in k'ajoolt.

—Chen a naats'kabaj ulaak' un p'iit, ti yaan k'iiwik.

—Maalo' tuun, ulaak' k'iin k'ilikbaa.

• • •

—Wey a taale' chan xiib, ba'ax ku máan u k'iin tech ka' taakech tiip'i walkila', tu'ux tukultik je' u pajtaj a bine'.

—Taan in máan in kaxtik Yum Kosonij Ja' tumen chen leti' je' u tsolt'antik ten le ba'ax k'abéet ka' koojken te' tu'ux in k'aat bin.

—Chan xiib naach wa p'aatáj te' tu'ux a k'aat bin.

—U jajile' ma' in woje tu'ux p'aatáj, in k'aat bini' tumen yaan un p'éel k'uben t'an k'abéet in k'ubik ti u Yum tsil X-La'Boon-Suumij, le oolaj tuun k'abéet in t'an yéetel Yum Kosonij Ja'. Je' wa ta t'an a waalik ten tu'ux aan leti'.

—Wey k'iiwik, ma' wa je' letio', yoje wa yaan a koojol a xinbaat béjlae' tumen ma' saansamal u jook'ol walkila'.

—Ma' tu pajtáj in waalik tech wa yoje, chen ba'ax in wojel in wa'atech, tene' ma' in túuxt t'an ti'.

—Le tie' ma' k'abéet u túuxta'a t'an ti' ka' yojéet un p'éel ba'a, yaan máax aalik u yich yéetel u xikin ku bino'ob xixinbáj tanxá kajil, yaan máax aalik xané yéetel bin aak'ab ku bino'ob yaan jujuntuul nojoch wiinik ku tsikbaatik, yaan bin nolo'ob u yilmajo'ob u'utúul mejen alux[7] yéetel aak'ab u tal u taaso'ob t'an ti' Yum Kosonij Ja; je' u tanajo', xen t'an yéetel.

—Jajal K'u kun u ts'atech kiimak oola yo'ola le tsol t'an ta ts'áj ten, je'e k-ilikbaa ti ulaak' k'iin.

—Xi'ik tech yéetel utsíl je' tu'uxak ka' xi'ikech.

—Kiimak oola u saasil k'iin tech nojoch máak.

—Yéetel kiimak oola xan tech chan xiib.

• • •

—Nojoch Yum, taan in máan in kaxtik Nojoch Yum Kosonij Ja', aaláb ten wey te' náj kajá'an, ma' wa tech ta t'an.

—Máax aaltech wey kaja'an.

—Leti' le chan máak wa'akbáj ti'its lak'iin k'iiwik.

—Chan xiipaal a k'aat a tusén wa ka tukultik ts'o'ok u bisa'a u saasil in wich.

—Ma' Nojoch Yum, ma' wa jeel wa wa'akbáj teé . . . ts'o'ok u bin tii' wa'akbalen yéetel, chen uuchik in taal ta wéete, jan binisa.

—Le ka waalik un p'éel ma' ka'anaj bakéj wiinik, ts'ookole' taan u che'e le ken u paktech bey xan le ken tsíkbanák ta wéete.

—Le ti', taan u ki' che'e ikil u tsikbáj, mix tin kaatáj ti' bix u k'aaba'.

—U k'abae' Yum Pik'Saastáj,[8] le béetik ts'o'ok u bin, saamáj u ka' suut.

—Nojoch Yum Kosonij Ja', taalen in wilech tumen in k'aat koojo X-La'-Boon-Suumij. Je' wa ta t'a a waanken ka' paaták in kojo in k'ajoolt.

—Ba'ax ten ma'. Wa jach taak a bin je' u yustál in waankech.

—Bix tuun je' u pájtal in kojo.

—Te' kan bina', tój nojol, jach yaabile' un luu' kan a xinbat ken nájkech ti' un wool k'anán ti xan kan a kaxant u Yum Chun Kanán.[9] K'abéet a t'an yéetel tumen leti' kun u tsol tech tu'ux kan bin.

—Chen le k'abéet ka' kojken te' tu'ux ka waalik ten.

—Chen le jeelo', mina'an tu'ux a sa'ataj. Wa ba'ax sájkech chen a waalik ten ka' in tuux tech kaxbíj wa ma' ta seé suut.

—Ma' sájkeni' chen in k'aat in láj wojéet tulaka ba'a ku naktik ti' le xinbaj kin beetik ka' seé kojken, Le in k'aaba' ta k'aata ten, Súulub in t'anaj.

—Ma' k'as a k'aaba' chen ooli' jela'an, ma' taan in jo'oskech wa a k'aat kojo béjlae' te' tu'ux ka bino' k'abéet a seé bin.

—Jajal K'u ku kalantech yoola le nojoch ántaj ta ts'áj ten, chen kin waalik, jee' k'ilikbaa ti' ulaak' k'iin.

—Xi'ik tech yéetel ya'abach útsil chan Súulub.

• • •

—Tu'ux ka bin chan xiipaal bey aalkabanbil a beeta'a, wa chen ts'i in wool.

—Ma' ts'i a wooli', seéba'a in bin tumen k'abéet in kaxtik un wóol K'anán aaláb ten kin kaxtéj.

—Ma' wa ta much je'elej ka' t'anako'on tumen teche' ma' weyilech, le oola kin tukultik yaan tsol t'an kun k'abéjtáj tech.

—Jáj a t'an ts'o'ok bakáan in kojo. Máaxech bey taan a k'aastik in bel.

—Tene' p'ata'anen weye' tia'al in k'amik tu laka máak ku taal u xinbato'on, yane' u k'aat bin u k'ajoolt "CH'E'EN-LEN-TUN" ulaak'oobe' ka' bisa'ak u kaxto'ob u "SAAKAL-JA'" yaan xan le "OOKOL TS'ON KEEJ KU TAALO'OB" yéetel áak'ab. Yaan xan ku taal u kaxto'ob "CHAK-SIINIK-CHE'." Chen wa ba'ax k'iin ku kaxta'al "P'ISTE'-CH'E'EN" wa u "SABAK-CHE'." Ts'o'ok a wuuyik tene', ma' taan in k'a'astik a bel, chen in k'aat in wojéet tu'ux a k'aat bin, kin wil wa je' u yustal in waakech.

—Mi jáj le ba'ax ka waalik ten, chen baale ma' ta waaten a k'aaba'.

—Jáj bakáan, ma' ch'i'ik ten yoola k'aasíj, a woje, tene' cheen u x-ka'aabilen "Nojoch Yum Chun-K'anán." Tulakal le kaja'ano'on te' un woola' láj láak'o'on yéetel le yaan wey te' noj lu'uma'.

—Wa ma' ta k'uuxíj, ma' ta much aalik ten tu'ux kaja'an Yum Chun K'anán k'abéet in tsikbal yéetel.

—Wa jach k'abéet a tsikbal yéetel xan tu paach le nojoch najo' walkila' ki' kulukbáj tu jáal le ch'e'en yaan téelo'.

—Maalo' pa' in bin tuun.

—Ts'aari', tumen wa ma' ta chukpáaxtik walkila' aan a páatik ook'iin ka' t'anakech yéetel.

—Nojoch Yum, kiimak ool u ts'atech jajal K'u ti' le k'iina'.

—Jajal K'u ku yu'ub a t'an chan xiib je' tuuxak ka' taakech.

• • •

—Nojoch Yum, taan u máan in kaxtik Yum Chun K'anán, aalab ten tumen u x-ka'abil wey bin kulukbáj tu jáal le ch'e'en jeela' ma' wa ta t'an tech tumen chen tech yaanech weye'.

—Ten máax taan a kaxtik, ts'ookole' ma tin na'atik ba'axten tuuxta'abech a kaxten, tumen in p'atmáj in paala in waabilo'ob yéetel in x-ka'abilo'ob utia'al u ts'aiko'ob t'an je' ti' máaxak ka taak u xinbato'on.

—Nojoch Yum Chum K'anán a woje, tene' yaab un teene ts'o'ok in wayak'tik in k'ajooltik X-La'-Boon-Suumij le oola taalen tsikbal ta weete.

—Wa ma' nojoch ba'a k'abéet a wojeltik, ko'ox jan tsikbal un suutuk tumen k'abéet in bin meyáj.

—Mina'an in wool in xaankuns-kech, yaax kin in waatech in k'aba', Súulub Chan Ek', chen taalen ka waaten wa ka' paatak bix je' in kojo X-La'-Boon-Suumij tume in k'aat in k'ajoolt.

—Le cola bakáan tuuxtabech tin wiknáj, ma' talam a kojo tumen ma' yaab u bin, chen ba'ax kin in wa'atech, wa tak'iin péeksik a wool ki' suut a paach ka' suunáj kech, tumen Baalame' ku tsi'iktik tulakal máax péeksa'an yool tumen tak'iin, u k'aat u k'ajoolt X-La'-Boon-Summij. Tuukult tu beel tumen wey kan a ch'a'jo'olt a suut ka paach wa ka bin a k'ajoolt le ch'e'eno'. Wa ts'aab a wayak'tik oxlajun paak (trece veces), ts'aab xan t'an ti' Yum Baalam[10] ma' u béetik tech loob, wa ma' beyi', ts'ook in tsolik ba'ax je' u yuuchuj tech.

—U jajile' ya'ab un teen ts'o'ok in wak'tik, ma' in xokla'anmáj jay paak, bix je' u pajtaj in woje ltik jay paak ts'o'ok.

—K'a'antech wa u ts'ook un paak ka' ts'aab a wayak'téj ba'ax sén ba'alo'ob ya wiláj, wa ma' k'aja'antech mix a chen tuus.

—Bix kin in tu'ubse, jats'uts' ba'a tin wayak'táj le aak'abo' kajik yéetel kan tuul máak jach ma' jach ka'anlobí, je'ex le mejen p'uus[11] ku yaala'a, taan u chen t'ankeno'ob: Ko'ox ko'ox a k'ajoolt X-La'-Boon-Suumij, ko'ox ka wuk' u ja'i Suju'uy Ch'e'en[12] ka kan ulaak' un p'iit ba'a, u yox paak u t'ankeno'ob tu chacho'ob in k'ab ka' jelpájnáj in wayak', jo'op' in wilik tuun un p'éel jach taax jánka', chen k'usu'uk jok'a'an, chuumuk tuune' ox p'éel nojoch ki'ichkelen Ya'axche' jok'a'an, yaana ti'ob tii' ku bo'oyankij ox tuul nukuch sak néj keej, ma' naach ti'obi' ox tuul koson ku maan u ts'its'iyankij, u ts'ook k'aja'an ten un p'éel xoolte' in machmáj yéetel in xts'iik, ma' taan u tuubuj ten oxp'éel u xa'ay yaan, jach bey tin wayak'tilak. Taan in chen cha'antik tulakal le ba'axo' ka' tiip' un p'éel nojoch Baalam ka' naats' iknáj le Sak Néj Keejo'ob, mix ba'a tu beetaj ti'ob naats' xan tin wiknaj, tu baa'pach ten ka' ka bini sa'ataj tu beeta ka' aajen xan.

—Wa jáj tulakal le ba'ax ta tsikbaata ten, ma' tun u tsi'ik tech Baalam. Ba'ax kan a beete', le ee' béj yaan áktaan nojol ku bin le kan a bisej, un luu' kan a xinbaatej tii' kan pa'atbi tumen Aj Kuuch,[13] le ti' kalantik u kuuch Baalam[14] k'iin ku ts'oon. Jeelo' je' u pájtáj a bin.

—Kiimak in wool kojken, kiimak in wool in bin, Jajal K'u ku kalante'ex "Yum Chun-K'anán." Je'e k-ilikbaa ti' ulaak' k'iin.

• • •

—Máax le chan xiipaal ku chen xuuxub ikil u taj. Chan xiipaal a woje waa máax lu'umil taan a péechk'tik, wa chokoj pool paalech tumen weye', u kajál Baalam, wa ka' k'uchúk u yiléch je' u tsi'ik kech kex paalech.

—Tech wa k'aaba'ta'anech Aj Kuuch. Taan in kaxtik tumen k'abéet in tsikbá yéetel.

—Ten, chen ba'ax ma' tin na'atik máax tuuxtech tsikbáj tin weete.

—Bey tech Aj Kuuch, ma' tsáj a kaxkabáj a na'at máax tuux ten tsikbáj, yaaxe' in k'aaba' kin in wa'atech. Súulub Chan Ek' u ka'p'éele', mix máak tuuxten tsikbáj u jájile' wayak'bil uuchik in t'anaj ka' taaken in k'ajoolt X-La'-Boon-Suumij.

—Wa beyo' yéetel kiimak oola kin in biséch a k'ajooltéj, chen baale' yaan a patkabáj kiimen[15] u tia'al binbáj bey xan utia'al k-suut beyo' wa k-ilaale', u Kuuch Baalam kin bisik kun tuukulbi.

—Ma' wa tuun xinbali k-bin bin.

—Ma' Aj Kuuch mix un teen u bis u kuuch kuxa'an, le oola k'aéet a patkabáj kiimen, je' le baala' jii' ta nok'.

—Ba'ax le ba'a ta ts'aten kin jii' tin nok', jach yak u book.

—Ma' a k'ajooli' chan xiib, u book Kooj,[16] u book Baalam, k'ajolltéj tumen un p'éel ilie' beyo' mix máak kun naats'a to'on tumen u ch'a'amo'o saják ti' Kooj ti' Baalam, ko'ox kin biséch un puli' chen u yalab k'iin yaan ten.

—Ko'ox tuun, je' kin in tuusinbaa kiimen wale' chen baale' bik taa'kech a p'atén beyo'[17] tumen je' u tój kech Yum Kiin.[18]

—Chan Súulub, ma' tsáj a k'eyken tumen Yum Kiin ts'áj t'an ti' Baalam ka' bia'akech a wuk' u ja'i Suju'uy Ch'e'en yéetel ka kajoot X-La'-Boon-Suumij. Wey a taal wa'ataj ka' in pájkaltech, ma' ch'i'ik sájkij, un chan suutuk ts'ook koojo tu Ts'ek Koson Ja' p'aatáj te' lak'iin to'on, ma' u chuk chuumuk k'iin ken kojko'on.

—Uuye Aj Kuuch, wa ts'o'ok a ka'anáj eenseni', tumen ulaak' un paak ka' jeesteni' ka láj kachik in ch'ala'at.

—Ma' u jo'op'ol a chéechij, ts'o'ok kojo, much wa'alen ka' je'el kech un suutuk le jeelo' wa a k'aat, ma' taan k-bin xantáj.

—Jach jáj, ma' xanchájo'oni', uuye bix u k'aaba' le weya'.

—U Ts'ek Koson Ja' bin bey k'aaba'ta'an. Ka' xaak'a wey nojjol-lak'iin p'aatáj Suju'uy Ch'e'en, wa k-xinbatik ulaak' un p'iit te' nojola' k-kojo X-La'-Boon-Suumij. Tii' k-bin yaax bini' tumen k'abéet un p'iit u chuk chuumik k'iin ken kojko'on tu jool, beyo' le ken u chukéj taan a ch'éene' ka' láj ch'aabak un máal ti' tulakal ba'ax a woje.

—Bix kun ch'a'abij un máal ti' tulakal ba'ax in kanmáj, Aj Kuuch bix wa taan a tukultik a tuuch'iken ich X-La'-Boon-Suumij.

—Ma', bix a wool, tuuxtaaben in kalantech ma' u tia'al kin béj tech loob. Wa ka' k'uchúk a bin ichijle' ma' ti' ten kun u naktéj, wa túsnája'anech uuchik a koojo weye', ti' ka kolbi ka bisaakech ichil, ma' tuun taan ka'suut.

—Ma' tukultik Aj Kuuch, ma' ánchaj tuus uuchik in koojo ta wéete, wa mina'an ulaak'ba'a a tsolten, ki' ko'ox.

—Ko'ox tuun, wa'alen téetla' ka' in pájkaltech tu ka'aten.

• • •

—Seeba'an uuchik k-koojo tuun, ma' tin tukultáj wa jach naats' ko'ox éenseni'.

—Te' a wa'atáj, ma' naats'a tu jaal u chi', láj k'ajóolt u ba'paach, ten kin in t'anech ka ch'ene'etéj.

—Maalo' wey kin pa'at kech.

—Kóoten wey a taale', chen a pool kan a tip's tu jaal u chi' le ch'e'en ka' paatak u bisa'a un máal ti' tulakal ba'ax a woje tu yiit ch'e'en, tumen Yum K'iin. Ka' paatak a bin beyo' a wuk' u ja'i Suju'uy Ch'e'en, jeelo' ts'aabáj un puli'.

—Maalo' ánilen beya'.

—Chen un chan p'iit ubin a tip'sik a pool ma' ch'ik sájkij, in chaachmaj a wook wa ka' koola'a ka'atulo'on k-bin luubuj.

—Chich machén wale' tumen taan in wuuyik, u saaltaj in pool. Taan xan in wilik un p'éel chan sak mosón tu yiit le ch'e'ena' je'ex u bin u suut bey ubin u taantaj bey xan u bin saasiltaj yéetel u juul Yum K'iin.

—Le ken naakák a paakat ti' un p'éel saya' yaan u ja'il bey un p'éel chan woolis néen, ka' jan muts'ik a wich, ts'ookole' ka cha'ik in biseech tak tu'ux wa'akbalech saamák.

—Jeelo' biseni', ts'o'ok in mts'ik in wich.

. . .

—Jeelo' ts'o'ok koojo, je u pájtáj a p'ilik a wich.

—Baan uuchíj le weya' ma' X-La'-Boon-Suumij, bix uuchík a kosken weye'.

—Ma' u ja'ak'al a wool Chan Súulub le weya', Suju'uy Ch'e'en u kaaba' ts'o'okele' ti teche' un p'iit u ja'i ka wuk'éj, ya'abach saasil kun ts'iktech u tia'al a tsikbaatik jach ya'ab tsikbal t'an, ti' u noj lu'umil Maya T'an wiinik.

—Jach wa jáj le ba'ax ka waalik ten Aj Kuuch, tumen yaan suutuk bey wayak'bil in béetik, yan xan bey ajáj.

—Mix a chen tukultik, wey a taal a wil tu'ux xotnaja'an u suumij paay-ja', ya'ab un p'éel yaan tu bak'anpaach u jáal uchi' le ch'e'ena'.

—Le bey tuuna', ya'ab máak ku taal u paay-ja' ka'ach uuchíj.

—Le jeelo' mix bij k'iin kun ka' uuchuj. Naale' chen wa ba'ax k'iin ku koojo máax uk'ik un luuch[19] u ja'i yéetel u chupik u chuuj[20] u tia'al u yuk'ik béj.

—Jeelo' ma' xaantaj, much siiten un luuch ja' kin wuk'éj yéetel laak' un p'iit kin t'ój tin chuuj.

—Jeela', yaaxe' t'ój ta chuuj ka' chuupuk le ulaak' un p'éela' tia'al a wuk'éj, chen baale' u ts'ook un luuk' kan a luk'éj, eejoch'e'entaj kun u béet a wic, sa'ata kun u béet a wool ma' tan a wuuy bix kin in biséch ta taanaj, le ken ájkech ya'abach ba'a a woje, tia'al a béetik úts, wa ma' ta béetik beyo, tulakal k'as ka' woot a béet ti' yaanaj, ku suut ta wook'o, wa ka béetik úts, úts kun suut ta wook'o xan, tech kan a yéey ba'ax a k'aat a béet ti' a wéet kájnaalo'ob.

—Wa beyo' ts'aten in wuk'éj.

—Jeela', tulakal le un luucha' a tia'a.

Notes

1. At the end of the twentieth century the Mayan language or Yucatec Mayan was Mexico's second largest Indigenous language in number of speakers: nearly 1.5 million, living primarily on the Yucatán Peninsula, in the states of Campeche, Yucatán, and Quintana Roo, in addition to some areas of the Republic of Belize. The author uses without variations the Practical Literacy Alphabet for Adult Mayan Speakers, officially established by several government institutions in August 1984, in Mérida, Yucatán.

2. Tree belonging to the Bombaceas, particularly *Bombax ellipticum* and *Ceiba aesculifolia*. The latter reaches more than 90 feet in height.

3. *Ya'ax che'* is the Mayan name for the ceiba, which etymologically means "green tree," in recognition of its preeminence among all trees. It is of the masculine gender; therefore, it should be referred to in Spanish as "el Ceibo," rather than "la Ceiba." For that reason, it is given the reverential title "Yum" and not "Xunán."

4. *Nojoch* is "the greatest," "the oldest," or "the most ancient"; "Nojoch Yum" would be equivalent to "the Greatest Lord" or "the Venerable One."

5. Literally, "well." Present-day Mayas do not always relate this word to cenotes. Nevertheless, in the *Diccionario de Motul* it has the additional meaning of "water cavern," and in Tzeltal it means "cave" or "cavern." Here the Ceibo understands that the word is referring to a deep cenote accessible only through an opening in its overhead cavity, like a well.

6. Literally, "Place of Two Hollows"; according to the author, this is a place located near Chunkanán.

7. Grammatically, the plural form of *alux* is unnecessary here, in reference to the seven small *aluxo'ob* or *aluxes* (the hispanicized plural form). (See Appendix C.)

8. Literally, "Father Clear Dawn."

9. Literally, "Father Kanán Tree."

10. Reverential form; literally, "Lord" or "Owner Jaguar." (See Appendix E.)

11. Hispanicized plural form of the Mayan *p'uuso'ob.* (See Appendix D.)

12. Literally, "Virgin Well"; that is, the "Virgin" or "Sacred" Cenote that will cleanse the child, preparing him for the well or cenote that he seeks.

Notas

1. La lengua maya, o mejor, el maya yucateco, era a finales del siglo XX la segunda lengua indígena con más hablantes en México: cerca de millón y medio de individuos asentados primordialmente en la Península de Yucatán en los estados de Campeche, Yucatán y Quintana Roo, y también en algunas zonas de Belice. El autor emplea en su totalidad el Alfabeto Práctico para la Alfabetización de los Adultos Hablantes de Maya que diversas instituciones oficiales de México acordaron en Mérida, Yucatán, en agosto de 1984.

2. Árbol perteneciente a las Bombacáceas, particularmente *Bombax ellipticum* y *Ceiba aesculifolia,* que alcanza más de 30 metros de altura.

3. *Ya'ax che'* es el nombre maya de la ceiba, que etimológicamente significa "el árbol verde." La etimología del nombre subraya que se trata del árbol por excelencia. Es de género masculino, de manera que debe pensarse en él como "el Ceibo," no "la Ceiba," de ahí que se le anteponga "Yum," no "Xunán."

4. *Nojoch* es "el más grande," "más viejo" o "más antiguo"; "Nojoch Yum" equivaldría a "el Señor más grande" o "el Venerable."

5. Literalmente, "un pozo." Los mayas actuales no siempre relacionan esta palabra con los cenotes. Sin embargo, en el *Diccionario de Motul* significa también "caverna de agua" y en tzeltal "cueva" o "caverna." Por el contexto, el Ceibo entiende que se trata de un cenote profundo al que sólo se tiene acceso por una abertura en la cavidad superior; es decir, como "un pozo."

6. Literalmente, "Lugar de dos hondonadas," lugar situado, según el autor, cerca de Chunkanán.

7. Gramaticalmente, no es necesario aquí el plural de *alux* para aludir a los siete pequeños *aluxo'ob* o "aluxes." (Véase Apéndice C.)

8. Literalmente, "Señor del Claro Amanecer."

9. Literalmente, "Señor Árbol Kanán."

10. Forma reverencial; literalmente, "Señor" o "Dueño Jaguar." (Véase Apéndice E.)

11. Plural castellanizado del maya *p'uuso'ob.* (Véase Apéndice D.)

12. Literalmente, "Pozo Virgen." Es decir, el "Cenote Virgen" o "Sagrado" que limpiará al niño a fin de prepararlo para el pozo o cenote que busca.

13. Literalmente, "Señor Carga"; por extensión, "el que cuida la carga" o "el que carga."

13. Literally, "Lord Load"; and by extension, "he who watches over the load" or "he who carries."

14. The Mayan expression implies the meaning and parallelism of Aj Kuuch as *le ti' kalantik* (he who watches over) *u kuuch Baalam* (Jaguar's load).

15. To "play dead" reinforces the author's idea of Aj Kuuch as a personification of death and therefore of the child's journey as one through the realm of death.

16. Literally, "Leoncillo" (Spanish) or "Little Lion."

17. This request that he "not leave him dead" and the solar deity's protection reaffirm the notion of the child's temporary "death."

18. Reverential form: "Lord Sun."

19. Literally, "gourd": *Crescentia cujete.*

20. Literally, "calabash": *Lagenaria siceraria.*

14. La expresión en maya explica el sentido y paralelismo de Aj Kuuch como *le ti' kalantik,* "el que cuida," *u kuuch Baalam,* "la carga de Balam."

15. El "hacerte muerto" refuerza la idea que el autor tiene de Aj Kuuch como una personificación de la muerte y, por lo tanto, del viaje del niño como un viaje a través de los dominios de la muerte.

16. Literalmente, "Leoncillo."

17. Esta petición de que "no lo deje muerto" y la protección de la divinidad solar reafirma la noción de la "muerte" provisional del niño.

18. Forma reverencial: "El Señor Sol."

19. Literalmente, "jícara": *Crescentia cujete.*

20. Literalmente, "calabazo": *Lagenaria siceraria.*

Ancient Rope Marks

Jorge Echeverría Lope

Maya[1]

[From *X-La'-Boon-Suumij/Vieja huella de soga,* pp. 7–22, 45–61. Letras Mayas Contemporáneas, 3rd series, vol. 8, C. Montemayor, series ed. Mexico City: INI/TRF, 1998.]

"Hey, hey, where are you going, boy? Do you not realize you are far from home and the sun is setting? You had best go back where you came from. This forest at night makes the fearful suffer. It even makes the brave tremble."

"Great Earth, are you speaking to me," asked the boy, "or is it my imagination?"

"Do you not recognize my voice? Take a good look at me; I am the oldest of the Ya'ax Che', the ceiba trees."[2]

"What are you doing here? I remember that they gave you your place to live in town."

"What you say is not true . . . do you not know? Some of my children and grandchildren, and even several of my great-grandchildren, do live in towns. God delivered them unto the Mayas so that, through us, they may recognize the pathway to heaven. After all, you have not told me if you are searching for something; you have not even told me your name."

"Does it upset you that I call you Yum Ya'ax Che', 'Lord Ceiba'? Or should I call you U Nojoch Yum Ya'ax Che', 'Greatest Lord Ceiba'?"[3]

"You may call me Yum Ya'ax Che', Lord Ceiba; it does not sound bad. You have shortened my name, and you still have not told me yours. Or are you the man without a name?"

"I understand. I will tell you. My name is Súulub. My paternal surname is Chan, and Ek', from my mother's side. Therefore, my full name is Súulub Chan Ek', 'Little Star Bit.'[4] Everyone knows me simply as Súulub."

"You do not have brothers or sisters, correct?"

"No, I do not. Why?"

"I just guessed it was so."

"If you are a mind-reader, can you tell me what I am searching for?"

"What you are requesting is a little difficult because I do not have a crystal ball. You must tell me what you are doing here."

"All right, I will tell you. I am searching for a cenote[5] called X-La'-Boon-Suumij, 'Ancient Rope Marks,'[6] but not everyone is willing to give me information. Father Turtle[7] scolded me; but thanks to Father White-Tailed Deer, I arrived here. He also told me, 'If you make a good impression on him, good Lord Ceiba will help you advance a little more.' "

"Father White-Tailed Deer told you the truth; but first, you must give me some answers. If your answers are correct, I will gladly help you. If not, I will send you elsewhere, and there they will also give you good advice. First I will ask you: do you really know for what you are searching? Because if you do not, you are on the wrong path."

"Then I shall say aloud what I am thinking: I wish to come to know the Ancient Rope Marks Cenote."

"I must say you answered well. Can you remember who put into your head the idea of going to see that cenote?"

"No one advised me to go and see it; I heard it mentioned in my dreams. The third time, I told my father and he said, 'The day you turn thirteen, you will go in search of the Grandmother of Ka' Loot K'oom, "Place of Two Hollows."[8] Do not go, however, during rainy season if you cannot swim, because the grandmother of that place has two whirlpools as guardians.' I had not yet turned twelve when I was orphaned. By the time I turned thirteen, I had already learned to swim. That day, I set out to search for the Grandmother of the Place of Two Hollows, and I soon found her. It only took me four days to locate her since she does not live very far. The grandmother asked me some questions like those you are asking, and I answered them. She then said I must search for Father White-Tailed Deer, who advised me to consult with you because you are good and honest and would help me. The rest you already know."

"I know everything. You come from the west and need to go to the east in search of Father Water Swallow; he will tell you about the Ancient Rope Marks Cenote."

"Is that all you can tell me?"

"Is there something else you would like to know? I already told you who you must locate and where."

"I want to know when to visit him."

"Little Súulub, you are in luck: these are the right days, these days of northern storms. You must pay great attention. Where you are going is not far. When you awake, you will rise in search of the first star that appears in the east; when you find it, walk toward it, and in that way, no later than dawn, you will encounter Yum Kosonij Ja', 'Father Water Swallow.' "[9]

"I shall have to sleep here."

"Of course. You must wait for the first star to appear; there is no other way."

"Fine. Since night is falling, I shall tie my hammock up to these trees."

"Little Súulub, if you do not arrive where you want to go, stop here on your way back and tell me about everything that happened on your search."

"Fine, we will talk another day."

• • •

The day had just begun to awaken when Súulub arrived at a clearing. There he met the brother of Lord Ceiba and was told, "You are just two steps away from Father Water Swallow."

• • •

"Hey, little boy, where are you going? Are you lost? You are not from these parts."

"May you be happy, sir, and may your dawn be beautiful today. You also speak the truth: I am not from around here," replied the boy.

"What winds have brought you here?"

"I am looking for Father Water Swallow so that he may orient me, that I might arrive at the place I wish to come to know."

"Then step just a little closer; Father Water Swallow is in the square."

"Fine, you and I will see each other some other day."

• • •

"Come here, boy, what are you doing up so early? Where do you think you can go at this hour?"

"I am searching for Father Water Swallow because only he can explain to me what I need in order to get to where I wish to go."

"Say, boy, is that place you want to go very far away?"

"The truth is that I do not know where it is. I must go because I have a message to deliver to Father Ancient Rope Marks. That is why I must speak with Father Water Swallow. Can you tell me where to find him?"

"Here in the square. Look, there he is. He knows you are coming to visit him because it is not every day that he is out so early."

"I could not tell you if he knows. All I know for sure is that I did not tell him."

"He does not need to receive messages in order to know something. There are those who say that his ears and eyes go out and wander at night. There are also those who say thus: 'There are very few grandfathers who can swear they have seen the seven little *aluxes*[10] who carry messages by night to Father Water Swallow.' That is his house."

"May God bring you happiness for the help you have given me. We shall see each other some other day."

"I wish you well."

• • •

"May today's dawn find you content, sir."

"I wish you the same, little boy."

"Great Sir, I am searching for Father Water Swallow. They told me he lives in this house. Is it you?" asked the boy.

"Who told you he lives here?"

"The boy who is standing on the eastern corner, where the sun rises."

"Listen little boy: do not try to deceive me, thinking I cannot see well."

"No, sir, I am not trying to deceive you. Look! He is standing over there, well . . . he is gone now, he was standing there . . . could he have gone?"

"Is the person you mention a short boy who smiles when he talks or when he is looked at?"

"Yes, the one who smiles while he talks, that is him. I did not get to ask his name . . ."

"His name is Yum Pik' Saastal, 'Father Clear Dawn'; that is why he left. We will see him again at dawn tomorrow."

"Father Water Swallow, I have come to see you because I want to come to know the Ancient Rope Marks Cenote. Do you think you can help me continue my path toward my destination?"

"Why not? If you truly want to go, I can help you."

"Well then, how can I get there?"

"From here, head due south. You will walk, a league[11] at most, to get to the K'anán[12] grove where you will find Yum Chun-K'anán, 'Father K'anán Tree.' You must speak with him so that he will tell you how to arrive at the place you desire."

"Is that all I need to do, to get to where you say?"

"That is it; there is no way for you to get lost. If you are afraid, you had best give me your name. That way, if you do not return soon, we can look for you."

"I am not afraid; I only wish to know everything regarding the long walk I will take, to get there more quickly. I was given the name of Súulub, and that is what everyone calls me."

"Your name is not ugly, but it *is* a little different. I am not chasing you off, but if you wish to arrive where you are going today, you should hurry."

"May the true God care for you for having helped me. All I can say is that we will see each other another day."

"I wish you well, little Súulub."

• • •

"Where are you going, boy? You act as if they were chasing you; or is it my imagination?"

"No, it is not your imagination, I am running because I must find a beautiful K'anán grove."

"Please stop, boy, so that we may talk. Since you are not from around here, I believe you need some advice."

"It is true that I have arrived from another place. And who are you that you would wish to stop me?"

"I was placed here to receive those who come to visit us. Some come to get to know Ch'e'en-Len-Tun, the 'Stone Cenote';[13] others come asking about Saakal-Já, the 'Water of the Carrier Ant'; a few others come under the cover of night asking about Ookol-Ts'on-Keej, 'Clandestine Deer Poachers'; still others come searching for Chak-Siinik-Ché, 'Red Tree Ant'; and some come looking for P'iste'-Ch'e'en, 'Little Chile Pepper Well' or Sabak-Ché, 'Dark Tree.' You can see by now that my intention is not to stop you. To the contrary, I only want to know where you wish to go, to see if I can help you."

"Everything you have explained to me may be true; however, you have not told me who you are."

"Oh yes, it is true, and please do not take it the wrong way. I am just the great-grandson of the Great Father K'anán Tree. All of us who live in this forest are related to all the other trees of this great earth."

"Then if it is no bother, please tell me where Father K'anán Tree lives, that I may speak with him."

"If you must speak with him, you will find him behind that great house. He is always sitting there at this hour."

"Well, I am going to see him."

"Hurry, because if you do not find him now, you will have to wait until nightfall."

"Sir, may God help you today."

"Little boy, may God hear you, wherever you are from."

• • •

"Sir," said the boy, addressing the tree, "I am searching for Father K'anán Tree. His great-grandson told me that he should be sitting around here near the cenote. Is it you? Only you are sitting here."

"I am the one you are looking for," said Father K'anán Tree, "and I do not understand why they sent you to look for me. That is the role of my children, of my grandchildren, and of my great-grandchildren: to give information to all of our visitors."

"Father K'anán Tree, you know, on many occasions I have dreamed of being able to see the Ancient Rope Marks Cenote. That is why I have come to speak with you."

"I must go to work soon; but, if it is not much that you need to know, we can talk for a moment."

"My intention is not to make you late. I will tell you my name: it is Súulub Chan Ek', Little Star Bit. I wish only to know how to get to the Ancient Rope Marks Cenote, as I would like to come to know it."

"Now I understand why they sent you to see me. It is not hard to get there; it is not far away. I must tell you, however, that if you are motivated by ambition you had best return from where you came, because Baalam, 'Jaguar,'[14] destroys everyone who comes to the Ancient Rope Marks Cenote out of ambition. Think it over well; here you will decide whether to return or to come to know the cenote. If you dreamed of it thirteen times, they have already notified Yum Baalam, 'Lord Jaguar,' so he will do you no harm if it is so. I have now explained what may happen to you."

"The truth is, I have dreamed of it often, though I have never counted how many times. How could I know how many times it has been so far?"

"Do you remember well what you dreamed the last time, of what things and persons? If you do not remember, you had best not lie."

"How could I forget: I had a beautiful dream that night! It began with four little men, like the *p'uuses,*[15] as we know them. They were calling me: 'Let us go, let us go to the Ancient Rope Marks Cenote. Let us go, so that you may drink the water of Suju'uy Ch'e'en, the "Virgin Cenote,"[16] so that you may become wise and learn many things.' The third time they spoke to me, they took my hand. Then my dream changed: I began to see myself on a grass-covered plain; there were three large, beautiful ceiba trees in the center; beneath them, three beautiful white-tailed deer rested serenely, while, not far away, a number of swallows flew about very happily and swiftly. The last thing I remember is a staff I held in my left hand. I cannot forget it: it had three forks. In truth, that was my dream. I was enjoying this bewildering scene when a great jaguar appeared. It approached the deer but did nothing to them. It then approached me, turned, and left. When Jaguar disappeared, I woke up."

"If what you tell me is true, no jaguar will do you harm. What you will do is take that path in front of us, which will lead you south. You will walk one league in order to get to Lord Aj Kuuch, 'the Carrier';[17] he will take care of you. He carries and takes care of Jaguar's load on hunting days. Well, you may go now."

"I arrived content, and I leave content. May God look after you, Father K'anán Tree. Well, we shall see each other another day."

. . .

"Who could that boy be who is whistling?" wondered Aj Kuuch. "Say, boy, do you not know whose territory you are in, or are you half crazy? This is Jaguar's territory, and he will tear you apart if he catches a glimpse of you, even if you are a child."

"Are you the one they call Aj Kuuch, the Carrier?" asked Súulub Chan Ek'. "I have been looking for him because I need to speak with him."

"It is I. I just do not understand why they have sent you to speak with me."

"Just as you are the Carrier, do not be concerned; I will explain why. First, I will tell you my name: my name is Súulub Chan Ek', Little Star Bit. The truth is that in dreams I have been told to come to know the Ancient Rope Marks Cenote."

"If it is so, I shall gladly take you there; but you will have to 'play dead' when I carry you there and back; that way, if they see me with you, they will think that you are the load that Jaguar has given me to carry."[18]

"We will not be walking, then?"

"No. The Carrier has never carried a live load; that is why you must play dead. Take this and rub it all over your clothing."

"What is this that you give me to rub all over my clothing? Ugh, it smells horrible!"

"You are not familiar with it, boy. It is the scent of Kooj,[19] it is Jaguar's scent. Get to know it; he and it are one and the same. With this scent, no one will get near us because they fear Kooj. Now, let us go. I shall take you now, since I only have the remainder of this day to spend with you."

"Yes, let us go then, and I will play dead. Just do not leave me dead because Yum K'iin, 'Lord Sun,' will burn you."

"Little Star Bit, do not scold me: Sun informed Jaguar so that I may take you to drink the waters of the Virgin Cenote and come to know the Ancient Rope Marks Cenote. Be still! I will pick you up; do not fear. Before long we will arrive at Ts'ek Koson Ja', 'Place of a Bit of Swallow Water,'[20] which is in the east. We will arrive before midday."

"Say, Carrier, if you are tired, let me down. With another jolt like that, you will surely break my ribs."

"Do not start crying; we have arrived. Stand up and rest a moment if you wish; we will not be here long."

"That really was fast! Say, what is the name of this place?"

"We are in the Place of a Bit of Swallow Water, as it is known. Two steps toward the southeast is the Virgin Cenote; another two steps toward the south is the Ancient Rope Marks Cenote. We should be there by midday. At that hour, you may put your head out over the cenote and leave on its bottom a copy of all that you know."

"How will they make a copy of everything I know, Lord Carrier? Perhaps you are planning on pushing me to the bottom of the cenote?"

"No, do not even think that way. I am here to take care of you, not to do you harm. If you fall in, it will not be my fault. If you have lied in order to get here, you will be pulled in and will never return."

"Do not worry, Carrier, I did not lie in order to get here. If you have nothing else to explain to me, we had best go."

"Let us go then . . . climb up onto me so I may carry you again."

. . .

"I never thought it was so close. Let me down."

"Stay here and do not get close to the edge. Take in all that surrounds you; I will let you know when to get near."

"All right, I will wait."

"Come here; you must put just your head out over the edge of the cenote so that the sun may carry a copy of everything you know to the bottom. Afterward, I will take you to the Virgin Cenote, and I will give you a little bit of its water for you to drink. Come, lean over."

"Am I all right like this?"

"Put your head out a little more. Do not be afraid, I will hold onto your feet. If they pull you, both of us will fall in."

"Hold on to me tightly because I feel a little dizzy. I am now seeing a little white whirlpool down on the bottom. As it spins, it gets deeper, and at the same time it becomes brighter with the sunlight. Everything else is dark."

"When you see a waterhole like a round mirror, close your eyes and let me know so that I may take you back to where you were standing."

"Well, you can take me now, my eyes are closed."

. . .

"You are back now, you can open your eyes again."

"What happened? This is not the Ancient Rope Marks Cenote! Why did you bring me here?"

"Do not be afraid, Little Star Bit, this place is called the Virgin Cenote. Drinking a little water from this cenote will make you more intelligent, and you will learn many things, including the legends of this land."

"Could everything you tell me be true, Carrier? I ask because there are moments when I feel that I am dreaming. I also feel at times as if I am just waking up."

"Do not think about it. Come and see the rope marks where the water is pulled up. There are many; the entire edge of the cenote has these marks."

"Then many people would come here to pull up water to drink."

"Yes, many years ago. That will not come to pass again. Rarely now does anyone come to drink a *jícara*[21] of water and to fill his *calabazo*[22] to drink down the road."

"Well, do not be late; give me a *jícara* to drink and another bit for my *calabazo.*"

"Here it is, take it; first fill your *calabazo,* and now this water is for you to drink. With the last drink, your sight will become dim. You will pass out and will not notice as I carry you home. There you will awaken knowing much more than before drinking the water from the Virgin Cenote. From this time on, you must do only good; do not attempt to do evil because everything will turn on you. If you do good, things will be even better for you. You will know how to treat the people of your land."

"If it is so, bring it to me, I shall drink of it."

"Drink this entire *jícara:* it is for you."

Notes

1. At the end of the twentieth century the Mayan language or Yucatec Mayan was Mexico's second largest Indigenous language in number of speakers: nearly 1.5 million, living primarily on the Yucatán Peninsula, in the states of Campeche, Yucatán, and Quintana Roo, in addition to some areas of the Republic of Belize. The author uses in its totality the Practical Literacy Alphabet for Adult Mayan Speakers, officially established by several government institutions in August 1984 in Mérida, Yucatán.

2. Tree belonging to the Bombaceas, particularly *Bombax ellipticum* and *Ceiba aesculifolia.* The latter reaches more than 90 feet in height. *Ya'ax che'* is the Mayan name for the ceiba, which etymologically means "green tree," in recognition of its preeminence among all trees.

3. See Appendix E.

4. *Súulub* in Mayan refers to a left-over portion of a corn or henequen field; *chan* is "small," and *ek'*, "star."

5. Hispanicized version of the Mayan *dzono'ot,* which refers to the large deposits and currents of underground water, accessible through small to very large openings in the limestone crust that covers a large portion of the Yucatán Peninsula. Through association, this word is also used in present-day Mayan to refer to wells.

6. According to the author, a cenote located some 8 kilometers from his village, the former Hacienda de Chunkanán.

7. Regarding the multiple uses of the Mayan reverential "Yum," Echeverría Lope explained in a February 2002 interview that he conceived these characters—and some of the other dwellers of the forest that the young protagonist subsequently encounters along his way—to be the personification of real geographic locations and natural phenomena (though not deities). In English the most unequivocal rendering of these names might be "Respected Father (Elder) [of] + [place name or nature reference]." I have chosen to render such names as "Father + [place name or nature reference]." When the character pos-

sesses divine attributes recognized by the Mayas, I employ the alternate equivalent "Lord."

8. According to the author, a place located near Chunkanán.

9. The swallow that crosses the sea, in reference to the swallows that cross the Gulf of Mexico with the first cold northern winds of September and October. According to the author, the swallows come to nest among the cenotes located near his home, in the municipality of Cuzamá, Yucatán. As a place name, Cuzamá is a derivative of *koson já*, "water of the swallow."

10. Plural, Hispanicized form of the Mayan *alux*, a clay figure brought to life through the ceremonies of traditional Mayan priests and used to protect planted fields and parcels of land. (See Appendix C.)

11. According to the author, equivalent to 4 kilometers or 2.5 miles; the term in Maya is *hun luub*, "one fall," possibly in reference to the maximum distance a person can physically haul some object before setting it down or dropping it.

12. *Hamelia erecta*, a shrub belonging to the Rubiaceae family that produces an edible red fruit; its leaves are used for medicinal baths.

13. This cenote and others subsequently mentioned are located in the vicinity of Cuzamá.

14. *Felis onca*.

15. Hispanicized form of the Mayan plural *p'uuso'ob*. (See Appendix D.)

16. Literally, "Virgin Well." The term *suju'uy* is of great importance in the prayers of the *jmeno'ob* (see Appendix A) and may be applied to the Virgin Mary, to the ritual altar and offering, or to the candles and other ritual paraphernalia. In each case it means "the immaculate," "the sacred," "the virginal." In the case of water, there is one water for human use; another for consumption by birds; and yet another, "the virginal," which is reserved for ritual purposes.

17. Literally, "Lord Cargo"; and by extension, "he who watches over the load" or "he who carries."

18. According to the author, this entity corresponds to a personification of death, who "carries away" those who have died.

19. Literally, "small lion"; *Felis concolor*.

20. This name is related to that of "Father Water Swallow" (see note 9). The Mayan expression refers here to a "small amount of the water of the swallow" (i.e., surface water), which lies immediately above the sacred or "virgin" water (see note 16).

21. From the Nahuatl *xicalli*, "receptacle or house from the *jícaro* tree." Bowl or vessel made from the fruit of the *jícaro*, *Crescentia cujete*, a tree that reaches 30 to 75 feet in height. Its fruit is oval or nearly spherical, with a diameter of 6 to 12 inches; vessels or *jícaras* are made from its dried husk.

22. *Lagenaria siceraria*, also known as *calabaza de peregrinos*, "pilgrims' squash." In Spain it is known as *calabacino*. The fruit of this plant, which grows into a variety of shapes, is generally used as a vessel for storing liquids or foods.

Vieja huella de soga

Jorge Echeverría Lope

Maya[1]

[De *X-la'-boon-suumij/Vieja huella de soga*, pp. 45–61. Letras Mayas Contemporáneas, 3a serie, vol. 8, C. Montemayor, coord. de la colección. México, D.F.: INI/TRF, 1998.]

—Hey, hey, ¿a dónde vas, muchacho? ¿No te das cuenta de que estás lejos de tu casa y que el sol se está ocultando? Mejor te regresas por donde viniste; esta selva por las noches hace sufrir a los que sienten miedo, también hace temblar a cualquiera que se sienta bravo.

—Gran tierra, ¿tú me hablas o es mi imaginación?

—¿No reconoces mi voz? Mírame bien, soy el mayor de los árboles de Ceiba.[2]

—¿Qué cosa haces aquí? Recuerdo que te encomendaron vivir en el pueblo.

—Eso que mencionas no es así, ¿sabes? Algunos de mis hijos y otros de mis nietos y hasta varios de mis bisnietos viven en los pueblos porque Dios los entregó a los mayas para que conozcan el camino al cielo. Después de todo, no me has dicho si andas o vienes en busca de algo, ni siquiera me has dicho cómo te llamas.

—¿No te molesta que te llame "Señor de los Ceibos"? ¿O es necesario que te diga "Gran Señor de los Ceibos"?[3]

—Está bien que me llames "Señor de los Ceibos," no se escucha mal. Tú has reducido mi nombre y aun no me has dicho cómo te llamas. ¿O es que eres el hombre sin nombre?

—Mi nombre es Súulub, mi apellido paterno es Chan y

por parte de mi madre Ek'. Por lo tanto, mi nombre completo es Súulub Chan Ek'.[4] Todos me conocen por Súulub solamente.

—No tienes hermanitos, ¿verdad?

—No tengo, ¿por qué?

—Adiviné que así era.

—Si eres adivino, ¿puedes decirme qué ando buscando?

—Eso que quieres es un poco difícil, porque no tengo la bola de cristal, debes decirme qué haces aquí.

—Está bien, te diré. Ando buscando un cenote[5] llamado "X-La'-Boon-Suumij,"[6] solamente que hay quien no quiere darme información. El Señor de las Tortugas me regañó, no así el Señor de los Venados Cola Blanca; gracias a él llegué hasta aquí; también me dijo: "El buen Señor de los Ceibos, si le caes bien, te ayudará para que puedas avanzar un poco más."

—Te dijo la verdad el Señor de los Venados Cola Blanca, pero debes darme unas respuestas. Si me las das correctas, con mucho gusto te ayudaré; si no es así, te enviaré a otro lugar, donde te darán buenos consejos. Primero te preguntaré: ¿realmente sabes qué es lo que andas buscando? Porque si no sabes, estás mal.

—Estoy pensando y así lo digo: quiero conocer el cenote "X-La'-Boon-Suumij."

—Diré que contestaste bien. ¿Crees poder recordar quien te metió en la cabeza conocer ese cenote?

—Nadie me aconsejó conocerlo. En mis sueños oí mencionarlo; a la tercera vez que lo soñé se lo platiqué a mi padre y él me dijo: "El día que cumplas trece años, vas en busca de la abuela de Ka' Loot K'oom,[7] no en tiempo de lluvias si no sabes nadar, porque la abuela de allá tiene dos remolinos de agua como guardianes." No había cumplido los doce años cuando quedé huérfano. Al cumplir los trece años, ya había aprendido a nadar. Ese día me puse a buscar a la Abuela de Ka' Loot K'oom y no tardé en encontrarla, sólo cuatro días me llevó dar con ella, pues no vive tan lejos. La abuela me hizo unas preguntas como las que me haces también, y las contesté; después me dijo que debo buscar al Señor de los Venados Cola Blanca y él me aconsejó que acudiera a ti porque eres bueno y noble, y que me ayudarías. Lo demás lo sabes.

—Me lo sé todo. Vienes del poniente y necesitas ir al oriente en busca del Señor de la Golondrina del Agua; él te dirá de X-La'-Boon-Suumij.

—¿Sólo eso me explicarás?

—¿Algo más que quieras saber? Ya te dije a quien debes localizar y dónde.

—Quiero saber cuándo debo llegar con él.

—Pequeño Súulub, tienes suerte, estamos en los días exactos, días de nortes, debes de fijarte bien pues no lejos está a donde vas. Al amanecer te levantarás en busca del primer lucero que sale por el oriente; cuando lo encuentres camina hacia él, y así, a más tardar al amanecer llegarás con el Señor de la Golondrina del Agua.

—Tendré que quedarme a dormir.

—Claro, debes esperar que salga el primer lucero, no queda otra.

—Está bien, como la noche avanza, de una vez amarro mi hamaca a estos árboles.

—Pequeño Súulub, si no llegas a donde quieres ir, cuando regreses pasa a platicarme qué tantas cosas te sucedieron.

—Como sea que me vaya, pasaré a platicarte; tú estarás pendiente de mi regreso.

—No te preocupes, no pienso ir a vivir a otra parte.

—Está bien, ya platicaremos otro día.

• • •

Comenzaba a amanecer cuando llegó a un claro. Allá conoció al hermano de "Yum Ya'ax Che' " y así le dijeron: Dos pasos te faltan para llegar a Yum Kosonij Ja'.[8]

• • •

—Hey, hey, muchacho, ¿a dónde vas? ¿Estás perdido? Porque tú no eres de este rumbo.

—Que contento estés, Señor, y que tengas un bonito amanecer este día; también dices verdad, no soy de este rumbo.

—¿Qué aires te han traído por acá?

—Ando buscando a Yum Kosonij Ja' para que me oriente y pueda llegar a un lugar que quiero conocer.

—Sólo te acercas otro poco, él está en la plaza.

—Está bien, nos veremos otro día.

• • •

—Ven para acá, muchacho, ¿qué te sucede tan temprano? ¿A dónde crees que puedes ir a esta hora?

—Ando buscando a Yum Kosonij Ja' porque sólo él puede explicarme qué es lo que necesito para llegar a donde quiero ir.

—Oye, muchachito, ¿queda lejos ese lugar a donde quieres ir?

—La verdad es que no se dónde se encuentra, debo ir porque tengo un mensaje que entregar a Yum X-La'-Boon-Suumij. Por eso necesito hablar con Yum Kosonij Ja'. ¿Puedes decirme dónde lo encuentro?

—Aquí en la plaza. Mira, allá está él. Sabe que vienes a visitarlo, porque no todos los días se le ve tan temprano.

—No sabría decirte si él sabe. Lo único que puedo asegurar es que no le avisé.

—Él no necesita recibir mensajes para saber algo. Hay quien dice que sus orejas y sus ojos salen a pasear por las noches. También hay quien dice: "Son pocos los abuelos que aseguran haber visto a los siete pequeños *aluxes*[9] que por las noches traen los mensajes a Yum Kosonij Ja'." Aquélla es su casa.

—Que Dios te de felicidad por la ayuda que me has dado. Nos veremos otro día.

—Que te vaya bien.

• • •

—Contento te amanezca este día, Señor.

—Igualmente para ti, muchacho.

—Gran Señor, ando buscando al "Yum Kosonij Ja'." Me dijeron que en esta casa vive. ¿Eres tú?

—¿Quién te dijo que acá vive?

—El muchacho que está parado en la esquina oriente, donde se asoma el sol.

—Oye, muchachito, no trates de engañarme pensando que no puedo ver bien.

—No, Señor, no trato de engañarte. Mira, allá está él parado, en . . . ya se fue, allá estaba parado, ¿se habrá ido?

—¿Ése a quien mencionas es un muchacho chaparrito, sonriente cuando está platicando o cuando se le mira?

—Ése que sonríe mientras platica, sí, ése es, no alcancé a preguntarle cómo se llama.

—Su nombre es "Yum Pik' Saastal"[10]; por eso se fue. Hasta mañana lo veremos otra vez, al amanecer.

—Señor Yum Kosonij Ja', vine a verte porque quiero conocer X-La'-Boon-Suumij, ¿crees poder ayudarme a continuar mi camino hacia donde voy?

—¿Por qué no? Si de veras quieres ir, puedo ayudarte.

—Entonces, ¿cómo puedo llegar?

—Por acá te vas derecho al sur, máximo caminarás una legua para llegar al monte de K'anán,[11] donde encontrarás a Yum Chun K'anán.[12] Necesario es que hables con él y te diga a dónde irás, para que llegues a donde quieres.

—¿Sólo eso debo hacer para llegar a donde me dices?

—Sólo eso, no tienes donde perderte. Si tienes miedo mejor dame tu nombre, para que te busquen por si no regresas pronto.

—No tengo miedo, sólo quiero saber todo lo relacionado a la caminata que haré para llegar pronto. Me pusieron Súulub por nombre y así me hablan todos.

—No es feo tu nombre, un poco diferente. No te corro, si quieres llegar hoy a donde vas, debes darte prisa.

—Que el verdadero Dios te cuide por ayudarme, sólo te diré que nos veremos otro día.

—Que te vaya bien, pequeño Súulub.

• • •

—¿A dónde vas, muchacho, que parece que te persiguen? ¿O es mi imaginación?

—No es tu imaginación, voy corriendo porque necesito encontrar un bonito monte de K'anán.

—Détente, por favor, muchacho, para que platiquemos. Como no eres de por acá, creo que necesitas algunos consejos.

—Es verdad, ya llegué. ¿Y tú quién eres que andas queriendo detenerme?

—Aquí me dejaron para recibir a las personas que vienen a visitarnos. Algunos vienen a conocer "Ch'e'en-Len-Tun,"[13] otros se acercan preguntando por "Saakal-Ja' "[14] y otros pocos por "Ookol-Ts'on-Keej,"[15] que vienen a escondidas por las noches. También una parte viene buscando "Chak-Siinik-Che'."[16] Y otro día vienen a buscar "P'iste'-Ch'e'en"[17] o "Sabak-Ché."[18] Con esto podrás entender que mi intención no es detenerte; es todo lo contrario: solamente quiero saber a dónde deseas ir, para ver si te puedo ayudar.

—Puede ser verdad todo lo que me has explicado, sin embargo, no me has dicho quién eres.

—Oye, es verdad, no me lo tomes a mal. Sabes, solamente soy el bisnieto del Gran "Yum Chun-K'anán." Todos los que vivimos en este monte tenemos parentesco con los demás árboles de esta gran tierra.

—Si no es molestia, por favor dime dónde vive "Yum Chun-K'anán"; necesito platicar con él.

—Lo encontrarás detrás de esa gran casa, si es indispensable que hables con él. Siempre a esta hora está sentado allá.

—Bueno, voy a verlo.

—Apresúrate, porque si no lo alcanzas ahora, tendrás que esperar hasta por la noche.

—Señor, que Dios te ayude en este día.

—Muchachito, que Dios te escuche, de donde quiera que seas.

• • •

—Señor, ando buscando a "Yum Chun-K'anán." Me dijo su bisnieto que por acá debe estar sentado junto al cenote. ¿No eres tú? Pues sólo tú estás sentado aquí.

—Yo soy a quien buscas y no entiendo por qué te mandaron a buscarme. Para eso están mis hijos, mis nietos y mis bisnietos, para dar información a todos nuestros visitantes.

—Señor "Yum Chun K'anán," ¿sabes?, en muchas ocasiones he soñado que tenía la oportunidad de conocer a "X-La'-Boon-Suumij"; por eso vine a platicar contigo.

—Si no es mucho lo que quieres saber, platicaremos un momento, pues necesito ir a trabajar.

—No tengo intención de retrasarte; te diré mi nombre, Súulub Chan Ek', solamente quiero saber cómo llegar hasta X-La'-Boon-Suumij, porque me gustaría conocerlo.

—Ya entiendo por qué te mandaron a verme; no es difícil que llegues, te falta poco. Sólo te diré que si la ambición te ha motivado, mejor te regresas por donde viniste, porque Baalam[19] destruye a todo aquel que viene por ambición a conocer X-La'-Boon-Suumij. Piénsalo bien, porque aquí decidirás si regresas o vas a conocer el cenote. Si lo soñaste trece veces, también le avisaron a Yum Baalam[20] para que no te haga daño; si es así, ya te expliqué lo que te puede suceder.

—La verdad es que muchas veces lo he soñado; nunca conté cuántas. ¿Cómo podría saber cuántas fueron ya?

—¿Recuerdas bien qué soñaste la última vez, qué cosas y a quiénes? Si no recuerdas, mejor ni mientas.

—¡Cómo lo voy a olvidar, si tuve un bonito sueño esa noche! Comenzó todo con cuatro hombrecitos, como los *p'uuses*[21] que se conocen. Me llamaban: "Vamos, vamos a conocer X-La'-Boon-Suumij. Vamos para que tomes el agua de Suju'uy Ch'e'en[22] y te dé sabiduría y también aprendas muchas cosas." La tercera vez que me hablaron, tomaron mi mano; entonces cambió mi sueño: comencé a verme en un llano cubierto de zacate, había tres grandes y bonitos árboles de Ceiba en el centro; debajo de ellos, tres bonitos venados cola blanca descansaban tranquilamente; no lejos otras tantas golondrinas revoloteaban muy alegres y veloces; lo último que recuerdo es un bastón que tenía en la mano izquierda, y no se me olvida, pues tenía tres horquetas. De verdad así fue mi sueño. Estaba embobado disfrutando el paisaje cuando se asomó un gran Baalam, se acercó a los venados y nada les hizo; después se acercó a mí, me dio la vuelta y se fue. Cuando Baalam desapareció también desperté.

—Si es verdad lo que me platicaste, no te hará daño alguno Baalam. Lo que harás es irte por esa vereda de allá enfrente, que al sur te llevará; una legua caminarás para llegar con el Señor Aj Kuuch;[23] él cuida, lleva y trae la carga de Baalam el día de cacería. Bueno, ya puedes irte.

—Contento vine, contento me voy. Que Dios les cuide Yum Chun K'anán. Bueno, nos veremos otro día.

• • •

—¿Quién será ese muchacho que viene silbando? Oye, muchacho, ¿sabes en territorio de quién andas o estás medio loco? Porque aquí es la tierra de Baalam, te despedazaría si te alcanzara a ver, aunque seas un niño.

—¿Eres tú a quién llaman Aj Kuuch? Lo ando buscando porque necesito platicar con él.

—Yo soy, nomás no entiendo por qué te mandan a platicar conmigo.

—Como tú eres Aj Kuuch, no te desesperes, yo te diré por qué. Primero, mi nombre te diré: me llamo Súulub Chan Ek'. De verdad en sueños me dijeron que viniera a conocer el cenote de X-La'-Boon-Suumij.

—Si es así, con mucho gusto te llevaré a conocerlo, sólo que tendrás que hacerte el muerto cuando te lleve y también de regreso; así, si me ven llevarte, pensarán que eres la carga que Baalam me da para llevar.[24]

—Entonces no iremos caminando.

—No, Aj Kuuch nunca ha llevado viva su carga; por eso es necesario que te hagas el muerto. Mira, aquí tienes esto, úntatelo en la ropa.

—¿Qué es esto que me das para untar en mi ropa? Uf, apesta feo.

—No lo conoces, muchacho, es el olor de Kooj,[25] es el olor de Baalam; conócelo, que es uno solo. Con este olor nadie se nos acercará, porque le tienen miedo a Kooj. Vamos, te llevo de una vez, pues sólo tengo para ti el resto del día.

—Entonces vamos, ya me hice el muerto; nomás no me vayas a dejar así, porque Yum K'iin[26] te quemaría.

—Chan Súulub, no me regañes, el sol le avisó a Baalam para que te llevaran a tomar el agua de Suju'uy Ch'e'en y conozcas X-La'-Boon-Suumij. Párate aquí, te cargaré; no sientas miedo, en poco tiempo llegamos a Ts'ek Koson Ja',[27] que está al oriente, antes del medio día llegaremos.

—Oye, Aj Kuuch, si estás cansado, bájame, porque con otro sacudón como éste, sí me romperías las costillas.

—No comiences a llorar, porque ya llegamos. Anda, incorpórate y descansa un momento si quieres, no tardaremos acá.

—De verdad llegamos rápido. Oye, ¿cómo se llama este lugar?

—Es Ts'ek Koson Ja', así le llaman. Aquí, a dos pasos, al suroriente, está Suju'uy Ch'e'en; a otros dos pasos al sur está X-La'-Boon-Suumij. Allá debemos estar antes del medio día para que cuando ya lo sea asomes tu cabeza al cenote y dejes en el fondo una copia de todo lo que sabes.

—¿Cómo le harán para tomar una copia de todo lo que

sé, señor Aj Kuuch? ¿No estarás pensando en empujarme al fondo del cenote?

—No, ni lo pienses. Estoy aquí para cuidarte y no para hacerte daño. Si cayeras, no será por culpa mía; si has mentido para llegar acá, de allá mismo te jalarán y nunca regresarás.

—No te preocupes, Aj Kuuch, no mentí para llegar acá. Si no tienes otra cosa que explicarme, mejor vámonos.

—Entonces nos vamos; súbete acá para cargarte de nuevo.

• • •

—No pensé que fuera tan cerca; bájame.

—Acá te quedas y no te acerques a la orilla, conoce bien todo el derredor, yo te hablaré para que te acerques.

—Bueno, esperaré.

—Ven para acá, sólo tu cabeza debes asomar en la orilla del cenote para que el sol se lleve al fondo una copia de todo lo que sabes. Después te llevaré a Suju'uy Ch'e'en y te daré un poco de su agua para que tomes. Ven, asómate.

—¿Estoy bien así?

—Asoma un poco más tu cabeza, no tengas miedo, yo te sujeto de los pies; si te jalan, los dos caeremos.

—Sujétame bien, porque siento que me da vértigo. Ahora veo un pequeño remolino blanco allá en el fondo, conforme gira se profundiza y al mismo tiempo se va aclarando con la luz del sol; todo lo demás es obscuro.

—Cuando veas un ojo de agua, como un espejo redondo, cierra tus ojos y me avisas para llevarte hasta donde estabas de pie.

—Bueno, ya puedes llevarme, ya tengo los ojos cerrados.

• • •

—Ya estás donde debes, puedes abrir los ojos nuevamente.

—¿Qué sucedió, éste no es X-La'-Boon-Suumij? ¿Cómo fue que me trajiste hasta acá?

—No te asustes, Chan Súulub, este lugar se llama Suju'uy Ch'e'en. Con un poco del agua de este cenote que tomes, serás más inteligente y aprenderás muchas cosas, también las leyendas de esta tierra.

—¿Será verdad todo esto que me dices, Aj Kuuch? Te pregunto, porque hay momentos en que siento que estoy soñando. También me parece que apenas voy despertando.

—Ni lo pienses; ven a ver las huellas de las sogas donde se saca el agua, son muchas, es decir, toda la orilla del cenote tiene esas huellas.

—Entonces mucha gente venía a jalar el agua para tomar.

—En tiempos pasados. Eso no volverá a suceder. Ahora rara vez alguien viene a tomarse una jícara[28] de agua y a llenar su calabazo[29] para tomar en el camino.

—Bueno, no te retrases y regálame una jícara para tomar y otro poco para mi calabazo.

—Aquí está, toma, primero llena tu calabazo; esta otra es para que tomes, en el último trago se te obscurecerá tu vista. Te desmayarás y no sentirás cómo te llevaré hasta tu casa, donde despertarás sabiendo mucho más que antes de tomar el agua de Suju'uy Ch'e'en. Ahora debes hacer el bien, no trates de hacer mal, porque todo se volverá contra ti; si haces bien, mejor te irá. Tú sabrás como tratar a tus coterráneos.

—Si es así, trae, me la tomo.

—Toma toda esta jícara, es para ti.

Notas

1. La lengua maya, o mejor, el maya yucateco, era a finales del siglo XX la segunda lengua indígena con más hablantes en México: cerca de millón y medio de individuos asentados primordialmente en la Península de Yucatán en los estados de Campeche, Yucatán y Quintana Roo, y también en algunas zonas de Belice. El autor emplea en su totalidad el Alfabeto Práctico para la Alfabetización de los Adultos Hablantes de Maya que diversas instituciones oficiales de México acordaron en Mérida, Yucatán, en agosto de 1984.

2. Árbol perteneciente a las Bombacáceas, particularmente *Bombax ellipticum* y *Ceiba aesculifolia*, que alcanza más de 30 metros de altura. *Ya'ax ché* es el nombre maya de la ceiba, que etimológicamente significa "el árbol verde." La etimología del nombre subraya que se trata del árbol por excelencia.

3. En maya Yum Ya'axché y Yum Nojoch Ya'axche'. (Véase Apéndice E.)

4. *Súulub* es en maya parte del terreno sobrante en las milpas o henequenales; *chan* es "pequeño" y *ek'*, "estrella."

5. Castellanización de la voz maya *dzono'ot*, que se refiere a la grandes depósitos y corrientes de agua subterránea accesibles a través de aberturas pequeñas o inmensas en la capa de piedra caliza que cubre una amplia zona de la Península de Yucatán.

6. Literalmente, "Vieja huella de soga." Según el autor, cenote que se localiza a 8 kilómetros de su aldea, la ex Hacienda de Chunkanán.

7. Literalmente, "Lugar de dos hondonadas," lugar situado, según el autor, cerca de Chunkanán.

8. Literalmente, "Señor de la Golondrina del Agua," es decir, la golondrina que cruza las aguas del mar, en referencia a las golondrinas que cruzan el Golfo de México en ocasión de los primeros vientos fríos del norte de septiembre a octubre. Según el autor, las golondrinas anidan en los cenotes que se extienden cerca de donde él vive, en el municipio de Cuzamá, Yucatán, cuyo nombre proviene precisamente de *koson já*, "agua de la golondrina."

9. Plural castellanizado de *alux*. (Véase Apéndice C.)

10. Literalmente, "Señor del Claro Amanecer."

11. *Hamelia erecta,* arbusto perteneciente a la familia de las Rubiáceas. Su fruto es rojo y comestible; sus hojas se emplean para baños medicinales.

12. Literalmente, "Señor Árbol Kanán."

13. Éste y los siguientes cenotes se encuentran situados en las cercanías de Cuzamá. Literalmente, "Cenote de piedra."

14. Literalmente, "Agua de la Saakal," es decir, de la hormiga arriera.

15. Literalmente, "Cazadores nocturnos o clandestinos de venados."

16. Literalmente, "Árbol de la hormiga roja."

17. Literalmente, "Pozo del pequeño fruto picante," es decir, del "chile" o "ají."

18. Literalmente, "árbol oscuro" o "sucio."

19. Literalmente, "Jaguar": *Felis onca.*

20. Forma reverencial; literalmente, "Señor o Dueño Jaguar." (Véase Apéndice E.)

21. Plural castellanizado del maya *p'uuso'ob.* (Véase Apéndice D.)

22. Literalmente, "Pozo Virgen." El término *suju'uy* tiene una gran importancia en los rezos de los *jmeno'ob* (véase Apéndice A) y puede aplicarse a la Virgen, al altar, a la ofrenda, al cirio y a otros enseres rituales. En todos los casos significa "lo inmaculado," "lo sagrado," "lo virginal." En el caso del agua, hay una para el hombre, otra para las aves y otra más, "la virginal," que es la ritual.

23. Literalmente, "Señor Carga"; por extensión, "el que cuida la carga" o "el que carga."

24. Según el autor, esta entidad corresponde a una personificación de la muerte, que "carga" con los que han fallecido.

25. Literalmente, "Leoncillo."

26. Literalmente, "El Señor Sol."

27. Este nombre se relaciona con el de "Señor de la Golondrina del Agua" (véase nota 8). La expresión maya se refiere aquí a una "poca del agua de la golondrina," es decir, a la que está inmediatamente antes del agua sagrada o "virgen" (véase nota 22).

28. Del náhuatl *xicalli,* "recipiente o casa del jícaro." Tazón o vasija hecha del fruto del jícaro, *Crescentia cujete,* árbol de 10 a 25 metros de altura. El fruto es oval o subgloboso de 15 a 30 centímetros; con la cáscara seca del fruto se hacen las vasijas o jícaras.

29. *Lagenaria siceraria;* se llama también "calabaza de peregrinos." En España es el calabacino. El fruto de esta planta, que adopta formas variadas, suele utilizarse como vasija para contener líquidos o alimentos.

Miguel Ángel May May

Maya

Miguel Ángel May May. Photographed at Casa de la Cultura, Mérida, Yucatán.

Miguel Ángel May May was born in Izamal, Yucatán, in 1959. In 1987 he joined the staff of the magazine entitled *U Tzikbalo'ob Xunáan Kaab,* to which he contributed translations and copy editing. That same year he worked as editor and writer for the newspaper *U Yajal Maya Wiiniko'ob.* He also collaborated in the editorial work for the first series of Colección Letras Mayas Contemporáneas. May May has worked as a researcher and as coordinator of the Mayan Language and Literature Program for the Yucatán Regional Popular Cultures Office; he has also worked as a cultural promoter and member of the State Commission of the Mayan People's Cultural Center. Presently he is assistant director of Mayan Language and Culture at the Institute for the Development of Mayan Culture (INDEMAYA) in Mérida, Yucatán, and is the organizational secretary for the Advisory Board of Indigenous Language Writers, Inc. In the first series of Colección Letras Mayas Contemporáneas (C. Montemayor, series ed.) May May published *Jump'eel tzikbaal yo'olal u kaajil Kimbilá* (vol. 27; Mexico City: INI/Sedesol/TRF, 1993) and *Breve reseña de Kimbilá* (A Brief Overview of Kimbilá) (vol. 28; Mexico City: INI/Sedesol/TRF, 1993). In the third series he published the volume *Lajump'éel maaya tzikbalo'ob/Diez relatos mayas* (Ten Mayan Tales) (vol. 10; Mexico City: INI/TRF, 1998) and *U pik' ilju'unil u ka'ansa'al xook yéetel dzíib ich maaya* (vol. 9; Mexico City: INI/TRF, 1998), a manual aimed at encouraging young people to write in the Mayan language.

Miguel Ángel May May nació en Izamal, Yucatán, en 1959. En 1987 formó parte del cuerpo de redactores de la revista *U Tzikbalo'ob Xunáan Kaab,* para la que hizo varias traducciones y correcciones de estilo. Ese mismo año participó como editor y colaborador en el periódico *U Yajal Maya Wiiniko'ob* y colaboró activamente en las tareas editoriales de la primera serie de la Colección Letras Mayas Contemporáneas. Ha trabajado de investigador y coordinador del Programa de Lengua y Literatura Maya en la Unidad Regional Yucatán de Culturas Populares y como promotor cultural y miembro de la Comisión Estatal del Centro Cultural de los Pueblos Mayas. Actualmente se desempeña como subdirector de Lengua y Cultura Maya del Instituto para el Desarrollo de la Cultura Maya (INDEMAYA), de Mérida, Yucatán. Es secretario de organización en el Consejo de la Asociación de Escritores en Lenguas Indígenas. Ha publicado, en la primera serie de la Colección Letras Mayas Contemporáneas (C. Montemayor, coord. de la colección), *Jump'eel tzikbaal yo'olal u kaajil Kimbilá* (vol. 27; México, D.F.: INI/Sedesol/TRF, 1993) y *Breve reseña de Kimbilá* (vol. 28; México, D.F.: INI/Sedesol/TRF, 1993). En la tercera serie publicó los tomos *Lajump'éel maaya tzikbalo'ob/Diez relatos mayas* (vol. 10; México, D.F.: INI/TRF, 1998) y *U pik' ilju'unil u ka'ansa'al xook yéetel dzíib ich maaya* (vol. 9; México, D.F.: INI/TRF, 1998), un importante manual para iniciar a jóvenes en la escritura en lengua maya.

Jump'éel tzikbaal yo'olal Yum Tzilo'ob[1]

Miguel Ángel May May

Maya[2]

[From *Lajump'éel maaya tzikbalo'ob/Diez relatos mayas,* pp. 39–44. Maya dziibo'ob bejla'e, 3rd series, vol. 10, C. Montemayor, series ed. Mexico City: INI/TRF, 1998.]

Anchaj juntéenake' juntúul óotzil máak kaja'an jo'okaaj ti' jump'éel su'ukil naj, le máaka' kaja'an be Itzmal;[3] leti'e' k'alk'alaak u t'aan ba'ale' ku na'ata'al je ba'axak ka u ya'ale'; láaj k'iin tu máane' táan u cha'achik k'úutz. U meyaje' chéen tusbeelil.

Jump'éel k'iin táan u je'elsikuba ti' u chan x-la' t'u'ut'u'uy k'aan, mi láas ocho ja'atzkab k'iin ka k'uch ilbil tumen juntúul nojoch máak ku k'aba'tik Yum Noolo, ka a'ala'ab ti' beya':

—Clavio je wa much beetik utz a bin a ch'akten junkúuch si'e', jach k'abéet ten.

—Je'ele', ba'axten ma', chéen ba'ale' yan a dzaik ten u nu'ukulil in meyaj.

—Ma'alob-ka núuka'ab ti'e' ka dza'ab u baat, u x-koorba yéetel u táabil u kuch si'.

Tu ch'a'aj u nu'ukulo'ob Clavioe' ka bin te ch'ak si'o'. Jach táan u ch'ak si'e' ka káaj u nookoytal ka'an, táan u líik'sikuba cháak. Ma' sáam ti' lelo' ka káaj u lúubul le ja'o'; ka'alikil Clavioe' táan u dzaik séebil u k'axik u si'; le ka tu yóotaj u kuche' ka tíip' tu yiknaal juntúul nojoch máak jach piim u me'ex chowaak yéetel saktake' ka a'ala'ab ti':

—Clavio, bix kéen a bisil le si' bey ch'uulilo', yéetel le ja'o' dzo'ok u aaltal, p'atej, sáamale' ka suut a ch'a'ej, bik xi'ik úuchul tech loob, ka'alikile' ko'ox a máans le cháak tin wotoch yan te naadzila'.

Ma' u yojel ba'axtene' ka tu núukaj Clavio beya':

—Mi jaaj a t'aan, ko'ox; wa ka u téek k'áat ten Yum Noolo tu'ux yan u si'e' kin wa'alik sáamal in bisik ti'.

—Ko'ox túun-ka a'ala'ab ti'e' ka bino'ob.

Ma' sen náajchajak u xíimbalo'obe' ka k'ucho'ob ti' jump'éel su'ukil naj; le ka ooko'ob ichile' ku yilik Clavioe' ti' yan u láak' oxtúul nojoch máako'ob je'ex le u yéet bino', le ba'ax je'ela' jela'an tu yilil, tumen chéen nukuch wíiniko'ob le kajakbalo'ob te najo'.

Ka ila'ab jela'an u paktik tuláakale' ka a'ala'ab ti' beya':

—Ma' ch'aik sajakilil, to'one' úuch kajlako'on weye', ka'alikil tya'anech t-éetele', je ba'axak kéen a wil ti'al jaantbile', jaantej.

—Ma'alob-tu núukaj.

Ka náadz Clavio te tu mayche'il le najo' ku yilike' ti' yan chakbil yéetel píibil nali', sa',[4] k'eyem,[5] ya'ach', tutil waaj, yéetel x-kaaxo'ob, óoli' je'ex le ku k'u'ubulo'ob ti'al le Ch'a' Cháak[6] wa ti' Wajil Koolo',[7] bey xan tuláakal le ba'axo'ob ku dzaiko'ob le koolo'obo'.

Ka ila'ab tu sen ch'antik le ki'iwajo'obo' ka a'ala'ab ti':

—Wa wi'ijeche' Clavio, ba'axten ma' ta ch'a'ik je je ba'ax a k'áat a jaante'.

—Ma', ma' wi'ijeni'—tu núukaj k'as su'ulakil yo'olal dzo'ok u yila'al.

Ma túun wa ma' wi'ijeche' much beet utz a chupik le kamp'éel chúuj ch'uyukbalo'ob te pak'lu'umo', le ja'o' te yan te táankabo'.

—Ma'alob-tu núukaj Clavioe' ka jóok'ij.

Tu ch'a'aj le kamp'éel chúujo' ka jo'op' u chupiko'ob; ikil u láalik le ja'o' tu yu'ubaj u wéekel tu k'ab chéen ba'ale' ku yilike' ma' tu ch'u'ulul u k'abo'obo', le ba'ax tu yilaja' le beet u ja'ak'al u yóole' ka tu ya'alaj:

—Ba'ax ja'il le je'el ma' tu ch'ulik in k'aba'.

Ma' sáam ti' lelo' ka tu yu'ubaj u taal u xíimbal tzíimino'ob, ka tu sutaj u yiche' ku yilike' leti'ob le kantúul nojoch máako'ob ku k'uchulo'ob yóok'ol u ki'ichkelem sak tziimino'obo',[8] tu ch'a'ajo'ob le chúujo'obo' yéetel u chikoote'obe' ka bino'ob tak ka sa'ato'ob chúumuk ka'an, ti' jump'éel tu'ux boox.

Chéen p'el sa'atiko'ob le nukuch wíiniko'ob yéetel u tziimino'obo' ka u'uya'abe' "kilili'im, si'in ta'aw," "kilili'im, si'in ta'aw." Ka dzo'oke' "to'ox" ka káaj u taal le cháako'.

Clavio ka tu yu'ubaj táan u k'áaxal le cháako' ka ook te ich najo'. Ma' sáam ti' le je'el ka ka' ch'eene'naje' ku yilike' mix junch'áaj ja' ku lúubul te tu'ux yan le najo', ba'ale' tu báak'paache' k'a'am u k'áaxal, ka tu yilaj beyo' ka júup u la'acht u pool, tumen ma' tu k'uchul u na'at tuláakal ba'ax ku yúuchul. Chéen ti' lelo' ka tu yu'ubaj Clavioe', u juum le cháako' táan u bin u náachtal tak ka sa'atij.

Jach táan u máan le cháako' ka suunajo'ob le kantúul nukuch wíiniko'obo', ka k'ucho'obe' ka tu ya'alajo'ob ti' Clavio beya':

—Le cháak ta wilaj u k'áaxalo', u ja'ilo'ob le chúujo'ob ta chupiáatajo'obo', le u juum le cháako' leti' t-beetilak u yáalkab le ba'alche'obo', le jaadz ta wu'uyaj u yúuchulo' leti' t-jadzilak le tzíimino'obo'.

—Máaxe'ex túun beya'—tu k'áataj Clavio.

—To'one' Yumtzilo'on—núuka'ab ti'—Le meyaj k-beetika' u ti'al ma' u pe'ertik u jooch le j-kolnáalo'obo', yo'olal lelo' k-t'oxikbáa tu kanti'itzil ka'an.

Le ka oorachaj u yúuchul janale' ka jaano'obij, ka dzo'oke' ka k'áata'ab ti Clavio:

—Ma' wa a k'áat a kan a beet a J-meenili'?[9] je'el k-ka'ansikeche'.

—Ma', ba'ax u chéen beelal ten ka in kanej, tene' ki'imak in wóol je bix yanikena'—tu núukaj.

—Mo'oten túun weye', nuka'ajo'on k-'o'o a pool—a'ala'ab ti'.

Le ka tu nadzubae' ka láala'ab u ja'il le chúuj tu poolo', le ka tu yu'ubaj síise' ka tu mudzaj u yich, le ka tu p'ilaje' ku yilike' te yan te k'áax tu'ux tu yilaj le nojoch máak ka káaj u ch'u'ulule', u si'e' tu yiknaal yan, ku dzo'okole' ma' ch'uuli'. Yo'olal ma' tu na'atik ba'ax úuche' ka tu ya'ach'taj u yich, ka tu ka' p'ilaje' ku yilike' leyli' tu yiknaal u si' yane'.

Yo'olal túun dzo'ok u yu'ubik wi'ij yéetel uk'aaje' ka tu kuchaj le si'o' ka suunaj te kaajo'.

Clavio ka k'uch tu yootoch'. Ka tu yu'ubaj Yum Nooloe' ka jóck' u yil máax le dzo'ok u k'uchul yéetel le si'o ka tu yilaje' leti' le Clavio dzo'ok u k'uchulo', chéen yo'olal u ki'imakil u yóol ikil tu ka' ililake' ka káaj u báan u ja'il u yich, ka tu ya'alaj beya':

—Clavio teech wa xi'ipal, tu'ux dzoka'anech beya', óolak a beet u chokotal in pool ikil sa'atikech le buka'aj k'iino'obo', ba'axten ma' ta wa'alaj ten wa yaan a bin tu yiknaal u láak' máaki'.

Ka túun tu núukaje':

—Je'el in tzikbatik tech tu jeel k'iine', beorae' wi'ij yéetel uk'aajen.

—Máanen túun janal, yan u yalab jump'íit ki'iwaj p'aatal ti' le chan kuum in dzaamaj te yóok'ol le báanketao'[10] a'ala'ab ti'.

Ka dzo'ok u ki' janal Clavioe' ka bin u je'elsuba tu yootoch.

Le k'iino'obo' bin u máano'ob tak ka tu chukaj mi jump'éel winaal úuchuk le ba'ax ti' le Clavioo', ka téek k'a'aj u tzikbatik ti' Yum Noolo.

Le nojoch máak ka tu yu'ubajo' ka tu ya'alaj beya':

—Jaaj leti' le Yumtzilo'ob bis le Clavioa', tumen k'aja'an ten tzibatik ten xan in nool le ka bisa'ab u láak máak xan, je bix le juntúulo', Clavioe yéeya'ab ti'al ka u beet u J-meenil ka'achij, chéen wa ka u yóot ka'ache', bejla' leti' u ma'alobil le J-meeno'obo'.

Notes

1. Plural of "Yumtzil" (God). A collective name for the Mayan protective entities, applied exclusively here to the rain entities. (See Appendix B.)

2. At the end of the twentieth century the Mayan language or Yucatec Mayan was Mexico's second largest Indigenous language in number of speakers: nearly 1.5 million, living primarily on the Yucatán Peninsula, in the states of Campeche, Yucatán, and Quintana Roo, in addition to some areas of the Republic of Belize. The author uses the Practical Literacy Alphabet for Adult Mayan Speakers, established by several government institutions in August 1984 in Mérida, Yucatán. The orthographic variations from this alphabet lie in the use of *tz* and *dz* rather than *ts* and *ts'*, respectively.

3. The city of Izamal. Some suggest that this name derives from the Maya *itzamatul*, "dew that falls from the sky." The legendary founder of this city was an Itzá priest called Zamná.

4. Mayan equivalent for the Spanish *atole.* (See Glossary.)

5. Mayan word that farmers translate into Spanish as *pozol* or *posol.* Dough made from cooked corn kernels that have burst open; it is dissolved in water for consumption.

6. Agricultural rain-petitioning ceremony. (See Appendix E.)

Notas

1. Plural de "Yumtzil" (Dios). Se trata de un nombre colectivo de las entidades protectoras mayas. Aquí se aplica fundamentalmente a las entidades de la lluvia. (Véase Apéndice B.)

2. La lengua maya, o mejor, el maya yucateco, era a finales del siglo XX la segunda lengua indígena con más hablantes en México: cerca de millón y medio de individuos asentados primordialmente en la Península de Yucatán en los estados de Campeche, Yucatán y Quintana Roo, y también en algunas zonas de Belice. El autor emplea el Alfabeto Práctico para la Alfabetización de los Adultos Hablantes de Maya que diversas instituciones oficiales de México acordaron en Mérida, Yucatán, en agosto de 1984. Las diferencias ortográficas con el alfabeto acordado institucionalmente son dos: el empleo de *tz* en lugar de *ts* y el de *dz* en lugar de *ts'*.

3. Ciudad de Izamal. Algunos sugieren que el nombre se deriva del maya *itzamatul*, "rocío que cae del cielo." El legendario fundador de la ciudad fue un sacerdote de los itzáes llamado Zamná.

4. Palabra maya para "atole." (Véase Glosario.)

5. Palabra maya que los campesinos traducen al español como "pozol" o "posol." Masa de maíz cocido y reventado que se deslíe para ser comido.

6. Ceremonia agrícola de petición de lluvias. (Véase Apéndice E.)

7. Agricultural ceremony to give thanks for the harvest. (See Appendix E.)

8. Plural of *tzíimin,* a word originally used for the tapir and, since the conquest, for the horse. The color white is characteristic of the rain gods' horses. (See Appendix B.)

9. *Jmen,* traditional Mayan priest. (See Appendix A.)

10. From the Spanish *banqueta,* "small bench," usually three-legged, where the Mayas prepare their corn dough and a variety of foods.

7. Ceremonia agrícola de agradecimiento por la cosecha. (Véase Apéndice E.)

8. Plural de *tzíimin,* palabra que originalmente designaba al tapir y a partir de la conquista al caballo. El color blanco es esencial en el caballo de los dioses de la lluvia. (Véase Apéndice B.)

9. *Jmen,* sacerdote maya tradicional. (Véase Apéndice A.)

10. Del español *banqueta,* "banco pequeño," generalmente de tres patas, donde los mayas preparan la masa de maíz y diversos alimentos.

A Story about Yum Tziles[1]

Miguel Ángel May May

Maya[2]

[From *Lajump'éel maaya tzikbalo'ob/Diez relatos mayas,* pp. 39–44, 121–125. Letras Mayas Contemporáneas, 3rd series, vol. 10, C. Montemayor, series ed. Mexico City: INI/TRF, 1998.]

There was a person who lived in a thatched-roofed house on the outskirts of town in the direction of Izamal.[3] He stuttered greatly when he spoke, but he managed to make himself understood. He always chewed tobacco and ran errands to make a living.

He was resting in his house one day in his old hammock, around eight in the morning, when Don[4] Nolo came to see him and said, "Clavio, would you do me a favor? Go out and cut for me a bundle of firewood, for I am in great need."

"I will gladly go. All I need is for you to give me some tools," responded Clavio.

"Fine," responded Don Nolo, and he gave Clavio a hatchet, a spade, and a *mecapal.*[5]

Clavio took the tools and departed to cut firewood. He was cutting wood when it began to cloud up; rain was approaching, and, within a matter of moments, it began to fall. Clavio rushed to bundle up the firewood. When he was about to load it up, there appeared before him an old man, dressed in white with a long white beard, who said to him: "Clavio, how are you going to carry wet firewood? With all the water, it must weigh a lot more. Leave it until tomorrow; do not injure yourself. Meanwhile, let us go to my house until the rain passes."

Without knowing why, Clavio responded: "I believe you are right, let us leave now. If Don Nolo asks me for the firewood, I shall tell him I will deliver it to him tomorrow."

"Let us go then," the other man said, and together they left the woods.

It was not long before they arrived at a thatched-roofed house. When they entered, there were three other old men there. It seemed odd to Clavio that only old men lived in that place. They noticed his surprise and said to him: "Do not fear, we have lived here for some time. As long as you are with us, you may eat any foods that you see."

"Fine," Clavio responded.

Clavio approached the table and saw ears of corn that had been cooked underground, *atole*[6] and *pozol;*[7] the soup and the bread that are used for the Ch'a' Cháak ceremonies,[8] chickens, and all the produce of the fields. The old men noticed how Clavio was staring at the food and said: "If you are hungry, why do you not take whatever you would like to eat?"

"No, I am not hungry," replied Clavio, embarrassed that they had noticed him staring.

"Well then, if you are not hungry, do us the favor of filling up the four water gourds hanging on the wall. The water is outside."

"Fine," Clavio responded, and he went out.

He took the four gourds and began to fill them. He felt water falling on his hands, but they did not get wet. That surprised him, and he thought: "What kind of water is this that does not make my hands wet?"

A few moments later, he heard the sound of horses approaching. He turned around to see the four old men arriving on four beautiful horses.[9] They took the four gourds and their whips and departed. They soon disappeared as black spots in the middle of the sky.

The men and their horses had barely vanished, when one could hear: *Kilili'im, si'in, ta'aw, kilili'im, si'in, ta'aw.* Then, *to'ox!* The rain began to fall.[10]

When Clavio heard this, he went inside the thatched-roofed house, but moments later he stuck his head outside. He realized that not a drop of water was falling where he was, even though it was raining very hard all around. He scratched his head because he could not understand what had happened. He then heard the sound of the rain grow fainter and finally disappear.

The rain had ceased when the same old men arrived on horseback and said to Clavio: "The rain that you saw falling is the water from the gourds you filled. The thunder is the sound that the horses produce when we make them gallop, and the lightning is made when we strike them."

"Just who are you, then?" Clavio asked.

"We are the Yum Tziles, the waterers of the fields. We carry out this labor so that the farmers do not lose their crops; that is why we divide ourselves up among the four cardinal directions."

When it was time to eat, everyone ate; they then asked Clavio: "Would you not like to become a *jmen?*[11] We can teach you."

"No, what good would it do me to learn? I am happy just as I am," he responded.

"Well then, come here, we are going to wash your head," they said to him.

He approached, and they emptied the water from one of the gourds on his head; it felt cold, and he closed his eyes. When he opened them, he realized that he was once again in the forest where he had seen the old man and that his firewood was no longer wet. He rubbed his eyes because he was unable to comprehend what had really taken place. Upon opening them again, he found himself next to the firewood. Since he was hungry and thirsty, he loaded up the firewood and returned to town.

Clavio arrived at the house of Don Nolo and dropped the firewood on his patio. Don Nolo came out to see who had arrived with the firewood and saw that it was Clavio. He was so glad to see him again that tears began to fall from his eyes, and he said: "Clavio, boy, it is you, where have you been? I almost lost my mind. Why did you not tell me that you had to visit with someone?"

Clavio then replied: "Oh, I will explain some other day. Right now, I am really hungry."

"Well then, come in and eat; there is still a little bit of food in the pot over on the *banqueta.*"[12]

When Clavio finished eating, he went home to rest.

The days went by, and soon a month had passed; Clavio then told Don Nolo the entire story.

Once the man heard the tale, he said: "Yes, it was the Yum Tziles who took you away. I now remember my grandfather told me that they had taken another person away. Just like you, they had chosen him so that he would be a good *jmen,* but he did not accept. He would have been the best of the *jmenes.*"

Notes

1. Hispanicized version of the Mayan plural noun "Yumtzilo'ob," literally, "the full, complete, or integral Lords," from "Yumtzil," "God" (the full, complete, or integral Lord). Collective name of the Mayan protective entities; in this story, the name is applied exclusively to the protective rain entities, the Cháako'ob. (See Appendix B.)

2. At the end of the twentieth century the Mayan language or Yucatec Mayan was Mexico's second largest Indigenous language in number of speakers: nearly 1.5 million, living primarily on the Yucatán Peninsula, in the states of Campeche, Yucatán, and Quintana Roo, in addition to some areas of the Republic of Belize. The author uses the Practical Literacy Alphabet for Adult Mayan Speakers, established by several government institutions in August 1984 in Mérida, Yucatán. The orthographic variations from this alphabet lie in the use of *tz* and *dz* rather than *ts* and *ts'*, respectively.

3. Municipality and city of some 15,000 inhabitants in the northern part of the state of Yucatán. In ancient times Izamal was an important worship site for the supreme deity Itzamná and the solar god Kinich-Kakmó. The author's home community of Kimbilá is located within the Municipality of Izamal. See also note 3 of the Mayan-language text.

4. A Spanish title of respect used before the names of older men.

5. From the Nahuatl *mecapalli,* "rope leaf." A wide band of rope that is strapped to the forehead for carrying bundles on one's back.

6. From the Nahuatl *atolli,* "diluted"; a thick beverage prepared from corn meal or flour dissolved in water and boiled.

7. From the Nahuatl *potzol,* "froth," or *potzolli,* "frothy"; its Mayan language equivalent is *k'eyem.* Dough made from corn kernels that have been cooked and have burst open; it is dissolved in water in a half-sphere gourd (*jícara*) for consumption. The farmer usually carries the dough in a shoulder bag and water in a gourd.

8. Agricultural rain-petitioning ceremony practiced by the Mayas

of the Yucatán Peninsula. It is conducted by a *jmen* or Mayan ritual priest (see Appendix A); various foods are placed on the ceremonial altar as offerings (see Appendix E).

9. The white horse is associated with the Rain Lords or Protectors, the Cháako'ob. *Tzíimin* is now the Mayan word for horse, but it originally referred to the tapir. (See Appendix B.)

10. Onomatopoeic terms that approximate the sounds of the colliding winds that bring on the rain; lightning bolts; thunderclaps; and the sudden unleashing of a downpour.

11. Traditional Mayan priest. (See Appendix A.)

12. Small, elongated bench, usually three-legged, where the Mayas prepare their corn dough and a variety of foods.

Una narración sobre Yum Tziles[1]

Miguel Ángel May May

Maya[2]

[De *Lajump'éel maaya tzikbalo'ob/Diez relatos mayas,* pp. 121–125. Letras Mayas Contemporáneas, 3a serie, vol. 10, C. Montemayor, coord. de la colección. México, D.F.: INI/TRF, 1998.]

Hubo una persona que vivía en una casita de paja, a la salida del pueblo, rumbo a la ciudad de Izamal;[3] tartamudeaba mucho al hablar pero se daba a entender; siempre mascaba tabaco y trabajaba haciendo mandados.

Un día que descansaba en su casa, en su vieja hamaca, como a las ocho de la mañana, don Nolo llegó a verlo y le dijo:

—Clavio, ¿me puedes hacer un favor? Ve a cortarme un tercio de leña, que me urge mucho.

—Cómo no he de ir, sólo que me tienes que dar mis herramientas.

—Está bien—le contestó y le entregó una hacha, una coa y un mecapal.[4]

Clavio tomó las cosas y se fue a leñar. Estaba cortando la leña cuando comenzó a nublarse, la lluvia estaba próxima; momentos después comenzó a llover. Clavio se apuró para amarrar su leña y al disponerse a cargarla apareció ante él un viejito vestido de blanco y con largas barbas blancas, que le dijo:

—Clavio, ¿cómo vas a cargar la leña toda mojada? Con el agua debe pesar más. Déjala y mañana regresas a buscarla, no te vayas a lastimar. Mientras tanto, vamos a mi casa para que pase la lluvia.

Sin saber por qué, Clavio respondió:

—Creo que tienes razón, vamos. Si don Nolo me llega a preguntar en dónde está la leña, le digo que mañana se la llevo.

—Vamos entonces—dijo el otro y se fueron.

No tardaron en llegar a una casa de paja. Cuando entraron, se encontraban otros tres viejitos ahí. Le pareció extraño que sólo viejitos vivieran en ese lugar. Ellos notaron que se extrañaba y le dijeron:

—No temas, hace tiempo que nosotros vivimos aquí. Mientras estés con nosotros, todo lo que veas de comer, cómelo.

—Está bien—contestó Clavio.

Clavio se acercó a la mesa y vio elotes que se habían cocido bajo la tierra, atole,[5] pozol,[6] la sopa y los panes que se utilizan para las ceremonias de Ch'a' Cháak[7] y Wajil Kol,[8] pollos y todos los productos de las milpas. Se dieron cuenta que estaba mirando mucho la comida y le dijeron:

—Si tienes hambre, ¿por qué no tomas lo que quieras comer?

—No, no tengo hambre—contestó apenado porque lo habían descubierto.

—Entonces, si no tienes hambre, haznos el favor de llenar los cuatro calabazos que están en la pared; el agua está afuera.

—Está bien—contestó Clavio y salió.

Tomó los cuatro calabazos y los comenzó a llenar; sintió que se le caía agua en las manos, pero éstas no se mojaban para nada; esto lo asombró y pensó:

—¿Qué agua será ésta que no me moja las manos?

Momentos después escuchó que venían caminando unos caballos. Se volvió a mirar y eran los cuatro viejitos que llegaban sobre cuatro hermosos caballos;[9] tomaron los cuatro calabazos y sus látigos y se fueron; pronto desaparecieron en un punto negro en el centro del cielo.

Apenas desaparecieron los señores con sus caballos se escuchó *kilililí'im, si'in, ta'aw, kililililí'im, si'in, ta'aw;* después de eso, *to'ox,*[10] comenzó a caer la lluvia.

Cuando Clavio escuchó esto, se metió a la casita de paja, pero momentos después se asomó y se dio cuenta que ninguna gota de agua caía en donde se encontraba, pese a que a la redonda llovía muy fuerte. Se rascó la cabeza porque no alcanzaba a entender lo que estaba sucediendo. Luego escuchó que el sonido de la lluvia se iba alejando hasta que desapareció.

Se había calmado la lluvia cuando los señores llegaron en sus caballos y le dijeron a Clavio:

—Esta lluvia que viste caer es el agua de los calabazos que llenaste; los truenos eran el sonido que producían los caballos cuando los hacíamos correr; los relámpagos era cuando les pegábamos.

—Entonces, ¿quiénes son ustedes?—preguntó Clavio.

—Nosotros somos Yum Tziles, los regadores de las milpas. Estabamos haciendo este trabajo para que el milpero no pierda su cosecha; por eso nos dividimos en los cuatro puntos cardinales.

Cuando llegó la hora de comer, todos comieron. Después le preguntaron a Clavio.

—¿No deseas convertirte en *jmen?*[11] Te podemos enseñar.

—No, ¿de qué me serviría aprenderlo? Estoy contento como estoy—respondió.

—Entonces, ven acá, vamos a lavarte la cabeza—le dijeron.

Se acercó y le echaron el agua de uno de los calabazos en su cabeza. La sintió fría y cerró los ojos; cuando los abrió se dio cuenta de que se encontraba otra vez en el monte donde había visto al viejito y su leña ya no estaba mojada. Se restregó los ojos, porque no alcanzaba a comprender qué era lo que había sucedido realmente. Al abrirlos de nuevo, estaba junto a la leña. Como estaba hambriento y sediento, cargó con la leña y regresó al pueblo.

Clavio llegó a la casa de don Nolo y tiró la leña en el patio. Don Nolo salió a ver quién había llegado con la leña y vio que era Clavio; por la alegría de volverlo a ver, le comenzaron a caer lágrimas y le dijo:

—Clavio, muchacho, eres tú, ¿dónde había estado? Por poco me vuelvo loco. ¿Por qué no me dijiste que tenías que ir con otra persona?

Entonces, él respondió:

—Ah, te lo cuento otro día, ahora tengo mucha hambre.

—Entonces, pasa a comer, queda un poco de comida en la ollita que está sobre la banqueta,[12] sobre esa mesita con tres patas.

Cuando Clavio terminó de comer fue a descansar a su casa.

Los días fueron pasando, hasta que transcurrió un mes; entonces Clavio le contó todo a don Nolo.

Cuando el señor lo supo, le dijo:

—Sí, son los Yum Tziles quienes te llevaron. Ahora recuerdo que mi abuelo platicaba que se habían llevado a otra persona. Como a ti, lo habían elegido para que fuera un buen *jmen,* pero no lo aceptó; hubiera sido el mejor de los *jmenes.*

Notas

1. Pluralización castellana de la voz maya "Yumtzilo'ob," literalmente, "los Señores plenos," de "Yumtzil," "Dios" (el Señor pleno). Nombre colectivo de las entidades protectoras mayas. En este cuento se aplica el nombre exclusivamente a las entidades protectoras de la lluvia, los Cháako'ob. (Véase Apéndice B.)

2. La lengua maya, o mejor, el maya yucateco, era a finales del siglo XX la segunda lengua indígena con más hablantes en México: cerca de millón y medio de individuos asentados primordialmente en la Península de Yucatán en los estados de Campeche, Yucatán y Quintana Roo, y también en algunas zonas de Belice. El autor emplea el Alfabeto Práctico para la Alfabetización de los Adultos Hablantes de Maya que diversas instituciones oficiales de México acordaron en Mérida, Yucatán, en agosto de 1984. Las diferencias ortográficas con el alfabeto acordado institucionalmente son dos: el empleo de *tz* en lugar de *ts* y el de *dz* en lugar de *ts'*.

3. Municipio y ciudad de unos 15,000 habitantes de la parte norte del estado de Yucatán. En tiempo antiguos, Izamal fue un importante lugar de culto a la deidad suprema Itzamná y el dios solar Kinich-Kakmó. La comunidad del autor, Kimbilá, está en el municipio de Izamal. Véase también nota 3 del texto en maya.

4. Del náhuatl *mecapalli,* "hoja de cuerda." Faja ancha de una soga que se coloca en la frente para llevar carga en la espalda.

5. Del náhuatl *atolli,* "agüita" o "aguado," bebida espesa preparada a base de masa o de harina de maíz disuelta en agua y hervida.

6. Del náhuatl *potzol,* "espuma," o *potzolli,* "espumante." En maya *k'eyem.* Masa de maíz cocido y reventado que se deslíe en agua para ser comido. El campesino suele portar la masa en su morral y el agua en un calabazo; deslíe la masa en una jícara.

7. Ceremonia tradicional de petición de lluvias entre los mayas de la Península de Yucatán. Es conducida por un *jmen* o sacerdote maya y en el altar de la ceremonia hay ofrendas de diversos alimentos. (Véase Apéndice A.)

8. Ceremonia agrícola de agradecimiento por las cosechas. (Véase Apéndice E.) Es conducida también por un *jmen* o sacerdote maya y en el altar de la ceremonia hay principalmente panes y ofrendas obtenidas de la milpa.

9. El caballo está asociado a los Señores o Protectores de la lluvia, a los Cháako'ob. *Tzíimin* es ahora el nombre maya del caballo, pero originalmente lo fue del tapir. (Véase Apéndice B.)

10. Términos onomatopéyicos que se aproximan al sonido de los vientos cruzados que traen la lluvia, los rayos, los truenos y el aguacero que súbitamente se suelta.

11. Sacerdote maya tradicional. (Véase Apéndice A.)

12. Banco alargado, generalmente de tres patas, donde los mayas preparan la masa de maíz y distintos alimentos.

Santiago Domínguez Aké

Maya

Santiago Domínguez Aké. Photographed in Mérida, Yucatán.

Santiago Domínguez Aké was born on July 25, 1951, in Muxupip, Yucatán. He studied bookkeeping in 1973–1974. Since 1981 he has worked as a bilingual cultural promoter for the Yucatán Regional Popular Cultures Office. He completed course-work for the bachelor's degree in anthropology with a concentration in history at the Universidad Autónoma de Yucatán. In 1993 Domínguez Ake participated actively as a proofreader and translator for the first series of Colección Letras Mayas Contemporáneas (C. Montemayor, series ed.). Within this collection, he authored *Felipe Carrillo Puerto, u kuxtal yéetel bix u k'a'ajsa'al tu kaajil Muxupip* (vol. 7; Mexico City: INI/Sedesol/TRF, 1993); *La vida de Felipe Carrillo Puerto y su memoria en Muxupip* (The Life of Felipe Carrillo Puerto and His Legacy in Muxupip) (vol. 8; Mexico City: INI/Sedesol/TRF, 1993); *U múuch'kabil ejido'ob tu kaajil Muxupip* (vol. 29; Mexico City: INI/Sedesol/TRF, 1993); *La historia de la sociedad ejidal de Muxupip* (A History of Muxupip's Ejido Society) (vol. 30; Mexico City: INI/Sedesol/TRF, 1993); *Ba'ax ku tukultiko'ob maya wiiniko'ob ku yuuchul* (vol. 19; Mexico City: INI/Sedesol/TRF, 1993); *Creencias, profecías y consejas mayas* (Mayan Beliefs, Prophecies, and Traditional Advice) (vol. 20; Mexico City: INI/Sedesol/TRF, 1993). Within the same collection, he co-authored *U Yum Santísima Kruuz Tuunil Xocén* (vol. 25; Mexico City: INI/Sedesol/TRF, 1993) and *Yum Santísima Cruz Tun* (The Very Holy Lord *Tun* Cross of Xocén) (vol. 26; Mexico City: INI/Sedesol/TRF, 1993). In 1997 he published *La milpa en Muxupip* (The Cornfield in Muxupip) (Colección Letras Indígenas Contemporáneas, Mexico City: DGCP, 1996), a broad exploration of the Mayan worldview. In the third series of Colección Letras Mayas Contemporáneas he published *Siljil yéetel kuxtal/Ciclo de vida en Muxupip* (The Life Cycle in Muxupip) (vol. 14; Mexico City: INI/TRF, 1998).

Santiago Domínguez Aké nació el 25 de julio de 1951 en Muxupip, Yucatán. Estudió la carrera de tenedor de libros entre 1973 y 1974. Desde 1981 trabaja como promotor cultural bilingüe en la Unidad Regional Yucatán de Culturas Populares. Es pasante de la licenciatura en ciencias antropológicas, en la especialidad de historia, de la Universidad Autónoma de Yucatán. En 1993 participó activamente como revisor y traductor de la primera serie de Colección Letras Mayas Contemporáneas (C. Montemayor, coord. de la colección). Fue autor de los siguientes tomos de esta colección: *Felipe Carrillo Puerto, u kuxtal yéetel bix u k'a'ajsa'al tu kaajil Muxupip* (vol. 7; México, D.F.: INI/Sedesol/TRF, 1993); *La vida de Felipe Carrillo Puerto y su memoria en Muxupip* (vol. 8; México, D.F.: INI/Sedesol/TRF, 1993); *U múuch'kabil ejido'ob tu kaajil Muxupip* (vol. 29; México, D.F.: INI/Sedesol/TRF, 1993); *La historia de la sociedad ejidal de Muxupip* (vol. 30; México, D.F.: INI/Sedesol/TRF, 1993); *Ba'ax ku tukultiko'ob maya wiiniko'ob ku yuuchul* (vol. 19; México, D.F.: INI/Sedesol/TRF, 1993); y *Creencias, profecías y consejas mayas* (vol. 20; México, D.F.: INI/Sedesol/TRF, 1993). Dentro de la misma colección fue co-autor de *U Yum Santísima Kruuz Tuunil Xocén* (vol. 25; México, D.F.: INI/Sedesol/TRF, 1993) y *Yum Santísima Cruz Tun* (vol. 26; México, D.F.: INI/Sedesol/TRF, 1993). En 1997 publicó *La milpa en Muxupip* (Colección Letras Indígenas Contemporáneas, México, D. F.: DGCP, 1996), obra donde desarrolla la amplia cosmovisión maya. En la tercera serie de Colección Letras Mayas Contemporáneas publicó *Siljil yéetel kuxtal/Ciclo de vida en Muxupip* (vol. 14; México, D.F.: INI/TRF, 1998).

U pa'ak'al Ixi'im

Santiago Domínguez Aké

Maya[1]

[From *La milpa en Muxupip*, pp. 63–67. Colección Letras Indígenas Contemporáneas. Mexico City: DGCP, 1996.]

Kex tuláakal u meyajil kool k'abéete', k-tukultike', u pa'ak'al nale' leti' u jach k'abéetil; tumen nale', u táabal u kuxtal j-kolnáal. Le beetike', j-kolnáale' k'abéet u yantal ti' junp'éel k'ajóolal ti'al ka páajchajak u na'atik ba'axo'ob ku dzaik ojéeltbil che'ob, ba'alche'ob, u "xook k'iin,"[2] yetel u chukáan ba'alo'ob ba'pachmilo'ob. Bix ken talak u dzaik cháak yetel ba'ax i'inajil ixi'im yetel u chukáan pak'alilo'ob ken ma'alob najmata'ak ichil kool.

Tu yo'olal bix u yojéelta'al ba'ax i'inajil ixi'im ken u dza ma'alobe', yum "Lool" (Florencio) Gorosica Cruz juntúul nojoch máak yan ti' ochenta ja'abo'obe' ku ya'alik:

—U'uch ka'ach bine', ti'al u yojéelta'al ba'ax i'inajil ken u dza ma'alobe', ti u oknaj k'iinil treintiuno ti disieembre ku yoxo'onta'al jejeláas i'inajilo'ob ti'al dzaabil jujun p'úut ti' leti'ob ichil junjáaw leek[3] ku dza'abal ti' junp'éel pe'et[4] ch'uykíinta'an tu yáanal junp'éel k'óoben mina'an u kolóojche'il ti'al ka páajchajak u ki' salta'al tumen iik'. Ken éemsa'ak le i'inajo'ob dzo'ok le "xook k'iino'"—ku ch'unpajal tu yáax junp'éel k'iinil eneero ti'al ka talak dzo'okol tu dzook k'iinil eneero le winala' le ku si'ip'il u puksi'ik'ale',[5] leti' le ma'alob ken u dzaik u jéek te ja'abo'. Le beetik j-kolnáale' u ya'abil u k'aanilo'ob u kool ku pak'ik yéetel le i'inaj je'ela'. Bey u tzikbaltmajil ten in nool-tu ya'alaj yum Florencio.

U "xook k'iine'," ku dzaik xan ojéeltbil wa "kabal ja'ab" wa "ka'anal ja'ab" ken u beetej. Ku ya'ala'al "kabal ja'ab" wa ku chu'unpajal u "lúubul" cháako'ob ma' k'uchuk u winalil mayoi'; "ka'anal ja'ab" wa ku chu'unpajal u "k'áaxal" cháako'ob dzo'ok u máan óoxlajun k'iinil juunio.

U jit'ik jach táaj chawak u k'u' x-yuuya[6] yéetel chéen tikin aak' yetel ch'ilibo'obe', u chíikul yan u xáantal ken u dza cháak. Wa ku jit'ik ma' chawak yéetel jéejentikin jéejenya'ax aak'o'obe', u chíikul yan u beetik ja'aja'al yáaxk'iin.

U yila'al u lool ja'abin[7] chéen p'óop'ot anik ichil u le'obe', chéen p'óop'ot xan ken "tza'ayak" nal, chéen tu'ux síis u lu'umil ken u dza u jéek. U sen chawaktal yetel u poloktal u yich beelsíinikche'e',[8] u chíikul yan u nuuktal u jéek nal; ba'ale', wa bek'ech u yich yetel jéejen tikine', bey xan ken p'áatak u jéek nal, ma' táan u nuuktal mix táan u ma'alob k'antal.

U yila'al xan u pe'et uj yetel u pe'et k'iine', u chíikul nuka'aj u dza cháak; wa kóoche pe'eto', k'a'am cháak ken u dzae, wa bek'eche', chéen x-tóosja' ken u dzae.

U yu'uba'al u k'aay ch'och'lin bey ma'as u kaal yetel k'alk'alake', u chíikul nuka'aj u dza cháak; wa ku yu'uba'al u dzirintik u k'aay ma' k'alk'alake', u chíikul ma' táan u séeb dzaik cháak.

U yila'al u máan saakal,[9] xuulab,[10] yetel síinik u kuchmajo'ob u k'eeyemo'ob[11] yetel u yaalo'ob ti'al u kaxáantiko'ob junp'éel kajtalil ti' junp'éel p'úus lu'ume', u chíikul nuka'aj u dza u cháakilo'ob xamán, ku "talik" wa ku máan tak ka'ap'éel k'iin leeyli' táane'.

Ku ya'alik nukuch máako'ob kaja'ano'ob tu kaajil Muxupiipo', Dioose'[12] u dzaaman ka e'esa'ak tumen le ba'alo'ob ba'pachmilo'on ba'ax ku taal u k'iin. Ba'ale' u toopil bine', yan k'iine kex ka u yilo'ob táan u jelpajal ba'ax suuka'an u beetik ba'alche'ob, u jelpajal bin u lool yetel u dzaik u yich che'obe', ya'ab ti' le ba'alo'oba' ma' bin u yojéeltmajo'ob ba'ax chíikulil ku ye'esiko'obi', tumen mina'an ti'ob le táaj ya'ab k'ajóolalo'ob je bix yan ka'ach ti' u úuchben j-kolnáalilo'ob Muxupiipe'.

Ti'al k-suut k-ch'a'chi'it tu ka'atéen u pa'ak'al nale', k-a'alike', le táan u chu'unpajal le siiglo je'ela', wa tu ye'esaj "xook k'iin" yan u beetik "kaabal ja'abe," j-kolnáale tu winalil maarzo ku yoxo'ontik le nal u yéeyman ti'al i'inajilo', beyo' chéen u yilik dzo'ok u dzaik junp'éel wa ka'ap'éel nuxi' k'a'amk'am cháak tu winalil aabrile ku ki' pak'al u puli'; tumen u yojel ma' táan u chukik u winalil u "lúubul" cháako'ob ken chu'unpajak u "k'áaxal" cháako'ob. Wa u "xook k'iin" tu ye'esaj tu winalil u dzaik cháako'ob ken chu'unpajake', j-kolnáale' ku yoxo'ontik i'inaj táan u taal u dzo'okol u winalil aabril, tumen beyo', je u pak'al tu jo'lajun k'iinil mayoe'[13] wa tu óoxlajun k'iinil juunio,[14] kex ma' u dza cháaki', kex tikin lu'um, tumen u yojel óoli' ma' táan u kipik u dzaik junp'éel nuxi' k'a'amk'am cháak te ka'ap'éel k'iino'ob je'ela', ti'al u chu'unsik u "ch'a'ik yook" cháak (dzo'ok u xáantal u "ch'a'ik yook" cháak wa ka chu'unpajak u dzaik cháak tu óoxlajun k'iinil juunio). Ka'ap'éel bix u yúuchul pa'ak'al nal: junp'éele', leti' le k'ajóolta'an "k'óoben pak'alilo'," u láak'e', k'ajóolta'an "síit' kéejil'."

Wa ma' pak'anak j-kolnáal dzo'ok u máan u winalil juunioe', kex ka okok u tuukulil ti'e', u yojel ma' p'áatak ma' u páajtal u pak'ali', tumen ma' máanak beintisinko ti' juulioi'.[15] Máame k'iin je'ela', ma' táan u jóok'ol le ixi'im ku pa'ak'alo', ku janta'al yáanal lu'um tumen x-lukúumkanil yetel ku páana'al jaantbil tumen u ch'o'il k'áax, tu yo'olal dzo'ok u ka'antal tzáab.[16] Ma u yojelo'ob le nukuch máako'ob kaja'ano'ob Muxupiip ba'ax yan u yil le tzáab yéetel x-lukúumkanil yetel le ch'o' jaantiko'ob le ixi'im ku pa'ak'alo'. Ba'ale', ku ya'aliko'ob le nukuch máako'oba', tzikbalta'an ti'ob tumen u taata'ob yetel u noolo'obe',[17] le dzo'ok u ka'antal le tzáab ka'ano', je jaytéenak ka pa'ak'ak ixi'ime' ku jaanta'al tumen x-lukúumkanil yetel ch'o'. Ba'ale', ma' a'ala'ab ti'ob wa yan wa mina'an ba'ax u yil tzáab yéetel u yantal le x-lukúumkanil yetel le ch'o'o', Muxupiipe' ma' ojéelta'ani'.

Notes

1. At the end of the twentieth century the Mayan language or Yucatec Mayan was Mexico's second largest Indigenous language in number of speakers: nearly 1.5 million, living primarily on the Yucatán Peninsula, in the states of Campeche, Yucatán, and Quintana Roo, in addition to some areas of the Republic of Belize. The author uses the Practical Literacy Alphabet for Adult Mayan Speakers, established by several government institutions in August 1984 in Mérida, Yucatán. The orthographic variations from this alphabet lie in the use of *tz* and *dz* rather than *ts* and *ts'*, respectively.

2. Literally, "day count," known in Spanish as *cabañuelas;* refers to the climatic conditions present during the month of January. It is believed that the weather of the coming twelve months may be predicted by observing the climatic conditions present during these days.

3. "Calabash": *Lagenaria siceraria.*

4. Type of net that is attached to a ring and hung from three strings tied in a knot; it is used to store foods.

5. Literally, "the heart" (i.e., the core).

6. Bird known in the Spanish of Yucatán as *oropéndula,* characterized by yellow and orange feathers and black spots on its head and wings.

7. *Piscidia piscipula.* (See note 8 of the English-language text.)

8. *Alvaradoa amorphoides.* (See note 9 of the English-language text.)

9. Black carnivorous ant, of the type known in Mexico as *hormiga arriera* or "carrier ant" because it travels at night in groups and carries food back to its nest; it is capable of devouring other insects, including bees.

10. Another type of black "carrier ant" that travels in large groups and is less destructive.

11. Plural of *k'eyem,* known in Spanish as *pozol* or *posol.* Dough made from cooked corn kernels that have burst open; it is dissolved in water for consumption. The plural is a way of referring to the ant's food or "provisions."

12. That is, "Christ."

13. The feast of Saint Isidore the Farmer (San Isidro Labrador), considered to be the first day for the first sowing of corn (a.n.).

14. The feast of Saint Anthony of Padua (San Antonio de Padua), considered to be the final day for the first sowing of corn (a.n.).

15. The feast of Saint James the Apostle (Santiago Apóstol), considered to be the final day for the second sowing of corn (a.n.).

16. The Constellation of the Pleiades. This term in Mayan also refers to the rattlesnake's rattle.

Notas

1. La lengua maya, o mejor, el maya yucateco, era a finales del siglo XX la segunda lengua indígena con más hablantes en México: cerca de millón y medio de individuos asentados primordialmente en la Península de Yucatán en los estados de Campeche, Yucatán y Quintana Roo, y también en algunas zonas de Belice. El autor emplea el Alfabeto Práctico para la Alfabetización de los Adultos Hablantes de Maya que diversas instituciones oficiales de México acordaron en Mérida, Yucatán, en agosto de 1984. Las diferencias ortográficas con el alfabeto acordado institucionalmente son dos: el empleo de *tz* en lugar de *ts* y el de *dz* en lugar de *ts'*.

2. Literalmente, "la cuenta de los días" o "Cabañuelas"; sistema por el cual los campesinos mayas pronostican las condiciones climáticas de los doce meses del nuevo año, mediante la observación de las condiciones presentes durante el mes de enero.

3. "Calabazo": *Lagenaria siceraria.*

4. Especie de red que se fija en un aro y se cuelga por tres hilos unidos en un nudo; en ella se guardan comestibles.

5. Literalmente, "el corazón"; es decir, el cotiledón.

6. Ave conocida en el español de Yucatán como "oropéndula," pero de plumaje amarillo y anaranjado con manchas negras en la cabeza y en las alas.

7. *Piscidia piscipula.*

8. *Alvaradoa amorphoides.*

9. Hormiga arriera y carnicera: es negra, anda en grupo y entre los insectos que es capaz de devorar se halla la abeja. Se llaman "arrieras" por su costumbre de transportar durante las noches, en grupos, sus alimentos a sus nidos.

10. Otro tipo de hormiga arriera, también negra y que anda en grandes grupos, menos destructiva.

11. Plural de *k'eyem,* "pozol" o "posol"; masa de maíz cocido y reventado que para ser comido se deslíe en agua fría. El plural es una forma de aludir al alimento o "bastimento" de las hormigas.

12. Es decir, "Cristo."

13. Día de San Isidro Labrador, considerado el día que debe iniciarse la primera temporada de siembra del maíz (n.a.).

14. Día de San Antonio de Padua, considerado el día en que termina el primer período de siembra del maíz (n.a.).

15. Día de Santiago Apóstol, considerado el último día del segundo período de siembra del maíz (n.a.).

16. Constelación de las Pléyades. También se refiere al cascabel de la serpiente.

17. Abuelos. Proviene de *nol* y *nola,* "abuelo" y "abuela." Es prob-

17. Grandparents. From the Mayan *nol* and *nola*, "grandfather" and "grandmother," which in turn probably derive from the endings of the Spanish words *señor* (sir, gentleman) and *señora* (ma'am, lady).

able que se derive de las terminaciones de las palabras españolas *señor* y *señora*.

The Sowing of Corn

Santiago Domínguez Aké

Maya[1]

[From *La milpa en Muxupip*, pp. 63–67, 180–184. Colección Letras Indígenas Contemporáneas. Mexico City: DGCP, 1996.]

Without underrating the other produce of the fields, we can definitely affirm that corn is the most important of all crops since it is the country people's staff of life. To grow it, the farmer must interpret the messages of plants, of animals, of the *cabañuelas*,[2] and of other natural elements. Through such messages, he learns which corn kernels and other crops will grow well in his field and when the seasonal rains[3] will fall.

Don[4] "Lool," Florencio Gorosica Cruz, a man of eighty years of age, explains how to determine which type of corn kernels will grow best in the field:

> One must remove the different types of kernels from the cob and place a little pile of each in the middle of a *leek*.[5] On the night of December 31, the *leeks* are placed on a *pe'et*[6] that hangs in a straw-roofed shack without siding, so that the breeze may reach them freely. On the morning of February 1, once the *cabañuelas* have ended, one takes the *leeks* down, and the kernel that has a swollen core[7] will give the year's best crop. Therefore, the farmer should allow more space for it in his field. That's how my grandfather explained it to me.

The *cabañuelas* also reveal whether a year will be "low" or "high." A year is "low" when the seasonal rains begin to fall before the month of May, and "high" when they begin to fall after June 13.

When the golden oriole weaves a long nest with just lianas and dry twigs, it is a sign that the dry season will be prolonged. If it weaves a short nest using lianas and dry twigs as well as green ones, it is a sign that it will rain periodically during the dry period and the rainy season.

When the branches of the *ja'abín*[8] have only clusters of leaves and flowers, it is a sign that in the fields the corn will only grow well in clusters; that is, there will be a good crop only within those parts of the earth that retain moisture.

If the *belsinikche'*[9] fruit becomes elongated and thick, it is a sign that there will be a good corn crop. On the other hand, if the fruit does not grow and remains thin with dry parts, the corn crop will have the same fate: it will not produce large ears and will dry before having ripened well.

If the moon and the sun have a luminous halo surrounding them, it is a sign that it will soon rain; if the halo appears wide, it will rain hard; if it looks thin, it will only drizzle.

To hear the raucous song of the cicada at intervals is a sign that it will soon rain; if its song sounds too long and sharp, it will not soon rain.

If the large ants known as *xulab*[10] and *saakal*[11] and other ants with their young are carrying their *pozole*[12] (provisions) in search of high ground, it is a sign of imminent "bad weather."[13]

According to the elderly residents of Muxupip, God determined that nature itself would provide the messages that He would send to His children. But we no longer possess all the vast knowledge held by the ancient inhabitants of

Muxupip. Therefore, no matter how much the farmers now observe the animals' and the insects' behavior, the flowering of the trees, or the *cabañuelas,* they are no longer able to interpret those messages.

Returning to the topic of planting corn, at the beginning of this century the corn farmer would remove the grain from the cob[14] according to the *cabañuelas;* if a "low year" had been predicted, he prepared his seed beginning in March to be sown with the first heavy rain or two in April since the rainy season would arrive early. In the opposite case, he prepared his seed at the end of April and planted it on May 15[15] or June 13,[16] even if it had not rained and the earth was dry; he knew that between those two dates the possibility was great that a heavy rain would fall, starting the rainy season. (The season is delayed if the rains have not begun to fall by June 13.) The planting of corn can be carried out in two different ways; one is known as *k'óoben pak'al* or "three round stones,"[17] and the other is called *síit' kéej* or "deer hop," which consists of taking intentionally long strides, and with each one perforating a hole with a *xúul*[18] and depositing the seeds.

The corn farmer who has not planted his field after the month of June due to lack of rain in a high year knows he can sow without problem as long as he does not go beyond July 25.[19] Tradition dictates that after this date, given that the Pleiades constellation (known as Tzáab in Mayan)[20] is already high in the sky, the kernels sown will not sprout, because the earthworm will eat their core and the wild rat will dig them up. The elders in Muxupip do not know what relationship may exist between the position of the Pleiades and the earthworm's and rat's destruction of corn. They simply act upon the knowledge that their fathers and grandfathers imparted to them: that when the Pleiades constellation is high in the sky, corn that is sown is corn that will be eaten by the earthworm and the wild rat. It is not known in Muxupip if the Pleiades actually have anything to do with this phenomenon.

Notes

1. At the end of the twentieth century the Mayan language or Yucatec Mayan was Mexico's second largest Indigenous language in number of speakers: nearly 1.5 million, living primarily on the Yucatán Peninsula, in the states of Campeche, Yucatán, and Quintana Roo, in addition to some areas of the Republic of Belize. The author uses the Practical Literacy Alphabet for Adult Mayan Speakers, established by several government institutions in August 1984, in Mérida, Yucatán. The orthographic variations vis-à-vis this alphabet lie in the use of *tz* and *dz* rather than *ts* and *ts',* respectively.

2. In Maya, *xook k'iin,* literally, "the day count." A system by which Mayan farmers predict an entire year's weather patterns, by observing the climatic conditions present during the month of January.

3. Rains that generally fall from May until September.

4. A Spanish title of respect reserved for older men, corresponding to "Yum" in Mayan.

5. *Lagenaria siceraria,* also known as *calabaza de peregrinos,* "pilgrims' squash." In Spain it is known as *calabacino.* The fruit of this plant, which grows into a variety of shapes, is generally used as a vessel for storing liquids or foods.

6. Type of net that is attached to a ring and hung from three strings tied in a knot; it is used to store foods.

7. Known in Mayan as *puksi'ik'al ixi'im,* "the corn's heart."

8. *Piscidia piscipula,* a poisonous tree that reaches a height of up to 45 feet; it flowers during the dry season and is very useful for making frames and doors.

9. *Alvaradoa amorphoides,* a tree that reaches a height of up to 60 feet; its wood is used to build the traditional Mayan house: thatch-roofed, with walls made from narrow planks covered with a mixture of earth and shredded red hay.

10. Black carnivorous ant, of the type known in Mexico as *hormiga arriera* or "carrier ant" because it travels at night in groups and carries food back to its nest; it is capable of devouring other insects, including bees.

11. Another type of black "carrier ant" that travels in large groups and is less destructive.

12. From the Nahuatl *potzol,* "froth," or *potzolli,* "frothy"; its Mayan-language equivalent is *k'eyem.* Dough made from corn kernels that have been cooked and have burst; it is dissolved in water in a half-sphere gourd (*jícara*) for consumption. The farmer usually carries the dough in a shoulder bag and water in a calabash.

13. A nearly steady rain that usually comes from the north and lasts two days or more (a.n.).

14. Only the kernels from the center of the cob are sown; if the kernels from the tip and the stem are sown, the corn plants branch out and do not produce (a.n.).

15. The feast of Saint Isidore the Farmer (San Isidro Labrador). Some men in Muxupip recognize May 15 as the beginning of the first corn-sowing period. Until the 1960s it was virtually assured that a heavy rain would fall by this date (a.n.).

16. The feast of Saint Anthony of Padua (San Antonio de Padua). Some men in Muxupip recognize June 13 as the end of the first corn-sowing period. Until the 1960s it was unusual if a heavy rain had not fallen by this date (a.n.).

17. This is accomplished by walking through the field at normal strides in a straight line. With each pace, one makes three holes, resembling the triangular placement of the three firestones used in cooking; the corn seeds are sown into these holes. The kitchen fire is known as *k'óobenil k'áak',* from which the noun *k'óoben pak'al* or "three round stones" is derived (a.n.).

18. Stick or cane some four and a half feet long used for planting.

19. The feast of Saint James the Apostle (Santiago Apóstol). This date is known as the last day to sow corn; that is, it marks the end of the second and final corn-sowing period (a.n.).

20. *Tzáab* also refers to the rattlesnake's rattle.

La siembra del Maíz

Santiago Domínguez Aké

Maya[1]

[De *La milpa en Muxupip*, pp. 180–184. Colección Letras Indígenas Contemporáneas. México, D.F.: DGCP, 1996.]

Sin menospreciar los demás productos de la milpa, podemos afirmar que el maíz es el más importante por ser la base principal de la dieta alimenticia del milpero. Para sembrarlo deben interpretarse los mensajes de plantas, animales, Cabañuelas[2] y otros elementos de la naturaleza, a fin de saber qué semillas de maíz y qué cultivos se producirán bien en la milpa y cuándo caerán las lluvias de temporal.[3]

Don "Lool," Florencio Gorosica Cruz, un señor de ochenta años de edad, nos dice cómo saber la clase de semillas que se producirá mejor en la milpa:

—Hay que desgranar las diferentes clases de semillas que uno tenga, poner un montoncito de cada una en la mitad de un *leek*[4] y depositarlas el treintiuno de diciembre por la noche en un *pe'et*[5] que cuelgue en un jacal de techo de zacate sin bajareque para que les dé libremente la brisa. Se baja el *leek* con las semillas la mañana del primer día de febrero, cuando hayan terminado las Cabañuelas, y la semilla que tenga el cotiledón[6] hinchado será la de mejor cosecha ese año. Por lo tanto, el milpero debe destinarle más espacio en su milpa. Así me lo platicó mi abuelo—dijo don Florencio.

Las Cabañuelas también dan a conocer si el año será "bajo" o "alto." Se dice que un año es "bajo" cuando las lluvias de temporal comienzan a caer antes del mes de mayo y "alto" cuando comienzan a caer después del 13 de junio.

Cuando la oropéndula teje su nido largo, solamente con bejucos y palillos secos, es señal que se alargará la temporada de secas. Si teje su nido corto, utilizando bejucos y palillos secos y verdes, es señal que lloverá a intervalos durante la época de sequía y durante la temporada de lluvias.

Cuando los ramajes del *ja'abín*[7] tienen manchones de hojas y flores es señal que sólo por manchones producirá bien el elote en la milpa; es decir, solamente en las partes del terreno donde se conserva más la humedad habrá una buena cosecha.

Si se alarga y queda grueso el fruto del *belsinikche*[8] es señal que habrá una buena cosecha de elote. En cambio, si el fruto del *belsinikche* no crece y queda delgado y con partes secas, lo mismo sucederá con el elote: no tendrá mazorca grande y se secará sin haber sazonado bien.

Si la luna y el sol tienen a su alrededor un halo luminoso es señal que lloverá pronto; si el halo se ve ancho lloverá fuerte; si se ve delgado solamente lloviznará.

Escuchar el canto ronco y a intervalos de la cigarra es señal que pronto lloverá; si su canto se escucha demasiado alargado y agudo no lloverá pronto.

Si los hormigones conocidos como *xulab*[9] y *saakal*[10] y las hormigas con sus crías cargan su "pozole"[11] (bastimento) en busca de un terreno alto es señal que está próximo un "mal tiempo."

Según las personas de edad avanzada del pueblo de Muxupip, Dios dispuso que la propia naturaleza fuera portadora de los mensajes que él envía a sus hijos. Pero como ya no se poseen todos los vastos conocimientos que tenían los antiguos pobladores de Muxupip, por más que ahora los campesinos observen el comportamiento de los animales, el florecimiento de los árboles o las cabañuelas, no pueden interpretar ya esos mensajes.

Volviendo al tema de la siembra de maíz diremos que a principios de este siglo el milpero desgranaba las mazorcas[12] de acuerdo con las cabañuelas; si habían predicho un "año bajo," preparaba su semilla desde el mes de marzo, para sembrar apenas cayeran una o dos lluvias fuertes en abril, ya que se adelantaría la temporada de lluvias; en caso contrario, preparaba su semilla a fines de abril y sembraba el 15 de mayo[13] o el 13 de junio[14] aunque no hubiera llovido y estuviera seca la tierra, pues sabe que entre esas dos fechas es muy remota la posibilidad de que no caiga un fuerte aguacero y se inicie la temporada de lluvias (se atrasa la temporada si hasta el 13 de junio no han comenzado a caer las lluvias). La siembra de maíz se puede realizar de dos maneras, una se conoce como *k'óoben pak'al*[15] o tres bolillo, y la otra como *síit' kéej* o salto de venado, que consiste en dar pasos largos, forzados, abriendo cada vez un hoyo con *xúul*[16] y depositando las semillas.

El milpero que no ha sembrado su milpa después del mes de junio por falta de lluvia en un año alto sabe que puede hacerlo sin problema alguno mientras no pase el 25 de julio;[17] después de esta fecha, debido a que ya se encuentra en lo alto del firmamento la constelación de la Pléyades, conocida como *tzáab*[18] en maya, el maíz que se siembra no brota porque la lombriz de tierra come su cotiledón y lo escarba la rata de monte. Los viejitos de Muxupip no saben qué relación existe entre la posición de las Pléyades y la destrucción del maíz a cargo de la lombriz de tierra y de la rata de monte, solamente les platicaron sus papás y abuelos que cuando ya se encuentran las Pléyades en lo alto del firmamento, maíz que se siembre es maíz que come la lombriz de tierra y la rata de monte. Si en esto influyen o no las Pléyades, en Muxupip no se sabe.

Notas

1. La lengua maya, o mejor, el maya yucateco, era a finales del siglo XX la segunda lengua indígena con más hablantes en México: cerca de millón y medio de individuos asentados primordialmente en la Península de Yucatán en los estados de Campeche, Yucatán y Quintana Roo, y también en algunas zonas de Belice. El autor emplea el Alfabeto Práctico para la Alfabetización de los Adultos Hablantes de Maya que diversas instituciones oficiales de México acordaron en Mérida, Yucatán, en agosto de 1984. Las diferencias ortográficas con el alfabeto acordado institucionalmente son dos: el empleo de *tz* en lugar de *ts* y el de *dz* en lugar de *ts'*.

2. El sistema mediante el cual los campesinos mayas pronostican las condiciones climáticas de los doce meses del nuevo año, mediante la observación de las condiciones presentes durante el mes de enero.

3. Lluvias que generalmente caen de mayo a septiembre.

4. *Lagenaria siceraria.* Se llama también "calabaza de peregrinos." En España es el calabacino. El fruto de esta planta, que adopta formas variadas, suele utilizarse como vasija para contener líquidos o alimentos.

5. Especie de red que se fija en un aro y se cuelga por tres hilos unidos en un nudo; en ella se guardan comestibles.

6. En maya *puksi'ik'al ixi'im,* "corazón de maíz."

7. *Piscidia piscipula,* planta venenosa. El árbol llega a alcanzar los 15 metros de altura. Florece durante la estación seca y es muy útil para la elaboración de marcos y puertas.

8. *Alvaradoa amorphoides:* la madera de este árbol, que llega a alcanzar hasta 20 metros de altura, se emplea para construir la casa tradicional maya de techo de zacate y bajareque con embarro.

9. Hormiga arriera y carnicera: es negra, anda en grupo y entre los insectos que es capaz de devorar se halla la abeja. Se llaman "arrieras" por su costumbre de transportar durante las noches, en grupos, sus alimentos a sus nidos.

10. Otro tipo de hormiga arriera, también negra y que anda en grandes grupos, menos destructiva.

11. Del náhuatl *potzol,* "espuma," o *potzolli,* "espumante." En maya *k'eyem.* Masa de maíz cocido y reventado que se deslíe en agua para ser comido. El campesino suele portar la masa en su morral y el agua en un calabazo; deslíe la masa en una jícara.

12. Se siembran solamente los granos del centro de la mazorca; si se llegara a sembrar los granos de la punta y el tronco, las plantas de maíz se ramificarían y no producirían (n.a.).

13. Día de San Isidro Labrador. Algunos señores de Muxupip conocen el 15 de mayo como el día que se inicia la primera temporada de siembra de maíz. Todavía hacia los años sesenta del siglo XX, era casi seguro que cayera una fuerte lluvia para esta fecha (n.a.).

14. Día de San Antonio de Padua. Algunos señores de Muxupip conocen el 13 de junio como la fecha en que termina el primer período de siembra de maíz. Todavía hacia los años sesenta del siglo XX, era raro que no cayera una fuerte lluvia para esa fecha (n.a.).

15. Se recorre en línea recta el terreno haciendo a cada paso tres hoyos como la posición triangular que guardan las tres piedras del fogón de cocina (*k'óobenil k'áak',* del cual deriva el nombre *k'óoben pak'al*) para depositar las semillas del maíz (n.a.).

16. Palo o bastón de un metro y medio de altura que se utiliza para la siembra.

17. Día de Santiago Apóstol. Se considera esta fecha como el último día que se puede sembrar maíz; es decir, que termina el segundo y definitivo período de siembra del grano (n.a.).

18. *Tzáab* también se refiere al cascabel de la serpiente de cascabel.

Isaías Hernández Isidro

Tabasco Chontal (Yokot'an)

Isaías Hernández Isidro. Photographed outside of Nacajuca, Tabasco.

Isaías Hernández Isidro is a Chontal writer born in Mazateupa, Nacajuca, Tabasco, in 1966. He was an instructor for the first generation of actors in the Laboratorio de Teatro Campesino e Indígena de Tabasco. He translated into Chontal works by Emilio Carballido, Elena Garro, and Federico García Lorca. Hernández Isidro is the author of *La gatita enamorada* (The Enamored Kitten) (Mexico City: Editorial Corunda, 1993); *Cha' jop'e t'ok chap'e älkan/Las doce verdades* (The Twelve Truths) (Mexico City: CONACULTA-DGCP, 1997), and *Furia de Mar/Käräxle nab'* (The Fury of the Sea) (Mexico City: ELIAC-SEP-UNESCO, 2000). He is co-author of *Relatos chontales* (Chontal Stories) (Mexico City: CONACULTA-DGCP, 1994) and *Cuentistas jóvenes* (Young Short-Story Writers) (Mexico City: Editorial Tierra Adentro, 1995). He has contributed to the magazines *Blanco Móvil, Hojas de Utopía,* and *Nuni.* In 1993–1994 he was a grantee of the National Fund for Culture and the Arts. Hernández Isidro is a founding member of Indigenous Language Writers, Inc. He has participated in the Gatherings of Indigenous-Language Writers at the regional, peninsular, and national levels and in the Gatherings of Poetry and the Short Story in different parts of the country, including Aguascalientes, San Luis Potosí, and the Federal District.

Isaías Hernández Isidro es un escritor chontal. Nació en Mazateupa, Nacajuca, Tabasco, en 1966. Fue maestro de la primera generación de actores del Laboratorio de Teatro Campesino e Indígena de Tabasco. Tradujo al chontal obras de Emilio Carballido, Elena Garro y Federico García Lorca. Es autor de *La gatita enamorada* (México, D.F.: Editorial Corunda, 1993), *Cha' jop'e t'ok chap'e älkan/Las doce verdades* (México, D.F.: CONACULTA-DGCP, 1997) y *Furia de Mar/Käräxle nab'* (México, D.F.: ELIAC-SEP-UNESCO, 2000). Es co-autor de *Relatos chontales* (México, D.F.: CONACULTA-DGCP, 1994) y *Cuentistas jóvenes* (México, D.F.: Editorial Tierra Adentro, 1995) y colaborador de las revistas *Blanco Móvil, Hojas de Utopía* y *Nuni.* Recibío el becario del Fondo Nacional para la Cultura y las Artes, 1993–1994 y es miembro fundador de Escritores en Lenguas Indígenas, A.C. Ha participado en Encuentros de Escritores en Lenguas Indígenas a nivel regional, peninsular y nacional, así como en Encuentros de Poesía y Cuento en diferentes entidades del país, como Aguascalientes, San Luis Potosí y el Distrito Federal.

U ch'ujlom k'ajalin ta Zutz'baläm[1]

Isaías Hernández Isidro

Tabasco Chontal (Yokot'an)[2]

[From *Cha' jop'e t'ok chap'e älkan/Las doce verdades*, pp. 25–28. Mexico City: DGCP, 1997.]

Ix Tok'[3] u yankärezi nu ch'oko' k'a mach u ni' che patan. Jinchich k'in u nume tä päpä' otote u zakän kone u chen k'a bintik ump'e k'ux k'o numzen ni k'in. Ump'e izapan u numzi ump'e yok'ja' bixi tunxe kaj. Tantu zamba u chänuba pänte' ump'e otot ka'awälä u juntuma. Ziztonan numi tu yak'o.

—Ochen mu'cha kä pitänet' t'oko'.

Bäk'ta, mach u chäne ni mu'u lotämba cha' otot'ba it'oban tama. Ya'i ze' u chajuba jit' otot ump'e noj yetz' jink'in yäliba u nikuba ni ka'.

—Mach bäk'taket', ixik, jinda na wotot. Kä na' ya'an tä jamäle, zamcha kälbi ke' ya' anet'da.

—Mäx it'oban. ¿Mach a känänta bak'ät'? Mach utz' ajniket a juntuma. Naj jutijo'ba mach u chäne kone uxe u dz'ibajteza une.

—Mach kä känänta bak'ät, kä na' yuyi ke' ko ajnikon tan it'o'ni.

Tan ch'ok otot pazi untu ix ch'upim pok'om, ix dz'apa', t'ok u pämi dz'e'ne u jut' ta käräx mut'.

—Na', une ni ixik a kält'benet'ba. Uxe tä kolan t'ok no'onla. Mach'an kabala'u ajnik nu ch'oko' u pa'zijo' päti.

Ya'jini koli ix Tok', chumka tan ump'e chumte' ch'ejpa ni pech'te' ta juch'i', tan ch'ok otot, t'ok u chaná baja tä ka'. Xäbä u k'ajalin, bäk'ta, mach u che t'an, Mach yuyi kachka untu o'i' aj lo' yuyi un k'aba' yu dz'aji zinko chänen oni.

Jink'in u bixe k'in u cha'tuma ni ixik k'uxijo' k'ä' mixix[4] k'a nix Tok' u yäli u bizan ump'e pulatu[5] ni p'i' aj lo' nix ch'upim u jätz'k'ejpi.

—Mach. Une u k'uxnan u yoche ak'ä'.

Tu k'ote ni ak'ä'ba nix ch'upim u yälbi ix Tok' kio täzen untu aj tz'o' tan kum, u cha'tumajo' u ch'uy kächijo' tä jäyte' tani oto. U na' p'i' aj lo' ch'i ump'e ixoni', u zekbi nu pam ix Tok' woyi ni ch'ich tan ump'e pulatu. Ya'i nix ch'upim u kat'bi ko bizben pete jini k'ux u yaj lo'. Tama ni otot an ump'e ni pech'te' ta wop',[6] t'ok cha'pe pulbänil ko t'e'e' yutz'u ta pom,[7] ya'jini, pam unk'e yokoto',[8] yäk'ti ni k'ux k'a ni p'i'aj lo' ze' pazi bixi.

Tä izapam, jink'in tä patan tan ch'ok otot, nu na' uchänen ix Tok' ko ya'ch'in an.

—Anet' mäx ch'ijka', ixik. ¿Mach a na'taba utz' t'ok no'ont'oko'? Kä chänenet mäx toxi'.

—Mach kuyi kone kä känäntan, ka' mach u nämton. ¿Re'i bäk'tet? Ma'kuyi kat'ok anomba. Na wajlo' kuxu tan it'o'ni, mach kuyi kachka, mach kuyi kani.

—Chänen Tok', idaba kuxu untu Zutz'baläm; mäx p'i'to jink'in u dz'äk'tezan ch'jo'p'e t'ok chap'e tamäl k'ino'ba xe tä bixe. Une u chi ke tiket k'a a känäntan jink'in no'on kä chen patan tä jamäle. A kälbenet ke niuntu mach u yuyna'tan nindaba. Ni Zutz'balämjo' u dz'ämzenjo' machka u chen jop'ojti'ba.

Ump'e k'in nix ch'upim bixi nat' ix Tok' koli tu k'ä' ni otot. Tu it'oban ni p'i' aj lo' pazi päti yu täk'i ak'ot'. Uneba u ch'ukän tu jut' ni bojte' ta ch'ok otot. Ni p'i' aj lo' tech'i u k'ä' t'ok une ump'e noj re'i yich', ta Zutz'. Ni p'i' aj lo yili nu awät' ta baläm uchi u nikänuba ni otot. Ump'e ik' muk' u täk'i u yuztan yu woye' ni buklajo'. Ni izki zut' wäni aj bätezia yocheda nix ch'upim u täk'i ni ja'a ko zujwäni ump'e no'aj ik' a jäläk' ni k'en k'ino. Ni jamäle koli xilawu. Ump'e ak'ä' ni p'i' aj lo' pazi tama noj ja'a ankäri u xoyän u pete ni päti; ni te'ejo' u nok'tä tu pänte'. Tu junch'äk'nan naj ik'a ona ch'ä'ti.

Ump'e junch'äk'nan u'ki ump'e ch'uyu' nätz'ä t'ok ni otot. Tojchich na''tinti ka' ump'e kua'chichka wa'wäni pan ni otot. Ix Tok', bäk'ta, p'izi nix ch'upim ko yälbi mäx käräx.

—Awubin kona wubin tan ni ak'ä' mach bäk'taket mach täkä ch'oyiket. Jin ni kajlo' ke mu' u k'ote.

Dz'idz'ita' a dz'dz'ita' ix Tok' xi tä nämtan t'ok nix ch'upim t'ok ni p'i' Zutz'baläm. Nu xek'ita xi tä kolan pati k'a ubada u känäntan bajka aj nik'. Ump'e izapan, tu juch'e'o ixim ta ni wajo', Ix Tok' u yäli:

—Ayan, jink'in a k'ote zäpäk'nan tä jamba, Na wajlo' u paze tä ak' ot' ak'ä'. Ankäran yu yile. Tan k'enchu muk' ke ni ik' ko päyeba ka' awälä uxo yacen ni otot.

—Jink'in ninda u chemba mu'u yälbenonla une koxe tä ajtä ump'e dz'ibajtezia. Ziu xe tä ajtä ump'e noj aj ik'aba, päpä' ak'ot u yä'ben; ump'e jitz'o: ankäran ajta kolak zop'; k'en k'ux: ak'ot', dz'e'ne yiyizt ch'uyu'.

Ze' ni ixik' u täk'i ajnik ch'ox u jut':

—U peta na chäniba axe a ch'ujnanune. Che' k'otiket a dz'aykun zinko yälbenet ni zutz'balämba, xe u dz'ibajtezanet, ch'e' chämiket'.

Ump'e k'in, ix Tok' t'äbi tan makän tau jäk'zen ixim yu chäni ump'e t'u' t'ok tak'in. Ankäri u dz'aykäben nux noja ko yälbi:

—Ma' xiket a täle' ni tak'in jini. Kajlo' u täzen u pete yuxk'in.[9] K'o neba mach u xup' ni k'ux tan ni otot'da.

Jini tamäl k'in jini xi ni xiwäl jitz'o ko känäntijo' tan k'en k'ino'. Ni tikäw k'in mach u ni' k'älka. Ni ätäk'ijo' ano' chokch'ok chämen, ni ka'o dz'alijo'. Ni ja' ch'ä'ti. Ni te'o ka' awälä chämenjo', ni päk'äbijo' ka' uxe tä zäto. Ni p'i' aj lo' pazi tä ankäre päti yäzuba tä ka'. U kukänuba mäkä tan ump'e noj k'uxita. Ka' awälä ke jochen tä chämo.

—¡A mach kä tz'onä une!—yäli nix ch'upim wa'a.—Ik'ä uxe tä tile ni jamäle k'a mäx tikin ke an ni ka'. Xe kä japänla ni päkäbi.

Ni ixik'tako' pazijo' tä junch'äk'nan. K'ajijo' u chijo' ump'e dz'ik t'ok ixim tänxin ni choj. Ya'i u bäk'ijo' t'ok chäk to'.[10] Mu'to u dz'upzemba u täk'i u ch'e' k'ak ni p'ozt. Laj puli u pete ni jamäle. Tok'a ni dz'i'tan naj yumnajo' tan ni ka'o jini. Ni muto' ni äläk'ijo' u numzijo' k'en k'in t'ok jitz'o k'a mach'an k'ux. Y kälbenet' ke nix Tok' nu yumo'ba mach ch'ä'tijo'.

Numijo' ni tamäl k'ino yump'e k'in ni p'ii Zutz'baläm jok u cha'tuma ni ixik'tako':

—Tä' ch'a'a kä jin ke nix Tok' u täk'lonla k'en. Ik'ä kä dz'äk'tezan cha'jo'p'e t'ok chap'e tamal k'ino' kä bixe bajka kä xe tä ajtä.

Chäni u na':

—Na'tankäba kolaket a juntuma. Ix Tok' u bixe dali t'ok u ch'oko' kio pitäno' t'ok ch'a'äljino'. Pete ni k'ino'daba u k'ajti'ijo' nu tanä, jimuk'a uxe tä zujtä t'ok unejo'.

Ix T'ok' yäli u chen t'an, naj lo' mach u yä'bi u chen.

—Kuyi kone axe a wäle' a kälbenet' ke ona dz'äk'tezi na patan. Na', ben u p'och' bixik ze' ma' it'o'nak. Mach ajniket xek'e. Tok'. Jink'in a na'tan re'I alt' pat' a wotot mach bäk'taket, no'on a numon une käktäbenet undz'ita' p'och'.

Ix Tok' ch'ubiji ta zut'wänik. Zätä an tan ni päpä' bij. ¡A numi k'en k'ino'! Ya'i u un'tuba t'ok untu aj k'ech'buch' ke ze'chich u k'ajna'ti. Chunwänijo' tä bo'oy ta untek pata[11] ni yinik u dz'aykäbi na numi tan ni kaj jink'in mach ajni.

—Niuntu yuyna'ti u yäle' kada anet'.

—Ajnon tä patan nat'. Naj k'ech' buch' u loti Ix Tok' ajta kan yotot. Nu ch'oko', ch'a'a u jino' k'a u chánen u na' u chijo' ump'e noj re'i jobäle yu jok'ijo' u pete ni kajo'. U pukijo' k'ä' chibälte'.[12] Popijo' k'elän aj tz'o' tänxin kaj. Ni ch'oko' u xoyijo' nu cherbinte u jobäle, yojo' u yubin kada ajni k'a mach u yo u chen dz'ajiba, u yä'bijo' noj k'elän chij ke k'ak'a chibäni.

Jinuk'a une u dz'ayki ni dz'aji ta p'i' aj Zutzbaläm jink'in u chen ak'ot u yäle' koxe tä ajtä lup', jitz'o ni k'ak ko pule' ni jamälejo. U yäli täkä koxe tä nume u yä'ben p'och' u pete yuxk'ino'. Yako k'ak'a' päpäychi ni t'an tanu chiba u k'ajna'ti ke' onu zäti t'ok nu loto' k'a mach u ch'ujni tan u pixan. Ump'e aj titz'om ik' u p'änuba. Um xim jut' k'ak wani tan u pik' ix Tok' u ch'i k'ak. Niuntu u chi trebe u täpe' une täkä machu u japuba t'ok ni toji' tänä. Tz'ozijo' ump'e nobena k'o jäk'zäbenjo' u käräxte ni p'i' Zutzbaläm. K'atbijo' ko najyezben u tanä ix Tok' yu nejo' takä k'a mach u tz'onäjo'.

Notes

1. Literally, "bat-jaguar": a deity.

2. The Chontal language in the state of Tabasco is known by its speakers as Yokot'an. By extension, this term also refers to any Indigenous language, possibly because *yoco* means "native" and *t'an,* "language," "regional form of speech." At the end of the twentieth century there were 72,000 Tabasco Chontal speakers. The author uses the alphabet that has been promoted since the 1980s by the Tabasco State Department of Indigenous Education. This alphabet was the result of the unification efforts carried out by a team of experts, in which Isidro García García, from Tamuelté de las Sabanas Centro, was an important figure.

3. "Teófila" (*ix* is the Chontal feminine prefix).

4. Chontal name for a fowl known regionally as *pijije. Dendrocygna*

Notas

1. Literalmente, "murciélago-jaguar": una deidad.

2. La lengua chontal del estado de Tabasco es designada por sus propios hablantes como *yokot'an;* por extensión, significa también cualquier lengua indígena, posiblemente por la derivación de *yoco,* "criollo," y *t'an,* "lenguaje," "modo de hablar de una región." La lengua chontal de Tabasco contaba a finales del siglo XX con más de 72,000 hablantes. El autor emplea el alfabeto impulsado desde la década de los ochenta por el Departamento de Educación Indígena del estado de Tabasco. Este alfabeto fue resultado de las tareas de unificación emprendidas por un cuerpo colegiado en el que destacó de manera esencial Isidro García García de Tamuelté de las Sabanas Centro.

3. "Teófila" (*ix* es el prefijo de género femenino).

4. Nombre chontal del ave conocida regionalmente como *pijije.*

autumnalis, a web-footed, edible fowl of the Anatidae family, similar to a duck, though smaller.

5. Chontal word derived from the Spanish *plato,* a bowl or dish.

6. Chontal name for a palm known regionally as *jaguacté* or *jahuacté: Bactris baculifera.*

7. Chontal name for *estoraque: Styrax argenteus.*

8. Literally, "white leaf": *Calathea grandifolia.*

9. Literally, "three days ago." The author suggests that the *yuxq'in* or *yuxk'in* was a Monday.

10. Literally, "lagoon or marsh leaf": *Calathea lutea.*

11. Literally, "guayabo tree": *Psidium guajava.*

12. Literally, "drunken wood"; that is, fermented sugar-cane juice.

Dendrocygna autumnalis, ave palmípeda de la familia de los Anátidos, parecida al pato pero de menor tamaño. Es comestible.

5. Palabra chontal aplicada a una escudilla o cajete, derivada del español "plato."

6. Nombre chontal de la palma conocida regionalmente como *jaguacté* o *jahuacté: Bactris baculifera.*

7. Nombre chontal del *estoraque: Styrax argenteus.*

8. Literalmente, "hoja blanca": *Calathea grandifolia.*

9. Literalmente, "hace tres días." El autor sugiere que ese *yuxq'in* o *yuxk'in* era un lunes.

10. Literalmente, "hoja de laguna" o "de estero": *Calathea lutea.*

11. Literalmente, "mata de guayabo": *Psidium guajava.*

12. Literalmente, "palo borracho"; es decir, jugo de caña fermentado.

The Secret of the Zutz'baläm[1]

Isaías Hernández Isidro

Tabasco Chontal (Yokot'an)[2]

[From *Cha' jop'e t'ok chap'e älkan/Las doce verdades,* pp. 25–32. Mexico City: DGCP, 1997.]

Teófila's children ran her off because she could no longer work. Thereafter, she would go from house to house looking for something to do in exchange for a mouthful to survive the day. One morning she crossed a river and went to another town. After much walking, she found herself in front of an abandoned-looking house. A chill ran through her body.

"Come in, we were expecting you," a voice called to her.

Nervous, she did not see who was speaking to her since the room was very dark. A large figure fell from the ceiling; the ground shook.

"Do not be afraid, Señora,[3] this is your house. My mother is in the fields; I have already notified her that you are here."

"It is so dark. Are you not you afraid? It is dangerous for you to be alone. The evil ones do not care about their victims' size."

The child laughed. Teófila could not make out his face in the darkness.

"Do not be afraid; I like the darkness," replied the child.

From the kitchen appeared a short, elderly, robust woman with a happy face and the gaze of an eagle.

"Mamá, this is the woman I told you about. She has no place to live because her children threw her out on the street."

There was Teófila, sitting on a tree trunk next to the grinding board in the kitchen, with her gaze riveted to the ground: confused, frightened, without words, unable to comprehend how a child could know her name and her background without ever having seen her. The women ate *pijije*[4] soup, and when Teófila was about to bring the child a plate of food, the old woman stopped her.

"He eats at night."

When it became dark, the old woman ordered Teófila to bring a turkey from the pen. Both women hung it from a beam in the kitchen. The child's mother took a knife and cut off its head, and Teófila collected the blood in a clay dish. The old woman asked her to take all of that food to her son. Within the house, there was an altar made of *jaguacte*[5] with two incense burners that spread the aroma of *estoraque.*[6] There, atop a *toj*[7] leaf, she placed the child's food.

At dawn, as they were working in the kitchen, the

mother observed Teófila, who was pensive: "You are very quiet, woman. Are you not happy here with us? You look very sad."

"I do not know what is wrong with me. It is as if I do not know where I am, or whom I am with. Your son lives in the darkness; I do not know what he is like. I do not know him."

"Look, Teófila, a Zutz'baläm lives here; he is still small, but when he turns twelve years of age he will leave. He made you come here to take care of him while I work in the fields. I strongly recommend to you that no one else learn of this. Zutz'baläms are cruel with traitors and the unfaithful."

Once, when the old woman had to go far away, Teófila took charge of the house. At nightfall, the child came out onto the patio and began to dance. She spied on him through a crack in the kitchen wall. The little one extended his arms and, along with them, huge bat wings. The child rose up into the air, and his jaguar roar shook the house. A strong wind began to blow, and clouds began to build. The sky became threatening, and just as the old woman arrived, it began to rain. A storm ensued that lasted several days; the fields were destroyed. Several nights later, the child came out and ran circles all around the patio in the downpour; the trees bent over as he passed. At dawn the storm had disappeared.

One early morning, a whistle was heard near the house, and it clearly felt like something had landed on the roof. Frightened, Teófila woke the old woman, who said to her in an annoyed tone: "No matter what you hear at night, do not be afraid and do not think about getting up. It is only my son arriving."

Teófila gradually became accustomed to the old woman and the small Zutz'baläm. Her sadness faded since she now had another family. One morning, while they were grinding corn for tortillas, Teófila said: "At times, when you arrive late from the fields, your child goes out to dance in the night. He runs and even flies. He is so powerful, it seems that the air he stirs is going to knock the house down."

"When that happens, he is warning us that something terrible will happen. If it is a storm, he dances furiously; if it is a drought, he runs until he is out of breath; if it is to be a big crop, he runs, laughs, and whistles softly."

The woman suddenly became serious: "Everything you have seen here you must keep secret. If you ever tell about this without the Zutz'baläms' permission, they will punish you; you might die."

One day Teófila climbed up into the house's storage loft to get some corn, and she saw a gourd with money in it. She ran to tell her mistress.

"Do not touch that money because my son brings it on Mondays.[8] Thanks to him, there is food in this house."

That year marked the worst drought they had lived through in many years. The heat was unbearable. The animals were choking, and the earth cracked open. There was no water. The trees appeared dead, and the crops were practically lost. The child came running out onto the patio, and he threw himself upon the ground. He squirmed about as if he were in great pain. It seemed as if he were dying.

"No, it can not be!" said the old woman, concerned. "Tomorrow the fields will go up in flames since the earth is so dry. We must save the crops."

They went out at dawn. They harvested the corn and in the middle of the field piled up the ears and covered them with *chäk to'*.[9] They had barely finished when the grass began to burn. The entire savannah burned, and only ash remained. The birds and the animals suffered from lack of food for several months; nevertheless, Teófila and her patrons did not perish.

The years went by, and one day the child Zutz'baläm called the two women together: "I am happy that Teófila has helped us so much. Tomorrow I turn twelve years of age and must go to my proper place."

He looked at his mother: "It saddens me that you will remain alone. Today Teófila will return to her children, who anxiously await her. All this time they have thought about their ingratitude, so she must return to them."

Teófila attempted to speak, but the little one stopped her: "I know what you are going to say, but you have completed your task. Mother, give her some money and make sure she leaves before nightfall. Do not be sad, Teófila. When you are under a great burden at home, do not be afraid; I will bring you some money."

She began her return. She became lost along unfamiliar pathways. It had been so long! A fisherman who was passing by immediately recognized her. They sat down in the shade of a *guayabo*[10] tree, and the good man filled her in on what had gone on in town during her absence.

"No one knew what had happened to you."

He accompanied her to her house. Her children, happy to see her, organized a big fiesta and invited the whole town. They served a lot of *guarapo*.[11] They roasted numerous turkeys in the town square. People gathered around the celebrated woman, wanting to hear of her adventures, but as they could not get her to tell them anything, they served her so much alcohol that she got drunk.

She then told them the story of the Zutz'baläm and how, when he danced and flew, he predicted storms, droughts, and the fires that char the fields. She also said that he promised to bring her money every Monday. After talking for hours in her drunken state, she realized she had betrayed the trust of her friends because she had failed to keep their secret. A terrible wind rose up. A spark from the cooking fires fell upon Teófila's clothing, setting it aflame. No one could extinguish the flames, and she did not even protest her punishment. Her children gathered up her ashes and took them to the cemetery. They built an offering to placate the ire of the young Zutz'balām. They begged him to pardon Teófila and themselves for their carelessness.

Notes

1. Literally, "bat-jaguar": a deity.
2. The Chontal language in the state of Tabasco is known by its speakers as Yokot'an. By extension, this term also refers to any indigenous language, possibly because *yoco* means "native" and *t'an,* "language," "regional form of speech." At the end of the twentieth century there were 72,000 Tabasco Chontal speakers.
3. A title used to address married women ("Mrs." or "ma'am").
4. *Dendrocygna autumnalis,* a web-footed, edible fowl of the Anatidae family, similar to a duck, though smaller. It is easily domesticated and is prized as a guardian, since it emits a long squawk when it sees strangers.
5. *Bactris baculifera,* a spiny palm that produces a spherical red fruit and reaches heights of up to 18 feet. Its wood is very hard and is good for making canes. It is common in the states of Tabasco and Chiapas.
6. *Styrax argenteus,* a tree that reaches heights of up to 60 feet; its trunk produces an aromatic resin that is used as incense. The name *estoraque* is also used in reference to *Liquidambar styraciflua,* which produces another type of aromatic resin.
7. From the Mayan *to',* "to wrap." *Calathea grandifolia,* known in Spanish also as "bijagua" or "hojablanca."
8. Day on which offerings are placed for the Zutz'balām, to obtain something in return.
9. *Calathea lutea,* known in Tabasco as *popal* leaf; that is, pertaining to a lagoon or marsh (this is the literal meaning of the Ch'ontal expression *chäk to'*). Since these leaves are generally used to wrap foods, other authors suggest that the word *to'* comes from Yucatec Mayan, where it means "to wrap."
10. *Psidium guajava,* a tree belonging to the Mirteaceae family. Its bark is reddish, smooth, and scaly; its edible fruit is aromatic and pyriform or oval in shape.
11. Fermented sugar-cane juice.

El secreto del Zutz'baläm[1]

Isaías Hernández Isidro

Chontal de Tabasco (Yokot'an)[2]

[De *Cha' jop'e t'ok chap'e älkan/Las doce verdades,* pp. 29–32. México, D.F.: DGCP, 1997.]

A Teófila la corrieron sus hijos porque ya no rendía en el trabajo. Desde entonces andaba de casa en casa buscando qué hacer a cambio de un bocado para pasar el día. Una mañana cruzó un río y se fue a otro pueblo. Después de mucho caminar se vio frente a una casa de apariencia abandonada. Un escalofrío recorrió su cuerpo.

—Entra, te estábamos esperando.

Nerviosa, no veía al que le hablaba, pues la habitación estaba muy oscura. Un gran bulto se desprendió del techo; el suelo se cimbró.

—No te asustes, señora, ésta es tu casa. Mi madre anda en el campo, ya le avisé que estás aquí.

—Está muy oscuro. ¿No tienes miedo? Es peligroso que te quedes solo. Los malos no ven el tamaño de sus víctimas.

El niño se rió. Teófila no podía distinguir su rostro en la oscuridad.

—No tengo miedo, me gusta la oscuridad.

De la cocina apareció una anciana robusta, de baja estatura, con rostro alegre y mirada de águila.

—Mamá, ella es la mujer de quien te hablé. No tiene dónde vivir, pues sus hijos la echaron a la calle.

Allí se quedó Teófila, sentada en un tronco junto a la tabla de moler en la cocina, con la mirada clavada en el suelo. Confundida, asustada, sin palabras. Sin entender cómo un pequeño podía saber su nombre y su historia sin haberla visto nunca. Las mujeres comieron caldo de *pijije*,[3] y cuando Teófila se disponía a llevarle un cajete[4] al niño, la anciana la detuvo.

—Él come entrando la noche.

Cuando oscureció, la anciana ordenó a Teófila que trajera un guajolote del gallinero. Entre las dos lo colgaron de una viga de la cocina. La madre del niño tomó un cuchillo, le cortó la cabeza al guajolote y Teófila recogió la sangre en un plato. La anciana le pidió que llevara toda esa comida a su hijo. Dentro de la casa había un altar de *jaguacte*[5] con dos sahumerios que esparcían el aroma del *estoraque*.[6] Allí, sobre una hoja de *toj*,[7] puso la comida para el niño.

Al amanecer, mientras trabajaban en la cocina, la madre observaba a Teófila, que estaba pensativa.

—Estás muy callada, mujer. ¿No estás a gusto con nosotros? Te miro muy triste.

—No sé qué me pasa, como que no me hallo, no sé con quién estoy. Tu hijo vive en la oscuridad, no sé cómo es, no lo conozco.

—Mira, Teófila, aquí vive un Zutz'balăm; aún es pequeño, pero cuando cumpla doce años se marchará. Él hizo que vinieras para cuidarlo mientras yo trabajo en el campo. Mucho te recomiendo que nadie más sepa esto. Los Zutz'balăm son crueles con los traidores e infieles.

Una vez que la anciana salió lejos, Teófila se hizo cargo de la casa. Al oscurecer el niño salió al patio y empezó a bailar. Ella lo espiaba por la rendija del seto de la cocina. El pequeño extendió sus brazos y con ellos unas alas enormes, de murciélago. El niño se alejó y su rugido de jaguar hizo temblar la casa. Un viento fuerte empezó a soplar y a juntarse las nubes. El cielo se volvió amenazador y justo al llegar la anciana comenzó la lluvia, que se convirtió en una tormenta que duró muchos días. El campo quedó destruido. Noches después el niño salió y corrió en círculos por todo el patio bajo el aguacero; los árboles se inclinaban a su paso. Al amanecer la tormenta había desaparecido.

Una madrugada se escuchó un silbido cerca de la casa. Claro se sintió que algo se posó sobre el techo. Teófila, asustada, despertó a la anciana, que le dijo muy molesta:

—Oigas lo que oigas en las noches, no te asustes ni mucho menos te levantes. Es mi hijo que va llegando.

Poco a poco Teófila se acostumbró a la anciana y al pequeño Zutz'balăm. Su tristeza iba quedando atrás, pues ahora tenía otra familia. Una mañana, mientras molían maíz para las tortillas, Teófila dijo:

—A veces, cuando llegas tarde del campo, tu hijo sale a bailar en la noche. Corre y hasta vuela. Es tan poderoso que parece que el aire que agita va a tirar la casa.

—Cuando esto sucede es que nos avisa que sucederá algo grave. Si es una tormenta, baila desesperado; una sequía: corre hasta sofocarse; mucha cosecha: baila, ríe y silba muy suave.

De pronto la mujer se puso seria:

—Todo lo que has visto debes guardarlo. Si llegas a contarlo sin permiso de los Zutz'balăm, te castigarán, puedes morir.

Cierto día subió al tapanco para bajar maíz y vio una jícara con dinero. Corrió a contárselo a su patrona.

—No vayas a tocar ese dinero, pues mi hijo lo trae los lunes.[8] Gracias a él no falta el alimento en esta casa.

Ese año fue la peor sequía que habían vivido en mucho tiempo. El calor era insoportable. Los animales estaban sofocados, la tierra agrietada. El agua desapareció. Los árboles parecían muertos; las siembras estaban a punto de perderse. El niño salió corriendo al patio y se tiró al suelo. Se retorcía preso de un gran dolor. Parecía que estaba agonizando.

—¡Ay, no puede ser!—dijo la anciana preocupada.—Mañana arderá el campo de tan seca que está la tierra. Hay que salvar la cosecha.

Salieron de madrugada. Tapiscaron e hicieron un montón de mazorcas en medio de la milpa y las cubrieron con *chăk to'*.[9] Apenas habían terminado empezó a arder el pasto. Se quemó toda la sabana; sólo la ceniza reinaba en esos parajes. Los pájaros y los animales sufrieron varios meses por falta de alimento; sin embargo, Teófila y sus patrones no perecieron.

Pasaron los años y un día el niño Zutz'balăm llamó a las dos mujeres:

—Me da gusto que Teófila nos haya ayudado tanto. Mañana cumplo doce años y debo ir al lugar que me corresponde. Miró a su mamá:

—Me entristece que te quedes sola. Teófila se irá hoy con sus hijos, que la esperan ansiosos. Todo este tiempo han pensado en su ingratitud, así que debe regresar con ellos.

Teófila quiso hablar, pero el pequeño se lo impidió.

—Sé lo que vas a decirme, pero ya cumpliste con tu deber. Madre, dale dinero y que se vaya antes que oscurezca. No estés triste, Teófila. Cuando sientas gran peso en tu casa no te asustes, seré yo que paso a dejarte unas monedas.

Emprendió el regreso. Estaba perdida en caminos desconocidos. ¡Había pasado tanto tiempo! Un pescador que pasaba por ahí la reconoció de inmediato. Se sentaron a la sombra de una mata de *guayabo*[10] y el buen hombre le contó lo que había pasado en el pueblo durante su ausencia.

—Nadie supo dar noticias tuyas.

La acompañó hasta su casa. Sus hijos, felices de verla, organizaron una gran fiesta e invitaron a todo el pueblo. Repartieron mucho *guarapo.*[11] Asaron muchos guajolotes en la plaza. La gente rodeaba a la festejada, querían escuchar sus aventuras, pero como no conseguían que les contara nada, le sirvieron tanto trago que se emborrachó.

Entonces ella contó la historia del niño Zutz'baläm, que cuando danza y vuela predice la tempestad, la sequía y el fuego que arrasa los campos. También dijo que él prometió dejarle dinero todos los lunes. Después de hablar por horas en su borrachera se dio cuenta que había traicionado la confianza de sus amigos porque no guardó el secreto. Un viento terrible se desató. Una chispa de la fogata cayó sobre la ropa de Teófila, incendiándola. Nadie pudo apagarla y ella ni siquiera se lamentó por su castigo. Los hijos recogieron sus cenizas y las llevaron al cementerio. Levantaron una ofrenda para aplacar la ira del niño Zutz'baläm. Rogaron que perdonara a Teófila y a ellos por su imprudencia.

Notas

1. Literalmente, "murciélago-jaguar": una deidad.

2. La lengua chontal del estado de Tabasco es designada por sus propios hablantes como *yokot'an;* por extensión, significa también cualquier lengua indígena, posiblemente por la derivación de *yoco,* "criollo," y *t'an,* "lenguaje," "modo de hablar de una región." La lengua chontal de Tabasco contaba a finales del siglo XX con más de 72,000 hablantes.

3. *Dendrocygna autumnalis,* ave palmípeda de la familia de los Anátidos, parecida al pato pero de menor tamaño. Se domestica fácilmente y es valiosa como guardián, pues cuando ve gente extraña, lanza un largo chillido. Es comestible.

4. Del náhuatl *caxitl,* "recipiente," "escudilla."

5. *Bactris baculifera:* palma espinosa que llega a una altura de 6 metros con fruto globoso y rojo. Su madera es muy dura, propia para hacer bastones. Común en Tabasco y Chiapas.

6. *Styrax argenteus:* árbol que alcanza alturas de 20 metros y cuyo tronco produce una resina aromática que se emplea como incienso. También se llama *estoraque* al *Liquidambar styraciflua,* que produce otro tipo de resina aromática.

7. Del maya *to',* "envolver." *Calathea grandifolia,* también conocida como "bijagua" u "hojablanca."

8. Día en que se ofrenda al Zutz'bälam para obtener algo a cambio.

9. *Calathea lutea.* En Tabasco se le conoce como hoja del *popal,* es decir, de laguna o estero. Esto significa literalmente la expresión chontal *chak to'.* Como estas hojas suelen emplearse para envolver alimentos, otros autores sugieren que la palabra *to'* proviene del maya peninsular, donde significa "envolver."

10. *Psidium guajava:* árbol perteneciente a la familia de las Mirtáceas, de corteza rojiza, lisa y escamosa, de fruto comestible y aromático piriforme u oval.

11. Jugo fermentado de la caña de azúcar.

Enrique Pérez López

Tzotzil

Enrique Pérez López. Photographed at Na Bolom Museum, San Cristóbal de las Casas, Chiapas.

Enrique Pérez López was born in San Pedro Chenalhó, Chiapas, on April 25, 1964. He is a speaker of the Tzotzil and Tzeltal languages. Some of his published works are *Chamula, un pueblo indígena tzotzil* (Chamula, a Tzotzil Indigenous Town), 3rd ed. (Tuxtla Gutiérrez, Chiapas: Gobierno del Estado de Chiapas/Instituto Chiapaneco de Cultura, 1998) and *El K'ox: El niño que se transformó en sol* (K'ox: The Child Who Became the Sun) (San Cristóbal de las Casas, Chiapas: Universidad Nacional Autónoma de México/Centro de Investigaciones Humanísticas de Mesoamérica y el Estado de Chiapas, 1995). Within the second series of Colección Letras Mayas Contemporáneas: Chiapas (C. Montemayor, series ed.), Pérez López published *Nichimal k'op ta k'in tajimoltik/La palabra florida del carnaval* (The Flowered Words of Carnival; transcription and translation) (vol. 9; Mexico City: INI/TRF, 1996); *Sk'opnel ch'ul vitz/Palabras para la sagrada montaña* (Words for the Sacred Mountain; transcription and translation) (vol. 10; Mexico City: INI/TRF, 1996); and the book of short stories entitled *Alperes: Te'tikal mut/El pájaro alférez* (The Standard-Bearer Bird) (vol. 11; Mexico City: INI/TRF, 1996). He was a founding member of the Mayas-Zoques Writers Group, Inc., and of Indigenous-Language Writers, Inc. Pérez López has worked as a consultant to the Office for the Strengthening and Promotion of Cultures, Undersecretariat of Indigenous Affairs; as a researcher for the Center for Humanistic Research on Meso-America and the State of Chiapas (CIHMECH-UNAM); and as director of publicity and cultural promotion, Secretariat for the Care of Indigenous Peoples. In 1992 he received the Rosario Castellanos Chiapas Prize for Literature and in 1994 was a grantee of the National Fund for Culture and the Arts.

Enrique Pérez López nació en San Pedro Chenalhó, Chiapas, el 25 de abril de 1964. Es hablante de las lenguas tzotzil y tzeltal. Entre sus trabajos publicados se encuentran *Chamula, un pueblo indígena tzotzil,* 3a ed. (Tuxtla Gutiérrez, Chiapas: Gobierno del Estado de Chiapas/Instituto Chiapaneco de Cultura, 1998) y *El K'ox: El niño que se transformó en sol* (San Cristóbal de las Casas, Chiapas: Universidad Nacional Autónoma de México/Centro de Investigaciones Humanísticas de Mesoamérica y el Estado de Chiapas, 1995). En la Colección de Letras Mayas Contemporáneas: Chiapas (C. Montemayor, coord. de la colección), publicó *Nichimal k'op ta k'in tajimoltik/La palabra florida del carnaval* (transcripción y traducción, vol. 9; México, D.F.: INI/TRF, 1996); *Sk'opnel ch'ul vitz/Palabras para la sagrada montaña* (transcripción y traducción, vol. 10; México, D.F.: INI/TRF, 1996); y el libro de cuentos *Alperes: Te'tikal mut/El pájaro alférez* (vol. 11; México, D.F.: INI/TRF, 1996). Fue miembro fundador de la Unidad de Escritores Mayas-Zoques, A.C., y de la Escritores en Lenguas Indígenas, A.C. Fue técnico en la Dirección de Fortalecimiento y Fomento a las Culturas de la Subsecretaría de Asuntos Indígenas, investigador en el Centro de Investigaciones Humanísticas de Mesoamérica y el Estado de Chiapas (CIHMECH-UNAM) y director de difusión y promoción cultural de la Secretaría para la Atención de los Pueblos Indígenas. En 1992 recibió el premio Chiapas "Rosario Castellanos" en literatura y en 1994 fue becario del Fondo Nacional para la Cultura y las Artes.

K'ox xchi'uk yajval vo'

Enrique Pérez López

Tzotzil[1]

[From *Alperes: Te'tikal mut/El pájaro alférez,* pp. 47–58. Colección Letras Mayas Contemporáneas: Chiapas, vol. 11, Carlos Montemayor, series ed. Mexico City: INI/TRF, 1996.]

Jun k'ak'al ti K'oxe[2] ibat xchi'uk sme' ta uk'um, ba la slupik tal vo' yu'un la ja'o yorail k'epelaltik, takijan xa o la skotol ti jok'etik xchi'uk sat vo'etik bu nopol no'ox xil ta snaike ja'yo mu'yuk xa ox ya'alik ti bu nakalike, batz'i jeche' xa la tik'ich'ojan ikoman ti jok'etike, ti banamile jeche' xa la takichijan sat, jatemik xa la ta jyalel, ti vomol a'male kantzikanik xa ti yanaltake ja' ti mu xa jutuk vo' cha'yike. Yanuk ti kirixanoetik une te la chil svokolik ta takiti'il ek, ja'yo la ti K'ox xchi'uk sme' une batik la k'alal muk'ta uk'um ta slupel ti vo' yuch'ike.

Te la sul chik tal yalel ta vitz ti K'oxe, abol xa la sba talel oy ta smatz'ulan tal pajal vomol sventa xmak jutuk cha'ay ti takiti'ile xchi'uk pasbil tal yaxib yu'un sme', ja' yaxibinoj be tal ti smochibe, te la oy svokolik talel un.

K'alal ik'otik ta uk'ume ep la kirixanoetik la yilik te, oy la antzetik sbatz'ilik chuk'om, yantike slupel vo' ta ka' no la chbat yu'unik, oy la bik'tal keremetik jun yo'onik ta xnuxik ti ta uk'ume, batz'i jun la yo'onik ta xa'ybeik smuil ti lek xa sik tz'ijan ti vo'e, yanuk ti pore K'ox une te la abol sba ta k'ok', te la ta xchik'inaj ta jyalel, k'alal yil te oy svokol yol ti me'ile xi la la yalbe:

—¿Me cha'atin K'ox?

—Ja' xa tzk'an ko'on ta jaylel, ta xichik'un ta jaylel yu'un ti jch'ul totike, k'ok' xa ta jyalel ti jole oy nan yik'al k'alal ta jch'ich'al k'ixnajem ya'el, xi la ti K'ox une.

—Ja' chavi ti ech' no'ox k'ux ta jaylel jtotike K'ox, ja'yo ja' lek ta xkatintasot, yo'to k'ichoj talel jutuk kuni ch'upak'tik,[3] me chamala jlikeluke ta jnoy ta ton k'uchal xak' lek yuni vok tanae.

—Xu' ka'aytik un cha'e, xi la ti K'oxe, te la ba chotkluk ta uni ton tzmala ak'o xlaj jnoy xch'upak' ti sme'e.

Ti sme' uni kerem une la la sa' jun yuni volvol ton sventa jnoy o ti ch'upak'e, yanuk ti K'ox une ta la xixtan vo' xchi'uk yakan, ja' no'ox yu'un oy k'usi batem xch'ulel ta sk'elel un, ja' la ch'ayem yo'on ta sk'elel k'u x-elan ta xnuxinik ti yantik keremetike, ti lek stz'et yo'ontonik ta yut vo' ko'ol xa la xchi'uk choyetik xkajajetik ta vo', ja' no jech batem xch'ulel ta sk'elel ti bik'tal chonetik oy ta yut vo'e, yu'un la oy uni choyetik, kuchulchinetik, bus, xchi'uk xa k'usitik yan, ja' no'ox yu'un ti juju likel te te xch'ulel ta sk'elel k'u x-elan ta xnuxik ti yantik keremetike, toj jk'ol o xa chil ti xkajetik ta ba vo'e, ti mu xmukik ochele. Jech te baten xch'ulel o, ja' to k'uxi xi la yich' albel yu'un ti sme'e:

—K'ox, lok'eso me ak'u'e ta xa xkatintasot, laj xa ko'on ta snoyel ti ch'upak'e.

Ti K'oxe une la la slok'es ti yuni k'u'e, jechuk bik'it to chava'ay une, uni tz'irim k'u'il to la slapoj, k'alal slok'esoj xa ti sk'u'e la yich' chotanel ta ba ton yu'un sme' k'uchal xich' lek atintasel, ta boch la yich' lek lupbel ti ya'lele, la yich' lek pokel xchi'uk ch'upak', ta ton la yich' le juxbel spat yo' k'uchal xlok' lek' ti yik'ubale, ja' no jech ta ton la yich' juxbel snuk' xchi'uk yakan, te chotol lek tzmala ya'ay ti atintasele.

Jun yo'on chotol chich' atintasel ti K'oxe, mu k'usi chal yo'on yilel, ja' no'ox yu'un te xvulvun ti sjole, ti yo'ontone, ja' te xnopnun o ta sk'elel ti yantik keremetik sbatz'ilik nuxele, xi la chalbe sba une:

—Oyuk no la k'uxi jchan ka'aytik ek ti nuxulajele, batz'i jun xa no'ox yo'onik yilel ti le' keremetik sna' xnuxike, ko'ol xa xchi'uk muk'ta choyetik ti xnuxtenuxteik no'ox ta yut vo'e.

K'alal laj yo'on ta atintasel ti K'ox une, xi la yal ti me'ile:

—Jechuk la atin xa vo'ote K'ox, ta me xamalaun jlikeluk ek un, yu'un ta to xi tzebin yo'to li jtal.

—Xu' yaya, li' to ta jcha'ay ko'on ta sk'elel k'u x-elan chnuxik le' keremetike.

—¡A me chalaban ek le'e! batz'i jun yo'onik chavi mu no sna' xi'ik yilel me xjik'oike.

—Ja' chkal. ta jk'an yilel ek ti oyuk k'uxi jchan nuxinele.

—Me chak'an ya'el ek xanmuxet ta vo'e yajtot.

—Tana yaya.

Jech la te xvullajetik ta lo'il xchi'uk sme' ti K'ox une. K'alal laj yo'onik ta atimole, ti me'ile la snojes batel ta vo' ti sk'ibe, jech ek ti K'oxe oy tal jbej yuni tzu,[4] la yich' nojesbel batel ta vo' ek un, te la xpitet batel ta spat ti stzue, ja' no jech oy svokolik muyel ta vitz un, sul chik'ik' xa ta jyalel ja' ti ven k'ixin ti jotike, k'alal ik'ot ta snaike kux xi yo'onik, bal to ti k'ot jutuk vo' yuch'ike, te xa la patal ta ti'na la staik ti Maxe, jech sbi yak'ojbeik ti stz'i'ike, sbitzbun xa la sne ti k'alal la yil yajvale:

—Li talkutik xa un Max, me la chabi lek jnatike ¿me mu'yuk la xi'?, xut la stz'i' ti K'oxe.

—K'usi ta xi' avu'un, le'e ja' stu jchabie na ak'bil tal yu'un yajval, xi la ti me'ile.

La xkux jikeluk yo'onik, va'ay un xi no xtok ti me'ile:

—¿K'ox me chavuch' matz'?[5]

—Tana yaya, ja' xa me tzk'an ko'on ya'el, xi xa jun lek yo'on la stak' ti K'oxe.

La yuch' ti smatz'ik une, va'ay un ti me'ile lik sk'el yil ti k'usi sk'an pasel ta snae, smesel xch'ubael yut na, spat xokon. Smaklinel yalak', ja' ti k'usitik sk'an pasel chile. Yanuk ti K'ox une lik ta tajimol ta amak', yo stuktuk chatjin ja' ti mu'yuk te sbankiltake, batemik ta abtel xchi'uk stotik, ja'yo te to stuk xpikpun xvulvun ta tajimol ti K'oxe.

—Li'e ja' muk'ta uk'um, li' ta xnuxinik ti kemetike ta xnuxinik xchi'uk choy, kuchulchin, jk'eltikik me mu xlajik ta ti'el yu'un bus tana, xi la xvulvun stuk ti K'oxe.

La slok'ta uk'um ti ta banamile, va'ay un te vul xi ta sjol jna' ti sk'eoje, te lik k'ejinuk, vul xi no ta sjol ya'el ti k'usi chale, ja' ti yu'un bijil olol o no'oxe, xi xa ti sk'ejimole:

Koxkox avakan bolom chon
kilkil avisin bolom chon
lukluk apat bolom chon
xkajet ta vo' kuchulchin
xkajet ta vo' choyetik
xmuket ta vo' busetik
la, la, la . . .
xkajet ta vo' kuchulchin
xkajet ta vo' choyetik
xmuket ta vo' busetik
la, la, la . . .

Ja' xa o me lik spasbe sk'ejimolal ti k'usi la yil ta uk'um une, ja' ti te to xvulvun ta yo'on ti ta sk'an xchan nuxinele, va'ay un te och ak'ubal, te ba vayikuk xchi'uk stot sme' ti K'oxe, ja' no'ox yu'un ti stuke te xvulvun o vayel ti yo'one, mu ja'uk bu ich'ay ta yo'on ti k'usi la yile.

Nax xa lek ti ak'ubaltike, jechuk bik'it to xch'ulel ti K'oxe, jechuk bik'it to chav'ay ti yajval ek une lok' la ta xanubal mu sventauk me oy k'usi snuptan ti bu ilok' batel ta xanovele, te la isut batel ta uk'un ti xch'ulel K'ox ta xvayeche, ja' la ba sk'el yil me oy to ta xnuxinajan ti yantik ololetike, ja' no'ox yu'un ti mu'yuk k'usi la sta te une, ja'yo te la yat yo'on ek ti ch'ulelale, ta xa ox la sut tal yilel un, manchuk xa k'uxi te la ba lok'uk tal jun mol yilel ti ta yut vo'e, xi la:

—¿K'usi chapas un le'e K'ox? ¿K'u yu'un ti chavat a avo'one?

—Muy'uk ta xkat ko'on, ja' no'ox yu'un li tal uni jt'abeluk ta paxyal, xi la itak'av ek ti xch'ulel K'oxe.

—Mo'oj, le'e yu'un mu xak'an xaval oy k'usi ma ti yatel avo'on yu'un avu'une jna'oj skotol, me mu jechuk xkal ti chak'upin lek ti vi k'u x-elan jnae, ¿me mu ja'uk tal ak'el me oy to bu xnuxtenuxte ta vo' ti bik'tal keremetik la avil naxe?

Ti K'oxe pilajtik to la k'otel sat, k'uxi la sna' xi xa la.

—Jech ox un bi yu'un batz'i toj lek chkil ti vi k'u x-elan ta xnuxike ¿mu jna' k'usi chutik chkale?

—¡Aaa . . . ! na' le'e, vu'un ta xkak' tajinikuk li' ta kamak'e, lek chka'ay me jech lek chich'ikun ta muk'e, me ta xich'ik ta k'ux ti jtz'unubtak oy li' ta jnae, me mu smilbikune, yanuk me ta xutz'intabikun, ta xilbajinbikun ti kamak'e ta me xi ilin stuk un bi, ta jxibtasan ti keremutike ta jnitanbe ta yakanik sventa xich' jutuk yo'onik, oy bak'intik mu xa sutik o tal oy bak'intik jun chib no'ox k'ak'al ta xch'ay sbaik.

—Me yu'un vo'ot yajvalot[6] un vo'e.

—Li' vi k'u yepal chavile ja' ku'un o skotol, ja'yo me chich'ikun ta k'uxe, jech ta xi ich'van ta k'ux ek, yanuk me mo'oje mu'yuk me stuk un bi, k'elvil oy ta muk'tik lum bu ch'ech'anan jk'obk'obtake ta snojesikun ta k'a'ep, mukulun xa yu'uni, xituẹt xitzijet xa, mu xa xi ik'in ta jyalel toj j-ech' no'ox ya'el ti ilbajinele, mu xa no xkuch ya'el, ja'yo oy bak'intik mu'yuk xa chiech' te te ak'o yil sbaik, mu xa jventaanuk me oy svokolik ku'une.

—¿Me yu'un vo'ot ti yajvalot vo'o une? Oy me ka'yoj yu'un jtot ti oy la yajval ti vo'e, xchi'uk ti kuxulot la la, xi chka'ay.

—Vu'un yajvalun ti vo'e, te oyun o ti butik oy vo'e, ja' ku'un skotol, ja' jna jk'uleb.

—¿K'u yu'un ti mu xak'ot ta jnakutik une? Vu'unkutike mu'yuk ta xakilbajinotkutik, oy jvokolkutik avu'un ta takiti'il, xi la tik K'oxe, vul xi la ta sjol ti oy svokol ta xkuchel vo' ti sme'e.

—Yu'un mu k'u xkut ximuy, toj jtoyol ti bu oyoxuke, xchi'uk ti vi ta yorail k'epelaltike ta xik'unib, chisayub mu xano xchi chka'ay ti muyel ta vitze, yanuk me ech' ti k'epelaltike ta no jcha' ich' kip xtok un, chimuy ta vinajel chisut no tal xtok, ta no xlik xanavanuk ti kok jk'obtak ta yut banamile, ja' ti mel mu xk'otatan ta lok'ele.

—Me yu'un chakux avo'on xkaltik un.

—Mo'oj, ja' ta skoj ti chavilbajinbeik sk'u' spok' ti jme'e, chatz'etik te'etik, vomol a'mal, ta xachik'ik ak'ajbenik, ja'yo te ta xitakij batel o un, snopuk to xtok ti boch'o solel chiyilbajinune.

—Ja' no'ox yu'un ti vu'unkutike ta xakich'otkutik ta muk', jech yalojbun ka'ay jtot jme'.

—¿K'usi yalojbot ti atot ame'e?, alo' ka'aytik.

Ti K'oxe te lik xchol ta alel ti k'usi albil yu'un stot sme'e, xi la likel:

—Ti jtot jme'e yalojbun ka'ay ti sk'an la xavich' ich'el ta muk'e, vo'ote mu xu' xavich' mukel ta ka'ep, oy atoyel axi'el ku'unkutik, ta xavich' pasbel ak'inal ta jujun abil oy atoyel axi'el, ta xavich' k'opanel ta ana, ta ak'uleb, ta jujun vitz, ta jujun ojov anjel, ta asat, ta avelo xkejet xpatetik, ta xavich' k'anel ta stojol jmuk'ta jtojvanej jmanvanej k'uchal te to xa nixnuxnun, ta xnovel, xa bajlajet ta yalel muyel ta yak'el jkuxlejkutik, k'uchal mu xilajkutik ta takiti'il xchi'uk kovol jtz'unubkutik, k'uchal te to kuxul batel ti k'usi lajal machal li' ta sba osil banamile.

Ti yajval vo'e tze' xi to la ti k'alal la ya'ay oy to boch'o ta x-ich'at ta muk' yu'une, ti yaloje ta skotol kirixano jipbil tenbil, k'alal la ya'ay ti k'usi la yich' albel yu'un ti K'oxe jun yo'on ik'ot, ta to sk'an xkuxi, xano ta sba osil banamil vinajel, va'ay un ti K'oxe xi to xtok:

—Me mu oyuk ava'yoj ti oy li' xvokoletik ta sti' ana ak'uleb cha'e.

—Oy,—xi la ti yajval vo'e—oy o no'ox ka'yoj ma ti li' xvokolajetik un bi, ja'yo ta to xkich'oxuk ta k'ux, mu xa vat avo'on te chik'ot ta ana le' ok'om cha'eje, ta xa me x-ech' ti k'epelaltike ta xa no jcha' ich' kip xtok . . . Ja' no'ox yu'un jot xa bat chka'ay ti ka'yejtik une, ¿vo'ote yan k'usi tal ak'el me mu jechuk?

—Jech ox un bi.

—Ja' chak'el ox batz'i ti jnuxolajeletike ¿me yu'un batz'i jechan ava'ay ek?

—Jech ox ta kaloj, yu'un batz'i toj lek no'ox chkil ti ko'ol xa xchi'uk choy xkajtekajte, xnuxuxetik no'ox ta ana ti jchi'iltake.

—Le'e mu tzotzuk ta chanel stuke, ja' no'ox venta me yu'un jech xal avo'one, yanuk me mu xak'an o me chaxi'une, mu me xchan avu'un un bi, jechuk lek avo'on chkile, ja' lek ta jkoltaot a'yo lek ti k'usi chkalbote.

Ti K'oxe te xa la pitajtik yuni sat xchi'uk bijbij xa xchikin ta smakel ti k'usi chich' albele.

—Me la tal no ta jna ok'om cha'eje, xa tzak' oxlajun kot uni bik'tal choyetik, ja' me kuni tz'unubtak ma va'ay une, ja' no'ox me oxlajunkot xa tzak, va'ay un xa bik'anan, ja' smetz'ul sventa xachan nuxinajel ti va'aye.

—Me mu me sti'ikun u, k'u xkaltik me sjombikun jbikile, ¡ay! oy to la k'uxi sti'ikune, me li cham yu'unike.

—Mu'yuk ta xa sti'anan, te ta xkalanbe.

—Lek oy un cha'e, me xu' xkak'be sbik' oxlajunkotuk ek ti Jmaxe, ta jk'an ak'o xchan nuxinel ek, me oy aviloj jtz'i' Max sbie.

—Le'e mu xavat avo'on yu'un stuk le'e, sna' xa xnux ak'bil tal stuke, jech pasbil manbil tal yu'un yajval.

—¿Sna' xa xnux ti tz'i'e? mu'yuk bu ka'yoj me sna' xnux.

—Ja' lek mu xabik' ti choy k'alal me la bat ta jnae, ja' lek ta xkak'bot xch'a ta jyalel li'e, xi la ti yajval vo'e.

Ti smuk'ta ajval vo' une nit xut la tal lok'el jun yuni tzu, ja' la te tik'ajtik tal yu'un ti uni choyetike, la la slok'essan tal ti oxlajun kot une:

—Ilo bik'an li'e, xut la ti K'oxe.

Ti xch'ulel K'oxe la la sbik' ti uni oxlajun kot choye, batz'i jk'ol xa o la ya'ay, ko'ol xa xchi'uk te ta xnuxan ta yut xch'ut ti uni choyetike, chikiltik xa la ti yut xch'ute, va'ay un xi la ti yalval vo 'une:

—Ja' me jech chachan o ti nux une, li' tana une batan xa un, nax no li' xij jvochvun ta lo'il chka'aye, bak'in xa tal ta jnae te xa och' mu xa xi', mu k'usi ta xkutot xchi'uk lek xa xkotkinot, jna'oj ti lek avo'ontone.

—Jechuk un cha'e te ta xi tal xchi'uk ti Max me tal ta lup vo' jme'e, oy nan yik'al tana no'ox, xi la ti K'oxe.

—Ja' ti bak'in xu' chava'ye . . . a te to me xavalbe atot ame' ti jechukikuk to me batel ka'aytik ti ta to x-ich'vanik ta muk'e, balto me li' xkilulan jbatik jun chibuk k'ak'ale, xi la komel ti yajval vo'e.

Te la sak ch'ay o batel yilel un. Yanuk ti xch'ulel K'oxe isut tal ta sna, jechuk xch'ulel no'ox K'ox ti ay ta uk'ume, mu jaluk xanav, ti ch'ulelale mu jechuk xva'vun ta banamil ta xbein, oy yik'al xvilet xkajet ta ik' ja'yo oy ven nom ta xbat ta paxyal.

Sak xa ox nan lek osil k'alal ijulov ti K'oxe, va'ay un itotz ta aniltik no'ox, la yanil jak'be sme' me ta xtalik ta ich'vo' k'alal to uk'ume, ja' xa yu'un ti oy k'usi la xvaychin cha'ay une, ta sk'an spas ya'ay poroval me jech ti xu' xa xnuxinaj yu'un ti ak'bat sbik' choy ta svayeche, ja'yo mu xa stz'ik cha'ay smalael un, xi la:

—¿Yaya me ta xijbat ta lup vo' tana ta uk'ume?

—Tana ta xijbat me laj ko'on ta lich'ume, xi la ti me'ile.

—Ta me xkik'tik batel ek un Maxe, ak'o ba nuxijuk stuk, oy nan yik'ak chik'il cha'ay ek ma le'e.

—Me yu'un sna' xnux ta avaloj ek le' pore tz'i'e.

—Sna' xnux jech xa la jvaychin samel, xi la ti K'oxe.

K'alal laj yo'on ta spasel k'u spasel ta sna ti sme' K'oxe italik ti ta uk'um une, te o no'ox oy svokolik tal yu'un ti ven k'ux jtotike, ta xa xchik'inik tal ta jyalel manchuk me yaleltik pisi ti sbeike. K'alal ik'otik ti ta uk'ume, xi la yal ti K'oxe:

—Yaya ta xi och ta uk'ume ta jtz'ajilan jba jutuk, ta jchi'in ti jmaxtike.

—Mo'oy oy me yik'al xajik'o, ja' lek ch'an uto.

—Mu xi jik'o xchi'uk mu natuk ta jtik' jba ochel, ja' no li ta yuni ti'e.

Ti sme' une te la yak' ochuk ta uk'um ti yole, va'ay un ti K'oxe kux xi to la yo'on, mu la k'usi jech cha'ay o xi xa la ta xale:

Ta xinux ta vo'
ta xi atin ta vo'
ko'ol xa xchi'uk choyun tana
ko'ol xa xchi'uk kuchulchinun tana
xi kajet ta vo'
xi tz'ajet ta vo' . . .

Yanuk stuk ti stz'i'e, ti Maxe te xa la xnuxet ta vo' stuke, ja'yo la ti K'oxe la xch'un ti k'usi la yich' albel yu'un yajval vo' ta svayeche. K'alal och ta vo' ti K'oxe mu'yuk ixi', mu la k'usi la yal yo'on, ko'ol xa no la xchi'uk te xkajajet ya'el, te la xchi'inan ta nuxel ti choyetike, ti kuchulchinetike, jun xa la yo'on ¡Vokol aval un ch'ul yajval vo'! la vak' jchan, k'ot ta jbek'tal jtakopal ya'el ti xitz'ajet ta vo'e.

Ja' to la ya'ay un oy boch'o ik'opoj tal ya'eluk, xi la:

—Jech pisine, ti chaxi' xavich' ti'bel abikil yu'un ti choy la kalbot chabik'ane, mo'oj mu xa xi', ja' no'ox yu'un ich'un me ta k'ux ek' un, mu xavilbajin ti kuni tz'unubtake, mu xa vik'ubtasun ek un. Te me kuxetuk ajol avo'nton xchi'uk atz'i' un cha'e K'ox, xi la la ya'ay un.

—Jech kani xal ti ja' yajval vo'e, batz'i ja' snuk' chka'ay, ja' kani lek ti ta jk'eltik, ta jchabitk skotol k'usi lajal machal ta sba osil banamile k'uchal jmoj lek jun ko'on kuxulutike, xi la.

Yu'un ti va'ay K'ox kereme lek la bij, xvul no la ta sjol yo'on ti k'usitik lek xk'ot ta kuxlejale, ta jujun jna jk'ulebtike oy jk'oxaltik ek, te o no'ox oy ti K'oxe.

Notes

1. Tzotzil speakers call their language Batz'i K'op, "true language." At the end of the twentieth century there were more than 514,000 Tzotzil speakers, living primarily in the state of Chiapas. The alphabet the author uses is among the Indigenous-language alphabets in Chiapas that resulted from the practice and the exchange of experiences among the members of Sna Jtz'ibajom (House of the Writer) and the Mayas-Zoques Writers Group. In the early 1990s the writers belonging to these independent organizations held a series of work sessions in Tuxtla Gutiérrez with the National Institute for Adult Education (INEA) and the Department of Ethnic Cultures of the State Government of Chiapas. The objective was jointly to establish practical alphabets in languages of interest to the INEA: Tzeltal, Tzotzil, Tojolabal, Chol, and Zoque.

2. Literally, "the smallest one," "the youngest child" of a family. (See Appendix F.)

3. *Ch'upak':* the Tzotziles use this word to refer to *Polygala floribunda,* a climbing plant belonging to the Polygonaceae. The roots contain saponin and are macerated to produce foam that is used as soap. Other authors identify this plant as *Cyclantera langaei.* The Tzotziles usually translate the word *ch'upak'* into Spanish as *amole.* (See also note 3 of the English-language text.)

4. Literally, a calabash (for storing water). Similarly, the Tzotzil people usually translate the word *tzu* into Spanish as *tecomate.* (See also note 5 of the English-language text.)

Notas

1. Los hablantes de tzotzil llaman a su lengua *batz'i k'op,* "idioma verdadero." A finales del siglo XX esta lengua contaba con más de 514,000 hablantes localizados principalmente en el estado de Chiapas. El alfabeto que emplea el autor es uno de los alfabetos en las lenguas indígenas de Chiapas que surgieron de la práctica y del intercambio de experiencias entre los integrantes de Sna Jtz'ibajom (Casa del Escritor) y de la Asociación de Escritores Mayas-Zoques. A principios de la última década del siglo XX los escritores de estas organizaciones independientes sostuvieron varias reuniones de trabajo en Tuxtla Gutiérrez con el Instituto Nacional de Educación para Adultos (INEA) y el Departamento de Culturas Étnicas del Gobierno de Chiapas, a fin de alcanzar acuerdos en el establecimiento de alfabetos prácticos en las lenguas de interés para el INEA: tzeltal, tzotzil, tojolabal, chol y zoque.

2. Literalmente, "el más pequeño," "el hermano menor" de una familia. (Véase Apéndice F.)

3. *Ch'upak':* se llama así entre los tzotziles a la *Polygala floribunda,* planta trepadora de las Poligonáceas. Las raíces contienen saponina y se les macera para usar la espuma como jabón. Otros autores identifican esta planta como la *Cyclantera langaei.* Suelen traducir al español la palabra *ch'upak',* por paralelismo, como *amole.* (Véase también nota 3 del texto en español.)

4. Literalmente, *calabazo* (para agua). Suelen traducir al español la palabra *tzu,* por paralelismo, como *tecomate.* (Véase también nota 4 del texto en español.)

5. *Matz'* is the Tzotzil equivalent for the Mayan *k'eyem,* known in Spanish as *posol* or *pozol,* dough made from cooked corn kernels that have burst open; it is dissolved in water for consumption.

6. *Yajval* (or *-ajual*), or its indefinite form *'ajvalil* or *yajvalil,* means "the owner," "the antagonist," or "the responsible one." To its basic root *'ojov* (or *'ajav*), "owner," one adds the so-called suffix of beneficent possession, forming *-ajval,* The word *kajval* would literally mean, therefore, "the owner" or "the person who possesses me" or "controls me" or "threatens me." (See Appendix E.)

5. *Matz'* es el término tzotzil para la voz maya *k'eyem.* Se trata del *posol* o *pozol:* masa de maíz cocido y reventado que se deslíe en agua para ser comido.

6. *Yajval* (o *-ajual*), o su forma indefinida, *'ajvalil* o *yajvalil,* significa "el dueño," "el antagonista" o "el responsable." A su raíz básica, es decir, *'ojov* (o *'ajav*), "dueño," se le agrega el sufijo llamado de "posesión benefactora" para formar *-ajval.* Así, la voz *kajval* significaría, literalmente, "el dueño" o "la persona que me posee" o "me controla" o "me amenaza." (Véase Apéndice E.)

K'ox[1] and the Lord of the Water

Enrique Pérez López

Tzotzil[2]

[From *Alperes: Te'tikal mut/El pájaro alférez,* pp. 47–58, 142–151. Colección Letras Mayas Contemporáneas: Chiapas, vol. 11, C. Montemayor, series ed. Mexico City: INI/TRF, 1996.]

One day, K'ox and his mother went to the river for water because it was the dry season. All the wells and springs were bone dry of thirst. The earth was cracked beyond imagination. The leaves on the plants had turned yellow since their roots were unable to find any water. People were suffering greatly because of their thirst. Therefore, K'ox and his mother went to the big river to bring back drinking water.

They sweated their way down the hill. K'ox was suffering greatly; he would chew on bitter-tasting leaves to mitigate his hunger. They had made him a parasol from his mother's head wrap; still, he suffered from the heat.

When they arrived at the river, they saw many people. Some women were washing; others were hauling water home on horses. There were also small children swimming and enjoying the river's cool waters. Poor K'ox was sweating heavily, and his mother asked him: "Would you like to bathe, K'ox?"

"That is what my heart most desires!" he responded. "The sun is burning me. My head is very hot. I think that even my blood is hot."

"Yes, the sun is very hot, I had best bathe you. I brought a little *amole*[3] along; I will crush it so that it will make a lot of foam. Wait just a moment."

"Fine," said K'ox, and he sat down on a rock to wait.

The little boy's mother looked for a round stone with which to crush the amole. Meanwhile, K'ox played in the water with his feet, and he entertained himself by watching the other children enjoying themselves, swimming around like big fish in the water. He also entertained himself by watching the little water animals: little fish, water bugs, crabs, and many others. But what most caught his attention was how the other children were swimming—floating on the water or submerging themselves; this was very strange to him. Suddenly his mother spoke: "Take off your shirt, K'ox, I am going to bathe you now, I have finished grinding the *amole.*"

Little K'ox took off his shirt. Since he was still very young, she sat him upon a rock to bathe him well. Using a gourd, she poured water on him, washed him well with the *amole,* and with a stone scrubbed his back to get off all of the dirt. She also scrubbed the nape of his neck and his feet with a stone. K'ox was very happy to be bathed, and his heart seemed to think about nothing else. But his head and his heart were speaking of many things as he watched the other children swim. He said to himself: "If only I could swim too! I can see that they are very happy to know how to swim; they look like big fish swimming in the water."

When K'ox's bath was complete, his mother said: "Now wait for me awhile; I also want to wash my head since we have come this far."

"Yes, mamá, I will be here entertaining myself watching those children swim. See how happy they are! They seem to have no fear of drowning."

"Would you like to glide through the water, *papacito?*"[4]

"Yes, mamá."

Once they had finished bathing, the mother filled her water jug. K'ox was carrying a small *tecomate,*[5] and they also filled that with water. He carried it slung on his back, even though it swung back and forth. Once again, they had to endure the climb, sweating copiously as the sun beat down upon their backs. They were happy once they arrived home since they now had a little drinking water. Max,[6] as they called their dog, was lying by the door, and he wagged his tail when he saw that his owners had returned.

"We are back, Max. Did you take good care of the house? You were not afraid, were you?" the child asked.

"What do you mean 'afraid'? It is his job to watch over the house. That is why the Lord created him," the mother said.

After resting a moment, the mother asked: "Would you like to drink some *pozol,*[7] K'ox?"

"Yes, mamá, my heart now desires it," the little one responded.

They drank their *pozol.* The woman then began to see what chores there were to do around the house. K'ox began to play alone on the patio since his brothers were not around; they had gone off to work with their father. The little one played alone and talked to himself. "This is the big river: here are the children swimming like fish and water bugs. Let us see if a crab does not bite them now," the little one would say to himself.

On the ground he drew a river; he then decided to start singing. Since he was a child prodigy, it suddenly occurred to him what to sing, and his song went like this:

You are lame in one foot, jaguar,
you have long whiskers, jaguar,
your back is twisted, jaguar.
The water bugs swim on top of the water,
the fish swim in the water,
the crabs are under the water,
lalala . . .
The water bug floats on top of the water,
the fish float in the water,
the crabs are under the water,
lalala . . .

He had already made up a song about what he had seen in the river, because his yearning to learn how to swim remained in his heart. Then night fell. Everyone went to sleep, but K'ox kept thinking. His heart continued to speak; it could not forget what it had seen. Very late at night, K'ox's little spirit (which was as little as its owner) went out for a walk. It was not worried that something might happen to it, and it returned to the river. K'ox traveled in his sleep; he went to see if the other children were still swimming, but he found nothing. That made him sad, and, as he was about to return, an old man suddenly emerged from the water and asked him: "What are you up to, K'ox? Why is your heart so sad?"

"I am not sad, I only came here for a moment," K'ox's spirit replied.

"No, that is not it. You do not want to tell me why your heart is sad, but I know everything. You are here because you like my house. You came to see if the children you saw today were still swimming, right?"

K'ox's eyes opened wide in astonishment. "Yes, it is true, I really like the way they swim. How do they do it?"

"I let them play here, on my patio. I am pleased if they respect me, if they take care of the things I have here in my house, if they do not kill them on me. But if they disturb them, if they mistreat my patio, then I get angry, I frighten them, I pull them by the feet so that their hearts feel fear. Sometimes they no longer return; other times they stay away for two or three days."

"Are you the Lord of the Water?"[8]

"Everything you see here is mine. When they respect me I also respect them; but if not, I am not kind either. Sometimes my legs or arms pass through the big cities, and all they do is fill me with trash; at times I have vanished or I stink and smell. My suffering has become great; that is why at times I can no longer endure it, and I no longer pass by. Let them work things out on their own; what do I care if they now suffer on my account?"

"But are you the Lord of the Water? I have heard some things from my parents, that water has its lord and that it has life."

"Yes, I am the Lord of the Water. I am present wherever there is water; it is all mine, it is my house, my dwelling."

"And why do you not come to our house? We have not mistreated you; we suffer a lot because of our thirst for you," K'ox said, remembering his mother's suffering while hauling water.

"It is because I cannot climb. It is very high where you live, and in the dry season I become depleted, I become very weak; I feel that I can no longer make it up the hill. But when the dry season passes, I regain my strength. I rise to the heavens and descend again; my arms and legs begin to walk the earth once more and manage to appear in many places."

"Then it is because you are resting, let us say."

"No. It is because they greatly damage my mother's clothing; they cut down the trees and plants and burn away the stubble; that is why we are drying up. If only those who mistreat me would think a little!"

"But we take care of you and respect you; my parents have told me so."

"Just what have your papá and mamá told you? Let us see, tell me."

K'ox began by saying: "My parents have told me that you are to be respected and esteemed, that you are not to be filled up with trash. We respect and fear you; we hold a fiesta for you every year; we praise and implore you; we pray and make offerings to you in your house, in your dwelling, whether on a hill or at a sacred site; on your surface, on your face, they kneel and humble themselves. We beg the great Creator and Shaper on your behalf so that you may still walk, circulate, trickle, as you climb and descend, delivering life so that we do not die of thirst along with our crops and plants; so that everything that exists upon the earth may continue to live."

The Lord of the Water smiled because there were still those who respected and feared him; he had thought that everyone had forgotten and humiliated him. Listening to K'ox, his heart grew large; he desired to continue to exist and to walk in heaven and on earth. K'ox went on to say: "Have you not heard by chance that at times, we are imploring you here before your house?"

"Yes," said the Lord of the Water. "I have heard you imploring here, that is why I respect you still. Do not be sad. I shall come to your house tomorrow or the next day. The dry season will be over and I will regain my strength once again . . . but it seems that our conversation has gotten off track . . . because you came for another purpose, is it not so?"

"Yes, it is so."

"You came to see the swimmers. Do you really want to be one also?"

"That is what I have desired; I believe it is very good; they look like fish in the water; they glide about through your house."

"It is not very difficult to learn if your heart desires it. If you do not wish to, or if you fear me, you will not learn. But since your heart is very good, I will help you. Listen carefully."

K'ox opened his eyes to listen to what he would be told.

"If you return to my house tomorrow or the next day, catch thirteen little fish, just thirteen, and swallow them; that is the secret for you to learn how to swim."

"And if they eat me? What if they eat through my intestines and I die? They will kill me."

"They will not eat you; I will tell them."

"Can I also give thirteen little fish to Max? I also want my dog to learn to swim, and his name is Max."

"Do not worry about him, he already knows how: his Creator made him so."

"My dog already knows how to swim?"

"I believe I had better give you the fish right now," said the Lord of the Water.

The great Lord of the Water produced a small gourd with a number of fish, from which he removed thirteen small ones.

"Take them, swallow them," he told K'ox.

In his dreams K'ox swallowed the thirteen little fish. He felt something very strange; it seemed that the fish were swimming about within his stomach and tickling him. The Lord of the Water then added: "Thus, you will learn to swim. Now go, we have been talking a long time. When you come to my house, enter with confidence; I will not do anything to you. Besides, I now know you well, I know that you have a good heart."

"Fine. I shall come with Max when my mother comes for water, maybe today," K'ox said.

"Come whenever you can. Tell your parents to continue to take care of me. At least we will be able to see each other for some days to come."

The Lord of the Water then disappeared. K'ox's spirit returned home. That did not take long. Spirits do not walk, they perhaps fly, they go with the wind; at times they travel great distances.

It was already daytime when K'ox awoke. He got up and quickly asked his mother if they would go to the river for water. He wanted to find out if he could really swim and could no longer stand to wait.

"Yes, we will go when I finish making tortillas," the mother responded.

"We will take Max along so that he can swim a little; perhaps he is really hot also."

"Do you believe that poor dog knows how to swim?"

"Yes, he knows how, I dreamt it last night," the little one replied.

When the mother had finished her chore, she and K'ox went to the river, once again under the ravages of the heat. When they arrived, K'ox said: "Mamá, I am going to into the river with Max to get a little wet."

"No, do not, what if you drown?"

"I will not drown. Besides, I am not going to go into the deep part; I will stay near the bank."

The mother allowed her child to go into the river, and K'ox felt great happiness; the feeling was incomparable, and he said to himself:

I shall swim in the water,
I shall bathe in the water,
I shall look like a fish now,
I shall look like a water bug now,
I shall float on the water,
I shall move through the water . . .

Since the dog was already swimming in the water, K'ox believed what he had heard in his dream. When he entered the water, he was not afraid, his heart said nothing. He saw how he floated, that he was swimming with the fish and the water bugs. His heart was happy.

"Thank you, sacred Lord of the Water, I have learned; the joy of floating on the water has come to my body and to my essence!"

All of a sudden, he heard someone speak to him and say: "Ah, remember how you were afraid that the fish that you had to swallow would eat your intestines? Now fear not, all I ask is that you respect me, that you do not mistreat my little animals, that you do not dirty me. May your heart and head be happy along with your dog."

K'ox said to himself: "It was true what the Lord of the Water told me. It is he who spoke to me. It is his voice. It is best that we care for and respect everything that exists here upon the earth, so that we may all live with one heart."

This little one, K'ox, was very intelligent; the things that are good for life came to blossom in his head. At home we have a little one; the latest in the family. He is our K'ox.

Notes

1. Literally, "the smallest one" or "the youngest brother" of a family (see Appendix F); approximately pronounced "kosh," as in the English word "kosher," with a strongly pronounced *k* (i.e., a *k* followed by a glottal stop, indicated by the apostrophe).

2. Tzotzil speakers call their language Batz'i K'op, "true language." At the end of the twentieth century there were more than 514,000 Tzotzil speakers, residing primarily in the state of Chiapas. See also note 1 of the Tzotzil-language version.

3. From the Nahuatl *amolli,* "soap," a foam produced by the maceration of Amarilidaceas plants, such as *Manfreda pringlei rose; Prochnyanthes viridescens;* and particularly, in northern Mexico, several varieties of *Agave: hartmanii, mayoensis,* and *schotii.* (See also note 3 of the Tzotzil-language version.)

4. A term of endearment.

5. From the Nahuatl *tecomatl,* "drinking cup," "pot." Receptacle made from a natural husk, such as that of the gourd, coconut, or calabash.

6. Literally, "monkey," pronounced "mosh" (rhyming with the English word "posh").

7. From the Nahuatl *potzol,* "froth," or *potzolli,* "frothy"; its Mayan-language equivalent is *k'eyem,* dough made from corn kernels that have been cooked and have burst; it is dissolved in water in a half-sphere gourd (*jícara*) for consumption. The farmer usually carries the dough in a shoulder bag and water in a gourd.

8. In Tzotzil, Kajval, a generic name for the protective entities or guardians of the hills, springs, or rivers. (See Appendix E.)

K'ox[1] y el Dueño del agua

Enrique Pérez López

Tzotzil[2]

[De *Alperes: Te'tikal mut/El pájaro alférez,* pp. 142–151. Colección Letras Mayas Contemporáneas: Chiapas, vol. 11, C. Montemayor, coord. de la colección. México, D.F.: INI/TRF, 1996.]

Un día el K'ox y su mamá fueron al río para traer agua, porque era temporada de sequía. Todos los pozos y ojos de agua estaba resecos, sedientos. La tierra estaba cuarteada a más no poder. Las plantas tenían ya hojas amarillentas porque no encontraban agua sus raíces. Las personas sufrían mucho por la sed. Por eso el K'ox y su mamá fueron hasta el río grande a traer agua para beber.

Iban sudando al bajar por el cerro. El K'ox sufría mucho; masticaba hojas medio agrias para mitigar su hambre. Le habían hecho una sombrilla con la toca de su mamá, pero padecía por el calor.

Cuando llegaron al río vieron que había mucha gente ahí. Había mujeres lavando, otros acarreando agua para sus casas con caballos. Había también niños pequeños que nadaban y disfrutaban de las aguas frescas del río. El pobre K'ox sudaba copiosamente y la mamá le preguntó:

—¿Te quieres bañar, K'ox?

—¡Eso es lo que más desea mi corazón!—respondió el K'ox—. Me quema mucho el sol. Ya está bien caliente mi cabeza. Creo que hasta la sangre la tengo ya bien caliente.

—Sí está muy fuerte el sol, por eso mejor te bañaré. Traje un poco de amole;[3] lo machucaré para que haga bastante espuma. Espera un momentito.

—Está bien—dijo el K'ox, y fue a sentarse sobre una piedra a esperar.

La mamá del niñito buscó una piedra redonda para macerar bien el amole. Mientras tanto, el K'ox jugaba con sus pies en el agua y se distraía mirando cómo los otros niños se divertían dentro del agua, como grandes peces que nadaban. También se distraía mirando los pequeños animales del agua: pecesillos, cucarachas de agua, cangrejos y otros muchos más. Pero lo que más le llamaba la atención era cómo nadaban los otros niños, porque flotaban en el agua y no se sumergían, era algo muy raro para él. De pronto le habló su mamá:

—Quítate la camisa, K'ox, ya te voy a bañar; terminé de machucar mi amole.

El pequeño K'ox se quitó la camisa. Como era muy niño aún, lo sentaron sobre una piedra para bañarlo bien. Con huacal le echaban el agua, lo lavaban bien con el amole y con una piedra le frotaban la espalda para que saliera bien la mugre; con piedra le frotaron también la nuca y los pies. Estaba feliz el K'ox de que lo bañaran y su corazón parecía no pensar en nada. Pero su cabeza y corazón hablaban de muchas cosas al mirar a los otros niños que nadaban. Se decía entre sí:

—¡Cómo pudiera yo nadar también! Veo que están muy felices porque saben nadar, ya parecen unos pecesotes nadando en el agua.

Cuando terminaron de bañar al K'ox, la mamá dijo:

—Ahora espérame un rato, también quiero lavarme la cabeza aprovechando que vinimos hasta acá.

—Sí, mamá, aquí estaré distrayéndome viendo cómo nadan esos niños. Mira qué felices están. No parecen tener miedo a ahogarse.

—¿Te gustaría deslizarte en el agua, papacito?

—Sí, mamá.

Una vez que terminaron de bañarse, la mamá llenó su cántaro de agua. El K'ox traía un tecomate[4] pequeño y se lo llenaron de agua también. Lo llevaba cargando en su espalda, aunque iba de un lado a otro. Nuevamente tuvieron que sufrir en la subida, sudando copiosamente porque el sol caía a plomo sobre sus espaldas. Cuando llegaron a la casa se sintieron felices porque ya tenían un poco de agua para beber. Ahí estaba echado en la puerta Max,[5] que así se llamaba su perro, que movía la cola al ver que sus dueños ya estaban ahí.

—Ya venimos, Max. ¿Cuidaste bien la casa, no tuviste miedo?—preguntó el niño.

—¡Qué va a tener miedo! Sirve para cuidar la casa. Así fue creado por el Señor—dijo la mamá.

Después de descansar un momento le preguntó la mamá:

—¿Quieres tomar pozol,[6] K'ox?

—Sí, mamá, mi corazón ya lo desea—respondió el pequeño.

Tomaron su pozol. Luego la señora se dedicó a ver qué pendientes había por hacer en la casa y el K'ox se puso a jugar a solas en el patio, porque sus hermanos no se encontraban, habían salido a trabajar con el papá. El pequeño jugaba y hablaba solito.

—Éste es el río grande: aquí están nadando los niños como peces y cucarachas de agua. Vamos a ver si no los muerde un cangrejo ahora—decía en su monólogo el pequeño.

En el suelo dibujó un río, después se le ocurrió cantar y comenzó a hacerlo. De repente le llegó a su cabeza lo que debía cantar, porque era un niño prodigio; en su canción decía:

Estás cojo de una pata tigre
tienes bigotes largos tigre
tienes la espalda torcida tigre
nadan sobre el agua las cucarachas
nadan en el agua los peces
están dentro del agua los cangrejos
lalala . . .
Flota en el agua la cucaracha
flotan en el agua los peces
dentro del agua están los cangrejos
lalala . . .

Ya había inventado un canto sobre lo que vio en el río, porque en su corazón seguía la inquietud de aprender a nadar. Luego entró la noche. Se fueron a dormir todos, pero el K'ox seguía pensando. Su corazón aún continuaba hablando, no se olvidaba de lo que había visto. Ya muy noche, como era muy pequeño todavía el espíritu del K'ox (tan pequeño como lo era el dueño), entonces se fue a caminar; no le importó si le podía suceder algo por ahí y volvió nuevamente al río. El K'ox viajó en su sueño, había ido a ver si todavía estaban nadando los otros niños, pero no encontró nada; por eso le entró tristeza y ya se regresaba cuando de pronto salió del agua un viejo y le preguntó:

—¿Qué haces, K'ox, por qué está triste tu corazón?

—No estoy triste, sólo vine a pasearme un momentito—respondió el espíritu del K'ox.

—No, no es eso. No me quieres decir el motivo por el cual tu corazón está triste, pero yo lo sé todo. Estás aquí porque te gusta mi casa. Viniste a ver si todavía estaban nadando los niños que viste hoy, ¿verdad?

Al K'ox se le saltaron los ojos de asombro.

—Sí, es cierto, me gusta mucho cómo nadan. ¿Cómo lo harán?

—Yo los dejo que jueguen aquí, en mi patio. Me agrada si me estiman, si cuidan mis cositas que tengo aquí en mi casa, si no me los matan. Pero si me los molestan, me maltratan mi patio, entonces me enojo, los espanto, les jalo los pies para que tenga miedo su corazón; a veces ya no regresan, otras se van en dos o tres días.

—¿Tú eres el Dueño[7] del agua?

—Todo lo que ves aquí es mío. Cuando me estiman, yo también los estimo; pero si no, yo tampoco soy complaciente. A veces pasan mis pies, mis manos, en las grandes ciudades, y lo único que hacen es llenarme de basura; a veces he desaparecido, apesto y hiedo, es mucho ya mi padecer. No aguanto por eso en ocasiones y ya no paso, que se las arreglen solos, qué me importa si ahora sufren por mí.

—¿Pero tú eres el Dueño del agua? He oído algo de mis padres, que el agua tiene dueño y que tiene vida.

—Sí, soy el Dueño del agua, estoy presente en todos los lugares en donde hay agua, es mío todo, es mi casa, mi morada.

—¿Y por qué no llegas a nuestra casa? Nosotros no te hemos maltratado, sufrimos mucho de sed por ti—dijo el K'ox, recordando el sufrimiento de su madre para transportar el agua.

—Es porque no puedo subir, es muy alto donde ustedes viven y en temporada de sequía me agoto mucho, me debilito, siento que ya no puedo caminar en el cerro. Pero cuando pasa la temporada de sequía vuelvo a tomar fuerzas; subo al cielo y regreso de nuevo, mis manos y mis pies comienzan a caminar otra vez dentro de la tierra y alcanzan a salir en muchos lugares.

—Entonces es porque descansas, digamos.

—No, es porque maltratan mucho la ropa de mi madre; cortan los árboles y las plantas, queman su rastrojo; por eso nos vamos secando. ¡Si al menos pensara un poco aquel que me maltrata!

—Pero nosotros te cuidamos y respetamos, así me lo han dicho mis padres.

—¿Qué te han dicho tu papá y tu mamá? A ver, dime.

El K'ox comenzó diciendo:

—Mis padres me han dicho que se te debe respetar y estimar, que no se te debe llenar de basura. Nosotros te respetamos y tememos, se te hace tu fiesta cada año, se te ensalza y ofrenda, se te ruega e implora en tu casa, en tu morada, ya en un cerro, ya en un lugar sagrado; en tu faz, en tu rostro, se hincan y postran, se te pide ante el gran creador y formador para que todavía estés caminando, circulando, gotees subiendo y bajando, repartiendo vida para que nosotros no muramos de sed con nuestras siembras y plantas, para que sigan viviendo todas las cosas que existen sobre la tierra.

El Dueño del agua sonrió porque todavía había quien le respetara y temiera; él pensaba que todas las personas lo habían olvidado y humillado. Al escuchar al K'ox se puso grande su corazón; todavía quería seguir existiendo, seguir caminando en el cielo y en la tierra. El K'ox continuó diciendo:

—¿De casualidad no has escuchado que a veces están suplicando aquí ante tu casa?

—Sí—dijo el Dueño del agua—, sí he escuchado que están suplicando aquí, por eso los estimo todavía. No te pongas triste, llegaré a tu casa mañana o pasado, porque ya pasará la temporada de sequía, ya volveré a tomar fuerza de nuevo . . . Pero parece que nuestra plática ya se desvió, porque tú habías venido por otra cosa, ¿no es así?

—Sí, así es.

—Venías a ver a los nadadores . . . ¿En verdad tú también quieres serlo?

—Yo había deseado eso, siento que es muy bueno; parecen peces dentro del agua, se deslizan por tu casa.

—No es muy difícil de aprender si lo dispone tu corazón. Si no quieres o me tienes miedo, no aprenderás. Pero como es muy bueno tu corazón, te ayudaré, escucha bien.

El K'ox abrió los ojos para escuchar lo que le dirían.

—Si vuelves a mi casa mañana o pasado, pesca trece pecesillos, sólo trece, y te los tragas; ése es el secreto para que aprendas a nadar.

—¿Y si me comen? Qué tal que me perforan la tripa y me muero. Me matan.

—No te comerán; yo les diré.

—¿Le puedo dar también trece pecesillos a Max? Porque también quiero que aprenda a nadar mi perro, que se llama Max.

—Por él no te preocupes, él ya sabe nadar, así fue formado por su creador.

—¿Ya sabe nadar el perro?

—Creo que será mejor darte los peces ahora mismo—dijo el Dueño del agua.

El gran Señor del agua sacó un pequeño tecomatito con varios peces; de ahí sacó trece pescaditos.

—Toma, trágatelos—le dijo al K'ox.

En sus sueños el K'ox tragó los trece pecesillos. Sintió algo muy raro; parecía que nadaban los peces dentro de su estómago y le causaban cosquillas. Luego agregó el Dueño del agua:

—Así aprenderás a nadar. Ahora vete, porque ya nos tardamos platicando. Cuando vengas a mi casa entra con confianza, no te haré nada. Es más, ya te conozco bien, sé que es bueno tu corazón.

—Está bien. Vendré con el Max cuando venga mi mamá por agua. Puede ser hoy mismo—dijo el K'ox.

—Cuando puedas le dices a tus padres que sigan cuidándome, algo será que nos sigamos viendo unos cuantos días más.

Luego desapareció el Dueño del agua. El espíritu del K'ox se regresó a la casa. No tardó mucho. El espíritu no camina, tal vez vuela, anda entre el viento, a veces se va muy lejos a pasear.

Ya era de día cuando el K'ox se despertó. Se levantó y preguntó rápidamente a su mamá si irían por agua hasta el río. Quería probar si era cierto que podría nadar y ya no aguantaba la espera.

—Sí, iremos cuando termine de hacer las tortillas—respondió la mamá.

—Llevaremos al Max para que nade un poco, tal vez sienta mucho calor también.

—¿Crees que sepa nadar el pobre perro?

—Sí sabe nadar, lo soñé anoche—contestó el pequeño.

Cuando la mamá terminó de hacer el quehacer doméstico, el K'ox y ella fueron al río, nuevamente bajo los estragos del calor. Cuando llegaron el K'ox dijo:

—Mamá, voy a entrar al río para remojarme un poco y acompañaré al Max.

—No, ¿qué tal que te ahogas?

—No me ahogaré. Es más, no me voy a meter en lo profundo, sólo aquí en la orillita.

La mamá dejó que su hijo entrara en el río y el K'ox sintió una gran felicidad; era incomparable su sentimiento y sólo decía:

Nadaré en el agua
me bañaré en el agua
pareceré pez ahora
pareceré cucaracha ahora
flotaré en el agua
andaré en el agua . . .

Como el perro ya estaba nadando en el agua, el K'ox creyó lo que había oído en su sueño. Cuando entró en el agua no tuvo miedo, su corazón no dijo nada; vio que flotaba, que nadaba con los peces y las cucarachas de agua. Estaba alegre su corazón.

—¡Gracias, sagrado Señor del agua! Aprendí, llegó a mi cuerpo y a mi esencia la dicha de flotar en el agua.

De pronto escuchó que alguien le hablaba y le decía:

—Ah, ¿no que tenías miedo de que te comieran las tripas los peces que debías tragar? Ahora no tengas miedo, sólo te pido que me respetes, que no maltrates a mis animalitos, que no me ensucies. Que tu corazón y tu cabeza estén contentos junto con tu perro.

El K'ox se dijo para sí mismo:

—Era cierto lo que me dijo el Dueño del agua. Es él quien me habló. Es su voz. Es mejor que cuidemos y respetemos todo lo que existe aquí sobre la tierra, para que todos vivamos con un solo corazón.

Este pequeño, el K'ox, era muy inteligente; a su cabeza llegaban a florecer las cosas buenas para la vida. En casa tenemos un pequeño, el último de la familia. Ahí está el K'ox.

Notas

1. Literalmente, "el más pequeño," "el hermano menor" de una familia. (Véase Apéndice F.)

2. Los hablantes de tzotzil llaman a su lengua *batz'i k'op*, "idioma verdadero." A finales del siglo XX esta lengua contaba con más de 514,000 hablantes localizados principalmente en el estado de Chiapas.

3. Del náhuatl *amolli*, "jabón," espuma producida por el maceramiento de plantas Amarilidáceas como las de *Manfreda pringlei rose*, *Prochnyanthes viridescens* y, particularmente en el norte de México, las variedades de *Agave hartmanii*, *mayoensis* y *schotii*. En el texto en lengua tzotzil el autor se refiere a la *Polygala floribunda*. (Véase tambien nota 3 del texto tzotzil.)

4. Del náhuatl *tecomatl*, "vaso," "olla." Recipiente hecho de cáscara de frutas como los guajes, cocos y calabazas.

5. Literalmente, "mono."

6. Del náhuatl *potzol*, "espuma," o *potzolli*. "espumante"; en maya *k'eyem:* masa de maíz cocido y reventado que se deslíe en agua para ser comido. El campesino suele portar la masa en su morral y el agua en un calabazo; deslíe la masa en una jícara.

7. En tzotzil Kajval, nombre genérico de entidades protectoras o guardianes de montes, manantiales o ríos. (Véase Apéndice E.)

Jacinto Arias Pérez

Tzotzil

Jacinto Arias Pérez. Photographed at his home in San Cristóbal de las Casas, Chiapas.

Jacinto Arias Pérez is a Tzotzil researcher and writer from San Pedro Chenalhó, Chiapas. He is the founder and first president of the Mayas-Zoques Writers Group, Inc., based in the state of Chiapas and a founding member of Indigenous Language Writers, Inc. He holds an M.A. in anthropology from the Catholic University of America (Washington, D.C.) and has completed his studies for the doctorate in anthropology at Princeton University. Arias Pérez has written a variety of essays on Chiapas Indigenous languages and cultures. He has published, among other books, *San Pedro Chenalhó, algo de su historia, cuentos y costumbres* (San Pedro Chenalhó, Some of Its History, Stories, and Traditions) (Tuxtla Gutiérrez, Chiapas: Gobierno del Estado de Chiapas/Instituto Chiapaneco de Cultura, 1990) and *El mundo numinoso de los mayas* (The Numinous World of the Mayas), based upon his master's thesis.

Jacinto Arias Pérez es investigador y escritor tzotzil de San Pedro Chenalhó, Chiapas. Es fundador y primer presidente de la Unidad de Escritores Mayas-Zoques, A.C., del Estado de Chiapas y miembro fundador de Escritores en Lenguas Indígenas, A.C. Ha escrito diversos ensayos sobre lengua y cultura de los pueblos indígenas de Chiapas. Cursó la maestría en antropología en la Catholic University of America (Washington, D.C.) y terminó los estudios para el doctorado en antropología en Princeton University. Ha publicado, entre otros libros, *San Pedro Chenalhó, algo de su historia, cuentos y costumbres* (Tuxtla Gutiérrez, Chiapas: Gobierno del Estado de Chiapas/Instituto Chiapaneco de Cultura, 1990) y *El mundo numinoso de los mayas,* que fue su tesis de maestría.

Xch'unel sk'op kajvaltik ta ch'ul na xchi'uk li jtsotsil jtseltaletike

Jacinto Arias Pérez

Tzotzil[1]

[From *El mundo numinoso de los mayas,* pp. 69–80. Spanish trans. Jorge Ferreiro Santana. México, D.F.: Colección SepSetentas, 1975. The 2nd edition was published in Tuxtla, Gutiérrez, Chiapas, by the Gobierno del Estado de Chiapas/Instituto Chiapaneco de Cultura, 1991.]

Ti ta ba'yi abteletike, kojtikinoj ti k'u x'elan ta xalik, ta spasik li ta slumal jtsotsiletik xchi'uk li jtseltaletike, xchi'uk ti k'usitik oy jelel k'u cha'al li vinike, k'u cha'al jelel ti k'usi chal ta jujuntal, ja' nox yech jelel k'u cha'al ta tsobolik; ja' yech k'u cha'al xkaltik li sts'unel ixime xchi'uk li ta jtuk'ulan jba jtuktike, ti k'usi xvinaj k'usi mu xvinaj. Taj va'i x'elan ti abtel iyich' pasele, iyich' ojtikinele, yu'un ja' skuenta ta xich' ak'el ta ilel ta stojol ti buch'utik mu xk'opojik ta bats'i k'op tsotsil xchi'uk ta tseltale; jutuk nox xcholbel smelol ti k'u x'elan xvinaj xch'iel sk'opojel ti vinik ants jtsotsil jtseltaletike, ti k'u x'elan ista ti stalel sjol yo'onik ti li' oyik ta sba balamile; yech noxtok iyich' chanbel smelol ti k'u x'elan xu' spoj xchabi sbaike.

Xcha'kojol abtel tey xvinaj li' ta vune, ja' tey ta xkiltik ti k'u x'elan iyich' ojtikinel ti sbats'i sjol yo'on xchi'uk xch'ulelik,[2] li ach' jch'ieletike, mu xa xko'olaj k'u cha'al sna'ik to ox ta sjol yo'onik xchi'uk xch'ulelik ti vo'ne jtotik jme'tik Mayaetike. Li abtel iyich' meltsanel li'e oy iyich' t'ujel cha' tos ti k'usi yiktaojik komel li namal krixchanoetike; ja' li k'usi k'otem ta ch'unel yu'un li krixchanoetike xchi'uk li poxiletik lavie. Li ta xchan kojol abtele, ja' tey xal ti k'u x'elan iyich' chanbel sk'oplal jchop bats'i vinik antsetik ti yolel ta sjelel ti stalel skuxlejike. Li abtel li'e ja' skuenta xchanel ti k'uxi sk'oplal li ach' k'opetike xchi'uk ti k'u xi stsakoj sba ta juchop ti k'uxi xk'ot o k'uxi xka'ibetik o smelol ti stalel skuxlejike.[3]

Li xch'unel li sk'op kajvaltik ta Ch'ul nae, yu'un ak'batik ti bats'i vinik antsetik li' ta vitstike, ja' to ox ti k'alal iyul tal ti jkaxlanetik vo'nee.[4] Va'i un ja' yech ista sba cha' tos ti k'usi i'ak'batike; li buch'utik ichanubtasvanik ta sk'op kajvaltike toj ep no ox iyak'beik yipal tajmek yo' la ti xmeltsaj o yo'onike. Li namal krixchanoetike yak'ojbeik yipal k'usitik yo' stak' xch'unik o ti sk'op kajvaltike, ja' ma'uk ta sjak'ik mi oy to k'usi yan o smelol k'usi stak' xch'unik o. Ja' yech jmoj sk'oplal yalojik ti k'u x'elan stak' xka'ibetik o smelole, ma'uk ti k'u onox cha'al xa'ibeik smelole; ja' xkaltik; ja' yech kom yu'unik ta xcha' tosol ja' nox ti mu snopojikuk lek ta sjol yo'onike. Le'e chopol ibat, yu'un iyak' ch'unuk ti k'usi yatel yo'onike mu xa xko'olaj k'u cha'al onox sna'ojbeik smelole, ti lek to ox smelol ta slo'iltabe sbaike, ja' yech k'u cha'al, chal li Paul Tillich, ti k'usi stu li k'usi xka'ibetik o smelol, k'usi xvinaj oe, ja' la chal ka'itik ti stak' xka'ibetik tsots sk'oplal k'u cha'al jna'betik smelol jtuktike, yu'un oy yip ti k'usi ta xal ka'itik smelole, yo' la ti lek xvinaj x'osilaj ta komon, yo' la ti xa'ibe lek smelol ti buch'u mu to sna'e; ak'o la ya'i sp'ijilik ti jchi'iltaktike, ta melel mu'yuk bu lek jnopojtik ta jol ta ko'ontik.[5] Ali ta sjol ta yo'on li paleetike;[6] ja'ta xal ka'itik yo' xka'ibetik o smelol k'usi xvinaj o, k'usi stu, ti ep ta tos smelol ta xal ka'itike, a le'e ma'uk ti makal ke chikomotik yu'un ti k'usi xa k'otem ta pasele mo'oj. Taj va'i x'elan ta xal ka'itik yo' ti xka'ibetik o smelol ti k'usi ta xal ti paleetike, li jSanperoetike mu k'usi chopol ta xa'iik, li stukike ta onox spasik ti k'u onox x'elan komem yu'unike, ak'o me vokol ta pasel yu'un onox ta spasik, sna'ojik o nox k'u x'elan xa'ibeik smelol ti stalel skuxlejike.

Ti k'usi xk'ot ta pasel yu'unik ti buch'u jp'el ti k'usi yale, mu xyal mu xmuy ti sjol yo'onike; stsakoj xa sba xchi'uk ti k'u x'elan xojtikinik la ti jmoj stalel skuxlejik ti bu nakal ti juchop jchi'iltaktike, yu'un ja' yech tsots sk'oplal chalik, ch'abal bu lek chich' ta muk' li jchanubtasvanejetik ta sk'op kajvaltike, ti ja' ta xal stukik ti k'u x'elan yo' xka'ibetik o smelole; yu'un ja' ta sk'an ta xp'ol ech'el slo'ilik ta slumal ti bats'i vinik antsetike; xavale bats'i jun yo'onik ti k'alal mu k'usi x'albatik ti k'alal ta xalik ti sk'op kajvaltike;. K'usi un oy bak'intik ti k'usi k'otem ta pasel li ach'toe (ja' k'u cha'al li mol pale Franses ta San Pero, ta xlik yotes ech'el li sone, li ak'ote, ti k'alal ta spas li mixa skuenta li kajvaltik ta Ch'ul nae) mu'yuk to ox bu xkiltik k'usi oy xak'ik iluk ta mukul ti xka'ibetik o smelol xchi'uk ti k'u x'elan ojtikinbilik li bats'i vinik antsetike. Li mol paleetike mu bu xkiltik ti ta xak'beik yipal ta xchanel li bats'i k'op tsotsil mi ja'uk tseltal; lek nox cha'iik yilel ti naka ta kaxlan k'op ta xchanubtasik ta sk'op kajvaltik ti buch'u mu sna' kaxlan k'ope. Taj va'i x'elan smelol slikesojik ti mol paleetike, ja' to ox ti k'alal i'och tal ti jkaxlanetik vo'nee, lek to xvinaj k'alal tana ti naka kapal ta bats'i k'op tsotsil xchi'uk tseltal xchi'uk kaxlan k'op, ja' nox yech yich'oj sbaik ta muk' ta stojol ti j'iloletike, yu'un sna'beik lek smelol k'u x'elan ta sp'isik ta vinik.[7]

Li mol paleetike chalik ti mu persauk xa'ibeik smelol k'usi li ta snopik xchi'uk ti stalel skuxlej ti bats'i vinik antsetike, mu'yuk k'usi tsots stu cha'iik ta sk'opon sbaik xchi'uk li jkaxlanetike. Taj x'elan mu'yuk ta xich'ik ta muk' ti talel kuxlejal yu'unik ti bats'i vinik antsetike, bats'i ja' yech lek xk'ot o k'u cha'al xkaltik jun ajvalil xchi'uk j'abteletik nox, ja' yech chal li Guillermo Bonfil,[8] ti mu bu lek jun yo'onik ta xcha' chopolike. jchop toyol jchop pek'el, ali Gonzalo Aguirre Beltrán ists'iba lek xka'itik tajmek smelol chalbe, ti sbalamilal buy isk'ej sbaike.[9] Sk'an xak' sbaik ta ojtikinel ti jchi'iltaktike, yu'un ja' tey joyol ta ch'ul vinajel ch'ul balamil ti xch'ulelike, yech onox slikelik tal ti oy xa jelavem ta chanib syen jabile, ti cha'ibeik smelol ta xcha' tosole. Ja' onox tey yak'oj sba ta stojol ti ajvaliletike, (ak'o mi oy onox jayvo'uk buch'utik lek skoltaoj sbaik, k'u cha'al li mol pale Bartolomé de las Casas, xchi'uk oy to jayvo'ik ti buch'utik tey ta x'abtejik lavie); ti ba'yie tey to ox xchi'uk ti buch'u oy ta yok ta sk'ob bats'i vinik antsetik k'alal iyul ti jkaxlanetik vo'nee; ta ts'akal ja' xa xchi'uk ti yajval osiletike, ti k'alal ta syu'elal li mol Porfirio Díaz, lavi une ja' xa xchi'uk li jkaxlanetike. Yech noxtok, k'u cha'al chal li Aguirre, li slumal bats'i vinik antsetike naka ja' sta o stak'inik li buch'utik oy tsots yabtelik ta sk'op kajvaltik ta Ch'ul nae, li stukike ja' slekilal stukik, yo' ti tey o ta sbatel osil ti k'u x'elan yilojik yojtikinojik ti stalel xch'ulelik li buch'utik nakajtik ta vitse, ma'uk ti yu'un ta skoltaik ta xchapanel ta lek ti xch'iel sk'opojelike.[10]

A taj jchi'iltaktike vokol to ta xvik' o satik ti k'usi sk'otel sbatel ti svayichike li k'u cha'al chal ali Karl Marx, ja' ti ta jlajesjbatik ta stojol ti ajvaliletike, ja' ti lek sjol yo'onik ti jchi'iltaktik xchi'uk ti sme'analike, li k'op taje ja' onox yech yabtelik o ta yalel ti k'uxi yo' xnijanvanik o li paleetik ta Ch'ul Nae, Ja' yech k'u cha'al xkaltik, ta xkak'tik ta a'yel jayp'eluk ti k'usi iyich' tabel ta sts'ib li mol Ovixpo Francisko Orosko (Ovixpo ta Ch'ul na ta Guadalajara), xchi'uk k'usuk ak'o me tsots albil sk'oplal k'alal ja' to ox va'al ta ajvalilal li Díaz, yu'un onox sna'ojbeik to xch'ulel ti paleetik ta vitstike.

> K'u cha'al li buch'utik oy yabtelike tey onox likem tal ta kajvaltik. Li j'abtel krixchanoe ta sp'is sat, bats'i tsots sk'oplal cha'i ti xch'unoj k'op, chak' sba ta stojol ti kajvaltik xchi'uk sbektal stakopal; ti k'alal tey xchi'uk ti ajvalile; taj va'i x'elan smelole, ti jch'unej k'ope, ma'uk ti yu'un ta sbik'tajes sbae xchi'uk ma'uk ti toj vokole. Ma'uk chitunotik yu'un li vinike, chitunotik yu'un li kajvaltike, ti buch'u chak' sba ta tunesel yu'un li kajvaltike ma'uk ti yu'un mu k'usi ta x'ak'bate. Me'on, k'ano ti k'u xa elane xchi'uk lavabtele, ta xcha' k'el muyel li vinajele. Ja' me tey li bats'i lekil kuxlejal une.[11]

Ja' tey xvinaj li b'uch'utik k'otem ta ch'unel yu'une xchi'uk li svinajesbel sk'oplale, ma'uk nox stukik ti sva'anoj sbaik oy yabtelike, yu'un oy to yan ti buch'utik yak'ojbeik yipal ta stael ti k'usi ta staik yo' ta skoltaik o ti jchi'iltaktike, yech noxtok k'u cha'al k'uxi ta sta stak'inik, yu'un ta melel a le'e tsots stunelik yo' ti mu xlaj o yabtel li jchanubtasvanejetik ta sk'op kajvaltike. Ja' yech lavi une sk'an ta xka'ibejbatik lek smelol, ka'ibetik smelol li sk'op kajvaltik k'u cha'al oy ta Ch'ul na li' ta yosil Chyapae; ja' xkaltik ti ja' yech stak'obil yu'un li vinik antsetik li' ta sba balamile.

Li buch'utik sna'ik kajvaltik ta Ch'ul na li' ta Chyapae, yech k'u cha'al ta xa'ibeik smelol li buch'utik va'ajtik oy yabtelike (k'usi un ja' jutuk k'u cha'al li pale frances ta Ch'enal vo'e), yu'un ja' tsots yip xch'ulel, li k'usi yak'oj ta yo'one ja'uk la lekuk ti xch'ulele, li sbek'tal stakopale jutuk nox yak'oj ta yo'on. Ali ants viniketik stak' xbak'ik xkiltike stak' xk'ataj ti mu xa xkiltik k'usi ta spase. Mu a'yibaj cha'i li paleetike, k'usi un toj tsots sk'oplal cha'iik, bats'i xp'ejte p'ejte sk'oplal yu'unik li xchanubtasel sk'op kajvaltik Kristoe, ja' skuenta chalbeik li buch'utik me'onetik xnijet xchimetike yu'un la ja' mu xlaj xkuxlejik ta sbatel osil. Taj x'elan xch'unel yu'unike bats'i tsots to sk'oplal yu'unik, mu to xko'olaj k'u cha'al naka ja' ta yo'onik ti k'usi oy mu'yuk staik ta balamil ti jchi'iltaktike, le'e chopol li k'usi x'elan ta sba balamile, jot o chak'be ma'uk xa ta xch'ulelik, xi'el sba skuenta li jch'uleltike, chalik ti k'usi leke ja' xa nox la ti chak namajuk taje. Ti k'usi chalik tajmeke, ti k'alal ta xk'opojike, yu'un la ja' ta "spojik ti xch'ulelike" yech noxtok "ta la xbatik k'alal vinajel," tsots ta sk'anik ta lekil k'op ti smulike, xchi'uk noxtok ja' yech ta staik o ti slajesel smulik ta kajvaltike; ta stam sbaik, ta xat yo'onik ta skotol k'ak'al, k'usi un ja' jutuk nox stuk'ulanoj sbaik ta slekubtasel ti xch'ulelike.

Ja' chak'beik yipal ta smantalil li k'usi jutuk nox sk'oplale, ma'uk li k'usi tsots sk'oplale. Li k'usi ta xojtikinbeik lek k'u x'elan slikeb li k'usi oye, ja' k'u cha'al li slikeb sts'unbal vinik antsetik, slikeb yibel snopbenal yu'un ti jchi'iltaktike, slikeb yabtel k'usi ta staik o stak'inik ti jchi'iltaktike, slikeb yibel stalel xch'iel ti jchi'iltaktike, oy to yan ti ja' chalik ti ja' ta xlekub o ech'el stalel skuxlej ti viniketike; mu x'ak'bat xch'unobil yu'un ti jchi'iltaktik taje, yu'un ja' xvinaj ti toj ech' xa nox ta sk'an stuk ma'uk xa yech ti stalel skuxlej stukike. Ta jp'el cha'p'el nox xkaltik, li paleetik taj va'i buy sbalamilale yu'un lek chapanbil yu'un ta sk'op kajvalktik ti ba'yi tajmeke, yu'un ja' yech chanubtasbil k'u cha'al ti svo'ne k'op li kajvaltike, ja' yech ta xchanubtasvan ti stak' la xich' pojel ti jch'uleltike ja' ma'uk li jbek'tal jtakopaltike. Xchi'uk k'usuk ti mi ixch'unik ti ja' ta xpoj o xch'ulelike yu'un xa ja' sk'an ti ochemot xa ta xchanbel sk'op kajvaltik ta Ch'ul na, ti buch'u sna' kajvaltik ta Ch'ul nae ja' xkaltik ti jutuk nox sk'oplale, ja' nox ti ak'o yich' vo'e (ti bu oy yan smelol taj va'i x'elan li'e, tey ta tael ta k'elel ta *Summa Theologica,* ja' smeltsanoj Tomás de Aquino, bats'i k'uuk nox svunal skuenta li slikeb yibel ti sk'op kajvaltike, le' to ox ts'ibabil k'alal sk'an to ox stsob sbaik ta xcha' kojol ti buch'utik oy yabtelik ta sk'op kajvaltike).

Ja' yech un, va'i un, xvinaj ti k'usi naka xa nox ja' xvinaj ta xch'ulelik ti stalel skuxlej ti jchi'iltaktike (ja' yech ti sk'opik une), ja' jutuk yich'ojik ta muk' li sbats'i talel ta sba balamile. Tey xtal noxtok ta xkak'tik iluk jutuk k'usi x'elan iyich' a'yibel smelol skuenta li ba'yi abteletike.

Ti k'u x'elan oy chapal sk'oplal stak' xilbeik smelol li ta xch'ulelik li buch'utik sna'beik sk'op kajvaltik ta Ch'ul na li jnaklomaletik ta yosilal Chyapae; oy smelol ta alel ti k'u x'elan ta xalik, k'u x'elan chil slumalik li viniketike, ti k'usi ta xalike tsots sk'oplal (chalik), ochem kajvaltik ta yo'onik, tey ta stsak sba ech'el ta yut xch'ulelik. Li k'usi ta xalik li jtsotsiletik xchi'uk li jtseltaletike yan o k'u x'elan chalik cha'ibeik smelol; xchi'uk k'usuk ja' ti jmoj ti stalel sts'unbalike ma'uk cha'ibeik smelol ti ja' tey xbat smelole, mo'oj yu'un chalik ti ja' yeche; ti k'u x'elan chalik cha'ibeik smelol li ta xch'ulelik ti bu mu xkiltike, ja' ta xalik ti oyuk lekilal ti buy xvinaj nakalik ti jchi'iltaktike.

Oy to yan ti k'usi jelel ta spasik ti buch'utik sna'beik sk'op kajvaltik ta Chul nae, taj va'i buy lumetike, mu'yuk k'usi yatel yo'onik taj va'i skuenta jch'uleltike; sna'ojik xa stukik k'u x'elan kuxulik ja' nox ti mu xkiltike; ja' nox yech k'u cha'al kuxulik ta xkiltike. Li xch'ulele kuxul onox ta xkom ak'o me chamemuk xa; ti k'alal tey xa ox ta jk'ol o balamil une mu epuk jelel k'u cha'al kuxul ta sba balamil li' toe, li k'u x'elan xkuxlejal ta ba'yie ja'tik nox la stsakalul yech xbat ta xcha' jotol balamil. Ti k'u x'elan yak'ojbeik yipal xkuxlej sk'opojelik ti jchi'iltaktik ta jujuntale ja' nox yech li k'alal ta tsobole, chalbe sbaik ti k'usi lek stak' spasike, ja' yech k'u cha'al bu xkiltik xchi'uk k'alal mu xkiltik.

Ti k'alal sta xch'iel sk'opojel k'u cha'al jun bats'i vinik, jun bats'i ants, yu'un ta xchan ti k'u x'elan stalel xkuxlej ti yan xchi'iltake; Ti k'u x'elan chal chak'beik yipal spasele yu'un ta xak'ik iluk ta melel, ma'uk ti mu xvinaje. Ali tsitsele ti k'usi ta xlaj o li smulike li' nox la ta staik ta sba balamile, ma'uk to ta yan o balamil. Oy to yan slo'ilal, lek chalbe smelol li Mircea Eliade, stak' xkaltik ti chalbe sba stukike yu'un ja' toj ech' nox toyol xa'i sbaik xchi'uk ti sp'ijil sjol yo'onike, ja' nox yech noxtok toj toyol xa'i sbaik ta yabtelik ti k'usi ta spasike. Bats'i lek yak'oj sbaik ta ojtikinel k'u x'elan kuxul chamalik, ma'uk ti ta makal ti k'u x'elan ti sjol yo'on kuxulike. Li k'u x'elan kuxul chamalike, lek vinajem ta sba balamil, ja' nox yech li sba balamile ojtikinbilik uk. K'alal tey nakajtike ma'uk ti stukike, oy li k'usitik oy ta sba balamile tey xchi'ukik; ja' nox yech li k'usitik oy ta sba balamile jtunel yu'unik uk, yu'un ja' oy o li balamil uke; ja' yech stak' xkaltik ti tey kuxulik o ta xvik' satik xchi'uk ti vinajel balamile xchi'uk stukik.[12]

Yech noxtok ali jchope ja' li paleetike, li jchope ja' li buch'utik tey nakajtik ta vitstike, oyik ta k'op xchi'uk jun jteklum ja' xch'unojbeik sko'op cha'vo' *Weltanschauung,* yan o snopobil yu'unik k'u cha'al li jtsotsiletik xchi'uk li jtseltaletike, ali vinike ta xich' sp'ijilik xchi'uk ti vinajel balamile, yan mi ja' li vinik jkaxlan une, naka ta sa'be ech'el smelol ta xch'ulel. Yech'o lavi une, lek xa na'bil skotol li k'usitik ta xch'ulelike, stak' skopon sbaik, stak' spasik, ja' tey ta xtal ta sjol ta yo'on ti jchi'iltaktike, ta xkoltaatik yu'un svokolik ta komon ti buch'utik xch'unojik ti k'usi xa'ibeik o smelole, mi jun mu'yuk buch'u yech yan o stalel; ti mi ch'abal li yane, li k'usi ta xch'ulelike tey, k'usi un ja' mu xvinaj xchi'uk ti k'usi xka'ibetik o smelole, ja' yech k'u cha'al li balamil li'e ch'abal k'usi oy xch'ulel. Ali k'usi oy xch'ulele toj p'ij, ta xu'unin ti k'usi sk'an yo'on spase yu'un ta xal ech'el ti k'usi smelole. Taj x'elan ta xalbe ech'el smelole,oy yik'al xvinaj ta sbats'i stalel skuxlej, mi mo'oje ta yan o ta sta talel.

Iyich' xa alel ti k'usi xka'ibetik o smelol k'usi xvinaj o ti stalel skuxlej li bats'i vinik antsetik ta sba'yi xchi'uk ta xcha' kojol li jpok abtel li'e. Ja' xa ta jk'eltik noxtok li k'usi xka'ibetik o smelol li yan o stalel skuxlejike, ti yu'un ta persa ochem ech'el te yo' buy xch'ulel ti Mayaetike.

Ich' Vo'

Ali ich' vo'e, chalik li paleetik teyik ta Chul nae, ja' k'u cha'al chkaltik to ox ta ba'yie, ja' xch'unel ti chi cha' ayanotik ta ach'e, ti ta x'och ta stojol kajvaltik li vinike; taje ja' ta xka'ibetik o smelol ti yu'un ta x'och yan xch'ulel li xch'ulele. Ti yu'un ja' jtos oy smelol staojik ti yu'un ja' xa ta xlaj o, ta xch'ay o ti k'u x'elan bu oy ti viniketike; le'e ja' yolel ta spasel ta yosilalik, ja' chbat sk'oplal yu'unik li k'u cha'al, lavie xchi'uk li ta ts'akal ti ma'uk xa ta skuenta ti vinike. Ja' yech k'u cha'al li *Weltanschauung,* taj jchi'iltaktik taje ta sk'an ta sk'opon sbaik li k'u cha'al xa'ibeik o smelol, xvinajik o ti k'alal xich'ik vo'e; yu'un ja' yech snopojik ta slikebal, ta xbatik ta jujun jteklum, ja' toj tsots sk'oplal yu'unik li ta sk'in yajvalik ta jujun jteklume, ta xak'beik yich' vo' ti k'oxetike, yu'un la ak'o pasuk ta xch'amal kajvaltik, ti k'u cha'al sna'ik li kajvaltik ta Chul nae.

¿K'u x'elan cha'iik li jSan Peroetike,[13] ti k'u x'elan xa'ibeik o smelol xvinajik o xchi'uk stalel skuxlej li jkaxlanetike? le'e naka ja' yech stalel skuxlejalik ti ja' yech xvinajik o li jkaxlanetike. Ja' nox xu' ta spasik ti k'u x'elan stak' pasel cha'iik ta xch'ulelike. K'u cha'al chal li sk'op kajvaltike, ta xich'ik ak'bel ja' nox li k'oxetike, ja' yech cha'ibeik smelol ti ta x'och xch'ulel yu'unik li k'oxetike. Ali buch'u ta sk'el li vune ak'o syules ta sjol ali xch'ulel xchi'uk sbek'tal stakopale ch'akal, mu xnaki ta anil ta jbek'tal jtakopaltik, ta xkom ta k'unk'un to, ja' ti k'u x'elan ta xch'i ech'el li k'oxe, ta xchan ech'el sp'ijil stsail; ja' yech k'u cha'al taj une. Ti sme' jun k'ox naka to ta x'ayane lek yich'oj ta muk' mi mu k'usi spas, yo' ti mu xch'ay o xch'ulel ti yole. Ti k'u x'elan stak' stuk'ulanike, chalik ti mu la stak' nom xbat te yo' buy snae, mu stak' xbat ti bu mu xojtikinik ti balamile, yu'un ja' chalik ti yik'al xch'ay ta be xch'ulel li k'oxe, mu xa teuk ta sbek'tal stakopal ta xkom. Ti mi o bu xlok'ik ech'el ta xanbale, ti me'ile tey nox ta sk'el julikel mi ta xich' ik' ti yole, oy yech noxtok ti bu xchoti xchi'uk ti yole, ta sk'as ni' yanal te' ta svelbe o ech'el ti xch'ulele, yo' la ti mu xkome, ak'o la xchi'in ech'el ti sbek'tal stakopale.

Taj x'elan smelol yich'ojik ta muk' ta xik'beik ech'el ti xch'ulele, yu'un la ja' chalik ti mu to bu tsots nakal ti xch'ulel ta spat ta xokone, tey onox nopola'a, ja' nox ti mu to toj tsotsuk tey une. Iyich' a'yibel smelol ali ich' vo'e ja' xa ta xkoltavan skuenta ta xtuk'ib o, ta stao yip, yu'un ja' ti mu to bu tsots ti xch'ulele. Koliyal taj x'elan smelole, ti k'oxe yu'un lek xa tsots ti xch'ulel ta xkome, mu xa toj xtae ta chamel, ti k'alal x'och lek xch'ulel ta sbek'tal stakopale, yu'un ja' smoton ta x'ak'bat k'alal ta xich' vo'e, yu'un xa ja' slekilal ta xkom, xkuch xa yu'un ti k'usitik tsots palta snuptan ta spat ta xokone. Oy to skoltael ta k'op yu'un stot li k'oxe, ti k'alal xlaj ti ich' vo'e li stot li k'oxe xi ta xalbe smelol ta sk'opon ti ch'ul totile:

> . . . Lavi ilaj xa ti smelole
> Och xa xch'ulel,
> Och xa yanima
> Ti yaj anjel ryoxe. (ja' li k'oxe)[14]

Skuenta li bats'i jnaklejetike, oy to yan k'usi xka'ibetik o smelol li ich' vo'e, ja' k'u cha'al li k'oxe, yu'un sk'an to koltael yu'un ti stot sme'e, ja' li' ta sba balamile, taj va'i x'elan koltael ta stae yu'un xa tey ta xkom ta yu'un, ja' nox ti mu xa xkiltike. Ati smelol ti k'usi xtun o li ich' vo'e, yu'un onox tey ta xkoltavan yu'un kajvaltik, ko'ol xch'unel k'u cha'al jpojvanej jchabivanej ali (jpetum-jkuchum). Ali k'usi sk'an chal li jp'el k'op petumajel, ja' chal a'yuk ti yu'un ta spet li k'oxe, li k'op le'e ko'ol xk'opojik ta skotolik jayibuk jteklum, yu'un ja' yech ti stak' xkalbetik smelol k'u x'elan ta spasik ich' vo' li buch'utik sna'ik kajvaltik ta Chul nae.

[Translation from Spanish: Juan de la Torre López]
[Traducción del español: Juan de la Torre López]

Notes

1. Tzotzil speakers call their language Batz'i K'op, "true language." At the end of the twentieth century there were more than 514,000 Tzotzil speakers, living primarily in the state of Chiapas. The alphabet the author uses is among the Indigenous-language alphabets in Chiapas that resulted from the practice and the exchange of experiences

Notas

1. Los hablantes de tzotzil llaman a su lengua *batz'i k'op,* "idioma verdadero." A finales del siglo XX esta lengua contaba con más de 514,000 hablantes localizados principalmente en el estado de Chiapas. El alfabeto que emplea el autor es uno de los alfabetos en las lenguas indígenas de Chiapas que surgieron de la práctica y del intercambio

among the members of Sna Jtz'ibajom (House of the Writer) and the Mayas-Zoques Writers Group. In the early 1990s the writers belonging to these independent organizations held a series of work sessions in Tuxtla Gutiérrez with the National Institute for Adult Education (INEA) and the Department of Ethnic Cultures of the State Government of Chiapas. The objective was jointly to establish practical alphabets in languages of interest to the INEA: Tzeltal, Tzotzil, Tojolabal, Chol, and Zoque.

2. The translators have opted to translate *numinoso* (numinous) with the Tzotzil word meaning "sacredness" or "spirituality"; from the Tzotzil *ch'ul,* "sacred," from which derives *ch'ulel,* "soul," "spirit," "sacred force." The term "numinous" was coined by the German theologian Rudolf Otto (1869–1937) in reference to an awareness of the sacred. For him, the "numinous" is the object of religion, something superior to reason, goodness, or beauty. "Numinous" is derived from the Latin word *numen,* "divinity" or "divine will."

3. There are very few publications that deal with this chapter's content. With regard to religion, there is only one systematic study: Dr. John Early, "The Sons of San Lorenzo in Zinacantán" (Ph.D. dissertation, Cambridge, Mass.: Harvard University, 1965); in the area of medicine, William R. Holland's book *Medicina maya en los Altos de Chiapas* (Mexico City: INI, 1963) is the only existing study; the reader must consult these two sources for more information. To understand the type of relationship that exists between Indians and *ladinos* in the Chiapas Highlands (examined in Arias' first chapter), one must consult Gonzalo Aguirre Beltrán, *Regiones de refugio: El desarrollo de la comunidad y el proceso dominical en Mestizoamérica* (Mexico City: INI, 1967); Pierre Van den Berghe has also written on this topic: "Ladino-Indian Relations in the Highlands of Chiapas, Mexico," *Social Forces* 40 (1961): 63–67. There is a good doctoral dissertation on shamanism: Daniel Silver, "Zinacanteco Shamanism" (Cambridge, Mass.: Harvard University, 1966). A good example of an outsider's perspective regarding the transformation of the Tzotziles and Tzeltales is Henning Silverts' study "Social and Cultural Changes in a Tzeltal (Mayan) Municipie, Chiapas, México," in *Proceedings of the Thirty-second International Congress of Americanists, Copenhagen, 1956* (1958). (a.n.)

4. See Henry R. Wagner, *The Life and Writing of Bartolomé de Las Casas* (Albuquerque: University of New Mexico Press, 1967). (a.n.)

5. Paul Tillich, "Theology and Symbolism," in *Religious Symbolism,* ed. F. Ernest Johnson (New York: Institute for Religious and Social Studies, 1955), p. 109. (a.n.)

6. Priests are called *jtotik pale* or *jalaltotik.* Here *jtotik* or *jalal-* denotes numinosity. A *jtotik pale* is, in fact, considered to be a numinous being: it is believed that he does not eat, drink alcohol, or sleep with a woman. Like God, he only partakes of their soul. But Indigenous people have recently begun to form a more realistic idea of priests, as the relationship between them broadens. This new awareness has resulted, for example, in the expulsion of a priest from a certain community because his behavior did not meet local expectations. (a.n.)

7. These prayers have been maintained because it is believed that their lack of intelligibility is highly powerful against invisible enemies, particularly the devil (*pukuj*); just like human beings, those enemies understand no language other than Tzotzil and Tzeltal. This idea perhaps originates with lower-class *ladinos,* who possess analogous beliefs; for example, they believe that prayers in Latin constitute powerful exorcisms again the devil. (a.n.)

8. Guillermo Bonfil, "Del indigenismo de la Revolución a la antropología crítica," in *De eso que llaman antropología mexicana* (Mexico City: Editorial Nuestro Tiempo, 1970), pp. 39–65. (a.n.)

9. Gonzalo Aguirre Beltrán, *Regiones de refugio: El desarrollo de la comunidad y el proceso dominical en Mestizoamérica* (Mexico City: INI, 1967). (a.n.)

10. Ibid., p. 44. (a.n.)

11. Francisco Orozco y Jiménez, "Carta pastoral del arzobispo Fran-

de experiencias entre los integrantes de Sna Jtz'ibajom (Casa del Escritor) y de la Asociación de Escritores Mayas-Zoques. A principios de la última década del siglo XX los escritores de estas organizaciones independientes sostuvieron varias reuniones de trabajo en Tuxtla Gutiérrez con el Instituto Nacional de Educación para Adultos (INEA) y el Departamento de Culturas Étnicas del Gobierno de Chiapas, a fin de alcanzar acuerdos en el establecimiento de alfabetos prácticos en las lenguas de interés para el INEA: tzeltal, tzotzil, tojolabal, chol y zoque.

2. Los traductores han optado por traducir "numinoso" con la voz tzotzil "sacralidad" o "espiritualidad," de *ch'ul,* "sagrado," de donde se deriva *ch'ulel,* "alma," "espíritu," "fuerza sagrada." El termino "numinoso" fue acuñado por el teólogo alemán Rudolf Otto (1869–1937) para referirse a la conciencia de lo sagrado; para él, lo "numinoso" es el objeto de la religión, algo superior a la razón, la bondad y la belleza. *Numinoso* se deriva de la palabra latina *numen,* "divinidad" o "voluntad divina."

3. Existen muy pocas publicaciones acerca del contenido del presente capítulo; a decir verdad, por lo que toca a la religión, sólo hay un estudio sistemático, que es el del doctor John Early, "The Sons of San Lorenzo in Zinacantan" (tesis de doctorado, Cambridge, Mass.: Harvard University, 1965); en el campo de la medicina sólo existe el libro de William R. Holland, *Medicina maya en los altos de Chiapas* (México, D.F.: INI, 1963). Para mayores detalles, el lector debe remitirse a esas dos fuentes. Para comprender el tipo de relación que existe entre indios y ladinos de las tierras altas de Chiapas, se debe consultar a Gonzalo Aguirre Beltrán, *Regiones de refugio: El desarrollo de la comunidad y el proceso dominical en Mestizoamérica* (México, D.F.: INI, 1967); Pierre Van den Berghe, "Ladino-Indian Relations in the Highlands of Chiapas, México," *Social Forces* 40 (1961): 63–67, también ha escrito acerca de ese tema. Hay una buena tesis de doctorado que trata del chamanismo: Daniel Silver, "Zinacanteco Shamanism" (Cambridge, Mass., Harvard University, 1966). Henning Silverts, "Social and Cultural Changes in a Tzeltal (Mayan) Municipie, Chiapas, México," en *Proceedings of the Thirty-second International Congress of Americanists (Copenhagen, 1956)* (1958) es un buen ejemplo del punto de vista de un extraño acerca de la transformación de los tzotziles y los tzeltales. (n.a.)

4. Véase Henry R. Wagner, *The Life and Writing of Bartolomé de Las Casas* (Albuquerque: University of New Mexico Press, 1967). (n.a.)

5. Paul Tillich, "Theology and Symbolism," en *Religious Symbolism,* comp. F. Ernest Johnson (New York: Institute for Religious and Social Studies, 1955), p. 109. (n.a.)

6. A los sacerdotes se les llama *jtotik pale* o *jalaltotik.* En ese caso, *jtotik* o *jalal* denotan numinosidad. A decir verdad, un *jtotik pale* es considerado como un ser numinoso; por ejemplo, se cree que no come, ni bebe alcohol, ni duerme con una mujer, etc.; lo mismo que Dios, sólo toma el alma de esas cosas. No obstante, últimamente y debido al hecho de que los indígenas tienen mayor relación con los sacerdotes, empiezan a formarse una imagen más realista de ellos. Una de las consecuencias de esa conciencia es el hecho de la expulsión de un sacerdote de cierta comunidad porque su comportamiento no iba de acuerdo con el que se esperaba de él. (n.a.)

7. Se han conservado esas oraciones porque se considera que su falta de inteligibilidad es sumamente poderosa contra los enemigos invisibles, especialmente el diablo (*pukuj*), ya que, como seres humanos, dichos enemigos sólo comprenden el tzotzil y el tzeltal pero no otras lenguas. La idea quizás haya sido tomada de los ladinos de clase baja que poseen creencias análogas; por ejemplo, creen que las oraciones en latín constituyen poderosos exorcismos contra el diablo. (n.a.)

8. Guillermo Bonfil, "Del indigenismo de la Revolución a la antropología crítica," en *De eso que llaman antropología mexicana* (México, D.F.: Editorial Nuestro Tiempo, 1970), pp. 39–65. (n.a.)

9. Gonzalo Aguirre Beltrán, *Regiones de refugio: El desarrollo de la comunidad y el proceso dominical en Mestizoamérica* (México, D.F.: Instituto Nacional Indigenista, 1967). (n.a.)

cisco Orozco y Jiménez de Guadalajara," in *Liberalismo en México, 1857–1929*, ed. Ardí Callcott (Stanford, Calif.: Stanford University Press, 1931). (a.n.)

12. Mircea Eliade, *The Sacred and Profane: The Nature of Religion* (New York: Sheed & Ward, 1959). (a.n.)

13. That is, the Tzotzil people of San Pedro Chenalhó. (a.n.)

14. Early, "The Sons of San Lorenzo in Zinacantán," p. 81. (a.n.)

10. Ibídem, p. 44. (n.a.)

11. Francisco Orozco y Jiménez, "Carta pastoral del arzobispo Francisco orozco y Jiménez de Guadalajara," en *Liberalismo en México, 1857–1929*, coord. Ardí Callcott (Stanford, Calif.: Stanford University Press, 1931). (n.a.)

12. Mircea Eliade, *The Sacred and Profane: The Nature of Religion* (New York: Sheed & Ward, 1959). (n.a.)

13. Es decir, los tzotziles de San Pedro Chenalhó. (n.a.)

14. Early, "The Sons of San Lorenzo in Zinacantán," p. 81. (n.a.)

Catholic Beliefs among the Tzotziles and Tzeltales

Jacinto Arias Pérez

Tzotzil[1]

[From "The Numinous World of the Maya: Contemporary Structure and Change," pp. 63–65. M.A. thesis, Dept. of Anthropology, Catholic University of America, Washington, D.C., 1973.]

In the previous chapters I have analyzed the interaction of the Tzotzil-Tzeltal people with their environment and beings-other-than-human, both at the individual and at the social level, using as frames of reference the production of maize and the preservation of the "self" in its tangible and intangible aspects. The analysis was aimed at providing non–Tzotzil-Tzeltal speakers with a brief presentation of the concept of the ideal Tzotzil-Tzeltal man and woman and the conception of human existence; the techniques used for their preservation were also discussed.

The following two chapters are concerned with an analysis of phenomena which take place when the modern "numinous" clashes with the Maya "numinous."[2] Two main Western cultural heritages have been chosen for the present chapter: Christian beliefs and modern medicine . . . Some modern principles related to each set of cultural symbolics will be discussed in the present chapter.[3]

Catholic Beliefs

Catholic beliefs have been forced onto the native Highlanders since the outset of the conquest.[4] Since then, two very different kinds of outlook have been in conflict; efforts at reconciling the two outlooks have been ignored by the missionaries. Westerners have continued to impose their religious symbols regardless of any philosophy of symbolism; they maintain a static concept of relationship between the symbol and the symbolized, that is, a deterministic relationship between the two is unconsciously held. Such a misunderstanding obviously goes against the nature of the symbol, which is a dynamic communicative instrument, since as Paul Tillich states, the great function of symbols is "to point beyond themselves, in the power of that to which they point, to open up levels of reality which otherwise are closed. And to open up levels of the human mind of which we otherwise are not aware."[5] But in the mind of the "priest"[6] there seems to be only one possible message capable of communication by an already established immutable set of symbols. In this respect, the priests' conception of symbols and that of the Indigenous people do not differ a bit; both defend static and exclusive attitudes toward symbols, which makes the fusion of cultural symbolics very difficult, if not impossible.

The consequence of such static minds combined with a

very strong ethnocentrism is the lack of interest among the missionaries in implanting "meaningful symbols" in order to convey their message to the native communities; they seem quite satisfied when they have the chance to function only as ritual technicians. Except for spasmodic attempts very recently (for example, the French priest in San Pedro is starting to introduce local music and dance in his Catholic ceremonies), there have been no attempts to use native symbols and images in order to make people grasp their message. The diocesan priests, especially, show no interest in learning the Tzotzil and Tzeltal languages; they appear to feel satisfied to continue the tradition of teaching prayers in Spanish to people who do not know that language at all. This tradition, started by missionaries of the colonial period, is still apparent in some prayers which contain a mixture of Tzotzil and Tzeltal and Spanish; these prayers are kept as part of the repertory of shamans since they enhance their sophistication.[7]

Priests believe that it is worthless to try to understand the native mind and culture and work through them to communicate *ladino* values. This contempt for native cultural values fits well the patron-slave relationship that Guillermo Bonfil talks about[8] or the asymmetrical relationship of superior and inferior which Gonzalo Aguirre Beltrán eloquently writes about in his *Regiones de refugio*.[9] One has to note that these persons surrounded by a numinous atmosphere have been functioning for more than four centuries as intermediaries for these kinds of relationship. They have always been on the side of the patrons (except some outstanding personalities such as Fray Bartolomé de Las Casas and a few of these presently working in the area); first with the encomenderos in the colonial period, then with the hacendados in the Porfirio Díaz regime, and now with the "lord *ladinos*." Furthermore, Indian communities are, as Aguirre states, the source of income for Catholic cult specialists who, for their own advantage, perpetuate the numinous outlook of the Highlanders instead of helping them to "rationalize" their existential situation.[10]

It will take a long time for those people to wake up from the soporific effect of the "opium" that Karl Marx talked about, since submission to the patrons in the virtuous form of humbleness and poverty is still a dominant theme of these priests' sermons in the churches. By way of example here are some words extracted from the pastoral letter of Archbishop Francisco Orozco (Archdiocese of Guadalajara), which, although pronounced during the Díaz regime, still express the Highlander churchmen's spirit:

> Since authority is derived from God, the Christian workman sanctifies and makes sublime his obedience by serving God in the person of his masters; in this way obedience is neither humiliating nor difficult. We do not serve man; we serve God, and he who serves God will not remain unrewarded . . . Poor, love your humble state and your work; turn your gaze toward Heaven. There is the true wealth.[11]

Hence, fanaticism and proselytism are not the only factors in maintaining the status quo; social and economic interests are also very important incentives for the continuation of such missionaries' activities. But now we have to turn to a deeper understanding of the Chiapanecan Catholic religion, considering that it is an existential response to the world.

Catholicism in Chiapas as understood by its leaders (with few exceptions, such as the French priest in San Pedro) is highly supernaturalistic: what matters most is the supernatural health of the soul; the body matters little. The tangible human being is outranked by the intangible "supernatural aspect of it." Subconsciously, priests take quite seriously and quite literally the teaching of Christ which refers to the blessed poor because they will possess eternal life. They still do not believe in the accomplishment of individuals as dynamic beings capable of realizing their potential. The belief is still very strong that the material part of humankind is bad and that "the mundane," as opposed to "the spiritual," is a dangerous milieu for the spirit; perfection is understood to be possible only by running away from this milieu. The most constant slogans used whenever preaching are "to save the soul" and "to go to heaven." A strong emphasis on sin and means to gain God's forgiveness is a constant preoccupation, with little worry for the means to make the soul better; negative rather than positive commandments are emphasized. Sciences, deemed primarily to lead to improvements in the worldly aspect of humankind, such as sociology, psychology, economics, anthropology, etc., are abjured by these persons as a sign of exaggerated ambition and inappropriate to their status. Briefly, priests in this area have been prepared in the old style and brought up on the old theology which teaches that the soul can be saved without the salvation of the body. They further believe that in order to be saved it is necessary to be Catholic; being Catholic means little more than being baptized. (For further information on this matter see the *Summa Theologica* of Thomas Aquinas and any of the theological textbooks written before Vatican Council II.)

Such is, then, the supernaturalistic outlook of human life which (ideally) underestimates the natural aspect. Next is a brief existential analysis of the content of the foregoing chapters.

In the existential framework the supernaturalistic outlook of Chiapanecan Catholics is an explanation of human interaction with the world; interaction which, sublimated (they say) by grace, becomes a channel for supernatural life. The Tzotzil-Tzeltal's interaction with the world and fellow humans, on the contrary, is not taken as a means but as an end in itself; interaction with the invisible world is aimed at maintaining the harmony of the tangible habitat of humankind.

Another difference from Catholic attitude is that among these people there is no preoccupation with supernatural life; they already live in the invisible world at the same time that they live in the visible one. The soul persists after death, but its existence in the "other world" is not very different from its existence in "this world"; the former is just a continuation of the latter. The efforts of the individual and the society are directed toward their own welfare in both the visible and the invisible worlds.

To become a real man or woman is to adjust oneself to the traditional ideal; the struggle for accomplishment is aimed at the actual visible fulfillment, not at the invisible one. Sanction and reward take place in "this world" not in the "other world." In other words, and paraphrasing Mircea Eliade, it can be said that these people look at themselves with "transhuman structure" just as everything surrounding them has a "transstructure." They have an open existence, for they are not strictly confined to their mode of being. Their existence is open to the world just as the world's existence is open to them. In living they are never alone; part of the world lives in them just as the world is nothing without them since the world lives in them. That is, they live in a constant "existential awakening" of the Cosmos and themselves.[12]

Hence, the priests, on the one hand, and the Highlanders, on the other hand, deal with numinosity, which follow opposite antagonistic *Weltanschauungen:* the Tzotzil-Tzeltal people are worldly oriented, while *ladinos* are supernaturally oriented. Now, it is well known that each "numinous" communicates, actualizes, and awakens itself in people's minds and existence through certain approved sets of symbols; neither one has any existential meaning without the other; the "numinous" is existentially inactive without the symbol, just as the symbol is mute without the "numinous." The "numinous" is dynamic; it draws to itself any attractive channel to communicate its content. This attractive channel can be one which is discovered within the culture or introduced from outside.

. . . Now let us look at what happens to foreign cultural symbolics after they have been forced into the Maya "numinous."

Baptism

Baptism, according to the churchmen discussed above, is the sacrament of rebirth and incorporation of humans into the kingdom of God; it is a symbol of the "supernatural transformation" of the soul. Rather than an event designed to cope with humankind's worldly situation, it is a worldly event designed to cope with what is deemed (by them) to be humankind's unworldly present and future. Such is the *Weltanschauung* that these persons want to communicate by means of the symbol that is called baptism; with such a principle in mind they go to each pueblo, especially at the time of each patron saint's feast, and baptize children in order to make them Catholics.

How do the natives[13] receive these *ladino* cultural symbolics? It can only be according to their own numinous outlook. Since this sacrament is mainly administered to children, baptism has been taken as a symbol of the act of "giving a soul to the baby." The reader must recall that the soul is detachable and does not abide in the body at once but enters bit by bit as the child grows and acquires education and wisdom. For this reason the mother of a newly born child takes precautions in order to avoid any danger that would cause the loss of the child's soul. Some of these precautions include not going far away from home or walking in unfamiliar places which would cause the soul of the child to lose track and not follow its body. On a journey, whenever the mother (with the child) stops and sits for a while to catch her breath, she must take some branches to sweep the place where she was sitting with the baby so that the soul will not stay there but follow its body.

The idea that these precautions give is that the soul of the child is not quite fixed to this body as yet; it is close to the body but not firmly attached. To correct this defect baptism has been found appropriate. Thanks to this ceremony the child will be protected strongly against illness; by the entrance of the soul to the body (through the rite of baptism) the child becomes better equipped to resist dangerous attacks against his or her person. The words of the child's father addressed to the godfather after the ceremony support this statement:

With this ceremony,
there has entered the spirit
there has entered the soul
of the Angel of God (the child).[14]

Another meaning of baptism for the natives is that a child needs the support and protection of elders in the visible world so that this same support and protection may exist in the invisible abode of the child. The idea and function of baptism also enhance the general belief in "supporter-protectors" (*jpetum-jkuchum*). Hence the term *petumajel,* which denotes the act of embracing a child, is a common expression in some communities to denote the Catholic rite under discussion.

Notes

1. Tzotzil speakers call their language Batz'i K'op, "true language." At the end of the twentieth century there were more than 514,000 Tzotzil speakers, living primarily in the state of Chiapas. The alphabet the author uses is among the Indigenous-language alphabets in Chiapas that resulted from the practice and the exchange of experiences among the members of Sna Jtz'ibajom (House of the Writer) and the Mayas-Zoques Writers Group. In the early 1990s the writers belonging to these independent organizations held a series of work sessions in Tuxtla Gutiérrez with the National Institute for Adult Education (INEA) and the Department of Ethnic Cultures of the State Government of Chiapas. The objective was jointly to establish practical alphabets in languages of interest to the INEA: Tzeltal, Tzotzil, Tojolabal, Chol, and Zoque.

2. The term "numinous" was coined by the German theologist Rudolf Otto (1869–1937) in reference to an awareness of the sacred. For him, the "numinous" is the object of religion, something superior to reason, goodness, or beauty. "Numinous" is derived from the Latin word *numen,* "divinity" or "divine will."

3. There are very few publications that deal with this chapter's content. With regard to religion, there is only one systematic study: Dr. John Early, "The Sons of San Lorenzo in Zinacantán" (Ph.D. dissertation, Cambridge, Mass.: Harvard University, 1965); in the area of medicine, William R. Holland's book *Medicina maya en los Altos de Chiapas* (Mexico City: INI, 1963) is the only existing study; the reader must consult these two sources for more information. To understand the type of relationship that exists between Indians and *ladinos* in the Chiapas Highlands (examined in Arias' first chapter), one must consult Gonzalo Aguirre Beltrán, *Regiones de refugio: El desarrollo de la comunidad y el proceso dominical en Mestizoamérica* (Mexico City: INI, 1967); Pierre Van den Berghe has also written on this topic: "Ladino-Indian Relations in the Highlands of Chiapas, Mexico," *Social Forces* 40 (1961): 63–67. There is a good doctoral dissertation on shamanism: Daniel Silver, "Zinacanteco Shamanism" (Cambridge, Mass.: Harvard University, 1966). A good example of an outsider's perspective regarding the transformation of the Tzotziles and Tzeltales is Henning Silverts' study "Social and Cultural Changes in a Tzeltal (Mayan) Municipie, Chiapas, México," in *Proceedings of the Thirty-second International Congress of Americanists, Copenhagen, 1956* (1958). (a.n.)

4. See Henry R. Wagner, *The Life and Writing of Bartolomé de Las Casas* (Albuquerque: University of New Mexico Press, 1967). (a.n.)

5. Paul Tillich, "Theology and Symbolism," in *Religious Symbolism,* ed. F. Ernest Johnson (New York: Institute for Religious and Social Studies, 1955), p. 109. (a.n.)

6. Priests are called *jtotik pale* or *jalaltotik.* Here *jtotik* or *jalal-* denotes numinosity. A *jtotik pale* is, in fact, considered to be a numinous being: it is believed that he does not eat, drink alcohol, or sleep with a woman. Like God, he only partakes of their soul. But Indigenous people have recently begun to form a more realistic idea of priests, as the relationship between them broadens. This new awareness has resulted, for example, in the expulsion of a priest from a certain community because his behavior did not meet local expectations. (a.n.)

7. These prayers have been maintained because it is believed that their lack of intelligibility is highly powerful against invisible enemies, particularly the devil (*pukuj*); just like human beings, those enemies understand no language other than Tzotzil and Tzeltal. This idea perhaps originates with lower-class *ladinos,* who possess analogous beliefs; for example, they believe that prayers in Latin constitute powerful exorcisms again the devil. (a.n.)

8. Guillermo Bonfil, "Del indigenismo de la Revolución a la antropología crítica," in *De eso que llaman antropología mexicana* (Mexico City: Editorial Nuestro Tiempo, 1970), pp. 39–65. (a.n.)

9. Gonzalo Aguirre Beltrán, *Regiones de refugio: El desarrollo de la comunidad y el proceso dominical en Mestizoamérica* (Mexico City: INI, 1967). (a.n.)

10. Ibid., p. 44. (a.n.)

11. Francisco Orozco y Jiménez, "Carta pastoral del arzobispo Francisco Orozco y Jiménez de Guadalajara," in *Liberalismo en México, 1857–1929,* ed. Ardí Callcott (Stanford, Calif.: Stanford University Press, 1931). (a.n.)

12. Mircea Eliade, *The Sacred and Profane: The Nature of Religion* (New York: Sheed & Ward, 1959). (a.n.)

13. That is, the Tzotzil people of San Pedro Chenalhó. (a.n.)

14. Early, "The Sons of San Lorenzo in Zinacantán," p. 81. (a.n.)

Las creencias católicas entre los tzotziles y los tzeltales

Jacinto Arias Pérez

Tzotzil[1]

[De *El mundo numinoso de los mayas,* trad. Jorge Ferreiro Santana, pp. 69–80. México, D.F.: SepSetentas, 1975. La segunda edición fue editada en Tuxtla Gutiérrez, Chiapas, por el Gobierno del Estado de Chiapas/Instituto Chiapaneco de Cultura, 1991.]

En los capítulos anteriores he analizado la interacción de los pueblos tzotziles y tzeltales con su medio y los seres distintos del hombre, tanto en el nivel individual como en el social, valiéndome de estructuras de referencia como el cultivo del maíz y la protección del yo en sus aspectos tangibles e intangibles. Dicho análisis tuvo como fin proporcionar a quienes no hablan ni tzotzil ni tzeltal una breve descripción del concepto modelo del hombre y la mujer tzotzil-tzeltal y de su concepción de la existencia humana; también se estudiaron las técnicas empleadas para su protección.

Los dos capítulos siguientes abordan el análisis de los fenómenos que tienen lugar cuando lo numinoso[2] moderno choca con lo numinoso maya. Para el presente capítulo se han escogido dos de las principales herencias de la cultura occidental: las creencias cristianas y la medicina moderna . . . En este capítulo se estudiarán algunos principios modernos vinculados a cada conjunto de símbolos culturales.[3]

Las creencias católicas

Las creencias católicas han sido impuestas a los indios serranos desde el principio de la conquista.[4] Desde entonces se han opuesto dos tipos muy distintos de perspectivas; los misioneros han pasado por alto los esfuerzos para conciliarlas. Los occidentales han seguido imponiendo sus símbolos religiosos sin tomar en cuenta otros simbolismos. Mantienen un concepto estático de la relación entre el símbolo y lo simbolizado, es decir, se sustenta inconscientemente una relación determinista entre ambas. Este error se opone obviamente a la naturaleza del símbolo, que es un instrumento comunicativo dinámico, puesto que, como afirma Paul Tillich, la gran función del símbolo consiste en "señalar más allá de sí mismo, con el poder de aquello que señala, para abrir niveles de realidad que de otra manera permanecerían cerrados, y para abrir niveles del intelecto humano de los cuales, de otra manera, no estaríamos conscientes."[5] Pero en la mente de los sacerdotes[6] sólo parece haber un mensaje posible capaz de lograr la comunicación mediante una serie de símbolos inmutables ya establecidos. A ese respecto las concepciones del símbolo de los sacerdotes y los pedranos no diferen en nada; uno y otros defienden actitudes estáticas y exclusivas ante los símbolos, que hacen muy difícil, si no imposible, la función de los símbolos culturales.

La consecuencia de ese estatismo mental, combinado con un etnocentrismo sumamente pronunciado, es la falta de interés, por parte de los misioneros, por implantar símbolos significativos, a fin de transmitir su mensaje a las comunidades indígenas; parecen totalmente satisfechos cuando tienen la oportunidad de actuar sólo como técnicos rituales. Salvo por intentos esporádicos hechos muy recientemente (por ejemplo, el sacerdote francés de San Pedro empieza a introducir la música y las danzas locales en sus ceremonias católicas), no ha habido indicios de que se empleen el simbolismo y las imágenes de los indios a fin de hacer que éstos capten su mensaje. Los sacerdotes diocesanos, especialmente, no muestran interés alguno por aprender las lenguas tzotzil y tzeltal; perecen sentirse satisfechos de seguir enseñando oraciones en español a personas que desconocen totalmente esa lengua. Esa tradición, iniciada por los misioneros de la época colonial, sigue siendo evidente en algunas oraciones que contienen una mezcla de tzotzil, tzeltal y español y que se conservan como parte del repertorio de los chamanes, toda vez que les dan mayor refinamiento.[7]

Los sacerdotes creen que no vale la pena tratar de comprender la mentalidad y la cultura indígenas, ni valerse de ellas para comunicar los valores ladinos. Ese desagrado por los valores culturales indígenas encaja bien en la relación de patrón a esclavo de que habla Guillermo Bonfil,[8] o en la relación asimétrica de superior a inferior, acerca de la cual Gonzalo Aguirre Beltrán escribe muy elocuentemente en sus *Regiones de refugio.*[9] Debe notarse que esas personas, rodeadas de una atmósfera numinosa, han venido actuando, durante más de cuatro siglos, como intermediarios en dicho tipo de relaciones. Siempre han estado del lado de los patrones (salvo algunas destacadas personalidades como fray Bartolomé de las Casas y unas pocas más que actualmente trabajan en aquella región); primero estuvieron con los encomenderos de la época colonial; luego, con los hacendados durante el régimen de Porfirio Díaz, y ahora están con los señores ladinos. Más todavía, como afirma Aguirre, las comunidades indígenas son fuente de ingresos de algunos especialistas del culto católico quienes, en beneficio propio, perpetúan la perspectiva numinosa de los serranos en vez de ayudarlos a racionalizar su situación existencial.[10]

A esas personas le llevará mucho tiempo despertar del efecto soporífero del opio de que hablaba Karl Marx, puesto que la sumisión a los patrones, en la virtuosa forma de la humildad y la pobreza, todavía es tema predominante de los sermones de esos sacerdotes en las iglesias. A manera de ejemplo, presentamos a continuación algunas palabras tomadas de la carta pastoral del arzobispo Francisco Orozco (arquidiócesis de Guadalajara) que, aunque pronunciadas durante el régimen de Díaz, todavía expresan el espíritu de los eclesiásticos serranos.

> Como la autoridad deriva de Dios, el trabajador cristiano santifica y hace sublime su obediencia sirviendo a Dios en la persona de sus amos; de esa manera, la obediencia no es ni humillante ni difícil. No servimos al hombre; servimos a Dios, y aquel que sirve a Dios no quedará sin recompensa . . . Pobre, ama tu humilde estado y tu trabajo; vuelve la mirada hacia el cielo. Allí está la verdadera riqueza.[11]

De allí que el fanatismo y el proselitismo no sean los únicos factores que mantienen el *status quo;* los alicientes sociales y económicos también son muy importantes en la continuación de las actividades de dichos misioneros. Pero ahora debemos orientarnos hacia una comprensión más profunda de la religión católica chiapaneca, considerándola como respuesta existencial del hombre al mundo.

El catolicismo en Chiapas, tal y como lo entienden sus dirigentes (salvo contadas excepciones, como el sacerdote francés de San Pedro) es por excelencia sobrenaturalista; lo que importa es la salud del alma, el cuerpo importa poco. El ser humano tangible es desplazado por su aspecto sobrenatural intangible. Subconscientemente, los sacerdotes toman muy en serio y muy literalmente las enseñanzas de Cristo que se refieren a los bienaventurados pobres porque de ellos será la vida eterna. Dicha creencia es todavía tan fuerte que la parte material de la humanidad es mala y lo mundano es oposición a lo espiritual, es un medio peligroso para el espíritu; se considera que la perfección sólo es posible alejándose de ese medio. Los lemas más constantes, empleados siempre que se reza, son "salvar el alma" e "ir al cielo." El fuerte hincapié en el pecado y los medios de obtener el perdón de Dios constituyen una preocupación constante, con escaso cuidado por los medios de mejorar el alma; se insiste en los mandamientos negativos y no en los positivos. Las ciencias, como la sociología, la psicología, la economía, la antropología, etc., de las que primordialmente se considera que dan lugar al mejoramiento del aspecto terreno de la humanidad, son abjuradas por esas personas como signo de ambición exagerada e impropia de su condición. En pocas palabras, los sacerdotes de aquella región han sido preparados según los cánones antiguos y educados de acuerdo con la vieja teología, que enseña que se puede salvar el alma sin salvar el cuerpo. Además, creen que a fin de salvarla es necesario ser católicos; ser católico significa muy poca cosa además de estar bautizado. (Para mayor información acerca de este tema véase la *Summa Theologica* de Tomás de Aquino y cualquiera de los textos de teología escritos antes del Concilio II Vaticano.)

Tal es, entonces, la perspectiva sobrenaturalista de la vida humana que (idealmente) subestima el aspecto natural. A continuación presentamos un breve análisis existencial del contenido de los capítulos anteriores.

En la estructura existencialista de la perspectiva sobrenaturalista de los católicos chiapanecos existe una explicación de la interacción del ser humano y el mundo; interacción que, sublimada (dice) por la gracia, pasa a ser un conducto hacia la vida sobrenatural. Por el contrario, la interacción de los tzotziles y los tzeltales con el mundo y sus congéneres no se considera como un medio sino como un fin en sí; su interacción con el mundo invisible se orienta hacia el mantenimiento de la armonía en el *habitat* tangible de la humanidad.

Otra diferencia respecto de la actitud católica radica en que, entre esos pueblos, no existe preocupación alguna por la vida sobrenatural; ya viven en el mundo invisible al mismo tiempo que viven en el visible. El alma subsiste después de la muerte, pero su existencia en el otro mundo no es muy distinta de su existencia en este mundo; el primero es sólo una continuación del segundo. Los esfuerzos del individuo lo mismo que de la sociedad se orientan hacia su propio bienestar tanto en el mundo visible como en el invisible.

Llegar a ser un verdadero hombre o una verdadera mujer es adaptarse al ideal tradicional; la lucha por la realización se orienta hacia la realización visible verdadera, no hacia lo invisible. El castigo y la recompensa tienen lugar en este mundo y no en el otro mundo. En otras palabras, y parafraseando a Mircea Eliade, se puede decir que esas personas se consideran a sí mismas como una estructura transhumana, del mismo modo que todo lo que les rodea posee una transestructura. Llevan una existencia abierta, pues no se hallan estrictamente confinadas en su modo de ser. Su existencia está abierta al mundo del mismo modo que la existencia del mundo está abierta a ellas. Al vivir nunca están solas, una parte del mundo vive en ellas lo mismo que el mundo no es nada sin ellas, puesto que en ellas vive el mundo. Es decir que viven en un constante despertar existencial al cosmos y a sí mismas.[12]

Así, los sacerdotes, por una parte, y los serranos, por la otra, se enfrentan a una comunidad que obedece a dos *Weltanschauungen* contrarios: entre los tzotziles y los tzeltales la gente se orienta hacia el mundo, mientras los ladinos lo hacen hacia lo sobrenatural. Ahora bien, es bien sabido que todo lo numinoso se comunica, se realiza y surge en la mente de las personas y la existencia merced a cierto conjunto aceptado de símbolos; ninguno de ellos tiene significado existencial alguno sin los otros; lo numinoso es existencialmente inactivo sin el símbolo, lo mismo que éste es mundo sin lo "numinoso." Lo numinoso es dinámico; hace suyo cualquier conducto interesante para comunicar su contenido. Dicho conducto puede ser alguno descubierto en la cultura misma o tomado del exterior.

. . . Veamos ahora lo que sucede con los símbolos culturales extraños cuando se los ha introducido por la fuerza en lo numinoso maya.

El bautizo

El bautizo, según los eclesiásticos de que hablamos anteriormente, es el sacramento del renacimiento y la incorporación del ser humano al Reino de Dios, es un símbolo de la transformación sobrenatural del alma. En vez de ser un acto concebido para acabar con la situación terrena del ser humano es un acontecimiento terreno, destinado a hacer frente a lo que es considerado por ellos como el presente y el futuro no terrenal del ser humano. Tal es el *Weltanschauung* que esas personas desean comunicar mediante el símbolo de lo que se llama bautizo; pensando en ese principio, van de pueblo en pueblo, especialmente en la época de la fiesta de cada santo patrón, y bautizan a los niños a fin de hacerlos católicos.

¿Cómo reciben los pedranos[13] esos símbolos culturales ladinos? Sólo pueden hacerlo de acuerdo con su propia perspectiva numinosa. Como dicho sacramento se imparte principalmente a los niños, se ha considerado como un símbolo del acto de "dar el alma a los niños." El lector debe recordar que el alma es separable y no mora en el cuerpo de manera inmediata sino que entra en él paulatinamente, a medida que el niño crece y adquiere educación y sabiduría. Por ese motivo, la madre de un niño recién nacido toma precauciones a fin de evitar cualquier peligro que pudiera causar la pérdida del alma de su hijo. Entre dichas precauciones se cuentan la de no alejarse mucho de la casa ni ir a lugares desconocidos que pudieran hacer que el alma del niño perdiese el camino y dejase de seguir al cuerpo. Durante un viaje, siempre que la madre se detiene con el niño y se sienta un rato para tomar aliento, debe tomar unas ramas para barrer el lugar en que se sentó a manera de que el alma no se quede allí sino que siga al cuerpo.

La idea que evoca esas precauciones es que el alma del niño todavía no se halla totalmente fija a su cuerpo; está cerca de él pero no firmemente sujeta. Se ha encontrado que el bautizo es apropiado para corregir esos defectos. Gracias a dicha ceremonia, el niño quedará poderosamente protegido contra las enfermedades, al entrar su alma en el cuerpo, merced al rito del bautizo, pasa a estar mejor dotado para resistir los ataques peligrosos en contra de su persona. Apoyan nuestra afirmación las palabras que el padre del niño dirige al padrino después de la ceremonia:

> . . . con esta ceremonia,
> ha entrado allí el espíritu,
> ha entrado allí el alma
> del Ángel de Dios (el niño).[14]

Para los nativos, otro significado del bautizo consiste en que el niño necesita el apoyo y la protección de sus mayores en el mundo visible para que ese mismo apoyo y esa misma protección puedan existir en su morada invisible. La idea y la función del bautizo ha propiciado igualmente la creencia general en los protectores-defensores (*jpetum-jkuchum*). De ahí el término *petumajel,* que denota el acto de abrazar al niño y es una expresión común en algunas comunidades para describir este rito católico.

Notas

1. Los hablantes de tzotzil llaman a su lengua *batz'i k'op*, "idioma verdadero." A finales del siglo XX esta lengua contaba con más de 514,000 hablantes localizados principalmente en el estado de Chiapas. El alfabeto que emplea el autor es uno de los alfabetos en las lenguas indígenas de Chiapas que surgieron de la práctica y del intercambio de experiencias entre los integrantes de Sna Jtz'ibajom (Casa del Escritor) y de la Asociación de Escritores Mayas-Zoques. A principios de la última década del siglo XX los escritores de estas organizaciones independientes sostuvieron varias reuniones de trabajo en Tuxtla Gutiérrez con el Instituto Nacional de Educación para Adultos (INEA) y el Departamento de Culturas Étnicas del Gobierno de Chiapas, a fin de alcanzar acuerdos en el establecimiento de alfabetos prácticos en las lenguas de interés para el INEA: tzeltal, tzotzil, tojolabal, chol y zoque.

2. El termino "numinoso" fue acuñado por el teólogo alemán Rudolf Otto (1869–1937) para referirse a la conciencia de lo sagrado; para él, lo "numinoso" es el objeto de la religión, algo superior a la razón, la bondad y la belleza. *Numinoso* se deriva de la palabra latina *numen*, "divinidad" o "voluntad divina."

3. Existen muy pocas publicaciones acerca del contenido del presente capítulo; a decir verdad, por lo que toca a la religión, sólo hay un estudio sistemático, que es el del doctor John Early, "The Sons of San Lorenzo in Zinacantán" (tesis de doctorado, Cambridge, Mass.: Harvard University, 1965); en el campo de la medicina sólo existe el libro de William R. Holland, *Medicina maya en los altos de Chiapas* (México, D.F.: INI, 1963). Para mayores detalles, el lector debe remitirse a esas dos fuentes. Para comprender el tipo de relación que existe entre indios y ladinos de las tierras altas de Chiapas, se debe consultar a Gonzalo Aguirre Beltrán, *Regiones de refugio: El desarrollo de la comunidad y el proceso dominical en Mestizoamérica* (México, D.F.: Instituto Nacional Indigenista, 1967); Pierre Van den Berghe, "Ladino-Indian Relations in the Highlands of Chiapas, México," *Social Forces* 40 (1961): 63–67, también ha escrito acerca de ese tema. Hay una buena tesis de doctorado que trata del chamanismo: Daniel Silver, "Zinacanteco Shamanism" (Cambridge, Mass., Harvard University, 1966). Henning Silverts, "Social and Cultural Changes in a Tzeltal (Mayan) Municipie, Chiapas, México," en *Proceedings of the Thirty-second International Congress of Americanists (Copenhagen, 1956)* (1958) es un buen ejemplo del punto de vista de un extraño acerca de la transformación de los tzotziles y los tzeltales. (n.a.)

4. Véase Henry R. Wagner, *The Life and Writing of Bartolomé de Las Casas* (Albuquerque: University of New Mexico Press, 1967). (n.a.)

5. Paul Tillich, "Theology and Symbolism," en *Religious Symbolism*, coord. F. Ernest Johnson (New York: Institute for Religious and Social Studies, 1955), p. 109. (n.a.)

6. A los sacerdotes se les llama *jtotik pale* o *jalaltotik*. En ese caso, *jtotik* o *jalal* denotan numinosidad. A decir verdad, un *jtotik pale* es considerado como un ser numinoso; por ejemplo, se cree que no come, ni bebe alcohol, ni duerme con una mujer, etc.; lo mismo que Dios, sólo toma el alma de esas cosas. No obstante, últimamente y debido al hecho de que los indígenas tienen mayor relación con los sacerdotes, empiezan a formarse una imagen más realista de ellos. Una de las consecuencias de esa conciencia es el hecho de la expulsión de un sacerdote de cierta comunidad porque su comportamiento no iba de acuerdo con el que se esperaba de él. (n.a.)

7. Se han conservado esas oraciones porque se considera que su falta de inteligibilidad es sumamente poderosa contra los enemigos invisibles, especialmente el diablo (*pukuj*), ya que, como seres humanos, dichos enemigos sólo comprenden el tzotzil y el tzeltal pero no otras lenguas. La idea quizás haya sido tomada de los ladinos de clase baja que poseen creencias análogas; por ejemplo, creen que las oraciones en latín constituyen poderosos exorcismos contra el diablo. (n.a.)

8. Guillermo Bonfil, "Del indigenismo de la Revolución a la antropología crítica," en *De eso que llaman antropología mexicana* (México, D.F.: Editorial Nuestro Tiempo, 1970), pp. 39–65. (n.a.)

9. Gonzalo Aguirre Beltrán, *Regiones de refugio: El desarrollo de la comunidad y el proceso dominical en Mestizoamérica* (México, D.F.: Instituto Nacional Indigenista, 1967). (n.a.)

10. Ibídem, p. 44. (n.a.)

11. Francisco Orozco y Jiménez, "Carta pastoral del arzobispo Francisco orozco y Jiménez de Guadalajara," en *Liberalismo en México, 1857–1929*, coord. Ardí Callcott (Stanford, Calif., Stanford University Press, 1931). (n.a.)

12. Mircea Eliade, *The Sacred and Profane: The Nature of Religion* (New York: Sheed & Ward, 1959). (n.a.)

13. Es decir, los tzotziles de San Pedro Chenalhó. (n.a.)

14. Early, "The Sons of San Lorenzo in Zinacantán," p. 81. (n.a.)

Diego Méndez Guzmán

Tzeltal

Diego Méndez Guzmán. Photographed at Na Bolom Museum, San Cristóbal de las Casas, Chiapas.

Diego Méndez Guzmán was born October 12, 1967, in the hamlet of Ch'ixaltontik, municipality of Tenejapa, Chiapas. He is a speaker of Tzeltal and Tzotzil. As a child he was initiated into agriculture; he later studied nursing in the municipal seat of Tenejapa for the purpose of assisting his community in the area of health concerns. He joined Sna Jtz'ibajom, A.C. (House of the Writer) in 1983 and has served several times as its president. As a Tzeltal writer Méndez Guzmán has published many works in local and national newspapers, magazines, and books. In the second series of Colección Letras Mayas Contemporáneas (C. Montemayor, series ed.) he published *A'yejetik yu'un jtzeltaletik ta Tenejapa/Relatos tzeltales de Tenejapa* (Tzeltal Tales from Tenejapa); his first novel appeared in the third series of the same collection, *Kajkanantik jch'ulta tiketik te leke sok te chopole/El Kajkanantik: Los dioses del bien y el mal* (Kajkanantik: The Gods of Good and Evil) (vol. 5; Mexico City: INI/TRF, 1998). In 2002 he studied theatre directing with Mexico's Luis Tavira.

Diego Méndez Guzmán nació el 12 de octubre de 1967 en el paraje Ch'ixaltontik, municipio de Tenejapa, Chiapas. Es hablante tzeltal y tzotzil. Desde su infancia se dedicó a la agricultura y después estudió enfermería en la cabecera municipal de Tenejapa con el fin de ayudar a su comunidad en problemas de salud. Ingresó en Sna Jtz'ibajom, A.C. (La Casa del Escritor) en 1983, para la cual ha fungido como presidente durante varios períodos. Como escritor tzeltal ha publicado diversas obras en periódicos locales y nacionales, revistas y libros. En la segunda serie de Colección Letras Mayas Contemporáneas (C. Montemayor, coord. de la colección) publicó *A'yejetik yu'un jtzeltaletik ta Tenejapa/Relatos tzeltales de Tenejapa* y en la tercera serie de la misma colección su primera novela: *Kajkanantik jch'ulta tiketik te leke sok te chopole/El Kajkanantik: Los dioses del bien y el mal* (vol. 5; México, D.F.: INI/TRF, 1998). En el año 2002 estudió dirección escénica con Luis de Tavira.

Lok' ta beel te Kajkanantike[1]

Diego Méndez Guzmán

Tzeltal[2]

[From *A'yejetik yu'un jtzeltaletik ta Tenejapa/Relatos tzeltales de Tenejapa,* pp. 9–12. Colección Letras Mayas Contemporáneas: Chiapas, 2nd series, vol. 7, C. Montemayor, series ed. Mexico City: INI/TRF, 1996.]

Ay la jun k'aal k'ot jtul pale te ta Tenejapae jich lajla yil te bit'il ay stalel te lume p'is la rominko ba spas k'in te a sok ba la yak'labe yich' ja' te uni alatike. Ta patil te k'alal ayix k'aal sk'oel te ae ay la jch'oj te ch'ay beel ta jk'axele, lajla xkuch beel te Kajkanantike, ja' jich ya yalik te mamaletike. Ma la mach'a la sna'ix stojol yu'unik a bayel la k'aal ch'ayal ja'to la te ay jun k'aal k'ot jtul jkaxlane,[3] ja' la jul yal te ta yanto lum ayix ae ma la la sna'ik binti a yu'la yakalix ta chonel la sta a te Kajkanantike, lijk la sna'be sba ta ora yu'la ta Tenejapa ay ek, te la yu'un a te ya sna'be sba ta leke.

Ba la yalbe te mach'a ya xchone te yakuk la x'ak'bet tal sujtele, pere ma la xyak' ta jk'axel, lajla yal te la xcha' manbe yan kirsianoe jich yu' nanix la ja' yu'un ta jk'axel a. Te jkaxlane lajla yak'be tak'in, pere ma la lok' yu'un a te bi yipal ya sk'an te mach'a ya xchone, ma la bi yan la spas laj nanix la sk'anbe ta jk'axel. Ta patil la te k'alal yakalik ta k'ope, lajnix la stajtal ta pojel ts'in te Kajkanantike, speto la tal ta anel, lok' la tal ta ti' lum ja' la jich bayel la ora animajtal ja' to la te jil yu'un te mach'a nutzojon tale; lajla xkux yo'tan j'ajk' yu' la jich k'unk'un ya xbenix a, k'ot la ta jun kolonia ja' la te ta asiento sbiile te ba sk'inalikix Samperoetike ya'tike.

Te la jul ta a'tel che' oxe k'aal a, te la jul slebe sna a te Kajkanantike yu' la jich te ya xba yich' ich'el ta muk' a oxe la ja'wil la en te a. Ta ora la la ya'yik te mach'atik tijil te ayik ae sok te mach'atik najt ayike, melel lom lek la ya xkoltawan ts'in, pujk la ta spisil lum te slekilale; ay la ya xk'ot jpayxaletik ta sk'anel wokol, ya nanix la skolta a. Lajla sna'ik stojol ts'in, jich la ek te Samperoetike xtaluk la spasbeik sk'in ek sok lijk la slebeik yaj martoma, yaj kaptan lajla xchajpanik ta lek, yu' la jich lek ya spasbeik a te sk'ine.

Te k'alal la asujtal te jkaxlane jul la yal te bit'il la stajal te Kajkanantike, sok te bit'il abajt te a te ta yan lume, jich la te kirsianoetike ta ora la abajtik te a te banti la yich'ik alele ba la xcha'ik'ik tal te ta lume. Ma la ba wokol la yalbe te kirsianoetik te ja' yu'unik te Kajkanantike jich ak'a la swentainikix a. Ja' la la yik'ik bel ta restiko te jkaxlane te mach'a la spojtal ta chonele jich ba la yak' ta ilel stukel, te banti sleobe jilel snae jich k'ax la bel k'aal yu'un te a te banti ak'bil jilele.

Pere te Kajkanantike k'aemix la sok a te kirsianoetike, sok te banti aye jich ma la la sk'an asujtix tal a. Te bi la ut'il ma la sk'an asujtal te Kajkanantike, te mach'atik ayik ta Tenejapae ok'ik la ta sk'anel wokol lajla yalbeik te ya xju' yu'nik spisil te binti ya sk'an yo'tane, pere ma la la xch'un ta jk'axel, awa'y la ts'in ma la bin yan la spasik laj nanix la yik'ik tal a jk'axel, bananix la xcha' ak'beik sta te snaktibe.

Ta yan la k'aal, chajpto la la yilik ta spisilik a, te k'alal la sjamik te sti'nelul ch'unae ja'to la xyilik ma'yukix chikan te a te Kajkanantike jich ba la stijik ta ora kampanaetik lajla yalbeik spisil kirsianoetik te lok'em ta anel te Kajkanantike. Lajla spuk sbaik ta sleel juju ch'ix be jich ja' la la staik te mach'atik abajtik ta sbelal bel asientoe, jakalto la la yilik bel te ja' te toj bel a te banti la yik'ik tale. Te k'alal la la yil te yakal bel ta nutsele, lajla yak'be xan bel yipal, jich la ek te jtsakawaletike lajla yak'beik xan bel animal ek yu' la jich ya staik ta ora a; te k'alal la nopol ya staik kix ae, te Kajkanantike lajla sk'ojchin la beel yakan ta tontikil t'uxa la koel ta yan be yu' la lom chujkul te bee.

Ja' to la jich la staik ta tsakel a, ma la la skoltaikix a. Te k'alal la at'uxa te Kajkanantike, la jaw la lok'el yejk'echil yakan, awa'y la ts'in lijk la stsob lajla smuk ta lum, ja' jich ya yalik te bit'il ay te stalele.

Jich lek nax la sba la stsakik sok lajla sk'anbeik perton te bit'il ja' smul stukel te t'uxae, sok te ejchina yakane, lajla yik'ik bel te ta xch'unae, te banti la la yalbeik mantar jtebuke lajla slebeik lek te bit'il ya xmuk'ub k'inal ya ya'y yu'un a te binti la spas j'ajk'e, lajla xchajpanbeik lek sk'in oxe la k'aal la spasbeik.

Te k'alal la junix yo'tanik a te yajwal lume jich la ek te Kajkanantike junix la yo'tan jtebuk ek a, te k'alal la yil te ay bayel atal yantik paraje ich'otok ta muk'e, ja' la lek la ya'y yu'un jich lajnix xch'un ajil yu'nik, te k'alal la spasbeik te oxe k'aal sk'ine lajla yak'beik lek bayel skantela laj to la stabeik ta chik'el sk'u' a.

K'ax la bel che' oxe k'aal, te banti la smuk jilel yejk'ech te Kajkanantike, ch'i lok'el ta lekil kaxlan chenek', ja' la jich awejt te kaxlan chenek'e jich lajla xcha' tz'unik xan te bit'il jich ma xtup' a te bit'il ak'atp'o te yejk'ech Kajkanantike, ja' jich ta ora ya to xlok' yu'unik bayel te ja'in lekil Kaxlan chenek'e, te ya xlok' yich chonel ta ch'iwiche.

Notes

1. From *kajkanan*, "protector," "caretaker." The ceremonial formula Kajkanantik, "Our Protector," is used in reference to the patron saint of every Tzeltal town. The author uses this term here in reference to the *kajkanan* of Tenejapa.

2. The Tzeltal people also call their language Batz'il K'op, "true language" or "true voice." At the end of the twentieth century there were more than 547,000 Tzeltal speakers, living primarily in the state of Chiapas. The alphabet the author uses is among the Indigenous-language alphabets in Chiapas that resulted from the practice and the exchange of experiences among the members of Sna Jtz'ibajom (House of the Writer) and the Mayas-Zoques Writers Group. In the early 1990s the writers belonging to these independent organizations held a series of work sessions in Tuxtla Gutiérrez with the National Institute for Adult Education (INEA) and the Department of Ethnic Cultures of the State Government of Chiapas. The objective was jointly to establish practical alphabets in languages of interest to the INEA: Tzeltal, Tzotzil, Tojolabal, Chol, and Zoque.

3. That is, someone who is not recognized as Indigenous, but rather *ladino*, a Spanish-language term used in Chiapas meaning "Spanish-speaking." The word *jkaslan* means "mestizo" in Tzeltal and Tzotzil, but among the Tzotzil people the word *kaxlan* (that is, without the prefix of agent *j*) means "hen," thus allowing for hilarious jokes at the expense of the mestizos.

Notas

1. De *kajkanan*, "protector," "cuidador." La fórmula ceremonial Kajkanantik, "Nuestro protector," se aplica a los santos patronos de cada pueblo. El autor da por sentado que en este caso se trata del *kajkanan* de Tenejapa.

2. Los tzeltales también llaman a su lengua *batz'il k'op*, es decir, "idioma verdadero" o "voz verdadera." A finales del siglo XX contaba esta lengua con más de 547,000 hablantes localizados fundamentalmente en el estado de Chiapas. El alfabeto que emplea el autor es uno de los alfabetos en las lenguas indígenas de Chiapas que surgieron de la práctica y del intercambio de experiencias entre los integrantes de Sna Jtz'ibajom (Casa del Escritor) y de la Asociación de Escritores Mayas-Zoques. A principios de la última década del siglo XX los escritores de estas organizaciones independientes sostuvieron varias reuniones de trabajo en Tuxtla Gutiérrez con el Instituto Nacional de Educación para Adultos (INEA) y el Departamento de Culturas Étnicas del Gobierno de Chiapas, a fin de alcanzar acuerdos en el establecimiento de alfabetos prácticos en las lenguas de interés para el INEA: tzeltal, tzotzil, tojolabal, chol y zoque.

3. Es decir, alguien no reconocido como indígena, sino *ladino*, de habla española. La palabra *jkaslan* significa "mestizo" tanto en tzeltal como en tzotzil, pero entre los tzotziles la palabra *kaxlan* (es decir, sin el prefijo agente *j*) significa "gallina," lo que permite en las comunidades bromas jocosas a costa de los mestizos.

Saint Ildefonso's Pilgrimage[1]

Diego Méndez Guzmán

Tzeltal[2]

[From *A'yejetik yu'un jtzeltaletik ta Tenejapa/Relatos tzeltales de Tenejapa*, pp. 9–12, 51–54. Colección Letras Mayas Contemporáneas: Chiapas, 2nd series, vol. 7, C. Montemayor, series ed. Mexico City: INI/TRF, 1996.]

Once upon a time, a priest came to Tenejapa.[3] He began to visit the town every Sunday, performing religious duties and baptizing newborn children. Having visited the place for some time, he one day disappeared forever and, according to the elders, took with him Tenejapa's statue of Saint Ildefonso. Much time passed, and the town heard nothing about the statue of Saint Ildefonso. Finally, one day a mestizo[4] arrived in Tenejapa with the news that in a certain town (no one can remember which), the statue of Saint Ildefonso was for sale in the plaza. The mestizo said that he had recognized it immediately since he was from Tenejapa and was perfectly familiar with it.

He tried to convince the merchant to return it, but the merchant refused, claiming that he had bought it from another person and therefore was the sole owner of the statue. The mestizo offered him money; but since he did not meet the price the merchant was asking for the statue, he had no choice but to take it by force. After quite a struggle, he finally managed to seize the statue and, with it in his arms, ran for the outskirts of town. He ran a long time until his pursuer was no longer in sight. He then rested a little and continued his trek, arriving at a place called La Hacienda, in the municipality of Chenalhó.[5]

Since he planned to work in Chenalhó for some time, he placed the statue in the town's little church so it would be venerated, and there it remained for three years. The saint soon made a name for himself among the locals and even in other far-away places. His fame as a worker of good miracles spread throughout the region. Pilgrims would arrive from everywhere to request favors, which the saint always granted. Aware of this, the residents of Chenalhó also came to worship him, and soon they undertook the task of creating a *mayordomo*[6] with *principales*,[7] to organize the saint's veneration better.

The mestizo returned to Tenejapa and told of how he had recovered the saint's statue and why it was now in that other place. The townspeople immediately prepared to go to La Hacienda to bring the saint back to Tenejapa. It took no small amount of effort to convince the residents of La Hacienda that the people of Tenejapa were the legitimate owners of the statue and that it therefore belonged to them. They had to bring the mestizo along to testify that he had recovered it from the merchant and that he had placed the statue in the church during his stay there.

However, Saint Ildefonso had already grown fond of the people and the place and for that reason would not accept going back. Faced with the saint's refusal, the people of Tenejapa begged him until they were in tears, promising him everything he desired; still he refused. Therefore, they had no choice but to take him away by force to place him once again upon their altar.

To everyone's surprise, when Tenejapa's church doors were opened the following day, the saint was gone. They quickly rang the bells to inform the town of his escape. The townspeople split up into several groups to search for him along every road. The group that took the path leading to La Hacienda had the good fortune of sighting the saint from a distance, heading for the place from which he had been recovered. Feeling himself pursued, he quickened his pace as his pursuers began to run to catch up with him. When they were near, the saint tripped on some rocks and tumbled some yards down the road, which was very steep.

This gave the townspeople the advantage, and they pounced on the saint so that he could not escape. In falling, the saint broke some toenails, which they carefully buried according to custom.

With great respect, they took him prisoner and begged his pardon, since it was their fault that he had fallen and hurt his feet. They led him to the church at Tenejapa, where they organized a grandiose celebration for him that lasted three days; this was done to console him and to brighten the sad spell he had experienced.

Soon the town's spirits were soothed, and the saint was a bit calmer. He felt pleased, having seen that people from remote hamlets came to honor him. He consented to remain in Tenejapa, despite the fact that during those three days of fiesta the people lit so many candles for him that they burned part of his clothing.

Some time later, in the place where Saint Ildefonso had buried his toenails, robust peanut plants began to sprout. The peanuts were harvested and resown to propagate the plants that had emerged from the saint's nails. To this day, large quantities of these delicious peanuts are still harvested and are sold in the plaza during market days.

Presently, the saint no longer gives signs of wanting to escape from his niche, since all the residents venerate and honor him with a multitude of celebrations that keep him quite amused and content.

Notes

1. In Tzeltal, the author uses Kajkanantik, "Our Protector." See note 1 of the Tzeltal-language text.

2. Like the Tzotzil people, the Tzeltal people also call their language Batz'il K'op, "true language" or "true voice." At the end of the twentieth century there were more than 547,000 Tzeltal speakers, living primarily in the state of Chiapas.

3. Tzeltal town and municipality in the state of Chiapas located some 18 miles northeast of San Cristóbal de las Casas. At the end of

the twentieth century this municipality had a population of 33,217 and comprised 50 localities or communities; 31 of these had less than 500 inhabitants, and the rest had between 500 and 2,000. Tenejapa's patron saint is Saint Ildefonso, whose feast is celebrated on January 23.

4. Someone who is not recognized as Indigenous but rather as *ladino* or Spanish-speaking. (Also see note 3 of the Tzeltal-language text.)

5. Town and municipality of San Pedro Chenalhó, Chiapas, located some 28 miles north of San Cristóbal de las Casas; at the end of the twentieth century its population was 30,876.

6. Traditional office rotated annually among different members of a community; the *mayordomo*'s main responsibilities include providing funds and material goods for a saint's celebrations.

7. Group of officials who share in the responsibilities of the *mayordomo.*

Peregrinar de San Ildefonso[1]

Diego Méndez Guzmán

Tzeltal[2]

[De *A'yejetik yu'un jtzeltaletik ta Tenejapa/Relatos tzeltales de Tenejapa,* pp. 51–54. Colección Letras Mayas Contemporáneas: Chiapas, 2a serie, vol. 7, C. Montemayor, coord. de la colección. México, D.F.: INI/TRF, 1996.]

Cierta vez llegó a Tenejapa[3] un sacerdote y tomó la costumbre de visitar el pueblo todos los días domingos para celebrar los oficios religiosos y bautizar a los niños recién nacidos. Después de cierto tiempo de visitar el lugar, un día desapareció para siempre, llevándose la imagen de San Ildefonso, según cuentan los viejos. Nadie volvió a saber de San Ildefonso durante mucho tiempo, hasta que un día llegó a Tenejapa un mestizo[4] que les trajo la noticia de que en cierto pueblo (ya nadie recuerda cuál) se estaba vendiendo en la plaza la imagen de San Ildefonso, la cual reconoció al momento, ya que él era de Tenejapa y la conocía perfectamente.

Trató de convencer al comerciante de que se la devolviera, pero éste se negó, alegando que la había comprado a otra persona y que por lo tanto era el dueño absoluto de la imagen. El mestizo le ofreció dinero, pero como no cubría el precio que pedía el vendedor, no tuvo más remedio que arrebatárselo a la fuerza. Después de muchos forcejeos, pudo al fin apoderarse de la imagen y con ésta en brazos salió corriendo hacia la salida del pueblo; corrió así mucho tiempo hasta que perdió de vista a su perseguidor. Entonces descansó un poco y luego continuó su marcha hasta un lugar llamado "La Hacienda," que pertenece al municipio de Chenalhó.[5]

Como él tenía que trabajar en ese lugar durante algún tiempo, colocó la imagen en la pequeña iglesia de aquel lugar para que fuera venerada, y allí permaneció durante tres años. Pronto se dio a conocer entre los lugareños y hasta en otros distantes lugares como buen cumplidor de milagros y se extendió su fama por toda la región. Llegaban peregrinaciones de todas partes a implorarle favores, que él siempre concedía. Sabedores de esto, los residentes de Chenalhó también acudieron a rendirle culto, y pronto se dieron a la tarea de formar mayordomo[6] y principales[7] para organizar mejor el culto del santo.

Cuando este mestizo regresó a Tenejapa y les contó cómo había recuperado la imagen del santo y por qué estaba en ese lugar, la gente se dispuso de inmediato a ir a La Hacienda para volver a traerlo a Tenejapa. No poco trabajo les costó convencer a las gentes de que ellos eran los legítimos dueños de la imagen y que por lo tanto les pertenecía. Tuvieron que llevar como testigo al mismo mestizo que lo había rescatado del vendedor y comprobar por su medio que la imagen había sido puesta en ese templo mientras transcurría su permanencia en ese lugar.

Pero San Ildefonso ya se había encariñado con las gentes y con el lugar, y por lo mismo no aceptaba el regreso. Ante la negativa del santo, los pobladores de Tenejapa le rogaron hasta el llanto, prometiéndole todo lo que quisiera, pero éste se negaba, por lo cual no tuvieron más remedio que llevárselo a la fuerza, para colocarlo nuevamente en su altar.

Para sorpresa de todos, al otro día, cuando se abrieron las puertas del templo, notaron la ausencia del santo y rápidamente tocaron las campanas para dar aviso a la gente de su fuga. Se dividieron en varios grupos para ir a buscarlo por todos los caminos y tocó en suerte al grupo que se encaminó por el sendero que conducía a La Hacienda verlo a distancia, encaminándose hacia el lugar de donde lo habían rescatado. Sintiéndose perseguido, apresuró el paso. Ellos empezaron a correr para darle alcance; cuando ya estaban cerca de él, el santo tropezó con unas piedras y rodó unos metros abajo del camino, que era muy empinado.

Esto les dio ventaja a ellos, que se abalanzaron sobre él, para que no pudiera escaparse. En su caída, el santo se rompió algunas uñas de los pies, las cuales enterró cuidadosamente, siguiendo las costumbres que así lo recomiendan.

Con mucho respeto lo tomaron prisionero y disculpándose de que por su culpa él se hubiera caído, lastimándose los pies, lo condujeron al templo de Tenejapa, donde le organizaron una grandiosa fiesta que duró tres días, para consolarlo y alegrarle el triste rato que había pasado.

Ya calmados los ánimos del pueblo y el santo un poco más tranquilo, al ver que había venido gente de lejanos parajes para honrarlo, se sintió halagado y aceptó quedarse con ellos, a pesar de que en esos tres días de fiesta le encendieron tantas velas que llegaron a quemarle parte de sus ropas.

Pasado algún tiempo, en el lugar donde el Santo había enterrado sus uñas empezaron a brotar robustas matas de cacahuate, los cuales fueron cosechados y vueltos a sembrar para propagar esta planta, en la cual se habían convertido las uñas del Santo, y hasta ahora se siguen cosechando grandes cantidades de estos sabrosísimos cacahuates, que se venden en los días de plaza.

Actualmente el Santo ya no da muestras de quererse escapar de su lugar, pues todos los habitantes lo veneran y honran con multitud de festejos que lo tienen muy entretenido y contento.

[Traducción de José Alfredo Melo de la Rosa y Francisco Álvarez Q.]

Notas

1. El autor emplea en tzeltal la voz Kajkanantik, "Nuestro protector." Véase nota 1 al texto tzeltal.

2. Los tzeltales también llaman a su lengua *batz'il k'op*, es decir, "idioma verdadero" o "voz verdadera." A finales del siglo XX contaba esta lengua con más de 547,000 hablantes localizados fundamentalmente en el estado de Chiapas.

3. Pueblo y municipio tzeltal del estado de Chiapas ubicado a unos 30 km al noreste de San Cristóbal de las Casas. A fines del siglo XX este municipio contaba con 33,217 habitantes, y comprendía 50 localidades o comunidades, 31 de las cuales tenían menos de 500 habitantes y el resto entre 500 y 2,000 habitantes.

4. Es decir, alguien no reconocido como indígena, sino *ladino*, de habla española. (Véase también nota 3 al texto tzeltal.)

5. San Pedro Chenalhó es una cabecera municipal situada a 45 kilómetros al norte de San Cristóbal de las Casas. A finales del siglo XX el municipio de Chenalhó contaba con 30,876 habitantes.

6. Cargo tradicional que se turna anualmente entre diferentes individuos de una comunidad, cuyas responsabilidades incluyen proveer fondos y bienes materiales para la celebración de un santo.

7. Grupo de oficiales que comparten las responsabilidades del mayordomo.

Domingo Gómez Gutiérrez

Tzeltal

Domingo Gómez Gutiérrez. Photographed at his home in Las Margaritas, Chiapas.

Domingo Gómez Gutiérrez is a Tzeltal writer born in San Jerónimo Tulijá, Chilón, Chiapas. He presently works in the Coordinating Center of the National Indigenist Institute (INI) in Las Margaritas, Chiapas. In the Colección Letras Mayas Contemporáneas: Chiapas (C. Montemayor, series ed.) he published a volume of oral history and narrative entitled *Juan López: Héroe Tzeltal/Jwan Lopes: Bats'il Ajaw* (Juan López: Tzeltal Hero) (2nd series, vol. 4; Mexico City: INI/TRF, 1996).

Domingo Gómez Gutiérrez, escritor tzeltal, originario de San Jerónimo Tulijá, Chilón, Chiapas. Actualmente labora en el Centro Coordinador del Instituto Nacional Indigenista de las Margaritas, Chiapas. En la Colección Letras Mayas Contemporáneas: Chiapas (C. Montemayor, coord. de la colección) publicó una colección de historia y narrativa oral titulada *Juan López: Héroe Tzeltal/Jwan Lopes: Bats'il Ajaw* (2a serie, vol. 4; México, D.F.: INI/TRF, 1996).

Bats'il Ajaw Jwan Lopes, Kanan Chij (Jman Enantes, Swijlibja, Chilón)[1]

Domingo Gómez Gutiérrez

Tzeltal[2]

[From *La voz profunda: Literatura mexicana en lenguas indígenas,* pp. 98–104. Carlos Montemayor, prologue, literary selection, and notes. Mexico City: Joaquín Mortiz, 2004.]

Te winike lok' ta paxyal sjok bael yinam sok jtuul yantsil nich'an, ta sujtelix a ijk'ubik ta be, yo ochik ta wayel ta ye'tal lejch ch'en,[3] te ochik ta wayel a, ba xtal komo te sjok yaiyel a te yantsil nich'ane, k'alal te sakub k'inal cha' jachik k'axel ta beel, pero jaxan ayix yal a te ach'ixe, ayix yal a ja' te waiy Rey Jwan Lopes.[4]

Komo ma ba ilin te state, te snane, ya sna'ik binut'il jajch talel yaiyel te alale, ja' nax te k'alal k'ax tal ta wayel te ta ch'ene, k'alal te mukubtal te ants sok te yale, muk'ubtal te alale, ka'alal ayin la yil, la skanantay. Pe te komo ayin ta k'inale ma laj ba la stsak xchu' te k'alal ayin ae, awil abot laj swayichtay, te alale ma me ba ya xchu'un, ma ba ya xba stsak xchu', pe tenix xa wik' bael a te ta banti jajch talele, tenix xa wik' bael a, ka'alal ya xk'ojt ya me xchu'un xchilaj sk'ojlal te snane; bajtnilaj a te ta Ts'ulanbile, k'alal k'ojt a te waiye; ja' nax tek'alal k'ojt sok te snane skojtesbelaj te skuchoj te yale, skojtesbele, ya'bebel laj xchu', ora laj chu'un te alale. Komo k'alal teay yaiyel a, chu'un laj ta ora te k'alal a'bot te xchu'e, laj ta chu'a te waiye och ta jeltayel yu'un te snane, ay ton te laj bajt sjukan sba a, muk'ul pechpech ton laj, yakaltolaj ta chu' te alal k'alal te och sjeltaye, komo t'uxem yaiyel. Yo jich laj kajal ta yakani, yo ja' nax te k'alal la snik sbae; bal xchilaj koel, balch'ujnax koel sok te sojmile. Te jilix abi, te snane bajt stsak ta ora te ya yal te yale pero ma ba ipajix ta sk'ab, ja' xan lajix te skujchile, jipxan lajix sp'atbeyojix jielel a, pe te alale, bajt, te bajtix a stukel, te jilix a, jip a te chu'une bajt ta yutil te ch'ene.

Ayin ta na stukel, ja' laj yu'un te ma ba la stsak xchu'e, ja' yu'un bajt ta ik'el te ta banti jachem talel yaiyele, jichlaj abot swayichin te tenix ya yik' bael a e. Te jil a te alale, sujt te snane, mayukix ba alal te jilix a. Ma xkil ay laj wan lajunebuk yabilal a te k'alal lok'talele, jul ta st'unel xchajol te snane, komo ya yil stukel, ya yil ya sna'be sba. Jich te ayin te waiy ajaw Jwan Lopese.

K'alal la st'un te snane ya x-a'tej sok, ya laj sts'unik tumin, puro tumin laj ya sts'unik, yo pe ya sta kontrainel che. Meba alal xchi ka waiy te kristianoetike, ya slabanik. Ta Bajch'ajon te kole, ja' me ta na wakax ya kaltike, te laj ya x-abot skanantay chij a me ine, pero ya laj xtal te waiye, te laj ya xtal sjachbe bael jimuch' a te chije, paaak' xhilaj ya xk'ojt ta sjol te chije, teenax laj ya xcham yu'un abi; ja' laj yu'un och ta jkanan chij yu'unik.

Weno muk'ubtalel bayel ay yaiyel te miltanbae. Bajtiklaj la stsob sba ja' me swinkilel lume. Konkik te ta miltanbae xchiiklaj. Ya laj xtal solaroetik, yakik lajix ta sojlel talel ta San Kristobal. Komo ay toyol ch'en te a me ta Chakte'e, toyol me ine, tenix ya sojlotik ta ye'tal a; jichwan stoyolil binut'il alaxax ini, ja' ich stoyolil te nix ya soj ta ye'tal a te kristianoetik te nameye. Mato ayuk stuj'ik a te waiye, ma bin ay yu'unik, ja' yu'un la stsobik ton, ina busil te ta bajch'ene, komo jich ya xbeen tal te solaro ta xch'ujt yaiyel te ch'ene, jich laj yak ta sojlel ai ya laj sbusk'inik koel te ya yalike. Te Jwan Lopese, me ine ma lekuk, ma jichuk ya sk'an pasel, ilawilik ja'i binti ya jpastiki ma jichuk ya sk'an pasel; mero ya nax k'ak' jbatik ta lajel a, mero obol abaik xchi ta yalel te Rey Jwan Lopese. Pee bi yu'un, ja'at tut alalat ja'at mero ka na' yaiyel xchilaj sk'oalal, bi mauk ya jna' obol a baik. Jichuk abi binti ya sk'an ya jpastik che, te me ay binti ya sk'an pasele jalame abi jpaskiltik xchi te mamaletike. Yo, ay bal te atulanilike; ay, tulanotkotik[5] xchiik laj, weno jichuk abi.

Lok'esaik kiltik che, ya xwiil lumto ya xk'ojt ta yan tsejle. Jejch uk'um, jejch ja', ja te ya'lel Chakte' e. Weno ya xjachik ta wilel ta banti la tsobik te tone yato xk'ojt ta jejch te ja'e, namal te ya xwijlike. Laj ta sojlel: yan laj jkots, yan laj choj, yantiklaj yilel te yok te ta tone, ay spimikil ya sta sbai ma ba pajal ya xk'ojt.[6] Weno laj yo'tan a te waiye, melel nimati a alko aytonix atulailik jiche, ay xchijik laj. Jaxanat aybal awu'un ek, ak'ame ta ilel abi, komo jo'otkotik la wilbotkotikix te ku'unkotike, xchiiklaj. Jichuk abi; komo ay laj snabate' stukel sts'apbel junax welta ta lum, t'ojt'oj la jyil k'axel te sjamalil bajlumilale, stsapbel koel, jichlaj la syuk'ilani; pee stukel te mamaletike xlamet laj ta lum sk'echtiklanbel yokik ta yajlel; nijk te bajlumilale, nijkel, ya laj syuk'ilan, mero xtichlajan laj ta lum te mamaletik k'alal ma slijlin sba ta syuk'el te snajbate'e, lok'emix slabik abi.

Weno laj a te waiye, la stam jachel sbaik, och laj xcha' yalbeik te batsíl ajaw Jwan Lopese, yo'tik la jkiltikix te yu'unix mero k'ax tulanat[7] ae, la jyutik, ja'at mati p'ijat, ja'at nimati toyolat a; te jo'otkotike mayuk binti xu' ku'unkotik jich binut'il me ine xchiik laj. Weno ja' te waiye la jyal xchajol te Reye, ini talix te solaroetike, xchilaj, talix lok'ix tal ta San Kristobal, pero te me li' ya x-ayinexe, ya xbojon jo'on ya xba jta talel xchilaj; ja'nix sk'ojlal a bajt te ta ye'tal K'ankujke. Bajt laj te waiye, bajt, pero te jkotse ya kik' stukel, ya kik'i jkotsi xchilaj. Weno ja' laj xchejchon bael ta spat k'alal yak ta bael, bajt laj, bajt la sta k'oel, komo koel tal me ta ye'tal K'ankujke, weno poch'ol te bee, weno poch'ol, yo'tik te laj a te waiye, la jyil kojtal te solaoetike, ora laj na'bot sba te ajaw Jwan Lopese, orita bats'il ajaw[8] ja'at xchilaj sk'olal, jo'on xchilaj ta sjak'el. Ochlaj ta abeyel bala te waiye, komo te jkotse la laj spots ta tulan tak'in, la laj spots, k'alal ya xtal ta abeyel te balae, jich laj la yak' te xike, jich ya slich te xik'e xchitet ta julal ta sik' te balae, weno pe tenax laj yak ta p'olel a, jich laj ya stejk'ani, ya laj smak te Reye, xchitetlaj ta abeyel te balae, k'alal laj ta t'omel stujk' te solaroe. Weno la jyalix abi, lajix te bala mayukix, lajix te balae, weno xchilaj, yo'tik uts k'elel jilel a te ajaw Jwane. Komo ay laj te snajbate' stukele, ja' nax laj ya sjoptal te sbalae, te busulixe, ya sjoptalel jich laj ya sjimimin a te ta snajbate'e, powre solaro, lamal laj ta lum, laj te solaroetike.

Ja' yu'un te Rey kuxul ya yalik ini, kuxul. Ja' yu'un jich binut'il ya yalik che, te me ya xjach miltanba ini ya xlok' tal te ajawe, te me ya laj xjach te miltanbae, ya laj xlok' tal te bats'il ajaw Inyo tseltal.[9]

Oxeb welta la smilik te ta K'ankujke, been laj komo rey che, kojt k'alal Oxchuk', Witstan bayuk laj k'ojt komo rey ka waiyche. Li' kol ta Bajch'ajoni, jich binut'il ya kaltik che, te ya sts'un te tumine, yu'un laj spak'; te meiltatilnix a te nameye jalbil pak' te ya slapike. Ya sts'un te tumine jich swotsili pe bayel laj ya xlok' yu'un a, pero ya xkontrainot laj yu'un te swinkilel te lume.

Ta Ts'ulanbil[10] te ta banti jachtalele, te anyij a, sna te waiye ay ta Kante'elja',[11] te swinkilel lume ma xyal, ma xyak'ik ta ilel k'uxultaybil komo sna Reyche, aynix leot, pee ma'yuk mach'a la jyal banti stojol.

Notes

1. This tale is one of seven predominant traditional narratives that have survived regarding a person of great magic and social power. It originated in the community of Swijlibjá, in the Municipality of Chilón, Chiapas. The tale was a conversation held at the beginning of the 1990s with Señor Manuel Hernández. The original tale was partly in Tzeltal and partly in Spanish; this presented a sizable challenge for the author and Carlos Montemayor to achieve a text entirely in Tzeltal with a literal translation in Spanish.

2. The Tzeltal people also call their language Batz'il K'op, "true language" or "true voice." At the end of the twentieth century there were more than 547,000 Tzeltal speakers, living primarily in the state of Chiapas. The alphabet the author uses is among the Indigenous-language alphabets in Chiapas that resulted from the practice and the exchange of experiences among the members of Sna Jtz'ibajom (House of the Writer) and the Mayas-Zoques Writers Group. In the early 1990s the writers belonging to these independent organizations held a series of work sessions in Tuxtla Gutiérrez with the National Institute for Adult Education (INEA) and the Department of Ethnic Cultures of the State Government of Chiapas. The objective was jointly to establish practical alphabets in languages of interest to the INEA: Tzeltal, Tzotzil, Tojolabal, Chol, and Zoque.

3. *Ye'tal* (at the foot of or within) *lejch ch'en* (the cave). Before beginning his tale, the narrator pointed out that this is a specific cave within the sacred hill called Ts'ulanbil, located near the Kante'elja' River, as he later clarifies and reiterates. Even though it does not appear in the

Notas

1. El presente relato constituye una de las siete narraciones tradicionales principales que se recuerdan acerca de un personaje de gran poder mágico y social. Proviene de una comunidad de Chilón llamada Swijlibjá; fue una conversación sostenida en los inicios de la década de los noventa del siglo XX con el señor Manuel Hernández. Parte del relato original fue en tzeltal y parte en español, lo que dificultó grandemente al autor y a Carlos Montemayor lograr un texto único en tzeltal con una traducción literal en español.

2. Los tzeltales también llaman a su lengua *batz'il k'op*, es decir, "idioma verdadero" o "voz verdadera." A finales del siglo XX contaba esta lengua con más de 547,000 hablantes localizados principalmente en el estado de Chiapas. El alfabeto que emplea el autor es uno de los alfabetos en las lenguas indígenas de Chiapas que surgieron de la práctica y del intercambio de experiencias entre los integrantes de Sna Jtz'ibajom (Casa del Escritor) y de la Asociación de Escritores Mayas-Zoques. A principios de la última década del siglo XX los escritores de estas organizaciones independientes sostuvieron varias reuniones de trabajo en Tuxtla Gutiérrez con el Instituto Nacional de Educación para Adultos (INEA) y el Departamento de Culturas Étnicas del Gobierno de Chiapas, a fin de alcanzar acuerdos en el establecimiento de alfabetos prácticos en las lenguas de interés para el INEA: tzeltal, tzotzil, tojolabal, chol y zoque.

3. *Ye'tal* (al pie o dentro) *lejch ch'en* (de la cueva). El narrador advirtió antes del registro de su relato que se refiere a una cueva (*lejch ch'en*) específica, en un cerro sagrado llamado Tsulanbil, que se encuen-

Tzeltal text, we have decided to include the name of the river in the translations from the beginning, since the native listeners understand that it is a reference to *that* particular cave and not an undetermined one. The ambiguity here, however, maintains the cave's secrecy.

4. The expression Rey Jwan Lopes (King Juan López) is generally used to refer to this historical character, who symbolizes the social struggles of the Mayan peoples of the Chiapas Highlands, particularly in the area surrounding the town of Bachajón. The tale's title is significant: Bats'il Ajaw (Lord, Angel, or True Owner) Jwan Lopes (Juan López) Kanan Chij (Shepherd). The tale uses the terms *rey* and *ajaw* synonymously, though the semantic value of *ajaw,* from the formula Bats'il Ajaw, surpasses the narrator's specific intentions. For that reason, we have decided to use the word *ajaw* rather than reduce it to one of its possible meanings of "lord," "owner," or "angel." Given that the Tzeltales refer to themselves as Bats'il (true), Bats'il Ajaw might be interpreted as "The Tzeltal *Ajaw.*"

5. The reiteration of the idea of "strength" or "power" in this passage (*tulanilike,* "truly powerful"; *tulanotkotik,* "we, the powerful") suggests that "power" corresponds to a magical authority and not a political one.

6. Here we learn of the elders' "power": their ability to transform themselves into a variety of animals capable of leaving tracks, even upon stone. In other words, they are elders who possess the power of their *nahuales.* (See Appendix G.)

7. The expression *k'ax tulanat,* "you are more powerful," is also the recognition of his magical power; therefore, the Spanish word *rey* (king) is used more in a magical than a political context. He is "king" since he is Bats'il Ajaw and not Ajaualil or Muc'ul Ajwalil, terms commonly used to refer to "governors" or "presidents."

8. The soldiers recognize Juan López as "Bats'il Ajaw," not as "king"; that is, the tale underlines his nature as "lord" or "owner."

9. This designation sums up the essence of Juan López' name and his nature as Bats'il Ajaw and, specifically, as *inyo tzeltal,* "Tzeltal Indian"; that is, he is not a "king" who reigns over the Tzeltal people but rather the "lord" who protects them. He is not only the "True Angel" *of* the Tzeltal people; he himself *is* a Tzeltal Indian.

10. Here Ts'ulanbil is recognized as a sacred "hill" or "mountain"; it is understood that within it is found the cave where Juan López was conceived.

11. The name places the hill in Kante'elja' (i.e., in the vicinity of the river).

tra por el río Kanteljá, que después aclara y reitera. Decidimos, aunque no aparece en el texto tzeltal, incluir el nombre del río en las traducciones desde el inicio, aunque los oyentes nativos saben que se trata de *esa* cueva, no de una cueva indeterminada. Sin embargo, la ambigüedad asegura su secreto.

4. Con la expresión "Rey Jwan Lopes" (El Rey Juan López) suele designarse a este personaje histórico y a la vez simbólico de las luchas sociales de los pueblos mayas de los Altos de Chiapas, particularmente en la zona que tiene como eje regional el pueblo de Bachajón. El título del relato es significativo: Bats'il Ajaw (el señor, ángel o dueño verdadero) Jwan Lopes (Juan López) Kanan Chij (cuidador de ovejas). El relator emplea los términos *rey* y *ajaw* como sinónimos, pero la carga semántica de la voz *ajaw* y de la fórmula "Bats'il Ajaw" rebasa la intención específica del relator. Por ello hemos decidido utilizar la palabra *ajaw* sin reducirla a uno de sus posible sentidos de "señor," "dueño" o "ángel." Como los tzeltales se denominan a si mismos con la voz *bats'il* (verdadero), Bats'il Ajaw puede entenderse como "el *Ajaw* Tzeltal."

5. La reiteración de la idea de "fuerza" o "poder" en este pasaje (*tulanilike,* "verdaderamente poderosos"; *tulanotkotik,* "poderosos nosotros") sugiere que el "poder" no es de autoridad política, sino mágica.

6. Aquí se ilustra sobre el tipo de "poder" de los ancianos: el de convertirse en esta variedad de animales que son capaces de dejar huellas incluso en la roca viva. En otras palabras, son ancianos que tienen el poder de sus "nahuales." (Véase Apéndice G.)

7. Esta expresión *k'ax tulanat,* "eres más poderoso," es el reconocimiento también a su poder mágico, de manera que la voz española *rey* está empleada más en un contexto mágico que político. Es el *rey* como Bats'il Ajaw, no como Ajaualil o Muc'ul Ajwalil (Gran Señor), términos habituales estos dos últimos para referirse a los "gobernadores" o "presidentes."

8. Los soldados reconocen a Juan López como Bats'il Ajaw, no como "rey"; esto es, el relato recalca su naturaleza de "señor" o "dueño."

9. Esta designación es el resumen esencial del nombre y naturaleza de Juan López: reitera su carácter Bats'il Ajaw y especifica: *inyo tzeltal,* "indio tzeltal." Es decir, no se trata del "rey" que impere sobre los tzeltales, sino del "señor" que los protege: éste es el "ángel verdadero" no sólo *de* los tzeltales, sino esencialmente que *es* indio tzeltal.

10. Aquí Ts'ulanbil es reconocido como un "cerro" o "montaña" sagrada, entendiendo que en sus entrañas se encuentra la cueva donde fue engendrado Juan López.

11. El nombre sitúa al "cerro" en Kanteljá (es decir, en la vecindad del río).

Juan López, the Tzeltal *Ajaw* and Shepherd (Manuel Hernández, Swijlibjá, Chilón)

Domingo Gómez Gutiérrez

Tzeltal[1]

[From *La voz profunda: Literatura mexicana en lenguas indígenas*, pp. 98–105. Carlos Montemayor, prologue, literary selection, and notes. Mexico City: Joaquín Mortiz, 2004.]

A man, with his wife and daughter, went to visit some relatives. As they were returning home and just as they reached the Kanteljá River,[2] night fell upon them, short of their town. Fortunately, there was a cave on the riverbank that was good for spending the night. There they relieved themselves of their cargo and spread their few blankets to rest upon. The following day, as they set out for home, the girl began to feel pain in her abdomen, and she had a premonition that something was about to occur. Those were the symptoms of her pregnancy with the future King Juan López.

Her parents were not suspicious since they had been witnesses to the origin of her pregnancy. The child developed and was born in due time. It was a boy. The young girl was a good mother to him, and the grandparents were pleased with the baby, but the child did not seek his mother's breast. One night, the mother was told in a dream that when she returned with her child to the place where she had been impregnated, the problem would be resolved. The mother obeyed and took her baby to that place, to the cave at Tsulanbil.[3] There the child accepted his mother's milk without any difficulty. But the little one wet himself, and the mother went to change his damp clothing, which consisted of a piece of old, patched skirt. She sat down on a rock and stretched her legs. She reached for some clean clothing, and, as she did so, the child slipped from his mother's shawl and fell into the river, shawl and all. The mother tried to reach him, but the child disappeared in the current's white foam.

Unfortunately, the child did not return. Several years passed before he returned to his mother's side; he was perhaps ten years old when he returned, in search of his mother. During the time of his absence, he did not lose sight of who his mother was. That is how the king and *ajaw*[4] Juan López was born and grew up.

He became a hard-working man at his mother's side. He worked in the countryside and planted his field. One of his usual chores was planting cotton. What little he harvested multiplied in his hands. People became aware of this and grew envious. They would say: "How can it be that this fatherless boy has plenty of clothing, and his mother always has cotton to make it for him?"

He was born in Bachajón,[5] and that was where he grew up with his mother. In the place presently know as the "Shepherd's House," he hunted sheep. There he would wait; and when he saw an animal, he would place a stone into his sling, and with two or three twirls he would hurl it directly at the sheep's head. Each throw meant one dead sheep. That is why people called him *cananchij* or shepherd.

In those old times, the soldiers were trying to exterminate the Tzeltal people. On one occasion, thousands of soldiers set out from their barracks to wipe out the people of Bachajón. The elders knew that the army was coming to kill them and that it had already passed through San Cristóbal. They prepared a roadblock[6] to prevent the soldiers from entering their territory. They placed the first roadblock at Chacté,[7] a very high hill the pathway crosses; everyone who travels that route must go that way. They thought that they would be able to take the soldiers by surprise there as they grew weary in their ascent. Since the people lacked arms, they gathered stones to hurl down upon the enemy once they were climbing. Juan López, pondering this, said that he thought it would be better to look for a different strategy.

"Why do you say that?" the elders asked. "What do you know? You are just a boy. We are older than you, and we believe this way is correct."

"Ah," Juan López responded, "it may be. I am seeing the soldiers on their way; they are now heading for Cancuc."[8]

"If it is necessary to prepare something different, tell us what to do," the wise elders said.

"First, I need to know what you have to fight with," King Juan López explained.

"Yes, we are whole men, truly powerful men," the town's guardians insisted, "and we shall demonstrate this to you right now."

At that moment, jaguars, turkeys, horses—many animals—leapt from one hill to another, next to the river, next to the current, crossing the Chacté River canyon and leaving tracks even upon the stones.[9] Juan became concerned.

"Yes," he said, "you do have something, but it is not enough to defeat the enemy."

"Well then, what do *you* have, Juan? Are you stronger than us? We need to see what you have," the elders insisted.

"Ah," said Juan López, "this is what accompanies me."

He picked up his staff as if it were nothing, and he held it in both hands. He began to move it lightly from side to side, and a strong quake shook the earth. Even those who were gathered in a circle fell to the ground.

Once their fright had passed, he spoke with the Tzeltal wise men. The elders, barely having regained their composure, spoke to the True Ajaw Juan López and recognized he was the most complete man.

"You are stronger than us," they said. "Next to you, we are nothing at this moment."

"This time," said Juan López, "I shall see to it that the soldiers return to their barracks, because they have already passed San Cristóbal. You all head back to town. The soldiers are already near Cancuc; I shall go face them, but the turkey may come in handy; I shall take him with me."

And the turkey followed behind him, leaving his tracks atop Juan's footprints. The soldiers had not yet entered the town when they realized that the Ajaw Juan López was there.

"There comes the true *ajaw,* it is he," the commander said.

At that moment, the bullets began to resound. The turkey, now covered in steel, extended his wings and shielded the king so that they would not wound him. Once the bullets had run out, Juan López raised his staff, which then turned into a rifle. He gathered the bullets and, taking aim at the army, fired one shot. His one shot was all that was needed to leave all of the soldiers lifeless. It was just him against thousands of soldiers. None of the bullets wounded the king.

The elders say that the *ajaw* lives on: he is alive. That is what they still say; and if they try to exterminate the Indigenous people again, he will return: the *ajaw* will return to save them. And if war breaks out and they try to kill the people, the True Tzeltal Indian Ajaw will return.

Three times he was killed in Cancuc, but he never died. Before being killed, he visited several places, including Huixtán and Oxchuc.[10] He was a man born in this very town of Bachajón. Here he lived with his mother. He worked in the fields. He raised cotton. The people in those times took notice of Juan López, and some envied his intelligence.

Tsulanbil is the name of the cave where he grew up. It is his home. It is in Kanteljá.[11] The people respect it and worship there during each fiesta. It is a sacred place for them. On one occasion, strange people arrived, asking about the cave. Everyone refused to show it to those people. It cannot be revealed to outsiders because it is the Indian king's home. Those people departed without having seen it.

Notes

1. Like the Tzotzil people, the Tzeltal people also call their language Batz'il K'op, "true language" or "true voice." At the end of the twentieth century there were more than 547,000 Tzeltal speakers, living primarily in the state of Chiapas.

2. Tributary of the Tulijá River; the Paxiljá River joins it at Yax Ha' (Agua Azul). It has calm portions only in the vicinity of Bachajón; otherwise it is characterized by whitewaters and numerous falls.

3. Name of a sacred hill. This region is rich in caverns of different dimensions located in large cliffs; since pre-Hispanic times, they have played an important religious and magical role. The cave mentioned in the narration, as we shall see further on, is kept secret so that no one will locate it and defile it. See also note 3 of the Tzeltal-language text.

4. The author applies the titles "king" and *ajaw* synonymously to Juan López. The word *ajaw* has a very broad religious and magical meaning that surpasses the concept of a civil governor. See notes 4, 8, and 9 of the Tzeltal-language text and Appendix E.

5. Tzeltal community in the state of Chiapas located in the municipality of Chilón, some 80 miles northeast of San Cristóbal de las Casas. At the end of the twentieth century Chilón had a population of 77,633.

6. The author states in Tzeltal that "they gathered stones to defend themselves," but in Spanish he repeatedly employs the word *retén,* "checkpoint" or "roadblock"; this choice of words is surely influenced by the militarizing of the state of Chiapas following the 1994 Zapatista uprising.

7. Name of a hamlet located along the cliffs of the Kanteljá River, near Bachajón.

8. Tzeltal town and municipality in the state of Chiapas, located some 20 miles northeast of San Cristóbal de las Casas. At the end of the twentieth century Cancuc had a population of 21,074.

9. Here it becomes clear that the elders' "power" was magical and not political. Certain individuals, according to Indigenous belief, may

transform themselves or maintain a conscious relationship with certain animals that are their doubles or *nahuales*. (See Appendix G.)

10. Tzeltal towns and municipalities in the state of Chiapas. Huixtán is located some 15 miles northeast of San Cristóbal de las Casas and had a population of 18,689 at the end of the twentieth century. Oxchuc is located some 25 miles northeast of San Cristóbal de las Casas and had a population of 37,895 at the end of the twentieth century.

11. The ambiguity in describing the location of the cave is intentional; see note 3 of the Indigenous-language text.

El Ajaw Tzeltal Juan López, el Pastor (Manuel Hernández, Swijlibjá, Chilón)

Domingo Gómez Gutiérrez

Tzeltal[1]

[De *La voz profunda: Literatura mexicana en lenguas indígenas*, pp. 99–105. Carlos Montemayor, prólogo, selección y notas. México, D.F.: Joaquín Mortiz, 2004.]

Un señor fue con su esposa y su hija a visitar unos familiares. Al regresar les alcanzó la noche justo a la altura del río Kanteljá,[2] antes del pueblo. Afortunadamente había una cueva a la orilla del río, con buenas condiciones para pasar la noche. Descansaron de las cosas que cargaban y tendieron sus pocas mantas para descansar. Al día siguiente, cuando se encaminaron a casa, la muchacha empezó a sentir dolor en el vientre y presintió que algo iba a suceder. Eran los síntomas del embarazo de lo que fue el Rey Juan López.

Los papás no desconfiaron de la joven porque fueron testigos del origen. La criatura se desarrolló y nació en fecha normal. Fue un niño. La joven cumplía como buena madre y los abuelos estaban contentos, pero el bebé no pedía el pecho. Una noche, a la madre se le dijo en sueños que eso se resolvería llevándolo al lugar donde ella se había embarazado. La madre obedeció y llevó a su bebé a ese lugar, a la cueva en Tsulanbil.[3] Allí, sin ninguna dificultad, el niño tomó la leche de la madre. Pero la criatura se orinó y la madre quiso cambiarle la ropa mojada, que era un pedazo de enagua vieja y remendada. Se sentó en una piedra y estiró los pies; con el movimiento que hizo para tomar la ropa limpia el niño se resbaló y cayó en el río con toda la manta. La madre trató de alcanzarlo, pero el niño se desapareció en la espuma blanca de la corriente.

Lamentablemente, ya no regresó. Pasaron varios años antes de que volviera al lado de su madre. Como a los diez años volvió en busca de su mamá. Durante el tiempo de su ausencia no perdió de vista quién era su madre. Así nació y creció el *ajaw*[4] Juan López.

Se hizo un hombre trabajador al lado de su madre. Trabajaba en el campo y sembraba su milpa. Una de sus labores cotidianas era plantar algodón. Lo poco que cosechaba se multiplicaba en sus manos. La gente se daba cuenta y comenzó a envidiarlo. Decían: "¡Cómo es posible, a este muchacho huérfano de padre no le falta ropa, siempre tiene su madre algodón para tejerle ropa!" En Bachajón[5] nació y ahí mismo creció con su madre. En el lugar que actualmente conocemos como "casa del pastor" cazaba borrego. Ahí se paraba y cuando veía al animal colocaba la piedra en su honda y con dos o tres vueltas la lanzaba directo a la cabeza; cada lance era un borrego muerto. Por eso la gente le llamó *cananchij* o pastor.

En aquellos viejos tiempos los soldados intentaban exterminar a los tzeltales. En una ocasión partieron de sus cuarteles miles de soldados para arrasar con la gente de Bachajón. Los ancianos supieron que venía el ejército a sacrificarlos y que ya había pasado por San Cristóbal. Prepararon un retén con piedras[6] en el camino para impedir que entraran en su territorio. Colocaron el primer retén con piedras a la altura del Chacté,[7] un cerro muy alto que atraviesa la vereda; toda persona que viaja por ese rumbo forzosamente cruza esa vía. Pensaron que en ese lugar podrían tomar por sorpresa a los uniformados, que se fatigarían por subir. Como carecían de armas, juntaron piedras para derrumbarlas sobre el enemigo cuando estuviera subiendo. Juan López, después de meditarlo, dijo que sería mejor buscar otra estrategia. "¿Por qué dices eso? Tú qué sabes, eres un simple chamaco. Nosotros tenemos más edad que tú y creemos que esto está bien."

"Ah, pero puede suceder. Yo estoy viendo que los soldados ya vienen en camino, que ya vienen a Cancuc,"[8] respondió.

"Si es necesario preparar otra cosa, dinos qué hacer," preguntaron los ancianos sabios.

El Rey Juan López explicó: "Para eso necesito saber qué tienen ustedes."

"Sí, nosotros somos hombres completos, hombres en verdad poderosos," insistieron los guardianes del pueblo. "Te lo mostraremos ahora mismo." En ese momento se vieron tigres, guajolotes, caballos—muchos animales—que saltaban de un cerro a otro, junto al río, junto a la corriente, cruzando la cañada del Chacté y dejando huellas incluso en la piedra.[9]

Juan se preocupó: "Sí, traen algo, pero no suficiente para vencer a los enemigos."

"Entonces, ¿qué es lo que tú traes, Juan? ¿Eres más fuerte que nosotros? Necesitamos ver lo tuyo."

"Ah, lo que me acompaña es esto," dijo. Sembró con mucha naturalidad su bastón y lo tomó con sus dos brazos; ligeramente comenzó a moverlo de un lado a otro y se sacudió la tierra con un fuerte terremoto. Hasta las personas reunidas en círculo cayeron al suelo.

Después de que les pasó el susto habló con los sabios tzeltales. Los ancianos, recobrando apenas su color, hablaron con el Verdadero Ajaw Juan López y reconocieron que era el hombre más completo. "Eres más fuerte que nosotros. No somos nada ante ti en este momento."

"En esta ocasión yo me haré cargo de que los ejércitos regresen a sus cuarteles, porque ya pasaron de San Cristóbal. Ustedes tomen su camino hacia el pueblo. Los soldados ya vienen hacia Cancuc. Iré a encontrarlos," explicó el Rey Juan López, "pero el pavo me sirve, lo llevaré conmigo."

Y atrás de él vino el pavo, encimando sus huellas a las de Juan. Todavía no entraban en el pueblo cuando los soldados supieron que era el Ahau Juan López.

"Ahí viene el Verdadero Ajaw, es él," dijo el comandante.

En ese momento comenzaron a sonar los balazos. El pavo, que se había cubierto con acero, extendió sus alas y cubrió al rey para que no lo hirieran. Al agotarse las balas, Juan López levantó su bastón, que se convirtió en un fusil, juntó las balas y apuntó hacia el ejército: un solo disparo fue suficiente para dejar a todos los uniformados sin vida. Sólo él contra miles de soldados. El rey no fue herido por ninguna de las balas.

Los ancianos dicen que el rey permanece vivo, que vive. Así es como dicen todavía, y que si trataran de exterminar de nuevo a la gente indígena entonces saldría, regresaría el *ajaw* para salvarlos; si comenzara la guerra y quisieran matar a la gente, entonces regresaría el Verdadero Ajaw Indio Tzeltal.

Tres veces fue asesinado en Cancuc, pero nunca murió. Antes de su sacrificio visitó varios lugares, como Huixtán y Oxchuc,[10] entre otros. Fue un hombre que nació en este pueblo de Bachajón. Aquí vivió con su madre. Trabajaba en el campo. Sembraba algodón. La gente de aquellos tiempos se dio cuenta de Juan López y algunos le envidiaban su inteligencia.

Tsulanbil se llama la cueva donde creció. Es su casa. Está en Kanteljá.[11] La población la respeta y adoran ahí en cada fiesta. Es lugar sagrado para ellos. En una ocasión llegaron personas extrañas preguntando por la cueva. Todos se negaron a mostrarla. No se le puede revelar a los que vienen de fuera, porque es casa del rey indio. Las personas regresaron sin ver ese lugar.

Notas

1. Los tzeltales también llaman a su lengua *batz'il k'op*, es decir, "idioma verdadero" o "voz verdadera." A finales del siglo XX contaba esta lengua con más de 547,000 hablantes localizados fundamentalmente en el estado de Chiapas.

2. Afluente del río Tuliljá; se le une el río Paxiljá en Agua Azul y sólo en los alrededores de Bachajón tiene tramos de calma, pues es tumultuoso y de numerosas cascadas.

3. Nombre de un cerro sagrado. La región es rica en cavernas de diversas dimensiones y en grandes acantilados, que desde tiempos inmemoriales han tenido un importante papel religioso y mágico. La

cueva del relato, como se verá más adelante, se mantiene en secreto para que nadie la identifique y mancille.

4. El autor emplea como sinónimo de "rey" la palabra *ajaw*, que tiene un muy amplio sentido religioso y mágico. (Véase notas 4, 8 y 9 del texto en lengua tzeltal y Apéndice E.)

5. Comunidad tzeltal del estado de Chiapas localizada en el municipio de Chilón, al noroeste de San Cristóbal de las Casas. A finales del siglo XX Chilón tenía 77,633 habitantes.

6. El relator decía en tzeltal que "reunían piedras para defenderse," pero en español empleaba repetidas veces la palabra "retén," influido seguramente por la militarización del estado de Chiapas a partir del levantamiento zapatista de 1994.

7. Nombre de un paraje de los acantilados por los que se desplaza el río Kanteljá, cerca de Bachajón.

8. Poblado y municipio del estado de Chiapas localizado a 32 km al noreste de San Cristóbal de las Casas. A finales del siglo XX contaba con 21,074 habitantes.

9. Aquí se aclara que el "poder" de los ancianos era mágico. Ciertos individuos, según creencias indígenas, pueden convertirse o tener una relación consciente con determinados animales que son sus *dobles* o *nahuales*. (Véase Apéndice G.)

10. Poblaciones y municipios del estado de Chiapas. Huixtán se localiza a unos 24 km al noreste de San Cristóbal de las Casas y a finales del siglo XX contaba con 18,689 habitantes. Oxchuc se localiza a unos 40 km al noreste de San Cristóbal de las Casas y a finales del siglo XX contaba con 37,895 habitantes.

11. La ambigüedad para ubicar la cueva es intencional; véase nota 3 al texto en lengua tzeltal.

María Roselia Jiménez

Tojolabal

María Roselia Jiménez. Photographed at Ixk'inib Mountain, Lomantam, Las Margaritas, Chiapas.

María Roselia Jiménez, Tojolabal writer and cultural promoter, was born in González de León, Comitán, Chiapas. She primarily writes stories for children and has been a grantee of the National Fund for Culture and the Arts. Jiménez has served as president of the Mayas-Zoques Writers Group, Inc., and coordinator of the Southern Mayan Writers Association. In 1996 she published the volume entitled *Jna'jeltik/Vivencias tojolabales* (Tojolabal Life Experiences) as part of the series Colección Letras Mayas Contemporáneas: Chiapas. She presently coordinates the Tojolabal Cultural Center near Comitán, Chiapas.

María Roselia Jiménez, escritora y promotora cultural tojolabal, es originaria de González de León, Comitán, Chiapas. Escribe cuentos para niños; ha sido becaria del Fondo Nacional para la Cultura y las Artes. Ha fungido como presidente de la Unidad de Escritores Mayas-Zoques, A.C., y coordinadora de los Escritores Mayas del Sur. Fue publicado en 1996 *Jna'jeltik/Vivencias tojolabales* en la segunda serie de la Colección Letras Mayas Contemporáneas. Actualmente coordina el Centro Cultural Tojolabal cerca de Comitán, Chiapas.

Jas lo'il ja statawelo, jtatawelotikoni

María Roselia Jiménez

Tojolabal[1]

[From *Jna'jeltik/Vivencias tojolabales,* pp. 20–21. Colección Letras Mayas Contemporáneas: Chiapas, 2nd series, vol. 5, C. Montemayor, series ed. Mexico City: INI/TRF, 1996.]

Ja najatei jela slo'ila jtatawelotikoni',[2] ja wax wajye a'teli, ti wax ch'ak yalawe jas lo'lei. Wax yalawe ke jas tataweloei b'a najate', yajni wax wajye a'teli, ja yajni wax kujlaji k'akui, wan b'ix ya'kan a'tel jas winikei, jaxa ye'nlei wan b'ix waj paxial.

Jaxa yajni wax yi'aj buelta, b'ut'elxa smoralei, ja ti b'i wax yalyab'a swinikei oj jijluk, ja ti wax ya elka sb'aal jas morralei, jun b'i tsamal k'aem, jun b'i mansana, jun b'i naranja, jun lima, jun papaya che'xtab'i.

—¡Lo'nik! wax yala.

Ja ti wax jo'b'jiyia:

—¿B'a waxa ta', tat jun? ¡Alaka'b'tikon! . . . ¡Lo'nik, Lo'nik! . . . tita wax a'jikia, yajb'al ti'itik. Jaxa tuk smoji, mi wax kan gusto, t'ilan wax k'an yila b'a lugaril wax k'ota'. Jaxa stataweloei mis sk'ana sjee'.

Jela slo'lei, masan ni iljiyea, le'jinia, mix ta'ji b'a wax ochyea yuxta k'ot k'ak'u iljiye'. Ja ti b'i wax k'otye b'a wits sb'iil, "IXK'INIB,"[3] wax yalawe ke yioj sb'aal, wan b'ix ochye ja b'a yojola witsi', ja ti b'i was ta'we sb'aali, yuxta mi yentoriluka winik was na'a, jun cha'b'e ma' wax ochi, ja ma' was na'a, ja ma' ay yi'oj sjakeli'.

Jachka slo'ila jtatawelotikoni'.

Ay b'i tuk winik ma' yi'oj sjakel, ja yajni chamta tuk tataweloi', wan b'ix yalawe; ke mi najka chameluk, najka ti ayea', wax yalawe: Ja juni' sna' guitarra, jacha juni sna' wajb'anel, ja juni sna' bigolin, jaxa juni sna' ajmay . . . ti naka ayea, mitox wajye', tsamala b'a ayei, tsamal lek.

Ja'ch wax yala ma' yi'oj sjakeli. Yuxta kechan ye'n wax yilawe, kechan ye'n sna'we.

Ja'chto wax ka'b'tikona slo'ila jtatawelotikona wego', ja'ch b'i wax yala stataweloei. Kechan yenle yilawe jas tsamalila ixk'inib'i, ja jasunka yioj ja b'a yojoli'.

Te'ya ixk'inib'i, wan smojtajel ja ma' kujlaji b'a lomantami. Ojma yi' chab' ora jk'otika b'a snii', ti chikan leka chonob'a, jel yi'oja k'uli, ti oj ta'ti b'ej jun sat ja' che'exta lek.

Notes

1. "Tojolabal" comes from *tojol,* "true," and *'ab'al,* "word," "language." As in the case of the Tzeltal and Tzotzil languages, Tojolabal is also referred to as a "true language." At the end of the twentieth century there were more than 78,000 speakers of this language, living primarily in the state of Chiapas. The alphabet the author uses is among the Indigenous-language alphabets in Chiapas that resulted from the practice and the exchange of experiences among the members of Sna Jtz'ibajom (House of the Writer) and the Mayas-Zoques Writers Group. In the early 1990s the writers belonging to these independent organizations held a series of work sessions in Tuxtla Gutiérrez with the National Institute for Adult Education (INEA) and the Department of Ethnic Cultures of the State Government of Chiapas. The objective was jointly to establish practical alphabets in languages of interest to the INEA: Tzeltal, Tzotzil, Tojolabal, Chol, and Zoque.

2. This tale from "our grandfathers" comes from Señora Trinidad Pérez García, who lives in the community of Lomantam, Municipality of Las Margaritas, Chiapas.

3. The original name was formed from *xk'inib',* "hill," and *yb',* "beneath." The present-day contraction lacks the original meaning.

Notas

1. Tojolabal proviene de *tojol,* "verdadero," y *'ab'al,* "palabra," "idioma." Es decir, como en el caso de la lengua de los tzeltales y tzotziles, la lengua de los tojolabales también es "idioma verdadero." A finales del siglo XX contaba esta lengua con más de 78,000 hablantes localizados fundamentalmente en el estado de Chiapas. El alfabeto que emplea la autora es uno de los alfabetos en las lenguas indígenas de Chiapas que surgieron de la práctica y del intercambio de experiencias entre los integrantes de Sna Jtz'ibajom (Casa del Escritor) y de la Asociación de Escritores Mayas-Zoques. A principios de la última década del siglo XX los escritores de estas organizaciones independientes sostuvieron varias reuniones de trabajo en Tuxtla Gutiérrez con el Instituto Nacional de Educación para Adultos (INEA) y el Departamento de Culturas Étnicas del Gobierno de Chiapas, a fin de alcanzar acuerdos en el establecimiento de alfabetos prácticos en las lenguas de interés para el INEA: tzeltal, tzotzil, tojolabal, chol y zoque.

2. Este relato de "nuestros abuelos" se debe a la señora Trinidad Pérez García de la colonia de Lomantam, Municipio de las Margaritas, Chiapas.

3. El nombre original se formaba de *xk'inib',* "cerro," y de *yb',* "debajo." Se trata, pues, de una contracción que carece del sentido original.

A Tale from Our Grandfathers and Great-Great-Grandfathers

María Roselia Jiménez

Tojolabal[1]

[From *Jna'jeltik/Vivencias tojolabales,* pp. 20–21, 48–49. Colección Letras Mayas Contemporáneas: Chiapas, 2nd series, vol. 5, C. Montemayor, series ed. Mexico City: INI/TRF, 1996.]

As told by Señora Trinidad Pérez García, from the town of Lomantam, Municipality of Las Margaritas, Chiapas.

This is what our grandfathers and great-great grandfathers would tell regarding Ixk'inib,[2] the mountain that accompanies the Tojolabal town of Lomantam, in the Municipality of Las Margaritas.[3] Many, many years ago, our grandfathers and great-grandfathers told that the elders of that time would leave their work and companions in the fields exactly at midday to take a walk. They would then return with their sacks full of fruit, which they would give to their fellow laborers: an apple, sugar cane, a papaya, an orange, a lime . . . all quite cold. That was the content of our grandfathers' sacks.

"Eat, eat!" they would say.

The rest would ask: "Grandfather, from whence do you bring all of this? Tell us, please, so that we too may go and obtain some."

The elders would only say: "Eat, eat! It is for your palates' delight. We obtain it nearby; we are given all of this not far from here."

Everyone wondered and wanted to know where those gifts came from. They wanted to discover and visit that place to enjoy such a delight. However, the elders would never say a thing. Speculation abounded, and, as they tell, one day they successfully followed the grandfathers and discovered that the elders entered a cave that led them inside the mountain, to the very tip of Ixk'inib'. That mountain possessed a treasure that could be enjoyed only by those gifted with wisdom and special powers. That mountain is Ixk'inib', located in Lomantam. There the chosen grandfathers enjoyed the mystery of its interior. Other men attempted it; they entered but never found anything. Nevertheless, the grandfathers said that they obtained all the gifts in a place that was picturesque, exuberant, and incomparable.

When some of the wise grandfathers died, the others would say that they were not dead; they were living in that lovely place, where they continued to see them. They would also say: "Grandfather so-and-so plays the violin; another plays the drum, another the reed flute, and they are always celebrating there quite happily. They are not dead."

That is what those who had a special gift such as that of the grandfathers would state. That is what our grandfathers' grandfathers or our great-great-grandfathers' grandfathers would tell. Only they saw and enjoyed that fantastic world. Ixk'inib' has its mystery, a mystery that only those wise grandfathers were able to discover and enjoy.

The mountain is there, keeping the Tojolabal town of Lomantam company, and preserving the memory of our grandfathers deep inside. It takes just two hours to climb to the peak and look out over Comitán.[4] Along the way, the hiker encounters exuberant vegetation and a cool flowing stream.

Notes

1. "Tojolabal" comes from *tojol,* "true," and *'ab'al,* "word," "language." As in the case of Tzeltal and Tzotzil, Tojolabal is also referred to as a "true language." At the end of the twentieth century there were more than 78,000 speakers of this language, living primarily in the state of Chiapas.

2. Literally, "under the hill"; from *xk'inib',* "hill," and *yb',* "beneath." The present-day name is a contraction that has lost its original meaning.

3. Las Margaritas is a municipality located in the Chiapas jungle, within the area known as Las Cañadas (the ravines). At the end of the twentieth century the population was 97,389; Lomantam is one of its communities.

4. Comitán de Domínguez is the *cabecera* or administrative seat of the *fronteriza* or "border" region of Chiapas. At the end of the twentieth century it consisted of 272 localities or communities, with a population close to 100,000.

Lo que contaron nuestros abuelos y tatarabuelos

María Roselia Jiménez

Tojolabal[1]

[De *Jna'jeltik/Vivencias tojolabales,* pp. 48–49. Colección Letras Mayas Contemporáneas: Chiapas, 2a serie, vol. 5, C. Montemayor, coord. de la colección. México, D.F.: INI/TRF, 1996.]

Narración de la Señora Trinidad Pérez García de la colonia Lomantam, Municipio de las Margaritas.

Esto contaban nuestros abuelos y tatarabuelos sobre el Ixk'inib',[2] cerro que acompaña al pueblo tojolabal Lomantam del municipio de las Margaritas.[3] Hace muchísimos años, nuestros abuelos y bisabuelos contaban que los viejos de aquel entonces, cuando se retiraban a trabajar al campo, exactamente al mediodía abandonaban las labores y a sus compañeros para ir de paseo. Regresaban luego con su morral lleno de fruta para regalar a los que se encontraban trabajando con ellos. Una manzana, una caña, una papaya, una naranja, una lima, bien fríos. Era el contenido del morral de los abuelos.

—¡Coman, coman!—decían.

Los demás les preguntaban:

—¿Abuelo, de dónde traes esto? Dinos, por favor. Así iremos nosotros y conseguiremos también.

Los abuelos sólo decían:

—¡Coman, coman!, que es para deleite del paladar. Lo consigo cerca, acá no más me lo dan.

Todos tenían dudas, querían saber de dónde procedían esos regalos, descubrir el lugar para visitarlo y disfrutar de ese deleite. Pero los viejos nunca decían nada. Surgieron muchos comentarios y, según cuentan, un día siguieron con éxito a los abuelos y descubrieron que se internaban en una cueva que los conducía al interior del cerro, a la punta del Ixk'inib'. Ese cerro poseía un tesoro del que únicamente podían disfrutar gentes dotadas de sabiduría y encantamiento. Ese cerro es el Ixk'inib' de Lomantam. Ahí, los abuelos escogidos disfrutaban de ese misterio del interior. Otros hombres lo intentaron, penetraron y nunca encontraron nada. Pero ellos decían que todo lo conseguían en un pintoresco y exuberante lugar, incomparable.

Cuando murieron algunos sabios abuelos, los otros decían que no estaban muertos, que vivían en ese lugar hermoso y que ellos los veían y le decían:

—El abuelo fulano toca el violín; otro abuelo toca el tambor; otro el carrizo. Y están siempre de fiesta ahí, muy contentos. No están muertos.

Eso afirmaban los que poseían un don como el de los abuelos. Esto contaban los abuelos de nuestros abuelos o de nuestros tatarabuelos. Sólo ellos vieron y disfrutaron ese mundo fantástico. El Ixk'inib' tiene su misterio, un misterio que pudieron descubrir y disfrutar únicamente esos sabios abuelos.

El cerro ahí está, haciendo compañía al pueblo tojolabal de Lomantam y conservando en su interior el recuerdo de nuestros abuelos. Sólo se necesitan dos horas para llegar a la cumbre y divisar Comitán.[4] A su paso, el caminante encuentra una exuberante vegetación y un arroyo de fresca corriente.

Notas

1. *Tojolabal* proviene de *tojol,* "verdadero," y *'ab'al,* "palabra," "idioma." Es decir, como en el caso de la lengua de los tzeltales y tzotziles, la lengua de los tojolabales también es "idioma verdadero." A finales del siglo XX contaba esta lengua con más de 78,000 hablantes localizados fundamentalmente en el estado de Chiapas.
2. Contracción de "Yb'xk'inib"; literalmente, "debajo del cerro."
3. Las Margaritas: municipio situado en la selva chiapaneca, en la zona conocida como "Las Cañadas." A finales del siglo XX contaba con 97,389 habitantes; una de sus localidades es la comunidad de Lomantam.
4. Comitán de Domínguez es la cabecera de la región de Chiapas llamada "fronteriza." A finales del siglo XX contaba con 272 localidades o comunidades y una población total cercana a los 100,000 habitantes.

Javier Castellanos Martínez

Sierra Zapotec

Javier Castellanos Martínez. Photographed at Monte Albán, Oaxaca.

Javier Castellanos Martínez was born on September 20, 1951, in the community of Yojovi, Sierra Zapoteca, Oaxaca. He is a cultural promoter for the Oaxaca Regional Popular Cultures Office. In 1982 he was declared winner of the "Monographs on Corn" contest sponsored by the National Museum of Popular Cultures. He has been a grantee of the National Fund for Culture and the Arts in Indigenous Languages. Castellanos Martínez has published several audio recordings of Zapotec-language songs. In 1994 he published the first Indigenous-language novel in Mexico, *Wila che be ze lhao/Cantares de los vientos primerizos* (Songs of Bezelhao) in Editorial Diana's Letras Indígenas Contemporáneas series. In 2002 he was awarded the national Nezahualcóyotl Prize for Indigenous-Language Literatures.

Javier Castellanos Martínez nació en el estado de Oaxaca, en la comunidad de Yojovi, de la Sierra Zapoteca, el 20 de septiembre de 1951. Es promotor cultural en la Unidad Regional de Culturas Populares en Oaxaca. Fue ganador del concurso "Monografías sobre el maíz" que realizó el Museo Nacional de Culturas Populares en 1982. Fue becario del Fondo Nacional para la Cultura y las Artes en Lenguas Indígenas. Ha editado varios audios con letra y música de cantos en idioma zapoteco. Publicó en 1994 la primera novela en lengua indígena de México, *Wila che be ze lhao/Cantares de los vientos primerizos* en la colección Letras Indígenas Contemporáneas de Editorial Diana. En 2002 recibió el Premio Nezahualcóyotl de Literatura en Lenguas Indígenas.

Wila che be ze lhao

Javier Castellanos Martínez

Sierra Zapotec[1]

[From *Wila che be ze lhao/Cantares de los vientos primerizos: Novela zapoteca*, selections from Chapter 5, "Ki Guneo Guchhope," pp. 88–89, and Chapter 6, "Ki Guneo Goyone," pp. 107–111. Colección Letras Indígenas Contemporáneas. Mexico City: Editorial Diana/CNCA/DGCP, 1994.]

Ku Guneo Guchhope

Kate xtawanda ka blerhe'e do nhirha kerhe nachho nha godee yelazi dan zjanhua benextirha[2] ka. Kerhe schaa goka kate blerhakze do nhite, ka nhan goka nha gozorhao chhaza nha chhosekorha da chhelyalljenhe lee, nha llda'on kate lee chhelyalljenhe nha chhelixjoen xlatje; nha kate kebe chhelyalljenhe kan teze chhelixjoen, kate nhan gochhe yane bia nagan chholchibe bedon llbian nha chholsebilleba nha chhelotoeba nha bextee cheba nha llda'o. Izanhe, llin kanhi belon xtaochhogorha ka kuenll goka banhe, nha nhigaxkan dekze yela ban, yogote yelli ki sjazuaze baya, la bene xtirha sjazuallwe gaka gaka yolsenhitie da nhaka yelachhjalirhalle chechho, nhakaxha: yogote beneyelle nabage'e gogawe' bxoze che ka; yogote bene yelle shiabeate yelonhe toxhen yelachhjalirhalle che bene xtirha ka, yogo lekze kebe nho zua wen chhaka ki.

Kan chhakallwa dote yelle, kate golen wedila yelle xhon[3] ka. Bene xhon[4] golechogorhalle tege yolrhage bene xtirha ka, bene yelle Ljaxilla,[5] len golebiarhao, belon tipe yichja-laxdawe nha be ze che da xtaochhon gokarhen lee, wentika ba zeja xbaba chen,ba goledee dote naga lla bene yelakarhen lee, ja'ke yelle xidsa[6] ka, ja'ke yelle rhache ka, kanhan goka kate belrhe'ee do nhite. Gaka tika golaka che xtaochho gorha ka, nhakaxha golenesnenhe gan lla yane bene brhao ka, bene wechogorhalleka. Danhan kate belrhaa Gobeza che ka, kebekze garha jke, to weli belonhe blerhe'e rhille da xtawa ka. Kanhan goka yela bene byo chie, nha bchixe kuinhe dan chaka lawe rhallie lo llan, nha benkze ka da gozekenhe yela chhakarhen ljuelle. Katekze godee wedila den chhaka kate nha.

Kate ba bebe shis kate nhachha belrhaa *soldado* che bene xtirha, kate nhachha dalexi'e da xtawa nha golechi'e lee Lachewize,[7] to shesherha belrhe, kege nho gokebe'e belvhise lee. Nha kuenll ka nho goserhaa lee tonheza nha bolche'e xhneze, lee xkan sjanalaga benan byinha nha da xtawanda zeje ni'aze; nha golke nhezan zeja yelle mixhe, belshinte Yarharhja[8] nha goledie yelle ka nazi Tabaa-Yaxhobe,[9] nha ba sjalla yeto kue *soldado* chelbeze lee che chjalesanhe lee Lachewize; nha kaze nhaka *costumbre* che yelle kanhi chhja'ke chhjaleyue bene kan chheleche xtirha ka. Kan goka nha bshin to ndogorha chhi'e lee: "Chhu'a yego chhe'la nha nhela lbaa naga chala techho che llinchho Lachewize, nhanche chakarhallo'o yerhao, sjalla chhu'a yego ka chhe'la bene yelakarhenhe lhue."

Kate golesa'ke yelle Tabaa-Yaxhobe nha bolozocheje lee, daxhen golesa'ke che bleshinhe chhu'a yego nagan nhela lbaa dan gonha benan kan. Ka to lenhida xhen nachheja lbaa ka nha nhelan nagan chholorheja bene kan chhelede nha yechopan sjanhela chala'a-chala'a naga chheloxo bene tee; che da nhan kate blellin bene kinga sjanache' bene xtawan, llnhan ka llnhan, goleselle lee che gaka tie. Lee xkan, zaakze chheshirhja rhalle'e gaka gonhe che yerhee.

Zaakze[10] chheshirhja rhalle'e gaka gonhe che yerhee. kate nha' jsaralle'e, dan golle ndogoran le' katen godie yelle Taba-yaxhobe, kate gozorawe godie to warazie lba dan nhela nha', kate bllinhe gachjalawe ba gochogo rhalle'e goxhonjoe, ka bllinhe nhi nha goge'e gozorawe bie dilla ki:

—Xhan gobilla zea natekana'a, len nezenhe che chhonha xlatje, kanga le'e nachere nheda wxe-willja, gateteze gaa llinle kate chjati' chere, weyekebe'kzerhe den chhosakare nheto na'a, kanhakan geyaxjon, lhente xhi'ne-xhezuare yeziakebe gozon dan na'a chhonle, rhawe da chhekere le'ze nhapare nhaka chere den nazi dali, hhekere che le'zen zaka, nha nheto llanto gorjanto kuita yixe, kebe bi zakanto, ware'ren, wxewillja, yereren.

Kate beyolle gonhe ki nha goxitie lo yego.

Gaakatica bre'e xtawadao yachen chhakate nhua yego le'. Cheze zua nho chhoyue chhi'o en axkaren xoze-xnachho gonabe chechho, to bi goke le', gozeke bsan yego xhen le'. Yexlayo che bene xidza-nhate[11] gozeke bechhoje, nha gozorao chjaxake bene, benhetega san kate llnabe gara zua rallie, kere nho neze kere nho ne yen gan zua rallie. Gokaze nha jaxake'e bene goka bchaljarenhe tochhu'a kan goka chie, kanhazen goka nha jxake bene yelle Rhacheyerha,[12] kanhan goka nha bllinhe yelle nhiga, kate beneyelle[13] gonezenhe kan goka chie, nha golezié lo nhe'e bene xtawan. Kanhan goka bllin xtawan yelle Rhe'ja,[14] gokazekze nha brebe nhiga nha goke bene Rhacheyerha.

Nhigan gorhja no'rhadaon gozua che Lia Kaxhon, xhesua benen chhenia kin goka chie. No'rhadon nhiga gaka tica goka leze bechise dilla che xtawen, kere nachho bchhoja chhua'a benenga kanhaka den bre'nhe che bllinhe yelle nagan gorja Lia Kaxhon, kon natescho to waraze no'rhen gozorhawe gonezenhe kanhaka da goka che yelle kan chhelerhen ka hhelerhen kate nha'; san kebe nhaka kan, zua nho chhen, zua nho llrhe'e, nha llda rhalle[15] ya'a-yego nha len nezen da nhaka xlatje da ka nhaka, nha lekzen nezen bata yanen gore'e kuinhe che da nhan xtilla bigoran bia yego che bene xhon kate nha' kebe benhiten, che danhakze yogote binne bechjo che bigoran goxite ego che xhon-ka[16] golezi'e xhon, nhakaxha no'rhadon nazie Lia Kaxhon. Kate bene don goke no'rha chhaban nha gozorhawe lldee lhawe yelle ka chhonhe wete zeya da ka'. Kan llde' bllintie rhalle zede, nagan nazi Yaze'e,[17] donhate chheje nha zenhu'e nho bela, beladao nha yezika da llrha do nhara. Lhawe llde kan gokaze bembi'e bene, kate golabea ba jaxake'e xtia to bene goke brao che yelle kan, xhi'ne xhesua Goziobe,[18] kanhan goka nha goshajani'nhe kan chhaka che yelle chechhon kate nha'. Kanhan goka nha goshjani'be gaxhan chharja dan chosaka zi bene lla nhiga kate nha', nha bchhojan sorao gon nheza che yenhite yoa kan chhoda bene xtira kollo bene waralle, nhakaxha den chhonhe chhozuallie bene warhalle che chhelaze da kebe dyalljenhe cheze dyallje bene xtira len, lagaze wesekora beyixe begora leze chhochinenhe, nha bedi lldanechho chhi'o gokaze benhiteben ka bedon chhelenhe nhaka ka bejaga,[19] lhawe le' kebe bledanenheba. Kanhan goka nha gozorao blla kanhaka le'eyixe, rhawe da gozorao chhaza da byora, nhakaxha bene xtira ki bledanellwenhe bexte che bedon bala chhelenheba bchhenbia,[20] bedon llbia rhawe yaga bia', lakze bene waralle chholchinenhe bextedao cheban, cheze to ni'a to bata. Nha bene xtira ki gakateran bledanechjeba nha sjaneze benan gaxha ta'oba, kanha goka nha kanhaka yexlayo ka gozoraollwa chholoxinje golazen yaga bia'. Cheze kate kebe llda'on xtaochho nhan chhelixjoe, nha lagaze kate lldao'llwan kere nachho nha kanteze kuen rhalljo bene waralle, gade, xtira kanhan chheleziébanheza. Kankze chhelonhe chholonhelljue do che chhelia no'rha waralle llnha dilla chjake rha'a, cheze kate ba de rhachhe gade rha'a, len chholoshiabe'e gaka yerhe'e totoe; lagaze snia za'ke chholonhelljue nho bllinha, nho coche, nho jeide, che chhosekorachhoba, kate llnhan che nha chhonhen rha'a, kate kebe dyalljenheba nha chhone bayen goyuechhoba nha kixjochhoba, en kere begora dyalljechhon, berha'gaze lla da chhaka.

Kanhan chaka kate nha'. Kan ben yela chhon doralle, yela chjali da chhon, yela kebe gokeshije da kobe da nallara, yela chhon dorhalle lhen bene zito. Zan tao iza gode goka ki kate golezorao bala bene ba jaletaralle'e, bene kan hhelekenhe zi da de che', gokaze bdile xtilla to kue bene ki nha gozorao chhaka wechalja che yebeja yoraga bene xtira ka. Gaka tika nhaka che Lia Kaxhon jxake bene ki nha bdanenhe kan nhaka dilla sjanose'e, ka nhan goka nha norhadaon besetie dilla kan chala'a chechho nhigara, rhadjo yelle rheja kan, nagan zua Lia Kaxhon yelle Rhacheyerha, kanhaze goka nha gozorao dshin dilla dan bchhoja chhua xtawe'e, benhetegan kate nha' yelle Rhacheyerha nha zuakze to xhesua bene xtira bcheje da xtao Lia Kaxhon nha', kon nazi'e Reynozo. Bene nhiga kate nha gakaterhan chharhallwa benan, ka yogote bene warall chie, anka nho chheyaxjeze nho chisa yichja ne'e benan a wawe sote chekan kebe gozexjoe shichje', cheze kere chhekebe'nhe bixhan llda chhon Lia Kaxhon. No'rha dao nhi kagaze llde chhoti'e da kan chhjaxie yelle zito kagaze nha chosie dilla llnhan: "kanteze yela chhozexjo yichja lhao bene xtira" torii ba lldile bene bllio kan chi'e le' "che le'e kebe geyaxjerhe sorhaorhe le goseni'a teze lo yo'o rhillechho, le goyue le'e bidao chechho, nheto no'rha goserhaonto kuinhachho, xhi'ne xhesuachho." Che lenan kate golenan nha gozorhaon yelle Yaze'e, Lia Kaxhon gozorawen yelle naga nazi Gawi,[21] btilen kate nha', lhillellia sjalla to kue bene chholode'nhe ja'ke jlesere' bllinha che benen rhe Reynoso, sjadaba rhatja che bene Rhacheyerha, che lenan kate Lia Kaxhon bllinhe yelle Gawi llnhe do gosera bene kan lla Lhillellia,[22] balanhozua gochebe, chadi beshinja yo'o Lhillellia zua nha'.

Bene xtira kan sjazua nhiga kate gonezenhe kan ba chhaka leze benan bloxhonjoe lhente bene warhalle ba sjanhonhe toxhen lhen leake, kanhaze goka beza bene xtira yelle Gawi. Kate bezua rhaze lla byorha, kate goneze benen chhenia zua chie Reynozo kan goka la gozatie nachi'e *soldado* xtirha, chhekenhe chjasillenhe nhoxhan ben kan, gade, nestayania katen blellinhe yelle Gawi, do yelle ba sjalla kuase chhelebeze nho llida, ba nachogoralle kebechha nho we rhatja yezorhaon ka zan, da nhan bene kebe nhoxo'e *machete*, nhoxoe docho'na, yaga laa, bene kebekze bi nhu'e nha nolle'e yija lo yixjo chie. Da nha kate blerhe'e *soldado* xtirha do yelle ba goyasa nhoan geyaxje kin *espada* kollo bene kan chhakateze kate nha'a. Reynozo lldile dsillenhe *soldado* chie' che chjake gonhe zi bene ka, llbelleye'e chhoshiabie che *soldado* chie kebe chhelegeyajenhe yelele'e bene warhalle; chala'a nagan lla bene warhalle lhawete ze Lia Kaxhon shlisa chi'be chhosarhallebe yogote da chholosaka benextirha chhi'o. Kan zee lebe chala'a, ye chala'a ze Reynozo lhen *soldado* chie kate chhoyue nito ni yeto kebe nho chheyaxje goxo ljuelle, godechjabe jsebe gagote nagan ze bllinha che Reynozo, gozorhaobe chhebe le'e ki: "¡Kuinho bexo nheto che chhekenho nhapo yela dali, che chhekenho xlatjen chhonho noda'o yelazi'i kollonto, lla!" Ka ben Reynozo ki golokochje la beyetjatie llhawe ben nalage'e, keberha ne sua ye chala'a ni'en lo yo katekze Lia Kaxhon dao nhi, goxhobeyochjabe le' godapatebe to xage'e bzalatebe le' nhate, kate nhan goyaze beneyelle kan, *soldado* xtirha kerhe nha golezie' wexhonjo, kate nhan gonha Lia Kaxhon chhi'e Reynozo: "¡Che nezerhe kerhe nachho kebe chhaka gonto kan chhonle le'e cheze kebe nhaka nheto rhea ka le'e, llbe nheto ba de yelanaban chento, le'e kebekze bi chhalere kon da ba chhirhja rhallerhe llbejarhe nheto, nika chhekebe'zerhe che chhonan nheto zi' che chholen nheto, che lenan ba jatarallento, kanteze, na'a le ka xnezare le chjaya'ka!"

Beyolle bebe dilla ku ye charasa goxhobeyobe le' jatatie xhan ni'a bllinha chie', nha ze beyixe yachen llbezaba le'e, llbeke Reynozo nha ne zeba chadi belage'ba, wexhonjo.

Kante bllin yela wechogoralle che Lia Kaxhon godabagabe kebechha nho goyerao benewenia kan, a toze dillan ba nhaka lhen bene rhalle zede, bene rhache, bene chala'a nhigara, cheze kan gonhakze lebe, dzirhenchho chhi'o ba nhapachho yelanaban, danhazen da llbezachho chhi'o, che lenan kate brhe'n ba beza xtirha kan rhalle totochho, nha gozi yela xhenlalle. Cheze bene xtirha kere gonha benan kan, ba neze benan katite daxhen gonhitie chekan chhi'o kebechha gonchho llin chie, danhan kebe gochhi'e llize gode goka kin. Golezorawe chhelirja rhalle'e gaka gonhe che geyo'o lo taken dan bnhitie, ka chholoyue kebe seke bi gon *soldado* chie kan nha ben llin xtilla la'ya che bxoze kan. Chheleda benan chhelenhe galarhallechho da goka, kebe cho'orhallechho biche ljuellechho, gokaze bene warhalle kan jlecho'e lo yaljan, nha bosorha lli dan nabeke che chhowian kate za'ka bene xtira kan. Beyolle goka ki nha goyaze *soldado* xtirha kan dabyorha. Kate golekebe'yanenhe kebecha bi seke bi gon bene warhale nhachha gozorhao chholozue do yogote bene brhao kan, rhadjo nha' zeja Lia Kaxhon, le tikabe godixjoben, kere nho gozixhen chebe lhawe da to iza kebe godago xtirhan che xtaochho, a lega daxhen godixjo Lia Kaxhon yela gozerhalle cho'na da gorhan da kollochho. Bene warhalle hechhon, kate nhatekzen zan kan, ka shloyue benan ba bezua bene xtirhan nhiga nho bi na', kate nhan brhe'e bido birhan: bloseye'e yish yichjabe, golechoge lollebe, golechoge nhabe dan godapa benan chhosaka zi ljuellebe, zeya da brhe'be lhen yezika bene brhao che yelle Yaze'e che yelle Rhacheyerha.

Ba gocha lhue kan brhe'e bidao birha waka, nheda nestan a xchenhan, che da nhan shle'nho nheda chawe, xlatje, che lenan la nheda la chhonha da nhaka gonha to gekenhan zede a da de'nhan; cheze ziten ba gonesda kan llrhe'chho, ba jatarhalla, kebechha bi llnhan, katenhite bebille rhallechho, yerha kanaze chheshiachho chhegorhachho, da nhan kebe chhakaralla'a gochixe chia gozua dilla ka nhaka da gonha. Tokze dlleba bi da zaa, bixhachha za, kanteze, jayue yelle chia.

• • •

Ki Guneo Goyone

Kate beyolle bchalja, Trhon Lia,[23] ki, nheda xkan, chhebanenha da llchaljabe, dlleba chhekenha nhoxha no'rha nhi, kan che'a chhonha xbaba chia katekze gonebe, nachho nhachha gokebe'be nha chherhenhabe.

—Nhi chhe'o.

—O'—chhapabe.

Nhachha gonachjabe nheda, nhakabea ba beyanebe, brhe'nha rhaoben ban llnhan dorhallebe nheda, kan yijrhaobe ba yo'n yelachheyache, dan to rhii llrheda yijrhaobe.

—Bize, ke?—gonhabe, gonechjabe yachegorha-gaxha la gonia ao, nha bsanha benechia, nha na'a, rhue a lega llbenho zezarhenho no'rha chio.

Gonhabe ki, beyasagabe, bechhojatebe rhille benen chhento. To chi'i daoze benha xbaba dan gonhabe, la goyasatea zeya'a kollobe, chjayexhenhabe chhekenha ze'.

Kate bllinha laneza chhaa ba zeyijabe, noxhonjochjabe, yeto chi'i gozea llna'be ka narhabe dzabe, nha chheyolle lldanechhenhabe, ka bekuasa nhiga, nha beyo'krha yecharhasa rhille Laria.

Ba chhe'a gozorhawa chhe'ja to warhazia, kebechha benteka xbaba che da ki chhochalja Trhon Lia towej; za'rha benha xbaba da chhekebe no'rha chia *antropologa,* nha chhe'a gozorhaowa chhirhjarhalla'a gakaxha gonha yenhe benen, bixha nee chekan yape "gako norhachia" chhon liza chhe'a nha. Kan zua kate blerha yeto chopa bi za'kakze we'e, nha gozorhaonto we'e, bi gokebe'nha bata beza'a, gaka benha bellinha nagan chhasento.

Lla yorha kate goyasa nha zeya'a nagan chhoseni'a Madarhen gorhan, nha ba chhee no'rha *antropologa,* chhi'e chhe'je *cafe,* ka brhe'nhe nheda la goneete' snia, chhi'e nheda:

—Gorhezagacha, xha; billchen kebe ne nao lnhi yo'o yellen zua nha'.—gonhee ki nha brhe'tenhe Lachelao.

—Na'lle chhan sorhao lanhi, se'—gocheteeze—za nodea yapa rhue che sa'o chejachho.

—Waza'a, lldanellwenhanda lanhi, bata saachho—gonhe, llbelwenhe.

—Ka tee rsirha nha saachho, xkan—chhape'e akerhe bi dekze bi gonhanda, nha kon leekzen gonrhenha llin.

Kan benan ze', ka godee rsirha nha gozanto zejanto lanhi, kate beyalanto bso da zua xhan yelle Lachelao, nha gozorhao no'rhadaon chhate ni'e, kanaze dzue benan, nha zeya rhen le shewerhalle. Nha zejanto nha dalexhen bene warhalle chechho nheto, chholxhille chento, katekze zejanto lanhi, bia bchhojakze bene gonha:

—Wenllwa chhon benedon, lldanenhe do nhigarha, chhala yega'narhe to chi'ze zuachho do nhigarha goncho llin.

—Kan gonto xha-chhapechaze'e, llbelwenha chhelekenhe no'rhachia antropologadao.

Kate bshinto yellen nagen yo'o lanhi, lldanto nhi, lldanto nha, goka to chi'dao nha jtarhalle no'rhan da chhowianto, chhekelja benan gakaterha nhaka da dee lanhi che yelledaon, kan golle Maderhen gorhan lee, ndogorhen xkan, bigaze chheke beneyache lanhi xhen, san no'rhadaon, yo'rhao benan da zan tao de da gowiachho nagan ze'e. kan lldanto nha gochekrawe j'nto to *refresco.*

Kate bllinto nagan llda'on, bene zan sjalla nhiga, nha benan chhelenabe gaxha zaa nheto, kate goche'e bene nhi nheto nha golezorhawe chhelone da chhe'janto, balan chhe'janda nha balan kebe chhe'ja, san no'rhadaon, yogolol dan chhe'je, rhawe da bchalja to bene golle lee:

—Chhala yi'jo yogoten dan chhelona bene ki, la she rhue ko yi'jon zejen chhonho *despreciar* nheto.

Nha goyjale'e no'rhadaon. kate gola ba dsollenhe nha bekuasakrhanto nhaa; goche'awe yodao jzenhaganto metin.[24] Rhawe lldanto ki nha goyijanto rhille comision[25] jatagonto xche' da chhonaze bene a lanhin sjazue; bezanto nhi nha jzento kuita nagan lla wekuelle, chhowianto chheye bellcoete,[26] nha zento nha chhelonakze da chhe'janto.

Nha da benha katen goyijanto je'nto refresco, kan bachete, nhate bkueza naga gasento, nhatee bchaljarhenha benan chhote, chhape'e gonee to rhatja naga gasento, "no'rha chia benen" chhape'e se', che lenan kate gocha no'rhadaon:

—Yeza'o chjatasechho.

—Gaxha—gonhee.

—Nheda nesta—goche'e.

—Balabide ba nokuezo, ke?—gonhe nha bxhille—yo'o xkan.

Nha beche'awe, godeza gozi'a yerhate da we'nto. Ka bllinto rhille benen nagan ba gonaba, ka brhe' benan nheto, la bchhojatee nha gochi'e nheto naga zua to yo'odao nagan gone gasento. Nha gosarhjen, nha' nhela *cama,* nakua shicha, nha goyo'nto ze'; nha nheda la goda'tea dan nhua nha gozorhaonto, nhachha goche'e dan zerhalla'a.

—Antropologadao, gakaxha gonho, rhue nhako to no'rhadao zaa Sita nha nheda nhaka bene gorhja do nhirha, indigena llnharhe le'e, gakaxha gonho kebe geyaxjenho gatarhenho nheda, ka nheda benebyo nha rhue ka yela no'rha chio.

Gokakze nallarha bene ki, ze'. charholledaoze gochhi'e shize, chhakate nhoxe'e dan chhe'je, la bechebetie.

—Ke, Jaime,—gonhe—bi nome'anda gaxha nachhen da nhonan rha' bene, che nachho bene nhiga nhake indio nha bene nharha nhake mexicano, nha bene kanharha nhake europeo. Nhedanda chhekenha yogotechho chhi'o beneache, nharhjatechho,rhebetee nhakachho; cheze yela chhaka wide che bene, lenan nhonan chhi'o . . .

Zerhallellwe gochalje ze', xdankzen llchalje, nhedanda xkan ba goyooa daxiwe kuinha kerhechha chhozenhaga, nha gochoga chen chhape'e:

—Weyaxjenho gonhelljo gusto kuinhachho xkan.

—Aan—nhe'—ba gokebe'nha gaxhan chhakarhallo'o chejo, karhe kanga dan, kerhe da nha dllebanda, da chhon yogote bene ban dan, cheze chhala wechho xlatje che a lega sichhon banheza kerhe lerha dan gosan yelazii chechho.

Chela goxhenhanda katen, kebechha birha gochalje naatege che waka che ka gaka, nha goche'e:

—Billchen gosan yelasii a lldanenhanda rhue.

—Chewerhalle, Jaime, Wakan, gorheza to chi'i—gonhe ki nha llchalje llchalje, yeto chi'kze bzenhaga che, katekze gozorhawa llganhawe, kan ba chhento, kate gozorhaollwe llbelleye'e.

—Shis, shis—chhonha.

Chhonhe benan gozorhaollwe chhaxhie nho gakarhen lee, kate gokebe'nha ba dyarhja *puerta* zua nhaa. Ka goyo'o bi nechho godela'achjabe, ba golokoan ze', ka belaze yezika bene ka, gozuakza, llgapa'a, shlibetea, kebechha bzuenha nhachha belelabe nheda. Lo lbeze beluabe nheda nha jlesambe nheda rhillellia, gade no'rha, gade lanhi, do yerha dea nha. Lla byorha nha golebeje nheda jchaljarhenha bene nhaka brhao che yelle, kate bshinha yorhawe nha ba zee no'rha antropologa dllallwa benan.

—Chhakarhalla'a gonho justicia chia, bene, billchekrhan bene nhiga bsake'e nheda kan, nhoxha chhekenhe nhaka; bene chhelon ki kebe chhala geledee kanhaze, bene kinga chhelekenhe nheto no'rha nhakanto ka to yaga, ka to beyixe, nha kon gakanto che kate llnhan che lee.

Gakaterhan dllachje, bene Brhao nhi, wa gozuakze gokarhalle'e gakarhenhe nheda chhi'e benan.

—Chhala gosakakzo rhate ze no'rha, bixhakze chhonho lldao nhite, bixhakze llnhaon jcho'o rhill to benebyo, to warhazio, dekze dilla llnhan: "narhakze rhe'ja chhe."[27]

Kate ben benen ki, yezisla golokochje, gozorhaoge llche'ne morraldaon nho'e, nha gorheje yishe che ka brhe'nhen benan nhaka brhao.

—Gonaa bene, llin che gobierno chhonha.

Kate brhe'e benen dan, nha gonie nheda.

—Gaxha rhue, kebe bi yishe chio nho'o.

Nhedanda, xkan, kerhe bi yishe nhua'nda a lega bene zeja lanhi za'nda. Kate gonezenhe kebe bi nhu'a nha besele'e nheda rhillellia, benchha kate golle no'rhen.

—Kerhe rhue goshiabe'o da chhala gonto, beyijateze, nheto goyuento bi gonento benen da benhe ka.

Gade sua lanhi, kanhaka lla kan, rhillellia yo'a. Godechha lanhi, nhachha blozue nheda doo, jlewe'e nheda Rhachewize, ka bllinha nhaa, da byorha rhillellia.

Notes

1. Sierra Zapotecs call their language Diflla Xhon, from *diflla,* "tongue," "word," "language," and *Xhon,* "peoples or settlements on the banks of the Cajonos River" (i.e., "the Zapotecs of the Xhon or Kaxhon Region"). Corresponds to the Isthmus Zapotec Didxazá, from *didxá* (another orthographic form of *diflla*) and *zá,* "cloud": the language of the Binnizá, from *binni,* "people," and *zá,* "cloud": the "People of the Cloud" (i.e., the Zapotecs). At the end of the twentieth century there were approximately 785,000 speakers of the different variants of Zapotec. The author uses the conventional alphabet that was declared official for the Sierra Juárez in 1988 by the Coordinadora para la Escritura del Zapoteco de la Sierra, an independent civil organization made up of teachers, musicians, writers, ritual dancers, Indigenous authorities, and workers from a variety of government agencies who participated as Zapotecs but not as government representatives.

2. Literally, "people of Castilla"; the term now applies also to the inhabitants of a large city, to underline that an individual is not from the countryside or a particular region.

3. The "Xhon towns." Refers to the towns located along the banks of the Cajonos or Kaxhon River. As a result of this geographic fact, this word in the Sierra Zapotec dialect has become the self-referential term for the Zapotecs themselves. "Xhon" is pronounced similarly to the English "shone."

4. Literally, "the people of the Xhon towns" (i.e., the Zapotecs).

5. Refers to the community of San Francisco Cajonos.

6. Literally, "the Xidsa towns" or the "Zapotecs of the Corner"; that is, the northern zone of Ixtlán, known as Xid Zá, "Zapotec Corner."

7. Refers to San Ildefonso Villa Alta, the first town settled by and for the Spaniards in the lower sierra.

Notas

1. Los zapotecos de la sierra llaman a su lengua *diflla xhon,* de *diflla,* "lengua," "palabra," "idioma", y *xhon,* "pueblos de la ribera del río Cajonos" (es decir, "los zapotecos de esa región," los *xhon* o *kaxhon*). En zapoteco del Istmo es *didxazá,* de *didxa'* (otra forma ortográfica de *diflla*) y *zá,* "nube," es decir, "el idioma de la gente de la nube" o *binnizá,* "los zapotecos." A finales del siglo XX la población zapoteca rebasaba la cifra de 785,000 hablantes. El autor emplea el alfabeto convencional que en 1988 fue declarado como oficial para la Sierra de Juárez por la Coordinadora para la Escritura del Zapoteco de la Sierra, organización civil independiente integrada por maestros, músicos, escritores, danzantes, autoridades indígenas y trabajadores de diversas dependencias oficiales que participaban en su calidad de zapotecos, no de representantes oficiales.

2. Literalmente, "gente de Castilla." Ahora se aplica también a los habitantes de una ciudad grande, para recalcar que alguien no es del campo o de la región.

3. "Los pueblos *xhon.*" Se refiere a los pueblos situados en la ribera del río Cajonos o Kaxhon. A partir de este dato geográfico se ha convertido en la variante dialectal del zapoteco de la sierra para referirse a los zapotecos mismos.

4. Literalmente, "la gente de los pueblos *xhon*" (es decir, los zapotecos).

5. Se refiere al pueblo San Francisco Cajonos.

6. Literalmente, "los pueblos de Xidsa," es decir, "los pueblos zapotecos del Rincón," zona situada al norte de Ixtlán, llamada Xid Zá, "Rincón Zapoteco."

7. Se refiere al primer pueblo fundado por y para españoles en las sierras bajas, San Ildefonso Villa Alta.

8. Refers to Yalálag (literally, "scattered hill"), a municipality of the region known as the Sierra Zapoteca de Villa Alta.

9. Refers to two Xhon communities: San Juan Tabá, municipality of the Sierra Zapoteca de Villa Alta, and Santo Domingo Yohovi.

10. Due to a publishing error, the final pages in Zapotec of Chapter 5 ("Ki Guneo Guchhope") that follow do not appear in the original edition cited. Once we became aware of this omission, we brought it to the author's attention, and he sent us the missing pages. Therefore, the complete text in Zapotec appears here for the first time.

11. Apocopated form of Benexidsa (i.e., the "Zapotecs of the Corner").

12. Region of the area known as Ixtepeji.

13. Literally, "people-town" (i.e., authority).

14. Region surrounding San Pablo Gelatao, which includes the communities of Ixtlán, Natividad, and Jalteanguis.

15. Literally, "soul." This is the core of an extensive clause that describes the "soul" of the rivers and the hills, which are patient and distinguish between the just and the unjust. This force that circles and protects the world was known to the ancient Zapotecs as Bezelhao (literally, "the wind that begins or moves forward," a sacred spirit that is always vigilant and close to humans).

16. Plural of Xhon; literally, "the Xhons."

17. One of the Xhon communities; literally, "Hill of Ashes."

18. Another sacred pre-Hispanic entity; literally, "lightning flash of air," from *gozio,* "lightning flash," and *be,* "air."

19. Sierra Zapotec name for *Coelogenys paca,* an edible rodent well known in Indigenous areas by the name of *tepescuintle* or *tepescuincle.*

20. Zapotec name for cochineal; literally, "prickly-pear paint."

21. San Mateo Capulalpan, one of the towns of the Rhe'ja region.

22. Literally, "iron house" (i.e., jail).

23. Zapotec form of the Spanish name "Petrona María."

24. Zapotec form for the Spanish *maitines.* (See note 32 of the English-language text.)

25. *Rhille comision:* literally, "Commission House." (See note 33 of the English-language text.)

26. Word formed by the Zapotec *bell,* "bull," and the Spanish *cohete,* "skyrocket." Name used for the portable pyrotechnic structure called *torito* or "little bull," which includes an imitation bull's head.

27. This is a Zapotec saying that might be rendered as: "You see the corral, but you don't take care?" The saying suggests that when people come near a corral, they should beware of the animals. This is a source of new irritation for the anthropologist, since the authority is telling her that she should have known that she was taking a chance with the man.

8. Se refiere a Yalálag (literalmente, "cerro desparramado"), municipalidad de la región conocida como sierra Zapoteca de Villa Alta.

9. Se refiere a dos poblados *xhon:* San Juan Tabá, municipalidad de la Sierra Zapoteca de Villa Alta, y Santo Domingo Yohovi.

10. Por un error de edición, las páginas finales en zapoteco del Capítulo 5 ("Ki Guneo Guchhope") que reproducimos a continuación no aparecen en el libro citado. Al darnos cuenta de este error, se lo hicimos ver al autor, y él nos envió las páginas faltantes. Por lo tanto, ésta es la primera vez que aparece el texto completo en zapoteco.

11. Apócope de *benexidsa* (es decir, los zapotecos del rincón).

12. Región de la zona conocida como Ixtepeji.

13. Literalmente, "gente-pueblo" (es decir, autoridad).

14. Región que está alrededor de San Pablo Gelatao, con poblaciones como Ixtlán, Natividad y Jalteanguis.

15. Literalmente, "alma." Es el eje de la amplia cláusula que describe "el alma" de los ríos y los cerros, que son pacientes y disciernen lo justo y lo injusto. A esta fuerza que recorre el mundo y lo cuida los antiguos zapotecos le llamaban Bezelhao (literalmente, "el viento que inicia o se adelanta," espíritu sagrado siempre vigilante y cercano a los seres).

16. Plural de *xhon* (es decir, literalmente, "los *xhon*").

17. Uno de los pueblos *xhon;* literalmente, "Cerro de Cenizas."

18. Otra entidad sagrada prehispánica. Literalmente, "relámpago de aire," de *gozio,* "rayo" o "relámpago" y *be,* "aire."

19. Nombre en zapoteco de la sierra del *Coelogenys paca,* roedor comestible muy conocido en las regiones indígenas con el nombre de *tepescuintle* o *tepescuincle.*

20. Nombre en zapoteco de la "cochinilla"; literalmente, "pintura del nopal."

21. San Mateo Capulalpan, uno de los pueblos de la región Rhe'ja.

22. Literalmente, "casa de fierro" (es decir, cárcel).

23. Forma zapoteca de los nombres castellanos "Petrona María."

24. Forma zapoteca de *maitines.* (Véase nota 26 al texto en español.)

25. *Rhille comision:* literalmente, "Casa de la Comisión." (Véase nota 27 del texto español.)

26. Palabra formada por la voz zapoteca *bell,* "toro," y la española *cohete.* Se designa así a la estructura portátil de fuegos artificiales llamada "torito," que se remata con la reproducción de una cabeza de toro.

27. Se trata de un refrán zapoteco; podría traducirse así: "¿por qué no te cuidas, si estás viendo el corral?" De aquí deriva la nueva molestia de la antropóloga, pues la autoridad le sugería que ella debió darse cuenta que se estaba arriesgando con el hombre. "Cuando uno pasa cerca de un corral, debe cuidarse de los animales."

Songs of Bezelhao[1]

Javier Castellanos Martínez

Sierra Zapotec[2]

[From *Wila che be ze lhao/Cantares de los vientos primerizos: Novela zapoteca,* selections from Chapter 5, "Ki Guneo Guchhope," pp. 88–89, and "Segunda Revelación," pp. 100–106, and Chapter 6, "Ki Guneo Goyone," pp. 107–111, and "Tercera Revelación," pp. 123–128. Colección Letras Indígenas Contemporáneas. Mexico City: Editorial Diana/CNCA/DGCP, 1994.]

Selection from Chapter 5, "Second Revelation"

My ancestors' arrival in these lands did not put an end to the poverty brought on by the arrival of the Spaniards. It was not long after my grandparents established themselves here that the foreigners arrived. At once, our activities came to depend upon the foreigners' needs. We grew the crops and bred the animals they needed. When the Spaniards were in great need, they paid us well; and when they were not, they paid us accordingly. It was then that *nopal*[3] was planted throughout this entire region. From it, they would remove the *cochinilla,*[4] place it to dry, and then grind it up. That powder was what the Spaniards would buy. The old Sa[5] had to do that type of work in order to subsist and survive during that period of destruction. When the Spaniards' strength increased, they tried to erase even our beliefs. With that as their goal, they forced us even to support their priests. As they gained still more power, they forced us to act and think like them. That is how things were in these communities when the fighting broke out in the Xhon[6] towns. Once the townspeople overcame their indecision, they decided to expel the Spaniards. The town of Ljaxilla[7] took the lead. Fortifying their hearts and minds, and with their ancestors' strength and breath, they temporarily met their goal. This they achieved by traveling throughout the Benexidsa[8] lands, visiting the towns on the plains in search of support. That is how they arrived in these towns. Those men were very intelligent: when their *gobeza*[9] arrived in a particular town, they headed straight to the homes of the most bold and resolute men. That is how they arrived at my old father's house. As a man, he accepted it as his duty to involve himself in the problem that his people were facing, and he did his best for the sake of fraternity.

When the conflict ended, when they felt confident in their peace and friendship (in the words of the foreigners) and everything was peaceful, the Spanish soldiers attacked. One dark night, they captured my old ancestor; and, without anyone noticing, he was bound and removed from his house to be taken to Villa Alta.[10] Fearing that he might be liberated along the way, they changed their course. With them riding on horseback and my father on foot, they crossed Mixhe[11] lands. At Yarharhj,[12] they changed course again until they arrived at the Tabaa-Yaxove[13] towns, where another group of soldiers was waiting to escort him to Villa Alta. It was customary in those towns to go visit the prisoners who were being led to Villa Alta. That is how an elderly woman came to visit my father. She said to him, in a way only he could understand, "Down below, there is a river that must be crossed using a bridge of lianas. If you have thought of escaping, that is where you can do it. Down-river there are people who can help you."

When they left the Tabaa-Yaxhove community headed for Villa Alta, my old father was bound once again. They walked for nearly half a day until they arrived at a great river. It was terribly swollen since it was the rainy season; and as the elderly woman had said, to cross it there was just a large bunch of lianas to walk across, and two or three hanging to either side to grasp hold of. Those who created this passage had sought out one of the narrowest sections of the river, one which was located in a canyon. As a result, the bridge was high over the river, and the river was very deep. Arriving at the river, my ancestor's guards, like it or not, had to untie him. Half of the party crossed first to await him on the other side. Once they had crossed, they made him cross alone, since only one person could cross at a time.

The poor prisoner, who still dreamed of his freedom, remembered the words of the old Zapotec woman. When he got to the middle of the liana bridge he stopped and, turning toward both sides, resolutely shouted: "This day will bear witness to my words. You who have brought me here will see that tomorrow—though it may be your last day, or you may have finally come to live in a place of understanding—you will suffer to see your descendants harvesting what you sow today by believing that your way is the only one, just because you see us growing up among the grasses; but even the grasses will rebel if you continue like this."

When he finished saying that, he hurled himself into the river.

Imagine what he must have seen as the river carried him along. If he did not lose his life in that turbulent river, it was only because there is someone who cares for us and because there was someone who had prayed for him since he was little. He was easily able to get back on solid ground once he was in the land of the Xidsa.[14] There he began to encounter people; and when he inquired about his town, no one was able to respond; they did not know that his town was far, far away, nor had they ever heard of it. He then found people in whom he could confide regarding his situation, and some appeared who were willing to help him. One of those persons was from Rhacheyerha,[15] and he went there and spoke with the *cabeza*[16] of that town, who in turn spoke with the townspeople. And that is how he remained in those parts, little by little finding his place until he forgot his own people; that is how my ancestors arrived in the Rhe'ja region.[17]

That was where Lia Kaxhon was born. She was a granddaughter of the person about whom I have been speaking. She was the first to put her grandfather's words to work. It is not that he instilled in her a hatred of the Spaniards because of what they had done to him. No, it was nothing like that. What really happened was that the great Bezelhao,[18] the mountains and the rivers, also listened on that occasion. They, too, can distinguish between right and wrong, and they decide when to express their opinion. Thanks to that, the words the old grandfather spoke when he hurled himself into the river were not lost.

His granddaughter's last name was Kaxhon[19] since she was a descendant of the man who was swept along by the river of the Xhon. When she became a young woman, she went to work buying and selling things. In the course of her business, she made numerous trips to Yaze'e,[20] and she would return with fish, shrimp, and other things of those lands. During those years, in the course of her work, she met the offspring of Goziobe.[21] Through them, she came to better understand their situation: that of living next to others who did not understand the reality of being different, and who took advantage of that difference to seize from those towns their means of survival. As a result, at that time in Yaze'e, the townspeople began to think up a way to cast off the wretched life that those men imposed by force. The Spaniards had forced the townspeople to plant whatever occurred to *them*, or to breed only animals that the Spaniards needed, and then they themselves decided what was good and bad. That is how they managed to rid all households of *bejaga*,[22] which in those times was kept just as one keeps pigs or turkeys today. Because *they* did not like it, they prohibited it. That is why today that animal lives only in the wild. In exchange, they practically forced the people to raise the *bchhenbia*,[23] which lives on the prickly-pear cactus. Our ancestors used it at times for painting; and, when the Spaniards discovered that, they began to demand that everyone raise it so it would not become scarce. The Spaniards always imposed the price that was best for them. The worst part was that sometimes they did not buy it; there were brothers whose entire effort had gone into raising prickly-pear cactus, which now brought them hunger rather than happiness. The Spaniards also began to give the women of the towns yarn to dye. They would promise to give the women half of the profits; but once the cloth was made, any pretext was sufficient for them not to divide things equally. Once again, the people's work was in vain. It was the last straw when they owed us and they would pay us with a burro or a horse, knowing that, as things were back then, there was no place to care for them, nor time to put them to work. So the people ended up giving them back, and the wages the Spaniards owed us for our work were lost.

Our people's suffering was so great because they were tolerant and resigned. They faithfully followed a path laid out by ancient knowledge that today seems so worn and beaten. Nevertheless, some men so felt the pain of their people that they began to organize themselves to expel the foreign evil. In her travels, Lia Kaxhon came to know these men, and it was she who carried and spread their ideas among the Zapotecs of Rhe'ja, mainly in her hometown of Rhacheyerha. In that way, the words of my ancestor were fulfilled. After some time, a descendant of one of the captains that took Lia Kaxhon's grandfather prisoner arrived in Rhacheyerha. This Spanish descendant's name was Reynozo. He felt very strong in those days because people did not dare raise their heads or turn to look when he passed by. But he did not know what Lia Kaxhon was up to while she peddled her fish and shrimp. In each town she visited, she now had people determined and in agreement that when the rebellion began in Yaze'e each town would follow suit. Therefore, when the moment arrived, people here in the sierra town known today as Capulalpan[24] also defended themselves. She had said: "It is time to end the Spanish domination." She challenged the men: "If you are not daring enough, go and prepare rations for us women; we will find a way to escape this rope that binds us and our children and our grandchildren." She chose this town to begin what had already occurred in Yaze'e because she knew that, at this time, there were some men in jail, accused of having untied Reynozo's animals which he had on Rhacheyerha lands. Therefore, when she said: "Let us get those men out of jail," the entire town went to tear down the prison.

When the Spaniards who lived in the town found out, they fled, along with those who had become their allies. That was how the Spaniards left the town of Capulalpan. The following day, when the one named Reynozo learned of what had happened, he immediately took his soldiers out to punish the people, though he achieved none of that. When they arrived in the town of Capulalpan, everyone was awaiting him, ready to resolve the situation. Those who were not carrying their machetes had a slingshot or some good club or at the very least a stone in their bag. Therefore, when the Spanish soldiers entered and saw that the townspeople were prepared to resist, they did not dare strike with their swords, as they were accustomed to doing. As much as Reynozo ordered his soldiers to arrest all the men, the people of the town were determined and prepared to defend themselves; leading them was that little woman named Lia Kaxhon, spurring her people on so that they would not be afraid. She boldly planted herself in front of Reynozo's horse and scolded him, saying: "You arrest them yourself if you believe that what you do is right in imposing these burdens upon us and causing us pain!" Infuriated, Reynozo immediately started to dismount. His foot had not yet reached the ground when Lia Kaxhon grabbed him and with her strength threw him a good distance. At that moment, too, the people began to attack. It was then that the foreign soldiers fled those lands, when Lia Kaxhon personally struck Reynozo in the face and spoke these words to him: "It is not that we cannot be like you; rather our hunger is not as great as yours. We are content with being alive. For what else can we ask? You have searched even your imaginations to find new needs which we have suffered to fulfill. Our will has now stood up to yours. So go find your path and leave us; we have decided we will tolerate you no longer!"

Upon so saying, she threw Reynozo so far that he landed at the feet of his horse, who had been standing by patiently. Reynozo no longer wanted to be there: he quickly mounted and left.

Lia Kaxhon's boldness reached those limits. She then believed our people would tolerate the Spaniards no longer because this had been agreed on by all in Yaze'e, in all the valley towns, and those on this side. But as she herself said, we gladly accept just being alive and are content with just that. However, the Spaniards remained dissatisfied with that turn of events and were determined to not lose us. We had been the ones feeding them; so as long as they were outside the region, they worked to find a way to return. Since they could not do so with their soldiers, they used their priests. The priests devoted themselves to traveling throughout our towns and inviting us to forget all that had happened because resentment is no good. They stressed that what had happened before would not be repeated and that peace must return. And thus it did. When our towns were peaceful again, the Spanish armies attacked us and, once again, revealed their true colors. Once they felt certain they had won, they arrested our leaders: among them was Lia Kaxhon. They unleashed upon them their fury and rage for having spent a year without eating off of our sweat. Lia Kaxhon's debt was great for attempting to achieve a life better for us than the one we had known under the Spaniards. Our compatriots, such as they were (and continue to be), seeing that the Spaniards were the winners, refused to commit themselves, while Lia Kaxhon paid. The soldiers set her hair afire, they burned her tongue, they cut off one of her hands and did many other things to her that made her suffer. The other leaders of Yaze'e and Rhacheyerha paid similarly.

Today I have told the story of my older sister, whose blood I still carry and along with it her character and her kindness, if I wanted to be kind. But I am not kind; nor will I be, because I know that since the arrival of the Spaniards we have been nullified; our seed no longer grows. I prefer to not anguish over fulfilling what is said to be my duty. And, though I know that punishment awaits me for not doing my duty, I do not care. I will forget my people.

Selection from Chapter 6, "Third Revelation"

When Trhon Lia[25] had finished telling this story, I remained thinking about it, fearfully, and I wondered about this woman. Then I heard her voice; she gave me the impression that she had just then noticed I was by her side, and she asked me: "Are you sitting here?"

"Yes, I am here," I answered.

She remained staring at me. I saw in her eyes that she had returned to her senses, that she was herself again, the one I knew; I could see in her pupils that hint of sadness she always carries with her.

"What little regard you have for others, huh?" she said, accentuating her sadness. "What if I had believed in your words and I had left my husband? I now see with just how much pleasure you brought your wife here and go about with her—damn you!"

She then got up and left the store. Her words shook me up, but I immediately stood up to follow her. When I got to the street, she was going uphill; the beautiful movements of her body as it swiftly walked made me forget what she had said; I smiled and realized that I liked her more with every passing day. With that idea in mind, I went back to Señora[26] Larhia's house to keep on drinking.

Alone and drinking, I could not think about Trhon Lia and her stories. Instead, another idea occurred to me: that the anthropologist was really my wife. I began to imagine how to make her my wife and to think about the possibility that she might accept. Other *paisanos*[27] arrived to drink, I bought a round, and the drinking spree became formal.

I do not know how I left or managed to get back to the room where we slept.

When I got up the next day, the first thing I did was head for the room where Doña[28] Madarhen cooks. The anthropologist was already there drinking a cup of coffee; and when she saw me she put on an angry face and said: "Why, you! Why didn't you tell me that there's a fiesta going on in that town?" as she pointed toward Lachelao.[29]

"It starts tonight," I responded. "I planned on telling you today, in case you might like to go."

"Yes, yes, let's go, of course, I'm fascinated by Indigenous fiestas!" she said happily.

"Fine, let's finish our *almuerzo*[30] and go," I answered. Since we were working together, I now had nothing to do.

And so it was: after our *almuerzo,* we set out walking toward the site of the fiesta. When we were in the uphill approach to Lachelao, the little woman began to tire, and we had to slow down so that she would last; it was around there that my *paisanos* who were also going to the fiesta began to catch up to us; they laughed kindly at us, and someone was even heard saying: "How pleasant that this woman likes to visit these parts; hopefully she'll stay in our town for good."

"That's the way it'll be," I said to them.

I felt happy and proud because they believed the anthropologist was my wife.

When we arrived in the town where the fiesta was taking place, we went to the church for a while and then to see the musicians and the few vendors' stands. Finally, that poor woman got bored; maybe she imagined a huge fiesta from what Doña Madarhen had told her. The truth is, to a *paisana*[31] who has never left the region, any little thing seems big; but the anthropologist, accustomed to numerous spectacles, soon became bored going from one spot to another; all I could think to say was: "Let's go have a refreshment."

When we arrived at the store, there were many people drinking; those who were from that town came forth and asked us where we were from. When we explained our work, they gladly began to offer us drinks. I drank a few, but not all; on the other hand, the beautiful little woman drank all they gave her, taking seriously what one of the men had said: "It's the custom here to drink all that one is given, because, if you do not, it means that you look down on us."

And believing that, the poor thing drank up everything. When we left there she was already fairly drunk, but we still went to listen to the *maitines*[32] the town band was playing. In a while, when we got hungry, we went to the Casa de la Comisión.[33] By then we felt the fiesta livening up, and the fireworks were set off. We went to stand near the band, and there also we were given drinks; by then she was looking tired. When we were having refreshments in that store, I had told the owner she was my wife and requested a place to rest. The storeowner had already said yes; therefore, I dared say to her: "Let's go sleep."

"Where?" she asked.

"I know a place," I responded.

"You are certainly prepared, aren't you?" she said and added: "Well, let's go."

And that is how I took her with me. Along the way, I stopped to buy more liquor in order to keep drinking. When we arrived at the store, the owner led us to a small room where he was going to let us sleep. It was, in fact, ready because there was a bed and some blankets folded on top of it. I immediately began to serve up what I had brought to drink and to make known my intentions.

"Beautiful anthropologist," said I, "whatever you decide, taking into account that you're from the city and I'm from these parts—'Indigenous,' as you say—I now want you to dare sleep with me, you as a woman and I as a man."

Although she became upset when she heard that, she

remained silent for just one moment and immediately responded.

"Look, Jaime," she said seriously, "I haven't seen any law written down that makes human beings different so that we might say 'this one is Indian, this one is Mexican,' or 'this other one is European.' As far as I'm concerned, from the moment we're born, we all have the same rights, except that human ambition is what has divided humanity . . ."

She was in the mood to talk, and what she was saying was interesting; but I, who already had the devil inside me, had no intention of further listening to her, and I abruptly cut the thread of her conversation: "What I am proposing is that you dare to join me in giving pleasure to our bodies."

"Ah!" she exclaimed. "Now I know what you're trying to accomplish, but that's the least of it; that doesn't frighten me, that's the most common thing between living beings; but everything has its place and time, and, for what you propose, there must be mutual attraction, which I feel is still lacking; and to act otherwise might cause us pain."

"Why should it bring us pain?" I said, already fairly aroused. "I like you a lot."

"Not so fast, Jaime, everything is possible; wait a moment," she said and kept on talking and talking.

I listened to her another while and finally began to caress her; for a moment she didn't say anything, but when she noticed that I wasn't just playing, she began to scream.

"Be quiet, please," I asked her insistently.

She began to scream louder, requesting help and calling for the police. It wasn't long before the door opened. Seeing that, I flew into a rage: I violently grabbed the first officer who came into the room. I punched him, and once he was on the ground I kicked him angrily. Suddenly I realized that there were now several of them trying to restrain me; and though I put up a lot of resistance, they overcame me and lifted me up into the air. And that's how they carried me off to jail. No woman, no fiesta, just jail, starting that night.

The following day, they pulled me out of jail and led me before the town authorities. When I arrived in front of them, I saw that the anthropologist was also there. She was very angry and became more angry when she saw me arrive: "I demand that justice be done, sir. Why did this individual treat me so? Who does he think I am? This type of person should not be free—those who believe that we women are objects and must be at their service whenever they desire. I demand justice!"

She said all of this very angrily; the authority tried to back me up a little.

"You should modulate the intensity of your voice a little," the *principal*[34] said to the anthropologist. "Just what is it you're looking for way out here? What did you expect when you went into that single man's room alone—or did someone make you do it?"[35]

When the woman heard that, she became even more furious and began to search for something in her bag. She began to pull out papers that identified her as working for the government; she displayed them to those present and said: "Look, gentlemen, I'm here working for a government agency."

The authority took a quick look at those papers and turned to me: "And aren't you carrying some paper to identify yourself?"

Well, as for me, why would I carry papers? I was just going to the fiesta. When I told that to the *principal,* the rest of the authorities laughed, saying that I looked just like them; why hadn't I told them I was from the neighboring town? They then decided to send me back to jail. When I was leaving, I overheard them tell the anthropologist: "You can go in peace now; we know how to punish, and no one is going to come and teach us differently."

Thus, I was unable to enjoy the fiesta those days, since I spent them all in jail. Once the fiesta was over, they tied me up and took me off to Villa Alta; and upon arrival, after an entire day of travel, I found myself once again in the "iron house."

Notes

1. Literally, "the wind that arises or moves forward," in reference to the Zapotecs' pre-Hispanic concept of a sacred spirit that is ever vigilant and that remains close to humans (see note 15 of the Zapotec-language text).

2. Sierra Zapotecs call their language Diílla Xhon, from *diílla,* "tongue," "word," "language," and Xhon, "peoples or settlements on the banks of the Cajonos River" (i.e., "the Zapotecs of the Xhon or Kaxhon Region") This corresponds to the Isthmus Zapotec Didxazá, from *didxá* (another orthographic form of *diílla*) and *zá,* "cloud": the language of the Binnizá, from *binni,* "people" and *zá* (*sá*), "cloud": the "People of the Cloud" (i.e., the Zapotecs). At the end of the twentieth century there were approximately 785,000 speakers of the different variants of Zapotec.

3. Prickly pear; name used for all cacti of the genuses *Platyopuntia* and *Nopalea.* The text refers to the variety *Nopalea cochinillifera.*

4. Cochineal; from the Latin *coccinus,* "scarlet" or "red." A hemipterous insect originating in Mexico that lives on the prickly-pear cactus

of the variety *Nopalea cochinillifera,* When dried and pulverized, it is used as a red dye for silk, wool, and other fabrics.

5. The ancient Zapotecs; see note 1 above.

6. Refers to the towns located along the banks of the Cajonos or Kaxhon River. As a result of this geographic fact, this word in the Sierra Zapotec dialect has become the self-referential term for the Zapotecs themselves. "Xhon" is pronounced similarly to the English "shone."

7. Refers to the community of San Francisco Cajonos.

8. In the Sierra Zapotec dialect, refers to the "Zapotecs of the Corner"; that is, the northern zone of Ixtlán, known as Xid Zá, "Zapotec Corner."

9. Literally, "messengers."

10. San Ildefonso Villa Alta was the first town founded by and for the Spaniards in the lower sierra lands. It borders upon Mixe and Chinantec lands. At the end of the twentieth century Villa Alta had a population of barely 1,000.

11. The Mixes or Mijes (their self-referential term is Ayook) make up one of the principal ethnic groups of the state of Oaxaca. Their communities extend throughout the Sierra Juárez, in the northern part of the state. At the end of the twentieth century there were approximately 188,000 Mixes.

12. Refers to Yalálag (literally, "scattered hill"), a municipality of the region known as the Sierra Zapoteca de Villa Alta. It is the number one weaving center in that part of the sierra.

13. Refers to two Xhon communities: San Juan Tabá, municipality of the Sierra Zapoteca de Villa Alta, and Santo Domingo Yohovi.

14. Apocopated form of Benexidsa (i.e., the "Zapotecs of the Corner").

15. Region of the area known as Ixtepeji.

16. The main town authority.

17. Region surrounding San Pablo Gelatao, which includes the communities of Ixtlán, Natividad, and Jalteanguis.

18. See note 1 above.

19. Plural of Xhon (literally, "the Xhons").

20. One of the Xhon communities; literally, "Hill of Ashes."

21. Another sacred pre-Hispanic entity; literally, "lightning flash of air," from *gozio,* "lightning flash," and *be,* "air."

22. Sierra Zapotec name for *Coelogenys paca,* an edible rodent well known in Indigenous areas by the name of *tepescuintle* or *tepescuincle,* from the Nahuatl *tepeitzcuintli,* "hill dog."

23. Zapotec name for cochineal (literally, "prickly-pear paint").

24. San Mateo Capulalpan, one of the towns of the Rhe'ja region.

25. Zapotec version of the Spanish name "Petrona María."

26. Mrs.

27. Other people from the same town or region.

28. Spanish title of respect used before the first names of older women.

29. Former Xhon town; today it is just a hamlet.

30. A late breakfast.

31. A woman from the same town or region.

32. In Catholic rites, the first of the canonical hours in which predawn prayers commence. Among the Sierra Zapotecs, musical pieces played by bands at evening or nighttime ceremonies, consisting of hymns to the Virgin, responses, and a *te deum* prayer.

33. Place where the fiesta organizers (La Comisión) feed all visitors for the duration of the fiesta.

34. The main town authority.

35. The original Zapotec-language text presents this idea with a good dose of humor. The authority recalls a Zapotec saying, which might be rendered as "You see the corral, but you don't take care?" The saying suggests that when people come near a corral, they should beware of the animals. This is a source of new irritation for the anthropologist, since the authority is telling her that she should have known she was taking a chance with the man.

Cantares de los vientos primerizos

Javier Castellanos Martínez

Zapoteco de la Sierra[1]

[De *Wila che be ze lhao/Cantares de los vientos primerizos: Novela zapoteca,* selección del Capítulo 5, "Segunda Revelación," pp. 100–106, y del Capítulo 6, "Tercera Revelación," pp. 123–128. Colección Letras Indígenas Contemporáneas. México, D.F.: Editorial Diana/CNCA/DGCP, 1994.]

Selección del Capítulo 5, "Segunda Revelación"

Cuando mis antepasados llegaron a estos lugares, no por ello terminaron las penurias provocadas por los de Castilla. Al poco tiempo de que se establecieron mis abuelos, hasta aquí llegaron los extranjeros y dependieron de sus necesidades desde entonces todas las actividades. Se sembraba y se criaban animales que ellos necesitaban; cuando era mucha su necesidad, pagaban bien, y cuando no, así era su precio. En ese tiempo toda esta región se llenó de nopales[2] del cual quitaban la cochinilla,[3] la ponían a secar y luego la molían y ese polvo era lo que compraban los de Castilla. Trabajos de este tipo tuvieron que hacer los viejos *sa*[4] para mantenerse y pasar esa época de destrucción. Cuando los de Castilla lograron fortalecerse, hasta nuestras creencias pretendieron borrar y nos obligaron incluso a mantener a sus sacerdotes; cuando tuvieron más poder, nos obligaron a que actuáramos y pensáramos como ellos. Así estaban las cosas cuando se inició la pelea allá en los pueblos *xhon*.[5] Ellos rompieron su indecisión y optaron por expulsar a los de Castilla. El pueblo de Ljaxilla[6] se puso a la cabeza y fortaleciendo su corazón y su mente y con la fuerza y aliento de sus antepasados lograron en un momento lo que querían y para lograrlo recorrieron la tierra de los *benexidsa*,[7] visitaron otros pueblos donde todo es llanura y en busca de ayuda llegaron a los nuestros. Cómo sería el conocimiento de aquellos hombres que cuando sus *gobeza*[8] entraron en este pueblo se dirigieron directamente a la casa de los atrevidos y decididos y de esa manera visitaron la casa de mi viejo padre; él, por su condición de hombre, aceptó inmiscuir su persona en el problema que enfrentaba su pueblo e hizo lo que le correspondía hacer y hasta donde pudo en aras de la hermandad.

Cuando terminó el conflicto, cuando estaban confiados en la paz y amistad, palabras que usa el extranjero, y todo parecía estar pacífico, fue entonces que cayeron los soldados de Castilla y en una oscura noche detuvieron a mi viejo antepasado y sin que nadie se diera cuenta fue amarrado y sacado de su casa, para llevarlo a Villa Alta.[9] Y teniendo miedo de que en el camino fuera liberado, cambiaron de rumbo, al cabo que ellos iban montados en bestias y el que caminaba era mi padre. Así atravesaron la tierra *mixhe*[10] hasta llegar a Yarharhj[11] y de allí se desviaron para llegar a los pueblos Tabaa-Yaxhove,[12] en donde los esperaba la partida de soldados que lo llevaría a Villa Alta. Se había hecho costumbre en esos pueblos visitar a los prisioneros de Villa Alta y así llegó una anciana y le dijo tratando que sólo él entendiera: "Hasta allá abajo hay un río que tienen que cruzar utilizando un paso de bejucos, ahí es que puedes escapar si lo has pensado; río abajo hay gente que te puede ayudar."

Cuando salieron del pueblo Tabaa-Yaxhobe, rumbo a Villa Alta, mi viejo padre fue nuevamente amarrado. Casi medio día caminaron para llegar al gran río que los esperaba, crecido terriblemente porque era tiempo de lluvias. Como le había dicho la anciana, sobre el río estaba tendido un gran manojo de bejucos para cruzar caminando; a fin de sostenerse con las manos, colgaban a los lados otras dos o tres tiras de bejucos. Las gentes que tendieron este paso habían buscado una de las partes más estrechas del río, por eso lo tendieron en un cañón; el puente quedó a una gran altura y el río estaba a gran profundidad. Por eso cuando llegaron al río, los custodios de mi antepasado, a querer o no, lo desataron; la mitad de la partida atravesó primero y luego lo hicieron pasar a él, ya que sólo podían pasar de uno en uno.

El pobre prisionero que aún pensaba en su libertad recordó las palabras de la vieja zapoteca y cuando llegó a la mitad del puente de bejuco, se detuvo con decisión y volviéndose hacia ambos lados les gritó:

—Este día será testigo de mis palabras: ustedes que me traen acá, verán que el día de mañana, aunque hayan concluido sus días o lleguen finalmente a morar a un lugar donde haya entendimiento, sufrirán al ver que la descendencia de ustedes recibirá los frutos de lo que hoy siembran por creer que lo de ustedes es único, porque nos ven a nosotros crecer junto a hierbas, pero hasta ellas se rebelarán si ustedes siguen así.

Cuando terminó de decir esto se lanzó al río.

Qué cosas no habrá visto mientras lo arrastraba el río. Sólo porque existe quien nos cuida y porque desde niño hubo quien hizo pedimentos para él, no perdió su vida en ese turbulento río. Fue ya en la región de los *xidsa*[13] donde pudo internarse tranquilamente en tierra. Ahí empezó a encontrar gente y cuando preguntaba por su pueblo nadie sabía darle razón; ignoraban que su pueblo había quedado totalmente en el otro extremo y ni siquiera habían oído hablar de él. Después encontró gente a quien le confió su situación y de ahí mismo surgió quien le ayudó; una de estas gentes era de Rhacheyerha[14] y hacia allá se fue y habló con la cabeza[15] de las autoridades del pueblo y él a su vez con la gente; así se quedó por esos lugares, poco a poco se adaptó hasta que olvidó a su gente y de esta manera mis antepasados llegaron a la región Rhe'ja.[16]

Aquí nació Lia Kaxhon, que fue una de las nietas de la persona de quien he estado platicando. Ella fue la primera en poner de pie las palabras de su abuelo y no es que él le haya inculcado el odio hacia los de Castilla por lo que le habían hecho, no, nada de eso, sino que el gran Bezelhao,[17] el alma de los montes y los ríos que también escucharon aquella vez y que también disciernen entre lo justo y lo injusto, decide el momento de expresar su parecer y gracias a ello las palabras del viejo abuelo no se desperdiciaron, las palabras que dijo cuando se arrojó al río. La nieta, la que tenía como apellido Kaxhon,[18] porque era descendiente del que arrastró el río de los *xhon,* cuando se hizo mujer joven empezó a trabajar comprando y vendiendo cosas; para eso viajaba a Yaze'e[19] y desde allí traía pescado, camarón y otros productos de esas tierras. Por esos años y andando en sus diligencias conoció a los retoños de Goziobe[20] y supo la situación que estaban padeciendo en la cercanía de gentes que no comprendían lo que era ser diferente y aprovechaban eso para arrebatar a los pueblos los medios de sobrevivir. En esa época, en Yaze'e, empezaron a pensar cómo contrarrestar la mala vida que estos señores a la fuerza imponían, obligando a la gente a sembrar lo que a ellos se les ocurría o a criar animales que ellos necesitaban, porque ellos decidían lo bueno y lo malo. Así desapareciera de las casas el *bejaga,*[21] ya que en esos tiempos ese animal se criaba como hoy se cría un cochinito o un guajolote; como a ellos no les gustó, lo prohibieron y ahora ese animalito sólo vive en el campo. En cambio, casi obligaron a la gente a que cuidaran al *bchhenbia,*[22] que vive en el nopal y que nuestros antepasados utilizaban a veces para pintar; cuando los de Castilla lo supieron, comenzaron a exigirle a todos que lo criaran para que no faltara, siempre imponiendo el precio que a ellos les convenía. Lo peor de todo es que a veces ni lo compraban y había hermanitos que ya todo su esfuerzo lo habían puesto en la siembra de nopales y esto en lugar de felicidad les traía hambre. También acostumbraban proporcionarles hilo a las mujeres para que tejieran, con la promesa de compartir la mitad de las ganancias; pero una vez hechas las mantas, les sobraban pretextos para no hacer la repartición igual y otra vez el trabajo era en vano. Llegaban al colmo, cuando nos debían, de entregarnos como pago algún burro o caballo, pero a como estaban las cosas entonces, no había tiempo ni lugar para cuidarlos ni trabajarlos, así que acabábamos regresando los pobres animales y el trabajo que nos debían quedaba perdido.

De ese tamaño fue el sufrimiento de nuestro pueblo por ser tolerante y resignado, por ser fiel a un camino trazado por el conocimiento antiquísimo que hoy parece demasiado trillado. Sin embargo, hubo hombres que les dolía lo que era suyo y empezaron a organizarse para expulsar al mal extranjero. Por donde anduvo Lía Kaxhon los conoció y llevó estas ideas y las regó entre los zapotecos de Rhe'ja, principalmente en su pueblo Rhacheyerha. De esta manera se iba cumpliendo la palabra, ya que con el tiempo al pueblo de Rhacheyerha también llegó un descendiente de uno de los capitanes que llevaron prisionero al abuelo de Lía Kaxhon. A este descendiente de Castilla le decían Reynozo. Se sentía muy fuerte porque nadie se atrevía a levantar la cabeza o a mirarlo cuando él pasaba. Pero no sabía en lo que Lía Kaxhon avanzaba mientras ofrecía su pescado y camarón. En cada pueblo que visitaba tenía a gentes decididas y había acordado con los de Yaze'e que cuando ellos empezaran, lo mismo harían por aquí. Por eso, cuando llegó el momento, también se defendieron aquí en la sierra, en el pueblo que hoy llaman Capulalpan.[23] Ella había dicho: "Ya es hora de que se detenga la dominación de los de Castilla." Reclamaba a los hombres: "Si ustedes no se atreven, preparen alimentos para nosotras y las mujeres veremos la manera de escapar de esta soga que nos sujeta a nosotras y a nuestros hijos y nietos." Ella escogió este pueblo para iniciar lo que también en Yaze'e había sucedido. Sabía que en ese tiempo estaban encarcelados unos hombres acusados de haber desatado las bestias de Reynozo, que las tenía en la tierra de Rhacheyerha. Por eso cuando dijo: "Vamos a liberar a los hombres que están en la cárcel," todo el pueblo acudió a derribar la prisión.

Cuando las gentes de Castilla que vivían en el pueblo supieron de eso, huyeron corriendo con los que antes ya se les habían unido; de esa manera se fueron del pueblo de Capulalpan. Al otro día, cuando se enteró de lo que había sucedido el que digo que le decían Reynozo, inmediatamente partió con soldados pensando en castigar a la gente, pero nada de eso logró. Cuando llegaron al pueblo de Capulalpan, allí estaban todos esperándolo, preparados para aclarar la situación: el que no traía su machete, traía su honda o algún buen palo y los más simples piedra en su morral. Por eso cuando entraron los soldados de Castilla y vieron aquello, no se atrevieron, como era su costumbre, a golpearlos con la espada, por más que el Reynozo les ordenaba detener a todos los hombres. Las gentes de ese pueblo ya estaban decididos y preparados para defenderse. Al frente de ellos estaba esa mujercita que se llamó Lía Kaxhon, incitando al pueblo para que no tuvieran temor, y resueltamente se fue a parar frente al caballo del Reynozo y le increpó así: "¡Deténlos tú, anda, si crees correcto imponernos carga y provocarnos dolor!" Enfurecido, Reynozo trató de bajar inmediatamente del caballo, pero todavía su pie no estaba en el suelo cuando Lía Kaxhon lo sujetó y lo arrojó con fuerza lejos. En ese momento el pueblo empezó a atacar. Entonces el soldado extranjero huyó de esas tierras, cuando Lía Kaxhon abofeteó personalmente a Reynozo y le dijo estas palabras: "No es que ustedes y nosotros no podamos ser iguales, pero entiende que nuestra hambre no es tan desmedida como la de ustedes. Nos basta con vivir, ¿qué más podríamos pedir? Ustedes con su imaginación buscan necesidades y nosotros sufrimos para complacerlos. Nuestra voluntad ya los enfrentó. Ahora encuentren su camino y váyanse, hemos decidido no tolerarlos."

Al decir esto, arrojó con tal fuerza al Reynozo que cayó bajo las patas de su caballo, que paciente allí esperaba. Él no quiso permanecer más, lo montó rápidamente y se fue.

A ese extremo llegó el atrevimiento de Lía Kaxhon. Creyó entonces que ya nadie iba a tolerar al de Castilla, porque era un acuerdo de todos, en Yaze'e, en los pueblos del valle y en los pueblos de este lado. Como ella misma dijo, nosotros aceptamos gustosos el hecho de tener vida y estamos contentos con ello. Sin embargo, los de Castilla, no satisfechos con lo que sucedía y dispuestos a no perdernos, porque para entonces nosotros los alimentábamos, mientras estuvieron fuera de la región meditaban en la manera de regresar. Como no podían hacerlo con soldados, utilizaron sacerdotes; ellos se dedicaron a recorrer los pueblos invitando a olvidar lo sucedido porque el rencor no es bueno; insistían que eso ya no iba a suceder y que volviera la paz. Y así sucedió. Cuando los pueblos se pacificaron, otra vez los ejércitos de los de Castilla cayeron sobre nosotros y de nuevo mostraron lo que en realidad eran. Cuando se sintieron seguros de ser los vencedores detuvieron a los principales, también a Lía Kaxhon, y sobre ellos descargaron el rencor y la furia de haber estado un año sin comer de nuestro sudor. Grande fue la deuda de Lía Kaxhon por haber luchado para que tuviéramos una vida mejor de la que llevábamos hasta entonces. Los paisanos, que así eran antes y así lo siguen siendo, cuando vieron que los de Castilla eran vencedores, no quisieron comprometerse mientras Lía Kaxhon pagaba. Le quemaron la cabellera aún estando viva, le quemaron la lengua, le cortaron una mano y tantas otras cosas que le hicieron sufrir. Así pagaron también los otros principales de Yaze'e y de Rhacheyerha.

Hoy platiqué la historia de mi hermana mayor, de la que aún traigo su sangre y por ello su carácter y bondad, en caso de que yo quisiera ser bondadosa. Pero no lo soy ni lo seré porque sé que desde que llegaron los de Castilla hemos sido anulados. Nuestra simiente ya no crece. No quiero afligirme en cumplir con lo que está dicho que es mi deber, aunque sé que me espere un castigo por no cumplir, pero no me importa, olvidaré a mi pueblo.

Selección del Capítulo 6, "Tercera Revelación"

Cuando Trhon Lía[24] terminó de contar esta historia, me quedé pensando en eso con miedo y me preguntaba sobre esta mujer. En eso estaba cuando oí su voz; me dio la impresión de que hasta entonces notaba que allí estaba yo, junto a ella, y me preguntó:

—¿Estás sentado aquí?

—Sí, aquí—le contesté.

Se me quedó mirando fijamente. Notaba en sus ojos que ya había regresado a su juicio, que ya era ella misma, la que yo conocía; pude ver en sus pupilas ese dejo de tristeza que siempre trae.

—Qué poco te parece la vida de los demás ¿verdad?—dijo resaltando su tristeza—Qué tal si yo hubiera creído en tus palabras y hubiera dejado a mi esposo. Porque ahora veo con qué placer te trajiste y te paseas con tu mujer, ¡carroña seas!

Después se paró y salió del tendajón. Me desconcertaron sus palabras, pero inmediatamente me incorporé para seguirla. Cuando llegué al camino, ella iba hasta arriba; los hermosos movimientos que hacía su cuerpo al caminar de prisa me hicieron olvidar lo que había dicho; sonreí y me di cuenta que cada día me gustaba más. Con esta idea regresé a la casa de la señora Larhia a seguir tomando.

Mientras estuve bebiendo solo no pude pensar en Trhon Lía y sus historias. En lugar de ella llegó a mi pensamiento la idea de que la antropóloga fuera realmente mi esposa. Empecé a imaginarme la forma de hacerla mi esposa y la posibilidad de que ella aceptara. Así estaba cuando llegaron otros paisanos a tomar. Los invité y la borrachera se volvió formal.

No sé cómo salí ni cómo pude llegar al cuarto donde dormíamos.

Al otro día, cuando me levanté, lo primero que hice fue dirigirme al cuarto donde cocina doña Madarhen. Ya estaba ahí la antropóloga tomando una taza de café. Cuando me vio, haciendo una mueca de enojo, me dijo:

—Vas a ver, ¿por qué no me has dicho que en ese pueblo hay fiesta?—y señalaba rumbo a Lachelao.[25]

—Hoy en la noche apenas empieza la fiesta—le contesté—, pensaba decírtelo hoy, por si te animabas a ir.

—Sí, sí vamos, claro. Me fascinan las fiestas indígenas—dijo alegremente.

—Está bien, terminando el almuerzo nos vamos—le contesté, pues a mí nada me apuraba, porque el trabajo lo íbamos a hacer entre los dos.

Y así fue, pasado el almuerzo nos echamos a caminar al lugar de la fiesta. Cuando íbamos en la subida, ya para llegar a Lachelao, la mujercita empezó a fatigarse y tuvimos que ir despacio para que ella aguantara. Ahí empezaron a alcanzarnos los paisanos que también iban a la fiesta, se reían de nosotros simpáticamente y no faltó quien se hiciera escuchar:

—Qué bonito que a esta mujer le guste venir a estos lugares, ojalá que se quede para siempre en nuestro pueblo.

—Así va ser—les decía yo.

Me sentía contento y orgulloso porque creían que la antropóloga era mi mujer.

Cuando llegamos al pueblo donde estaba la fiesta, fuimos un rato a la iglesia, luego a ver los músicos y los pocos puestos de vendedores que allí había. Así anduvimos hasta que se fastidió la pobre mujer. Tal vez ella se había imaginado una gran fiesta por lo que le contó Doña Madarhen. Es que a una paisana que nunca ha salido de la región cualquier cosita se le hace mucho, pero para la antropóloga, acostumbrada a una infinidad de espectáculos, ir de un lugar a otro pronto se le hizo aburrido y a mí sólo se me ocurrió decirle "vamos a tomar un refresco."

Al llegar a la tienda, había mucha gente tomando. Los que eran del pueblo se animaron a preguntarnos de dónde veníamos. Cuando les explicamos la actividad a la que nos dedicábamos, contentos nos empezaron a convidar de lo que ellos tomaban. Yo, por mi parte, algunas tomaba y otras no; en cambio, la linda mujercita tomaba todas, creyendo que era serio lo que uno de estos señores había dicho:

—Aquí la costumbre es que debes tomar todo lo que te dan, porque si no lo haces, quiere decir que nos desprecias.

Y creyendo eso, se tomaba todo, la pobrecita. Cuando salimos de allí ya iba bastante borracha, pero todavía fuimos a escuchar los maitines[26] que interpretaba la banda de música de ese pueblo, y al rato, cuando nos dio hambre, nos fuimos a la Casa de la Comisión.[27] A esa hora sentíamos que se estaba animando la fiesta. Quemaron fuegos artificiales. Nos fuimos a parar cerca de la banda y allí también nos regalaron de tomar. Ella mostraba cansancio ya. Por mi parte, cuando fuimos a tomar el refresco en esa tienda, le había dicho al dueño que ella era mi esposa, por lo que le pedí un lugar para descansar y él ya había dicho que sí, por eso me atreví a decirle:

—Nos vamos a dormir.

—¿Dónde?—preguntó.

—Yo sé donde—le contesté.

—Qué prevenido eres ¿eh?—dijo—Vamos, pues.

Y de esta manera me la llevé y en el trayecto pasé a comprar más licor para seguir tomando. Cuando llegamos a la tienda, el dueño nos condujo a un pequeño cuarto donde nos iba a dejar dormir y efectivamente ya estaba preparado porque allí había una cama y sobre ella unas cobijas dobladas. Yo inmediatamente empecé a servir lo que llevaba para tomar y a soltar las intenciones que traía.

—Linda antropóloga, qué decisión podrías tomar, teniendo en cuenta que tú eres gente de ciudad y que yo soy de estos lugares, soy indígena, como ustedes dicen, y ahora quiero que te atrevas a dormir conmigo, tú como mujer y yo como hombre.

Aunque se turbó cuando oyó esto, nada más un momento se quedó callada e inmediatamente me contestó.

—Mira, Jaime—dijo seriamente—yo no he visto donde esté escrita la ley que hace a los seres humanos diferentes como para que digamos éste es indio, éste es mexicano o este otro es europeo; para mí, desde el momento en que nacimos tenemos los mismos derechos, sólo que la ambición humana es la que ha dividido a la humanidad . . .

Ella tenía muchas ganas de platicar y su plática era interesante, pero yo, que tenía al diablo adentro, no tenía intenciones de escucharla, por lo que corté bruscamente el hilo de su conversación.

—Lo que yo te estoy proponiendo es que si te atreverías a que juntos le demos satisfacción a nuestros cuerpos.

—¡Ah!—exclamó—ya sé a dónde quieres llegar, pero eso es lo de menos, a mí eso no me asusta, eso es lo más común entre los seres vivos, pero cada cosa en su lugar y en su momento. Para eso debe haber mutua simpatía, cosa que yo siento que todavía no la hay, ya que de otra manera, nos puede causar dolor.

—¿Por qué nos va a traer dolor?—le dije, ya bastante excitado—Tú me gustas mucho.

—Despacio, Jaime, todo es posible, espera un momento —dijo y siguió plática y plática.

Todavía la escuché otro rato y de pronto la empecé a acariciar; por un momento no dijo nada, pero cuando notó que era en serio, empezó a gritar.

—Cállate, por favor—le pedía yo encarecidamente.

Y ella más fuerte empezaba a gritar, pidiendo ayuda y llamando a los policías. No pasó mucho rato y al poco se abrió la puerta. Al ver esto me enfurecí y al primero que entró al cuarto lo agarré violentamente, lo golpeé y ya tirado le di de patadas, bastante enojado. Cuando me di cuenta ya eran varios los que intentaban detenerme y aunque opuse bastante resistencia me vencieron, me levantaron en vilo y así me llevaron a la cárcel. Qué mujer ni qué fiesta, a la cárcel desde esa noche.

Al día siguiente me sacaron de la cárcel y me llevaron ante las autoridades del pueblo. Cuando llegué con ellos estaba allí también la antropóloga bastante enojada, y más cuando me vio llegar.

—Exijo que se me haga justicia, señor, ¿por qué este individuo me trató así?, ¿quién cree él que soy? Este tipo de personas no deben andar libres, creen que nosotras las mujeres somos objetos y que podemos estar a su disposición cuando a ellos se les antoje. Exijo justicia.

Decía todo esto muy enojada. La autoridad trató de apoyarme un poco.

—Debes calcular un poco la intensidad de tu voz—dijo el principal a la antropóloga—, porque, ¿qué es lo que buscas hasta estos lugares? ¿Alguien te obligó? ¿Qué esperabas al entrar sola al cuarto de un hombre solo?[28]

Cuando oyó la mujer todo eso más se enfureció y empezó a buscar algo de entre su morral, sacó papeles que la identificaban como una persona que estaba haciendo un trabajo para el gobierno y mostrándoselos a las personas que allí estaban dijo:

—Miren, señores, yo ando aquí trabajando para una oficina del gobierno.

La autoridad apenas le dio una ojeada a esos papeles y se dirigió hacia mí.

—¿Y tú no traes algún papel que te identifique?

Yo qué iba llevar papeles, pues de plano yo iba a la fiesta, y cuando se lo dije a la autoridad, los demás miembros se rieron diciendo que me parecía yo a ellos; porque nunca les dije que era yo del otro pueblo de enfrente. Entonces decidieron mandarme otra vez a la cárcel. Cuando iba saliendo todavía oí que le dijeron a la antropóloga.

—Ya te puedes ir tranquila, nosotros sabemos cómo castigarlos y nadie va a venir a enseñarnos.

Así fue que no pude disfrutar de la fiesta durante esos días, todos los pasé en la cárcel. Cuando acabó la fiesta me amarraron, me condujeron a Villa Alta y después de todo un día de camino, al llegar, otra vez a la casa de fierro.

Notas

1. Los zapotecos de la sierra llaman a su lengua *diílla xhon,* de *diílla,* "lengua," "palabra," "idioma," y *xhon,* "pueblos de la ribera del río Cajonos" (es decir, "los zapotecos de esa región," los *xhon* o *kaxhon*). En zapoteco del Istmo es *didxazá,* de *didxa'* (otra forma ortográfica de *diílla*) y *zá,* "nube," es decir, "el idioma de la gente de la nube" o *binnizá,* "los zapotecos." A finales del siglo XX la población zapoteca rebasaba la cifra de 785,000 hablantes.

2. Nombre de todas las cactáceas de los géneros *Platyopuntia* y *Nopalea.* El texto se refiere a la variedad *Nopalea cochinillifera.*

3. Del latín *coccinus,* "escarlata" o "grana." Insecto hemíptero originario de México; vive sobre el nopal de la variedad *Nopalea cochinillifera.* Seco y reducido a polvo es muy útil para teñir de rojo la seda, lana y otras telas.

4. Se refiere al descendiente de la nube o *sa* (*zá*), el antiguo zapoteco, los antiguos pueblos. En zapoteco del Istmo se dice *binnizá,* "gente de la nube."

5. Se refiere a los pueblos situados en la ribera del río Cajonos o Kaxhon. A partir de este dato geográfico se ha convertido en la variante dialectal del zapoteco de la sierra para referirse a los zapotecos mismos.

6. Se refiere al pueblo San Francisco Cajonos.

7. Variante dialectal del zapoteco de la sierra para referirse a la gente "zapoteca" del "rincón," es decir, la zona norte de Ixtlán, llamada Xid Zá, "Rincón Zapoteco."

8. Literalmente, "mensajeros."

9. San Ildefonso Villa Alta fue el primer pueblo fundado por y para españoles en las sierras bajas. Colinda con territorios mixes y chinantecos y a finales del siglo XX contaba con apenas mil habitantes.

10. Los *mixes* o *mijes* (ellos se autodenominan *ayook*) constituyen uno de los principales grupos étnicos del estado de Oaxaca. Sus pueblos se extienden por la sierra de Juárez, al norte del estado. A finales del siglo XX su población ascendía a un total aproximado de 188,000 personas.

11. Se refiere a Yalálag (literalmente, "cerro desparramado"), municipalidad de la región conocida como sierra Zapoteca de Villa Alta. Es el primer centro de producción de tejidos de esa zona de la sierra.

12. Se refiere a dos poblados *xhon:* San Juan Tabá, municipalidad de la Sierra Zapoteca de Villa Alta, y Santo Domingo Yohovi.

13. Apócope de *benexidsa:* es decir, los zapotecos del rincón.

14. Región de la zona conocida como Ixtepeji.

15. Principal autoridad del pueblo.

16. Región que está alrededor de San Pablo Gelatao, con poblaciones como Ixtlán, Natividad y Jalteanguis.

17. Literalmente, "el viento que inicia o se adelanta," espíritu sagrado siempre vigilante y cercano a los seres. (Véase la nota 15 del texto en lengua indígena.)

18. Plural de *xhon* (es decir, literalmente, "los xhon").

19. Uno de los pueblos *xhon;* literalmente, "cerro de cenizas."

20. Otra entidad sagrada prehispánica. Literalmente, "relámpago de aire," de *gozio,* "rayo" o "relámpago," y *be,* "aire."

21. Nombre en zapoteco de la sierra del *Coelogenys paca,* roedor comestible muy conocido en las regiones indígenas con el nombre de *tepescuintle* o *tepescuincle,* del náhuatl *tepeitzcuintli,* "perro de cerro."

22. Nombre en zapoteco de la "cochinilla" (literalmente, "pintura del nopal").

23. San Mateo Capulalpan, uno de los pueblos de la región Rhe'ja.

24. Forma zapoteca de los nombres castellanos "Petrona María."

25. Pueblo desaparecido perteneciente a los *xhon.* Ahora es sólo un paraje.

26. En el ritual católico, primera de las horas canónicas en que comienzan los rezos previos al amanecer. Entre los zapotecos de la sierra, obra musical que las bandas tocan en ceremonias vespertinas o nocturnas compuesta de un himno a la virgen, responsos y un rezo de *te deum.*

27. Casa de la Comisión: lugar donde los organizadores de la fiesta ("la Comisión") dan de comida a todos los visitantes durante los días de fiesta.

28. El original en zapoteco maneja esta idea con especial buen humor. La autoridad recuerda un refrán zapoteco. El pasaje sería más o menos así: "Como dice el refrán: ¿Ves el corral, pero no te cuidas?" (Véase nota 27 del texto en lengua zapoteca.)

Joel Torres Sánchez

Purepecha

Joel Torres Sánchez. Photographed at Tzintzuntzan, Michoacán.

Joel Torres Sánchez was born in San Jerónimo Purenchécuaro, Michoacán. He is a graduate of the Rural Teacher Training School in La Huerta, Michoacán, and of the Autonomous University of Tlaxcala. He also completed an enrichment program for Purepecha teachers at the National Autonomous University's Centro de Enseñanza de Lenguas Extranjeras (CELE). Torres Sánchez has taught in several primary and secondary schools in the Purepecha area, where he learned to value and promote his people's culture through historical research, narrative, and music. He has been a grantee of the National Fund for Culture and the Arts and is a member of the Scholarship Commission of the Undersecretariat of Middle and Higher Education. His work entitled "Lo que el lago me contó" (What the Lake Told Me) was the winner of the Second Purepecha Short Story Competition. In 1995 Torres Sánchez was awarded the National Prize for Narrative in the Literary Composition on National Symbols contest with his "Origen p'urhepecha de la bandera nacional" (The Purepecha Origin of the National Flag). Both compositions appeared in volume 1 of his two-volume personal anthology: *P'urhepecha Uandatskuecha/Narrativa P'urhepecha* (Purepecha Narrative). The second volume of this work was published in 2001 by the Secretariat of Public Education for use in Purepecha bilingual schools.

Joel Torres Sánchez es originario de San Jerónimo Purenchécuaro, egresado de la Escuela Normal Rural de la Huerta, Michoacán, y de la Universidad Autónoma de Tlaxcala, así como de un diplomado de formación para profesores de purépecha del Centro de Enseñanza de Lenguas Extranjeras (CELE) de la Universidad Nacional Autónoma de México. Se desempeñó como profesor en varias escuelas primarias y secundarias de la zona purépecha, donde aprendió a valorar y promover la cultura de su pueblo en aspectos como la investigación histórica, la narrativa y la música. Fue becario del Fondo Nacional para la Cultura y las Artes. Forma parte de la Comisión de Becas de la Subsecretaría de Educación Media y Superior. En el Segundo Concurso del Cuento Purépecha premiaron su trabajo "Lo que el lago me contó." Obtuvo el Premio Nacional de Narrativa en el certamen de Composición Literaria sobre los Símbolos Patrios 1995 con "Origen p'urhepecha de la bandera nacional." Ambas composiciones aparecen en el primer tomo de su antología personal en dos tomos: *P'urhepecha Uandatskuecha/Narrativa P'urhepecha.* El segundo tomo de esta obra fue publicada en 2001 por la Secretaría de Educación Pública para uso en las escuelas bilingües purépechas.

Ji no xukuamiska, ¡ji xurhijkirhiska! (Mindakata)

Joel Torres Sánchez

Purepecha[1]

[From *P'urhepecha Uandatskuecha/Narrativa P'urepecha,* vol. 1, pp. 157–164. Morelia: INI/PACMYC, 1997.]

Ka niarasïpti ma jurhiani enga xarhintku uandajpapka Delfinani ka arhisïpti eska jikuarapiringa, ka:

—Tatsekuarhini tepetsikuaka ka jatsikuntarini sïrijtakua turhipitini, jichiti inchanikua enga k'erati tsïtsïkichani jukanarhiaka, juchiiti jongüarhikuani, imani engarini intsikuarhika uarhiti P'urhenchekuaru anapu. ¡Joo! ima enga uekampka mitini nani jamasïambi uajpa, miasïndi na xani tsipeni p'ikuarherapka ekaksï xentapka uajpani; indenisïni uejka jukantani ka tatsunarhikuani engani ji untapka, isï engarini na jurhendapka juchaari nandi; ka jirinachintarini k'uanindikua turhipitini, imani engatsïni jauirani ueratini juacheka.

Ka nana Delfina k'urhamarhisïpti:

—Andirisï uejki xukuparhani eska k'uinche ambeeni?

—¡Jimboka k'uinchekuegüaka!—mokukuarhisïpti nana Simona.

Menderu k'urhamarhisïpti nimakua jembanana Simonani:

—¿Kanigüa k'uinchikua?

Ka nana Simona arhisïpti:

—Era inchatiru jimbo jugüati ma uarhiti "K'eri eratakata,"[2] ka uekasïnga eskarini sesi xukuparhatini xentaaka, ka no ima tatsekua ikiani, jimboka inde uarhiti kanikua ikiasïnga enga no sesi jasï xentaaka k'uiripuni enga nirajka p'urhembeni; ka eka k'uiripu enga nirajka p'urhenbinanini: tsipikua jingoni erokajka, sesi xukuparhatini ka sesi jikuarhini (jupatsïtini), sesi eratasïndi, ka isï jimbo ji uekajka sesi erokani, ¡Turini kurhangucheejka!

—Eka isïka, uaka ambe engarini kurhaachijka—uandasïti nana Delfina.

Ka isi usïti na enga nana Simona kurhakupka, ka tatsekua terupinirhu uaxajtasïtpti, ka eka na Tata Jurhiata[3] inchatsikuntani jamanga, janosïpti nana Uarhikua,[4] ka nana Simona kanikua tsipikua jingoni erokasïpti, ka nana Simoneri tsipikua ima jingoni niraspti.

Pauandimakua jimbo jatsïnantasïpti, ka najkirukua uarhiperakua notku k'amakurhiampka, uanikua k'uiripu pambintasïpti, eratsiparini esïka inde jurhitikua no nema uarhiperapiringa, jimboka nana Delfina nanita jemba, jindesïpka ma k'uiripu enga uanikua iretarhu anapuechani jarhuatapka ka maruteruechani ambakerantapka.

Ka inde jurhitikua jimbo, iamendu k'uiripuecha enga nipka uandanuentani nana Simonani, eratsïsptiksï eratani nana Delfinani eska k'eri xurhijki, ka ninantanani jamani arhisïptikisï nana Delfineri arhinakua, joperu jananarhikua jingoni, ka eska jucha na mitika uandakua "Cha"[5] jindesïti ne mani uandajpani jananarhikua jingoni, ka isï jiimbo jimajkantki ueratini undasïpti arhinani "Cha Nana Delfina."[6]

Ka uarhiperakua pauani pauani sanderu k'epasïpti, ka pauani pauani sanderu k'uiripu uarhisïampti ka sanderu iurhiri tsïncheni, ka no anaxurhini uarhiperakua, ka nana Delfina uamba pauani ka pauani uekasïampti eska nana Delfina, sanderu ambe jurhendapiringa, jimbokana ambe enga ima mitipkia no kanekuesïpti, isï jimbo uekampti eska sanderu jurhendapiringa, ka jimbosï mentku no kejtakuampti nani enga ima p'ikurhpentani japiringa.

Ka inde uarhiperakua enga metku chuxapani japka, uenasïpti k'arhingua jarhani, ka k'uiripu noteru jatsïspti nani p'irani t'irekua ka undasïptiksï nirani kurhakuni nana Delfinani, noksï mitisïpti nanina, joperu no meni kueratanchasïampti t'irekua, menisï jatsisïampti k'uiripita auaniri, menisï kuarakiri, menichani karichiri, ka meni axuniri ambe; enga jimbo uatsotakuarhu exeantauampka uarhiriksï.

Ka ma jurhitikua jimbo nana Delfineri uamba[7] arhisïpti eska ima noteru uekampka erokani, ka ima uekampka eska arhipiringa nani nirasïambi; eska ima uandamindu erangüsipka na enga ima churhikua jimbo jauarampka, turhipiti xukuparhenga ka kuerajtsïtini, juatarhu jurhibitku niranga ka enga nierampka juatarhu jandukutini uenampka perentsïni ka tatsïkua ma k'eri tarhiata echeriri jauarampka, enga na anaxurhiampka, jima xarharasïampti ma k'eri jiuatsï enga kapindikuarhu uiriauampka ka nirasïampti jurajkuni k'umanchikua uatsotakuarhu ma auani, ma kuaraki, ma karichi ka menisï ma axuni, ka enga ima pauandimakua xarhintku jimbo ambakerauampka ka angunakua urani ka ijtu intsïmbini imani k'uiripuechani engaksï nirampka kurhakuni t'irekua ambe, iamendu ini ambeniha ima mitisïpti, joperu eskana no uandaniapiringa imana no nemani eiangupiringa, imana imatkusï uekampti eska nana Delfina sanderu ambe jurhendapiringa, jimbokana ima uambesïpka.

Ka nana Delfina arhispti eska ini ambe jurhengüarhini, kanekua iondakuarhiampka, ka tsunapikua jukasïpti ka no iamendu k'uiripuecha usïampti jurhenani,[8] ka uetarhisïampti esïka ima k'uiripuecha no kuatantapiringa, eska no uiriakuarhujku jamapiringa ka upiringa no ma ambe miani jarhani enga jurhendanani japiringa, ka no epurhperakua jimbo uekani jurhenguarhini, ka no jimboka uekapiringa no sesi utsïpini, ka eska ma k'uiripu enga jurhengüarhipiringa ini ambe, uekapiringa jarhuani k'uiripuechani.

Joperu ima no uekasïpti ini ambe kurhanguni, ka metku arhisïampti nana Delfinani eska jurhendapiringa, ka xani kurhajchatini ma jurhiani jimbo arhisïpti eska ima no jakajkusïampka eska upiringa jurhengüarhini ka eska ima chesïampka eska indeni jurhengüarhikua jimbo ima no sesi utsïpini jamapiringa.

Nana Delfina kurhakusïpti eska eiakupiringa eska ima jurhengüarhikua no, sesi utsïpitarapiringa ka jananarhipiringa arhijtsïperatani, ka isï ueenasïpti jurhendani, ka xexapti na enga ima no kurhajchani jarhanga enga ima jurhendani japiringa, mentkisï tamu erani jarhasïampti, ka metku sonichani meni k'urhangurhini imani ambe enga t'uini arhijtanimenga, jimboka sontkusï mirikuarhiampka ambe enga arhijtanimenga, ka najkiruka ini ambe exeni japka nana Delfina, niarasïpti jurhitikua engaksï tsa tsimani nipiringa kuanitarhu xarhatani jurhengüarhikuani ka isï jimbo ma inchatiru, arhisïpti uandamindu arhijtakuni nasïptiksï uandakuecha enga ima uenapiringa arhiani, ka ambe jatsïspka uni tatsekua ka uni jiuatsi ukuarhintani ka menderu nakisï jindesïpi uandakuecha enga jimbo ima upiringa menderu k'uiripu ukuarhintani, ima achaati undasïpti iamendu ambe sesi kurhanguni ka miani jarhani andarhierani.

Uenani jamani iamendu ambe sesi ueraspti usïptiksï jupiani juatarhu anapu irekuarhirichani, joperu erandu isï ma ambe no sesi uerasïpti, achaati no usïampti k'uiripu ukuarhintani, mentku janguarhintasïampti mandani ambe miantani ambe enga arhijtaminapka, ka nana Delfinajtu arhijtakusïampti, ka najkirukaksï kanikua jangüarhintapka, no usïpti k'uiripu ukuarhintani nana Delfineri uamba.

Ka enga na xarharapka tata jurhiata, nana Delfina arhisïpti jiuatsïni eska jirikuarhipiringa k'umanchikuarhu, nani enga no nema exepiringa, enga jamberi niarapiringa churekua. Inde jurhitikua jimbo sanderu k'uiripu nierasïpti exeni nana Delfinani ka no xantku eska na p'indekuepka, ka maru k'uiripuechani imeri uichuecha chuxapasïpti, ka engaksï na niarampka nana Delfinoo uenasïamptikisï k'uangunchini ka mentkuksï k'umanchekuani uanotantani, ka ini ambe exeparini ma k'uiripu terekuarhiparini arhispti:

—Ambejtsï jatsïski incharini, andisï uichu xani mintsïtajki?, inajki sïpiruni jaki jiuatsïni ambe.

Ka nana Delfina mokukuarhisïpti terekuarhiparini:

—Iurhiri auanicheri ambe jindeeti.

Ka menderu k'urhamarhihasïpti:

—¿Ka chari achati[9] nani jarhaski?

Ka nana Delfina kurhakuarhisïpti:

—Lasï k'oru uekasti nirani juatarhu ch'akari iuini.

Ka sontku nitamasïpti jurhitikua, ka churekua janosïpti, ka eka na jindepka terojkani churi, jangüarhintasïptiksï eska uamba nana Delfineri menderu k'uiripu ukuarhintapiringa, najkiruka nana Delfina kuatantapka arhijtakuni ambenga uandapiringa ka najkirukajtu achaati janguarhintapka noksï usïpti. Ka isïksï usïpti mandani churhichani, joperu ima achaati noteru usïptia k'uiripu ukuarhintani ka isï jimbo nana Delfina arhisïpti uambani eska inde jindepiringa imeri irekuarhikua ka eska nipiringa irekuarhini juatarhu.

Ka enga na jurhitikuechana nitamapenga ka nema k'urhamarhiampka nana Delfinani nani jarhasïpi uamba, ima arhisïampti eska kuatantasïpka jima jarhani ka k'uanatsintapka imeri iretarhu, joperu jiajkani ueratini undasïpti exenani ma k'eri jiuatsï enga inchatiruechani niarampka nana Delfina, ka menichani xarhintkuechani niarasïampti jurajkuni ma auanini, ma kuaraki, ka menchani ma tsikata ambe, enga jima iretarhu tsïnchiampka.

Ka irekuarhikua nitamapaxapti, ka ima jingoni mamaru ambe uenasïpti mojtakukuarhini iretarhu, ka enga nitamapkia iumu t'amu uexurhinicha enga inde ireta arhukuarhipka, k'eri juramukuecha eratsïsptiksï inchakuni ka anaxutani indeni uarhiperakuani; materu xanaru jimboksïni eiangüaka na enga japka inde uarhiperakua. Ka isï jimbo inde uarhiperakua sangani arhini ahaxurhisïpti, ka no ioni jimbo menderu mamaru intsïpikurhiricha uenasïpti inchakuni inde ireta tsïpinarhi jimbo, maruksï uenasïpti paani motsïtarakuechani engaksi jiajkani isï uenapka xarharani. Ka isï mamaru jasï ambeksï inchatasïpti ini iretarhu, jimaksï mitikuarhisïpti uandakua p'ikutarakuecha engaksï ueenapka xarharani; ka iasï miantaxaka ma ambe enga upka tata Nacho Ramos: ima uekasïampti uandikuni ma uandakua p'ikutarakuani, ma uandikutarakua tiamueri jingoni, jimbokana uandakua p'ikutarakua no uekasïampka menderu k'ujtakuni inde pirekuani enga k'amatapka kusïkani.

Kanikua tsunapikua jingoni kurhangutarasïpka tata Nachuni eska tsa engaksï pireni japka noksï uandakua p'ikutarakuarhu jatarini jarhasïpka; eska ima pirericha jiniksï jarhasïpka ireta k'erirhu: Tsakapuo jima jarhasïpti uaxajtakata inde uandakua etsakutarakua enga ima kurhani japka, ka eka na juchiiti taati ka ji papkaksï miiurani indeni uandakua etsakutarakuani, jiajkani k'oru jakakusïpti.

Ka enga terujkanisï nirani japka inde uexurhini 1959; uenasïptiksï anchekurhitecha enga marhuapiringa erajkutarakua peerani inde iretarhu, ka engaksï na anasïkuapka k'erati chikarichani, apirhukupasïptiksï imani enga jimbo upiringa niarani erajkukua.

Ka ma jurhiani enga maru achaaticha nirani japka juatarhu xarhini jimbo, exesïptiksï ma ambe engaksï no meni exepka, ka ma achaati uiriasïpti eianguni tata jurhentpirini engajtu jindepka tata kaarari iretarhu anapu, tatsekua tata jurhentpiri chuxapasïpti achaatini, ka pajtasïpti uajpani enga jatiripka ma tembini uexurhinisï.

Ambe enga exekuarhipka, ma no jakajkukuarhisïampti, joperu jima jarhasïpti opsarhukutini xasïku nana Delfina, ka jajkicharhu maru k'uirakua karukukatechani tirhixurhatini, ka ekatsïni erokapka, kurhajkuarhisïpti eskaksï keskuntapiringa, ka jindijtsïni arhisïpti eskani k'ejtakupiringa, ka tsïmani achaaticha nirasïpti kuanditkurhiani maru karharatarakuechani engaksï jatsïkuapka ka unksï kesïkuntani nana Delfinani ka nema k'uanitasïpti ma t'arhahikua enga jingoni xukuparhapka ka eska na keskuhantapka, no ma ambe arhiasïpti ka chuxapasïpti nintani imeri k'umanchikuarhu; jiajkani exesïpka ma xanaru uni jamani, jimboka jima no iauani nitamasïpka engani ji japka, ka najkiruka uandamindu kurhapka imeri ambe uandanani, no meni usïpka exeni jimajku no iauani.

Jindesïpti ma uarhiti k'eri enga jauiri iorhati ka merekasï jukapka, tatsekuani andarhierasïpka taatini enga uandontsïkuarhini japka achaaticha jingoni ka maru urhiiticha engaksï jima janopka.

¿Iamenduecha k'urhangurhisïampti nanina karharapi nana Delfina? ¿Ambena uni karharapi? ¿Andisïna karharapi?

Ka ma achaati uandasïpti:

—Jimboka nana Delfina sanderu k'erati ambe usïna, no inde sanderu k'erisïkia, sanderu jurhenasïti, sanderu iauani isï nirasïndi eska maruteru iretecharhu k'uiripuechani exeani, engaksï jurhajka exeni; ka isï jimbo churichani tukuru[10] ukuarhintajti ka iapurisï jamajti ka iasï enga jungüani japka mirikuarhipti eska inde anchikurhita ukata japka ka isï jimbo opsarhukuti.

Ka materu achaati sanderu sapichu, sanderu jahasikati, ka enga no jakajkuampka ini ambe uandasïpti:

—Nombe, nema jarhuajti karharani jini jimboka noteru nema nirasïnga exeni ka jini karhakua iamenduecha upiringa exeni ka jakajkuhksï ambe enga ari achati uandajka, joperu no sïkuami o xurhijki ambesïti, ji no kani jakajkusïnga eska nana Delfina kárajka.

Jiajkani juchiti taati uandasïpti, nije iamenduecha chaari anchekorhitecharhu, tatsekuaksï xejperantaka; ka arhisïptirini juia, ka ji chuxapasïpka taatini, metku eratsïparini ka engani iasï jamberi no ujka mitini, ambesï ukuarhipi: isïpi eska nana Delfina karapungüempka ka opsarhukutini pakarapka, no jakajkukueni jasïsïti; nema jarhuatapi karharani; sanderu no jakajkukueni jasïsti, jimboka nana Delfina no uetarhinchasïampka eska mitinapiringa, ka imajtu no meni uekapirindi xasïku karharani ka isï jarhani, nandi xani jatakuechani ka xani tsïrakuarhikua jingoni ka isï jimbo no k'amatajka kurhanguni ambesï ukuarhipi.

Notes

1. For a long time, the Purepecha language was erroneously called "Tarasco." This language's origins and linguistic family remain un-

Notas

1. Durante mucho tiempo, de manera errónea, se llamó a la lengua purépecha "tarasca." Se trata de una lengua cuyo origen y familia lin-

known. As in the case of Euskera, the language of the Basques in Spain, Purepecha is a linguistic island on the continent. At the end of the twentieth century there were more than 204,000 speakers of Purepecha, living primarily in the state of Michoacán. The author uses the alphabet established in Pátzcuaro in 1979 by the Secretariat of Public Education and the Michoacán University of San Nicolás Hidalgo as the result of a Centro de Cooperación Regional para la Educación de Adultos en América Latina y el Caribe (CREFAL) working group.

2. Literally, "High-Ranking Woman." (See note 4.)

3. Literally, "Father Sun."

4. Literally, "Lady Death."

5. A Purepecha form of addressing both men and women with the highest level of respect and prestige; similar to "thou" in Old English or *vuestra merced* in Old Spanish.

6. "Nana": a title for older females who have borne children; Cha Nana Delfina: "Thou, Mother Delfina."

7. Literally, "husband." The author chose to translate this word into Spanish as *señor,* used in Spanish to refer to a mature man, which in Purepecha would be *achámari* or *tatáchi.*

8. "Prepare oneself" or "be initiated into knowledge." The author translated this ambiguous concept into Spanish as *don,* a "talent" or "gift."

9. Literally, "man" or "sir"; that is, "husband."

10. "Owl," which, curiously, in Mayan is *tunkuruchu.*

güística no se ha podido identificar. Como la lengua vasca, el euskera, en Europa, el idioma purépecha es en nuestro continente una isla lingüística. A finales del siglo XX esta lengua contaba con 204,000 hablantes que residían principalmente en el estado de Michoacán. El autor emplea el alfabeto acordado en Pátzcuaro el año 1979, durante una reunión de trabajo del Centro de Cooperación Regional para la Educación de Adultos en América Latina y el Caribe (CREFAL), entre la Secretaría de Educación Pública y la Universidad Michoacana de San Nicolás Hidalgo.

2. Literalmente, "Señora Principal." (Véase nota 4.)

3. Literalmente, "Padre Sol."

4. Literalmente, "Señora Muerte."

5. Forma purépecha de dirigirse a los hombres y mujeres con el más alto nivel de respeto. Similar a "Vuestra Merced" en el castellano antiguo o al *thou* en el inglés arcaico.

6. "Nana": título para mujeres mayores que han sido madres; Cha Nana Delfina: "Usted, Madre Delfina."

7. Literalmente, "esposo." El autor quiso traducir esta palabra al español como "señor," que sería *achámari* o *tatáchi.*

8. "Prepararse" o "iniciarse en el conocimiento." El autor tradujo este concepto ambiguo como "don."

9. Literalmente, "hombre" o "señor"; es decir, "esposo."

10. "Tecolote," "lechuza"; en maya, curiosamente, *tunkuruchu.*

I'm Not a Witch, I'm a Healer! (Selection)

Joel Torres Sánchez

Purepecha[1]

[From *P'urhepecha Uandatskuecha/Narrativa P'urepecha,* vol. 1, pp. 157–164, 180–188. Morelia: INI/PACMYC, 1997.]

As they worked, Delfina noticed that with each passing day her grandmother grew more and more weary; she was no longer steady on her feet; she no longer ate well; she spent a lot of time looking at her granddaughter and making numerous recommendations regarding what she should do once she had left this world.

One day her grandmother spoke to her very early and said: "I want you to bathe me. Then comb my hair and dress me in my black *nahuas,*[2] my cross-stitched *huanengo*[3] with purple flowers, my engraved sash—the one the woman from Purenchécuaro gave me—the woman who wanted to know where her son was. How happy she was when we located him! I also want to put on the apron I embroidered just as my mother taught me; and please look for the black striped *rebozo*[4] they brought me from Ahuirán."[5]

"Why do you want to dress up as if there were a fiesta?" asked Delfina.

"Because there is going to be a fiesta," answered her grandmother.

"When?" Delfina asked.

"This afternoon a high-ranking woman is going to come, and I want her to find me well dressed; she gets angry when the person she goes to visit is dirty and complaining. On the other hand, when she finds one smiling, in fresh clothing and without fear, she treats one better. That is why I want to be prepared; do you understand me?"

"Well, if that is what it is about, then I will do everything you want," Delfina responded to her grandmother.

Delfina took care of everything that her grandmother had ordered. When she was ready, she sat her in the center of her *choza.*[6] As Father Sun was about to depart, Nana[7] Simona received the visit of Lady Death, who carried away her soul, leaving upon her face a smile full of satisfaction.

She was buried the following day; and despite the ongoing dispute between "those from up above" and "those from down below,"[8] people from both groups showed up at the burial. They decided that out of gratitude for the *señora*[9] who had healed so many, it was proper that there be no fighting much less killing that day, out of respect for her memory.

In the graveyard, Delfina was virtually promoted; as they were leaving, everyone who approached to give her the "hug of consolation" added "Cha"[10] to her name, which in our language is a symbol of respect. From that day on, she became "Cha Nana Delfina."[11]

Nevertheless, the town conflict was growing, and the desire for revenge was on the rise. Nana Delfina also began to feel pressure from her husband, who admitted that he already had learned some things but wanted to know more and constantly observed her in everything she did.

Due to the scarcity of food in town, many people called on Nana Delfina to give them something to eat. They did not know how, but she always had some meat: rabbit, squirrel, mutton, and at times even deer; they appeared on her fence always in the morning, with puncture wounds on their necks.

One day her husband said that he could wait no longer: she had to share her knowledge with him. He often had seen her get up at night, leave the house wrapped in a black tunic with her hair untied, and head for a place at the foot of the hill, where she would roll about in the loose dirt. He would then see a cloud of dust rise, from which an enormous she-coyote would emerge and run off into the dark of night. The same animal would later return and leave on their fence the animals, which Delfina would begin to clean early the next day. They would eat only a little of those animals, and she would give most of the meat to the people who came begging. Her husband assured her that she need not worry: everything was fine; he just wanted to learn more, and since he was her husband she had the obligation to teach him.

Nana Delfina told him that he needed time to learn those things and that not everyone possessed the "gift";[12] those who desired to learn needed much patience and had to be able to concentrate and clear their mind. They could not be motivated by envy or the desire to harm others but only by need or the desire to help.

The husband kept on insisting until one day Nana Delfina told him she would teach him. She was not confident, however, that he would learn well because she did not see the "gift" in his eyes. She also feared he would use his newly acquired knowledge—along with the little that he already possessed—to cause harm.

Once he had promised to use what he would learn to do good, Nana Delfina began to teach him. She then realized that the man did not pay proper attention, was not steadfast, and often forgot things. Despite it all, the night arrived when they made their first trip to the hill together. Beginning that afternoon, she prepared her husband with her final suggestions; she repeated several times to him the words to pronounce in the beginning; what to do immediately following; then the words and actions he had to remember to recover his normal shape. At nightfall, when he said he was ready, they left for the place of loose earth.

Everything went well at the beginning and in collecting the animals that would provide them with meat and hide; but in the early morning something went wrong. The man could not recover his form no matter how hard he struggled, even with Nana Delfina's advice. When Señor Sun awoke, she told her husband to hide inside the house so that no one would see him, and they would await nightfall to fix the problem.

That day, more people than usual went to visit Nana Delfina; some of them were followed by their dogs, who, when they approached the place, barked and encircled the house. In a laughing tone, one person said: "What do you have hidden inside, Nana Delfina? My dog is barking and running about as if he sensed a coyote."

"It must be the animals' blood," she answered with a smile.

"And your husband?"

"Ah! He decided to go to the hill for firewood today."

Day became night, and when it reached its mid-point, the attempts began once again for the husband to recover his form; but they could not achieve their objective: neither she with her advice nor he through his struggling. Having made an effort for several nights, they realized that they would accomplish nothing; therefore, she told him to resign himself to his fate and to go off to the hill and live his life.

Days later, when someone would ask about her husband, she would simply say that he had grown tired of being there and had gone back to his home town. But from then on, many people would see an enormous coyote in the afternoons or very early in the day. It would approach Nana Delfina's house to leave a rabbit, a squirrel, or, mistakenly, a hen that had foolishly gotten lost right in town. "How foolish!" Nana Delfina would say.

Father Time continued his journey, and with it things began to change in town. After nine years the government, "the big law" as they called it, finally decided to intervene to halt the conflict; arresting the leaders of each group imposed order. At some other time, I will tell how these truly unique events transpired. The important thing is that, little by little, the division among the people came to an end. Outsiders once again were coming to town, and merchants brought the first automobiles ever seen there. They would bring many new things; that was when we saw the first battery-powered radios. I remember how Tata[13] Nacho Ramos wanted to "kill" a radio with his pistol because it would not repeat a song it had just played. It was very difficult to make him understand that those who were singing were not inside the radio but rather in a transmitting station in Zacapu. Once he was convinced, my papá and I took him to see the radio station.

In mid-1959 work began to bring electricity to town. Once the posts were up, they began to hang the wires on them. The first men to head to the hill early one day saw something out of the ordinary. One of them went to notify the teacher who was serving as secretary of land tenure, who headed out to tend to the matter along with his ten-year-old son: me.

What we saw was astonishing indeed: stuck up among the four electric wires was Nana Delfina, whose only article of clothing consisted of pieces of an old *petate*.[14] She asked us to get her down. I was requested to step back; two of the men went to get a ladder to help her get down. Someone loaned her an overcoat; and, wrapped up in it, she headed off toward her house without saying a word. That was the first time I saw her, since she passed near where I was standing. I knew of her existence because I often had heard tell of her, but I had never seen her up close. She was elderly, and that was why my eye was drawn to her hair: very long, black, and shiny. I then approached my papá, who was talking with the men and some women who had come around. Everyone was asking each other just how, and why, she had gotten up there.

Then a very confident man said: "The thing is, Nana Delfina is much older now; she knows more; she now travels further; she goes off to other towns to see people who request favors. Now at night she turns into a *tecolote*[15] and flies everywhere. Therefore, as she was returning, she forgot they had just put up the wires and she got stuck."

A younger man, more modern, more skeptical, said: "No, the thing is that she has already lost a lot of people, and many no longer visit her; with someone's help she climbed up there so that we would think what this man just said. But I do not believe it is true that she can fly."

My papá ended the discussion: "Well, it is getting late: let us get back to our chores and later on we shall see. Let us go!"

I followed my papá while thinking and thinking. From that day on, I have not been able to find a reasonable explanation. Did she really get stuck while flying? That is hard to believe. Or did she allow someone to help her get up among the wires? That is even harder to believe; she did not possess, as we would say today, the need for publicity. It is even less likely that she would decide to climb up there naked; besides, at her age, it was difficult to endure who knows how many hours in such an uncomfortable position. Well, the truth still eludes my scant knowledge.

Notes

1. For a long time the Purepecha language was erroneously called "Tarasco." This language's origins and linguistic family remain unknown. As in the case of Euskera, the language of the Basques in Spain, Purepecha is a linguistic island on the continent. At the end of the twentieth century there were more than 204,000 speakers of Purepecha, living primarily in the state of Michoacán.

2. Apocopated form of the Old Spanish *enaguas;* a woman's exterior garment that hangs from the waist. From the Taino *naguas*, "cotton skirt."

3. Traditional white cotton blouse adorned with embroidered flower motifs.

4. A woman's exterior garment used to cover the shoulders and upper torso; a shawl.

5. Purepecha town where high-quality *rebozos* are produced.

6. A rustic house or hut.

7. A Purepecha title of respect reserved for older women who have borne children.

8. A reference to those living in the elevated and nonelevated zones of the region.

9. A Spanish title used to refer to or address married women.

10. A Purepecha form of addressing both men and women with the highest level of respect and prestige; similar to "thou" in Old English or *vuestra merced* in Old Spanish.

11. "Thou, Mother Delfina."

12. *Jurhenani,* in Purepecha: to "prepare oneself" or "be initiated into knowledge." The author translated this ambiguous concept into Spanish as *don,* "talent" or "gift."

13. A Purepecha title of respect reserved for older men.

14. From the Nahuatl *petlatl,* a weaving of palm or reeds used as a mat for sitting or sleeping or as a funerary wrap.

15. From the Nahuatl *tecolotl,* "owl." The Purepecha word is *tukuru,* closer to the Mayan *tunkuruchu.*

No soy hechicera, ¡soy curandera! (Selección)

Joel Torres Sánchez

Purépecha[1]

[De *P'urhepecha Uandatskuecha/Narrativa P'urepecha,* vol. 1, pp. 157–164, 180–188. Morelia: INI/PACMYC, 1997.]

Mientras trabajaban, Delfina notaba que su abuela cada día se cansaba más, sus pasos no eran firmes, no comía bien, se le quedaba mirando y le daba muchas recomendaciones sobre lo que debía hacer cuando ella faltara.

Un día, muy temprano, le dijo:

—Quiero que me bañes, luego me peinas y me pones mis naguas[2] negras, mi huanengo[3] de punto de cruz con flores moradas, mi faja grabada, la que me regaló la señora de Purenchécuaro, aquélla que quería saber dónde andaba su hijo. ¡Quedó tan contenta cuando lo encontramos! . . . También quiero ponerme el delantal que bordé como me enseñó mi madre. Y por favor, búscame el rebozo negro rayado, que me trajeron de Ahuirán.[4]

—¿Por qué quieres vestirte como si fuera fiesta?—preguntó Delfina.

—Porque habrá fiesta—contestó su abuela.

—¿Cuándo?—volvió a preguntar Delfina.

—Por la tarde vendrá una señora muy principal y quiero que me encuentre bien arreglada, porque ella se enoja cuando a la persona que llega a visitar está mugrosa y quejumbrosa. En cambio, cuando lo encuentra a uno sonriendo, con ropa limpia y sin miedo, lo trata a uno mejor. Por eso quiero estar preparada, ¿me entiendes?

—Si es por eso, haré lo que quieres—respondió Delfina a su abuela.

Delfina cumplió lo ordenado por su abuela y cuando estuvo lista la sentó en el centro de la choza. Cuando el Señor Sol estaba por irse, doña Simona recibió la visita de la Señora Muerte, quien se llevó su ánima dejando en su cara una sonrisa plena de satisfacción.

Fue sepultada al siguiente día y pese al conflicto que existía entre "los de arriba" y "los de abajo,"[5] acudió a su entierro gente de ambos bandos; consideraron que en agradecimiento a la Señora que a tantos había curado, era bueno que ese día no fuera de pleito y menos hubiera muertos, por respeto a su memoria.

En el panteón, Delfina prácticamente fue ascendida, pues todas las personas que se acercaron a darle el "abrazo de consuelo," al retirarse le agregaron a su nombre el término de "Cha,"[6] que en nuestro idioma es símbolo de respeto, por lo que a partir de ahí fue "Cha Nana Delfina."[7]

Sin embargo, el conflicto del pueblo fue creciendo y los

deseos de venganza aumentaban. También Nana Delfina sentía la presión de su señor que reconocía que ya sabía algo, pero quería saber más y constantemente la observaba en lo que hacía.

Debido a la escasez de alimentos en el pueblo, muchos acudían con Nana Delfina por algo de comida. No sabían cómo, pero ella siempre tenía carne de conejo, ardilla, borrego, a veces de venado, pues aparecían siempre por la mañana cerca de su casa, con el cuello mordido.

Cierto día, su señor le dijo que ya no aguantaba más y tenía que compartirle lo que ella sabía; que muchas veces la había visto levantarse en las noches, salir de la casa envuelta en una túnica negra con el pelo suelto y dirigirse a un lugar de la falda del cerro; ahí empezaba a revolcarse en la tierra suelta y se levantaba una nube de polvo de la cual salía una enorme coyota que corría hacia lo oscuro de la noche, que después regresaba a depositar en la cerca de la casa los animales que muy temprano ella se ponía a limpiar para comer un poco de carne y regalar la mayor parte a la gente. Él le dijo que no se preocupara, que todo estaba bien, que sólo quería saber más, que por ser su señor ella tenía la obligación de enseñarle.

Nana Delfina le dijo que era necesario mucho tiempo para aprender eso y que no todas las personas poseían el "don." El que deseara aprenderlo debía tener mucha paciencia, concentrarse, poner la mente en blanco, no hacerlo por envidia, ni para causar males a nadie, sino por necesidad o por ayudar a los demás.

El señor siguió insistiendo hasta que un día Nana Delfina le dijo que le enseñaría, pero que no estaba segura de que él aprendiera bien porque no le veía el "don" en los ojos y temía que él utilizara ese conocimiento, y con los otros pocos que ya tenía, para causar males.

Bajo la promesa de que usaría lo aprendido para bien, Nana Delfina empezó a enseñarle, pero se dio cuenta de inmediato que el señor no ponía la atención debida, era inconstante y olvidaba las cosas. Pese a todo, llegó la noche en que juntos hicieron el primer viaje al monte. Desde la tarde preparó a su señor con las últimas recomendaciones, le repitió las palabras que tenía que pronunciar al principio y lo que debía hacer en seguida; luego, las palabras y acciones que debía recordar para recuperar su figura normal. Al caer la noche, cuando él dijo estar listo, salieron al paraje de tierra suelta.

Todo salió bien al principio y en la recolección de animales que les proporcionarían su carne y su piel. Pero en la madrugada algo resultó mal, pues el señor no podía recuperar su forma por más lucha que hacía, aún con los consejos de Nana Delfina. Cuando despertó el Señor Sol, ella le dijo que se escondiera dentro de la casa para que nadie lo viera y esperaran la noche para solucionar el problema.

Ese día fue más gente que de costumbre a visitar a Nana Delfina. A algunos los siguieron sus perros y al acercarse al lugar ladraban y corrían alrededor de la casa. En tono de risa, uno de ellos le dijo:

—¿Qué tienes escondido, Nana Delfina? ¿Por qué mi perro ladra y corre como si olfateara a un coyote?

—Ha de ser por la sangre de los animales—contestó ella con una sonrisa.

—¿Y tu señor?

—Hoy decidió ir al cerro por leña.

El día cedió paso a la noche y cuando llegó a su mitad se reanudaron esfuerzos para que el señor recobrara su forma. Pero no lo pudieron lograr ni una con sus consejos ni el otro con su empeño. Después de varias noches comprendieron que nada lograrían y ella le recomendó que se resignara a su suerte y regresara al cerro a vivir su vida.

Días después, cuando alguien preguntaba por su señor, ella simplemente explicaba que él se había cansado de estar allí y había vuelto a su pueblo. Pero a partir de entonces mucha gente vio un enorme coyote que por las tardes o al amanecer se acercaba a la casa de Nana Delfina a dejar un conejo, una ardilla o una gallina que se había perdido en el mismo pueblo malamente. Decía Nana Delfina, malamente . . .

El señor tiempo siguió su camino. Con él, las cosas empezaron a cambiar en el pueblo. El gobierno, "el ley grande," como ellos decían, después de nueve años decidió intervenir para que terminara el conflicto de la división. Puso orden deteniendo a los cabecillas de cada bando; en otra oportunidad narraré cómo sucedieron esos hechos verdaderamente especiales. Lo importante es que poco a poco la división del pueblo fue acabando y nuevamente empezó a entrar a la comunidad gente de fuera y los comerciantes llevaron los primeros automóviles. Llevaban muchas cosas nuevas. Entonces conocimos los primeros radios de pilas. Por cierto, recuerdo que don Nacho Ramos quería "matar" con la pistola a un radio porque el aparato no quería tocarle otra vez la canción que acababa de terminar. Nos costó mucho trabajo que entendiera que los músicos no cantaban dentro del radio, sino en una estación transmisora de Zacapu. Cuando se convenció, mi papá y yo lo llevamos a conocer la estación de radio.

A mediados de 1959 comenzaron en el pueblo a introducir la luz eléctrica. Después de colocar los postes tendieron los cables sobre ellos. Un día, muy temprano, los madrugadores que iban al cerro vieron algo fuera de lo común. Uno de ellos fue a avisarle al profesor que fungía como secretario de tenencia, el cual salió a atender el caso con su hijo, que era yo, de diez años de edad.

Lo que vimos era en realidad asombroso. Atorada entre los cables de los postes estaba Nana Delfina. Como única vestimenta colgaban de sus brazos pedazos de petate[8] viejo. Ella pidió que la bajaran. A mí me dijeron que me retirara y dos de los señores consiguieron unas escaleras para ayudarle a bajar. Alguien le prestó un gabán y envuelta en él se marchó a su casa sin decir nada. Fue la primera vez que la vi, pues pasó cerca de donde yo estaba. Ya sabía de su existencia porque con frecuencia oía hablar de ella, pero nunca la había visto de cerca. Era una señora de edad y por eso me llamó la atención su cabello: muy largo, negro y brilloso. Luego me acerqué a mi papá que platicaba con los señores y varias señoras que ya se habían acercado. Todos se preguntaban cómo se había subido o para qué se había subido.

Un señor dijo, con mucha seguridad:

—Es que Nana Delfina ya es muy grande, sabe más, va más lejos, llega a otros pueblos a ver gente que le pide favores. Ahora por las noches se convierte en tecolote[9] y vuela a todas partes. Por eso, cuando regresaba se le olvidó que acababan de tender los cables y se atoró.

Otro más joven, más moderno, más incrédulo, replicó:

—No, lo que pasa es que ya perdió mucha gente y no la visitan. Con la ayuda de alguien se subió para que pensáramos lo que tú dices. Pero no creo que sea cierto eso de que vuela.

Mi papá terminó la discusión:

—Bueno, se hace tarde. Vaya cada quien a sus quehaceres y luego veremos. ¡Vámonos!

Yo seguí a mi papá, piense y piense. Desde entonces no he podido encontrar algo razonable. ¿En verdad venía volando y se atoró? Difícil de creerlo. ¿Permitió que alguien le ayudara a subirse a los cables? Más difícil de creer; ella no tenía, como dijeramos hoy, necesidad de publicidad ni se animaría a subirse desnuda. Luego, a su edad, era difícil aguantar no sé cuántas horas en posición tan incómoda. En fin, la realidad sigue escapando a mis pocos conocimientos.

Notas

1. Durante mucho tiempo, de manera errónea, se llamó a la lengua purépecha "Tarasca." Se trata de una lengua cuyo origen y familia lingüística no se ha podido identificar. Como la lengua vasca, el Euskera, en Europa, el idioma purépecha es en nuestro continente una isla lingüística. A finales del siglo XX esta lengua contaba con 204,000 hablantes que residían principalmente en el estado de Michoacán.
2. Apócope del español antiguo *enaguas*, prenda exterior femenina que cuelga desde la cintura. Del taíno *naguas*, "falda de algodón."
3. Blusa tradicional hecha de algodón blanco y adornada de motivos florales bordados.
4. Pueblo purépecha donde se producen rebozos de gran calidad.
5. En referencia a los habitantes de las zonas altas y zonas bajas de la región.
6. Forma purépecha de dirigirse a los hombres y mujeres con el más alto nivel de respeto. Similar a "Vuestra Merced" en el castellano antiguo o al *thou* en el inglés arcaico.
7. "Nana": título para mujeres mayores que han sido madres; Cha Nana Delfina: "Usted, Madre Delfina."
8. Del náhuatl *petlatl*, tejido de palma o de carrizos que se emplea como estera para sentarse y dormir o como envoltura funeraria.
9. Del náhuatl *tecolotl* (de *col*, "doblar," "curva"): lechuza. La voz purépecha es *tukuru*, más cercana a la maya *tunkuruchu*.

Gabriel Pacheco

Huichol

Gabriel Pacheco. Photographed in Guadalajara, Jalisco.

Gabriel Pacheco Salvador was born on November 21, 1963, in Guadalupe Ocotán, La Yesca, Nayarit. He holds a bachelor's degree (*licenciatura*) in literature and a master's (*maestría*) degree in applied linguistics from the University of Guadalajara. He has worked as a bilingual promotor in Jalisco. He is presently a professor and researcher in the Department of Indigenous Languages Research, University of Guadalajara. Pacheco is a founding member of Indigenous Language Writers, Inc., and has served as its secretary for organization and relations. On two occasions he has been a grantee of the National Fund for Culture and the Arts. He has taught a variety of courses on linguistic development to young Huicholes aspiring to the teaching profession. Since 1994 he has been engaged in the project entitled Phonological, Grammatical, Lexical, and Literary Guide for the Development of Bilingual Huichol Teachers. Pacheco is a co-author of several texts, including *Reflexiones sobre la identidad étnica* (Reflections on Ethnic Identity) (Guadalajara: Universidad de Guadalajara, 1995); *Relatos huicholes* (Huichol Tales) (Mexico City: SEP/DGCP, 1995); *Políticas lingüísticas en México* (Linguistic Policy in Mexico) (Mexico City: UNAM/La Jornada, 1997); and *Función gramática didáctica del huichol* (The Didactic Grammatical Function of Huichol) (Guadalajara: Universidad de Guadalajara, 1999). He is the author of *Tatei Yurienaka y otros cuentos huicholes* (Tatei Yurienaka and Other Huichol Stories) (Mexico City: Editorial Diana, 1994). He received the national Nezahualcóyotl Prize for Indigenous-Language Literatures in 1998.

Gabriel Pacheco Salvador nació el 21 de noviembre de 1963 en Guadalupe Ocotán, La Yesca, Nayarit. Es licenciado en letras y maestro en lingüística aplicada por la Universidad de Guadalajara. Ha laborado como promotor bilingüe en Jalisco y actualmente es profesor e investigador del Departamento de Investigación de Lenguas Indígenas de la Universidad de Guadalajara. Es miembro fundador de Escritores en Lenguas Indígenas, A.C., y ha fungido como su secretario de organización y relaciones. Ha sido becario del Fondo Nacional para la Cultura y las Artes en dos ocasiones. Impartió diversos cursos sobre desarrollo lingüístico a jóvenes huicholes aspirantes a la docencia. Desde 1994 realiza el proyecto Guía Fonológica, Gramatical, Lexical y Literaria para Formación de Maestros Bilingües Huicholes. Es coautor de varios textos, entre ellos: *Reflexiones sobre la identidad étnica* (Guadalajara: Universidad de Guadalajara, 1995); *Relatos huicholes* (México, D.F.: SEP/DGCP, 1995); *Políticas lingüísticas en México* (México, D.F.: UNAM/La Jornada, 1997) y *Función gramática didáctica del Huichol* (Guadalajara: Universidad de Guadalajara, 1999). Es autor del libro *Tatei Yurienaka y otros cuentos huicholes* (México, D.F.: Editorial Diana, 1994). Recibió el Premio Nezahualcóyotl de Literatura en Lenguas Indígenas en 1998.

Tatei Yurienaka

Gabriel Pacheco

Huichol[1]

[From *Tatei Yurienaka y otros cuentos huicholes*, pp. 147–152. Colección Letras Indígenas Contemporáneas. Mexico City: Editorial Diana/CNCA/DGCP, 1994.]

Yurienaka[2] rɨ xɨka katiuyeikanike keteyɨakake netiku’eriwatɨ tuaxatɨa nemutika ne’uxipietɨ. Yɨwikɨta mukawiyexɨ, ‘aimieme hikɨ kuxi mɨya mɨtiuhawi. Neteukari tsiere kauka tɨkarikɨ witari niu’eni kwitɨ ximeri mewayetɨa heumamawetɨ, nai takwa yukiwarie makukexiyaxɨ. Kwitɨ meri nehanukukeka nai nemuhaɨtsiwatɨya ‘aimieme hikɨ ne’uxipietɨ mɨya tuaxatɨa nemɨreukuka; kename haɨtsi mɨ’uaye kename kwie mɨ’uaye neteukari neti‘ɨxatsitɨwakaku nekaniutiyɨneni neumamawetɨ, hikɨ neweruxi kwi netatunatɨkaitɨ nekatineukukani. Nai neteukari mɨnetixaxatɨwa, kename yakɨ tekau’uwa, kename texeiyarietɨ tete’ane mɨnetihɨawe . . . ‘Ikɨ hetsiena temu’uwa waniu mɨtatei, Tatei Yurienaka memimamate Tatuutsima.[3] Haɨtsi tɨtɨ ta waniu Wiyekate memɨ’ane, nɨ’arixi memeuyɨa. Neteukari herie mɨnetsihanenetɨwa mɨya tixatsikayarikɨ. Kepai kwie Tɨkarixa paɨ mu‘ɨa kanixatsiwani, puwari ‘ukari paɨ mɨ’ane kanixatsiwani meta Takutsi Nakawe[4] mɨhayatɨni paɨ tsiere kani’uayeni; ‘akuxi ta titamama, titatuutsi, ‘imatɨrieka titatei Yurienaka. Haɨtsi tsiere tsimɨ’ane mɨtukaɨye, mɨxawatɨ Tawexikɨa hɨrɨpa. ‘Ikɨ waniu ‘ɨkatetsie kwinie mɨti’uaye manuyetsetse’inikɨ, ‘aimieme ‘emuwietsie pai ne kwinie nemɨtitemawie, newarie xeikɨa haɨtsi tsimɨkakanetɨyeikani nemɨtimaika; mɨya muwietsie ‘aixɨa nemɨtimate kwitɨ ne’anatutsaxɨanikɨ. Turatemai mɨnetikuhɨawe rawaritsie waniu waɨka mɨka’uaye haɨtsi. ‘Ari tsɨari ‘ukiratsi tɨtɨ mutainekai, mɨya tɨtɨ kuxi ‘iitsɨ mɨkaku’eriwakai. Mɨkɨ hikɨ nai mɨnetixaxatɨwa, xɨka ri ‘uyɨwini yapauka tai ‘aurie mɨnetsiutiyeka tsepa ne’ayexɨkeme mɨnetsiutiyuruwa. Mɨkɨ ya mɨkatiu’eriwa ‘etsiwa teiwari[5] paɨ nemuyɨneni. Tsɨ kuta neteukari ka’utaineka xeikɨa neti’erieme ‘iyaritana yanemɨtikayani. Mɨya tɨtɨ rikɨ ‘etsiwa nemɨti’eni, hikɨ niukieya nekaniyeweiyani kuxi. Keteyɨatɨ teɨteri temuhekɨarixɨ, kemeyɨatɨ tatuutsima takakaɨma memuku’uixɨa, mɨkɨ nai mɨnetiutaxatɨa. Hikɨ kuxi niukieya nemɨku’eniwa, ‘ena nekanetikekani netei Yurienaka nehayexeiyatɨ. Mɨkɨ mɨnetimikwa ya netikuxaxatɨwatɨ mɨnetsiukateika me kani’aneni, ‘aimieme hetsiena nekawietɨ ‘ena nekaniuyeikani, tsɨ yeme mɨkɨtsie nekaneuwaɨreni mɨkɨtsie nekaniuyeikani. Tatei Yurienaka tɨtɨ tsiere mɨtakutsi, Takutsi Nakawe temimamate tanaitɨmatɨ. Meyuniitɨ memɨtatsi‘ɨwiya memɨtatsikuwima. Mɨpaɨ ‘aimieme waniu memuhekɨarixɨ. ‘Aimieme ne hikɨ tsinemɨkatiwatemawie: nemɨkaukakai kwi newa’utɨamɨtɨ neketatekɨ, tsepa kemupauku wahetsie ‘aixɨa nemɨtiukukutsu. Hau’erietɨ ‘iteɨrite mɨreuxuawe ya tewatsiekate memɨteu’uwa mɨkɨ Tatei Yurienaka waniu mɨtipinieya. Kepauka ke ta maye’ani ha kakaɨyarita pai nehanimieme nemuyeikani: Tatei Yurienaka haya, Takutsi Nakawe haya ya tatuutsima waha nemɨyurieneni. Heiwa muwa pai nemɨkauyeneni, hawai hura xeikɨa nemetihanɨni muwa pai tinakemekɨ mayani. Hatsuaku wana tɨma nemɨkawareukaxɨrie ya nemɨtiwarayexeiya ya nemɨtiwaharitɨa. Hipatɨ meniutiyuanenikeṭɨ takie waniu ‘axa tiniu’aneni: niukukuni, niu’aiyaka, niuyemuriyaka meniutiyuaneni. Ne kakaitsie nemɨkauwe yanekatineumamaweni. Hipatɨ teiwarixi takie memuta’axe ‘axa metatenikumamateni mɨya temɨ’anenekɨ. Mɨya neti’enakarekaku neteukari nemɨtitixatɨani. Mɨkɨ mɨyɨni waɨka tɨma mɨkanetsi’enieni. Yɨkɨ pɨta mɨnetitixatɨani mɨya ranuyɨneme kati’eniemɨtɨ. Mɨkɨ mɨ’ane ‘etsiwa tɨma mɨkanetsikweriwayurie kwinie waniu mɨnereuyehɨwa mutaine. Kepauka maye’akani, ‘ana tsɨ ‘aku Tatewari[6] ‘aurie netsiutiyetɨ nai nereuyexatɨaneni mutiyɨne, wamɨrahane kemɨtiutaine ya kemɨti’ane mɨkɨ mɨnereuyexatɨaneni. Waɨka waniu nemɨtiuyemaikakɨ mɨnetsiutiyuruwa, tietɨ tɨtɨ waniu teiwari paɨ netinekuhɨawetɨ nemɨnatɨa ‘utaitɨ mɨkanetsihayewani. Heiwa waniu, kuxi nemɨnunutsitɨkaitsie, nemamatɨkai mɨnetsiutatɨmai tɨma, ‘ayɨweka waniu mɨkɨ neheima meukatɨa nemutawikwei. Ne ‘etsiwa tɨma nemɨkahane’eriwa kepauka mɨya nemɨranuyemie. Xɨka kuta mɨkɨ yuri kanetixaxatɨwanike yuri nemɨkati’eririekake. Hatsuaku tɨma mɨkanetsihate’ani, xɨka netsitiemɨkɨni heitserie pɨta xeikɨa mɨnetitaxatɨani mɨtiuka'iyari. Mɨya ri neteukari nemɨtiuweiyakaikɨ teiwarixi waɨka memɨkanetsixɨamayakai. Tsɨ mɨkɨ xapatuxi kemɨtitsutsuikatsie meheu'utɨ mekaniyɨakakuni, meta wapai karetatsie pai xeikɨa mekahipitetɨ. Me'utikwiemarekɨ waniu mɨya pai memɨteyukuwawakai. Mɨya tari mɨkɨ memɨnetexeiyakɨ ne waɨka nekatiwatemawie. Kepai kuta rikɨ yutei tɨme tɨtɨ pɨkahauyehɨwa, titayari yu'ɨkate kwinie tiku'eimani; karikɨ matsi mɨkɨkɨ kwiepa tekaniwikweka, mɨya tiniketɨ rikɨ ta'ɨkate Tatei 'iwemeya kanakɨkani. Tanaime ketemeupaɨme ya ketemɨteutei katanikuwimani, mɨpaɨ xeikɨa metsɨ tekateniwikweka 'ayɨweka. Nai ne'ɨkama nekanikexiyani, tixaɨ mawiwe, kawaya, xapatuxi nereuyehɨaka, hau'erietɨ 'ɨtsita, yemuritsie, teikɨmana, kɨatsata nekanikexiyani. Teiwarixi memɨnetsitawe'erie kawayatsie waniu xɨka hakani xeiya muyeiweni, xapatuxitsie waniu ya xɨka tiweni tsepa hakewa meuyene mɨyɨweni, tsɨ waniu teté, xuya mɨkarakutseweni. Xɨka ta waniu 'eekatsie 'uyewieka mɨ'aixɨa, 'aimieme waniu ki 'e'utɨtɨme memɨwewiwa, mɨkɨ 'aku waniu tsepa yekɨritana pai 'atikaitɨ 'eeka hɨkɨame mɨrakwa'a me mekaniutiyuaneni; 'aimieme waniu mawiwetsie xeikɨa mekaniyaxetɨweni, me'utikwiemarekɨ . . . Heiwa rikɨ xewitɨ teiwari kwi mɨnetsikuxeiyatɨya. Merikɨ tɨ kwi netsiheu'ɨkimɨkɨ. Kepauka nehakɨ'etɨ nekie nemeuyekekaneni 'ana tsɨ 'aku yu'ɨkeme netixeistɨaka. Netsinenimayatɨ waniu mɨnetsiutiyuruwakai mɨpaɨ ke 'arike mɨnetiuxatɨa. Tsepa nekemari mɨtitsani, nekɨpate tsepa mɨtitsitsini ya tsepa mɨtitɨtɨ mɨpai ne'aneme mɨnetsiye'ɨkirɨmeni. Tsipu me tewa mɨniu'ɨa mɨpaɨ yeme mɨkɨ muku'ɨarekai newarita mɨnetsihaxeiyatɨyeikanitsie. Ne tsiere ta hapaɨna netikaxeiyatɨyeikani. Heiwa kwi yeme ne'itemawieneme kapɨta'eriekai, neteukari kie pai neuyekekaneni kemɨrenaneka. Mɨkuyɨre 'ana tsɨ 'aku Tatewari 'aurie tiutikani kɨye 'epametsie hakaitɨ, tame ri kwiepa tetekumaka: nekutsi, neteukari, nee ri. Kepauka ri mɨti'uxe mekakumɨkatɨyani yukaretatsie pai mɨyemie, tatsɨ ri tatsiti'ɨkeme mɨyɨaneni. Neteukari nekutsi matɨ nawitsie kuxi memuhixime kutsinata. Tame ta Tsinari matɨ karetatɨa pai teteyehipitetɨ tematahɨtɨwa. Tsinari yeme nehepaɨ tsiere mɨtiyukuhɨawe Tatei Yurienaka 'iyarieya muyemate; kepauka xatsika maye'ani kwiepa heumu'utɨ yuhuka mɨxɨriyani. Tsinari 'aixɨa mɨtiuka'iyari xɨka ka'ihaxɨatɨaka, xɨka ta 'iyehaxɨatɨani mɨranayeketɨyani; 'aimieme teiwarixi mɨkawatexie hau'erietɨ memeihɨawetɨwenitsie . . . Neteukari tewamama memɨku'u tsiere tahepaɨ memɨtewikwe, tahepaɨ memɨ'ane, tahepai memɨtehaare. 'Akuxi memɨkamɨire memɨyu'auxuwi ke: Mɨtɨxi, Tsimanixi, Yeuka, Haɨtsi, 'imatɨreme Nauxi mɨtitewa. Neteukari maine 'ikɨ waniu Takutsi Nakawe memɨtewamama, mɨkɨ waniu Tatei Yurienaka mɨrakawima yuhetsie mɨwahɨ memɨwakaitsiximama. Netsɨkɨ tsiere mɨtiuyemate hau'erietɨ mɨkatikewekare, tsepa wakaitsixi tahamatɨ karetatɨa memɨteyehe mɨkawatakeni mɨwahayewani xeikɨa. Ke tipaɨmetɨ kwiepa mɨtihekɨa waniu mɨkatinanaimariwa mɨpaɨ neteukari maine. 'Aimieme 'iku, muume, hatsí hawaikɨ mɨkahexɨrietɨyeikani tɨma mi'ɨwiyani xeikɨa, tinakemekɨ ke mika'eni. Waɨka kuxi waniu mɨnereuyeɨwa 'utaitɨ mɨkanetsihayewa. Mexi waniu 'uyeika mɨya mɨnetsiutiyuruwani, ne ta xeimieme yanemɨtikamieni. Mɨkɨ waniu nunutsiyari mɨpaɨ mewati'itɨarietɨya, papayatɨkai Pariyatsie[7] mɨixa mewakanuitɨa yu'ɨkama; 'arike tari nekutsi matɨ xeikɨa meheta'axetɨ memakɨ, hikɨ tsɨari waniu kemete'ukɨne mekani'ukiratsixietɨkani, ne xeikɨa ri hikɨ nekaniyeikaneni hipame mara'akate[8] wahamatɨa. Tsɨ ne'ɨkate kwinie kwinie mɨtitemawietsie nekaniyɨaneni, kepauka yeiya tuukarieya maye'akani kaniyu'uitɨakuni Tatei Yurienaka 'eniekutɨ. Mɨkɨ Tatei, Takutsi memɨwa'enie meniyɨaka, wa'iyari kemɨtikuyuane mɨpaɨ xeikɨa tiniku'uwekuni, mɨpaɨ wahuye reuhanekaku. Tatei Yurienaka ta'ɨkate mɨpaɨ katinewiyani, 'aixɨa 'anekɨa 'iyenenetɨwatɨ. Xɨka 'iyaritana tekateku'uweni xaitsie pɨta mɨtatsiuyenetɨani, kwi temɨtekwine. Tamɨ Tatei huyeya temuweiyani tsepa ke'anekɨa mɨtatsiuyenetɨa. Tsɨ mɨkɨ nai ta'ɨkate kani'ɨwiyani, 'aimieme 'etekaneuneneka temɨteukanenewiekakɨ, tsiere ta'ɨkatetsie tekananatsinikeni waɨka temanayɨyɨranikɨ, ya tsiere 'etekaneuyeyeuka waɨka takeetate mukuhekɨkɨarenikɨ huyeta. Tatei Yurienaka yamɨkatiu'eriwa waɨka ta'ɨkate temɨti'eimani, 'aimieme kwitaxi tsihatayeyeumekɨ takakai tekanawɨwɨtɨwani mɨtikwiemarikenikɨ . . . Kepauka 'ixɨarari maye'ani kwiepa pɨta xeikɨa teetɨ temumaka, ya ri matsi Tatei mɨtatsitinenimayata kwiepa mɨtatsikutuani. 'Aixɨa mɨtatixeiya, tahɨkɨame tɨma mɨkatatsihayewa. Mɨkɨ tayɨyu: xeime ya yumɨireme mɨwaka'uxipitɨani yuhetsie mɨwahɨni wakɨpuripieme . . . Nekutsi Hamaima nunutsiyari waniu yu'ɨkatetsie meuhaixɨa tikwewiyarietɨ. Weiya maye'atsie ke waniu mɨtiutimawaxɨ, 'ana tineinetɨ mukatariyarie. Kwitɨ waniu meuhaipiexɨa Tatei Yurienaka tiutimawirieku . . . Teiwarixi hau'erietɨ memeu'uwa heitserie yeiya memɨkakumaitɨwe, xeikɨa memeuye'utɨweni memɨteu'iyari. Mɨya meuyɨatɨ heiwa kakaɨyarita pai memuyeneikani, mexɨka tɨni memɨtatsitiyuriya. Tewa 'axa 'anekɨa waniu Tatuutsima, Tateteima temɨwaruku'uitɨatɨka, kari waniu takie hurawa tepɨkawareukitɨaku, ya tɨ waniu teerɨta temɨtewareu'awieta mɨpaɨ waniu mɨkati'anekaku memutiyuane teiwarixi. Mɨkɨ waniu wawewiekame ki tsi'anemeta mayewe, wapai waniu mɨkɨ mɨwarakaxeiya, hatsuaku waniu kwieta ya teerɨta memɨkaheihɨatɨkɨka, mɨpaɨ waniu mɨkati'ane. Ya waniu hipatɨ yukiekari heima menuatɨ memeutakwixɨa mɨkɨ teerɨta, hayukarita ya yemuritsie waniu memɨkawaruyetuatɨkɨka, wapai waniu xeikɨa memɨwakuyayatsa me'utikwiemarekɨ, mɨpaɨ memutiyuane teiwarixi. Ne ta neteukari nemu'eni yɨkɨ pɨta nemɨtikamaitɨyeika: ‘ikɨ Tatei mɨ'ane, Takutsi ‘ayeikame meuyɨane, nai yuhetsie mɨtiwima, tanaime mɨtatsiwima. Hɨkɨa meukahane Tatuutsima,[9] Takakaɨma[10] memuketɨkɨ; Tatei Yurienaka mɨwarupitɨa naitsarie memeuku'uixɨa: yemuritsie, haixata, teerɨta, ‘aitsie, harakunapa, ‘akitsie, yetata, haramaratsie, maxatsi wahetsie, wikixi wahetsie, hikuritsie, ‘ikutsie, tukipa[11] ya tahetsie. Naitsarie mɨwarupitɨa, naitsarie memuhekɨarixɨ; hikɨ temanukɨka, wakietata temɨwaranuhɨawetɨkɨka. Mɨkɨ tixaɨ ki meteku'iwawatɨ mete'aneka tinakemekɨ tatɨ mɨya mekateniukuxɨriyaxɨani . . . Tɨma tsɨxi neheuwakitɨ ne'utaineka, ‘akuxi mɨya nereukwaranitɨ tuaxatɨa ne'utikaitɨ nekaniutaineni. Ne‘ɨkatetsie yaxeikɨa nekatineumumunani, tsɨ mɨkɨkɨ ‘ɨxa mɨhaɨtsimatɨka nekaniuwatɨyani, . . . " ‘Uxamɨire[12] hakewa Tsinari, ‘ena mepɨte'uti'axe" mɨrehiwaxɨ neteukari Turatemai, xeimieme temekɨ Tsinari tanaitɨ.

Notes

1. "Huichol" is possibly derived, through corruption or Spanish adaptation, from "Wixárika," the Huichol people's self-referential term. Some authors believe that this archaic word comes from the now-extinct Guachichil language. According to Karl Lumholtz, *wixárika* meant "doctors" or "healers." At the end of the twentieth century there were more than 55,000 speakers of Huichol in the states of Nayarit, Durango, Zacatecas, and Jalisco. The author uses the Sole Huichol Language Alphabet, established in 1990 by the Department of Indigenous Language Studies at the University of Guadalajara.
2. Yurienaka or Tatei Yurienaka, "Our Mother Earth."
3. Literally, "our great-grandparents"; that is, the eldest members of the family of pilgrims that founded the world.
4. Takutsi, "Our Grandmother," meaning "Our Germinated Seed" (i.e., the life produced upon all the earth). This positive deity can become transformed into a dark entity known as Nakawe. In the story, the author refers only to Takutsi's virtues.
5. Literally, "neighbor," used in reference to non-Huichol people and therefore applied here to mestizos and foreigners.
6. Literally, "Our Grandfather," in reference to fire.
7. Abbreviated form of the expression *páriyatsié yeyá,* "pilgrimage feast or celebration," in reference to the pilgrimage made from the mountains of the states of Jalisco and Nayarit, where the Huichol people reside, to the desert surrounding Real del Catorce in the state of San Luis Potosí, where they harvest peyote.
8. Plural of *mara'akame,* a healer and priest; literally, "he who sings" or "the singer."
9. See note 3.
10. Literally, "the Lords of Midnight," in reference to the sacred entities of darkness and the underworld.
11. Ceremonial centers that are believed to have preserved, since remote times, the world's design and the steps of creation; the *tukipa* remain active with groups of *mara'akate* who must remain within them for a period of five years. In Spanish, the Huichol people refer to the *tukipa* as *calihuey,* from the Nahuatl *calli,* "house," and *huey,* "great"; that is, "great house" or "temple."
12. The narrator's proper name, meaning "he who has many writings or drawings on his face." During ritual pilgrimages, Huichol pilgrims paint their faces with sacred solar and peyote motifs; this name reflects the narrator's desire to communicate with the gods as a ritual officiant through many face-drawings.

Notas

1. La palabra *huichol* posiblemente se deriva, por corrupción o adaptación castellana, de *wixárika,* término con que los huicholes se autodenominan. Algunos autores creen que esta voz arcaica proviene de la lengua Guachichil, ya desaparecida. Según Karl Lumholtz, *wixárica* significaba "doctores" o "curanderos." A finales del siglo XX contaba esta lengua con más de 55,000 hablantes en los estados de Nayarit, Durango, Zacatecas y Jalisco. El autor emplea el Alfabeto Único de Lengua Huichola que desde 1990 impulsó el Departamento de Estudios en Lenguas Indígenas de la Universidad de Guadalajara.
2. Yurienaka o Tatei Yurienaka, "Nuestra Madre Tierra."
3. Literalmente, "bisabuelos nuestros"; es decir, los integrantes más viejos de la familia de peregrinos que fundaron el mundo.
4. Takutsi, "Nuestra Abuela," con el sentido de "Nuestra Semilla Germinada" (es decir, la vida que se produce en toda la tierra). Esta deidad positiva puede convertirse en oscura y llamarse Nakawe. En el relato, el autor se refiere solamente a las virtudes de Takutsi.
5. Literalmente "vecino," en referencia al que no es huichol; por eso se aplica ese nombre a los mestizos y extranjeros.
6. Literalmente, "Nuestro Abuelo," en referencia al fuego.
7. Forma abreviada de la expresión *páriyatsié yeyá,* "fiesta o celebración de la peregrinación"; se refiere al peregrinaje desde las montañas de Jalisco y Nayarit, donde viven las comunidades huicholas, hasta la sierra de Real del Catorce en San Luis Potosí, que constituye el territorio donde recolectan el peyote.
8. Plural de *mara'akame,* curandero y sacerdote; literalmente, "el que canta" o "el cantor."
9. Véase nota 3.
10. Literalmente, "los Señores de la Medianoche," en referencia a las entidades sagradas de la oscuridad y del inframundo.
11. Centros ceremoniales que, se supone, conservan desde una remota antigüedad el diseño del mundo y los pasos de su creación; se mantienen activos con grupos de *mara'akate* que deben permanecer en ellos por período de cinco años. En español llaman al *tukipa* con la palabra *calihuey,* del náhuatl *calli,* "casa," y *huey,* "grande"; esto es, "casa grande," o sea, "templo."
12. Nombre propio del narrador, que significa "el que tiene muchas escrituras o dibujos en su rostro." Durante peregrinaciones rituales, los peregrinos huicholes se pintan la cara con motivos solares y de peyote; este nombre refleja el deseo del narrador de comunicarse con los dioses a través de muchas pinturas faciales como oficiante ritual.

Our Mother Yurienaka[1]

Gabriel Pacheco

Huichol[2]

[From *Tatei Yurienaka y otros cuentos huicholes*, pp. 147–159. Colección Letras Indígenas Contemporáneas. Mexico City: Editorial Diana/CNCA/DGCP, 1994.]

If it were not for Yurienaka, what would become of us? What would become of this oak tree, from whose branches droplets of water continue to fall? It rained hard last night. The earth is very wet. My grandfather went out early to walk around his house without his *huaraches.*[3] He is making his way through all the green, grassy areas around his house. I also got up early to walk among the tall grasses. I am now taking a short rest under this old oak tree. My grandfather tells me that the dew, as well as the earth, is medicinal; that is why I take these walks daily without *huaraches* and with my breeches rolled above the knee. My grandfather tells me everything: how we should behave as humans, why we appear upon the earth, and why the gods watch over us every day . . . The earth upon which we live is Our Mother. That is why Our Great-Grandparents call her Tatei Yurienaka. The dew represents the different gods who make it rain, those who are the messengers of the principal gods. My grandfather never ceases to explain these things to me.

The earth has a pleasant smell like the *tikarixa*[4] flower. It also has the color of the female *cempasúchil*[5] flower and is medicinal like the sacred water of Takutsi Nakawe.[6] The dew is also lovely; bright and fresh like clear spring water, transparent and sparkling when, in the morning, Tawexikia[7] looks upon it from the other side of the horizon. My grandfather tells me that dew is a good remedy for strengthening the feet and legs. Therefore, I always try to walk through the tall grasses that cover me completely to receive from them an infinite number of dewdrops that roll down my back. It is good that the dew falls on my back. That way, it will remain strong and firm and will never become hunched over. I always go out with that intention as long as the rainy season lasts. Turametai[8] says that dew on one's back is not as medicinal as dew on the feet and legs. Turatemai is very old but still has no need of a cane. He talks to me about everything. When night falls quickly, he sits me down next to him at the fire. He never agrees with my dressing like a *teiwari.*[9] He constantly recommends that I do certain things, and I nearly always do as he says. I have been following his advice and continue to do so. Why humans appeared and how it was that Our Grandparents and all of Our Ancestors came to inhabit sacred places; my grandfather tells me all of this. I listen to and follow all of his advice and, as a result, I have become more fond of Tatei Yurienaka. She gives me life. She talks to me and embraces me when night falls. That is why I always depend upon her: I recover my strength through her and always walk upon her. Tatei Yurienaka is also Our Grandmother; therefore, we also know her as Takutsi Nakawe. Together, they protect and care for us in their bosom. For that purpose, they were born and live with us and for us. That is why I love them very much and treat them with great tenderness: without *huaraches,* I walk with them, and with them I sleep peacefully. Everything that exists upon the earth depends upon them. Therefore, when the time comes to go to the sacred sites, I am extremely delighted to go and bring them their sacred water: the blessed water of Tatei Yurienaka and that of Takutsi Nakawe.

Many times, I do not make it to the sacred site and must return from wherever I can get water; that is, from wherever the gods allow me to take it, but the water is taken only with the use of the proper prayer. At no time in my life do I forget them. I always think about them, always giving them their blessed water to drink. Many people say that it is quite ugly around here, that it is full of ravines, cliffs, and hills; that the only thing lacking is plateaus. Nevertheless, I do not wear *huaraches.* I always walk barefoot. People who come to our houses from afar make fun of the way we dress. I have heard so much of that, I once mentioned it to my grandfather. He did not pay any attention to that, however. He began to speak of other things so as not to hear me. My grandfather has always loved me very much. He has never allowed anyone to do me harm. As soon as nighttime arrives, he quickly sits me down next to Tatewari.[10] He tells me everything: how I should behave with others and how to find out what is happening in other places. He always says that he does this so that I may learn and know more about my people's customs. He says that even though I may dress like a *teiwari,* that is still not so dangerous. But, my grandfather tells me, it is when I begin to think like one that I will be ruined. This is what he tells me at night. He tells me that when I was still a child, my mother almost lost me from this world and that if it were not for my grandfather I would be no longer be alive. I do not remember any of that. Nevertheless, since my grandfather always tells me the truth, I believe him fully. As far as I can remember, he has never scolded me; he always tries to speak to me straight and with reason. Since I follow in my grandfather's footsteps, the *teiwaris* do not think well of me. They always walk around wearing thick shoes. They try always to sleep up high, upon carts or on something comfortable so that they will not get dirty. Even where there are no such amenities, they always seek comfort upon carts or on something that resembles a bed. And, since they do not look kindly upon me, neither do I look kindly upon them. How can one deny one's mother? Why, then, do they cover up their feet as they do? Do they not know that it is through our feet that we are attached to Our Mother Earth?

It is through our feet that we take in Tatei Yurienaka's vital breath. Her cloak continually covers all who exist upon her. When I take long walks, I need neither a horse nor shoes for walking; I walk barefoot through thickets, hills, up and down. The *teiwaris* always look at me strangely; they say, "On horseback, one moves quickly and with shoes on one can make it anywhere, since with shoes rocks and thorns are of little consequence." The *teiwaris* say that the higher up one is, the more one enjoys life. They make very tall houses so that from high up they can breathe pure air, and they always take airplanes, so that the earth will not get them dirty . . . Once a *teiwari* would not take his eyes off me. He kept taking pictures of me. When he saw me arrive home with firewood on my back, he quickly took a look at me through his dark camera. I think he felt sorry for me and thought I looked quite comical. He said he wanted to photograph my shirt and pants where they were torn, that is why he took so long taking photos of me. Goats smell from afar, and this man did not smell much better. When he walked around me, I was surrounded by a cloud of odor from which I could only escape by distancing myself from him. When he stared at me, I also looked him up and down. I think that it is because of how I looked at him that he believed that I was already his friend. Because he then came home with me, sporting a wide grin. For a few days, he would accompany us, sitting on a tree trunk as my grandfather, grandmother, and I sat on the ground around Tatewari. When he got drowsy, he would go back where he came from to sleep, but he would first photograph us. My grandfather and grandmother sleep in the kitchen on a piece of cowhide. Tsinari[11] and I stay underneath the cart. Tsinari thinks just as I do; he also knows Tatei Yurienaka's advice very well. That is why, whenever he gets sleepy, he puts his head upon the ground, besides always warming his belly upon Our Mother Earth. Tsinari is well behaved and respectful when no one harms him; but if someone tries to harm him, he is quick to defend himself with his sharp teeth; that is why the *teiwaris* have the luck they do when they provoke him . . .

My grandfather's friends also eat, think, and live as we do. Just like us, they need to drink a lot of water. There are not many of them, only five: Mitixi, Tsimanixi, Yeuka, Haisi, and finally Nauxí.[12] My grandfather tells me that these animals belong to Nakutsi Nakawe. She entrusted them to Tatei Yurienaka, who takes great care of them, because they are her cows. My dog is very intelligent, like me; that is why he never thinks of biting these cows. He does not bite them, so that they will sleep under the cart with us. On the contrary, he watches over them. Nothing that exists upon the earth should experience harm. That is what my grandfather tells me. Therefore, when it comes to grains like corn, beans, or squash seeds, my grandfather does not waste them. To the contrary, he guards them as he would a great treasure and only deposits them in the earth when the gods have allowed him to do so through prayers. He tells me I still have many things to learn; that is why he never stops telling me important things. He says that as long as he lives, he will not stop telling me things, that he will always teach me new things. Meanwhile, I quickly obey his orders. He tells me that he teaches me the same things that were taught to him. His deceased father took him on foot from an early age to get to know Pariyatsie.[13] Later he and my grandmother would go alone to Pariyatsie. They think that they can no longer make it there; so now, in the company of some *marakames,*[14] I must do it for them and for myself. After all, my feet are very happy treading on the earth, so they come and go, to and fro. When one's feet learn that the day has arrived to leave for Pariyatsie, they quickly get happy because they want to feel and caress Tatei Yurienaka's body. Our feet hear Tatei and Takutsi's heart and breathing; that is why they choose to walk upon the earth; they know that is their pathway. Therefore, Tatei Yurienaka is the owner of walking feet and does not let loose of them in any case; she always guides them along a good pathway. But if one does not step as Tatei would like, she takes it upon herself to provoke bad or false steps so that we suffer some mishap.

The best thing is always to follow her good steps, no matter where they lead us. As my grandfather says, she is the mistress of walking feet and nonwalking feet. Therefore, she gave us the gift of very fat feet in order to resist long walks, cracked feet so that Tatei Yurienaka's breath may penetrate there and give us more life and health, and she extended our feet so that our steps may leave good marks as we take our long walks. Tatei Yurienaka never likes us to walk with our feet too covered. Thus, we only wear a few strips of leather so not to cover our entire foot; that is what she wants because she always wants to feel the warmth of our feet . . . When fiesta day arrives, we all sit upon Our Mother Earth; and when she begins to feel affection for us, she puts us to bed in her cloak. She always looks fondly upon us; that is why she lays us all down equally in her cloak. She never leaves us alone; she always remains with us. She decides when to take one or more persons to her world; there she receives them in their whole body and soul. My grandfather tells me that when my grandmother was small her feet swelled up because she owed a promise. And, at the Holy Week fiesta, she had to make offerings and sacrifices and begin dancing at dawn. That is how Tatei Yurienaka reduced the swelling of her feet, because it was to her she owed the promise . . . Many mestizos move about just to move about, without knowing where they will end up. With such boldness, they once arrived at a sacred site and made fun of the place and of what they found there. They asked why we had Our Great-Grandparents and Our Mothers so far from our homes, and why we did not make them a house closer to ours, rather than keeping them in such far away places and hidden away in caves. The *teiwaris* say that the gods should not be treated in such a way. They keep their God in a very pretty house, and he is always watching them from above. They cannot conceive of a God that is on the ground, much less in a cave; that is why they would never wish their God to be on the ground. They also say that heroes should not be at ground level, but rather placed on high so that they do not get dirty; never in springs or in the hills.

I, who know some of the things my grandfather tells me, think very differently from the way they talk. To start with, the Earth is Our Mother and Our Grandmother—everything that exists upon her belongs completely to them; therefore, we also depend upon them. Many years ago Tatutsima[15] and Takakaima[16] took their places in the hills, springs, caves, cliffs, streams, plateaus, seas, deer, birds, peyote, corn, *tukipa*,[17] and in ourselves. That is why our gods appear in the different places we are always going to visit without thinking about distance. They never asked us to make them a house. From the beginning, their house was made for them thus . . . I have not yet dried off and I am still sitting with my breeches wet beneath this oak here. My feet still look soaked; it is because the dew bathed me from head to toe when I walked through the tall grasses. I certainly opened up many little paths among the grasses, but the day after tomorrow they will have disappeared again . . . "Uxamiire,[18] where is Tsinari? People are arriving," I heard my grandfather Turatemai call to me. At once, Tsinari and I come to his aid.

Notes

1. Yurienaka or Tatei Yurienaka, "Our Mother Earth."

2. "Huichol" is possibly derived, through corruption or Spanish adaptation, from "Wixárika," the Huichol people's self-referential term. Some authors believe that this archaic word comes from the now-extinct Guachichil language. According to Karl Lumholtz, *wixárika* meant "doctors" or "healers." At the end of the twentieth century there were more than 55,000 speakers of Huichol in the states of Nayarit, Durango, Zacatecas, and Jalisco.

3. From the Purepecha *kwarachi*, a rustic leather sandal.

4. One of the ornamental herbaceous species cultivated in various parts of Mexico, generically known in Spanish as *manto*, "cloak" or "blanket." Its flowers are of many colors, particularly purple, pink, red, blue, and white. It is common in hot and temperate climates; in this story, the reference is to *Ipomoea purpurea*.

5. Marigold flower; *Tagetes erecta*, a herbaceous plant with uneven leaves, penetrating aroma, and yellow flowers. From the Nahuatl *cempoalxóchitl*, "twenty flowers, many flowers"; also written *sempasúchil*.

6. Takutsi, "Our Grandmother," meaning "Our Germinated Seed" (i.e., the life produced upon all the earth). This positive deity can become transformed into a dark entity known as Nakawe. In the story, the author refers only to the virtues of Takutsi.

7. Religious name with which a small bird named Meterui Tewiyari baptized the sun (a.n.).

8. Proper name of the narrator's grandfather.

9. Literally, "neighbor," used in reference to non-Huicholes and therefore applied here to mestizos and foreigners.

10. Literally, "Our Grandfather," in reference to fire.

11. Name of the narrator's dog.

12. Names of Turametai's five cows.

13. Abbreviated form of the expression *páriyatsié yeyá*, "pilgrim-

age fiesta or celebration," in reference to the pilgrimage made from the mountains of the states of Jalisco and Nayarit, where the Huichol people reside, to the desert surrounding Real del Catorce in the state of San Luis Potosí, where they harvest peyote.

14. Hispanicized plural version of the Huichol noun *mara'akame* (pl., *mara'akate*), traditional healer and ritual officiant; literally, "he who sings (chants)" or "the singer (chanter)," in reference to the music, dance, prayers, and songs or chants that he must know in order to officiate in a variety of ritual ceremonies.

15. Literally, "Our Great-Grandparents," in reference to the first creators of the world.

16. Literally, "the Lords of Midnight," in reference to the sacred entities of darkness and the underworld.

17. Ceremonial centers that are believed to have preserved, since remote times, the world's design and the steps of creation; the *tukipa* remain active with groups of *mara'akate*, who must remain within them for a period of five years.

18. The narrator's proper name, meaning "he who has many writings or drawings on his face." During ritual pilgrimages Huichol pilgrims paint their faces with sacred solar and peyote motifs; this name reflects the narrator's desire to communicate with the gods as a ritual officiant through many face-drawings.

Nuestra Madre Yurienaka

Gabriel Pacheco

Huichol[1]

[De *Tatei Yurienaka y otros cuentos huicholes*, pp. 153–159. Colección Letras Indígenas Contemporáneas. México, D.F.: Editorial Diana/CNCA/DGCP, 1994.]

Si no fuera por Yurienaka,[2] ¿qué sería de nosotros? ¿Qué sería de este roble de cuyas ramas siguen cayendo todavía gotas de agua? Anoche llovió fuerte. La tierra está muy mojada. Mi abuelo salió muy temprano a caminar sin huaraches[3] alrededor de su casa. Anda recorriendo todas las partes cubiertas de zacate verde en torno de su casa. Yo también me levanté muy temprano para caminar entre las altas hierbas. Ahora me vine a tomar un breve descanso debajo de este viejo roble. Mi abuelo me cuenta que tanto el rocío como la tierra son medicinales; por eso hago estos paseos a diario sin huaraches y con mi calzón arremangado hasta por encima de la rodilla. Todo me platica mi abuelo: de qué manera debemos comportarnos como humanos, por qué surgimos en la tierra y por qué a diario nos vigilan los dioses . . . La tierra en la que vivimos es Nuestra Madre, por eso Nuestros Bisabuelos la llaman Tatei Yurienaka. El rocío viene representando a los diferentes dioses que hacen llover, que son los mensajeros de los dioses principales. Mi abuelo nunca deja de explicarme sobre estas cuestiones.

La tierra tiene un olor agradable como la flor de Tikarixa.[4] Además tiene colores como la flor de cempasúchil[5] hembra; es también medicinal como el agua sagrada de Takutsi Nakawe.[6] Pero sobre todo es Nuestra Madre Yurienaka y también Nuestra Bisabuela. El rocío también es hermoso, brillante y fresco como el agua clara de manantial, transparente y centellante cuando Tawexikia[7] lo mira por la mañana desde el otro lado del horizonte. Mi abuelo me platica que el rocío es un buen remedio para el fortalecimiento de los pies y las piernas; por eso yo siempre trato de caminar por las altas hierbas, que me tapen y cubran todo, para de ellas recibir infinidad de gotas de rocío que me resbalen por la espalda. Es bueno que por mi espalda me llueva el rocío, para que se mantenga fuerte y maciza y nunca me quede jorobado. Con esta finalidad lo hago siempre, mientras dura la época de lluvia. Turatemai[8] dice que el rocío en la espalda no es tan medicinal como en los pies y las piernas. Turatemai es grande de edad, pero aún no piensa en el bastón. Él me platica de todo, en cuanto va oscureciendo rápido me sienta a un lado de él y del fuego. Él nunca está de acuerdo que yo me vista como un *teiwari*.[9] Continuamente me aconseja que haga tal o cual cosa, y casi siempre le hago caso. He estado llevando a cabo sus consejos y hasta la fecha todavía los sigo ejerciendo. Por qué fue que apareció el hombre, cómo fue que Nuestros Bisabuelos y todos Nuestros Ancestros se colocaron en lugares sagrados, esto me lo platica mi abuelo. Oigo y sigo todos sus consejos, por eso ahora me he encariñado más con Tatei Yurienaka. Ella me da la vida, me platica y me acurruca cuando llega la noche. Por eso siempre dependo de ella, en ella recobro mis fuerzas y en ella siempre ando. Tatei Yurienaka también viene siendo Nuestra Abuela, por eso la conocemos como Takutsi Nakawe. Las dos juntas nos cuidan y nos miman en su seno. Con esta finalidad nacieron y viven con nosotros y para nosotros. Yo por eso las quiero mucho y las trato con mucha ternura: sin huaraches ando con ellas y duermo tranquilo con ellas. Todas las cosas que existen en la tierra también dependen de ellas. Y cuando llega el plazo para ir a los lugares sagrados, muy encantado de la vida voy y vengo para traerles su agua sagrada: agua bendita de Tatei Yurienaka y la de Takutsi Nakawe.

Muchas veces no llego al lugar sagrado y me regreso de donde pueda agarrar agua, es decir, de donde los dioses me permitan que la tome, pero sin dejar de pronunciar su respectivo rezo. En ningún momento de mi vida me olvido de ellas, siempre pienso en ellas, siempre dándoles de beber su agua bendita. Mucha gente dice que por estos rumbos está muy feo, que está lleno de barrancas, peñas, cerros. Sólo las mesetas escasean. A pesar de esto, yo no uso huaraches, siempre ando con los pies descubiertos. Las gentes de lejos que vienen a nuestras casas se burlan de nosotros por como andamos vestidos. De tanto que les escuchaba así, se lo platiqué a mi abuelo. Pero él no le dio ninguna importancia. Sólo se ponía a platicarme otras cosas con tal de no escucharme. Mi abuelo siempre me quiso mucho, nunca permitía que nadie me dañara. Cada vez que llegaba la noche pronto me sentaba a un lado de Tatewari.[10] Todo me lo platica, cómo debo actuar con la demás gente y cómo había que enterarse de lo que sucedía en otros lados. Él siempre dice que lo hace para que yo sepa y conozca más sobre la costumbre de mi pueblo. Porque dice que bien me puedo vestir como un *teiwari,* que todavía no es tan peligroso, pero que si agarro idea de ellos me echo a perder por completo; eso me platica en las noches. Él me platica que cuando yo aún era niño mi mamá casi me perdía de este mundo; que si no fuera por mi abuelo, ya no estuviera vivo. De eso yo no me acuerdo nada. Pero como mi abuelo siempre me platica la verdad, siempre le creo todo. Que yo me acuerde, jamás me ha regañado, siempre procura hablarme derecho y con razón. Por seguir los pasos de mi abuelo, los *teiwaris* no me ven bien. Es que ellos siempre andaban con zapatos gruesos y además procuran dormir en lo alto, como en los carretones o en algo cómodo, para que no se ensucien. Ellos, aún en lugares donde no se cuenta con comodidades, buscan comodidad en los carretones o en algo que se parezca a una cama. Y como ellos no me ven bien, yo tampoco los veo bien. Pero ¿quién puede rechazar a su madre? ¿Por qué entonces forran tanto sus pies? ¿O acaso no saben que con nuestros pies estamos prendidos de Nuestra Madre Tierra?

Por los pies respiramos el aliento vital de Tatei Yurienaka. Todos los que existimos en ella estamos siempre cubiertos por su manto. Cuando hago largas caminatas no necesito de un caballo ni de zapatos para andar; descalzo ando por los matorrales, cerros, subidas y bajadas. Los *teiwaris* siempre me ven con extrañeza, dicen: en caballo se anda rápido y con zapatos se llega a donde sea, pues las piedras y espinas no lo molestan a uno. Ellos dicen que entre más alto esté uno mejor goza la vida; que por eso se hacen casas muy altas, para desde lo alto respirar aire puro; que por eso mismo andan siempre en aviones, para no ensuciarse con la tierra . . . Una vez, un *teiwari* no me despegaba la vista. A cada rato me tomaba fotos. Cuando él me veía llegar a mi casa con leños a mi espalda, rápido me miraba por su oscura cámara. Yo creo que me tenía mucha lástima y que me veía muy chistoso. Decía que le interesaba fotografiar las partes donde yo tenía rota mi camisa y mi pantalón; por eso tardaba mucho tomándome fotos. Los chivos huelen de lejos, pero éste no se quedaba atrás; cuando caminaba alrededor de mí, me envolvía en una nube de olor de la que sólo me podía desprender cuando me alejaba de él. Cuando él se me quedaba viendo, yo también lo miraba de arriba abajo. Yo pienso que por como lo miraba creyó que ya era su amigo, porque luego llegó hasta mi casa con una sonrisa de oreja a oreja. Por las noches solía sentarse en un tronco junto con nosotros alrededor de Tatewari; mientras tanto nosotros permanecíamos sentados en el suelo: mi abuelo, mi abuela y yo. Cuando le daba sueño se iba a dormir al lugar de donde había llegado, pero después de fotografiarnos. Mi abuelo y mi abuela duermen en la cocina sobre un pedazo de piel de vaca. En cambio, Tsinari[11] y yo nos quedamos debajo del carretón. Tsinari también piensa igual que yo; él también conoce bien los consejos de Tatei Yurienaka. Por eso cada que le da sueño, pone su cabeza sobre el suelo, y además en Nuestra Madre la Tierra calienta siempre su barriga. Tsinari es educado y respetuoso cuando no se le hace daño, pero si lo tratan de dañar, rápido se defiende con sus filosos dientes; por eso a los *teiwaris* les va como les va cuando lo cucan . . .

Las amigas de mi abuelo también comen, piensan y viven como nosotros; ellas como nosotros necesitan beber mucha agua. Aún no son muchas, apenas cinco: Mitixi, Tsimanixi, Yeuka, Haitsi y por último Nauxí.[12] Mi abuelo me platica que estos animales son pertenencias de Takutsi Nakawe. Ésta los dejó en manos de Tatei Yurienaka, quien los cuida mucho, porque son sus vacas. Mi perro es demasiado inteligente, como yo, por eso nunca piensa en morder a estas vacas. Aunque ellas duerman debajo del carretón con nosotros no las muerde. Al contrario, las vigila. Nada de lo que en la tierra existe debe sufrir daño. Así me platica mi abuelo. Por eso, granos como maíz, frijol o semilla de calabaza, mi abuelo no los anda desperdiciando, sino al contrario, los cuida más que un tesoro, solamente los deposita en el suelo cuando a través de los rezos los dioses así se lo hayan permitido. Él me dice que todavía me faltan muchas cosas que aprender y por eso no me deja de platicar cosas importantes. Él me dice que mientras él viva no me va a dejar de platicar cosas, que siempre me va a enseñar cosas nuevas. Yo obedezco sus órdenes. Él me cuenta que lo que me enseña ahora, eso mismo se lo enseñaron a él; su fallecido padre fue quien desde muy chico y a pie lo llevó a conocer varias veces Pariyatsie[13] y que más tarde él y mi abuela iban solitos a Pariyatsie. Ahora piensan que ya no pueden llegar hasta allá; ahora, en compañía de unos *marakames,*[14] lo tengo que hacer yo por ellos y por mí mismo. Al fin mis pies son muy felices pisando tierra y así van y vienen de allá. Cuando los pies de uno se enteran de que ya llegó el día para salir a Pariyatsie, pronto se alegran por querer sentir y acariciar el cuerpo de Tatei Yurienaka. Los pies escuchan el corazón y la respiración de Tatei y de Takutsi, por eso así eligen las pisadas en la tierra, porque saben que así es el camino de ellos. Por eso Tatei Yurienaka es ama de los pies andadores y no los suelta por nada, siempre los conduce por un buen camino. Pero si no se pisa de acuerdo como Tatei quisiera, ésta se encarga de provocar malos pasos o pasos falsos para que suframos algún percance.

Lo conveniente es siempre seguir los buenos pasos de ella, sin importar hasta dónde nos conduzcan. Como dice mi abuelo, ella es la dueña de los pies andadores y no andadores. Ella nos dio el don de tener los pies muy gordos para resistir las caminatas; los pies agrietados para que por ahí penetre la respiración de Tatei Yurienaka y para que así siga recobrando más vida y salud; por eso también nos extendió los pies, para que se marquen bien las pisadas en el momento de las caminatas. Tatei Yurienaka nunca está de acuerdo que andemos con los pies muy forrados; por eso sólo nos ponemos unas cuantas tiras de correas para no cubrir todo el pie; así lo quiere ella, porque siempre quiere sentir el calor de los pies . . . Cuando llega el día de la fiesta, todos nos sentamos en Nuestra Madre la Tierra; cuando a ella le entra ternura por nosotros, nos acuesta en su manto. Ella siempre nos ve bien, por eso en su manto nos acuesta a todos por igual. Ella nunca nos deja solos, siempre se queda con nosotros. Ella decide cuándo llevarse a una o a varias personas hacia su mundo; ella las recibe de cuerpo y alma enteros . . . Me platica mi abuelo que a mi abuela de chica se le hincharon los pies por deber una manda. Y que en la fiesta de Semana Santa tuvo que hacer ofrendas y sacrificios, y que entonces se amaneció bailando con música. De este modo fue como Tatei Yurienaka le deshinchó los pies, porque a ella era a la que le debía la manda . . . Muchos mestizos andan sólo por andar, sin saber a dónde van a parar. Una vez, con estos atrevimientos, llegaron hasta un lugar sagrado y se burlaron del lugar y de lo que ahí había. Decían que por qué tenemos muy lejos de nuestras casas a Nuestros Bisabuelos y a Nuestras Madres, que por qué mejor no les hacemos casa muy cerca de nuestras casas, para no tenerlos en lugares tan lejanos ni escondidos en cuevas. Dicen los *teiwaris* que eso no debe suceder con los dioses. Que el Dios de ellos lo tienen en una casa muy bonita y que los está mirando desde arriba. Ellos no pueden concebir como Dios a uno que está en el suelo ni mucho menos en cuevas, que por eso nunca quisieran que su Dios quedara en el suelo. También dicen que los héroes no deben de quedar al ras del suelo, sino siempre en lo alto, para que no se ensucien; nunca en los ojos de agua ni en los cerros.

Yo que conozco algo de lo que me platica mi abuelo, pienso muy diferente de lo que ellos dicen. Para empezar, la Tierra es Nuestra Madre y Nuestra Abuela. Todo lo que en ella existe es completamente de ellas y por lo tanto nosotros también dependemos de ellas. Hace muchos años que Tatutsima[15] y Takakaima[16] ocuparon sus lugares en cerros, ojos de agua, cuevas, peñas, arroyos, mesetas, mares, venados, pájaros, peyote, maíz, *tukipa*[17] y en nosotros mismos. Por eso nuestros dioses aparecieron en distintos lugares y los estamos visitando y saludando sin tomar en cuenta las distancias. Ellos jamás nos piden que les hagamos su casa. Desde un principio así les hicieron su casa . . . No me he secado todavía; aquí debajo de este roble sigo sentado con mi calzón mojado. Mis pies siguen bastante remojados. Es que el rocío me bañó de pies a cabeza cuando yo caminaba por las altas hierbas. Por cierto, hice muchos caminitos entre las hierbas, pero pasado mañana se borrarán nuevamente . . . " 'Uxamiire,[18] ¿dónde está Tsinari, que aquí van llegando gentes?" Así oí que me gritó mi abuelo Turatemai. Enseguida Tsinari y yo acudimos en su auxilio.

Notas

1. La palabra *huichol* posiblemente se deriva, por corrupción o adaptación castellana, de *wixárika,* término con que los huicholes se autodenominan. Algunos autores creen que esta voz arcaica proviene de la lengua Guachichil, ya desaparecida. Según Karl Lumholtz, *wixárika* significaba "doctores" o "curanderos." A finales del siglo XX contaba esta lengua con más de 55,000 hablantes en los estados de Nayarit, Durango, Zacatecas y Jalisco.
2. Yurienaka o Tatei Yurienaka, "Nuestra Madre Tierra."
3. Del purépecha *kwarachi,* sandalia rústica de cuero.
4. Es una de las especies herbáceas que se designan en varias zonas de México con el nombre genérico de *manto.* Se cultivan como ornamentales. Las flores son de diversos colores, particularmente del morado y rosa, al rojo, azul y blanco. Es común en climas cálidos y templados. En el caso de este relato, se trata de la *Ipomoea purpurea.*
5. *Tagetes erecta,* planta herbácea de hojas recortadas, olor penetrante y flores amarillas. Del náhuatl *cempoalxóchitl,* "veinte flores, muchas flores"; se escribe también *sempasúchil.*
6. Takutsi, "Nuestra Abuela," con el sentido de "Nuestra Semilla Germinada" (es decir, la vida que se produce en toda la tierra). Esta deidad positiva puede convertirse en oscura y llamarse Nakawe. En el relato, el autor se refiere solamente a las virtudes de Takutsi.
7. Nombre religioso con el que un pájaro pequeño llamado Meterui Tewiyari bautizó al sol (n.a.).
8. Nombre propio del abuelo del narrador.
9. Literalmente "vecino," en referencia al que no es huichol; por eso se aplica ese nombre a los mestizos y extranjeros.
10. Literalmente, "Nuestro Abuelo," en referencia al fuego.
11. Nombre del perro del narrador.
12. Nombres de las cinco vacas de Turatemai.
13. Forma abreviada de la expresión *páriyatsié yeyá,* "fiesta o celebración de la peregrinación"; se refiere al peregrinaje desde las montañas de Jalisco y Nayarit, donde viven las comunidades huicholas, hasta la sierra de Real del Catorce en San Luis Potosí, que constituye el territorio donde recolectan el peyote.
14. Plural castellanizado de *mara'akame* (pl., *mara'akate*), curandero y sacerdote; literalmente, "el que canta" o "el cantor," en referencia a la música, danza, rezos y cantos que debe saber para oficiar en una variedad de ceremonias rituales.
15. Literalmente, "Nuestros Bisabuelos," en referencia a los primeros creadores del mundo.
16. Literalmente, "los Señores de la Medianoche," en referencia a las entidades sagradas de la oscuridad y del inframundo.
17. Centros ceremoniales que se supone conservan, desde una remota antigüedad, el diseño del mundo y los pasos de su creación; se mantienen activos con grupos de *mara'akate* que deben permanecer en ellos por período de cinco años.
18. Nombre propio del narrador, que significa "el que tiene muchas escrituras o dibujos en su rostro." Durante peregrinaciones rituales, los peregrinos huicholes se pintan la cara con motivos solares y de peyote; este nombre refleja el deseo del narrador de comunicarse con los dioses a través de muchas pinturas faciales como oficiante ritual.

Librado Silva Galeana

Nahuatl

Librado Silva Galeana. Photographed in his study in Tlalpan, Distrito Federal.

Librado Silva Galeana was born in the Indigenous community of Santa Ana Tlacotenco, now part of the Federal District's Milpa Alta Delegación, located to the southeast of Mexico's capital. He is a professor of primary and secondary education with a specialization in the English language. He holds a bachelor's degree in Latin American Studies from the National University's Division of Philosophy and Letters. In his native region he has promoted and carried out eight *encuentros,* "gatherings" of Nahuatl speakers at which Dr. Miguel León-Portilla has coordinated a group of distinguished scholars. In October 1995 Silva Galeana received the Nezahualcóyotl Prize for Indigenous-Language Literatures. With Natalio Hernández he co-authored *Flor y canto de los antiguos mexicanos* (Flower and Song of the Ancient Mexicans) (Nayarit State Government and El Día, 1990). The piece we include here was also published in *Yancuic Nahuasasanili/Narrativa náhuatl contemporánea* (Contemporary Nahuatl Narrative) (Mexico City: Editorial Diana, 1994). He is presently collaborating with Miguel León-Portilla on a bilingual edition of *Cantares mexicanos* (Mexican Songs) by pre-Hispanic poet King Nezahualcóyotl of Texcoco.

Librado Silva Galeana nació en la comunidad indígena de Santa Ana Tlacotenco, Delegación de Milpa Alta, en el sureste del Distrito Federal. Es profesor de educación primaria y secundaria en la especialidad de lengua extranjera en inglés. Cursó la carrera de Estudios Latinoamericanos en la Facultad de Filosofía y Letras de la UNAM. En ocho ocasiones ha promovido y llevado a cabo, en su tierra natal, "Encuentros" de hablantes de náhuatl en donde han estado presentes connotados investigadores bajo la coordinación de Miguel León-Portilla. En octubre de 1995 recibió el Premio Nezahualcóyotl de Literatura en Lenguas Indígenas. Es coautor, con Natalio Hernández, de *Flor y canto de los antiguos mexicanos* (Gobierno del Estado de Nayarit y El Día, 1990). El relato que incluimos aquí apareció publicado también en *Yancuic Nahuasasanili/Narrativa náhuatl contemporánea* (México, D.F.: Editorial Diana, 1994). Actualmente está preparando, en colaboración con Miguel León-Portilla, una edición bilingüe de *Cantares mexicanos* del Rey Nezahualcóyotl de Texcoco.

In temazcalli

Librado Silva Galeana

Nahuatl[1]

[From *La voz profunda: Literatura mexicana en lenguas indígenas*, pp. 190–194. Carlos Montemayor, prologue, literary selection, and notes. Mexico City: Joaquín Mortiz, 2004.]

Ihcuac mocalquetza in temazcalli[2] quichihuiliah icuayolicpac zan ica tezontli ihuan motzicoa in tetzontemeh[3] ica zoquitl. In temazcalli ahmo huel huehyi mochihua, zan onaqui nahui ahnozo chicuacen tlacah.

Achtotipa quitlaliliayah in ixic ica campa quizaz in poctli. Inon itlatlacoyocton quichihuiliayah inacacic, axcan zan mocoyonia ica campa quizaz in tzoatl. No quichihuiliah in itlexic.[4] Nican tlepitzalo ica mototoniz in temazcalli ihuan motlecuiltia in tlecuahuitl ica ocototon.

Ihcuac ye oquitlanqueh, ye oquichiuhqueh in temazcalli, motemoah in teoyoticatahtli ihuan monotza in teopixqui.

Ipan tonalli ihcuac moteochihuaz, no motocayotia. Ahci in teopixqui temazcalco, quiteochihua ica popochtli ihuan quito-cayotia ica in quixtianotocaitl quemen Jose, Xuan, Luis ihuan occequintin. Yece, in teoyoticatahtli achto quitlamahuichih-chihuah in temazcalli ica xochitl, chinaamatl, quilacatzoa ica xochicuzcatl ihuan quimahmana in xochitl icehcecac, ica campa calacoah. No itech monequi in teoyoticathatli quitema-caz, quitetlacuiliz galletahtoton, necuhtli,[5] pahchichic ihuan tlacueponiz.

In ahquin iaxca in temazcalli quitemaca tlacualli: alozmolli, ayohhuachmolli, yemolli, quemmanian tlemolli ica yeta-malli ahnozo ahuaxtamalli. Quemmanian no motemaca in tepach-necuhtli.[6]

Ihcuac aca motemaz, tlepitzalo ihtic in tlexictli. Intla monequi huel totonqui yez in temazcalli motlalilia in ahua-cuahuitl ahnozo tamazquicuahuitl; intla ahmo monequi cenca totonqui zan motlalilia ococuahuitl. Ihcuac ye netemaloz achto mototonia in atl ihtic in temazcalli, itech in itlexic. Intla ye tlacuauhtotonqui motzacua in tlexictli ica centetl tepatlachtli, inin motzicoa ica zoquitl ihuan mixtilinaltia ica tetoton.

Aquihuan mopacazqueh quinechicoah in tecapolxihuitl[7] ah-nozo capolxihuitl,[8] mochinin cenca yamanqui, ica mototonia in tonacayo. Icanin xihuitl nexiuhhuilo. Quemanian nexiuhhuilo ica ahhuiyayalizxihuitl itoca teyahuitl,[9] poleoxihuitl.[10]

Ihcuac ye ototonix in temazcalli ihtic aca calaqui, qui-quixtia in tlecohcotoccuahuitl, tlen oc popoca, ihuan quitla-xilia in atzintli ipan tlexihcotezontli ica tleconexquizaz.

Ihcuac inin ye omochiuh mocalaquia in yamancazacatl, mozohhua ihuan ye cualli calacoaz, netemaloz.

Mihtoa quimmach ye huehcauh, ihcuac yancuic in temazcal-li, achto calaquia ce tlacatl, quicalaquiaya centetl chichi. Mihtoaya quimmach intla itech in temazcalli itla ahmo cualli oyeya ipan inon chichi motzicoaya ihuan quiquixtiaya. Icanin inon ahmo cualli ahmo motzicoa ipan tlatlacah ihuan ahmitla impan mochihuaz.

No achtotipa impan tlatlacah inin omomat: otzinnehnemoa-ya inic calaquia ihtic in temazcalli (ihcuac inin yancuic), quimmach intla ahmo yuhqui calacoaz micoazquiani.

No yuhqui mihtoa quimmach quemmanian cequi tlacah ihuan cihuameh ompa yahuih michtacahuizqueh. Intla yuhqui, ahqui-huan zatepan ompa motemah imicpac tlayohua, cochhuetzih ihuan ihcuac tlahtlachia quincocoah intzontecon. Inin teihtitia acameh ompa quichihuato impitzoyoh, ompa omopacmacatoh.

Ihcuac tlacati in conetl, ipan chicuey ilhuitl ye motema in nantli. Yahuih quitlanehuizqueh in temazcalli (ahmo nochtlacah quipiah). In ihcuac ayahmo motlecuiltia, ihtic motlalia in popochtli ihuan cecerahtoton, tlahtlanihua quen itoca in temazcalli ihuan quinotzah, quilhuiah: "Xiquihta, Jose (intla inin itoca), nican nimitztlalilia in popochtli ihuan cera, nimitztlatlauhtia, nican tictemazqueh inin cone-atzintli, xic-huapahua cualli, ma totahtzin quimixotili, ma mochipa quimopalehuili, ayc ma quemman ipan huetziz in cocoliztli, ma nemi miec xihuitl, ma pacta muchipa. Timochin-tin tipahpaquizqueh intla cualli quizaz in inemiliz." Immanon mocuacualatza in atl ica teyahuitl ihuan motema in nantli ica icoconeton.

Zatepan, in ye onetemaloc, in inamic quimama in mixiuh-qui, ahmo quicahua in nehnemiz, quimamahtiuh ichan. Quemmani-an, intla huehyi in cihuatl, intla tomahuac ihuan yetic, quiayaxiquipililpiayah[11] (in mixiuhqui moteca nepantla in ayatl ihuan inin monacazilpia), mocalaquia in cuauhpitzactli ihuan moquechpanoa. Yuhqui momama.

Ihcuac ye quihuica in mixiuhqui ichan, ipan ohtli qui-cehcemmantihuih in tecapolxihuitl in ica omoxiuhhuihqueh ahnozo zacatl in omozouh; intla yuhqui mochihua ahtle ahmo cualli ipan mochihuaz in conetl.

Ihuan no ihcuac tlacati in conetl in tahtli quitemaca in xopacatl.[12] Inin quihtoznequi in tetahtzin quimmaca mochintin ahquihuan quihtlanilia techichic, necuhtli ihuan occequi tlamantli.

Notes

1. Nahuatl is the Mexican Indigenous language with the largest number of speakers. At the end of the twentieth century there were more than 2,563,000 Nahua people distributed among the states of Puebla, Veracruz, Hidalgo, Guerrero, San Luis Potosí, Tlaxcala, Morelos, and México and the Federal District. The author is a native of Milpa Alta. He writes in the Nahuatl alphabet regarded as "classic," since numerous texts from the colonial period were written in it, including legal documents, correspondence, and literary works.

2. "Bath house"; a small stone structure of pre-Hispanic origin still in use today for ritual and medicinal steambaths.

3. *Tezontle,* a porous stone. From *tetl,* "stone," and *tzoneua* or *tzoneuhqui,* "overflowed" or "softened." The verb *tetzonuia,* "to wipe with a sponge," is derived from *tetzontli.*

4. Literally, "navel of fire"; that is, the fire's center or heart.

5. Literally, "honey." It is understood that this is the fermented *aguamiel* or "honey water." In present-day Nahuatl it is more commonly known as *neutli.*

6. Literally, "pressed" or "crushed honey," because of the process of extraction that yields the *miel de tepache* or "tepache honey" from the fruit.

7. Small reddish fruit of *Schinus molle,* a tree originating in Peru and consequently known as *perú, pirú,* or *pirul.*

8. From the Nahuatl *capolin,* a name applied to several plants of the Mirsinaceae, Tiliaceae, Mirteaceae, and Rosaceae families that produce spherical edible fruit measuring 5 to 10 mm in diameter. In this story, the author is referring to *Prunus capuli,* a tree that reaches heights of 30 to 45 feet; its small fruit is black or reddish, with a single seed.

9. *Pericón: Tagetes florida.*

10. *Poleo* leaf: *Hedeoma palmeri.*

11. Literally, "an *ayate* tied as a *xiquipil*"; that is, used as a shoulder bag or carrying sack.

12. Literally, "to wet one's foot"; equivalent to *el remojo* in Mexican Spanish. An obligatory toast to commemorate having obtained something new.

Notas

1. El náhuatl es la lengua indígena con mayor número de hablantes. A finales del siglo XX contaba con una población de más de 2,563,000 individuos distribuidos en los estados de Puebla, Veracruz, Hidalgo, Guerrero, San Luis Potosí, Tlaxcala, Morelos y México y el Distrito Federal. El autor es originario de Milpa Alta y escribe con el alfabeto de náhuatl llamado "clásico" porque con él se escribieron los numerosos textos, documentos legales, correspondencia y obras literarias de la época colonial.

2. "Casa de bañarse" (por tratarse de una pequeña construcción de piedra). Baño de vapor prehispánico todavía utilizado ahora con propósitos rituales y medicinales.

3. Tezontle: piedra porosa. De *tetl,* "piedra," y *tzoneua* o *tzoneuhqui,* "desbordada" o "reblandecida," "suave." De *tetzontli* se deriva el verbo *tetzonuia,* "pasar una esponja," "enjuagar con una esponja."

4. Literalmente, "ombligo de fuego"; es decir, el centro o corazón del fogón.

5. Literalmente, "miel." Se entiende que se trata del "aguamiel" fermentado. En el náhuatl contemporáneo es más común *neutli.*

6. Literalmente "miel prensada," "aplastada," por el proceso de maceración o prensado de la fruta que produce la "miel de tepache."

7. Pequeño fruto rojizo del *Schinus molle,* árbol originario de Perú y por eso llamado indistintamente pirí, perú o pirul.

8. Del náhuatl *capolin.* Nombre que se aplica a diversas plantas que tienen frutos comestibles globosos de 5 a 10 mm y que pertenecen a las Mirsináceas, Tiliáceas, Mirteáceas y Rosáceas; en este relato, el autor se refiere al *Prunus capuli,* árbol que alcanza alturas de 10 a 15 metros; su pequeño fruto es negro o rojizo y con una sola semilla.

9. Pericón: *Tagetes florida.*

10. Hoja de poleo: *Hedeoma palmeri.*

11. Literalmente, "un ayate amarrado como *xiquipil*"; es decir, usado como "bolsa" o "morral."

12. Literalmente "mojar el pie." En el español de México, "el remojo." Se refiere al brindis que se considera obligatorio por estrenar algo.

The *Temascal*

Librado Silva Galeana

Nahuatl[1]

[From *La voz profunda: Literatura mexicana en lenguas indígenas,* pp. 190–195. Carlos Montemayor, prologue, literary selection, and notes. Mexico City: Joaquín Mortiz, 2004.]

When a *temascal*[2] is raised, the uppermost part is constructed solely of *tezontle*[3] stones joined with mud. A *temascal* is not very large. Only four to six persons fit inside.

Previously, *temascals* were given a "navel" so that the smoke would escape. The little opening was made above and to one side; now an opening is only made where the dirty water exits. They are also given a "fire navel," which is where the fire is placed to heat the *temascal.* The fire is ignited with *ocotitos.*[4]

Once the *temascal* has been completed, a godfather is sought and the priest is summoned. The day it is blessed, it is also given a name.

The priest comes to where the steambath is located. He blesses it, incenses it, and baptizes it with a Christian name, such as José, Juan, Luis, or some other. But first, the padrino adorns it with flowers and *papel de China;*[5] he wraps it in a flowery garland and spreads flowers on each side of its entrance. The padrino must provide cookies, *pulque,*[6] and liquor and light skyrockets.

The owner of the *temascal* provides the food: rice, green *mole,*[7] and beans; sometimes he provides *mole* and bean tamales; *tepache*[8] is also served at times.

When people are going to bathe, they place the fire in the "fire navel." If they want the *temascal* quite hot, they use oak or strawberry tree wood; if they do not want it so hot, they use pine. Before bathing, the water is heated inside next to the fire navel. Once the *temascal* is quite hot, the fire navel is covered with a flat stone that is attached with mud and tightly held in place with stones.

Those who are going to bathe collect *pirú*[9] or *capulín*[10] herbs, which are very hot. The bathers are "seasoned" with these herbs. At times, they are seasoned with aromatic herbs known as *pericón*[11] and *poleo.*[12]

Once the *temascal* is hot, someone enters, removes the firewood that is still smoking, and throws water on the *tezontle* stones by the fire navel so the ash will be washed away.

Once this has been done, grass is spread; and one can then enter to bathe oneself.

It is said that long ago, when a *temascal* was used for the first time, a dog was placed inside before any person would enter. And it was said that if there was something evil inside the bath, it would stick to the dog, who would remove it. That way the evil element would not stick to the people, and nothing would happen to them.

People also used to do the following: they would walk backward when entering the *temascal* (when it was new); they believed that if they did not enter thus, they would die.

It is also said that when men and women go there secretly to "do something," "darkness falls" upon those who subsequently bathe there: they faint or fall asleep and awake with a headache. This shows that some persons had already gone there to do their "dirty things"; they went there to give each other pleasure.

When a child is born, the mother bathes herself in the *temascal* one week later. The family members go and ask to borrow a temascal, since not everyone has one. Before lighting the fire, they place incense and candles inside, ask what its name is, and invoke it; they say to it: "Look, José (if it has been baptized as such), we are giving you incense and candles. I beg that you allow us to bathe this little baby here. Make him grow well. May our father care for him. May he always help him. May sickness never befall him. May he live many years and always be happy. We will all be happy if he lives well." Then the water is boiled with an aromatic herb, and the mother bathes herself with her little child.

Following the bath, the spouse carries the new mother. He does not allow her to walk; he carries her to their house. At times, if the woman is very tall or fat and heavy, she is carried in an *ayate*[13] tied like a *xiquipil*[14] (the mother lies down in the middle of the *ayate,* which is tied by its ends). A pole (one that is not too thick) is inserted in the *ayate* and is placed over the shoulders; that is how she is carried.

When the new mother is being carried home, the *pirú*

herb with which she "seasoned" herself or the grama that was spread in the bath is scattered in the street. If this is done, nothing bad will happen to the child.

Also, when a child is born, the parents provide *xopacatl.*[15] In other words, they give an alcoholic beverage, *pulque,* or other things to anyone who requests it.

Notes

1. Nahuatl is the Mexican Indigenous language with the largest number of speakers. At the end of the twentieth century there were more than 2,563,000 Nahua people distributed among the states of Puebla, Veracruz, Hidalgo, Guerrero, San Luis Potosí, Tlaxcala, Morelos, and México and the Federal District. See also note 1 of the Nahuatl-language text.

2. From the Nahuatl *temazcalli,* "bath house." A small stone structure of pre-Hispanic origin, with one entrance, still in use today for ritual and medicinal steambaths.

3. From the Nahuatl *tetzontli;* a porous, light-weight volcanic stone, reddish in color, used for construction during numerous periods of Mexican history.

4. From the Nahuatl *ocotl,* "torch." Small strips of wood from *Pinus montezumal,* a resinous pine.

5. Brightly colored tissue paper hung as an adornment during celebrations; it typically bears cut-outs featuring relevant slogans and motifs.

6. From the Nahuatl *poliuhqui,* "spoiled." A thick white beverage obtained through the fermentation of the juice or *aguamiel* (literally, "honey water") of certain magueys or agaves, particularly of the genus *Agave atrovirens.*

7. From the Nahuatl *molli,* "sauce." Green *mole* is a sauce that contains green tomatoes, poblano or serrano peppers, oregano, *epazote* (*Chenopodium ambrosioides*), parsley, and *hojasanta* (the leaf from a bush of the genus *Eriodictyon*); at times, it also contains squash seeds, Swiss chard, coriander, and lettuce.

8. From the Nahuatl *tepiatl,* "raw sugar water." Today the term is applied to a fermented drink made from pineapple and sugar.

9. Small reddish fruit of *Schinus molle,* a tree originating in Peru and consequently known as *perú, pirú,* or *pirul.*

10. From the Nahuatl *capolin,* a name applied to several plants of the Mirsinaceae, Tiliaceae, Mirteaceae, and Rosaceae families that produce spherical, edible fruit measuring 5 to 10 mm in diameter. In this story, the author is referring to *Prunus capuli,* a tree that reaches heights of 30 to 45 feet; its small fruit is black or reddish, with a single seed.

11. *Pericón: Tagetes florida,* a herbaceous plant one meter tall, with elliptical and serrated leaves; the aroma of its flowers is very similar to that of anis. It is common to the Valley of Mexico, the states of Hidalgo, Zacatecas, and Durango, and some regions of southeastern Mexico.

12. This name is used in reference to two varieties of labiated *Hedeoma* found in central Mexico and in the states of Hidalgo and San Luis Potosí: *Hedeoma palmeri,* mentioned here, and *Hedeoma drummondii.*

13. From the Nahuatl *ayatl,* a thin cloth made from maguey fiber.

14. In Nahuatl, literally, "shoulder bag" or "carrying sack." The author is suggesting that the *ayate* cloth takes on this shape to transport the woman.

15. In Nahuatl, literally, "to wet one's foot"; equivalent to "el remojo" in Mexican Spanish. An obligatory toast to commemorate having obtained something new.

El temascal

Librado Silva Galeana

Náhuatl[1]

[De *La voz profunda: Literatura mexicana en lenguas indígenas,* pp. 191–195. Carlos Montemayor, prólogo, selección y notas. México, D.F.: Joaquín Mortiz, 2004.]

Cuando se levanta un temascal[2] se construye su parte superior solamente con piedras de tezontle[3] que se pegan con lodo. El temascal no se hace muy grande. Solamente caben en él cuatro o seis personas.

Anteriormente le ponían un *ombligo* para que saliera el humo. Ese agujerito se lo hacían arriba, a un lado; pero ahora sólo le hacen un agujero por donde sale el agua sucia. También le hacen un *ombligo del fuego* donde se pone la lumbre para que se caliente el temascal. Se prende la lumbre con ocotitos.[4]

Una vez que se ha acabado de construir el temascal, se busca un padrino y se llama al sacerdote. El día en que se bendice también se le pone nombre.

Llega el sacerdote donde se encuentra el baño, lo bendice, le pone incienso y lo bautiza con un nombre cristiano, como José, Juan, Luis u otro. Pero antes, el padrino lo adorna con flores, papel de China,[5] lo rodea con una guirnalda florida y esparce flores a los lados, donde está su entrada. También está obligado el padrino a regalar galletas, pulque[6] y aguardiente y a tronar cohetes.

El dueño del temascal da la comida: arroz, mole verde,[7] frijoles, a veces da mole con tamales de frijol o de haba. Otras veces también se da *tepache*.[8]

Cuando alguien se va a bañar, pone la lumbre en el "ombligo del fuego." Si se quiere que esté bien caliente el temascal se le pone leña de encino o de madroño; si no se quiere muy caliente, nada más se le pone leña de ocote. Antes de bañarse se calienta el agua caliente, junto al "ombligo." Y cuando ya está muy caliente el temascal, se tapa el "ombligo del fuego" con una piedra plana, y ésta se pega con lodo y se aprieta al frente con piedrecitas.

Aquellos que se van a bañar juntan hierbas de pirú[9] o de capulín,[10] que son muy calientes. Con estas hierbas se "hojean." A veces se "hojean" con hierbas aromáticas que se llaman pericón[11] y poleo.[12]

Cuando ya está caliente el temascal, alguien entra en él, saca los tizones que todavía humean y arroja agua sobre los tezontles del "ombligo del fuego" para que salga la ceniza.

Cuando ya se hizo esto, se mete grama, se tiende y luego ya puede uno entrar para bañarse.

Se dice que hace mucho tiempo, cuando se iba a estrenar el temascal, antes de que entrara una persona, metían un perro. Y se decía que, en caso de que en el baño se hallara algo maligno, se pegaba al perro y éste lo sacaba. Con ello, lo malo no se pegaría en las personas y nada les ocurriría.

Anteriormente, las personas también acostumbraban lo siguiente: caminaban de espaldas para entrar al temascal (cuando este era nuevo), dizque porque, de no entrar en esta forma, se morirían.

También se dice que cuando hombres y mujeres se van ahí a "hacer algo" secretamente, quienes después se bañan "sobre ellos se hace la oscuridad" (se desmayan), se quedan dormidos, y cuando despiertan, les duele la cabeza. Esto demuestra que allá fueron antes algunos a hacer "su porquería," que allá fueron a darse placer.

Cuando nace un niño, a los ocho días ya se baña en el temascal la madre. Van a pedir prestado un temascal (no todas las personas lo poseen). Antes de encenderlo, adentro se ponen incienso y velas, se pregunta su nombre (del temascal) y lo llaman, le dicen: "Mira, José (en caso de que así haya sido bautizado), aquí te ponemos incienso y velas, te ruego que nos permitas bañar aquí a este bebecito, haz que crezca bien, que nuestro padre lo cuide, que siempre lo ayude, que nunca caiga sobre él la enfermedad, que viva muchos años y que siempre esté contento. Todos seremos felices si vive bien." Luego, se hierve el agua con una hierba aromática y se baña la madre con su hijito.

Después del baño, el marido carga a la parturienta. No permite que camine; la carga hasta su casa. A veces, si la mujer es de gran estatura o si es gorda y pesada, la cargan en un *ayate*[13] amarrado a manera de *xiquipil*[14] (la parturienta se acuesta en medio del ayate y éste se amarra por las puntas), se introduce un palo no muy grueso y se pone sobre los hombros. Así se carga.

Cuando ya llevan a la parturienta a su casa, en la calle van arrojando la hierba de pirú con que se "hojeó" o la grama que se tendió en el baño. Si así se hace, nada malo ocurrirá al niño.

Y también, cuando nace un niño, los padres dan el *xopacatl*.[15] Esto quiere decir que le dan, a todo el que lo pide, una bebida alcohólica, pulque u otras cosas.

Notas

1. El náhuatl es la lengua indígena con mayor número de hablantes. A finales del siglo XX contaba con una población de más de 2,563,000 individuos distribuidos en los estados de Puebla, Veracruz, Hidalgo, Guerrero, San Luis Potosí, Tlaxcala, Morelos y México y el Distrito Federal.

2. Del náhuatl *temazcalli*, "casa de bañarse" (por tratarse de una pequeña construcción de piedra). Baño de vapor prehispánico todavía utilizado ahora con propósitos rituales y medicinales.

3. Del náhuatl *tetzontli*. Piedra volcánica porosa y ligera, de color rojizo, empleada en construcciones a lo largo de muchas épocas de la historia de México.

4. Del náhuatl *ocotl*, "tea," "antorcha." Pequeñas rajas de la madera del *Pinus montezumal*, un pino resinoso.

5. Papel delgado de colores brillantes que se cuelga como adorno durante celebraciones; típicamente lleva recortes que representan dichos y motivos relevantes.

6. Del náhuatl *poliuhqui*, "echado a perder." Bebida obtenida por la fermentación del jugo o "aguamiel" de ciertos magueyes o agaves, par-

ticularmente del género *Agave atrovirens.* Se trata de un líquido blanco y espeso.

7. Del náhuatl *molli,* "salsa." El mole verde es una salsa que contiene tomates verdes, chiles poblanos o serranos, orégano, epazote, perejil y hojasanta; en ocasiones lleva pepitas de calabaza, acelga, cilantro y lechuga.

8. Del náhuatl *tepiatl;* agua de maíz crudo. Se aplica ahora a una bebida fermentada de piña y azúcar.

9. Pequeño fruto rojizo del *Schinus molle,* árbol originario de Perú y por eso llamado indistintamente pirí, perú o pirul.

10. Del náhuatl *capolin;* nombre que se aplica a diversas plantas que tienen frutos comestibles globosos de 5 a 10 mm y que pertenecen a las Mirsináceas, Tiliáceas, Mirteáceas y Rosáceas; en este relato, el autor se refiere al *Prunus capuli,* árbol que alcanza alturas de 10 a 15 metros; su pequeño fruto es negro o rojizo y con una sola semilla.

11. Pericón: *Tagetes florida,* planta herbácea de un metro de altura, de hojas elípticas y aserradas, con flores de marcado olor a anís. Es común en el valle de México, Hidalgo, Zacatecas, Durango y otras regiones del sureste de México.

12. *Poleo:* se designa con este nombre a dos variedades de *Hedeoma* labiadas en el centro de México, Hidalgo y San Luis Potosí: la *Hedeoma palmeri,* mencionada aquí, y la *Hedeoma drummondii.*

13. Del náhuatl *ayatl,* tela delgada hecha con fibra de maguey.

14. Literalmente, "morral," "bolsa," "talega." El autor sugiere que es la forma que adquiere el ayate donde se va a transportar a la mujer.

15. Literalmente, "mojar el pie." En el español de México, "el remojo." Se refiere al brindis que se considera obligatorio por estrenar algo.

Román Güemes Jiménez

Nahuatl

Román Güemes Jiménez. Photographed in Xalapa, Veracruz.

Román Güemes Jiménez was born on August 9, 1953, in the Indigenous community of Tecalantla, Municipality of Platón Sánchez, Veracruz. He has a bachelor's degree (*licenciatura*) in linguistics (1975) and the master's degree (*maestría*) in social anthropology (1979) from the Universidad Veracruzana and presently holds a full-time research post in that university's Anthropology Institute. Güemes Jiménez has carried out research projects in the Huasteca region on oral narrative, settlement patterns, ethnomusicology, and *huapango* lyrics. He was awarded the National and Central American Prize for Indigenous Short-Story (Puebla, 1985) and the National Prize for Oral Narrative (Mexico, 1987). He is a *huapango* musician and is proficient at improvising poetry. Güemes Jiménez is a founding member of the Amatlán Pro Huapango and Huasteca Culture Association, Inc., and also a founding member of the Association of Veracruz Indigenous Speakers and Writers, Inc.

Román Güemes Jiménez nació en la comunidad indígena de Tecalantla, municipio de Platón Sánchez, Veracruz, el 9 de agosto de 1953. Realizó estudios de lingüística (licenciatura) y de antropología social (maestría) en la Universidad Veracruzana, institución de la que egresó en 1975 y 1979. Actualmente se desempeña como investigador de tiempo completo en el Instituto de Antropología de la Universidad Veracruzana. Ha realizado proyectos de investigación en la región Huasteca sobre narrativa oral, patrones de asentamiento, etnomusicología y lírica popular del huapango. Obtuvo el Premio Nacional y Centroamericano de cuento indígena (Puebla, 1985) y el Premio Nacional de Narrativa Oral (México, 1987). Es músico de huapango y poeta improvisador. Es miembro fundador del Patronato Pro Huapango y Cultura Huasteca de Amatlán, A.C., y también miembro fundador de la Asociación de Hablantes y Escritores Indios de Veracruz, A.C.

Chikomexochitl: Ne konetsij tlen tiopamitl kikuajki

Román Güemes Jiménez

Nahuatl[1]

[From *Yancuic Nahuasasanili/Narrativa Náhuatl Contemporánea: Antología,* pp. 149–164. Colección Letras Indígenas Contemporáneas. Mexico City: Editorial Diana/CNCA/DGCP, 1994.]

Nimactilla Carlo Antonio Castro,
ihuan Crescencio Güemes

Ne Tlaixpantli uajkamelaualistli ika kauitl. Ne Tlaixpantli ne kuatitlamimej tlaxoxojko techijlamikiliaj tonatintekitl.

—Nochi monekis kitokasej inxopanmil . . .

—San ya mijlik nopaj noikni Ijuantsij,[2] pilyoliktsij nijkajki kejuak san uaya monojnotsayaya nopaj semanauaktli. Pampa tlakatki kitokaxtijkej Ijuantsij uan pampa ya tlacopochuijtinemij ya Tlapopochuijketl[3] yajaya tlayekantinemij nochi ipan ueyiluimej ueytlaneskayomej. Ya nojkia Tlamatijketl,[4] san ya tlauel tlamatl yajaya lajlamiki pan nopaj chinamitl. Kilt yoltok tlen ax uelis tipoasxiuitl. Ya ne Ixkejkelochtli.[5]

Ista ni uajkapaj-ista pan ni San Mikeltepexitl tlen ejekaselia uan sekuiselia pan diciembre metstli tlen pan ueyatl ualauij uan tlen iika kiajkukui nopaj chikometepetlatilistli-san sejko tikitaj nopaj poktlajchinoli then xiuitsakua, tlen pilkuatsitsij tsakua uan tlen ueyikuatsakua. Nikaj Temikiloyan: kampa nelnelia motemiki.

Neka katlani nejnemij maseualmej ¿Kanij?, ¿kanij yaui Juan Tsakualika?, ¿kanij yaui Pécoro Olivares Catarina?, ¿kanij yaui Mikel Antunyu Jose Ana?, ¿kanij yaui Abondio Xokixual María? . . . ¿kanij yauij nopaj maseualmej, kanij yauij . . . ? Nopaj nejnemilpamitl neka uajka nojkia kiyeknextia ne tlaltsokopil.

Ne katlani nojkia motlaltokaj ne tlakamej intemikilis tlen achtoui ualajkej Temikiloyan kikauakoj pan ni tlali intlamalxoyaualis uan kej nopaj mochiuas nopaj uajkamitl, tlen uajkatemikili polijtok. Nopaj uajkamitl, nopaj tlen axkeman titemiktokej, tlen axkeman tikitstokej yon axkeman timoijlijokej. Then ax motemiktok ax moixmati uan tlen ax moixmati uelis elis se tlejtlejya tlen toixpa motlatijtok, tlen tonakastla, ika to ikaj. Kej ni ax oui titemikis; ax oui kej ni ne uajkamitl.

Ne katlani eltoya ne nelneliantlali para kej nopaj ijlamikilistli ma asiki pan noikni Ijuantsij Tlapopochuijketl, Tlamatijketl, Ixkejkelochtli, kejuak se tlatlapankayo jtototl kejuak kuextekantlanexmej. Ne ka tlani pan ne kejuak tlaltsokopili ax mas ueyi tlen kej ne Sontekomatlan atentsokopili, motepasolchiuayaya Ijuantsij itlachial uan ilajlamikilis. Nopaj tlaltsokopili kitsaua iyejyejka pan ojtli uan apamitl. Nopayol ipan poktli ika uajka, petlaniyayaj pinauapanlaminanajkayojmej tlen sekij kalmej petlaniyayaj kejuak ateskamej kejuak ixpopoyotsij pepeyokanuixmej[6]—kuauimej tlen petlanij—pan se auiltilistli ke kinixkuapolouayayaj ika mixpoktli.

Neka katlani ax tlen molinia, nochi san ken tlaeltok mas ke ni axmolinilistli kipia ijlamikilintosuij uan mas ke ax kinekiskia techkamouiaj: techkamouiaj ika iyamankatos uan kema tikualanij yaja techajuaj ika itlatomontosulj . . . Kiijtokej ika nopayoj uajkajkia panojkej nopaj nauama seualmej uan nopaj tepeuajmaseualmej kitemojtinemiyayaj pan tonati uan ekauili inchinankoojuij.

Mololojtok pan se temikmixtli kistejki noikni Ijuantsij kiikankajtiyajki ipopochkoijyotl, se mixtli kisayaya pan imajuaj.

Ken yajki kiijtok:

—Tinomelauasej pan tonechkatemikilis pan ne tochinanko Kalkaual . . .[7]

Na nojuak nitemiktika pan ne uajkapantepexitl, ista Temikiloyan: pan ne tlali kampa se nelbelia temiktli uelis mitsitskis. Uankino elki keman se pilkonetsij tlen xoxokasoltik itlake uan itsonkaltonal monextik pan se tlauejchijkatototomej imakya uan pan se tlauejchijtokej etsamej, xikojmej uan masamej. Nechtlajtlanik ika noikni Ijuantsij Ixkejkelochtli, Tlamatijketl, Tlapopochuijketl:

—Uan moixkejkelochikni tlen ika ikopalpokuij kintotoniaj Auakej totiotsitsij,[8] tlen atekojmej uan Tepechanejkej,[9] tlen tepemej euanij tepekojmej ¿Kenke ax nojuaj temiktika keman kiita ni semanauaktli kampa ni nauatlakamej uan tepeuantlakamej panojkej? ¿Kenke ax nojuaj mixchijchiua, kopalmixmej . . . ?

Auamakya, imakya uipinxalamatl[10] imakya nopaj Kuauimej tlen petko[11] itoka nopaj tlen ika makojtik ixochio moita kejuak moixpantiaj ika eluikaktli ipan inilui, nikijlik nopaj konetsij tlen iixkopinka monextiyaya kuamakya, nikijlik nopaj konetsij:

—Noikni nechijlik timomelauasejyok pan seyok totemikilis nepaj tochankalkaual . . .

Nopaj kopalpopochtli tlen Ijuantsij kikajtejki no juaj mijyotia pan ne tepexitl uan nochi temikiloyan uan ijuaktsa kiualikayaya ijlamikilistli uejueyluimej uan xochisontli[12] intekuesontlatsotson . . .

Ya nechtlayekanas pan nomikya—kiijtok nopaj konetsij—; ya tlanauatis mijkasones[13] uakino kiuikas ikuika miyak ixayotl. Ya nechchoka kuikatias pa ijkino nias xitlauak uan nimokuapolos. San Ijuantsij uelis nechyekanas . . . ¿Ax tikita ax kemaj nikokoya más ki nama uan san notata Ijuantsij Ixkejkelochtli, Tlapopochuijketl uan ta nojkia ta tifanankero,[14] ta tlen tinotlayi, inomej uelis innechamakasej Auakej innejnenkaojuij, ika chan tepechanejkej, ika chan teskatlapetlanianij, ika chan teskatlatomoniajij? . . . Nopaj se chikauak ojtli uan ouij tipanos uan imojuantij innechmetsilpisej pan ne mijkan ojtli, uaukino tikitasej tlan ax niuasiti . . . pan san aki ueli ojtli tiasis ika tlatsotsontli ika ixayotl . . . Uankinono tikitasej tla axkana . . .

¿Ti ajkiya ta konetsij kejuak san totiotsij nimitsita?, ¿ajkiya ta ken motlajtol pantuetsi pan se Kelochtepexitl kejuak san moikni Ijuantsij?, ¿ta tiajkiya ista tikixmati ne Ixkejkelochtli ne tlen ika ipopochkopal kintotoniaj totiotsitsij Auakej uan inijuantij ika inyolpakilis peuaj maltiaj uan nopaj tlatioachiuatl uetsi ipan totlalnana uankinono onka tlakualistli para tojuantij timaseualmej? . . . ¿Ajkiya ta ista tinechijlia tlayi?, ¿atlak Ijuantsij ika ieuentepexitosuij mitsualikak pan ni tlaltipaktli ika itlajtol?

Nopal konetsij uetskak, kiiskik se axkaneli uan kitlajkoitak uan kiijlik:

—¡Nochipaj kej ni tieltos!

Kiitskik se xikojtli uan kostik kipanuasanik uan kiijlik:

—¡Kej ni tieltos!

Kiitskik se michi pan atl uan kiuitschijki pan ietl uan kiijlik:

—¡Kej ni tieltos!

Kiueytlasojtlachilik ne masatl uan kikuakuaajalaxok iueyikorona kiajaloxok; sanilok iuaya se tsana uan miitotik ipan miyak xochikoxualimej.

—¿Atlak ni tlamantli, fantankero, ax tlen mitsyomelaua. Atlak ni ax mitsixtiyoltlauilamama?

Teipa nechsaniluik ika aketspali, ne tlen kikixtilik inenepiltlauil uan nechkamauik ika tsitsimitenantsij, noipal xipeuantenentsij tlen nopaj konetsij kikalakik pan temaskali para uelis maseualmej itstosej, yoltosej.

Uankinono nikijlik:

—Aj, ta uelis ti Chikomexochitl,[15] ti Chikomexochitl tatitata Chikomexochitl, titiokichpil, ta ti Ueychikimexo chili, ta tinotata, notlakualis, ta tinotata.

—Melauak na ni Chikomexochitl . . . tlen ueyi ya yajke, tlen kintlamakak maseualmej, pero nama na nipilkonetsij uan ax niuelis nielis nitotata nielis ¿Ax tikita nechkuajki ni tiopamitl?, ¿ax tikita tlan san nechsemajkajkej ika itlanauatil ika se axkualkiatlajtoli?, ¿ax tikita tlan san moikni Ijuantsij nechijlamikilia uan san ipopoch kintotoniaj totiotsitsij Auakej uan ne Tepechanejkej? . . . Pero ne ipokyo nojkia tlamis; ne ya se ixkewjkelochtli, ya mikis uan na nimikis. Tla ax ika ni kopali ax uelis nitlakonanas. Tla ne mixtli tlen imajuaj paniuetsi ax eltok ax niuelis niyoltikas; tlan ax itstokej tlen ueli techtonalnotsaj ika inxochitlajtol ika inuajkatlajtol kejuak ni tepexitl ista kampa na nichikomexochitl nitemiktika. Tlan ax itstokej nopaj xochimijtotianij nitemiktika. Tlan ax itstokej nopaj xochimijtotianij ax nijmatis tlachketl nijchiuas san nimikis; tlan ni xochitlatsotsontli ax eltos ax uelis nitlakonanas . . . Nikaj Temikiloyan ista na nitemiki; nikaj temikij tlen kimatij tlachiasej, tlen kimatij kitlanisej se sintlayouajkamitl se uajkamajmajtli; nikaj motemiki ni temikilismej, nikaj axkana motemiki se tlejtlejya tlen ax melauak se tlejtlejya tlen ax melauak tijneki, nikaj motemiki temikilismej. San temikilismej. Yeka moixkejkelochiki notata, uan ta tifantankero, tinotlayi . . . ta ika mokuakauason tipixpias ne mijketl . . . ne Ixkejkelochtli kitsatsayatsas ne koyolxiuitl,[16] kimaxakualos ne xochiixuakentsij,[17] kisesentilis ijyajxochitl,[18] kitsontekis ika tepostlatsontejketl ne alaxoxiuitl, kichiuas ne xochikoskamej, ne akaseuasmej uan sanilos ista kemaj kechuakis. Naui tonati uan majuili yauali kamatis uan ijkia kamatitias ista kemaj kechuakis. Naui tonati uan makuili yauali kamatis uan ijkia kamatitias ista kemaj kiaxitis majtlaktli uan ome tonati. Majtlaktli uan ome maueyintonati, pampa na Chikomexochitl, tlen Chikomexochitl nimopoalkokoa, nimoilkakokoa, nimotatasokokoa, nimotlejtlelkakokoa, axnimonelitankokoa. Na, kejuak nitotata ni eltoya nitlaxtlajtika uan tlanankilijtika ika nomikilis. Xinechtlachili, nimikia, na, niueyitlanesyotata, nitemiktlakuali, nimikia . . .

Ni pilkonetsij tlen kejuak se totiotsij nesi, melauak nelia mikiyaya san kichixtoya noikni Ijuantsij Ixkejkelochtli, Tlamatijketl Tlapopochuijketl iteipantlajtol tlen ya nojkia mikisa; pero tlan timoyolijlisej ne Ixkejkelochtli, kilt nopaj uajka iikxipaxalojtinenki san kampa ueli, itlachial moskaltijkia ekauilonkanmakya, pan tla totoniamakya, ojmakya . . . pero ax tlauel miyak temiktok uan ax ueli asis ika ne ka nali . . .

Neka ka tlani patlantika ne Chicomexochikonetsij, ya nechyolkokoa uan nechtekipachoa, nechkuesolmaka, nojkia kichiua ki ixayotl manesika pan ne Ijuantsij itlajtol. Patlani kejuak se tototl uan nejnemi kejuak se maseuali uan motlalana kejuak se temikmej tlen nikaj yolij para ma onka yolistli. Patlani nopaj Chikomexochikonetsij yaui uan uala pan ne San Mikeltepexitl uan tlachixtia kampa yaui ika ne Postektitlantepetl, nopayo kampa moketsaj Auakej uan tlaauetsiltiaj uan kampa Tepechanejkej nojkia kipiaj incha. Ejekamauiltijtika nechtsajtsiliaj nopaj konetsij:

—Ika nopayo niya fantankero; ax nijneki xinechtemikikaua uan xitlejtos ki nimiktok. Nimokuapas nimitsitaki . . .

Ne Postektitlantepetl ne se ueytata, mokaua ika arrabes San Mikeltepexitl, ika Temikiloyan arrabes, kampa yon se temiktli ax uelis moompantis. Ne kuanextik uajkamitl yajaya ueytata Postektitla ixayak uan kejuak se kuatlatoktli iyakapa kinkuatopeua ne mixmej. Ika tiotlak siyoui imatojlo uan nopaj mixmej temoj kitlakentiyaj uan kichiuiliaj ikuaixuaktonkal. Nopayo patlantiyaui Chicomexochikonetsij, itsonkal kejual se mixtli tlen uimolijtika pan ne ueytata ixayak. Nopayo nojkia kioni chikaualistli, uan nopaj konetsij itlakual ya nopaj noixkejkelochikni ikopal.

Ax uajkajtika mokuapki nopaj konetsij pan nopaj tenexitl, nikaj Temikiloyan, kampa se temiktli ax kema mosemajkaua, kampa tonati uan xayaktli ax san se techchiuilia nopaj temikmej.

Sampa mokokoa ualajki nopaj konetsij, naman kena ax keman mokokoa ualajki . . . ax timatis tlachketl pano ika nopaj xopanmilmej . . . Nechechkauia nopaj konetsij uan nechtlajtlania ma nipaleui moketsas; ichipauauetskalis nesi ax miyak uetskilistli, ax mas tlauel kej se konetsij; kejuak se mikilistli nesi. Nikitskia pan iselmaj-se kentsij sisikiportik-para ma moeua itlakayo. Nechkualseualtlachilia uan nechtlajtlania ika Ijuantsij ne Ixkejkelochtli.

Uankino se pitsajatl kipaxaloua Temikiloyan. Nopaj totomej motlatiaj tejtsonkuamajkayo; teipa tlaejekak se kentsij. Nechiljuia nopaj konetsij:

—Nimachilia nimikisa, pero nopaj Ixkejkelochtli ax asi.

Para niseseltis se kentsij—uan nojkia para nimotemakas para nimochikaualis pan ni temikojmej—nikistlakauik, nikajkayaua. Nikijlia para axkana mikis, ki ya ax mikini, ki nopaj imets axkana moilpis pan nopaj ojtemikilistli mas ki moixkejkelochikni, Tlamatijketl, Tlapopochuijketl tochontik mixchijchijketl mas ki matlatskia pan nopaj mikojtli. Sesenxiuitl, nikijlia nopaj konetsij, mitsnotsaj ta tiueyijketl, ika naui tlamantli, para xitechtlakualmantikaj, para xitechyol makatikaj, para xiyolmakatika ni tlaltipaktli, nochi maseualmej tlen mochijchijtokej ika moselnakayo, moyamankanakayo uan kostik, kejuak ken se elotl titlalpaniuetsi, kejuak se yeksintli, para titlamakas nopaj chiyalistli, nopaj nekilistli, nopaj ualalistli:

—Sesenxiuitl—nikijlia nopaj konetsij—mitsiluikixtiaj ika inyolo mitstokiaj moxopanmil uan nopayo ika moxochio timotlakentijtok, ika mopayo, kuali timoyeknextia pan inakastla tlen motlaijtla nesi nopaj elosiuapiltsij[19] nopaj tlen nesi kejuak se siuatl uan tlen kitlaliaj monakastla pan se tlaixpamitl . . . sekij kiijtouaj ke nopaj situapil mouelti . . . na nijmati nopaj tlen ista kiuika se tlaxkalyoyomitl kichiuaj ika ome elotl kuamotskijtokej kuanechijtokej uan kejuak maseuali kitlakentiaj. Nopaj situapil seyok monexitilis, Chikomexochitl isiuanextilis . . . Chikomexochitl iasijka . . .

Uetska ne konetsij uan nechkuanajnaua kejuak san kikuanajnauayaya se tochikauaktata tekitijketl; uankino nijmachilia itlakensisikiporxoxoasoltik, isesektsonkal uan tsopelik uan ijyonxiuitl tlan pan itlalouala uan motemaka uan motemaka uankino nechiljuis ika itlatsotsonkantlajtol:

—Tlayi, fantankero, ¿Uankinono, ax nimikini? ¿Ax nipoliuini?

Yolpaktok mauiltia nopaj konetsij ika itlalyayauik tepexitl uan kimimiloa tepesili ika tepexiko uan piluitontiyauij kemaj mijmilojtiyauij ista kemaj tlalkomolasitij. Na nikita uan nitlachilpijpia, nijmati mauiltia ika imajmayo ika totiotsij tlen kitepexiuis uan kikuas nopaj Tiopamitl. Nijmati para nijkajkayajtok. Namaj ya mauiltia, pero na nikuesojtok, nimotekipachojtok. Nichoka ika san tlen iyojtsij mokaua nopaj ixtiyoli tlen nouajkauampojuaj; nichoka ika nopaj konetsij, ika ueyixketl, nichola ika se tiotlayamankatotonik tlen yaui. Nichoka ika nouajkaixtiyol noyankuikixayo, ni ixayotl tlen nimatki ika moixkejkelochikni. Nimoijlia ki nepaj chinanko, nepaj Kalkaual, ya nojkia ika iome ixtiyoltlapopochuijketl choka, taxtikixmatisixayotl.

—Se ixayotl nopaj se uajkamitl tlen mojmostlamopatla. Mojmostla kipa se iyankulkxayak uan se yankuik nejnenkaseyastli . . .

Nimoyolijlia Ixkejkelochtli itlajtol: "Se ixayotl nopaj kejual se Auakejmaltilistli tlen toyolpa tikinuikaj tlen ika kopalyolistli mototoniliaj uan maltiaj . . . no paj ixayomej kiatsejtselokij kiamakakij ualauij toxopanmi . . ."

Kemaj na nikijlamiki nopaj Ixkejkelochtli, nopaj konetsij yolpaktok tlamauiltijtika uan tepesilmimilojtika ika tepexiko. Kemaj san iyojtsij tepesili tlen kimimilok nopaj konetsij keman tlakomolasito, nikaj Temikiloyan, nichoka ika nopaj seyok noixtiyol nopaj tlen nechasiko ika Postektitlantepetl ipan Ijuantsij imaxko uan pan isanilotlajtol; uankino kena nopaj chokilistli mosansejkochijki mosansejtilik moolchok. Nopaj konetsij nechita ken nichoka uan mokuesoa, uan ax nechselia:

—Sesenmaseualmej monekis motokisej inxopanmil ¿axke?, ta moneki timotokilis, nojkia ne Ixkejkelochtli. Nochi monekis kitokasej inxopanmil. Uankino, ¿Kenke titlauelchoka, fantankero, uan tlan ta titlatsotsontlalilis nomikyo, ika noikxipa totiotsitsij intlatsili uan pan notlakayo ixayokuikalistli, chokauikalistli . . . ? ¿Atlak ta nojkia tiuayatias uan nojuaj tinekiskia titemikis nopaj nelnelintemikmej? ¿Tinekiskia nelnelia titemikis temikmej? ¿Ta tijpia mo ome ax san se ixtiyoli pero ya moixayo tlauel iuikal . . . ?

Sampa nichoka. Sesen ixayotl nopaj kejuak se temiktli tlen nech echolouia uan tlen choloa tlen motlaloua ika seja ken nopaj tepesili tlen ika tepexiko momimiloa, seja kej ne konetsij patlani ipan ne Postektitlantepetl . . . pero namaj nimoketsasneki uan nojkia nitsajtsisneki—kej chichi nitlaajuas—, pero se axkualtlamantli pano, ax ueli nimoketsa uan nijneki, mas ki ax kemaj, nitlamiltis nimiktlantlamantli. Nichokastlankia, nimoketsasneki . . . ne konetsij uetska, pan iuetskalis nesi se melaualistli uan se majkaualistli . . . ax kemaj uelisok timomelauasej, kejuak san pa iuetskalis kiijtoua: "Niyoua fantankero, namaj kena nijmati ki ta tikixmati ne maseualmej inkualnemilis inkualtlachialis uan tlen sesenxiuitl nechyolnotsaj ika nopaj naui tlamantli pa nojuak ma nikintlamatijikaj. Niyoua, san ne Ixkejkelochtli kimati keman nechnotsas . . . niyoltikas namaj kemaj nineltoka motlajtol uan nikitstok moixayo san se itlachialis. Namaj nikixmati moomeixtiyol: se tlen Postektitlantepetl uan se tlen touajkanpoyouaj."

Se tlanankilistli pankiski pan Postektitlantepetl; se ajkauaka atli uale ne ika tlaltsokopil. Totomej uan sayolimej kisokouijkej ne eluikaktli patlantiyauiyayaj se konetsij itepotsko mokajkayatlalouayaya moyolijliyaya ke yoltiskaskia; ki onkaskia nojuaj kopaltlapopochtli mas ki ne noixkejkelochikni mikis. Nopaj konetsij yajki uelis ika nochipaj . . . ¿Kemaj kiitasejyok ni noixtiyoljuaj? Uankino nimoketsasnejki kemaj nikitak yolpakto pankiski, kinextiyaya isesekchipauakuetskalis, ax niuelki; ouij nimoketsaskia uan nijchiuas nomets manejnemikaj. Ax uelki nimoketsak uan ax nijneki nimakauas ni Chikomexochokonetsij kemaj ax kimajtok nimelauaktlajtoli nimelauaktlamantli ni san keualmaseualtlamantli. Nitsajtsilik kemaj niyoltlamiyaya:

—Chikomexochitl, Chikomexochitl, nomachkoni, nomachkoni, ximokuapa, ximokuapa . . .

Ax nijnekiyaya ma itstlakayaui. Kemaj nikitak para ya yauia-motsonkaltonalejkamajkajti-nitsajtsilijki sampa. Sampa nitsajtsik:

—Chikomexochitl, Chikomexochitl, ximokuapa . . .

Nopaj konetsij polijtiyajki ika uajkamitl. Nopaj ikonetlajtlalonkalak san kentsij mokakiyaya, uankino nimoyolijlik para ni seyoktokaxtis nopaj konetsij ken titokaxtiaj ika sekinok chinankojmej uan kejuak nikajki Ijuantsij kitokaxtiyaya:

—Chikomexochitl, Sintektli, Pilsintektli, Sinteopiltsij,[20] ximokuapa, xiuala xinechpaleuiki nimoketsas, xinechmaka moselmaj xoxokasoltik; xinechpaleui . . .

Ax uelki nimoketski, kejuak se tlajkatl tlen ipan kuamakuayotl tlaki, kejual tlali ichichiktlajkakuamakuayo; kejual se tlen ayojkaka kineki uan tlen nochi kikokoliaj. Nopaj konetsij axkana mokuapayaya uan nomajmajyo uextijtiyajki pampa nimoijliyaya pampa niuetstikaskia pan nopaj yayauik uan apachtik tlali. Uankinono, kemaj yauali moixkuapolouasiyaya ika nopaj tlali kampa Chikomexochitl mauiltiyaya nimotemakak nitsajtsilis sampa ayojkana kejuak se totata tlen kinejki chikauaktlakatl elis tekitijketl elis, yon kej itlayi, yon kej nopaj fantankero tlen noyolkoajkokuitok, namaj kena kej nelnelia ni eli; se yamaxtekone uan, se Konekauali; kejuak se temikanmaseuali, tlen mojmostla kipaxaloua ne Temikiloyan, tlan ista ne San Mikeltepexitl kiita ni semanauaktli tlen kinekiskia kej nopaj ma eli nopaj semanauaktli . . . Kej ne maseuali tlen nochipaj tepexikonaualita para temikis nopaj nelnelia temikmej . . . Nitsajtsilik:

—Notaataaaa, notata, Chicomexochitata, amo xinechmajkajteua pan ni yayauik uan chikauak yauali; xinecheua, xinechtsontekontemiyolmaka ximochikajmaka para ax ma nimiki . . .

Chikauak tlailpitsayaya ne ejekatl kejual san nochchijchiuiliyaya se melauak tlajtoli. Tlaauetsiyaya kejuak se tlatetsajyotl; San Mikeltepexitl—tlen eltok pan Temikiloyan kampa temikilistla—nopaj kejuak san moxoyauayaya pan iapojyejui uan kejuak san tlaueloniskia. Tlaauetsiyaya, kena, pero pan noyolo ax moxoyauayaya nopaj auetsichialistli, moxoyauayaya nopaj etikyolistli. Uetstok kej nopaj, ika yon se ijyojtli axkana nieliyaya seyok mas ki tlen ne nojkia moneki ma mometsilpi pan ne mikojtli, ika ne Auakenojtli, ne chikauak uan ouij ojtli—tlen ne konetsij moijtliyaya—mas ki chikauak uan ouij san totiotsitsij inmikilis elis, pampa ni san tlen keualmaseualmej ni mikilistli ni ax ouij, pampa san ni mikilistli ax kemaj miki uan tlan pan tiasiti uan iijti tikalakisej ax timikinij tielisej.

Teipa ne auetsistli uan ejekamitl ualajki ne tonali ika itlililimekixtiyol nechixitio, nechixtlauiliko. Na nimoketstoya, kualinimochikaualijtoya, chikauak nitlatskitoya pan tlali uan nitlachixtoya ika ne eluikajtlamijyotl ika ne Piltepepantepetl iixko . . . Uankino, ne ika uajka, ne ika akuekueyochatlajtli, ne ika uejkapajtiokuatitla, nikitak ne tlapepetlantlauili tlen se tsonkaltonali tlen kinextiyaya ne tosxokojyatl, notata Chikomexochitl itsonteko eliyaya tlen chikauak motlalouayaya kiuimolojtiyauiyaya ne xoxokasoltik itlake. Ayojkana patlaniyaya kejuak se tototl, kimotlalouayaya kejuak se ejekatl kiuikayaya. Youiyaya ika ne totiotsitsij auakej inojuik, kampa ne Teskatlapetlanijuetstokej[21] uan ne Teskatlatomonianij[22] uetstokej, ika nepaj youiyaya notata iikxiika nepaj tlamanextiyaya iijsijkayo . . . ixochimijtotis kichijtiyouiyaya; ne xochimijtotili tlen na notechpoui nijchiuas itlatsotson, uankino nimoijlik: Moneki nijnotsas ne noixkejkelochikni; niitstojka pan ni tochinanko Kalkaual, nikaj timomelauaskiaj pan tonechkantemikilis . . .

Ista ne uajkapa, nitlachixki ika ne chinanko, noixtiyol uan ne sakakalltsonpamiti kichijkij se trato . . . ipan uejueyintekitl itlakojtia kampa san xochikamisajmej, xochikuexmej, tsonekauilmej uan chipauaktlakemej, ipan imojmostlanpoluij sesenkali imakya, ipan se siuasanili tlen ax kemaj tlamis uan metlakakalaktli, peuayaya tlayistli, ne kuatotlaminej yoliktsij kipolojtiyouiyayaj inkuatitlayo, nochi mouelpachouayayaj kemaj tepostlatsontejkitl pano, uan siuamej kiualikayayaj axokotl, tlayionilistli, uan tlakamej kioniyayaj pan pilatekontsij;[23] tlalchinoli ualajki, uan ne temikmili ipokuij xopanmili, ne achtoui poktli tlen nochi sintli, kipijki nochi ne chinamitl; sesenkali motiochijki ne sinxinachtli, pan sesentlaixpamitl, uan teipa ika tsajtsilistli motokaski. Ne tlakamej sinxinachtli kimakakej ne tlali uan pan insiyajkaualis kionikij ne seltemaxokiatoli, kikuajkej ebosali uan etixtli uan kikuikej nopaj pajpatlapikchilmichi. Sekij kikuayayaj torojtlakualij.

Nimantsij asiko nekualkiatl, ne auetstli asiko uan ne ejekatl kinuixouayaya ne piltoktsitsij ma ki pisiltsitsij kinkixtiliayayaj innenepil ne tsanemej; uankino mochijki ne kuauejuelolistli uan kuaketsalchiuistli. Ualajki opantlatokilistli.

Sampa asiko ne tlaauetstli, ne ejekatl kinajalaxouelpachouayaya ne tojkuauimej, pejki ne tlatoktlameualistli uan titlachilis ne tojkuauitl ika majtlaktli uan ome ipilkualneluayo tlen chikajtokej ika tlaauetsili, ika ayauitl, ika ajuechtli, ika tonati . . . nochi ni tlamantli Auajkej totiotsitsij kiualtitlanki, inijuantij pan ne tepeixko moketstokej, ijkatokej nojkia mototonilijkej ika ne noikni Ijuantsij ipopochkopal uan maltijkej uan tlaauetski pan tlali . . .

Ni ijkatok pan ni Piltepepantepetl nikitak ken moskaltik ni xopanmil uan sampa nikijlamiki noixkejkelochikni . . . kemaj elomej kuali motlanotsayayaj, kitlapoayayaj inxochimiyaual nopaj tokmej ipan tonati, kemaj ne mili eliyaya kejuak se chipauak tsonkali kejuak se ueyitlakemitl kipikiyaya ne sinmili uan ax tekauayaya ma kiitakj ne ixoxokasoltik uan sisikiportik tlakemitl, ika chokilistli uan tekipacholi sampa ne Chikomexochitl notata nitsajtsilik::

—Notata, notata . . . amo xinechsemajkaua . . . pampa nojuaj timotlaloua nimitsita uan tinechtlakakilijtok nijmati, ximokuapa, amo xinechsemajkaua . . . ista nikaj nikita nojuaj motsonkal itosxokojka . . .

Ne komontlakamej motekipachojkej, ne tostekipacholi kimixtenki ne Kalkaual. Ne tlakamej, ne siuamej tlen nojuaj seja inxayak, tetajtsitsij uan konemej, nechechkauijkej, ualajkej moixtiyolkauako ista pan ni Piltepepantepetl iixko uan nochi nechijlijke ayok ma nimokuesojto, ma nimoseselti, tlanestoyaya uan nimoketstoya ken nijnekiyaya, ayojkana niuetstoya kej se chichik kuamakuayotl, ki se pilkonetsij—tlen kejuak se tototl patlantiualajki—nechkajtejtoya nechtlalijtejtoya pan Piltepepantepetl uan nechtekimakajtejki ma nitlamokuitlaui nochi tekitl tlen kineki ni sintli para yoltos, pampa nopaj konetsij teijlijtejki youijya, iyauilis ika intotiotsitsij Auakej inojuij kampa ayojkemaj mokuapas. Ki namaj uan nochipaj nochi moneki motokisej inxopanmil . . .

¿Uan noixkejkelochikni?, ¿kanij mometstlalijtok, nopaj kejuak se totiositsij eli?, ¿ika kanij tlaltsokopili kititlani itlachilis ne tlen axkema siyaui? . . .

—Moikni miktojka—nechijlik se siuatl—tlami miktok uan ika nopaj mikilistli kiilpitok ne Chikomexochitl imikilis yon ika tlatsotsontli yon ika xochitl uan namaj ome miktokej.

Se tlen nopayo itstoya kipiuik:

—Ome miktokej, ne Ixkejkelichtli, tlamatijketl Ijuantsij Kokajtsintla,[24] tlen ajkokuikuitoya maseualtlajlamikilistli uan nopaj yejyekechikomexochitl elookichpitsij[25] tlen totatasinelotlanextil. Ome miktokej ika nochipaj, kiilpitokej imets pan ne mikojtli uan nopayo axkeman motojtomasej. San yoltosej nochipaj iuaya mikilistli . . .

Se telpokatl mokalakik:

—Moixkejkelochikni kitokia ixopanmil ika itlakayo. Kemaj kixpixkej ax onkak yon tlatsotsontli, ax onkakmijkasones, yon ki ichikontilis ax kipixki, san motiochijketl ualajki kilatintiochiuako uan kiuikiliko itiopanuikalis; uankinono moixkejkelochikni kiseuik ipokyo uan ika doctrina motojki majtlaktli uan ome tonati kipia, nopaj majtlaktli uan ome tonati kemaj ta fantankero tikochtoya ika majmajtli uan silsesekuistli ipampa ne temikchikauaktotonilistli . . .

Se tetajtsij asijo uan nechtlajpaloki, itlachialis nechijlamikiliyaya noikni Ijuantsij, ya nechijlik:

—Ta, noikni fantankero, tiitstoya ipan tekipacholi uan pan temikchokilistli ipan majtlaktli uan ome tonati, nopaj majtlaktli uan ome tonati teipa kemaj mijki moikni Ijuantsij Kokajtsintla. Tikijlamiktok ika Maria Angustina Tlalkuapa, tlen, eyi xiuitl kipia mijki; ika Juan Antunyu Lino, Ilimo eua. Pero achtoui tikinnonotski, tikamatki ika Pegro Simón, ika Tomás Ramírez Tekamaxochiko, ika Martín Santiago Kolatla, ika Leonardo Pochotl; pero moikni Ijuantsij Kokajtsintla, nochipaj tinonotski, tikijlamijke iuajkakualtlajlamikilis, ika ya tikamatki kejuak san nika itstoya pan monemilis uan pan moyolpanolis . . . Namaj xiuala, noikni, ne totajtsij tlen Chikome[26] kitiochiuaski ni toxopanmil ixochimiyaual, pampa namaj ayojkana tijchiuaj ni tlanesyotl tlen Chikomexochitl elotlamanalistli[27] tlen ne toelo titenkauiliyaya; namaj ne Tiopamitl technauatijtok ni xochimiyaualtiochiuali . . . ne konetsij, kitl, mijki; nochi techkotonilijkej . . .

Nochi kiualikayayaj pan imaj ne inxochimiyaualxopanmil, ne Tiopamitl kinnotsayayeyaj ika intepostlatsilimi ne tlen ista techkuanakasiliaj uan nochi kitokiliayayaj ne tepostli kejuak se sesek tlajkatl kuauiyontok pan ne tiopankuatetomitl . . . nochij techkotonilijkej . . . miyak xiuitl kipia mijtok ne konetsij . . . Nopaj tlajtoli tsilinij pan notsonteko tlen ax tlen kiilkaua, tlen ax kineki kipolos . . .

Ne motiochijketl nechechkauik uan nechijlik:

—Kena noikni, kiijtoua ne Tiopamitl ki nopaj kichijchijki tlauelilok, ki se istlakayotl, ax melauak ni sintli konetsij eli kemaj eltok elotl; pampa istlakayotl ki se konetsij uelis elis totiotsij; ki nopaj konetsij tlen tijchiuiliyaya ni tlanesyotl axkemaj yoltoya, ne la Biblianmochtli axkana ika kamatl; nopaj tlauelilok itekitl.

Nopaj yauali ax nikjnejki niyaski pan ne pakilistli tlen kikotonki tlen mopatlani uan kimiktik ne konetsij, uan tlen namaj kitokaxtiaj xochimiyaualtiochiuili, kampa tlen ika sekinok Tlamatinij uan tlapopochuianij tlen Kalkaual euanij nonotsineltokej uan motetsauilijtokej . . . Nitlapejpenki, nikamatki nitlatejtemojki tla nelia eltoya ne Temikiloyan: ne kampa nelnelia motemiki.

Telpantonati, Ijuantsij Ixkejkelochtli itonal sampa noixpa monextik, na tlen nifantankero, na tlen nitlatemojketl . . .

—Xikechkaui, xinechkaui moxayak kampa konetsij tlalauiltijki, fantankero kabrontik, xitlatopeua kej se mosisinijkaejekatl ika ne kuamachilistli kampa itstoya ne uajkamitl imets uan tikasitis nochi temikmej tlen tinektoya, tla ax ika ni tlamantintekitl ne chokilistli ax kisas pan motlakayo para mokuapas ken se yolpakilistli uan yolistli . . . Xikijlamiki: axkana ompa tinentimenis ne Temikiloyan . . .

Ista ken nikistejki ne Kalkaual uan ninejnenki ika Kuatlapechtla uan nopayo, ista pan kuatlapechmej, kampa tlamokuitlauia, ista ne ueyikuatlapechmej, pejki nikitak se ueyixopanmili kitoponijtika inxochimiyaual ika pan tonati kuamapelojtok pan se arrechtik tlankuitsiuili ixuitili. Nimoyolijlik; uan namaj, ¿Tlachketl kineti ni?, ¿kenke kejuak san uetskaya . . . ? Ne xochitlatsotsontli nechekauijtiajki pan se kali kampa se eyi ome kaltenpoyomaseualmejkichiuayayaj ne elotlamanalistli ne eloiluitl. Uelki tlamelauak nikajki ne tlaelokalakilistlison; nopaj tlatsotsontli sampa nechtopejki ni elis fantankero. Ne pilkuakakauatsij,[28] ne kuakikistli[29] uan ne ueyikuakakakauatl[30] Tlachijchiualijtoyaj ika akaseuasmej uan kichokiliyayaj ne Chikomexochikonetsij. Uankino sampa nielki finantankero. Nikitskik notlatsotson uan nikalajki pan kali, kampa Chikomexochitl mochantlalijtok uan nitlatsotsonki . . . teipa nochi uikakij:

—¿Kanij tiyajki, ta xochitl? ¿Kanij tiyajki nopilkonetsij? Amo ximokueso, nika timotlalis pampa nimitstemos hasta kampa tiitstos, mas ki ika ni son timoechkauijtiualas. Ni son nika eltok. Ta nika tiitstojka. Kej ni nimitsijlia, kej ni melauak: amo san kampa ueli xinentinemi, amo ximochokili, nika niitstok na. ¡Xiuala nokone, xiuala nokone . . . !

Sampa nieli nifantankero pampa ninejki niyolkuis uan nichikauilis Chikomexochitl itonal—mas ki san pan ni Kuatlapechtla— . . . perona nonekilis tlen kasis uelis nopaj Temikiloyantlali nojuaj itstok. Nopayo kampa uelis nelnelia titemikis . . .

Titemikis nopaj mas ueyitlamantli ki se uelpachouetskilistli ika ejekatl, nopaj mas ueyitlamantli ken tijnekis titlajtolajkokuis ken tijnekis ti ouij tekitl tiajkokuis, nika eli yejyektlaltikpak tlen kampa ueli tlachia ueli tlamati uan uelij, uelij kiitaj ne uajkapantlamantli, itlamachilis uan inemilis.

Ijuantsij Ixkejkelochtli, tlen ika ipopochkopal kinarrechmakayayaj totiotsitsij uan kintotoniyayaj, nochi ni tlamantli kimatiyaya.

Ne Temikiloyan ne tlali kampa eltok mokualnekilis . . .

Se pilkoneuetskistsij kinkuatotoniaj ista uankino ne tlapamimej uan chipauaknemilismej . . . nochi moneki motokisej inxopanmil . . . ne temikmili.

Notes

1. Nahuatl is the Mexican Indigenous language with the largest number of speakers. At the end of the twentieth century there were more than 2,563,000 Nahua people distributed among the states of Puebla, Veracruz, Hidalgo, Guerrero, San Luis Potosí, Tlaxcala, Morelos, and México and the Federal District. The author is a Nahuatl speaker from the state of Veracruz. He uses the Modern Practical Alphabet proposed in 1975 by the Organization of Nahua Professionals, Inc.

2. The Nahuatl form of the Spanish name "Juan."

3. By virtue of his function as *tlacopochuijtinemij,* he receives this name that literally means "incenser" or "incense bearer."

4. From *tlamati,* "intelligent," "skillful," "wise." In some Nahua areas the term *tlamatqui* refers to traditional healers or sorcerers.

5. Literally, "full of wrinkles"; that is, "old," "venerable," "respectable."

6. *Populus arizonica,* a variety of cottonwood tree known as "cimarrón."

7. Literally, "uninhabited," "where we no longer live."

8. Literally, "Ahuakej Gods"; that is, "Owner Gods of the water." (See Appendix E.) The author uses the form "Auakej," common in the Huasteca region. In other areas, such as in the Milpa Alta, the form "Ahuakej" is proper.

9. Literally, "the *chaneques* of the hills." *Chaneque* is the plural of *chane,* "inhabitant of a house," "owner of the house," or "inhabitant" or "owner" of some particular place, particularly a *tepetl,* "hill." (See Appendix E.)

10. *Ficus padifolia:* a large tree with milky sap and edible fruit. It is more commonly known as *jalamate.*

11. *Nissa sylvatica:* a tree of the Nisaceae family that reaches heights of up to 105 feet, producing bluish flowers and fruit. *Petko* is derived from the Zoque word *petcui.*

12. *Sones de costumbre:* ritual music played exclusively in traditional religious ceremonies.

13. Literally, *sones de muerto:* ritual music played exclusively in funeral ceremonies.

Notas

1. El náhuatl es la lengua indígena con mayor número de hablantes. A finales del siglo XX contaba con una población de más de 2,563,000 individuos distribuidos en los estados de Puebla, Veracruz, Hidalgo, Guerrero, San Luis Potosí, Tlaxcala, Morelos y México y el Distrito Federal. El autor es hablante náhuatl del estado de Veracruz y utiliza el Alfabeto Práctico Moderno propuesto en 1975 por la Organización de Profesionistas Nahuas, A.C.

2. Forma náhuatl de "Juan."

3. Por su función como *tlacopochuijtinemij,* recibe este nombre, literalmente, "incensador" o "portador del incienso."

4. De *tlamati,* "inteligente," "diestro," "sabio." En algunas zonas nahuas se le llama *tlamatqui* a los curanderos o brujos.

5. Literalmente, "lleno de arrugas"; es decir, "viejo"; o sea, "venerable," "respetable."

6. *Populus arizonica,* variedad de álamo llamado "cimarrón."

7. Literalmente, "deshabitado," "donde ya no vivimos."

8. Literalmente, "dioses Ahuakej," esto es, "dioses Dueños del agua." (Véase Apéndice E.) El autor emplea la forma "Auakej," común en la Huasteca. En otras regiones, como Milpa Alta, es propia la forma "Ahuakej."

9. Literalmente, "*chaneques* del cerro." *Chaneque* es el plural de *chane,* "habitante de una casa," "dueño de la casa"; o también "habitante" o "dueño" de cierto sitio, particularmente del *tepetl,* "cerro." (Véase Apéndice E.)

10. *Ficus padifolia:* árbol grande de jugo lechoso y fruto comestible. Es más usual llamarlo en español *jalamate.*

11. *Nissa sylvatica:* árbol de la familia de las Nisáceas que llegan a tener alturas de 35 metros con flores y frutos azulados. *Petko* deriva del zoque *petcui.*

12. "Sones de costumbre": música ritual que sólo se toca en ceremonias religiosas tradicionales.

13. Literalmente, "sones de muerto": música ritual que sólo se toca en ceremonias fúnebres.

14. Del español "fandanguero." Se le llama así, en la Huasteca, a los que saben tañer diversos instrumentos de cuerda para sones populares

14. From the Spanish *fandanguero.* In the Huasteca, this term refers to musicians who play a variety of stringed instruments for popular *sones* and *sones de costumbre.* In Spain *fandanguero* refers to a player and singer of *fandangos,* spirited musical compositions in three-quarters time originating in Andalucía.

15. Literally, "seven" (*chicome*) "flowers" (*xóchitl*). In this story, this character symbolizes the sacred child who successively is transformed into corn, the sun, and the sustainer of life. (See Appendix F.)

16. "Coyo palm": *Acrocomia mexicana;* according to other authors, *Acrocomia vinifera.*

17. From the Tenek *ichbequen,* a small flower used in a variety of ceremonies; known in Spanish as *manzanita* or *mazapán;* Corresponds to *Malvaviscus grandiflorus* and *Malvaviscus arboreus.*

18. "Fragrant flower": *Tagetes florida.*

19. Literally, "Woman of the Young Corn."

20. Sintektli, "Lord of Corn"; Pilsintektli, "Young Lord"; Sinteopiltsij, "Young God of Corn." Through these names, the narrator more broadly reveals the sacred nature of Chikomexóchitl as a corn entity.

21. Literally, "Shining Mirror," the ceremonial name for lightning.

22. Literally, "Mirror of Thunder," the ceremonial name for thunder.

23. Literally, "small vessel," from *tecontli,* "vessel."

24. Literally, "Abundant in Ears of Corn."

25. Literally, "Small Male Ear of Corn."

26. Apocopated name for the city of Chicontepec, not for Chikomexóchitl.

27. Literally, "He Who Spreads the Ears of Corn upon the Table," another of Chikomexóchitl's names.

28. The author translates this word into Spanish as *jarana,* which underlines its strictly regional usage. The prefix and suffix are the diminutives of *kuakakaua* (that is, "the little *kuakakaua*"). This word begins with the notion of *kua,* "wood" (from *kuahuitl*). This may be a fusion of Spanish *guitarra,* "guitar," and Nahuatl *kua* to give the name to this *guitarrita* or "small guitar." However, linguist Delfino Hernández explains that *kuakakaua* is composed of *kua,* "wood," and *kakaua,* "hollowness"; therefore, "the small hollow wood."

29. The author translates this word as *violín,* "violin"; this may be another regional usage of *kuakikiztli,* from *kikiztli,* "trumpet," "conch shell" (from *quiquitzoa,* "to sound a trumpet"), but which also means "to whistle," and *kua,* "wood"; the literal meaning therefore might be "whistling wood."

30. For the author, this word means *guitarra huapanguera,* "huapango guitar." The prefix *ueyi* is augmentative. In accordance with the information in note 28, we should understand this word as "the large guitar," once again a regional usage.

y para sones de costumbre. En España, *fandanguero* es el que sabe tocar y cantar *fandangos,* composiciones musicales animadas al compás de tres por cuatro, originarios de Andalucía.

15. Literalmente, "siete" (*chicome*) "flores" (*xóchitl*). En este relato el personaje simboliza al niño sagrado que se convierte sucesivamente en maíz, en el sol y en el sustentador de la vida. (Véase Apéndice F.)

16. "Palma de coyo": *Acrocomia mexicana;* según otros autores, *Acrocomia vinifera.*

17. Del tenek *ichbequen;* una pequeña flor que se emplea en varias ceremonias, conocida en español como "manzanita" o "mazapán"; corresponde al *Malvaviscus grandiflorus* y al *Malvaviscus arboreus.*

18. "Flor olorosa": *Tagetes florida.*

19. Literalmente, "La mujer del elote tierno."

20. Sintektli, "Señor de la Mazorca"; Pilsintektli, "Tierno Señor"; Sinteopiltsij, "Tierno Dios de la Mazorca." Con estos nombres el narrador revela más ampliamente la naturaleza sagrada de Chikomexóchitl como entidad del maíz.

21. Literalmente, "Espejo brillante," nombre ceremonial de los relámpagos.

22. Literalmente, "Espejo de Trueno," nombre ceremonial de los truenos.

23. Literalmente, "vasijita," de *tecontli,* "vasija."

24. Literalmente, "Abundante en Mazorcas."

25. Literalmente, "Pequeño varón mazorca."

26. Apócope no de Chikomexóchitl, sino de la ciudad de Chicontepec.

27. Literalmente, "El que extiende las mazorcas en la mesa," otro nombre de Chikomexóchitl.

28. El autor traduce esta palabra como "jarana," lo que recalca su acepción solamente regional. El prefijo y el sufijo son los diminutivos de *kuakakaua* (es decir, "el pequeño *kuakakaua*"). Esta palabra principia con la noción de *kua,* "madera" (de *kuahuitl*). Es posible que se trate de una fusión del español "guitarra" y del náhuatl *kua* para designar así a la "guitarrita." Sin embargo, el lingüista Delfino Hernández explica que *kuakakaua* se compone de *kua,* "madera," y de *kakaua,* "hoquedad"; sería, pues, "la pequeña madera hueca."

29. El autor traduce esta palabra como "violín" y quizás se trate de otro uso regional de *kuakikiztli,* palabra formada por *kikiztli,* "trompeta," "caracola" (de *quiquitzoa,* "hacer sonar la trompeta"), pero que también significa "silbar," y *kua,* "madera"; literalmente, podría significar, pues, "la madera que silba."

30. Para el autor esta palabra significa "guitarra huapanguera." El prefijo *ueyi* es aumentativo. Conforme lo expuesto en la nota 28, deberíamos entender esta palabra como "la guitarra grande" y su sentido también como una acepción regional.

Chikomexóchitl: The Child the Church Devoured

Román Güemes Jiménez

Nahuatl[1]

[From *Yancuic Nahuasasanili/Narrativa Náhuatl Contemporánea: Antología*, pp. 149–164, 165–180. Colección Letras Indígenas Contemporáneas. Mexico City: Editorial Diana/CNCA/DGCP, 1994.]

For Carlos Antonio Castro,
for Crescencio Güemes

There ahead, the profound encounter with time. There ahead, the mountains: tonal green. They remind us of our working hours.

"People must all now plant their summer crop," my brother, Ijuantsij,[2] said to himself. I heard him say it very quietly, as if he were addressing the countryside.

He received the name Ijuantsij by birthright, and because he performs the duty of "Incenser," he is the *tlapopochuijketl*,[3] the celebrant of all the great ceremonies.

He is also the Tlamatijketl,[4] the Wise One, of the ranch since he has lived countless years. He is the Wrinkled One.[5]

From here up above: from this San Miguel hillside that in December receives the wind and the cold from the sea, and on its back holds the secret to the seven hills; nearby we see the smoke from the *roza*[6] that envelops grasses, bushes, and trees. This is Temikiloyan,[7] the place where one truly dreams.

Down below, the Indians walk. But where? Where is Juan Tsakualika going? Where is Pedro Olivares Catarina going? Where is Miguel Antonio José Ana going? Where is Abundio Xokixual María going? Where are the Indians going? Just where are they going? They are a line off in the distance, adorning the ravine.

Down below are buried the dreams of the men who came before to Temikiloyan; those who left behind their outpourings of knowledge to create distance: the distance of dreams swallowed up. Distance is that which we have never dreamed, never seen, nor imagined. What has not been dreamed is the unknown, and the unknown can be something that conceals itself in front of us, at our side, or behind us. Not to dream is that simple; distance is that simple.

Down below was the perfect place for memory to reach my brother, Ijuantsij—the Incenser, the Wise One, the Wrinkled One—like a bird of many colors, like the Huasteca[8] dawns. Down below, his gaze and his thoughts were nesting in that irregular sort of canyon smaller than the Zontecomatlán River[9] canyon that weaves its beauty in pathways and streams. There in the distance amid the smoke, the timid sheet-metal roofs of some houses shone like water mirrors, like the tops of blind, shining *pepeyocal*[10] trees, in an interplay that confusingly blended them with clouds of smoke.

Down below, all is silence. Silence that holds the voices of thought and, without desiring it, speaks to us with its gentle voice. And when we become upset, it scolds us with its voice of thunder. They say that was the place through which, in times past, the Nahuas[11] and the Tepehuas[12] passed, searching through sun and shadows for the way to their ranches and their towns.

Entangled in a cloud of dreams, my brother Ijuantsij departed, leaving behind the smell of his censer, a cloud that flowed from his hands. Upon leaving, he said: "In our next dream, we shall meet again, on our ranch, Kalkaual, 'The Uninhabited.' "[13]

I continued dreaming from high upon the hillside, from Temikiloyan, the place where a true dream might seize one. Then, from among a commotion of birds and the uproar of wasps, *jicotes*,[14] and deer, a boy appeared in greenish-blue garb and with a mane like the sun.

He asked for my brother Ijuantsij, the Wrinkled One, the Wise One, the Incenser: "And your brother, the Wrinkled One, he who with his incense smoke warms the Auakej[15] gods, the dreams of the water; and the Tepechanejkej,[16] the

Lords of the Hills . . . why did he not continue dreaming when he saw this countryside through which Nahuas and Tepehuas passed? Why did he not continue creating clouds . . . clouds of incense?"

Among the oak trees, among thick *jalamantes;*[17] among the *petko*[18] trees, whose violet flowers seem to toast the sky in a feast all their own, I said to the child whose image was visible through the trees: "My brother said we would see each other in our next dream, there on our ranch, Kalkaual."

The incense smoke left behind by Ijuantsij still permeated the hillside and all of Temikiloyan. It brought back memories of magnificent ceremonies and the melancholy sound of the *sones de costumbre.*[19]

"He is the one who shall accompany me when I die," said the child. "He is going to arrange the *sones de muerto*[20] so that his song will bear more tears. He will sing, crying for me, so that I may go directly, without losing my way. Only Ijuantsij will be able to guide me. Do you not see that I am now even sicker and that only my father, Ijuantsij, the Wrinkled One, the Wise One, the Incenser, and you, *fandanguero*[21]—you who are my uncle—will be able to show me the pathway to the Auakej and the Tepechanejkej, to the mirrored lightning, and the mirrored thunder? It is a hard pathway and it is difficult to pass. You two will bind my feet to that pathway of death, and then we shall see if I do not make it there . . . One arrives at any pathway with music and weeping . . . So, we shall see . . ."

"But who are you, child, you who seem so divine? Just who are you . . . you, whose words spring from a ravine that appears as wrinkled as my brother Ijuantsij?

"Who are you, child? . . . You, who knows the Wrinkled One; he who, with his incense smoke, warms the Auakej gods? Gods who then, out of pure delight, begin to bathe themselves, and whose divine waters fall upon our mother earth, producing food for us humans? Who are you, child, that you call me *uncle?* Perhaps Ijuantsij, with his voice like an old ravine, brought you to this world with his words!"

The child[22] laughed, picked up an ant, and, squeezing its waist, said to it: "This is how you shall be forever!"

He grasped a *jicote,* painted yellow stripes on its back, and said to it: "This is how you shall be."

He pulled a fish out of the water, placed bones on its fins, and said to it: "This is how you shall be."

He looked at a deer with great tenderness and caressed the tip of its antlers: "This is how you shall be."

He spoke with a thrush and then danced across a multitude of turtles.

"Does this mean nothing to you, Fandanguero? Does this not charge your eyes with light?"

Afterward, he spoke to me of the lizard from whose tongue he removed the light, and of the Tsitsimitenanjtsij[23]—the old, skinless woman whom the child placed into the *temascal*[24] so that humans might live . . .

Then I said to him: "Oh, without a doubt you must be Chikomexóchitl,[25] Seven-Flower; you are Chikomexóchitl Elder, Divine Child. You, the great Seven-Flower . . . you are my Father, my Sustenance. You are my Father."

"Exactly. I am Chikomexóchitl, He who was great, He who gave sustenance to the humans; but now I am a child . . . and I can be no one's father. Do you not see that the Church devoured me? Do you not see that they abandoned me in a time lacking in words? Do you not see that only your brother Ijuantsij remembers me, and that only his smoke warms the Auakej gods and the Tepechanejkej? . . . Nevertheless his smoke will also end. He is already a Wrinkled One. He will die and I will die. I cannot continue without incense, without the cloud that sprouts from his hand; or the presence of those who know to name us with their speech, flowery and profound like this hillside where I, Seven-Flower, am dreaming. I cannot go on without those who perform the flowery dances; I will have no place to turn except to die. Without the flowery music, I cannot go on . . . Here in Temikiloyan, even I am dreaming, for this is where those who are able to see dream; here are those who are able to conquer the darkest and most fearful distance. Here dreams are dreamt; here one does not dream of insecurities or false desires. Here dreams are dreamt; just dreams . . . That is why your brother, the Wrinkled One, is my father; and you, Fandanguero, are my uncle. With the sound of your instrument, you will accompany the deceased. The Wrinkled One will separate the fibers of the *coyo* palm,[26] grind the *ixuakentsij*[27] flower, gather the *pericón*[28] flower, cut orange leaves with his machete, make the flowery necklaces and the flowery fans, and speak until his throat goes dry. He will speak for four days and five nights and will continue speaking until twelve days have passed, twelve long days because I, Chikomexóchitl, Seven-Flower, am sick with time, oblivion, oppression, ridicule, and contempt. I, as the Father I was, am paying and responding with my death. Look at me: I am dying. I, the Father of the greatest traditions, the sustenance of dreams, am dying . . ."

This child of divine appearance was truly dying. He

only awaited the final words of my brother Ijuantsij, the Wrinkled One, the Wise One, the Incenser, who was also on the verge of death. However, with respect to the Wrinkled One, well, he has already walked his feet over a great distance. His sight has already grown in the midst of so much shadow, so much sun, so many pathways; yet even he has not dreamed enough and is unable to arrive at the other shore.

Down below flies Child Seven-Flower. He grieves me and concerns me, he distresses me and makes the tears of Ijuantsij appear in his words. He flies like a bird and walks like a human and rises as the dreams that blossom here to give rise to life. Child Chikomexóchitl flies to and fro along the San Miguel hillside and sets his sights on Postektitla[29] Hill, the place where the Auakej stop to send the rains, and where the Tepechanejkej also dwell. Romping in the air, the child shouts to me: "I am going over there, Fandanguero. I do not wish you to stop dreaming of me or to say that I am dead, Fandanguero. I will return to see you."

Postektitla Hill is a large grandfather. It stands to the left of the San Miguel hillside and to the left of Temikiloyan, the place where no dream may be repeated. The gray distance is the face of grandfather Postektitla; like the point of a sowing stick, he pushes the clouds. In the afternoon, his fist grows weary, and the clouds come down to protect him and to create his white crest. Child Chikomexóchitl flies toward him: his mane is like a cloud that undulates in the grandfather's face. There the child also imbibes strength, and his nourishment is my brother the Wrinkled One's incense.

A short while later, the child returns to the hillside, here to Temikiloyan, the place where a dream is never abandoned, where dreams characterize the days and our faces. The child arrived sick again, now more sick than ever . . . who knows what might be happening with the summer plantings.

He approaches me and asks me to help him sit up; his white laugh seems less a laugh, less childlike, and more death-like. I take him by his tender, slightly rough hands so he may lift up his body. He looks at me gratefully and asks me about Ijuantsij, the Wrinkled One.

Meanwhile, a light, fine rain arrives in Temikiloyan. The birds hide among the thick branches of the trees; then a little bit of wind blows.

The child says to me: "I feel myself dying, but the Wrinkled One does not arrive."

To console him a bit, and to encourage myself on this pathway of dreams, I lie to him, I deceive him. I tell him that he will never die, that he is not mortal; that his foot will not be bound to the pathway of death even though my brother the Wrinkled One, the Wise One, the Incenser, the incorrigible Builder of Clouds, may attach himself to the road of death.

"Year after year," I confess to him, "through the four elements, they call to you, Great One, that you may continue to nourish us and give us life; that you may continue to give life to the earth and to all people made of your matter—young, soft and hard, white, purple, red and yellow—as if you had sprouted from the earth as a beautiful ear of corn to nourish hopes, desires, or destinies."[30]

"Year after year," I tell the child, "they perform your ceremony with the summer crop that is planted in your honor; and there, dressed in your flowers and your kerchief, you look wonderful next to Elosiuapiltsij,[31] she who could be your beloved. She who in the shape of a woman is placed at your side upon the altar. Others say she is your sister. I know that she, who even wears a shawl and is dressed as a human, is formed with two ears of corn joined together. She is your other presence, the feminine presence of Chikomexóchitl."

The child laughs and embraces me as if he were embracing a responsible and strong father; I then feel the roughness of his greenish-blue garb, his cold and sweet hair, and that vegetable smell that comes from his veins. He then dares to say in his harmonious speech: "Fandanguero, uncle, then I am not mortal? I will not perish?"

The child joyfully plays with the hillside's black earth and tosses little stones into the abyss; they perform tiny pirouettes along their way until touching bottom. I look at him, I contemplate him; I know he is playing with his own fears, those of a god about to be toppled, devoured by the Church. I know I have deceived him. He plays now, but I am sad, concerned.

I cry with the only eye I have remaining from my ancient race; I cry for the child, for the Great One, as if for a warm afternoon that is waning. With my ancient eye, I cry my recent tears, those I learned from my brother, the Wrinkled One. I think that, on the ranch at Kalkaual, his two Incenser eyes are also shedding his distant and unknown tears.

"A tear is a different distance every day. Each day has a new face and a new footprint."

I reflect on the words of the Wrinkled One: "A tear is the bath of our internal Auakej because of the heat that the incense of life produces for them . . . tears that water our summer crop."

While I remember the Wrinkled One, the child goes on happily playing with the earth and tossing little stones into the abyss. As the last stone touches the bottom of the hill-side here in Temikiloyan, I cry with my other eye, the one that came to me from Postektitla Hill in the hands and words of my brother Ijuantsij; then my weeping is whole and unique. The child sees me cry and becomes sad; he reproaches me: "People must all plant their summer crop, is this not so? You must plant yours, and the Wrinkled One must plant his as well. Everyone will have to plant the summer crop. Why are you wholly crying then, Fandanguero, if you are the one who will set music to my death, the sound of the gods to my feet, and the song of lament to my body? Might you not also go with us and even wish to go on dreaming, dreaming the true dreams? Might not you even want to go on truly dreaming dreams? You have two different eyes, but your tears are now completely identical."

I cry anew. Each tear is a dream that escapes from me and flees in the same way the little stones roll into the abyss, the same way the child flies to Postektitla Hill. But now I want to stand up on my feet and also I want to shout—or bark like a dog—but something serious is happening: I cannot stand up on my feet and I want, more than ever, to end this matter of death. I have stopped crying completely, I wish to stand up on my feet. The child laughs, in his smile announcing a farewell and an encounter; his little smile seems to say that it will be impossible to meet again.

"I am leaving, Fandanguero," says the child. "Today I have discovered that you are aware of the humans' good intentions and understand that, year after year, they call to me through the four elements so that I may continue to nourish them. I am leaving. The Wrinkled One will call me, he will know when. I will go on living today because I have believed in your words and I have seen your tears, the one completely identical to the other. I now know your two eyes: one from Postektitla and another from the ancient race."

A profound echo was heard from Postektitla; from the ravine came a roar of water. Birds and insects darkened the sky flying behind a child who, deceived, fled thinking he would go on living; that there would be more incense smoke, even though my brother, the Wrinkled One, were to die. The child went away, perhaps forever. When will my eyes see him again? Upon seeing him depart happily, showing off his white, fresh laugh, I tried to stand up on my feet but could not. It was impossible for me to get up and make my legs walk. I was unable to stand up, and I did not want to let Child Chikomexóchitl, Seven-Flower, leave without knowing the truth, the terrible human truth. I cried out to him in my agony: "Chikomexóchitl! Chikomexóchitl! Nephew of mine! Nephew Chikomexóchitl! Come back! Come back!"

I did not want him to go away deceived. Upon seeing him continue along his way, tossing his sun-colored hair to the wind, I shouted to him again. Once again, I shouted to him: "Chikomexóchitl, Sintektli, Pilsintektli, Sinteopiltsij,[32] come back, come help me get up; give me your young, greenish-blue hand, help me . . ."

Unable to stand up, I remained spread upon the ground like a fruit that grows in a cluster; like a cluster of the earth's most bitter fruit; like something that no one desires any longer and everyone shuns. The child was not turning back, and my fear of remaining there, spread out upon the black and humid earth, increased in magnitude. When night was falling, blending into the earth where Seven Flower had been playing, I decided to call out to him again. Not as a father trying to be responsible and strong; not as his uncle; and not even as the Fandanguero that sleeps within me; but rather as what I truly am: a weak and helpless child, a human dreamer, a devoted visitor to Temikiloyan who from the San Miguel hillside sees the world only as he wishes it to be; one who constantly arrives at the abyss to dream the true dreams. I shouted to him: "Faaaatherrrr, father . . . Chikomexóchitl Father, do not leave me lying here on this dark and hard night. Pick me up, fill my head with courage, attempt to save me from death."

The wind blew strongly as if preparing me for the inevitable. It rained strangely. The San Miguel hillside, located in the place of dreams—in Temikiloyan—seemed to slide and wash away in its own wetness. Yes, it was raining. But in my heart the rain of hope did not trickle. I felt only the heaviness of life. Spread out as I was, without breath, I was but he who also must bind his feet to the pathway of death, heading toward the Auakej, that hard and difficult pathway, according to the child. But death must be hard and difficult only for the gods, because only death is immortal; and if we arrive at her, and place ourselves within her womb, we shall be immortal.

Following the rain and the wind, day arrived with its fiery eyes to awaken me, to give light to my eyes. I was standing, steady on my feet, firmly gripping the earth and seeing the horizon over Piltepepa Hill.[33] Then, off in the distance, near Akuekueyoch Stream,[34] toward the old cedars, I saw the glow of a mane like the sun that announced the dawn: it was the head of my father Chikomexóchitl, who was running, his greenish-blue garb flapping. He no longer flew like a bird; rather, he ran as if he were being carried by the wind. He was heading toward the pathway of the Auakej gods, to the place where the Teskatlapetlanij,[35] the Mirrored Lightning, and the Teskatlatomonianij,[36] the Mirrored Thunder, are scattered. My father's foot was heading here, his haste pointed in that direction; he was doing the dance that it was my job to set to music. I then said to myself: "I must call to my brother, the Wrinkled One. I am now at our ranch, Kalkaual; we were to see each other here in our next dream."

From up high, I turned my gaze toward the ranch: the thatched roofs and my sight became entwined. In the midst of an overwhelming movement of blouses and layered skirts, of hats and white garb; within the vital smoke emanating from each house; among the never ending conversations of women and the sounds of *metates,*[37] the clearing of the fields had begun. The fields were gradually losing their growth; all gave way to the machetes. The women brought *axókotl,*[38] the drink for clearing the fields, and the men drank while sitting on *huacalitos.*[39] Afterward came the burning of the fields and the smoke of the field of dreams—the summer planting, the smoke that comes before any and all corn—completely enveloping the ranch. Afterward the seed was blessed in every house, on every altar, then to be sown among cries of encouragement. The men delivered the seed to the earth and, during their rest, drank fresh plum *atole,*[40] ate *bocoles,*[41] and removed roasted *chiltepín*[42] from the bundles of *papatla*[43] leaves. Others consumed beef broth.

The good weather quickly arrived. The rains came, and the wind swayed the little plants that in their smallness stuck their tongues out at the thrushes. Next came the cutting of firewood and the building of the *tareas.*[44] Replanting followed.

Once again, the rains came; the wind fondly tilted the stems of the plants. It was time to weed the fields and observe the stalks with their twelve good little roots strengthened by the rain, by the mist, by the dew, by the sun. The Auakej gods, standing atop the hills, were also warmed by the smoke of my brother Ijuantsij's incense and sent all of this; they bathed and rain fell to earth.

Standing here on Piltepepa Hill, I saw this summer crop grow and I again remembered my brother, the Wrinkled One. When the ears of corn promised to be good, and the plants sprouted their shoots to the sun; when the field was but one white head of hair that covered the corn crop like a giant blanket, blocking the view of the rough, greenish-blue garb, weeping and desperate I again shouted to my father Chikomexóchitl: "Father, father, do not abandon me. I still see you running and I know that you are listening to me. Come back, do not abandon me. From here, I can still see your dawn-like hair."

The town became concerned; the voice of desperation darkened Kalkaual. The men and the women, whose faces still remain the same, the old people and the children, all approached me. They came to the very top of Piltepepa Hill to leave their eyes, and everyone told me not to be sad, to console myself. It was daytime now, and I was on my feet as I had requested; I was no longer spread out like a bitter cluster of fruit. A child who had come flying like a bird had deposited me here on Piltepepa. He had charged me with watching over the tasks that corn requires for its existence, because he was departing on his journey to the pathways of the Auakej gods, from which he would never again return. Now and forever, everyone will have to plant the summer crops, the Child had told them.

"And my brother, the Wrinkled One? Where has the Divine One placed *his* feet? Toward which ravine has the Untiring One set his sight?"

"Your brother has died," one of the women told me. "He has completely died, and with that death, he left the death of child Chikomexóchitl without music or flowers. Now both have died."

One of those present added: "Both have died: the Wrinkled One, Wise Ijuantsij Kokajsintla,[45] the depository of knowledge, and the marvelous child Chikomexóchitl or Elookichpiltsij,[46] who is our representation of the Ear-of-Corn-Father. Both have died forever; they have bound their feet to the pathway of death, and they will never be released from it. They will now live forever, only with death."

One of the young persons added: "Your brother, the Wrinkled One, has already planted his summer crop with his body. At his wake, there was no music, there were no *sones de muerto;* nor did he have his ceremony seven days later; just the catechizer came to pray for him in Latin and to sing his eulogy; therefore your brother the Wrinkled One put out his smoke and was given a Christian burial exactly twelve days ago; twelve days during which you, Fandanguero, have been sleeping through the shakes and chills caused by the fever of dreams."

An elderly man came and greeted me. His gaze reminded me of my brother Ijuantsij. He said to me: "You, brother Fandanguero, have been amid the weeping and desperation of dreams for twelve days, the twelve days following the death of your brother, Ijuantsij Kokajtsintla. You have evoked the memory of María Agustina Tlalkuapa, who died three years ago, and Juan Antonio Lino, who lives in El Limón. But, before naming them, you spoke of Pedro Simón, Tomás Ramírez Tekamaxochiko, Martín Santiago Kolatla, and Leonardo Poóchotl. Further, the entire time you were evoking the memory of your brother, Ijuantsij Kokajtsintla. You remembered his good and profound knowledge, and you spoke of him as if he were present in your time and circumstance. Come now, brother, the priest from Chikón[47] will bless the shoots of our summer crop. You see, we no longer perform the Chikomexóchitl-Elotlamanalistli[48] ceremony that was dedicated to the ears of corn. Today the Church has imposed upon us the blessing of the shoots. The child has died, and everything has fallen to pieces."

They all carried in their hands the shoots from their summer crop as the church called to us with its penetrating bells; everyone followed that metallic voice that hangs like a cold fruit from the beams of the church. "Everything has fallen to pieces. The child died years ago." The old man's words resounded in my head that does not forget, in my head that refuses to give up . . .

The catechizer approached me and said, "Yes, brother, the Church says that the Chikomexóchitl-Elotlamanalistli ceremony was invented by the devil, and it is a lie that the ears of corn are children, since a child cannot be a god. The child to whom you performed the ceremony never existed; the Bible does not speak of him, he is the devil's creation."

That night I refused to attend the ceremony that supplanted and killed the child, that which today they call the Blessing of Shoots, in which the other Wise Ones and Incensers of Kalkaual remain silent and shocked. I preferred to inquire regarding the possible existence of Temikiloyan, the place where one can truly dream.

Days later, the shadow of Ijuantsij, the Wrinkled One, again appeared before me, the Fandanguero, the Seeker.

"Bring your face over to where he as a child played with the earth, damned Fandanguero; like the raging wind, attack the prints left behind by the foot of distance, and you will find all the dreams you have desired. Only then will weeping leave your body to return in the form of happiness and life. Remember: no more than twice will you pass through Temikiloyan."

I finally departed Kalkaual and walked to Kuatlapechtla.[49] There from the lookout platforms—from the enormous platforms—I looked out at a great summer crop, its shoots bursting with arms open to the sun in a crazed look of satisfaction. I thought: "And now what does it want? Why is it almost laughing?" The *son de costumbre* led me to a house where a small group of neighbors was performing the corn ceremony. I could clearly hear the song that is played at the moment the ears of corn are received into the house: music that pushed me to be a *fandanguero* again. The *jarana*,[50] the violin,[51] and the *huapanguera*[52] guitar showed off their decorations of flowered fans, and they cried for Child Seven-Flower. And I became a *fandanguero* again. I took hold of my instrument and I entered the house, into the child's room, and I played. Afterward, everyone sang: "Where did you go, flower? Where did you go, my little child? Do not be sad. Here you will settle down, because I will search for you wherever you may be . . . although the *son* will draw you near. The *son* is here. You are now here. So I am telling you as is proper. Do not go just anywhere . . . do not make yourself cry; I am here. Come my child, come!"

I became a *fandanguero* again in an attempt to revitalize and strengthen the presence—even if just in Kuatlapechtla—of child Seven-Flower. But my desire to find a possible Temikiloyan persists; there, where one may truly dream.

To dream is something more than a flexible little smile to the wind; something more than the simple desire to avoid words and difficulties. It is the paradise where those who are able to see may know and be able; there they manage to see distant things, their way and their means.

Ijuantsij, the Wrinkled One, he who with his incense smoke drove the gods mad and warmed them, knew all of this.

Temikiloyan is the place of the most desired eventuality.

Since then, a childish little laugh hounds both the *tapancos*[53] and the consciences . . . everyone must now plant the summer crop . . . the crop of dreams.

Notes

1. Nahuatl is the Mexican Indigenous language with the largest number of speakers. At the end of the twentieth century there were more than 2,563,000 Nahua people distributed among the states of Puebla, Veracruz, Hidalgo, Guerrero, San Luis Potosí, Tlaxcala, Morelos, and México and the Federal District. See also note 1 of the Nahuatl-language text.

2. The Nahuatl form of the Spanish name "Juan."

3. From the Nahuatl *tlapopoca,* "to smoke," in reference to his functions as incenser or incense bearer in ceremonies.

4. From *tlamati,* "intelligent," "skillful," "wise." In some Nahua areas the term *tlamatqui* refers to traditional healers or sorcerers.

5. Ixkejkelochtli in Nahuatl. Literally, "full of wrinkles"; that is, "old," "venerable," "respectable."

6. The act of cleaning the fields of brush and useless plants before tilling them.

7. Literally, "place of dreams," from *temictli,* "dream"; the physical world, according to ancient Nahua thought.

8. An extensive and varied region of the Eastern Sierra Madre encompassing parts of the states of Tamaulipas, San Luis Potosí, Veracruz, Hidalgo, and Puebla. In this story, the author is referring to the Veracruz Huasteca. From the Nahuatl *huaxteca,* inhabitant of Huaxtla, "place of many *huaxin,*" that is, *guajes* or calabashes (*Lagenaria siceraria).*

9. River located in the municipality of Zontecomatlán in the southern Huasteca region of state of Veracruz.

10. *Populus arizonica,* a variety of cottonwood known as "cimarrón"; its white leaves blend in or shine with the smoke.

11. Several ethnic groups inhabit the Huasteca regions; here the reference is to the Nahua groups residing in the northern part of the states of Veracruz and Hidalgo. See also note 1 above.

12. At the end of the twentieth century the Tepehua people numbered 17,000, distributed throughout the Huasteca region.

13. The name of this ranch in Nahuatl means "where we no longer live" or "uninhabited."

14. From the Nahuatl *xicotli,* a variety of wasp.

15. Literally, "the Lords of the Water." (See Appendix E.)

16. Literally, "the *chaneques* of the hills," magical beings of scant height who inhabit and keep watch over the hills; the belief in these beings of the invisible world extends throughout wide regions of central, southern, and southeastern Mexico. (See Appendix E.)

17. *Ficus padifolia,* a large tree with milky sap and edible fruit. It is more commonly known as *jalamate.*

18. *Nissa sylvatica,* a tree of the Nisaceae family that reaches heights of up to 105 feet, producing bluish flowers and fruit. *Petko* is derived from the Zoque word *petcui.*

19. Ritual music played exclusively in traditional religious ceremonies.

20. Ritual music played exclusively in funeral ceremonies, to help the soul depart and not to get lost.

21. In the Huasteca, this term refers to musicians who play a variety of stringed instruments for popular *sones* and *sones de costumbre.* In Spain, *fandanguero* refers to a player and singer of *fandangos,* spirited musical compositions in three-quarter time originating in Andalucía.

22. The anecdotes which follow in this story correspond to a variety of identities of a child deity, related to the solar deity throughout broad regions of Mesoamerica. (See Appendix F.)

23. Literally, "Mother of the Tsitsimi," harmful pre-Hispanic deities. According to the author, this is a reference to the grandmother of Chikomexóchitl, a skinless old woman who, due to her intrinsically evil nature, constantly attempts to kill her grandson. She is considered to be the source of all venomous animals, including the scorpion, the snake, and the wasp.

24. From the Nahuatl *temazcalli,* "bath house." A small stone structure of pre-Hispanic origin, with one entrance, still in use today for ritual and medicinal steambaths.

25. Literally, "seven" (*chicome*) "flowers" (*xóchitl*). In this story, the character symbolizes the sacred child who successively is transformed into corn, the sun, and the sustainer of life. (See Appendix F.)

26. *Acrocomia mexicana;* according to other authors, *Acrocomia vinifera.* Known as *coyo* or *coyol* (from the Nahuatl *coyoli,* "little bell") because of the shape of the fruit and because it resembles a small bell when shaken.

27. From the Tenek *ichbequen,* a small flower used in a variety of ceremonies; known in Spanish as *manzanita* or *mazapán.* Corresponds to *Malvaviscus grandiflorus* and *Malvaviscus arboreus.*

28. *Tagetes florida,* a herbaceous plant one meter in height, with elliptical and serrated leaves; the aroma of its flowers is very similar to that of anis. It is common to the Valley of Mexico, the states of Hidalgo, Zacatecas, and Durango, and some regions of southeastern Mexico.

29. One of the highest mountains in the Huasteca region; since ancient times, it has been used as a site for sacred ceremonies related to water, agriculture, and community life.

30. Refers to the Meso-American belief that human beings were created from corn; the colors correspond to the different varieties of that grain: white, yellow, red, and purple.

31. Literally, "Woman of the Young Corn."

32. Sintektli, "Lord of Corn"; Pilsintektli, "Young Lord"; Sinteopiltsij, "Young God of Corn." Through these names, the narrator more broadly reveals the sacred nature of Chikomexóchitl as a corn entity.

33. Located in Alahualtitla, municipality of Chicontepec, state of Veracruz; a sacred site where ceremonies related to corn and water are performed, as well as the healing of children.

34. Located in the community of Alahualtitla, state of Veracruz; literally, "water with toad eggs."

35. Literally, "Shining Mirror," the ceremonial name for lightning.

36. Literally, "Mirror of Thunder," the ceremonial name for thunder.

37. Plural Hispanicized form of the Nahuatl *metatl,* a flat, horizontal stone upon which corn is ground.

38. From the Nahuatl *axococ,* "sour water"; from *texócotl,* "tejocote": *Crataegus mexicana* or *Crataegus parryana,* a spiny tree or bush that produces a spherical fruit, whose thick yellow pulp is aromatic, sweet or acidic, and edible.

39. From the Nahuatl *huacalli,* a box or cage made from spaced wood strips used for transporting goods.

40. From the Nahuatl *atolli,* "diluted"; a thick beverage prepared from corn meal or flour dissolved in water and boiled.

41. Generic name for a typical food of the Huasteca region made from corn, salt, chile, and lard, particularly pork lard; *bocoles* take the shape of round and thick cakes.

42. *Capsicum frutesceus,* a shrub that produces an extremely piquant fruit.

43. *Heliconia schiedeana,* a herbaceous plant some four and a half feet tall; it resembles a small banana plant, producing oval, pointy leaves used to wrap foods.

44. A stack of firewood that conforms to a unit of measurement by volume used for wood; its length, width, and diagonal measurements correspond to an arm's length.

45. Literally, "Abundant in Ears of Corn."

46. Literally, "Small Male Ear of Corn."

47. Apocopated form of Chicontepec, from the Nahuatl Chicometepetl, "Seven Hills"; a town and municipality in the Veracruz Huasteca.

48. Literally, "He Who Spreads the Ears of Corn upon the Table," another of Chikomexóchitl's epithets.

49. Literally, "place of many platforms"; in reference to the platforms erected in the fields, from which a watchman protects the crops from being destroyed by birds. With this term, the author suggests a place of abundant or very large cultivated fields.

50. Small, five-stringed guitar used to accompany the *huapango* and *son jarocho.* The *huapango* is a traditional dance and its music from the Huasteca region of the northern part of the state of Veracruz and neighboring states; the *son jarocho* is traditional music for dance from

the southern Gulf coast region. *Huapango* comes from the Náhuatl *huapalli.* See also note 28 of the Nahuatl-language version.

51. See note 29 of the Nahuatl-language version.

52. Small, eight-stringed guitar used mainly to interpret the *huapango* in the Huasteca region; due to its high-pitched tonality, it is also known as *guitarra quinta* or "fifth (octave) guitar." See also note 30 of the Nahuatl-language version.

53. From the Nahuatl *tlapanco,* "on the roof"; horizontal planks used to divide a room into two levels to form a loft or attic.

Chikomexóchitl: El niño devorado por el templo

Román Güemes Jiménez

Náhuatl[1]

[De *Yancuic Nahuasasanili/Narrativa Náhuatl Contemporánea: Antología,* pp. 165–180. Colección Letras Indígenas Contemporáneas. México, D.F.: Editorial Diana/CNCA/DGCP, 1994.]

A Carlo Antonio Castro,
a Crescencio Güemes

Allá, enfrente, el encuentro profundo con el tiempo. Allá, enfrente, las montañas, de un verde tonal, nos recuerdan las horas del trabajo.

—Todos tendrán que sembrar ahora su milpa de verano . . . —dijo para sus adentros mi hermano Ijuantsij.[2] Lo oí decirlo muy quedamente, tal como si hablara con el paisaje.

Recibió el nombre de Ijuantsij por haber nacido. Y por ejercer el oficio de incensador es *tlapopochuijketl,*[3] que es el oficiante de todas las grandes ceremonias.

Es también *tlamatijketl*[4] sapiente del rancho, pues ha vivido años incontables. Es el Rugoso.

Desde aquí arriba, en esta ladera de San Miguel que recibe en diciembre el viento y el frío venidos del mar y que en sus espaldas guarda el secreto de los siete cerros, vemos juntos el humo de la roza[5] que envuelve hierbas, arbustos y árboles. Aquí es Temikiloyan:[6] el lugar donde se sueña verdaderamente.

Por allá abajo caminan los indios. ¿A dónde?, ¿a dónde va Juan Tsakualika?, ¿a dónde va Pedro Olivares Catarina?, ¿a dónde va Miguel Antonio José Ana?, ¿a dónde va Abundio Xokixual María? . . . ¿A dónde van los indios, a dónde van . . . ? Es una fila que adorna en la distancia la cañada.

Allá abajo se sepultan los sueños de los hombres que antes vinieron a Temikiloyan, que dejaron en este sitio el derrame de sus conocimientos para formar la distancia, la distancia de los sueños devorados. La distancia es lo que nunca hemos soñado, lo que jamás hemos visto ni imaginado. Lo que no se ha soñado no se conoce y lo que no se conoce puede ser algo oculto frente a nosotros, a nuestros costados o a nuestras espaldas. Así de fácil es no soñar: así de fácil es la distancia.

Allá abajo estaba el sitio exacto para que el recuerdo llegara a mi hermano Ijuantsij, el Incensador, el Sabio, el Rugoso, como un pájaro de múltiples colores, como los amaneceres huastecos.[7] Allá abajo, se anidaba su mirada a su pensamiento, en esa especie de cañada irregular, menos grande que la cañada del río Zontecomatlán,[8] que teje su belleza en caminos y arroyos. Allí, entre el humo, a lo lejos, brillaban los tímidos techos de lámina de algunas casas como espejos de agua, como copos de ciegos *pepeyocales,*[9] árboles que brillan, en un juego que los confundía con las nubes del humo.

Allá abajo todo es silencio; el silencio tiene las voces del pensamiento y sin querer nos habla, nos habla con su voz suave. Y cuando nos agitamos nos regaña con su voz de trueno. Dicen que por allí mismo transitaron desde tiempos idos los nahuas[10] y los tepehuas,[11] buscando entre el sol y las sombras el rumbo de sus ranchos y comunidades.

Enredado en una nube de sueños se ausentó mi hermano Ijuantsij, dejando tras de sí el olor de su incensario, una nube que fluía de sus manos. Al irse dijo:

—Nos encontraremos el próximo sueño en nuestro rancho Kalkaual.[12]

Yo seguí soñando desde lo alto de la ladera, desde Temikiloyan, el lugar donde algún sueño verdadero te puede apresar. Fue entonces cuando se presentó, entre una confusión de pájaros y una escandalera de avispas, jicotes[13] y venados, un niño de ropaje verde azuloso y cabellos de sol.

Me preguntó por mi hermano Ijuantsij, el Rugoso, el Sabio, el Incensador:

—¿Y tu hermano el Rugoso, el que con el humo de su incienso acalora a los dioses Auakej,[14] los Dueños del agua, y a los Tepechanejkej,[15] los habitantes de los cerros, por qué no siguió soñando al ver este paisaje por dónde pasaron nahuas y tepehuas? ¿Por qué no continuó elaborando nubes, nubes de incienso?

Entre los árboles de encino, entre tullidos jalamantes,[16] entre los árboles llamados *petko*,[17] que con sus flores violáceas parecen brindar con el cielo, en su propia fiesta, le dije al niño, cuya imagen se vislumbraba a través de los árboles:

—Mi hermano dijo que nos veríamos en nuestro próximo sueño, allá en nuestro rancho Kalkaual.

El humo del incienso dejado por Ijuantsij todavía inundaba la ladera y todo el Temikiloyan, y traía al momento los recuerdos de las ceremonias grandiosas y el melancólico sonido de los sones de costumbre.[18]

—Es que él me va a acompañar en mi muerte—dijo el niño—; él va a ordenar los sones de muerto[19] y llevará entonces más lágrimas su canto; él llorará cantando para mí, para que de esa manera me vaya derechito y sin perderme. Sólo Ijuantsij me podrá guiar . . . ¿No ves que ahora estoy más enfermo que nunca y sólo mi padre Ijuantsij el Rugoso, el Sabio, el Incensador, y también tú, fandanguero,[20] tú que eres mi tío, podrán darme la señal del camino rumbo a los Auakej, rumbo a los Tepechanejkej, rumbo a los relámpagos de espejo y rumbo a los truenos de espejo? . . . Ese es un camino duro y de difícil paso y ustedes amarrarán mis pies a ese camino de la muerte, y entonces veremos si no he de llegar . . . a cualquier camino se llega con música y con llanto . . . entonces veremos si no . . .

—Pero ¿quién eres tú, niño, que tan divino me pareces? ¿Tú quién eres que tus palabras brotan de una barranca que se me antoja rugosa como mi hermano Ijuantsij? ¿Tú quién eres que hasta conoces al Rugoso, el que con el humo de su incienso acalora a los dioses Auakej, y éstos, de puro gusto, empiezan a bañarse, y esa agua divina cae sobre nuestra madre tierra y entonces hay sustento para nosotros los humanos? . . . ¿Quién eres tú que hasta me llamas tío? ¿Acaso Ijuantsij con su voz de barranca vieja te trajo a este mundo con sus palabras?

El niño[21] rió, tomó una hormiga y le apretó la cintura y le dijo:

—¡Así serás para siempre!

Tomó un jicote y le pintó rayas amarillas en su espalda y le dijo:

—Así serás.

Tomó un pez del agua y le puso espinas en sus aletas y le dijo:

—Así serás . . .

Miró con gran ternura al venado y le acarició la corona de su cornamenta:

—Así serás . . .

Habló con el tordo y bailó sobre una multitud de tortugas.

—¿Esto acaso no te dice nada, *fandanguero?* ¿Acaso esto no te carga de luz los ojos?

Después me habló del lagarto, a quien quitó la luz de su lengua, y de la Tsitsimitenantsij,[22] la anciana despellejada que el niño metió en el temascal[23] para lograr que los hombres vivieran . . .

Entonces le dije:

—Ah, sin duda tú has de ser el niño Chikomexóchitl,[24] el Siete-Flor; Chikomexóchitl padre eres tú, niño divino, tú, el grandioso Siete-Flor . . . tú eres mi padre, mi sustento. Tú eres mi padre.

—Exacto, yo soy Chikomexóchitl, el que fue grandioso, el que le dio manutención a los hombres, pero ahora soy niño . . . y no puedo ser padre de nadie. ¿No ves que me devoró el Templo? ¿No ves que me abandonaron a fuerza de un tiempo malo en palabras? ¿No ves que sólo tu hermano Ijuantsij me recuerda y sólo su humo acalora a los dioses Auakej y a los Tepechanejkej? . . . Pero el humo de él también se acabará: él ya es un Rugoso, él morirá y yo moriré. No podré seguir sin el incienso. Sin esa nube que de su mano brota no podré seguir viviendo; sin la presencia de quienes saben nombrarnos con sus discursos floridos y profundos, como esta ladera hasta donde yo, el Siete-Flor, estoy soñando. No podré seguir sin los que saben ejecutar los bailes floridos, no sabré qué hacer más que morir; sin la música florida no podré seguir . . . Aquí en Temikiloyan, hasta que yo esté soñando; es que aquí sueñan los que saben ver, los que saben vencer a la distancia más oscura y temerosa; aquí se sueñan los sueños, aquí no se sueñan las inseguridades o los falsos deseos, aquí se sueñan los sueños. Sueños solamente . . . por eso tu hermano, el Rugoso, es mi padre y tú, *fandanguero,* eres mi tío. Tú con el son de tu instrumento acompañarás al muerto. El Rugoso deshebrará la palma de coyo,[25] macerará la flor *ixuakentsij,*[26] recogerá la flor pericón,[27] cortará con machete la hoja del naranjo, hará los collares floridos, los abanicos floridos y hablará hasta secar su garganta. Hablará cuatro días y cinco noches y seguirá hablando hasta completar doce días, doce largos días, porque yo, Chikomexóchitl, el Siete-Flor, estoy enfermo de tiempo, de olvido, de opresión, de burla y desprecio. Yo, como padre que fui, estoy pagando y respondiendo con mi muerte. Mírame, estoy muriendo, yo, el padre de las costumbres más grandiosas, el sustento del sueño, estoy muriendo . . .

Este niño con aspecto divino verdaderamente estaba muriendo, sólo esperaba las palabras finales de mi hermano Ijuantsij el Rugoso, el Sabio, el Incensador, que a punto está también de morir; pero si pensamos en el Rugoso, pues ese ya paseó su pie por mucha distancia, su vista ya creció en medio de tanta sombra, en medio de tanto sol, entre tanto camino, pero no ha soñado lo suficiente, y no puede llegar hasta la otra orilla.

Allá abajo vuela el niño Siete-Flor. Él me duele y me preocupa, me acongoja y hace también que las lágrimas de Ijuantsij asomen en sus palabras. Vuela como pájaro y camina como humano y se eleva como los sueños que aquí afloran para dar lugar a la vida. Vuela el niño Chikomexóchitl, va y viene por la ladera de San Miguel y apunta su destino al cerro Postektitla,[28] sitio donde los Auakej se paran para mandar la lluvia y donde los Tepechanejkej también tienen morada. Jugueteando en el aire me grita el niño:

—Para allá voy, *fandanguero;* no quiero que dejes de soñarme y que digas que estoy muerto. Regresaré a verte.

El cerro Postektitla es un abuelo grande, queda a la izquierda de la ladera San Miguel, a la izquierda de Temikiloyan, el lugar donde ningún sueño se puede repetir. La distancia gris es el rostro del abuelo Postektitla y como punta de palo sembrador empuja a las nubes. Por la tarde su puño se cansa y las nubes bajan a cobijarlo y a formar su copete blanco. Para allá va el niño Chikomexóchitl volando; su pelambre parece una nube que ondula en la cara del abuelo. Ahí también bebe fuerza el niño y su alimento es el incienso de mi hermano el Rugoso.

Al poco rato retornó el niño a la ladera, aquí, a Temikiloyan; al lugar donde un sueño jamás se abandona; donde los sueños nos diferencian los días y el rostro. Vino el niño nuevamente enfermo, ahora más enfermo que nunca, quién sabe qué estará pasando con las milpas de verano.

Se aproxima a mí y me pide que lo ayude a incorporarse; su risa blanca parece menos risa, menos infantil; más de muerte parece. Lo tomo de sus manos tiernas, un poco ásperas, para que levante su cuerpo. Me mira agradecido y me pregunta por Ijuantsij, el Rugoso.

En tanto, una lluviecita menuda visita Temikiloyan. Los pájaros se esconden entre las ramas tupidas de los árboles; después sopla un poco de viento.

Me dice el niño:

—Me siento morir, pero el Rugoso no llega.

Para consolarlo un poco y también para animarme en este camino de los sueños le miento, lo engaño. Le digo que él no morirá jamás, que él no es mortal, que no se atará su pie al camino de la muerte, aunque mi hermano el Rugoso, el Sabio, el Incensador, el incorregible constructor de nubes se prenda al camino de la muerte. Año con año, le confieso, a través de los cuatro elementos te llaman a ti, grandioso, para que sigas alimentándonos y dándonos vida, para que sigas dándole vida a la tierra, a todos los hombres hechos de tu misma materia tierna, blanda y dura,[29] blanca, morada, roja y amarilla, como si brotaras de la tierra en forma de elote, de maíz hermoso para alimentar esperanzas, deseos o destinos:

—Año con año—le digo al niño—hacen tu ceremonia con la milpa de verano que en tu honor se siembra, y ahí, vestido con tus flores y tu paliacate, luces bien al lado de la que podría ser tu novia, la Elosiuapiltsij,[30] ésa que en forma de mujer colocan a tu lado en el altar. Otros dicen que esa niña es tu hermana. Yo sé que a esa niña que lleva hasta rebozo se le forma con dos elotes mancornados, en pareja; que se le viste como a humano. Es tu otra presencia, la presencia femenina de Chikomexóchitl.

El niño ríe y me abraza como si abrazara a un padre responsable y fuerte; siento entonces la aspereza de su ropaje verde azuloso, sus cabellos fríos y dulces y ese olor vegetal que le viene de las venas. Se atreve entonces a decirme en su armoniosa lengua:

—*Fandanguero,* tío, ¿entonces yo no soy mortal? ¿No soy un perecedero?

Alegremente juguetea el niño con la tierra negra de la ladera y rueda piedrecitas al abismo, que van haciendo minúsculas piruetas a su paso, hasta tocar fondo. Yo lo veo, lo contemplo, sé que juega con sus propios temores de Dios a punto de ser derribado, devorado por el Templo. Sé que lo he engañado. Ahora él juega, pero yo estoy triste, preocupado.

Lloro con el único ojo que me queda de mi raza antigua; lloro por el niño, por el grandioso, como por una tarde cálida que se va. Lloro con mi ojo antiguo mis lágrimas recientes. Pienso que en el rancho, allá en Kalkaual, también él llora con sus dos ojos de incensador sus lágrimas lejanas y desconocidas.

—Una lágrima es una distancia distinta cada día. Cada día tiene un nuevo rostro y un nuevo rastro . . .

Pienso en las palabras del Rugoso: "Una lágrima es el baño de nuestros interiores Auakej por el calor que les produce el incienso de la vida . . . ellas vienen a regar nuestra milpa de verano."

En tanto yo recuerdo al Rugoso, el niño sigue jugando alegre con la tierra y rodando piedrecitas al abismo. Al momento en que la última piedrecita rodada por el niño toca el fondo de la ladera, aquí en Temikiloyan lloro con mi otro ojo, ése que me vino del cerro Postektitla en manos y en palabras de mi hermano Ijuantsij; entonces el llanto sí ya es íntegro y único. El niño me ve llorar y se entristece, me reprocha:

—Cada quien tendrá que sembrar su milpa de verano ¿verdad?; tú tendrás que sembrar la tuya, también el Rugoso. Todos tendrán que sembrar su milpa de verano. Entonces, ¿por qué lloras completamente, *fandanguero,* si tú serás el que le ponga música a mi muerte, a mis pies, el sonido de los dioses, y a mi cuerpo el canto con lágrimas? ¿Acaso tú también te irás con nosotros y quisieras aún seguir soñando, soñando los sueños verdaderos? ¿Querrás aún seguir soñando verdaderamente los sueños? Tú tienes dos ojos distintos, pero ya tus lágrimas son enteramente iguales.

Lloro nuevamente. Cada lágrima es un sueño que se me escapa y que huye de la misma manera en que las piedrecillas ruedan por el abismo o de la misma manera en que el niño vuela al cerro Postektitla, pero ahora quiero ponerme de pie y también quiero gritar—o ladrar como un perro—pero algo grave pasa, no puedo ponerme de pie y quiero, más que nunca, parar este asunto de la muerte. He dejado de llorar completamente, deseo ponerme de pie; el niño ríe, se anuncia en su sonrisa un despido y un encuentro, imposible volver a encontrarnos parece decir en su risita:

—Me voy, *fandanguero,* hoy que he sabido que tú conoces las buenas intenciones de los hombres y que año con año me llaman a través de los cuatro elementos para que los siga alimentando. Me voy, el Rugoso me llamará, él sabrá cuándo; seguiré viviendo hoy que he creído en tus palabras y he visto tus lágrimas enteramente iguales una y otra. Ahora conozco tus dos ojos; uno del Postektitla y otro de la raza antigua.

Un eco profundo salió del Postektitla; un rugir de agua vino de la cañada. Pájaros e insectos mancharon el cielo volando detrás de un niño que engañado huía pensando que seguiría viviendo; que habría más humo de incienso, aunque mi hermano el Rugoso muriera. El niño se fue, tal vez para siempre. ¿Cuándo mis ojos volverán a verlo? Quise entonces ponerme de pie al verlo partir feliz, exhibiendo su risa blanca y fresca, pero no pude, imposible era incorporarme y hacer que mis piernas caminaran. No pude pararme y no quise dejar ir al niño Chikomexóchitl, el Siete-Flor, sin que supiera la verdad, la terrible verdad humana, le grité desde mi agonía:

—Chikomexóchitl, Chikomexóchitl, sobrino mío, sobrino, Chikomexóchitl, regresa, regresa.

No quería que se fuera engañado. Al ver que seguía su camino echando al viento sus cabellos de sol, volví a gritarle. Nuevamente grité:

—Chikomexóchitl, Chikomexóchitl, regresa.

El niño seguía perdiéndose en la distancia. El ruido de su carrera infantil ya casi no se escuchaba. Pensé entonces en nombrarlo como se le ha nombrado en otros lugares y como le oí a Ijuantsij:

—Chikomexóchitl, Sintektli, Pilsintektli, Sinteopiltsij,[31] regresa, ven a ayudarme a incorporarme; dame tu mano tierna, verde azulosa, ayúdame . . .

No pude incorporarme y quedé tirado en la tierra como un fruto que en racimo crece; como racimo de fruto más amargo de la tierra; como algo que ya nadie quiere y que todos evitan. El niño no retrocedía y mi temor de quedarme ahí tirado en el suelo negro y húmedo era cada vez más grande. Entonces, cuando la noche llegaba confundiéndose con la tierra donde el Siete-Flor jugaba, decidí nombrarlo de nueva cuenta, ya no como un padre que quiso ser responsable y fuerte, ni como su tío, ni siquiera como el *fandanguero* que dentro de mí dormita, sino como lo que verdaderamente soy: un hijo débil y desamparado, como un humano soñador, visitante asiduo de Temikiloyan, que desde la ladera San Miguel ve al mundo como quiere que sea; como aquel que constantemente se asoma al abismo a soñar los sueños verdaderos. Le grité:

—Paaaadreeeee, padre . . . Chikomexóchitl Padre, no me dejes tirado en esta noche negra y dura; levántame, llena mi cabeza de ánimos, esfuérzate porque yo no muera.

El viento soplaba fuertemente como preparándome una verdad. Llovía de manera extraña; la ladera San Miguel, ubicada en el sitio de los sueños, en Temikiloyan, parecía escurrirse en su propia humedad y deslavarse. Llovía, sí. Pero en mi corazón no escurría la lluvia de la esperanza, sino la pesadez de la vida. Así tirado, sin ningún aliento, no era yo otro, sino aquel que también debería atar sus pies al camino de la muerte, rumbo a los Auakej, ese camino duro y difícil, según el niño, aunque dura y difícil será la muerte sólo para los dioses, porque sólo la muerte es inmortal y si llegamos a ella y nos metemos en su vientre seremos inmortales.

Después de la lluvia y el viento vino el día con sus ojos de fuego a despertarme, a darle luz a mis ojos. Estaba yo de pie, bien incorporado, firmemente aferrado a la tierra y mirando el horizonte en la superficie del cerro Piltepepa.[32] Entonces, allá a lo lejos, por el arroyo Akuekueyoch,[33] rumbo a los cedros viejos, vi el resplandor de una melena de sol que señalaba la aurora: era la cabeza de mi padre Chikomexóchitl que corría ondulando su ropaje verde azuloso. Ya no volaba como pájaro, sino que corría como llevado por el viento; iba en dirección al camino de los dioses Auakej, al sitio donde están tirados los Teskatlapetlanij,[34] relámpagos de espejo, y los Teskatlatomonianij,[35] truenos de espejo. Para allá iba el pie de mi padre, para allá apuntaba su prisa; iba haciendo la danza que a mí me correspondía musicalizar. Me dije entonces "debo llamar a mi hermano el Rugoso; estoy ya en nuestro rancho Kalkaual; aquí nos veríamos en nuestro próximo sueño."

Desde lo alto volví la vista al rancho: los techos de zacate y mi vista hicieron un compromiso. En medio de una actividad desbordante de blusas y enaguas, de sombreros y ropaje blanco, entre el humo vital de cada casa, entre una conversación sin fin de mujeres y ruidos de metates,[36] se iniciaba la roza, los terrenos paulatinamente iban perdiendo sus montes, todo se inclinaba al paso del machete y las mujeres traían el *axókotl*,[37] bebida para la roza, y los hombres bebían en los huacalitos.[38] Después la quema del terreno y el humo de la milpa soñada, la milpa de verano, el humo anterior a todo maíz cubrió por completo el rancho; después se bendijo la semilla en cada casa, en cada altar, para luego sembrarla entre gritos alentadores. Los hombres entregaron la semilla a la tierra y tomaron en su descanso el atole[39] de ciruela tierna, comieron los bocoles[40] y tomaron de los bultitos de hoja de papatla,[41] el chiltepín[42] asado. Otros comían caldo de res.

Rápidamente vino el tiempo bueno. Las lluvias llegaron y el viento mecía las pequeñas matas que minúsculas le sacaban la lengua a los tordos; se hizo entonces el corte de la leña y la construcción de las "tareas."[43] Vino la resiembra.

Nuevamente llegaron las lluvias, el viento inclinaba cariñosamente los tallos de las matas; se inició la temporada de limpiar la siembra y observar los tallos con sus doce buenas raicitas fortalecidas por la lluvia, por la neblina, por el rocío, por el sol. Todo esto lo mandaron los dioses Auakej que erguidos en la punta de los cerros también se acaloraron con el humo del incienso de mi hermano Ijuantsij y se bañaron y cayó la lluvia a la tierra.

De pie aquí en el cerro Piltepepa vi crecer esta milpa de verano y me acordé nuevamente de mi hermano el Rugoso. Cuando los elotes ya se anunciaban buenos, abriendo las matas sus espigas al sol, cuando la milpa era solamente una cabellera blanquecina que como una cobija gigante cubría el maizal y no dejaba ver el ropaje verde azuloso y áspero, volví a gritarle a mi padre Chikomexóchitl entre el llanto y la desesperación.

—Padre, padre, no me abandones, que todavía te veo correr y sé que me estás escuchando, regresa, no me abandones. Veo desde aquí todavía la aurora de tu cabello.

El pueblo se inquietó; la voz de la desesperación nubló a Kalkaual. Los hombres, las mujeres cuyos rostros son los mismos todavía, los ancianos y los niños, se acercaron a mí, vinieron hasta la punta del cerro Piltepepa a dejar sus ojos y todos me dijeron que ya no estuviera triste, que me consolara, que ya era de día y que estaba de pie como lo había pedido, que ya no yacía tirado como un racimo amargo; que un niño, que había venido volando como pájaro, me había depositado aquí en el Piltepepa y me había encomendado vigilar los trabajos que requiere el maíz para su existencia, porque el niño había anunciado su partida, su viaje a los caminos de los dioses Auakej de donde no retornaría jamás. Que ahora y siempre todos tendrán que sembrar sus milpas de verano.

—¿Y mi hermano el Rugoso? ¿Dónde ha puesto sus pies el divino?, ¿hacia qué cañada dirige su vista el incansable?

—Tu hermano ha muerto—me dijo una de las mujeres—, ha muerto completamente y con esa muerte ha atado sin música ni flores la muerte del niño Chikomexóchitl. Ahora han muerto los dos.

Uno de los presentes agregó.

—Han muerto los dos, el Rugoso, el Sabio Ijuantsij Kokajsintla,[44] el depositario del conocimiento y el maravilloso niño Chikomexóchitl o el Elookichpiltsij,[45] que es nuestra representación del elote-maíz-padre. Han muerto los dos para siempre, han atado a sus pies al camino de la muerte y de ahí no se soltarán jamás. Siempre con la muerte vivirán solamente.

Uno de los jóvenes intervino:

—Tu hermano el Rugoso ya sembró su milpa de verano con su cuerpo. Al velarlo no hubo ni siquiera música, no hubo sones de muerto, ni a los siete días tuvo su ceremonia; sólo vino el catequista a rezarle en latín y a cantarle sus alabanzas; así que tu hermano el Rugoso ya aplacó su humo y fue cristianamente sepultado hace exactamente doce días, doce días durante los cuales tú, *fandanguero,* has estado durmiendo entre temblores y escalofríos causados por la fiebre de los sueños.

Un anciano llegó y me saludó; su mirada me recordaba a mi hermano Ijuantsij; éste me dijo:

—Tú, hermano *fandanguero,* has estado entre la desesperación y el llanto de los sueños durante doce días, los doce días posteriores a la muerte de tu hermano Ijuantsij Kokajtsintla. Te has acordado de María Agustina Tlalkuapa, muerta ha tres años; de Juan Antonio Lino, que vive en El Limón, pero antes de nombrarlos a ellos, hablaste de Pedro Simón, de Tomás Ramírez Tekamaxochiko, de Martín Santiago Kolatla, de Leonardo Poóchotl; mas a tu hermano Ijuantsij Kokajtsintla todo el tiempo lo estuviste nombrando, recordaste sus conocimientos buenos y profundos. De él hablaste tal y como si estuviera presente en tu momento, en tu circunstancia. Ahora ven, hermano, el sacerdote de Chikón[46] bendecirá las espigas de nuestra milpa de verano, porque hoy ya no hacemos la ceremonia Chikomexóchitl-elotlamanalistli[47] que era dedicada a los elotes; hoy el templo nos ha impuesto la bendición de espiga. El niño, pues, murió; todo nos lo trozaron. Todos traían en sus manos las espigas de su milpa de verano, ya el templo los llamaba con sus campanas penetrantes y todos seguían esa voz de metal que como fruto frío cuelga de las vigas del templo. Todo nos lo trozaron. El niño murió hace años. Esas palabras resuenan en mi cabeza que no olvidan, que no quiere perder . . .

El catequista se me acercó y me dijo:

—Sí, hermano, dice el templo que eso fue inventado por el demonio; que es mentira que el maíz, cuando es elote, sea un niño; porque es mentira que un niño pueda ser un dios; que el niño ése a quien le hacíamos la ceremonia jamás existió, la Biblia no habla de él. Eso es un invento del diablo.

Esa noche me negué a asistir a la ceremonia que suplantó y mató al niño, a la que hoy nombran Bendición de espigas, en la que los otros sabios e incensadores de Kalkaual permanecen mudos y asombrados. Preferí indagar sobre la posible existencia de Temikiloyan: el lugar donde se puede soñar verdaderamente.

Días después, la sombra de Ijuantsij el Rugoso volvió a aparecer ante mí, el *fandanguero,* el buscador.

—Acerca tu rostro al sitio donde de niño jugó la tierra, *pinche fandanguero,* arremete como el viento embravecido contra la señal donde estuvo el pie de la distancia y encontrarás todos los sueños que has deseado; sin esta condición el llanto no saldrá de tu cuerpo para regresar en forma de alegría y de vida. Recuerda: no más de dos veces recorrerás Temikiloyan.

Por fin, partí de Kalkaual y caminé a Kuatlapechtla[48] y ahí, desde las plataformas vigías, desde las plataformas enormes, me puse a mirar una gran milpa de verano, reventando sus espigas con los brazos abiertos al sol, en una enloquecida mueca de satisfacción. Pensé: "Y ahora, ¿ésta qué quiere? ¿Por qué casi se ríe?" El son de costumbre me fue acercando a una casa donde un pequeño grupo de vecinos hacía la ceremonia del elote. Logré escuchar claramente el son que se toca al momento de recibir los elotes en la casa; esa música me empujó a ser nuevamente fandanguero. La jarana,[49] el violín y la guitarra huapanguera[50] lucían adornados con abanicos floridos y lloraban por el niño Siete-Flor. Entonces volví a ser fandanguero. Tomé mi instrumento y me introduje a la casa, al aposento del niño y toqué. Después todos cantaron:

—¿Dónde fuiste tú, flor?

—¿A dónde fuiste, mi pequeño hijo?

—No te aflijas, que aquí te asentarás, porque te buscaré hasta donde estés . . . Aunque con el son te vendrás acercando.

—El son está aquí. Tú ya estás aquí.

—Así te digo, así es correcto: no andes por donde quiera, no te hagas llorar, que aquí estoy yo.

—¡Ven hijo, ven hijo!

Volví a ser *fandanguero* en un intento por revitalizar y fortalecer la presencia—aunque sea en Kuatlapechtla—del niño Siete-Flor, pero mis deseos de encontrar el posible Temikiloyan persisten. Allí, donde se puede soñar verdaderamente.

Soñar es algo más que una flexible sonrisita al viento: algo más que el simple deseo de ahorrarse las palabras y las dificultades; aquí es el paraíso donde los que saben ver pueden saber y poder, logran ver las cosas de la distancia, su modo y su medio.

Ijuantsij, el Rugoso, el que con el humo de su incienso enloquecía a los dioses y los acaloraba, todo esto sabía.

Temikiloyan es el lugar de la posibilidad mejor deseada.

Una risita infantil acosa desde entonces los tapancos[51] y las conciencias . . . Todos tendrán que sembrar ahora su milpa de verano . . . la milpa soñada.

Notas

1. El náhuatl es la lengua indígena con mayor número de hablantes. A finales del siglo XX contaba con una población de más de 2,563,000 individuos distribuidos en los estados de Puebla, Veracruz, Hidalgo, Guerrero, San Luis Potosí, Tlaxcala, Morelos y México y el Distrito Federal. Véase también nota 1 al texto en náhuatl.

2. Forma náhuatl de "Juan."

3. Del náhuatl *tlapopoca*, "humear," en referencia a sus funciones de incensador o portador del incienso en las ceremonias.

4. De *tlamati*, "inteligente," "diestro." En algunas zonas nahuas se le llama *tlamatqui* a los curanderos o brujos.

5. Acción de limpiar las tierras de las matas y hierbas inútiles antes de labrarlas, bien para que retoñen las plantas o bien para otros fines.

6. Literalmente "lugar del sueño," de *temictli*, "sueño."

7. "De la Huasteca." Comarca muy extensa y variada de la Sierra Madre Oriental en Tamaulipas, San Luis Potosí, Veracruz, Hidalgo y Puebla. En este relato el autor se refiere a la Huasteca veracruzana. Del náhuatl *huaxteca*, habitante de Huaxtla, lugar donde abundan los *huaxin*, "guajes" o "calabazas" (*Lagenaria siceraria*).

8. Río ubicado en el municipio de Zontecomatlán, Veracruz, en la Huasteca meridional.

9. *Populus arizonica*, variedad de álamo llamado "cimarrón"; sus hojas blancas se confunden o brillan con el humo.

10. En las comarcas de las Huastecas viven varios grupos étnicos. Aquí se refiere a los grupos nahuas asentados fundamentalmente en el norte de Veracruz e Hidalgo. A finales del siglo XX los nahuas eran el grupo indígena más numeroso, con una población de 2,563,000 habitantes distribuida entre los estados de Puebla, Veracruz, Hidalgo, Guerrero, San Luis Potosí, Tlaxcala, Morelos y México y el Distrito Federal.

11. A finales del siglo XX la población tepehua era de 17,000 habitantes.

12. El nombre de este rancho significa en náhuatl "donde ya no vivimos"; es decir, "deshabitado."

13. Del náhuatl *xicotli*, una variedad de avispa.

14. Literalmente "Los Dueños del agua." (Véase Apéndice E.)

15. Literalmente, "los *chaneques* del cerro," seres mágicos de pequeña estatura que habitan y cuidan lo cerros; la creencia en estos seres del mundo invisible se extiende por amplias regiones del centro, sur y sureste de México. (Véase Apéndice E.)

16. *Ficus padifolia:* árbol grande de jugo lechoso y fruto comestible. Es más usual llamarlo *jalamate*.

17. *Nissa sylvatica:* árbol de la familia de las Nisáceas que llegan a tener alturas de 35 metros con flores y frutos azulados. *Petko* deriva del zoque *petcui*.

18. Música ritual que sólo se toca en ceremonias religiosas tradicionales.

19. Música ritual que sólo se toca en ceremonias fúnebres, para ayudar al alma a que se retire y no se pierda.

20. Se le llama así, en la Huasteca, a los que saben tañer diversos instrumentos de cuerda para sones populares y para sones de costumbre. En España, *fandanguero* es el que sabe tocar y cantar *fandangos*, composiciones musicales animadas al compás de tres por cuatro, originarios de Andalucía.

21. Las anécdotas que a continuación señala el relato forman parte de diversas atribuciones de una deidad infantil que se confunde con la deidad solar y que se extiende en amplias zonas de Mesoamérica. (Véase Apéndice F.)

22. Literalmente "Madre de las Tsitsimi," divinidades nocivas prehispánicas. Según el autor se refiere a la abuela de Chikomexóchitl, una anciana despellejada que por su maldad intrínseca intenta constantemente matar a su nieto. Es considerada la fuente de todos los animales venenosos, incluyendo el alacrán, la serpiente y la avispa.

23. Del náhuatl *temazcalli*, "casa de bañarse" (por tratarse de una pequeña construcción hecha de piedra). Baño de vapor prehispánico todavía utilizado con propósitos rituales y medicinales.

24. Literalmente, "siete" (*chicome*) "flores" (*xóchitl*). En este relato el personaje simboliza al niño sagrado que se convierte sucesivamente en maíz, en el sol y en el sustentador de la vida. (Véase también nota 31.)

25. *Acrocomia mexicana;* según otros autores *Acrocomia vinifera*. Se le llama *coyo* o *coyol* (del náhuatl *coyoli*, "cascabel") por la forma del fruto y porque se convierte en cascabel al sacudirse el fruto seco.

26. Del tenek *ichbequen;* una pequeña flor que se emplea en una variedad de ceremonias, conocida en español como "manzanita" o "mazapán." Corresponde al *Malvaviscus grandiflorus* y al *Malvaviscus arboreus*.

27. *Tagetes florida:* planta herbácea de un metro de altura, de hojas elípticas y aserradas, con flores de marcado olor a anís. Es común en el Valle de México, Hidalgo, Zacatecas, Durango y algunas regiones del sureste de México.

28. Una de las montañas más elevadas de la Huasteca que desde tiempos inmemoriales sirve como centro de ceremonias sagradas relacionadas con el agua, la agricultura y la vida comunitaria.

29. Se refiere a la tradición mesoamericana de que el hombre fue creado a partir del maíz; los colores corresponden a los diferentes tipos de este cereal: blanco, amarillo, rojo y morado.

30. Literalmente, "la mujer del elote tierno."

31. Sintektli, "Señor de la Mazorca"; Pilsintektli, "Tierno Señor"; Sinteopiltsij, "Tierno Dios de la Mazorca." Con estos nombres el narrador revela más ampliamente la naturaleza sagrada de Chikomexóchitl como entidad del maíz.

32. Ubicado en Alahualtitla, municipio de Chicontepec, Veracruz; lugar sagrado donde se efectúan ceremonias de maíz, agua y la curación de niños.

33. Literalmente, "agua con huevecillos de sapo."

34. Literalmente, "Espejo Brillante," nombre ceremonial de los relámpagos.

35. Literalmente, "Espejo de Trueno," nombre ceremonial de los truenos.

36. Forma plural castellanizada del náhuatl *metatl;* piedra plana y horizontal sobre la cual se muele el maíz.

37. Del náhuatl *axococ,* "agua agria"; de *texócotl,* "tejocote": *Crataegus mexicana* o *Crataegus parryana,* arbusto o árbol espinoso que produce un fruto globoso, con pulpa espesa aromática, dulce o ácida, amarilla y comestible.

38. Del náhuatl *huacalli,* caja o jaula formada con tiras de madera, separadas para transportar mercancías.

39. Del náhuatl *atolli,* "aguado" o "agüita," bebida espesa preparada a base de masa o de harina de maíz disuelta en agua y hervida. En este caso, con ciruela tierna.

40. Nombre genérico de un alimento típico de la Huasteca hecho a base de maíz, sal, chile y manteca de origen animal, particularmente de cerdo, en forma de un pan redondo y grueso.

41. *Heliconia schiedeana:* planta herbácea de un metro y medio, con aspecto de platanillo, con hojas ovales y agudas que se emplean para envolver alimentos.

42. *Capsicum frutesceus:* planta arbustiva que produce un fruto en extremo picante.

43. Medida de volumen de leña de una brazada de largo, otra de ancho y otra más de diagonal.

44. Literalmente, "Abundante en Mazorcas."

45. Literalmente, "Pequeño Varón Mazorca."

46. Chicón: apócope de Chicontepec, del náhuatl Chicometepetl, "Siete Cerros."

47. Literalmente, "El que extiende las mazorcas en la mesa," otro nombre de Chikomexóchitl.

48. Literalmente, "lugar de muchas tarimas"; en referencia a las plataformas erigidas en las milpas desde las cuales un guardián cuida que las cosechas no sean destruidas por las aves. Con este término, el autor sugiere un lugar de milpas abundantes o muy grandes.

49. Guitarra pequeña de cinco cuerdas que acompaña el *huapango* y *son jarocho. Huapango* es una danza y música de baile tradicional de la región Huasteca del norte de Veracruz y los estados vecinos; se emplea también para la música de baile tradicional de las costas sureñas del Golfo de México que corresponden al *son jarocho. Huapango* viene del náhuatl *huapalli.*

50. Guitarra de ocho cuerdas empleada principalmente en la región Huasteca para interpretar el *huapango;* por su tonalidad aguda se le llama también "guitarra quinta."

51. Del náhuatl *tlapanco,* "en la azotea." Tablas horizontales con que se divide una habitación en dos niveles para formar un desván o ático.

Appendices

The information contained in these appendices is primarily extracted from two works by Carlos Montemayor: *Arte y trama en el cuento indígena* (Mexico City: FCE, 1998) and *Arte y plegaria en las lenguas indígenas de México* (Mexico City: FCE, 1999).

Appendix A

The *Jmeno'ob,* Traditional Mayan Priests

Traditional literary forms found in Mexican Indigenous languages correspond to a worldview that Western culture has long forgotten: that the world is a living being. It is for this reason that some traditional prayers contain an interpretation of natural and community life whose origins may lie in pre-Hispanic times. One unique example is the prayers sung by Mayan priests during the agricultural ceremonies of the Yucatán Peninsula. These ceremonies are generally differentiated by function: Lol Corral is a blessing for a parcel of land or an animal pen; Wajil Kool is a farmers' offering of cornmeal cakes to the "invisible entities" in appreciation for a harvest or blessings received; Ch'a' Cháak is the rain-petitioning ceremony; and Jedz Lu'um is performed when one desires to initiate new chores on a plot of land. These prayers contain no moral references and do not seek to transmit doctrine. Nor are they necessarily understood by those in attendance. They are in effect formal, sacred instruments, directed exclusively toward spiritual entities. Their effectiveness depends upon those entities' attitudes and the wisdom of the officiant.

The altars used in these agricultural ceremonies reinforce the notion of the horizon as the foundation of the sky and of the four cardinal directions as the placement of the deities that watch over the entire world. Depending on the ceremony, the content of the offerings may be different foods; those prepared with corn, however, are fundamental. In the story by Miguel May May, for example, there are references to offerings given in the rain-petitioning ceremony, Ch'a' Cháak.

Apéndices

La información de estos apéndices proviene fundamentalmente de dos obras de Carlos Montemayor: *Arte y trama en el cuento indígena* (México, D.F.: FCE, 1998) y *Arte y plegaria en las lenguas indígenas de México* (México, D.F.: FCE, 1999).

Apéndice A

Los *Jmeno'ob,* sacerdotes mayas tradicionales

Las formas literarias tradicionales en las lenguas indígenas de México se corresponden con una concepción del universo que la cultura occidental ya ha olvidado: que el mundo es un ser viviente. Algunos rezos tradicionales contienen por ello una explicación de la vida natural y comunitaria que acaso proviene de los tiempos prehispánicos. El rezo del sacerdote maya durante las ceremonias agrícolas en la península de Yucatán es un ejemplo singular. Las ceremonias agrícolas en esta región se distinguen habitualmente por la función que desempeñan: son de Lol Corral cuando se procura la bendición de una parcela o de un corral; de Wajil Kool cuando los campesinos ofrendan panes de maíz a las entidades invisibles como agradecimiento por las cosechas o dádivas recibidas; de Ch'a' Cháak cuando fundamentalmente se trata de una petición de lluvias, o de Jedz Lu'um cuando se desea iniciar nuevas tareas en un terreno. Estos rezos no contienen referencias morales ni buscan una transmisión doctrinal; no necesariamente son comprendidos por los concurrentes, pues se trata de instrumentos formales en sí mismos sagrados que sólo se dirigen a entidades espirituales; su efectividad depende de la actitud de esas entidades y de la sabiduría del oficiante.

Por otra parte, los altares de estas ceremonias agrícolas reproducen la concepción del horizonte como cimiento del cielo y los cuatro puntos cardinales como la distribución de las deidades que custodian el mundo entero. Las ofrendas pueden ser alimentos diversos, según la ceremonia, pero los que se preparan a base de maíz son fundamentales. En

While the Mayan word *payalchi'* may be translated as "prayer," the Mayan villages of Yucatán never confuse the prayers of Catholic priests with those used by Mayan priests when petitioning for rain, blessing a parcel of land, or giving thanks for a harvest. Catholic priests are now called *k'iin* or *yum k'iin,* whereas Mayan priests are referred to as *jmen* or *jmeno'ob.* The expression *k'iin* means "sun" or "day," and *aj k'iin* historically referred to an officiant in solar ceremonies; however, the expression *aj k'iin* (or *yum k'iin,* "respected elder priest") has now come to denote a Catholic priest only. When *aj k'iin* is used to refer to the Mayan officiant, the expression must be made specific by adding the words *maya* or *maya'obo',* for only in this manner does the term refer to a Mayan priest.

The word *jmen* is most commonly used to identify the Mayan priest. This title presupposes a knowledge of ceremonies, prayers, and healing techniques. It reflects a special spiritual state that surely derives from a permanent connection with traditional invisible entities; the latter are able to "choose" their priests, as we also observe in the story by Miguel May May. The word *men,* among other uses, reaffirms a state of knowledge or a possession of the skills needed for some occupation or discipline. When it is used without qualifiers (with the exception of the prefix *aj* or its reduced form *j*), *jmen* means "Mayan priest" in common speech. Etymologically, it means "the one who knows," "the one who is informed," or "the one who is skilled at something."

No contemporary Mayan can mistake the religious category to which the various prayers belong, even though some Catholic prayers are integrated into the *jmen*'s *payalchi'ob* to strengthen traditional prayers. *U payalchi'ob jmeno'ob,* "the *jmen*'s prayers," are as abundant and varied as the number of recognized officiants. The majority are sung or recited in a unique manner; this makes it difficult to separate the way in which they are sung from the nature of the prayers' words themselves. By virtue of their formal qualities and form of recitation, they possibly constitute the most ancient art form of the Mayan language.

el relato de Miguel May May, por ejemplo, se alude a las ofrendas de la ceremonia de petición de lluvia, Ch'a' Cháak.

Por otra parte, si bien la palabra maya *payalchi'* puede traducirse como "plegaria" o "rezo," los pueblos mayas de Yucatán no confunden la plegaria de los sacerdotes católicos con las que los sacerdotes mayas emplean para pedir la lluvia, santificar un predio o agradecer la cosecha. Al sacerdote católico se le llama ahora *k'iin* o *yum k'iin;* a los sacerdotes mayas se les llama *jmen* o *jmeno'ob.* La expresión *k'iin* significa "sol" o "día" y la forma *aj k'iin* se remonta históricamente a un sacerdote del culto solar; la expresión *aj k'iin* ha pasado ahora a denotar solamente al sacerdote católico cuando aparece así o en la forma *yum k'iin* (señor sacerdote). Cuando se le emplea para designar al oficiante maya la expresión *aj k'iin* debe precisarse posponiéndole las voces *maya* o *maya'obo';* de esta manera sólo *aj k'iin maya* equivale al sacerdote de los mayas, no al sacerdote católico.

La voz *jmen* es la más empleada para identificar al sacerdote maya y supone, además del conocimiento de ceremonias, rezos y técnicas curativas, una cierta condición espiritual que proviene seguramente de su contacto permanente con las entidades invisibles tradicionales. Estas ciertas entidades pueden, pues, "escoger" a sus sacerdotes, como también observamos en el relato de Miguel May May. La voz *men* tiene, entre otras funciones, la de reafirmar la condición de conocimiento o destreza en algún oficio o disciplina. Cuando se emplea sin ningún otro término que limite su sentido, salvo el prefijo *aj* o su reducción *j,* entonces *jmen* significa en el lenguaje popular "sacerdote maya." Etimológicamente es "el que sabe," "el que está enterado," "el que es diestro en algo."

Ningún maya contemporáneo puede equivocarse en el orden religioso al que pertenecen las diferentes plegarias, a pesar de que algunos rezos católicos se integran en los *payalchi'ob* del *jmen* como un refuerzo para las peticiones propiamente tradicionales. *U payalchi'ob jmeno'ob* son tan abundantes y tan variados como el número de oficiantes reconocidos. La mayoría se entonan o recitan de manera peculiar, por lo que es difícil distinguir entre la naturaleza de su entonación y la naturaleza de las palabras del rezo mismo. Por su composición y recitado, posiblemente sea la forma artística de la lengua maya más antigua.

Appendix B

Cháak, the Mayan God of Rain

There are many traditional stories regarding invisible entities in the Indigenous languages of Mexico. They serve to reaffirm, describe, and recollect a broad range of evil and good entities and specific information regarding their attributes and functions. These stories sometimes contain Christian or European motifs; however, the latter are always assigned a subordinate position vis-à-vis Indigenous entities, since the objective is precisely the survival of unique cultural data. An extraordinary example is that which María Luisa Góngora Pacheco presents in "U tzíimin Yum Cháak"[1] (The Horse of the Lord of the Rain). The God of Rain, Yum Cháak, requests a swift animal of the Supreme God, to help him transport his calabash of water. It is easy to imagine how, with the arrival of the conquistadors, the god Cháak came to see just how useful the horse was as a mode of transportation. It also was natural that a deity who traveled throughout so many heavenly places, handling his whip of lightning and thunder, might also wish to make use of it. At the first attempt, the god falls from his saddle due to the distance between the two cultures. He will fall repeatedly because he faces the "risk" any rider assumes. Junab K'uj, the One or Supreme God, rejects the animal on the basis that it is dirty and too large. Washing it and endowing it with wings are two relevant motifs in its "Mayanization."

In "A Story about Yum Tziles," Miguel May May presents four elderly gods on horseback distributed among the four cardinal directions. He also shows the calabashes as being indispensable for transporting rainwater. In "Ancient Rope Marks," Jorge Echeverría Lope mentions the calabash as the receptacle in which the character will carry the sacred water.

The word *tzíimin* translates as "horse," but it originally denoted a much smaller animal, the tapir. Because of a resemblance between the two, the Maya applied the word *tzíimin* to the horse. The celestial *tzíimin,* then, seems a return to the smaller size, due to the traditional weight of its name and the visual dimension of the stars. With respect to its wings, Yum Cháak's little horse is not related to the Greek Pegasus but rather to another Mayan icon: the winged, or plumed, serpent. At some point in its sacred transformation, the serpent sprouts wings to depart for its

Apéndice B

Cháak, Dios maya de la lluvia

Los cuentos tradicionales de entidades invisibles son abundantes en las lenguas indígenas de México. A través de ellos se reafirma, describe y recuerda una enorme gama de entidades malignas y benignas y una precisa información sobre sus atributos y funciones. Aunque a veces contienen motivos cristianos o europeos, siempre se les subordina a los motivos de las entidades indígenas, ya que se trata justamente de la supervivencia de una información cultural distinta. Un magnífico ejemplo es el que María Luisa Góngora Pacheco ofrece en "U tzíimin Yum Cháak"[1] (El caballo del Señor Lluvia). El dios de las lluvias, Yum Cháak, le pide al Dios Supremo un animal veloz que lo ayude a transportar su calabazo de agua. Es fácil entender que con la llegada de los españoles el dios Cháak tuvo tiempo de ver lo útil que resultaban los caballos como medio de transporte y para una deidad que debía recorrer tantos sitios celestes y manejar su látigo de rayos y truenos era natural que quisiera utilizarlo también. El dios cae de su montura en el primer intento porque señala una distancia entre las dos culturas y caerá sucesivamente porque es un "riesgo" de todo jinete. El mismo Junab K'uj o el Dios Único o Supremo desconocía el caballo, pues objeta que está sucio y demasiado grande. Lavarlo y dotarlo con alas son motivos relevantes para su mayización. En "Una narración sobre Yum Tziles," Miguel May May presenta a cuatro ancianos dioses a caballo distribuidos en los cuatro puntos cardinales. También señala a los calabazos como indispensables para transportar el agua de las lluvias. En "Vieja huella de soga," Jorge Echeverría Lope menciona el calabazo como el recipiente donde el personaje transportará el agua sagrada.

La palabra *tzíimin* significa, ciertamente, "caballo," pero en su origen denotó al tapir; por semejanza, los mayas aplicaron la palabra al caballo. El *tzíimin* celeste parece retornar a un tamaño más pequeño que el original por la inercia del nombre y por la dimensión visual de las estrellas. En cuanto a las alas, no se relaciona el caballito de Yum Cháak con el Pegaso griego, sino con otra imagen maya: la serpiente alada o emplumada. En algún momento de su transformación sagrada, a la serpiente le brotan alas para que parta hacia su último destino y encuentro con Junab K'uj. Andrés Tec Chi escribió varios relatos sobre esta serpiente

final destination and its encounter with Junab K'uj. Andrés Tec Chi wrote several stories about this serpent, the caretaker of waterholes or cenotes, known interestingly as "the maned serpent."

There are important similarities between these stories primarily because the serpent's metamorphosis seems to turn it into a horse and then endow it with wings for the task of watching over the underground waters. Information provided by the *jmeno'ob* tells us that the Cháako'ob gather water precisely from the openings in the waterholes (cenotes). Therefore, a horse and a serpent—or a horse that later possesses wings—are tied to Yum Cháak. Traditional stories regarding the creatures that accompany Yum Cháak would be incomplete if they did not transmit, explain, or recollect the motifs of the horse, the serpent, a winged being, and water in the form of rain as well as sacred deposits to which the god turns to spread throughout the world as rain.

cuidadora de fuentes y cenotes, llamada, curiosamente, "de crines."

Son importantes las semejanzas entre estas historias. Sobre todo porque la metamorfosis de la serpiente parece convertirla en caballo y luego le concede alas por la tarea de custodiar las aguas subterráneas. Por las informaciones de los *jmeno'ob* sabemos que los Cháako'ob recogen el agua justamente en las grietas de los cenotes. Por lo tanto, con Yum Cháak se relacionan un caballo y una serpiente o un caballo que después posee alas. Los cuentos tradicionales sobre las criaturas que acompañan a Yum Cháak estarían incompletos si no transmiten, explican o recuerdan los motivos del caballo, la serpiente, un ser alado y el agua tanto en forma de lluvia como de depósitos sagrados a los que acude el dios para repartirla como lluvia sobre el mundo.

Note

1. "U tzíimin Yum Cháak," in María Luisa Góngora Pacheco, *U tzikbalilo'ob Oxkutzcab yéetel Maní,* Colección Letras Mayas Contemporáneas, 1st series, vol. 3, C. Montemayor, series ed. (Mexico City: INI/TRF, 1994), pp. 43–46. The Spanish-language version is in María Luisa Góngora Pacheco, *Cuentos de Oxkutzcab y Maní,* Colección Letras Mayas Contemporáneas, 1st series, vol. 4, C. Montemayor, series ed. (Mexico City: INI/TRF, 1994), pp. 39–42.

Nota

1. "U tzíimin Yum Cháak," en María Luisa Góngora Pacheco, *U tzikbalilo'ob Oxkutzcab yéetel Maní,* Colección Letras Mayas Contemporáneas, 1a serie, vol. 3, C. Montemayor, coord. de la colección (México, D.F.: INI/TRF, 1994), pp. 43–46. La versión española aparece en María Luisa Góngora Pacheco, *Cuentos de Oxkutzcab y Maní,* Colección Letras Mayas Contemporáneas, 1a serie, vol. 4, C. Montemayor, coord. de la colección (México, D.F.: INI/TRF, 1994), pp. 39–42.

Appendix C

The Mayan *Alux*

Of all the invisible entities in the Mayan world, the *alux* (pronounced "aloosh") is the only creature created by humans from the important ceremonial elements of *saka'*,[1] honey, and blood. Santiago Domínguez Aké emphasizes that *jmeno'ob* are the possessors of knowledge, and it is they who must transmit that knowledge to farmers who wish to protect their fields with the help of an *alux:*

> The *alux* is made by soaking clay with honey, forming a little doll. With the same clay, one makes a slingshot and a dog. To bring the *alux* to life, the corn farmer must offer the *saka'* drink thirteen times. The offering must be made at the center of the field. There the *alux* is also placed beneath a rock. This activity is performed on successive Tuesdays and Fridays, until the required thirteen offerings have been made. Once the farmer lowers the *saka'* from the branches of the trees where he has hung it, he does not drink it, but buries it beneath the altar where the offering was made. He then rubs nine drops of his blood on the *alux*'s mouth and that of its dog only on Tuesdays and Fridays, so that they may effectively guard the produce of the field.
>
> Should a thief desire to enter the field, the *alux* will whistle and throw stones at him as soon as he attempts to jump the field's stone wall. He will also hear the dog bark from inside the field, although he will not see it. Once the potential thief sees the stones shattering upon the stone wall he is attempting to cross, he decides to flee.
>
> When the farmer is done working that field, he destroys the *alux,* shattering it against a stone. In that way, the field may again be freely worked because it no longer has a guardian.[2]

Many *aluxo'ob* (plural) that are not destroyed continue to watch over their fields, attacking or attempting to ward off those who now live or work there. The *aluxo'ob* are a legacy of the past, ancient dwellers of the astonishing Mayan world. They must not be confused with European entities like dwarves or gnomes, whose scant height is the only characteristic they share with these beings of clay and honey.

Apéndice C

El *Alux* maya

De todos los entidades invisibles del mundo maya, sólo el *alux* es una criatura formada por el hombre, a partir de importantes elementos ceremoniales: el *saka'*,[1] la miel y la sangre. Santiago Domínguez Aké insiste que el conocimiento lo poseen los *jmeno'ob* y que ellos deben enseñarlo al campesino que desee cuidar su milpa mediante un *alux:*

> El alux se hace remojando barro con miel, dándole la forma de un muñequito y con este mismo barro le agregan su honda y su perro. Para darle vida al alux, el milpero ofrenda la bebida de *saka'* en trece ocasiones. La ofrenda debe hacerse en el centro de la milpa, donde también se pone al *alux,* debajo de una piedra. Esta actividad se efectúa los martes y viernes, hasta completar las trece ofrendas correspondientes. Al bajar la bebida de las ramas de los árboles donde la colgó el milpero, no la bebe y sólo la entierra debajo del altar en que hizo la ofrenda. Luego le unta nueve gotas de su sangre en la boca del *alux* y en el hocico del perrito. Después de haber completado las trece ofrendas, el milpero sólo alimenta con sangre al *alux* y su perrito los días martes y viernes, para que éste pueda cumplir como guardián de los productos de la milpa.
>
> Porque si alguien quiere entrar a robar en la milpa, apenas intente brincar el cerco le silbarán y tirarán piedras. Además escuchará ladrar al perro dentro de la milpa, aunque no lo vea. El presunto ladrón, al ver cómo se hacen pedazos las piedras que le arrojan sobre la barda donde quiere entrar, opta por huir.
>
> Cuando el milpero termina de trabajar el terreno, destruye el *alux,* estrellándolo contra una piedra. De esta manera, el terreno se puede volver a trabajar libremente, porque ya no tiene guardián.[2]

Muchos *aluxes* que no fueron destruidos siguen al cuidado de sus terrenos atacando o tratando de disuadir a los que ahora los habitan o trabajan. Los *aluxes* son legados del pasado, antiguos pobladores del mundo deslumbrante del Mayab, que no pueden confundirse con otras entidades europeas como los duendes o gnomos, que salvo la estatura, nada tienen en común con su naturaleza de barro y miel.

The etymology of the term *alux* is uncertain. The verb *ux* means "to pick the fruit of a tree" or "to harvest"; the verb *xob* means "to whistle." *Ox,* meaning "three," may also be related, while *al* refers to the child of a woman or female animal. The word *alux* may also derive from words or meanings that have fallen from use.

Su etimología es incierta. El verbo *ux* significa bajar los frutos de un árbol o de una mata, esto es, "cosechar." El verbo *xob,* por otra parte, significa "silbar" o "chiflar." Podría relacionarse también con *ox,* que significa "tres." *Al* se aplica al vástago o a la cría de una mujer o de un animal hembra. También la palabra *alux* podría proceder de voces o de sentidos caídos en desuso.

Note

1. Beverage similar to that which the Mayan farmer calls *k'eyem* (known as *pozol* in Spanish).

2. Santiago Domínguez Aké, "Alux," in Andrés Tec Chi, *Cuentos sobre las apariciones en el Mayab,* Colección Letras Mayas Contemporáneas, 1st series, vol. 6, C. Montemayor, series ed. (Mexico City: INI/TRF, 1994), pp. 57–59. The Mayan-language version is also titled "Alux," in Andrés Tec Chi, *Tzikbalo'ob yo'olal ja'asaj óolo'ob, k'aak'as ba'alo'ob yéetel aluxo'ob,* Colección Letras Mayas Contemporáneas, 1st series, vol. 5, C. Montemayor, series ed. (Mexico City: INI/TRF, 1994), pp. 57–59.

Nota

1. Una bebida semejante a la que el campesino maya designa como *k'eyem* (o "pozol" en español).

2. Santiago Domínguez Aké, "Alux," en Andrés Tec Chi, *Cuentos sobre las apariciones en el Mayab,* Colección Letras Mayas Contemporáneas, 1a serie, vol. 6, C. Montemayor, coord. de la colección (México, D.F.: INI/TRF, 1994), pp. 57–59. En maya es también "Alux," en Andrés Tec Chi, *Tzikbalo'ob yo'olal ja'asaj óolo'ob, k'aak'as ba'alo'ob yéetel aluxo'ob,* Colección Letras Mayas Contemporáneas, 1a serie, vol. 5, C. Montemayor, coord. de la colección (México, D.F.: INI/TRF, 1994), pp. 57–59.

Appendix D

The Mayan *P'uus*

In Yucatán's Mayan zone, the Flood and the Tower of Babel were linked to a typically Mayan element: the powerful builders who lived prior to present-day humanity, but who lacked intelligence and physical height. Their Mayan name is *p'uus* (sing., rhymes with English "loose") and *p'uuso'ob* (pl.), though they are referred to at times with the Spanish plural *puses.* Some researchers see them as hunchbacks or even dwarves, equivalent to entities of the European oral tradition. In folktales found throughout France, Belgium, Italy, Germany, and Ireland, hunchbacked dwarves serve to test the kindness and courtesy of the tales' heroes, to award or deny them riches, advice, or arms without which they cannot survive. In some cases, they reward kindness and straightforwardness; in others they punish arrogance with numerous and incredible disasters. The Mayan *p'uuso'ob* perform none of these functions; they are characterized by four basic attributes: their scant height (not a hunched back, which is never mentioned); their marked clumsiness; their skills as builders of great edifices; and having lived prior to "present-day" humanity. The meaning of the word *p'uus* is uncertain. Etymologically, it is related to removing dust from an object, though the *jmeno'ob* and, in general, most Mayas today use it as a synonym for "idiot" or "fool."

The *p'uuso'ob* are presented in this way in one of Irene Dzul's traditional tales, "The Turkey and the *Puus*."[1] Because of their scant intelligence, they were also turned into the heroes of a famous Indo-European folktale about a father and his son, who, concerned about what others will say, successively take turns riding their horse until they themselves end up carrying it. The *p'uuso'ob* were also immediately linked to the Tower of Babel and the Flood because of their building skills (their name is so recorded in the name of a town in southern Yucatán, near Oxkutzcab: Puustunich) and for having lived prior to present-day humanity. Both characteristics were the mortar that allowed the Mayas to combine the Tower of Babel and the Flood into one tale, hardly orthodox with respect to the Holy Scriptures.

From the Mayan perspective, the Flood tells us of the destruction of a prior humanity. First, the *p'uuso'ob* must

Apéndice D

El *P'uus* maya

En la zona maya de Yucatán, el Diluvio y la Torre de Babel se asociaron con un elemento típicamente maya: los poderosos constructores que vivieron antes de la actual humanidad, pero que tenían poca inteligencia y escasa estatura. El nombre maya es en singular *p'uus* y en plural *p'uuso'ob,* aunque a menudo se les llama en español los *puses.* Algunos investigadores quieren ver en ellos a corcovados, jorobados ("hunchbacks") o incluso enanos ("dwarfs"), equiparándolos a otras entidades de la tradición oral europea. En cuentos populares muy extendidos en Francia, Bélgica, Italia, Alemania e Irlanda, los enanos con jorobas tienen como función probar la bondad y cortesía de los héroes de los relatos a fin de concederles o negarles riquezas, consejos o armas sin los cuales no sobrevivirían; en unos casos premian la bondad y sencillez; en otros castigan la arrogancia con numerosas e increíbles calamidades. Ninguna de estas funciones desempeña el *p'uus* maya, que fundamentalmente está caracterizado por cuatro atributos: su pequeña estatura (no su joroba, que no se menciona); su gran torpeza; su habilidad como constructor de grandes edificios; y el haber vivido antes de la "actual" humanidad. El sentido de la palabra *p'uus* es incierto; aunque etimológicamente se relaciona con sacudir o limpiar de polvo alguna cosa, los *jmeno'ob* y, en general, la mayor parte de los hablantes mayas la utilizan como sinónimo de *bobos.*

Así se representa a los *p'uuso'ob* en uno de los cuentos tradicionales de Irene Dzul, "El pavo y el *puus*."[1] Por su poca inteligencia también se les convirtió en los héroes de un famoso cuento popular indoeuropeo: el del padre y el hijo que, para dejar satisfecha a la gente, sucesivamente van cediéndose uno al otro el caballo hasta que llegan a cargarlo ellos mismos. Se les relacionó de inmediato con la Torre de Babel y con el Diluvio por su capacidad de constructores (su nombre se registra así en un pueblo del sur de Yucatán, cercano a Oxkutzcab: Puustunich) y por haber vivido antes de la actual humanidad: ambos rasgos fueron la argamasa que les permitió a los mayas unir en un solo episodio a la Torre de Babel y al Diluvio bajo una lectura, por supuesto, poco ortodoxa de las Sagradas Escrituras.

Desde su perspectiva, el diluvio remite a la destrucción de una anterior humanidad. Los *p'uuso'ob* deben ser,

therefore be that human race referred to in the Bible, as the Mayas know that they constituted a prior human race. Second, the pyramids were built in their efforts to avoid destruction since, as builders, it is logical that they constructed great towers to save themselves. Third, as humanity now inhabits a post-Flood world, Adam and Eve were therefore the human couple who, along with many pairs of animals, took refuge in the Ark. The adaptation of biblical episodes is made possible by the very fabric of Mayan culture; rather than introducing new tales, they give coherence to those episodes from their own perspective.

Note

1. "El pavo y el *puus*," in Irene Dzul Chablé et al., *Cuentos mayas tradicionales*, Colección Letras Mayas Contemporáneas, 1st series, vol. 14, C. Montemayor, series ed. (Mexico City: INI/TRF, 1994) pp. 14–15. The Mayan-language version is "Tzo' yéetel p'uus," in Irene Dzul Chablé et al., *Tzikbalo'ob suuk u beeta'alo'ob I*, Colección Letras Mayas Contemporáneas, 1st series, vol. 13, C. Montemayor, series ed. (Mexico City, INI/TRF, 1994), pp. 16–18.

pues, primero, esa humanidad a que se refiere la Biblia, puesto que los mayas saben que constituyeron la humanidad anterior. Segundo, las pirámides son resultado de ese esfuerzo por no perecer, pues como constructores resulta lógico que edificaran grandes torres para salvarse. Tercero, como ahora vive en el mundo una humanidad posterior al Diluvio, entonces Adán y Eva fue la pareja humana que con muchas otras parejas de animales se refugió en el Arca. La adopción de estos episodios bíblicos es posible, pues, por el tejido mismo de la cultura maya. Más que introducir una nueva historia, le da coherencia desde su propia perspectiva.

Nota

1. "El pavo y el *puus*," en Irene Dzul Chablé et al., *Cuentos mayas tradicionales*, Colección Letras Mayas Contemporáneas, 1a serie, vol. 14, C. Montemayor, coord. de la colección (México, D.F.: INI/TRF, 1994), pp. 14–15. En maya es "Tzo' yéetel p'uus," en Irene Dzul Chablé et al., *Tzikbalo'ob suuk u beeta'alo'ob I*, Colección Letras Mayas Contemporáneas, 1a serie, vol. 13, C. Montemayor, coord. de la colección (México, D.F.: INI/TRF, 1994), pp. 16–18.

Appendix E

The Owners, Lords, or Guardians of the Earth and Water

The "Lords," "Owners," or "Guardians" of a site, the hills, an animal species, a river, the rain, or the thunder are known by a variety of names in Mexican Indigenous languages: Yum or Kanán (among the Mayas of Yucatán); Kajval, Yajval, or Kajwal (among the Mayas of Chiapas); Chikón (among the Mazatecs of Oaxaca); or Chaneque (among the Nahuas and other Indigenous peoples of Veracruz, Oaxaca, and Puebla). These entities live on as part of daily life in Indigenous communities. Often there are many tales describing how one may enter into contact with them and how some farmers enter into their service inadvertently or by force.

In Miguel May May's story, the Lords of the Rain are the Yum Tziles, and the main character collaborates with them. In Román Güemes' story, the Lords of the Water are the Auakej; and the Chaneques, or Lords of the Hills, are the Tepechanejkej, who act as the Guardians of Life. In the tale by Enrique Pérez López, the Lord of the Water is Yajval Vo', who teaches a child to relate to water.

In many other stories, Christian influence is very strong, as the "Lord" and the episodic motif may be confused with the "pact with the Devil" motif found in several European folktales. According to the Aarne-Thompson classification, in tale-types 314, 400, 502, 756b, and 810 the hero enters into the Devil's service. The adventures, risks, or benefits that the servant acquires are diverse but always result from fleeing, trickery, or the help of animals or bewitched individuals. It is only in the stories cataloged as types 475, 821a and b, and 361 (the latter perhaps better known as "Bearskin"), that the Devil helps those who enter into a pact with him; he makes them rich and "saves their lives" but carries others away in their place. The European episodic motif of "entering into the Devil's service" might well lead us to a misconception: that farmers who, in Indigenous tales, enter into the service of guardian entities—refashioned by Christianity as Devils—are assuming a similar type of relationship. In a Tzotzil tale, Yajval Balamil (the "Lord of the Property" or the "Lord of the Earth") has *ladino* characteristics and orders the young man on horseback to close his eyes. Here the Christian overlay operates principally in the introduction, but the entity is Indigenous: strictly speak-

Apéndice E

Los Dueños, Señores o Guardianes de la tierra y el agua

Los "Dueños", "Señores" o "Guardianes" de un sitio, un monte, una especie animal, un río, la lluvia o el trueno, llámense, en diversas lenguas indígenas de México, Yum o Kanán (entre los mayas de Yucatán), Kajval, Yajval o Kajwal (entre los mayas de Chiapas), Chikón (entre los mazatecos de Oaxaca) o Chaneque (entre los nahuas y otros pueblos indígenas de Veracruz, Oaxaca y Puebla), siguen siendo entidades constantes en las comunidades indígenas y a menudo muchos relatos describen la manera de entrar en contacto con ellos y la forma en que algunos campesinos se ponen a su servicio inadvertidamente o forzados a ello.

En el relato de Miguel May May los Señores de la lluvia son Yum Tziles, y con ellos trabaja el personaje principal. En el relato de Román Güemes los Señores del agua son los Auakej y los Chaneques o Señores del cerro son los Tepechanejkej, que actúan como guardianes de la vida. En el cuento de Enrique Pérez López el Dueño del agua es el Yajval Vo', que le enseña a un niño a relacionarse con el agua.

En algunos de muchos otros cuentos, la influencia cristiana es muy fuerte porque se descalifica al "Señor" o "Dueño" y el motivo episódico puede confundirse entonces con el "pacto con el Diablo" de varios cuentos populares europeos. En los catalogados en la clasificación Aarne-Thompson como tipos 314, 400, 502, 756b y 810, el héroe entra a trabajar al servicio del Diablo. Las aventuras, riesgos o beneficios que adquiere el siervo son diversos pero siempre a partir de la huida, el engaño, la ayuda de animales o de personas hechizadas. Sólo en los cuentos catalogados como tipos 475, 821A y B y 361—éste último acaso más difundido como Piel de Oso—el Diablo ayuda a quienes hacen un trato con él, los enriquece y les "salva la vida," pero se lleva a otros en su lugar. El motivo episódico europeo "entrar al servicio del Diablo," pues, podría conducirnos a una equivocación: creer que se trata del mismo "servicio" al que entran los campesinos en relatos indígenas con entidades guardianas que el cristianismo ha investido como demonios. En un relato tzotzil el Yajval Balamil (o "Señor del predio o la tierra") tiene aspecto de ladino y le ordena cerrar los ojos al joven que monta a caballo. La superposición cristiana opera fundamentalmente en la introducción, pero la entidad es propiamente indígena: el

ing, "the Lord or Guardian of the Hills." To enter into his service here is a blessing, not a danger.

There is another Christian reinterpretation of tales of this type found in the state of Chiapas: that of the farm or hacienda owner who exploits the Indian peons during long periods of work, after which he gives them their "pay." Yet another overlaying is illustrated in the confusion of Yajval with the exploitative land owner and the Devil. Yajval belongs to an invisible world that is a copy of the visible world. Some "owners" of a possible pre-Hispanic tradition were perhaps vengeful, inflicting punishment upon those who defiled their territories. As a result, in Chiapas, Christianity's interchange of the Devil and the landowners has produced a terror regarding these entities that in no way equals the reverential fear of them in other areas — not even in those cases where unfortunate hunters must experience the reprimands of the Owners of Animals.

In several Indigenous languages of Mexico, the Lord not only of Rain but of Lightning or Thunder wears a cape or a sleeve that holds the power to unleash and control storms. The attributes of these entities of lightning and rain do not always appear integrated in the tales themselves, as they do in the precise explanations of community experts; this perhaps reflects the reduction and conditioning that the oral tales have undergone throughout the processes of colonization and the imposition of Christianity and the Spanish language. For example, a Tepehua tale, "The Old Man of the Sea," calls the Lord of the Rain (who would annually flood and destroy the world) Siní, but it also employs its Christian "equivalent": Saint John (San Juan).[1]

Note

1. "El viejo del mar," called "Siní" or "San Juan, the Siren," who brings on the rains and the floods, in R. Williams García, *Mitos tepehuas,* Colección SepSetentas (Mexico City: SEP, 1972), pp. 77–78.

Señor o Guardián del monte. Aquí entrar al servicio de él es una bendición, no un peligro.

Pero hay una superposición más en los relatos de este tipo en el estado de Chiapas: el del finquero o hacendado que explota a los jornaleros indios durante largas temporadas al cabo de las cuales les da su "paga." A la confusión del Yajval con el hacendado explotador y con el demonio se liga otra superposición: el Yajval pertenece a un mundo invisible que es una réplica del mundo visible. Como algunos Dueños de la posible tradición prehispánica eran quizás vengativos e inflingían castigos a quienes profanaban sus territorios, la superposición cristiana del demonio y del finquero ha producido en Chiapas un pavor ante estas entidades que no equivale al temor reverencial que se les tiene en otras zonas, incluso en los casos en que cazadores desafortunados tienen que experimentar las reprimendas de los Dueños de los animales.

En varias lenguas indígenas de México el Dueño del rayo o del trueno, más que solamente de la lluvia, se viste una capa o manga que contiene el poder de provocar y controlar las tormentas. No siempre los atributos de estas entidades del rayo y la lluvia aparecen integrados en los relatos mismos, sino en explicaciones específicas de conocedores de las comunidades, lo que quizás refleja la reducción y condicionamiento que los relatos orales han experimentado a lo largo de los procesos de colonización, cristianización y castellanización. Un relato tepehua, "El viejo del mar," por ejemplo, llama al Dueño de la lluvia (entidad que anualmente inundaba y destruía el mundo) Siní, pero también emplea su "equivalente" cristiano: San Juan.[1]

Nota

1. "El viejo del mar," llamado Siní o "San Juan, el Sireno," que provoca las lluvias y las inundaciones, en R. Williams García, *Mitos tepehuas,* Colección SepSetentas (México, D.F.: SEP, 1972), pp. 77–78.

Appendix F

The Xut and the K'ox of Chiapas

In the Tzeltal and Tzotzil areas of Chiapas, several tales tell of the adventures of a Younger Brother, the Xut (pronounced "shoot") or the K'ox (pronounced "kosh," as in "kosher"). When harassed by his older brothers in some recurring episodes, he is forced to do away with them. He later becomes the sun, and his mother, the moon. This final transformation is an episodic motif that is relevant in numerous stories from other regions of Mexico. In a Popoloca tale, the sun and the moon were siblings; she was the elder sister, and the sun was her younger brother.[1] In the Tepehua story "For My Sake, the Moon Became the Moon,"[2] a little boy becomes the sun and an adult woman, the moon. The motifs of the sun (a little boy) and the moon (an adult, frequently a woman) who ascend from earth to sky are most likely indices of pre-Hispanic origin, even in the Tzeltal and Tzotzil versions, in which they are referred to as "the Virgin" and "the son of Saint Joseph." The Totonaco tale "The Origin of the Sun and the Moon" also affirms the Christian motif,[3] according to which, before the sun existed, "three kings" ruled the world. Let us remember that in the Kiliwa creation story the sun has its origin in a child, and the moon in the creator-coyote. Some episodic motifs surrounding the Xut and the K'ox are autonomous and are included within broader tales; such is the case of the hawk who comes to visit the sun in a Tzeltal story entitled "The Hawk and the Rooster";[4] or the attacks of the elder brothers in a Mochó story, "The Origin of the Sun."[5]

In the story by Enrique Pérez López, the character K'ox is not the sacred entity—rather, just a small boy. However, the uniqueness of the term *k'ox* provides an important cultural resonance to the relationship between the child and magical entities. Something similar occurs in the perspective of Gabriel Pacheco's story "Our Mother Yurienaka": a child narrates his encounter with the sacred Huichol entities. In the tale by Román Güemes Jiménez, conversely, the child Chikomexóchitl is the divine creator of life, the young corn, the sustainer; he is one of the principal manifestations of the divine child, the sacred K'ox or Xut.

Notes

1. "El sol y la luna," in K. Jäcklein, *Un pueblo popoloca* (Mexico City: INI/SEP, 1974), p. 284.

Apéndice F

El Xut y el K'ox de Chiapas

En las zonas tzeltales y tzotziles de Chiapas varios relatos refieren las peripecias de un Hermano Menor, el Xut o el K'ox, que acosado por sus hermanos mayores en ciertos episodios recurrentes se ve forzado a eliminarlos; posteriormente, se convierte en el sol y su madre en la luna. Tal transformación final es un motivo episódico relevante en muchos cuentos de otras regiones de México. En un cuento popoloca, la luna y el sol eran hermanos; ella la hermana mayor; el sol, el menor.[1] En el cuento tepehua "Por mí la luna se hizo luna"[2] un niño se convierte en el sol y una mujer adulta en luna. Los motivos del sol (un niño) y la luna (un adulto, a menudo mujer) que ascienden desde la tierra al firmamento posiblemente señalen su origen prehispánico, incluso en las versiones tzeltales y tzotziles en que se les llama la "Virgen" y "el hijo de San José." En el cuento totonaco "El origen del sol y la luna"[3] se afirma además el motivo cristiano de que antes del sol gobernaban en el mundo "tres reyes." Recordemos que en el relato kiliwa de la creación del universo un niño es el origen del sol y el creador coyote el de la luna. Algunos motivos episódicos del Xut y del K'ox son autónomos y se insertan en relatos más amplios; tal es el caso del gavilán que acude a visitar al sol en un cuento tzeltal llamado "El gavilán y el gallo"[4] o los ataques de los hermanos mayores en un cuento mochó llamado "El origen del sol."[5]

En el cuento de Enrique Pérez López el personaje K'ox no es la entidad sagrada; sólo se refiere a un niño pequeño. Sin embargo, la aplicación única del término *k'ox* implica una resonancia cultural importante para ver la relación del niño con las entidades mágicas. Algo similar ocurre en la perspectiva del relato de Gabriel Pacheco "Tatei Yurienaka": un niño va relatando el encuentro con las entidades sagradas huicholas. En el cuento de Román Güemes Jiménez, en cambio, el niño Chikomexóchitl es la divinidad creadora de la vida, el maíz tierno, el sustentador; se trata de una de las principales manifestaciones de la divinidad infantil, del K'ox o Xut sagrado.

Notas

1. "El sol y la luna," en K. Jäcklein, *Un pueblo popoloca* (México, D.F.: INI/SEP, 1974), p. 284.

2. "Por qué la luna se hizo luna," in R. Williams García, *Mitos tepehuas,* Colección SepSetentas (Mexico City: SEP, 1972), pp. 65–66.

3. "El origen del sol y la luna" ("Xa kilhtsukut chichi chu xa pap"), by Telésforo Hernández Hernández, collected by Rosa Isela Albarrán Serrano, trans. by Bartolo Ramos García, in *Relatos totonacos,* Colección Lenguas de México (Mexico City: CNCA/DGCP, 1995), pp. 9–13.

4. "El gavilán y el gallo," in *Relatos tzeltales,* Colección Lenguas de México (Mexico City: CNCA/DGCP, 1995), pp. 77–79.

5. "El origen del sol" ("We ts'a'ik"), collected by Perla Petrich, in *Relatos Mochó,* Colección Lenguas de México (Mexico City: CNCA/DGCP, 1995), pp. 52–57.

2. "Por qué la luna se hizo luna," en R. Williams García, *Mitos tepehuas,* Colección SepSetentas (México, D.F.: SEP, 1972), pp. 65–66.

3. "El origen del sol y la luna" ("Xa kilhtsukut chichi chu xa pap"), de Telésforo Hernández Hernández, recopil. de Rosa Isela Albarrán Serrano, trad. de Bartolo Ramos García, en *Relatos totonacos,* Colección Lenguas de México (México, D.F.: CNCA/DGCP, 1995), pp. 9–13.

4. "El gavilán y el gallo," en *Relatos tzeltales,* Colección Lenguas de México (México, D.F.: CNCA/DGCP, 1995), pp. 77–79.

5. "El origen del sol" ("We ts'a'ik"), recopil. de Perla Petrich, en *Relatos Mochó,* Colección Lenguas de México (México, D.F.: CNCA/DGCP, 1995), pp. 52–57.

Appendix G

The *Nahuales* or *Tonas*

Tales of transformations and bewitchings are numerous and frequent in present-day Indigenous communities and, as a religious concept, constitute a watershed. They are sustained by an important pre-Hispanic foundation of ideas regarding men and women of power; however, moral condemnation is a constant in these tales, resulting from Christianity's distorted perception of the power wielded by Indigenous healers.

For many years, during entire nights, I have heard tales regarding individuals who transform themselves into other beings to perform simple tasks (for example, some shopkeepers fly by night to a large city to obtain supplies; others carry out attacks or celebrate diabolical meetings).

The tales spring from the common idea that human beings have, throughout their entire lives, a vital relationship with an animal. This relationship is particularly heightened among sorcerers or powerful healers. This animal suffers, or becomes strengthened, as does the human twin; but the human is also affected by what occurs to the animal twin. These "companions" or "twins" are the *nahuales* (also written *naguales*) or the *tonas*. Everyone should therefore take care of "his or her *nahual*."

The term *nahual* is also applied to persons who are able to assume an animal form or summon to their aid their "animal companion," as occurs in the narrative by Domingo Gómez Gutiérrez, when King Juan López plans the defense of the area along with the town leaders, and in the piece by Joel Torres, where the healer is able to transform herself into an owl or an enormous she-coyote.

The term comes from the Nahuatl *nahualli*, which means "evasive" or "hidden" and alludes to that which camouflages or transforms itself to pass unnoticed. Nahuatl speakers now apply it to their neighbors who change according to present conditions or who are elusive. The *nahualli* lies in the other, the hidden, the invisible world. This type of power of transformation is a strictly Mesoamerican tradition, foreign to Christianity and to the folktales of Asia or Europe. Nevertheless, in the present day, we are able to identify a European strain of tales of transformation and bewitching with a Christian influence that classify truly Mesoamerican transformation as negative or

Apéndice G

Los *Nahuales* o *Tonas*

Numerosos y frecuentes son en las comunidades indígenas actuales los relatos de transformaciones y hechicerías, que constituyen un parteaguas como concepción religiosa. Los nutre un importante sustrato prehispánico de ideas acerca de los hombres y mujeres de poder, pero la descalificación moral es permanente a causa del cristianismo, que desnaturaliza el poder de los curanderos indígenas.

A lo largo de muchos años he escuchado durante noches enteras relatos sobre personas que se transforman en otros seres para realizar desde sencillas tareas (los dueños de algunas tiendas vuelan de noche a una gran ciudad para abastecerse de mercancías, por ejemplo) hasta la consumación de ataques o la celebración de reuniones diabólicas.

Los relatos parten de la idea generalizada de que los seres humanos tienen con un animal durante toda la vida una relación vital, particularmente consciente entre los brujos o curanderos poderosos. Ese animal padece o se fortalece conforme transcurre la vida del gemelo humano; pero también la persona se ve afectada por lo que le ocurre a su gemelo animal. Estos "compañeros" o "gemelos" son el *nahual* (también se escribe *nagual*) o la *tona*. Las personas deben cuidar, pues, a "su *nahual*."

También se le suele llamar *nahual* a la persona que es capaz de asumir la forma de otro animal o que es capaz de convocar en su ayuda la presencia de su "compañero animal," como ocurre en el relato de Domingo Gómez Gutiérrez cuando el Rey Juan López planea la defensa de la comarca en compañía de los dirigentes del pueblo; igualmente en el relato de Joel Torres, donde la curandera puede transformarse en un tecolote o en una enorme coyota.

El término proviene de la voz náhuatl *nahualli*, que significa "escurridizo" y "oculto": alude a lo que se mimetiza o se transforma para no ser visto. Los hablantes de náhuatl lo aplican ahora al vecino que cambia con las circunstancias o que es escurridizo. El *nahualli* está en lo otro, en lo oculto, en el mundo invisible. Este tipo de poder para transformarse es una tradición solamente mesoamericana y es ajena al cristianismo y a los relatos populares de Asia o de Europa. Sin embargo, actualmente podemos reconocer una corriente europea de cuentos de transformación y hechicería con el influjo cristiano que califica como negati-

"diabolic"; this European tradition basically condemns the thesis of the *nahual.*

Therefore, it is worthwhile to illustrate some characteristics of tales of transformation from the European oral tradition. The Aarne-Thompson *Index of Tale Types* includes, under types 551 to 554, a series of tales in which grateful animals lend support to a hero in his adventures and reward him with the ability to take on their form. In the case of folktales of type 552, another type of transformation shows up: the hero's in-laws are eagles, bears, or seagulls during certain hours of the day and afterward take on human form. In those of Type 545B, of considerable influence on the Yucatán Peninsula, as in "Puss and Boots," a giant or ogre transforms himself into a lion, rooster, and mouse, thus falling under the hero's dominion. At times, the hero receives the gift of transformation through other means; in stories of type 665, told in the Baltic countries and some areas of Hungry and Russia, the hero may receive it from an "old man" or from the spirit of a "grateful dead man."[1]

In the European tradition, the transformation may also appear linked to a Christian notion: that of male and female witches who surrender themselves to the devil on the *shabat* or witches' sabbath. This Christian notion has become overlaid in many areas upon Indigenous folktales for the purpose of "explaining" the content of the oral tradition from a non-Indigenous perspective. This occurs in certain Mayan tales from Yucatán and Chiapas regarding the *wáay* and the *chanul* that are not based upon the Mesoamerican notion of the *nahual* or the *tona* but upon European notions of diabolical transformations. In these tales, the transformations into goats, owls, or animals of the forest do not derive from a knowledge of the *nahual* but from evil and "from the devil." Therefore, it is worthwhile to consider that a large portion of present-day oral tradition has given way to or simply adopted European and Christian models of transformation. In many cases, however, the very values of transformation—based upon a complex tapestry of Mesoamerican beliefs relating to the *nahual* or the *tona*—may remain intact.

Note

1. Stith Thompson, *The Folktale* (Berkeley and Los Angeles: University of California Press, 1946; reprinted in 1977), pp. 57–58.

vas o "diabólicas" las transformaciones propiamente mesoamericanas. Es decir, se trata de una tradición europea que descalifica, en el fondo, la tesis del *nahual.*

Por ello conviene que precisemos algunos rasgos de los cuentos de transformaciones en la tradición oral europea. El *Index of Tale Types* de la clasificación Aarne-Thompson incluye en los tipos 551 a 554 una serie de relatos que se refieren a animales agradecidos que apoyan al héroe en sus aventuras y le *conceden* la capacidad de asumir la forma de ellos. En el caso de los cuentos populares del tipo 552, aparece otra clase de transformaciones: los cuñados del héroe son águilas, osos o gaviotas durante ciertas horas del día y después asumen la figura humana. En los del tipo 545B, de considerable penetración en la península de Yucatán, característico de "El gato con botas," un gigante u ogro se transforma en león, gallo y ratón, y así cae bajo el dominio del héroe. En ocasiones el héroe recibe el don de transformación por otros medios; en los cuentos del tipo 665, narrados en los países bálticos y en algunas zonas de Hungría y Rusia, el héroe puede recibirlo de un anciano o del espíritu agradecido de un muerto.[1]

En la tradición europea la transformación puede aparecer también ligada a una noción cristiana: las brujas y brujos que se someten al diablo en los *shabat* o aquelarres. Esta noción cristiana se ha superpuesto en muchas zonas y relatos populares indígenas para "explicar" contenidos de la tradición oral desde una perspectiva *no* indígena. Esto ocurre en ciertos cuentos de los mayas de Yucatán y de Chiapas conocidos como los *wáay* y el *chanul,* que no parten de la noción mesoamericana del *nahual* o la *tona,* sino de concepciones europeas de transformaciones diabólicas. En estos relatos, la transformación en chivas, tecolotes o animales de monte no provienen del conocimiento del *nahual,* sino de la maldad y "del diablo." Por tanto, conviene tomar en cuenta que en gran parte de la tradición oral actual se han abierto paso, o simplemente se han tomado, los modelos de transformación europeos y cristianos, aunque permanezcan intactos en muchos casos los valores propios de la transformación a partir del complejo de creencias mesoamericanas relacionadas con el *nahual* o la *tona.*

Nota

1. Stith Thompson, *The Folktale* (Berkeley y Los Angeles: University of California Press, 1946; reimpresión de 1977), pp. 57–58.

Appendix H

The Huicholes and the Celestial Deer

The Huicholes' main ritual ceremony ties together, as different faces of the same spiritual and life-giving force, the deer, peyote, and corn. A celestial deer, Káuyúmari, fertilizes the earth with its blood because its heart holds and sustains the life of Hikú (corn), which, at the same time, is Hikuri (peyote). Huichol villages undertake the hunting of deer or Marra to offer the heart to Tatei Yurienaka (mother earth), where it will resurrect as Hikuri and as Hikú. For this reason, they hunt deer and peyote, to help the world. From both of the celestial deer's hearts, man, woman, and the Huichol child are annually reborn.

This hunt takes place during a sacred pilgrimage: from the mountains of Jalisco and Nayarit, where the Huichol communities are located, to the sierra of Real del Catorce, in the state of San Luis Potosí. On this pilgrimage through the desert, through Wirikuta, the Huichol priests devotedly collect the sacred heart of peyote from the ground. This collection is another "deer hunt." In the Huichol language this Pilgrimage Feast is called Páriyatsié Yeyá and also 'Iweiyari, "the hunt." In the ritual feast the two hunts converge: that of Hikuri and that of Marra, the sacrificed deer —on one hand, the celestial deer, and, on the other, the heart of that sacred deer, the Hikuri. In Gabriel Pacheco's tale "Our Mother Yurienaka," the young narrator prepares himself for this feast and journey, assuming the name of the officiant who adorns his own body with ritual paint.

The celestial deer has a name: Káuyúmari. In the memory of the Huichol people are preserved many of his tales. In the stories, Káuyúmari also appears as a true Huichol priest, a *mara'akame.* One of the great tales of Káuyúmari is that of his struggle against a deceiving plant, another psychotropic plant called "Tree of the Wind" or Kiéri Téwiyari. During this struggle, it becomes obvious that the *mara'akame*'s training is very thorough: it continues for five years and requires six pilgrimages through the desert and involves the knowledge of certain dances, chants, melodies, and tales that do not withstand improvisation or subjective embellishment. For that reason, the word *mara'akame* means "the chanter" or "singer." Importantly, the tale points out that the sorcerers of the "Tree of the Wind" are individuals who did not complete their training as Huichol priests.

Apéndice H

Los Huicholes y el Venado Celeste

La principal ceremonia ritual de los huicholes enlaza, como distintos rostros de una misma fuerza espiritual y vivificante, al venado, al peyote y al maíz. Un venado celestial, Káuyúmari, fecunda con su sangre la tierra porque su corazón sostiene y alienta la vida de Hikú (el maíz), pero al mismo tiempo es Hikuri (el peyote). Los pueblos huicholes emprenden la cacería del venado o Marra para ofrendarlo a la madre tierra, a la Tatei Yurienaka, donde el corazón renacerá como Hikuri y como Hikú. Por eso cazan al venado y al peyote, para ayudar al mundo. De ambos corazones del venado celeste renacerá cada año el hombre, la mujer, el niño huichol.

Esta cacería ocurre en un peregrinaje sagrado: el viaje desde las montañas de Jalisco y Nayarit, donde viven las comunidades huicholas, hasta la sierra del Real de Catorce, en San Luis Potosí. En este peregrinaje por el desierto, por Wirikuta, los sacerdotes huicholes van recolectando del suelo, devotamente, los corazones sagrados de peyote. Esta recolección es otra "cacería del venado." En lengua huichola se llama a la Fiesta de Peregrinación Páriyatsié Yeyá y también 'Iweiyari, "La caza." En la fiesta ritual se funden las dos cacerías, la de Hikuri y la de Marra, el venado sacrificado. Esta conjunción sagrada es también una faceta mágica del maíz o Hikú: por un lado, es el venado celeste; por otro, el corazón de ese venado sagrado, el Hikuri. Por esta fiesta y recorrido se prepara el pequeño narrador del relato de Gabriel Pacheco, "Tatei Yurienaka," que asume el nombre del oficiante que se atavía el cuerpo con pintura ritual.

El venado celeste tiene un nombre: Káuyúmari. La memoria de los huicholes conserva muchos relatos suyos. En ellos Káuyúmari aparece también como un verdadero sacerdote huichol, un *marakame.* Uno de los grandes relatos de Káuyúmari es su lucha contra una planta engañosa, otra planta narcótica llamada "Árbol del viento" o Kiéri Téwiyari. Durante esta lucha se evidencia que la formación del *marakame* es muy minuciosa: se prolonga por cinco años y exige seis peregrinaciones por el desierto. La formación del *marakame* implica el conocimiento de ciertas danzas, cantos, melodías y relatos que no pueden quedar al azar ni al embellecimiento subjetivo. Por ello la palabra *marakame* significa "el cantor." El relato señala, significativa-

Kiéri may refer to *Datura meteloides,* a hallucinogen popularly known in Mexico as *toloache,* considered sacred among the Zunis and Hopis of the southwestern United States. They employ it in their designs, which at times blend in with the stylized squash blossom.

mente, que los brujos del "Árbol del viento" son personas que no completaron su formación como sacerdote huichol.

Posiblemente se designa como Kiéri a la *Datura meteloides,* un alucinógeno popularmente llamado en México *toloache,* considerado sagrado entre los zuñis y los hopis del suroeste de Estados Unidos y que emplean en sus diseños, confundidos éstos a menudo con la estilización de la flor de calabaza.

English Glossary

Ahuakej. In Nahuatl, "The Lords of the Water." (See Appendix E.)

Almuerzo. Spanish term used in Mexico to refer to a late breakfast.

Alux. Clay figure brought to life through the ceremonies of traditional Mayan priests and used to protect planted fields and parcels of land.

Amole. From the Nahuatl *amolli,* "soap"; foam produced by the maceration of Amarilidacea plants, including *Manfreda pringlei rose, Prochnyanthes viridescens,* and particularly several varieties of *Agave* found in northern Mexico: *hartmanii, mayoensis,* and *schotii.*

Anolar. From the Mayan verb *nóol;* to hold a candy or seed between the tongue and the hard palate without chewing it.

Atole. From the Nahuatl *atolli;* a thick beverage prepared from corn meal or corn flour dissolved in water and boiled.

Auakej. See *Ahuakej.*

Axókotl. From the Nahuatl *axococ,* "sour water"; from *texócotl, tejocote* in Mexican Spanish, *Crataegus mexicana* or *Crataegus parryana.* A drink made from this fruit.

Ayate. From the Nahuatl *ayatl;* a thin cloth made from maguey fiber.

Baalam. Mayan name for the jaguar, *Felis onca.* Also written *balam.*

Banqueta. Spanish term that the Mayas apply to an elongated bench, usually three-legged, used to prepare corn dough and a variety of foods.

Bchhenbia. Sierra Zapotec name for cochineal; literally, "prickly-pear paint." (See *cochinilla.*)

Bejaga. Sierra Zapotec name for *Coelogenys paca,* an edible rodent well known in Indigenous areas by the name *tepescuintle* or *tepescuincle;* from the Nahuatl *tepeitzcuintli,* "hill dog."

Belsinikche. Alvaradoa amorphoides, a tree that reaches a height of up to 60 feet. Its wood is used to build the traditional thatch-roofed Mayan house, whose walls are made from narrow planks covered with a mixture of earth and shredded hay.

Benexidsa. "Zapotecs of the Corner," in Sierra Zapotec; refers to the northern zone of Ixtlán, known as Xid Zá, "Zapotec Corner." (See *Zapotecs.*)

Bezelhao. In Sierra Zapotec, "the wind that begins or moves forward," in reference to the pre-Hispanic concept of a sacred spirit that is ever vigilant and close to humans.

Bocoles. Generic name for a typical food of the Huasteca region made from corn, salt, chile, and lard, particularly pork lard; *bocoles* take the shape of round and thick cakes.

Cabañuelas. Spanish term for the system by which Mayan farmers predict the climatic conditions for the twelve months of the new year, by observing the conditions present during each day of the month of January; in Maya, *xook k'iin;* literally, "the day count."

Calabazo. Lagenaria siceraria: the fruit of this plant, which grows into a variety of shapes, is generally used as a vessel.

Capulín. From the Nahuatl *capolin;* a name applied to several plants of the Mirsinaceae, Tiliaceae, Mirteaceae, and Rosaceae families that produce a spherical, edible fruit measuring 5 to 10 mm in diameter. The most common is the *Prunus capuli,* a tree that reaches heights of 30 to 45 feet; its small fruit is black or reddish, with a single seed.

Casa de la Comisión. Place where fiesta organizers (la Comisión) feed all visitors for the duration of a fiesta.

Ceiba. Tree belonging to the Bombacaceae family, particularly *Bombax ellipticum* and *Ceiba aesculifolia;* the preeminent tree in Mayan thought and spirituality.

Cempasúchil. Marigold flower; *Tagetes erecta,* a herbaceous plant with uneven leaves, penetrating aroma, and yellow flowers. From the Nahuatl *cempoalxóchitl,* "twenty flowers, many flowers"; also written *sempasúchil.*

Cenote. From the Mayan *dzonot;* deposits and currents of underground water accessible through openings in the Yucatán Peninsula's limestone crust.

Ch'a' Cháak. Traditional rain-petitioning ceremony practiced by the Mayas of Yucatán. It is conducted by a *jmen* or Mayan ritual priest; various foods are placed as offerings on the ceremonial altar. (See Appendix A.)

Chäk to'. Tabasco Chontal name for *popal* (*Calathea lutea*). Herbaceous plant belonging to the Marantaceae family, usually found in lagoons or marshes. It grows to three feet in height. Its large leaves have a whitish film containing wax on their underside. In Tabasco it is known as *popal* leaf and is generally used to wrap foods.

Chaneques. Magical beings of scant height who inhabit the mountains, forests, and hills. (See Appendix E.)

Chikomexóchitl. In Nahuatl, "seven" (*chicome*) "flowers" (*xóchitl*). Sacred child who successively is transformed into corn, the sun, and the sustainer of life.

Chikomexóchitl-elotlamanalistli. In Nahuatl, "He who spreads the ears of corn upon the table"; another of Chikomexóchitl's names.

Chiltepín. Capsicum frutesceus, a shrub that produces an extremely piquant fruit.

Chontal de Tabasco. See *Tabasco Chontal* and *Yokot'an.*

Choza. Spanish word designating a rustic house or hut.

Cochinilla. Cochineal. From the Latin *coccinus,* "scarlet" or "red"; a hemipterous insect originating in Mexico that lives on the prickly-pear cactus of the variety *Nopalea cochinillifera.* When dried and pulverized, it is used as a red dye for silk, wool, and other fabrics.

Coyo. Acrocomia mexicana; according to other authors, *Acrocomia vinifera.* Known as *coyo* or *coyol* from the Nahuatl *coyoli.* "little bell," because of the shape of the fruit and because it resembles a small bell when shaken.

Don. Spanish title of respect reserved for older men; corresponds to *tata* in Purepecha, and *yum* in Mayan.

Doña. Spanish title of respect used before the first names of older women. Corresponds to *nana* in Purepecha.

Elookichpiltsij. In Nahuatl, "Small Male Ear of Corn."

Elosiuapiltsij. In Nahuatl, "Woman of the Young Corn."

Estoraque. Styrax argenteus, a tree that reaches heights of up to 60 feet; its trunk produces an aromatic resin that is used as an incense. The name *estoraque* is also used in reference to *Liquidambar styraciflua.*

Fandanguero. In the Huasteca region, this term refers to musicians who play a variety of stringed instruments for *sones populares* and *sones de costumbre.* In Spain, *fandanguero* refers to a player and singer of *fandangos,* spirited musical compositions in three-quarter time originating in Andalucía.

Goziobe. A sacred pre-Hispanic entity of the Zapotecs; literally, "lightning flash of air," from *gozio,* "lightning flash," and *be,* "air."

Guarapo. Fermented sugar-cane juice.

Guayabo. Psidium guajava, a tree belonging to the Mirteaceae family. Its bark is reddish, smooth, and scaly; its edible fruit is aromatic and pyriform or oval in shape.

Huacal. From the Nahuatl *huacalli;* a box or cage made from spaced wood strips used for transporting goods.

Huanengo. Among the Purepechas, a traditional white cotton blouse adorned with embroidered flower motifs.

Huapango. A traditional dance and its music from the Huasteca region of the northern part of the state of Veracruz and neighboring states; the *son jarocho* is traditional dance music from the southern Gulf coast. *Huapango* comes from the Nahuatl *huapalli.*

Huapanguera. An eight-stringed guitar used mainly to interpret the *huapango* in the Huasteca region; due to its high-pitched tonality, it is also known as *guitarra quinta* or "fifth (octave) guitar."

Huarache. From the Purepecha *kwarachi;* a rustic leather sandal.

Huasteca. A broad and varied region of the Eastern Sierra Madre encompassing parts of the states of Tamaulipas, San Luis Potosí, Veracruz, Hidalgo, and Puebla. From the Nahuatl *huaxteca,* inhabitant of Huaxtla, "place of many *huaxin,*" that is, *guajes* or calabashes (*Lagenaria siceraria*).

Huaya. Talisia olivaeformis, a tree native to the Yucatán Peninsula and several regions of the states of Tabasco and Chiapas.

Huicholes (self-referential term, *Wixárika*). Important ethnic group residing primarily in the western states of Jalisco and Nayarit. At the end of the twentieth century the Huichol people numbered 55,000.

Ixuakentsij. From the Tenek *ichbequen;* a small flower used in a variety of ceremonies. Known in Spanish as *manzanita* or *mazapán. Malvaviscus grandiflorus* and *Malvaviscus arboreus.*

Ja'abín. Mayan name for *Piscidia piscipula,* a poisonous tree that reaches a height of up to 45 feet; it flowers during the dry season and is very useful for making frames and doors.

Jaguacte. Bactris baculifera, a spiny palm that produces a spherical red fruit and reaches heights of up to 18 feet.

Jalamante. Ficus padifolia, a large tree with milky sap and edible fruit. It is more commonly known as *jalamate.*

Jalamate. See *jalamante.*

Jarana. Small, five-stringed guitar used to accompany the *huapango* and *son jarocho.*

Jícara. From the Nahuatl *xicalli,* "receptacle or house of the *jícaro* tree." Bowl or vessel made from the fruit of the *jícaro, Crescentia cujete.*

Jicote. From the Nahuatl *xicotli;* a variety of wasp.

Jmen. Traditional Mayan priest. (See Appendix A.)

Kajkanantik. From *kajkanan,* "protector," "caretaker." A Tzeltal ceremonial formula meaning "Our Protector," used in reference to the patron saints of each Tzeltal town.

Kajval. In Tzotzil, a generic name for the protective entities or guardians of the hills, springs, or rivers. (See Appendix E.)

Kaxhon. Plural of "Xhon." Refers to the towns located along the banks of the Cajonos or Kaxhon River in the present-day state of Oaxaca. As a result, this word in Sierra Zapotec has become the self-referential term for the Zapotecs themselves.

Kokajsintla. In Nahuatl, "abundant in ears of corn."

K'ox. In Tzotzil, "the smallest one," "the youngest brother" of a family. (See Appendix F.)

Leoncillo. Felis concolor.

Maitines. In Catholic rites, the first of the canonical hours in which predawn prayers commence. Among the Sierra Zapotecs, musical pieces played by bands at evening or nighttime ceremonies, consisting of hymns to the Virgin, responses, and a *te deum* prayer.

Marakame. In Huichol, *mara'akame* (pl., *mara'akate*) is the title given to a traditional healer and ritual officiant; literally, "he who sings (chants)" or "the singer (chanter)."

Mayas. The Mayas of the Yucatán Peninsula are, after the Nahuas, Mexico's largest ethnic group. At the end of the twentieth century there were 1,490,000 Mayan people.

Mayordomo. Traditional office rotated annually among different members of a community; the *mayordomo*'s main responsibilities include providing funds and material goods for a saint's celebrations.

Mecapal. From the Nahuatl *mecapalli,* "rope leaf"; a wide band of rope that is strapped to the forehead and sustains a bundle carried on one's back.

Mestizo/Mestiza. (1) Someone recognized not as Indigenous but rather as *ladino* or Spanish speaking. (2) In Yucatán, a man or woman dressed in gala clothing. For men, this usually includes white pants and a white guayabera or filipina shirt; and for women, a three-piece dress (*terno*) with colorful and abundant embroidery.

Metate. From the Nahuatl *metatl;* a flat, horizontal stone upon which corn is ground.

Mixes or *Mijes* (self-referential term, *Ayook*). One of the principal ethnic groups of the state of Oaxaca. Their communities extend throughout the Sierra Juárez in the northern part of the state. At the end of the twentieth century the Mixes numbered 188,000.

Mole. From the Nahuatl *molli,* "sauce."

Naguales. Certain individuals who, according to widespread Indigenous belief, are able to transform themselves into specific animals or maintain a conscious relationship with the latter as their doubles or *nahuales.* (See Appendix G.)

Nahuales. See *Naguales.*

Nahuas. At the end of the twentieth century the Nahua people were Mexico's largest group of Indigenous people, numbering 2,563,000; they were distributed among the states of Puebla, Veracruz, Hidalgo, Guerrero, San Luis Potosí, Tlaxcala, Morelos, and México and the Federal District. Their native language is Nahuatl.

Nopal. Name for all the cacti of the genera *Platyopuntia* and *Nopalea.*

Numinous. Term coined by the German theologist Rudolf Otto (1869–1937) in reference to an awareness of the sacred. For him, "numinous" refers to the object of religion, something superior to reason, goodness, or beauty. "Numinous" is derived from the Latin word *numen,* "divinity" or "divine will."

Ocote. From the Nahuatl *ocotl,* "torch"; small strips of wood from *Pinus montezumal,* a resinous pine.

Paisano/Paisana. A man or woman originating from the same town or region as oneself.

Pak'al. Method of planting corn practiced by the Mayas of Yucatán; consists of perforating three holes into which the seeds are deposited, resembling the triangular placement of the three firestones used in cooking. The kitchen fire is known as *k'óobenil k'áak',* from which the noun *k'óoben pak'al* is derived.

Papatla. Heliconia schiedeana, a herbaceous plant some four and a half feet tall; it resembles a small banana plant and produces oval, pointy leaves used to wrap foods.

Pariyatsie. Abbreviated form of the Huichol expression *páriyatsié yeyá,* "pilgrimage celebration"; refers to the pilgrimage the Huicholes make from their place of residence in the mountains of the states of Jalisco and Nayarit to the desert surrounding Real del Catorce in the state of San Luis Potosí, where they gather peyote.

Pe'et. Type of netting attached to a ring and hung from

three strings tied in a knot; it is used by the Mayas to store foods.

Pepeyocales. Populus arizonica, a variety of cottonwood known in Spanish as *cimarrón.*

Pericón. Tagetes florida, a herbaceous plant three feet in height, with elliptical and serrated leaves; the aroma of its flowers is similar to that of anis.

Petate. From the Nahuatl *petlatl;* a mat woven from palm or reeds used for sitting or sleeping or as a funerary wrap.

Petko. Nissa sylvatica, a tree of the Nisaceae family that reaches heights of up to 105 feet, producing bluish flowers and fruit. *Petko* is derived from the Zoque word *petcui.*

Pijije. Dendrocygna autumnalis, a web-footed, edible fowl of the Anatidae family, similar to a duck though smaller.

Pilsintektli. In Nahuatl, "Young Lord"; one of Chikomexóchitl's names.

Pirul. Small reddish fruit of *Schinus molle,* a tree originating in Peru and therefore known as *perú, pirú,* or *pirul.*

Poleo. This name is used in reference to two varieties of labiated *Hedeoma* found in central Mexico and in the states of Hidalgo and San Luis Potosí: *Hedeoma palmeri* and *Hedeoma drummondii.*

Pozol. From the Nahuatl *potzol* or *potzolli,* a dough made from corn kernels that have been cooked and have burst; it is dissolved in water for consumption.

Principales. Group of officials who share in the responsibilities of the *mayordomo.* (See *mayordomo.*)

Pulque. From the Nahuatl *poliuhqui,* "spoiled"; a thick white beverage obtained through the fermentation of the juice or *aguamiel* (literally, "honey water") of certain magueys or agaves, particularly of the genus *Agave atrovirens.*

Purepechas. The most important ethnic group in the state of Michoacán. At the end of the twentieth century the Purepecha people numbered 204,000.

P'uus (Mayan pl., *p'uuso'ob*). According to the Mayas, the human race that existed prior to the Flood.

Rebozo. A woman's exterior garment used to cover the shoulders and upper torso; a type of shawl.

Roza. The act of cleaning the fields of brush and useless plants before tilling them.

Saakal. Mayan name for an *arriera* or "carrier" ant, less destructive than the *xulab.* (See *xulab.*)

Saka'. Beverage similar to that which the Mayan farmer calls *k'eyem* (known as *pozol* in Spanish); it is obtained by dissolving corn dough in a small amount of water. The corn kernels for *saka'* are cooked without salt and are ground with their skin intact; when dissolved, the dough is sometimes sweetened with honey.

Sempasúchil. See *cempasúchil.*

Señor. "Lord" or "sir" (a Spanish title of respect); also, "Mr."

Señora. "Lady" (a Spanish title of respect); also, "Mrs."

Sintektli. In Nahuatl, "Lord of Corn"; one of Chikomexóchitl's names.

Sinteopiltsij. In Nahuatl, "Young God of Corn"; one of Chikomexóchitl's names.

Sones de costumbre. Ritual music played exclusively in traditional religious ceremonies.

Sones de muerto. Ritual music played exclusively in funeral ceremonies, to help the soul depart and not to get lost.

Suju'uy Ch'e'en. In Mayan, "Virgin Well"; from *suju'uy,* "immaculate," "sacred," "virginal," and *ch'e'en,* "well." Water used for ritual purposes.

Tabasco Chontal. Ethnic group of the Mayan family that primarily lives in the state of Tabasco. At the end of the twentieth century the Tabasco Chontal people numbered 72,000. See *Yokot'an.*

Takakaima. In Huichol, "The Lords of Midnight"; the sacred entities of darkness and the underworld.

Takutsi. In Huichol, "Our Grandmother" or "Our Germinated Seed" (i.e., the life produced upon all the earth). This positive deity can become transformed into a dark entity known as "Nakawe."

Tapanco. From the Nahuatl *tlapanco,* "on the roof"; horizontal planks used to divide a room into two levels to form a loft or attic.

Tatei Yurienaka. In Huichol, "Our Mother Earth."

Tatewari. In Huichol, "Our Grandfather," in reference to fire.

Tatutsima. In Huichol, "Our Great-Grandparents," in reference to the first creators of the world.

Tecolote. From the Nahuatl *tecolotl,* "owl"; from *col,* "to bend," "a curve."

Tecomate. From the Nahuatl *tecomatl,* "drinking cup," "pot." Receptacle made from a natural husk, such as that of a gourd, coconut, or calabash.

Teiwari. In Huichol, "neighbor," used in reference to non-Huicholes (mestizos and foreigners).

Temascal. From the Nahuatl *temazcalli,* "bath house"; a small stone structure of pre-Hispanic origin, with one entrance, used for medicinal and ritual steambaths.

Tepache. From the Nahuatl *tepiatl,* raw sugar water; today the term is applied to a fermented drink made from pineapple and sugar.

Tepechanejkej. In Nahuatl, "The Lords of the Hills"; magical beings of scant height who inhabit and keep watch over the hills. (See Appendix E.)

Tepehuas. At the end of the twentieth century the Tepehua people numbered 17,000 and lived primarily in the state of Veracruz.

Tepescuintle (*tepescuincle*). From the Nahuatl *tepeitzcuintli,* "hill dog"; *Coelogenys paca.*

Teskatlapetlanij. In Nahuatl, "Shining Mirror"; the ceremonial name for lightning.

Teskatlatomonianij. In Nahuatl, "Mirror of Thunder"; the ceremonial name for thunder.

Tezontle. From the Nahuatl *tetzontli;* a porous, lightweight, reddish volcanic stone that has been used for building since pre-Hispanic times.

Tikarixa. Huichol name for one of the ornamental, herbaceous species cultivated in various parts of Mexico and generically known in Spanish as *manto,* "cloak" or "blanket." It is common in hot and temperate climates.

Tlamatijketl. From the Nahuatl *tlamati,* "intelligent," "skillful"; in some Nahua areas the term *tlamatqui* refers to traditional healers or sorcerers.

Tlapopochuyketl. From the Nahuatl *tlapopoca,* "to smoke"; the incenser or incense bearer in ceremonies.

Toj. From the Mayan *to',* "to wrap"; *Calathea grandifolia,* known in Spanish also as *bijagua* or *hojablanca.*

Tojolabales (self-referential term, *Tojolwinik Otik*). One of the most important ethnic groups in the state of Chiapas, belonging to the Mayan family. At the end of the twentieth century there were 74,000 Tojolabal people.

Tsitsimitenantsij. In Nahuatl, "Mother of the Tsitsimi," harmful pre-Hispanic deities.

Tukipa. Huichol ceremonial centers that are believed to have preserved, since remote times, the world's design and the steps of creation; the *tukipa* remain active, with groups of *mara'akate* who must remain within them for a period of five years.

Tzáab. Mayan name for the Pleiades constellation; also refers to the rattlesnake's rattle.

Tzeltales. One of the most important ethnic groups in the Chiapas Highlands, belonging to the Mayan family. At the end of the twentieth century the Tzeltal people numbered 547,000.

Tzíimin. The present-day Mayan name for the horse; originally, the name for the tapir. (See Appendix B.)

Tzotziles. One of the most important ethnic groups in the Chiapas Highlands, belonging to the Mayan family. At the end of the twentieth century the Tzotzil people numbered 514,000.

Xhon. Refers to the towns situated along the banks of the River Cajonos or Kaxhon in the present-day state of Oaxaca. As a result, this word in Sierra Zapotec has become the self-referential term for the Zapotecs themselves.

Xidsa. Apocopated form of "Benexidsa," that is, the "Zapotecs of the Corner."

Xiquipil. In Nahuatl, "shoulder bag" or "carrying sack."

Xopacatl. In Nahuatl, "to wet one's foot"; equivalent to *el remojo* (the wetting) in Mexican Spanish. An obligatory toast to commemorate having obtained something new.

Xulab. Mayan name for a highly destructive and carnivorous ant. In Spanish, it is known as *arriera* or "carrier" because it travels at night in groups and carries food back to its nest.

Xúul. Mayan name for a stick or cane some four and a half feet long used for planting.

Yokot'an. Self-referential term used by the Tabasco Chontals.

Yum. In Mayan, "Lord." Generic name for the Mayan protective entities.

Yum Tziles. From the Mayan "Yumtzil," "God" (integral Lord); collective name applied to the Mayan protective entities. (See Appendices B and E.)

Zapotecs. "Descendants of the Cloud" or *sa* (*zá*). In Isthmus Zapotec, "Binnizá" means "People of the Cloud." In Sierra Zapotec, "Benexidsa" means "Zapotecs of the Corner." At the end of the twentieth century there were 785,000 Zapotec people distributed among the Central Valleys, the Isthmus, and the Oaxaca Sierra.

Zutz'baläm. In Tabasco Chontal, "bat-jaguar": a deity.

Glosario español

Ahuakej. En náhuatl, "Los Dueños del agua." (Véase Apéndice E.)

Alux. Figura de barro que toma vida por ceremonias de sacerdotes mayas tradicionales para proteger sembradíos y terrenos.

Amole. Del náhuatl *amolli,* "jabón"; espuma producida por el maceramiento de plantas Amarilidáceas como las de *Manfreda pringlei rose, Prochnyanthes viridescens* y, particularmente en el norte de México, las variedades de *Agave hartmanii, mayoensis* y *schotii.*

Anolar. Del verbo maya *nóol;* mantener entre el paladar y la lengua, sin masticar, un dulce o una semilla.

Atole. Del náhuatl *atolli;* bebida espesa preparada a base de masa o de harina de maíz disuelta en agua y hervida.

Auakej. Véase *Ahuakej.*

Axókotl. Del náhuatl *axococ,* "agua agria," de *texócotl,* "tejocote"; *Crataegus mexicana* o *Crataegus parryana.* Bebida hecha a base de este fruto.

Ayate. Del náhuatl *ayatl,* tela delgada hecha con fibra de maguey.

Baalam. Nombre maya del jaguar, *Felis onca.* También se escribe *balam.*

Banqueta. Banco alargado, generalmente de tres patas, donde los mayas actuales preparan la masa de maíz y distintos alimentos.

Bchhenbia. Nombre en zapoteco de la sierra de la "cochinilla," literalmente "pintura del nopal." (Véase *cochinilla.*)

Bejaga. Nombre en zapoteco de la sierra del *Coelogenys paca,* roedor comestible muy conocido en las regiones indígenas con el nombre de *tepescuintle* o *tepescuincle,* del náhuatl *tepeitzcuintli,* "perro de cerro."

Belsinikché. Alvaradoa amorphoides: la madera de este árbol, que llega a alcanzar hasta 20 metros de altura, se emplea para construir la casa tradicional maya de techo de zacate y bajareque con embarro.

Benexidsa. Variante dialectal del zapoteco de la sierra para referirse a la gente "zapoteca" del "rincón," es decir, la zona norte de Ixtlán, llamada Xid Zá, "Rincón Zapoteco." (Véase *zapotecos.*)

Bezelhao. Literalmente, "el viento que inicia o se adelanta." Se refiere a la concepción prehispánica, entre los zapotecos, de un espíritu sagrado siempre vigilante y cercano.

Bocoles. Nombre genérico de un alimento típico de la Huasteca hecho a base de maíz, sal, chile y manteca de origen animal, particularmente de cerdo, en forma de un pan redondo y grueso.

Cabañuelas. El sistema mediante el cual los campesinos mayas pronostican las condiciones climáticas de los doce meses del nuevo año, mediante la observación de las condiciones presentes durante cada día del mes de enero.

Cajete. Del náhuatl *caxitl,* "recipiente," "escudilla."

Calabazo. Lagenaria siceraria: el fruto de esta planta, que adopta formas variadas, suele utilizarse como vasija.

Capulín. Del náhuatl *capolin;* nombre que se aplica a diversas plantas que tienen frutos comestibles globosos de 5 a 10 mm y que pertenecen a las Mirsináceas, Tiliáceas, Mirteáceas y Rosáceas. El más común es el *Prunus capuli,* árbol que alcanza alturas de 10 a 15 metros; su pequeño fruto es negro o rojizo y con una sola semilla.

Casa de la Comisión. Lugar donde los organizadores de las fiestas patronales ("la Comisión") ofrecen comida a todos los visitantes durante los días de fiesta.

Ceiba. Árbol perteneciente a las Bombacáceas, particularmente *Bombax ellipticum* y *Ceiba aesculifolia.* El árbol por excelencia en el pensamiento y espiritualidad mayas.

Cempasúchil. Del náhuatl *cempoalxóchitl,* "veinte flores," "muchas flores." Se escribe también *sempasúchil. Tagetes erecta,* planta herbácea de hojas recortadas, olor penetrante y flores amarillas.

Cenote. Del maya *dzono'ot,* depósitos y corrientes de agua subterránea accesibles a través de aberturas en la capa de piedra caliza de la Península de Yucatán.

Ch'a' Cháak. Ceremonia tradicional de petición de lluvias entre los mayas de la Península de Yucatán. Es conducida por un *jmen* o sacerdote maya y en el altar de la ceremonia hay ofrendas de diversos alimentos. (Véase Apéndice A.)

Chäk to'. Nombre chontal para *popal* (*Calathea lutea*).

Planta herbácea perteneciente a las Marantáceas, que suele crecer en lagunas o esteros. Llega a medir tres metros de altura y posee hojas grandes con una película blanquecina en la cara inferior que contiene cera. En Tabasco se le conoce como hoja del *popal* y suele emplearse para envolver alimentos.

Chaneques. Seres mágicos de pequeña estatura que se supone habitan en montañas, selvas y cerros. (Véase Apéndice E.)

Chikomexóchitl. En náhuatl, "siete" (*chicome*) "flores" (*xóchitl*). Niño sagrado que se convierte sucesivamente en maíz, en el sol y en el sustentador de la vida.

Chikomexóchitl-elotlamanalistli. En náhuatl, "El que extiende las mazorcas en la mesa," otro nombre de Chikomexóchitl.

Chiltepín. Capsicum frutesceus, planta arbustiva que produce un fruto en extremo picante.

Chontales de Tabasco. Grupo étnico de la familia mayense establecido principalmente en el estado de Tabasco. A finales del siglo XX su población era de 72,000 habitantes. (Véase *yokot'an.*)

Cochinilla. Del latín *coccinus,* "escarlata" o "grana." Insecto hemíptero originario de México; vive sobre el nopal de la variedad *Nopalea cochinillifera.* Seco y reducido a polvo es muy útil para teñir de rojo la seda, lana y otras telas.

Coyo. Acrocomia mexicana; según otros autores, *Acrocomia vinifera.* Se le llama *coyo* o *coyol* (del náhuatl *coyoli,* "cascabel") por la forma del fruto y porque se convierte en cascabel al sacudirse el fruto seco.

Elookichpiltsij. En náhuatl, "Pequeño varón mazorca." Otro nombre de Chikomexóchitl.

Elosiuapiltsij. En náhuatl, "La mujer del elote tierno."

Estoraque. Styrax argenteus, árbol que alcanza alturas de 20 metros y cuyo tronco produce una resina aromática que se emplea como incienso. También se llama *estoraque* al *Liquidambar styraciflua.*

Fandanguero. Se le llama así, en la Huasteca, a los que saben tañer diversos instrumentos de cuerda para sones populares y para sones de costumbre. En España, *fandanguero* es el que sabe tocar y cantar *fandangos,* composiciones musicales animadas al compás de tres por cuatro, originarios de Andalucía.

Goziobe. Entidad sagrada prehispánica de los zapotecos. Literalmente, "relámpago de aire," de *gozio,* "rayo" o "relámpago," y *be,* "aire."

Guarapo. Jugo fermentado de la caña de azúcar.

Guaya. Véase *huaya.*

Guayabo. Psidium guajava: árbol perteneciente a la familia de las Mirtáceas, de corteza rojiza, lisa y escamosa, de fruto comestible y aromático piriforme u oval.

Huacal. Del náhuatl *huacalli,* caja o jaula formada con tiras de madera, separadas para transportar mercancías.

Huanengo. Entre los purépechas, blusa tradicional hecha de algodón blanco y adornada de motivos florales bordados.

Huapango. Danza y música de baile tradicional de la región Huasteca del norte de Veracruz y los estados vecinos; se emplea también para la música de baile tradicional de las costas sureñas del Golfo de México que corresponden al son jarocho. *Huapango* viene del náhuatl *huapalli.*

Huapanguera. Guitarra de ocho cuerdas empleada principalmente en la región Huasteca para interpretar el *huapango;* se le llama también "guitarra quinta."

Huarache. Del purépecha *kwarachi;* sandalia rústica de cuero.

Huasteca. Comarca muy extensa y variada de la Sierra Madre Oriental en Tamaulipas, San Luis Potosí, Veracruz, Hidalgo y Puebla. Del náhuatl *huaxteca,* habitante de Huaxtla, lugar donde abundan los *huaxin,* "guajes" o "calabazas" (*Lagenaria siceraria*).

Huaya. Talisia olivaeformis, árbol de la península de Yucatán y de varias regiones de Tabasco y Chiapas.

Huicholes (ellos se autodenominan *Wixárika*). Importante grupo étnico del occidente de México. Asentado fundamentalmente en los estados de Jalisco y Nayarit. A finales del siglo XX su población era de 55,000 habitantes.

Ixuakentsij. Del tenek *ichbequen;* pequeña flor que se emplea en una variedad de ceremonias, conocida en español como "manzanita" o "mazapán." Corresponde al *Malvaviscus grandiflorus* y al *Malvaviscus arboreus.*

Ja'abín. Nombre maya para *Piscidia piscipula,* planta venenosa. El árbol llega a alcanzar los 15 metros de altura y florece durante la estación seca; es muy útil para la elaboración de marcos y puertas.

Jaguacte. Bactris baculifera, palma espinosa que llega a una altura de 6 metros con fruto globoso y rojo.

Jalamante. Ficus padifolia, árbol grande de jugo lechoso y fruto comestible. Es más usual llamarlo *jalamate.*

Jalamate. Véase *jalamante.*

Jarana. Guitarra pequeña de cinco cuerdas que acompaña el *huapango* y el *son jarocho.*

Jícara. Del náhuatl *xicalli,* "recipiente o casa del jícaro." Tazón o vasija hecha del fruto del jícaro, *Crescentia cujete.*

Jicote. Del náhuatl *xicotli,* una variedad de avispa.

Jmen. Sacerdote maya tradicional. (Véase Apéndice A.)

Kajkanantik. De *kajkanan,* "protector," "cuidador." Fórmula ceremonial tzeltal que significa "Nuestro protector," y que se emplea en referencia a los santos patronos de cada pueblo.

Kajval. En tzotzil, nombre genérico de entidades protectoras o guardianes de montes, manantiales o ríos. (Véase Apéndice E.)

Kaxhon. Plural de *xhon,* es decir, literalmente, "los xhon"; se refiere a los pueblos zapotecos ubicados en la ribera del río Cajonos o Kaxhon.

Kokajsintla. En náhuatl, "abundante en mazorcas."

K'ox. En tzotzil, literalmente, "el más pequeño," "el hermano menor" de una familia. (Véase Apéndice F.)

Leoncillo. Felis concolor.

Maitines. En el ritual católico, primera de las horas canónicas en que comienzan los rezos previos al amanecer. Entre los zapotecos de la sierra, obra musical que las bandas tocan en ceremonias vespertinas o nocturnas compuesta de un himno a la virgen, responsos y un rezo de *te deum.*

Marakame. En huichol *mara'akame* (pl., *mara'akate*), curandero y sacerdote ritual; literalmente, "el que canta" o "el cantor."

Mayas. Los mayas de la Península de Yucatán son, después de los nahuas, el grupo étnico más numeroso de México. A finales del siglo XX su población era de 1,490,000 habitantes.

Mayordomo. Cargo tradicional que se turna anualmente entre diferentes individuos de una comunidad, cuyas responsabilidades incluyen proveer fondos y bienes materiales para la celebración de las festividades de un santo.

Mecapal. Del náhuatl *mecapalli,* "hoja de cuerda." Faja ancha de una soga que se coloca en la frente para llevar carga en la espalda.

Mestizo/a. (1) Alguien *no* reconocido como indígena, sino como *ladino,* de habla española. (2) En Yucatán, hombre o mujer ataviados con ropa de lujo, usualmente, en el caso del hombre, pantalón blanco y guayabera o filipina blanca; en el caso de la mujer, un vestido de tres piezas con bordados coloridos y abundantes (*terno*).

Metate. Del náhuatl *metatl;* piedra plana y horizontal sobre la cual se muele el maíz.

Mixes o *Mijes* (ellos se autodenominan *Ayook*). Uno de los principales grupos étnicos del estado de Oaxaca. Sus pueblos se extienden por la sierra de Juárez, al norte del estado. A finales del siglo XX su población ascendía a un total aproximado de 188,000 personas.

Mole. Del náhuatl *molli,* "salsa."

Naguales. Ciertos individuos, según creencias de numerosos pueblos indígenas, que pueden convertirse o tener una relación consciente con determinados animales que son sus *dobles* o *nahuales.* (Véase Apéndice G.)

Nahuales. Vease *naguales.*

Nahuas. A finales del siglo XX los nahuas eran el grupo indígena más numeroso en México, con una población de 2,563,000 habitantes distribuidos entre los estados de Puebla, Veracruz, Hidalgo, Guerrero, San Luis Potosí, Tlaxcala, Morelos y México y el Distrito Federal. Su lengua materna es el náhuatl.

Nopal. Nombre de todas las cactáceas de los géneros *Platyopuntia* y *Nopalea.*

Numinoso. Término acuñado por el teólogo alemán Rudolf Otto (1869–1937) para referirse a la conciencia de lo sagrado. Para él, lo "numinoso" es el objeto de la religión, algo superior a la razón, la bondad y la belleza. *Numinoso* se deriva de la palabra latina *numen,* "divinidad" o "voluntad divina."

Ocote. Del náhuatl *ocotl,* "tea," "antorcha." Pequeñas rajas de la madera del *Pinus montezumal,* un pino resinoso.

Pak'al. Método de siembra entre los mayas de Yucatán que consiste en abrir tres hoyos en la tierra, como la posición triangular que guardan las tres piedras del fogón de cocina (*k'óobenil k'áak',* del cual deriva el nombre *k'óoben pak'al*) para depositar las semillas del maíz.

Papatla. Heliconia schiedeana, planta herbácea de un metro y medio, con aspecto de platanillo, con hojas ovales y agudas que se emplean para envolver alimentos.

Pariyatsie. Forma abreviada de la expresión huichola *páriyatsié yeyá,* "fiesta o celebración de la peregrinación"; se refiere al peregrinaje desde las montañas de Jalisco y Nayarit, donde viven las comunidades huicholas, hasta la sierra de Real del Catorce en San Luis Potosí, que constituye el territorio donde recolectan el peyote.

Pe'et. Especie de red que los mayas de Yucatán fijan en un aro y cuelgan por tres hilos unidos en un nudo; en ella guardan comestibles.

Pepeyocales. Populus arizonica, variedad de álamo llamado "cimarrón."

Pericón. Tagetes florida, planta herbácea de un metro

de altura, de hojas elípticas y aserradas, con flores de marcado olor a anís.

Petate. Del náhuatl *petlatl,* tejido de palma o de carrizos que se emplea como estera para sentarse y dormir o como envoltura funeraria.

Petko. Nissa sylvatica, árbol de la familia de las Nisáceas que llegan a tener alturas de 35 metros con flores y frutos azulados. *Petko* deriva del zoque *petcui.*

Pijije. Dendrocygna autumnalis, ave palmípeda de la familia de los Anátidos, parecida al pato pero de menor tamaño. Es comestible.

Pilsintektli. En náhuatl, "Tierno Señor." Otro nombre de Chikomexóchitl.

Pirul. Pequeño fruto rojizo del *Schinus molle,* árbol originario de Perú y por eso llamado indistintamente pirú, perú o pirul.

Poleo. Se designa con este nombre a dos variedades de *Hedeoma* labiadas en el centro de México, Hidalgo y San Luis Potosí: la *Hedeoma palmeri* y la *Hedeoma drummondii.*

Pozol. Del náhuatl *potzol* o *potzolli;* masa de maíz cocido y reventado que se deslíe en agua para ser comido.

Pozo Virgen. Entre los mayas de Yucatán, derivado del término *suju'uy,* "lo inmaculado," "lo sagrado," "lo virginal." Agua ritual.

Principales. Grupo de oficiales que comparten las responsabilidades del *mayordomo.* (Véase *mayordomo.*)

Pulque. Del náhuatl *poliuhqui,* "echado a perder"; bebida obtenida por la fermentación del jugo o "aguamiel" de ciertos magueyes o agaves, particularmente del género *Agave atrovirens.*

Purépechas. El grupo étnico más importante de Michoacán. A finales del siglo XX su población era de 204,000 habitantes.

P'uus (plural maya *p'uuso'ob*). Según los mayas de Yucatán, la humanidad anterior al diluvio.

Roza. Acción de limpiar las tierras de las matas y hierbas inútiles antes de labrarlas, bien para que retoñen las plantas o bien para otros fines.

Saakal. Nombre maya para una hormiga arriera, negra, menos destructiva que la *xulab.* (Véase *xulab.*)

Saka'. Una bebida semejante a la que el campesino maya designa como *k'eyem* (o "pozol" en español) y que obtiene al desleír la masa de maíz en un poco de agua. El nixtamal del *saká* se sancocha sin sal y se muele con la cascarilla misma; a menudo cuando se deslíe la masa, se endulza con miel.

Sempasúchil. Véase *cempasúchil.*

Sintektli. En náhuatl, "Señor de la Mazorca." Otro nombre de Chikomexóchitl.

Sinteopiltsij. En náhuatl, "Tierno Dios de la Mazorca." Otro nombre de Chikomexóchitl.

Sones de costumbre. Música ritual que sólo se toca en ceremonias religiosas tradicionales.

Sones de muerto. Música ritual que sólo se toca en ceremonias fúnebres, para ayudar al alma a que se retire y no se pierda.

Suju'uy Ch'e'en. En maya, literalmente, "Pozo Virgen." De *suju'uy,* "lo inmaculado," "lo sagrado," "lo virginal," y *ch'e'en,* "pozo." Agua para uso ritual.

Takakaima. En huichol, "Los Señores de la Medianoche," en referencia a las entidades sagradas de la oscuridad y del inframundo.

Takutsi. En huichol, "Nuestra Abuela," con el sentido de "Nuestra Semilla Germinada" (es decir, la vida que se produce en toda la tierra).

Tapanco. Del náhuatl *tlapanco,* "en la azotea." Tablas horizontales con que se divide una habitación en dos niveles para formar un desván o ático.

Tatei Yurienaka. En huichol, "Nuestra Madre Tierra."

Tatewari. En huichol, "Nuestro Abuelo," en referencia al fuego.

Tatutsima. En huichol "Nuestros Bisabuelos," en referencia a los primeros creadores del mundo.

Tecolote. Del náhuatl *tecolotl* (de *col,* "doblar," "curva"); lechuza.

Tecomate. Del náhuatl *tecomatl,* "vaso," "olla"; recipiente hecho de cáscara de frutas como los guajes, cocos y calabazas.

Teiwari. Literalmente, "vecino," en referencia al que no es huichol. Se aplica a los mestizos y extranjeros.

Temascal. Del náhuatl *temazcalli,* "casa de bañarse"; pequeña construcción de piedra, con una sola entrada, para baño de vapor. Su origen es prehispánico.

Tepache. Del náhuatl *tepiatl,* agua de maíz crudo. Se aplica ahora a una bebida fermentada de piña y azúcar.

Tepechanejkej. En náhuatl, "los Señores del cerro," seres mágicos de pequeña estatura que habitan y cuidan lo cerros. (Véase Apéndice E.)

Tepehuas. A finales del siglo XX la población tepehua era de 17,000 habitantes y habitaban fundamentalmente en el estado de Veracruz.

Tepescuincle. Véase *tepescuintle.*

Tepescuintle. Del náhuatl *tepeitzcuintli,* "perro de cerro"; *Coelogenys paca.*

Teskatlapetlanij. En náhuatl, "Espejo brillante," nombre ceremonial de los relámpagos.

Teskatlatomonianij. En náhuatl, "Espejo de Trueno," nombre ceremonial de los truenos.

Tezontle. Del náhuatl *tetzontli;* piedra volcánica porosa y ligera, de color rojizo.

Tikarixa. Nombre huichol de una de las especies herbáceas que se designan en varias zonas de México con el nombre genérico de *manto.* Se cultivan como ornamentales.

Tlamatijketl. De *tlamati,* "inteligente," "diestro." En algunas zonas nahuas se le llama *tlamatqui* a los curanderos o brujos.

Tlapopochuyketl. Del náhuatl *tlapopoca,* "humear," incensador o portador de incienso en las ceremonias.

Toj. Del maya *to',* "envolver"; *Calathea grandifolia,* también conocida como "bijagua" u "hojablanca."

Tojolabales (ellos se autodenominan *Tojolwinik Otik*). Uno de los grupos étnicos más importantes de Chiapas; pertenecen a la familia mayense. A finales del siglo XX su población era de 74,000 habitantes.

Tsitsimitenantsij. En náhuatl, "Madre de las Tsitsimi," divinidades nocivas prehispánicas.

Tukipa. Centros ceremoniales huicholes que se supone conservan, desde una remota antigüedad, el diseño del mundo y los pasos de su creación; se mantienen activos con grupos de *mara'akate* que deben permanecer en ellos por un período de cinco años.

Tzáab. Nombre maya de la constelación de las Pléyades. También se refiere al cascabel de la serpiente.

Tzeltales. Constituyen uno de los grupos étnicos más importantes de los Altos de Chiapas; pertenecen a la familia mayense. A finales del siglo XX su población era de 547,000 habitantes.

Tzíimin. Es ahora el nombre maya del caballo, pero originalmente lo fue del tapir. (Véase Apéndice B.)

Tzotziles. Uno de los grupos étnicos importantes de los Altos de Chiapas; pertenecen a la familia mayense. A finales del siglo XX su población era de 514,000 habitantes.

Xhon. Se refiere a los pueblos situados en la ribera del río Cajonos o Kaxhon. A partir de este dato geográfico se ha convertido en la variante dialectal del zapoteco de la sierra para referirse a los zapotecos mismos.

Xidsa. Apócope de *benexidsa,* es decir, los zapotecos del rincón.

Xiquipil. En náhuatl, "morral," "bolsa," "talega."

Xopacatl. En náhuatl, "mojar el pie." En el español de México, "el remojo." Brindis que se considera obligatorio por estrenar algo.

Xulab. Nombre maya para una hormiga muy destructiva y carnicera. Se le llama "arriera" por su costumbre de transportar durante las noches, en grupos, sus alimentos a sus nidos.

Xúul. Palo o bastón de un metro y medio de altura que los mayas de Yucatán utilizan para la siembra.

Yokot'an. Término con el que se autodenominan los chontales de Tabasco.

Yum. En maya, literalmente, "Señor." Nombre genérico de las entidades protectoras mayas.

Yum Tziles. De la voz maya "Yumtzil," "Dios" (el Señor pleno). Nombre colectivo de las entidades protectoras mayas. (Véase Apéndices B y E.)

Zapoteco. Descendiente de la nube o *sa* (*zá*). En zapoteco del Istmo se dice *binnizá,* "gente de la nube." En zapoteco de la sierra, *benexidsa,* "zapotecos del rincón." A finales del siglo XX su población era de 785,000 habitantes distribuidos en el valle, el Istmo y la sierra de Oaxaca.

Zutz'baläm. En chontal de Tabasco (Yokot'an), literalmente, murciélago-jaguar: una deidad.

www.ingramcontent.com/pod-product-compliance
Lightning Source LLC
Chambersburg PA
CBHW081327090726
47907CB00010B/2400

* 9 7 8 1 4 7 7 3 1 5 2 6 2 *